THE
260

**A Life-Changing Experience Through the
New Testament One Chapter at a Time**

journey

Tim Dilena

The 260 Journey: A Life-Changing Experience Through the New Testament One Chapter at a Time

ISBN: 978-1-94429-875-3

Cover Design by Josh Guilbeau
Interior Design by Niddy Griddy Design, Inc.

Printed in the United States of America

3 4 5 6 7 8 9 10 Printing / Year 25 24 23 22 21

I've said on numerous occasions when you sat in an audience to hear me speak:

"Everyone in the room is in black and white but I see you in color."

This book can only be dedicated to one person, my wife Cindy.

For the one I see in color. I love you.

Foreword

Early in our retirement, when we lived in Key Largo, Florida, I received an email from a man named Tim Dilena. He invited me to preach at his church—The Revival Tabernacle—in Detroit. I answered him ten minutes later—and said yes. My wife Louise said to me, "Do you know this man? How do you know you are not making a mistake?" I replied, "Because I'm not making a mistake." I have developed a way of knowing when to say yes and when I must say no, and I have not been disappointed so far. I began preaching for Pastor Tim some eighteen years ago. A deep friendship developed over the years. During this time Louise and I have entertained Tim and Cindy in Key Largo and I have preached for him several times, including when he was pastor of Our Savior's Church in Lafayette, Louisiana. He has endorsed at least two of my books; it is my honor to write the foreword for *260 Journey*—Tim's first book.

For those who don't know the story of Tim's father in David Wilkerson's book *The Cross and the Switchblade*, allow me to sum it up. When David Wilkerson began preaching in the streets of Brooklyn, the police stopped him. Paul Dilena, a police captain walked up, overruled them and said, "Let's hear what the man has to say." This event paved the way for David Wilkerson's future success on the streets of New York. That, of course, is an amazing story. But if anything is more extraordinary it is that sixty years later, Paul Dilena's son, Tim, is now the Senior Pastor of Times Square Church, founded by David Wilkerson.

Several years ago, Pastor Carter Conlon, who succeeded David Wilkerson at Times Square Church, gave Tim Dilena a prophetic word that Tim was about to undergo the greatest trial of his life. Tim recently took me to the restaurant—and showed me where they were seated—when Carter gave him this sobering word. But eight years later, ironically at the same table in the New York restaurant, Carter said to Tim: "You are to be my successor at Times Square Church."

> *God moves in a mysterious way His wonders to perform;*
> *He plants His footsteps in the sea and rides upon the storm.*
>
> *Ye fearful saints, fresh courage take; the clouds ye so much dread*
> *Are big with mercy, and shall break with blessings on your head.*
> —William Cowper (1731-1800).

It happens that my friendship with Tim was deepened during those five years. Tim visited us twice at our home in Hendersonville, Tennessee, where we now live. We also spent time together in New York, including traveling to the Baseball Hall of Fame in Cooperstown, New York. We are both New York Yankee fans! I will never forget that trip to Cooperstown. It was in Tim's darkest hour, at his lowest moment. I felt his pain. Few people of God have endured the kind of suffering Tim was put through. But God was in the middle of it all! It was an essential part of Tim's preparation for what God has called him to be and to do today. Dr. Martyn Lloyd-Jones, the man who put me in Westminster Chapel, once said to me: "The worst thing that can happen to a man is to succeed before he is ready." Those hard years helped ensure that Tim would not succeed before he was ready.

260 Journey is designed to take two hundred and sixty days to read a chapter a day. No more. You are supposed to stick to the "rule"—one chapter a day. However, you are going to have a problem reading this book, that is, sticking to the rule. A definite problem. You may not be able to read only a chapter a day. You will be sorely tempted to jump to the following chapter—which is supposed to be read the following day! These chapters read so easily and provide such interest that—if you are not careful—you will finish it too soon! I'm serious. I will only say to you, make yourself do two things (at least): (1) read the corresponding chapter in the New Testament first, then (2) read Tim Dilena's comments. I predict you will be rewarded more fully by heeding this rule.

You will also see quickly why Carter Conlon recommended Tim to Times Square Church and why the people there so eagerly welcomed him. Tim has an original mind, seeing things that will make you say, "Why didn't I see that?" or "Wow. I never thought of that." His sense of humor, his being widely read, his love for Jesus, his reverence for the Word and approachableness with people will be very apparent. The people of Times Square Church know that they are very blessed to have Tim Dilena as their Senior Pastor. Thank you, Carter Conlon, for recommending him. Thank you, Cindy, for being the kind of wife that Tim has needed. Thank you, Heavenly Father, for preparing Tim during these years and bringing him back home to New York for such a time as this.

—R. T. Kendall

Acknowledgements

Cindy and I pray with our children every single morning before they walk outside the door to school these words "Father, give them God-honoring relationships because Your Word says in I Corinthians 15:33 'Bad company corrupts good character.'" We make them say it out loud. I believe the inverse of that verse is true too: good company helps me towards good character.

Author and leadership expert John Maxwell said: "The people closest to me determine my level of success or failure. The better they are, the better I am. And if I want to go to the highest level, I can do it only with the help of other people. We have to take each other higher." I not only want exceptional people close to my children, Cindy and I know it's imperative to have exceptional people involved in every phase of our lives. Maxwell couldn't have said it any clearer that if I want to go to the highest level it is only possible with the right people. *The 260 Journey* represents one of those high-level places for us, so that means exceptional people played a huge role and gratitude is in order.

First, to Cindy, Christian, Anna, Grace, and Lauryn, you are my joy and my crown. I am the most blessed man alive. I don't do ministry alone, we do it as a team. Team Dilena makes me smile every day. I love you all. To my father, Paul Dilena, who is my hero. I am the person I am today because of your life and example. So many days I wish you were still here but know the next time we are together we will be singing together to the Lamb of God. Next, to the people that got the 260 off the starting line. Katie Wilbanks and Luke LaPrairie, for your constant edits and filming of the 260 as a daily devo. You both saw it to be something much more than I did. Sallie Guillory, I'm grateful for the day that Katie came in and said to me, "This is one of your greatest disciples and you don't even know it." You always seemed to make whatever project I was doing a priority and pushed it to the top of the list with your team. God is using you to make a difference in a big way.

To Jacob Aranza and the OSC family, I so appreciate your investment and encouragement to be better and to see further. And thank you, Ginger Kolbaba for using the quarantine to knock out a quarter of million words of tireless book editing. You are amazing.

In football, the red zone is the place where you are in striking distance of the goal line. Many teams can get your offense inside the 20-yard line but it doesn't mean you put points on the board. There is always a group of people that gets you to cross the goal line. There was a team that got the 260 project from the red zone into the end zone. Thank you to Michael Fratt and Taina Dougé for your consistent pushing and prodding and deadlines. Thank you, Luly McCoy for getting all the right people involved and your detailed Excel charts.

To Pastor Carter Conlon for his friendship and prophecy in Gallagher's restaurant in NYC—he knows the details. You have played a big part of our lives and still do. I love you my friend. And thank you, Times Square Church family for the joy you have brought to our lives—there is an amazing journey we have ahead.

But for now, let's take the journey through 260 chapters of the New Testament.

The 260 Journey Introduction

*T*he *260 Journey* is not a yearly devotional. It is a study tool for a pastor, a motivational tool for a devoted Christ-follower, and a starting point for a new Christian. It transcends New Year's resolutions and goes beyond a Bible commentary on a shelf. The 260 is a Bible companion that can be started in January or June or any other time. It is a strategy and a resource for believers at any phase in their Christian walk.

A senior church leader and personal friend once told me that a vision without a strategy is fantasy. Here is your strategy for not just reading the New Testament in a year but being challenged by each chapter of the New Testament.

Why call it the 260?

The New Testament contains 260 chapters, and there are 261 weekdays in every year.

The strategy is one chapter a day Monday through Friday with weekends off to finish the entire New Testament in a year.

The 260 will take a verse and sometimes a number of verses each day from that day's New Testament chapter and explain, inspire, and bring it to life. Personal stories, historical illustrations, quotes, and cross-references help make each chapter more easily understandable and applicable. Pastors will find a nugget to help them clarify a Bible verse for their sermon and new Christians will have the light go on in their comprehension of the Bible.

Though the 260 challenges you to read a New Testament chapter Monday through Friday, it isn't stuck in that method. You can use it for a small-group book study or for simply a personal devotional time. Though it isn't an exegetical commentary, it doesn't shy away from it when necessary.

Augustine said this about the Bible: "The Bible is shallow enough for a child not to drown, yet deep enough for an elephant to swim." The 260 reflects that. You will be able to wade in sections and swim in others. It's a reservoir for everyone.

Get ready for a life-changing journey called the 260.

Day 1

GETTING RID OF YOUR LABELS

Today's Reading: Matthew 1

The whole of the New Testament starts with today's reading in Matthew 1. This is the story of stories—and it starts off all wrong.

Most adventure stories begin with the wondrous "Once upon a time" so we know we're in for something truly amazing. That's the way the New Testament should begin, right? After all, what is more adventurous and exciting than the story of salvation, redemption, hope, and the keys to eternal life?

Instead, Matthew starts his book of the same name with a genealogy. Why in the world would he do that? Because this story is not a fairy tale; this story is true. And he wants you to know beyond a shadow of a doubt that it *is* true. The greatest story ever told starts like a phone book, a long list unpronounceable names. But this is important: Those names tell us that Jesus is real and that He can be traced. This is Jesus' ancestry.com.

What makes this list amazing is that some names in this long list belong to people who had sketchy pasts. Not only did Jesus associate with liars, cheaters, adulterers, murderers, and prostitutes—as we'll see throughout the Gospels—but Jesus had them in his lineage. And Matthew didn't even attempt to cover it up!

Why does that matter to you and me? Because it shows from the outset that Jesus wants to associate with all of us. No matter what we've done or have become, we aren't beyond His love or reach.

I know this is true. Throughout my years of ministry, I have seen hardened prostitutes changed. Too often prostitutes feel irredeemable because their past holds so tightly to them. And yet, no one shows a way out of a past like Rahab, the prostitute who shows up in Jesus' lineage. Her story is epic, and we see her name in that long list of names in Matthew: "Salmon was the father of Boaz by Rahab, Boaz was the father of Obed by Ruth, and Obed the father of Jesse" (Matthew 1:5, AMP).

This is the Rahab from the Old Testament book of Joshua whose act of saving Hebrew spies got her inducted in Hebrews' hall of faith (see Hebrews 11:31). She hid them, and when they returned Joshua and the Hebrews conquered Jericho when the walls came crashing down, the only family they saved was

Rahab's. Jesus is associated with a prostitute. Would you expect anything less? Not only was she saved, but she married a Jewish man.

Let's reread Matthew 1:5: "Salmon was the father of Boaz by Rahab, Boaz was the father of Obed by Ruth, and Obed the father of Jesse."

Salmon and Rahab had Boaz, who married Ruth—of the Old Testament book of Ruth. Boaz and Ruth had a son named Obed who had a son named Jesse. And Jesse had a son named David. Not just any David. "Jesse was the father of David the king" (Matthew 1:6 , AMP).

Guess who was the great-great grandmother of King David?

Rahab, the prostitute, the harlot.

A quick thought for today: Almost every time Rahab's name is mentioned, in both the Old and New Testaments, it says, "Rahab the harlot."

How would you like that, if every time someone said your name, they included with it the worst season of your life? Can you imagine that the worst season of your life is your label and tag line connected to your name?

What if it looked like this? (I'll use my name so I don't indict anyone!): Tim the thief. Tim the embezzler. Tim the adulterer. Tim the baby aborter. Tim the wife beater. Tim the divorcee. Tim the porn addicted. Tim the alcoholic. Tim the road rager. Tim the unemployed. Think about what label would be after your name. For Rahab, "harlot" connects the past to her.

If time heals all wounds, then we wouldn't need God. Time is not that strong, but God is. There is only one place in the entire Bible where "harlot" or "prostitute" is removed from Rahab's name: It's when her name is connected to Jesus in Matthew 1.

The only way the past lets go of us is when it is confronted with a future in Jesus. When you are connected to Jesus, the future is bigger and greater than your past. Rahab had a huge past. And could have easily driven her life by the rearview mirror, but something happened to her. She got a windshield bigger than her past. She got Jesus.

It's always easier to drive forward using the windshield than the rearview mirror. With Jesus, we can look ahead and no longer be held back by the labels of our past.

Day 2

ALWAYS ONE STEP AHEAD

Today's Reading: Matthew 2

Obedience to God is such a powerful tool. Obedience to God will always keep you one step ahead of the enemy. Obedience to God brings you blessing. And it brings protection and puts you in the right place at the right time—exactly where God wants you to be.

When we don't obey God, we withhold from ourselves all that God has in store for us. An old friend, Joy Dawson, said this: "Disobeying God is the same as telling Him to hold back all of the blessings that come with obedience. That is not only stupidity, it's insanity."

We find this idea of being obedient to God in today's Scripture reading. Jesus has been born, which is epic. But what happens after the Christmas story is epic as well. The magi were heading to the place where Jesus was. They'd come to worship Him and to bring Him gifts. One of my favorite descriptions of their arrival is in verse 10 in the Message paraphrase: "They were in the right place! They had arrived at the right time!"

Think about that. "They were in the right place. They had arrived at the right time." I want a life like that. I want to be in the right place—at the right time. We only get there one way: by being obedient to God.

Too many of us, though, believe we can handle things on our own. As John Maxwell said, "Most Christians are educated way beyond their level of obedience."[1]

I know many people who are (education) smart but not (obedient) wise. Education smart is good and helpful, but it isn't the same as obedient wise. You can't become obedient wise through education. When you are wise, you will be at the right place at the right time. And wisdom comes from obedience.

Joseph shows us this truth. After the magi leave, Joseph has a dream:

After the scholars [the magi] were gone, God's angel showed up again in Joseph's dream and commanded, "Get up. Take the child and his mother and flee to Egypt. Stay until further notice. . . . Joseph obeyed" (Matthew 2:13, MSG).

What happens next is monumental!

King Herod, who learned about the Messiah through the magi, when they initially arrived in the area, commanded that every little boy two years old and younger who lived in Bethlehem was to be murdered.

Here is the reality: Obedience to God keeps us one step ahead of the enemy. Think about it. Herod wanted to kill Jesus. Before that happened—first—God gave Joseph a dream that told him to leave. And then—second—Herod sends his men on a killing spree. Because God called Joseph to obedience before Herod's plan was enacted, *and because Joseph obeyed*, Joseph, Mary, and Jesus were able to flee Bethlehem and find safety in Egypt.

It was a forty-mile journey for the new family.[2] So they were forty miles ahead of death and destruction, because God is always a first responder. But we have to obey to reap the benefits.

As Brother Andrew said, "Whenever, wherever, however You want me, I'll go. And I'll begin this very minute. Lord, as I stand up from this place, and as I take my first step forward, will You consider this is a step toward complete obedience to You? I'll call it the Step of Yes."[3]

I have experienced this truth in my own life. I have watched it happen with a simple apology. I said something I should not have and the Holy Spirit convicted me and called me to go to that person and apologize. Conviction was my dream. And that apology kept that relationship forty miles ahead of the enemy's narratives to harm it and kill it. Obedience keeps you and me forty miles ahead of death.

Jesus said this about our enemy, the devil: "The thief [Satan] comes only to steal and kill and destroy" every child of God (John 10:10, MSG). That's his mission and his Herod-like plan every day. Obedience to God keeps us ahead of any steal-kill-and-destroy agenda. And when we are one step ahead, we are *always* in the right place at the right time.

HEARING THE MOST IMPORTANT VOICE

Today's Reading: Matthew 3

A little brother was jealous that his older brother was getting water baptized and he wasn't. As his father instructed the older brother on what it meant and how special it was, the little guy left the room in tears because he wasn't being baptized. His father followed him to find out why he was so upset. When the father asked the four-year-old what was wrong, the little boy said, "I want to be *advertised* too with my brother on Sunday."

When you get water baptized, you also get advertised. It is a public declaration. It announces to everyone who you are following. But it doesn't make you a Christian any more than saying that a wedding ring on your finger makes you married. My wedding ring doesn't make me married, but it shows people that I am married. The ring is a symbol. And baptism is a symbol. To make it anything more than a symbol is dangerous. Water baptism, whether a spoonful or a tankful will never save anyone. But it is an important second step in our faith journey. Being water baptized differentiates the serious from the casual follower of Jesus. As Max Lucado says, "Baptism separates the tire kickers from the car buyers."[4]

Some call them ordinances of the church, but really, communion and water baptism are mini-dramas of salvation using props—water, bread, and wine. Something very special happens every time one of these mini-dramas take place: they are not just events in the life of the church among believers; they are sacred moments for God to speak to us.

That's what happened to Jesus.

After being baptized, Jesus came up immediately from the water; and behold, the heavens were opened, and he saw the Spirit of God descending as a dove and lighting on Him, and behold, a voice out of the heavens said, "This is My beloved Son, in whom I am well-pleased." (Matthew 3:16-17)

God spoke after Jesus was water baptized: "This is My beloved Son, in whom I am well pleased." God confirmed family. God confirmed His love. And so when we participate (practicing obedience), we do it because we love God (the motive of our obedience) and to hear God speak to us. God responds, "I love you too." We all need that Voice out of heaven to speak to us.

We live in a world crowded with voices all shouting at us:

- You are not good enough!
- You are not skinny enough!
- You are not good looking enough!
- You don't make enough money!
- You are not married!
- You don't have kids!

Those voices label you over what *I'm not*. And yet God tells us, *You belong to Me and you are greatly loved.*

We need to listen to and hear the Voice that Jesus heard at His baptism. As Steven Furtick writes, "The voice you believe will determine the future you experience."[5] God's voice is where our identity is found and the searching stops. We can be assured that God's voice tells us that He loves us and that He is pleased with us.

The biggest temptation today is to seek an alternative identity to who God created us to be. We see it in the ways we answer the question, *Who am I?*

- I am what I do—my job and career define me.

But when I get old and can no longer do a job and I retire, I lose my identity.

- I am what others say about me—people's words about me have power, especially who is saying it.

So I'm good when the talk about me is good, but I lose my identity when it's negative.

- I am what I have—I have a degree, health, good parents, good children, good salary, and security.

But when I lose any of those things, I lose my identity.

When we participate in the mini-dramas of salvation, we answer the identity question by hearing and embracing God's voice. He says, *You are God's beloved.* Heaven says that about you today. One of my dear friends reminds us, "There's nothing you can do that will make God stop loving you because there was nothing you did that made God start loving you." And Proverbs 3:6 tells us: "Listen for GOD's voice in everything you do, everywhere you go; he's the one who will keep you on track" (MSG)—because you are His beloved.

Day 4

WHY YOU ARE A TARGET

Today's Reading: Matthew 4

It seems Jesus can't even towel off and get dressed after being water baptized in the Jordan River before Satan shows up and challenges what Jesus has heard.

We ended yesterday's reading in Matthew 3 with hearing God speak.

Today's reading in Matthew 4 opens with hearing Satan speak.

Remember that in Matthew 3 at Jesus' water baptism, God said, "This is My beloved Son, in whom I am well-pleased." And before Jesus could properly digest and process those words, Satan spoke. Satan's message: *Did God really say that?*

> Then Jesus was led up by the Spirit into the wilderness to be tempted by the devil. And after He had fasted forty days and forty nights, He then became hungry. And the tempter came and said to Him, "*If* You are the Son of God . . . ." (Matthew 4:1-3, emphasis added)

God the Father had just told him, "You are My Son" (Matthew 3:17). Now Satan was questioning what God had said to Jesus. In essence, he was asking, "Did God really say that . . . ?"

This is not new. Satan was just shooting the same bullet he always does.

Remember back to the beginning of the Bible. In Genesis 3, the devil did the same thing in the Garden of Eden with Eve. His first recorded words pose a question—but not just any question. He asked a question to humans about God. "Has God said . . . ?" (Genesis 3:1). In other words, "Did God really say that?"

This is what you need to know: *Whatever God backs, Satan attacks.*

Sometimes Satan's attacks are the confirmations that you *did* hear from God and God *did* speak to you. As clear as God's voice was for Jesus, Satan's voice came in fast and clear. He did the same to Adam and Eve. He'll do the same to you and me.

No one is off limits—not Jesus, not the first family (Adam and Eve), not a child in the womb, not a pastor's family. *No one* who follows God and tries to be obedient to Him. C. S. Lewis writes, "The enemy will not see you vanish into God's company without an effort to reclaim you."[6]

Why does Satan come after you? Not because you are bad, but because, as a child of God, you are valuable. If you are a thief, and that is what Satan is, you don't break into abandon houses; you break into places you know has valuable stuff. Thomas Watson puts it this way: "Satan doth not tempt God's children because they have sin in them, but because they have grace in them. Had they no grace he would not disturb them."[7]

A thief will not assault an empty house, but where he thinks there is treasure.

Several years ago Sotheby's auction house in New York City had an auction. Here are some of the items that sold:

- Napoleon's toothbrush: $48,000
- Jacqueline Kennedy Onassis's fake pearls: $256,000
- President John F. Kennedy's wood golf clubs: $750,000

In and of themselves, they had worth, but what made them so extravagantly valuable? Not what they were by themselves, but whom they belonged to. Just as you had worth before you became a Christian, the day you got saved, your value skyrocketed. You just went from being "abandoned property" to being owned by the Creator of the Universe.

Now since you are valuable, you are a target.

Day 5

JESUS' PRESCRIPTION FOR HAPPINESS

Today's Reading: Matthew 5

Several years ago, the *Wall Street Journal* reported a story on happiness in different nations around the world. The newspaper's title gave away the happiness level of people living in the United States: "Richest Country, Saddest People—Any Coincidence?"

According to a study jointly conducted by the World Health Organization and Harvard Medical School, and based on more than 60,000 face-to-face interviews worldwide, the richest country—the United States—has the saddest people and is regarded as one of the *unhappiest* places on earth. Out of the fourteen countries surveyed, we have the highest rate of depression. We have the highest standard of living and yet we take more tranquilizers than anyone. And it seems that the more people have, the angrier they are.

The happiest people on the planet? Nigerians.

And they have one of the lowest standards of living.[8]

I don't believe Nigerians have the corner on the market, though. Believers do. Not feeling it? Today's reading will help fix that. In Matthew 5, Jesus gives us His prescription for how to have happiness.

In the reading for today and the next two days (Matthew 5–7), we find the greatest sermon ever preached by the greatest preacher who ever walked the planet. It's called the Sermon on the Mount. In this sermon, Jesus tells us how to be happy. It's connected to eight verses, called the Beatitudes, which are structured this way: "Blessed are the . . . for they shall . . ." Some translations have it as, "Happy are those who . . ."

It's amazing that Jesus starts His first sermon with happiness. But what makes this crazy is that Jesus says what will make us happy or blessed are the very things we wouldn't expect. I once heard theologian N. T. Wright say in a sermon, "The beatitudes of Jesus tell us that all the wrong people are going to be blessed; they are counterintuitive. God is turning everything upside down."[9]

Let me read it to you from the Good News Translation:

Happy are those who know they are spiritually poor; the Kingdom of heaven belongs to them!

Happy are those who mourn; God will comfort them!

Happy are those who are humble; they will receive what God has promised!

Happy are those whose greatest desire is to do what God requires; God will satisfy them fully!

Happy are those who are merciful to others; God will be merciful to them!

Happy are the pure in heart; they will see God!

Happy are those who work for peace; God will call them his children!

Happy are those who are persecuted because they do what God requires; the Kingdom of heaven belongs to them!

Happy are you when people insult you and persecute you and tell all kinds of evil lies against you because you are my followers. (Matthew 5:3-11)

This is *not* what Jesus is saying in the Sermon on the Mount: Live like this and you will become a Christian. That's impossible. What He *is* saying: *Because* you are a Christian, you can live like this and experience happiness.

What to remember regarding the Beatitudes:

1. Happiness is found in character not in possessions.

Every one of these Beatitudes is something internal, not external; something you are, not something you have.

2. God would never ask you to do or be something that is not possible.

God never makes His Word, His promises, or His challenges unattainable. God never directs us into dead-ends.

3. God always leaves a gap (of dependency).

You can't practice the beatitudes without God. Which means you can't be happy without God.

These beatitudes are not natural for us. We need God to instill them into us and direct us. We look to God to help us. And He will.

Eight times Jesus says we can be happy. That tells me this is really important. Why? Because of the way He begins His sermon: "When Jesus saw his ministry drawing huge crowds, he climbed a hillside. Those who were apprenticed to him, the committed, climbed with him. Arriving at a quiet place, he sat down and taught his climbing companions" (Matthew 5:1-2, MSG).

The Sermon on the Mount is a challenge to us. It's a challenge to climb higher and go higher in our thinking, in our lives, and in our thoughts. There are huge crowds, but Jesus breaks away from them. And He is about to break these disciples out of their religious thinking into Kingdom thinking.

You want to be happy? Jesus shows us the way. It may take a little effort to get there, but it's doable with Jesus beside us, helping us. The committed are willing to break out of their religious thinking and embrace Kingdom thinking. That brings us true and ultimate happiness.

THE PAYCHECK IS REALLY GOOD—
SO SHOW UP

Today's Reading: Matthew 6

In the first part of chapter 6, Jesus spoke about three personal disciplines that are part of every Christian's life: *giving, praying,* and *fasting.*

Note that I said, these three disciplines are part of *every* Christian's life. If you are a Christian, then they are to be part of your life as well.

How do we know they should be part of our lives? Because as Jesus spoke about them, He used an important word before each of them. Jesus started off each of the three with the word *when,* which assumes we are already practicing them.

When you give . . .
When you pray . . .
When you fast . . .

As He discussed these disciplines, He wanted to guide us in the proper way to practice them. In each instance, Jesus used a second word that is an essential part: *secret* (see verses 4, 6 and 18). We are to do these things in secret. In other words, we aren't supposed to flaunt the fact that we practice them. Why? Because there's only to be one member of our audience who sees what we do: God.

We do these things in secret—and the aftereffects of them go public. That's the *power* of these disciplines, He explained. If we pursue them without anybody's knowledge, we will receive a reward and everyone will benefit—they will always go public, or "in the open," in their effect.

Let me explain by using prayer as an example.

Jesus said, "But you, when you pray, go into your inner room, close your door and pray to your Father who is in secret, and your Father who sees what is done in secret will reward you" (Matthew 6:6).

When we dissect this sentence, we see the *when* ("when you pray"), the *secret* ("go into your inner room"), and *in the open* (your Father . . . will reward you).

But I want you to see something else. Go back to the Scripture and count the number of times Jesus used the words *you* or *yours*. This is the only verse in the *whole* Bible that has the singular personal pronoun in it seven times: "But *you*, when *you* pray, go into *your* inner room, close *your* door and pray to *your* Father who is in secret, and *your* Father who sees what is done in secret will reward *you*."

Why is this important to note? Because Jesus was saying that you have a responsibility. *You*.

But—and here's the beautiful part of it—this responsibility is never a waste of time. Because your Father will reward you. *You*.

The word *reward* means to clock in and get a paycheck. Jesus was saying that every time you pray, you clock in—you expect a paycheck. God pays His workers well. You will come out with *way* more than you put in.

When Mother Teresa was alive, many who visited her and her missionaries of Charity in Calcutta were surprised that every lunchtime they left their life-sustaining work in dispensaries and in the home for the dying.

"Why do you go back so soon and not stay longer? Where do you go?"

Mother Teresa responded, "We go to pray. We have learned that to work without prayer is to achieve only what is humanly possible and our desire is to be involved in divine possibilities."[10]

We get to be involved in divine possibilities. *When* we give, *when* we pray, *when* we fast.

Let's show up today to our responsibilities. The pay-off is too good not to.

LOGS AND SPECKS

Today's Reading: Matthew 7

A concerned husband went to see the family doctor. "I think my wife is deaf," he said. "She never hears me the first time I say something. In fact, I often have to repeat things over and over."

"Go home tonight," the doctor suggested. "Stand about fifteen feet from her, and say something. If she doesn't reply, move about five feet closer and say it again. Keep doing this so we can get an idea of the severity of her deafness."

That night, the husband went home and did exactly as instructed. He stood about fifteen feet from his wife, who was standing in the kitchen, chopping vegetables.

"Honey, what's for dinner?" he said. When he received no response, he moved five feet closer and asked again. "Honey, what's for dinner?"

No reply.

So he moved another five feet closer and repeated his question. But still no reply.

Fed up and frustrated, he moved right behind her, and standing about an inch away, asked one final time, "Honey, what's for dinner?"

"For the fourth time," she said. "Chicken!"

Guess who had the problem? Guess who was the deaf one?

We can laugh over this story, but it tells a truth: we always assume it's the other person who has the problem.

Jesus addressed this issue in the last part of the Sermon on the Mount—and it gets really up close and personal. He called it logs and specks.

> Do not judge so that you will not be judged. For in the way you judge, you will be judged; and by your standard of measure, it will be measured to you. Why do you look at the speck that is in your brother's eye, but do not notice the log that is in your own eye? (Matthew 7:1-3)

Jesus was a carpenter so this illustration made sense. Jesus said, in essence, "How can you see the speck in others and yet miss your own log?" In other words, Jesus was saying that the little junk you see in other people and point out just reveals a lot of junk that's in you, which you choose to ignore.

Jesus called this type of person a hypocrite. I've heard a hypocrite described this way:

> A hypocrite is a person who is easy on himself but hard on others, but a godly man is hard on himself and easy on others.

It's much harder to judge yourself than to judge others.

Jesus' challenge is for us to keep our eyes on ourselves *first* and be especially sure to admonish ourselves before you and I admonish any of our friends. When practicing this, some good advice to start with is this:

- It would be wiser to accuse yourself and excuse others.
- If you want to be endured, learn to endure others.

The fault lies not in our inability to see ourselves but in our unwillingness to see ourselves. As the great nineteenth-century preacher Charles H. Spurgeon aptly put it: "None are more unjust in their judgments of others than those who have a high opinion of themselves."[11]

I have asked couples in marriage counseling to name their logs before telling me their spouse's specks. It's amazing how hard that is for them to think of their own.

We get in the way of ourselves. Instead we prefer to be the "Help and Speck Inspector."

If we go back to what Jesus was saying, He was showing us that logs are bigger than specks. Meaning that we have the bigger problem than those we judge. When we don't start with "I'm the problem," we have a long haul ahead of us in our relationships. Instead we must always start with ourselves not with the other person.

If you want to judge, judge *yourself first*, is what Jesus said. Logs before specks, and the logs take a long time to get rid of. You'll be so busy getting rid of the log that you won't have time for specks. Get this and you will build deep, meaningful, and long-term relationships.

London preacher (and one of the best Bible-character writers), F. B. Meyer, once said, "When we see a brother or sister in sin, there are three things we do not know and [must] keep in mind before we pass judgment:

> First, we do not know how hard he or she tried not to sin.

Second, we do not know the power of the forces that assailed him or her.

Third, we do not know what we would have done in the same circumstances.[12]

Good words to remember.

Day 8

EIGHT IS MONDAY

Today's Reading: Matthew 8

Her name was Agnes and she was from Albania. In 1928, at age eighteen, she went to Ireland and became a nun. Almost twenty years later, in 1946, she received what she described as a call within the call. As she was riding on a train, her heart heard the Lord tell her to help the most rejected people in society, the poorest of the poor—the throw-away people of Calcutta, India.

It took her two years of fighting through the bureaucratic red tape in order for her to pursue that call. But she remained committed, and in 1950, Agnes Bojaxhiu founded the Missionaries of Charity. Agnes Bojaxhiu, of course, is Mother Teresa.

Discussing that call within a call, she stated, "Stay where you are. Find your own Calcutta. Find the sick, the suffering, and the lonely right there where you are—in your own homes and in your own families, in your workplaces and in your schools. You can find Calcutta all over the world, if you have the eyes to see. Everywhere, wherever you go, you find people, who are unwanted, unloved, uncared for, just rejected by society—completely forgotten, completely left alone. Help one person at a time, and always start with the person nearest you."[13]

We just finished reading the greatest sermon ever preached by the greatest preacher—Jesus' Sermon on the Mount (Matthew 5–7). Now we turn our attention to chapter 8. What interests me is not just the sermon, but what took place the day *after* the sermon—what we learn about in today's reading of chapter 8.

This is when the crowd shrinks to the individual. The audience now has a name. And we see it immediately in Matthew 8:1-2, MSG: "Jesus came down the mountain with the cheers of the crowd still ringing in his ears. Then a leper appeared".

Life just got real. The worst disease came after the greatest sermon. You know what I'm talking about. After the singing and the preaching, there is debt, marriage problems, addictions, cancer, diabetes, divorce, and abuse.

Because chapter 8 is all about what happens on Monday—after the great and inspiring Sunday morning worship service. Chapter 8 is where there is no stage, no music, but people with a lot of problems who need help. Chapter 8 is about a lot of people—and *all* of them have an issue. And Jesus met every one—cleansing, healing, deliverance, words of truth.

Think about this with me:
- Chapters 5–7 is Sunday at church service
- Chapter 8 is Monday through Saturday
- Chapter 5–7 is about interacting with God
- Chapter 8 is about how we interact with people

No one did it better than Jesus:
- Chapters 5–7, He is the preacher-teacher
- Chapter 8, He is the doctor

In chapter 8, His Monday included four encounters:
- a leper
- a Roman captain with a paralyzed staff member
- His disciple Peter's sick mother-in-law who was stuck in bed with a fever
- two graveyard demoniacs who were causing havoc in town

But this is important to notice: Jesus had compassion and healed them. The key word with Jesus, and when He sees someone in need, is *compassion*. To know the Bible, to know how to sing Christian songs, is important, but that doesn't translate into making other people's lives better when we meet them in a tragedy.

You can't be compassionate without people. Compassion needs people to sacrifice for. No one is compassionate alone. Our Calcuttas are right next to us. And they need our compassion.

It's about touching your city, your community, your neighbors, your family and friends.

Every one of us has three resources to show compassion: time, treasure, and talents.

Time: The Bible says, "To redeem the time" (Ephesians 5:16, KJV). To "redeem" it means to see it as valuable and get the best bang for your buck. The New American Standard Bible translates it as making the most of our time, using it the best way we can.

Examine what you give your time to. Does it show others compassion? I heard someone once say, "You can see the priorities of a person's life by two documents: a checkbook and a calendar." Your time reveals your priorities.

Treasure: How you spend your money also reveals your priorities. Do you spend your money in compassionate ways? For instance, do you tithe regularly to the work of God's Kingdom? Tithing is a thank-you note to God for entrusting you with 90 percent of God's 100 percent. When we give to God, we are just taking our hands off what He already owns. Give to God what's right, not what's left. As Martin Luther once said, "I have tried to keep things in my hands and lost them all, but what I have given into God's hands I still possess."[14]

Talents: What is your talent? You have at least one—everybody does. The apostle Peter wrote in 1 Peter 4:10: "As each one has received a special gift, employ it in serving one another as good stewards of the manifold grace of God." You show compassion by using your talent well.

Jesus told a parable of those who were given talents (see Matthew 25). When they used them, they produced more with what they had. *Your talent produces something more.*

Your gift is your obligation to others. So if everyone has a gift, then everyone is to impact someone. You included. No exceptions. And it also surrounds using your gift for others.

Whether your gifting is loving people, helping people, serving people, giving to people, bringing people to church . . . it's always about people. That's how you show compassion. By meeting their needs.

Eight is Monday. Where is your Calcutta? Where does life get real for you? How might you show compassion during your Monday? That is today's challenge.

HOW BIG IS YOUR FAITH?

Today's Reading: Matthew 9

Matthew 9 is a chapter that is spilling over with healing and faith. A paralyzed man is brought to Jesus by his friends in verse 2 and Jesus sees the faith of the friends and the paralyzed man walks. A woman with a twelve-year disease is free in an instant. Jesus says to her, "Your faith has made you well" (verse 22). Two blind men finally see through their eyes after Jesus said to them, "It shall be done to you according to your faith" (verse 29).

Faith and healing. Those two things are inseparable.

So many people today need healing in their bodies. It seems that we want our healing, but we have never checked our faith.

We probably should get a handle on faith. This small word is huge. Let's see if we can unpack it in the next few minutes.

Faith has to be a huge thing, if in fact:
- It's how we get saved
- It's how people get healed
- It's how we please God
- It's how we walk the Christian life—even a little still does big things
- It's what makes prayer powerful

Almost everything we do as a Christian has faith involved. So I think we better get a handle on it and realize what it is. Faith . . .
- honors God and God honors faith.
- cashes God's checks.
- won't get you everything you want, but it *will* get you everything that God wants you to have.

Only two times does the Bible devote an entire chapter to one topic. This first is love in 1 Corinthians 13. The second is what we are discussing today—faith, which we find in Hebrews 11. Though we aren't there yet in our 260 journey, today's reading helps us understand the power of faith.

As we see in Matthew 9, God takes faith very seriously. As I've heard it said,

"Faith is like WiFi. It's invisible but it has the power to connect you to what you need!"

You exercise faith everyday. Let's take one example of the doctor and the pharmacist. You go to a doctor whose name you cannot pronounce and whose degrees you have never verified. He gives you a prescription you cannot read. You take it to a pharmacist you have never met. He gives you a chemical compound you do not understand. Then you go home and take the pill according to the instructions on the bottle. All in trusting, sincere faith.

When it comes to your spiritual life, you need faith to get over the hurdle of determining that God exists. You use faith for the next hurdle: Who is this God you gave my life to. Then you face another hurdle that takes faith—fighting the devil as he tries to mess you up on the greatness of God. Why?

Because biblical faith always depends upon its object.

You can have little faith in thick ice and still survive; you can have great faith with thin ice and drown—it's the object that is the issue. The Bible never says to believe only; it's says to believe *on the Lord Jesus Christ*. The Bible never says to have faith only; it says to "have faith *in God*" [Mark 11:22].

So if the God you put your faith in is misconstrued, then so is your faith. The best way to grow faith is to do as Peter tells us, to "in the grace and knowledge of our Lord and Savior Jesus Christ" [2 Peter 3:18]. And the best place to start that growth, in order to know God, is through reading and studying the Word of God.

The Bible is God's bio. The more we read it, the more our faith strengthens.

Faith needs an object. The object—the bulls eye—of our faith is God and who He is.

Your faith is only as great as the God you believe in. He must be the object of your faith. Since God does not change, your faith can still be strong in tough times. You don't need great faith, you need faith in a great God.

As Charles H. Spurgeon once said, "Oh, brethren, be great believers! Little faith will bring your souls to heaven, but great faith will bring heaven to you."[15]

If you grow, or feed, your faith through the Word of God and the knowledge of God, how does Satan attack your faith and try to squelch it? By messing up what you think about God. If you have faith in a small God, then you will have small faith.

How big is your God?

Take a page from this little guy . . .

A little boy was asked, "How many gods are there in the world?

"One God," he replied.

"How do you know that?" said the skeptic.

"Because there is only room for One. Since heaven and earth can't contain Him, how can anyone else fit?"

He is so right. "For our God is the best, far better than competing gods. Why, the skies—the entire cosmos!—can't begin to contain him" (2 Chronicles 2:5-6, MSG).

Tell me what other God can fit, if the entire cosmos is already filled up—with the one true God, Jesus!

Where is *your* faith today?

GOD'S PEOPLE ARE DIFFERENT AND THAT'S GOOD

Today's Reading: Matthew 10

I want to tell you the history of two groups of people who are in the New Testament—the tax collectors and the zealots. The tax collectors were Jews who collected taxes from fellow Jews for the Roman Empire. They made their living by charging an extra amount on top of what everyone owed. Some of them made more than a living. They exacted any amount they could and became well to do. The Jews considered tax collectors to be traitors, because they "stole" money, they became wealthy by collaborating with Roman authorities at the expense of their own people. And their own people hated them.

The Zealots strongly believed that the Romans should not rule their land—and they confronted any opposition directly, even considering violence an appropriate response. Within the Zealots were a subgroup called the Sicarii, or "dagger men." Sicarii were a group of rebels, most widely known today as the group who fought against the Roman authorities and took Masada, Herod's famous fortress in the desert. Today we would call them first-century terrorists. They murdered in the name of religion. And they hated traitors— more specifically, tax collectors.

Zealots were the terrorists. Tax collectors were the traitors. Put those two together, and it isn't going to be good. Call 911.

And that's where we find ourselves in today's reading:

Jesus summoned His twelve disciples and gave them authority over unclean spirits, to cast them out, and to heal every kind of disease and every kind of sickness. Now the names of the twelve apostles are these: The first, Simon, who is called Peter, and Andrew his brother; and James the son of Zebedee, and John his brother; Philip and Bartholomew; Thomas and *Matthew the tax collector*; James the son of Alphaeus, and Thaddaeus; *Simon the Zealot*, and Judas Iscariot, the one who betrayed Him. These twelve Jesus sent out after instructing them. (Matthew 10:1-5, emphasis added)

Think about that. Jesus put a zealot and a tax collector close to each other as His disciples. Out of the twelve disciples, two of them were from sworn enemies of each other: Simon the Zealot and Matthew the tax collector. Matthew 10 even labels them for us, so we know of the potential conflict. And Jesus specifically called each of them to follow Him and to work and live together. It wasn't an accident or a mistake. He did that *on purpose*!

What does that have to do with you and me? Our tendency is to hang out with people we like and who are like us. Think about your church. If you choose a church based upon the people whom you have stuff in common with, then you want a club not a church.

What I love about Jesus' disciple list is that it doesn't say, "Peter, a fisherman; John, a fisherman; Simon, a fisherman . . ." Their descriptions show us that Jesus chose people who couldn't be more opposite.

God can put you with people who irritate you. That is how sandpaper works. You get rubbed so the rough edges come off of you, you can be smooth, and you become more like Christ.

You don't grow by being with people who are just like you. (You become boring but you don't grow.) Oswald Chambers explained it this way: "God can never make us wine if we object to the fingers He uses to crush us with. If God would only use His own fingers and make us wine. But when He uses someone whom we dislike, and makes those the crushers . . . we object."[16]

God may have put the tax collector with the zealot in your church. Why? Because this is a church, not a club. Because the church is about making people become more like Christ. It represents Jesus' loves and not your likes. And He loves everyone—even the people you might think are the worst.

So the next time your zealot nature sits next to an irritating tax collector, think about how Jesus may have placed that person in your life to make you a stronger Christian. Or put another way, when your "I was raised in a Christian home all my life" sits next to a brand new saved person who smells like his struggle, don't think, *That person bothers me*. Think, *That person sanctifies me*.

Then rejoice over the fact that God is using *you* to sanctify somebody else.

How Exclamations Turn into Question Marks

Today's Reading: Matthew 11

Conditions or circumstances can affect perspectives. What goes on in our lives can determine our points of view and how we define important things—most seriously, our view and definition of God. Sometimes our circumstances can take us from living an exclamation-mark life to living a question-mark life.

Let me give you an example of what I mean. John the Baptist was an exclamation man. He was known as a prophet who called people to repent of their sins and baptized them. He's most well-known, however, as the one who baptized Jesus.

Read the following verses about him from the book of John—and pay close attention to John the Baptist's punctuation:

The next day he saw Jesus coming to him and said, "Behold, the Lamb of God who takes away the sin of the world! (John 1:29)

Again the next day John was standing with two of his disciples, and he looked at Jesus as He walked, and said, "Behold, the Lamb of God!" (John 1:35-36)

We see two exclamation-point verses here. He speaks with certainty and confidence. But then something happens. A change in John's circumstances began to change his perspective: "When John, while imprisoned, heard of the works of Christ, he sent word by his disciples and said to Him, "Are You the Expected One, or shall we look for someone else?" (Matthew 11:2-3).

What happened to the exclamation points? John went from an exclamation to a question. And it all hinged on two words—two *huge* words: "*John . . . imprisoned.*"

These two words changed his perspective on Jesus. His exclamation points got punched in the gut and doubled over into a question mark. That's what a question mark is—an exclamation point that got punched in the gut.

Here's what John needed to know and what we need to remember:
- We change, but God doesn't.
- Circumstances change, but God doesn't.
- Life changes, but God doesn't.

If Jesus was the Lamb of God two years earlier, John's imprisonment doesn't change who Jesus is. Our circumstances can't make God any different.

John let being in prison decide his definition of Jesus. Don't let whatever circumstances arise in your life define Christ.

I'm in trouble.
I'm in debt.
I'm in a divorce.
I'm in a wheelchair.
I'm in court today.
I'm in rehab.
I'm in hot water.
I'm in therapy.
I'm incarcerated.

Those are circumstances; those don't define who Christ is. Know that with all that going on, you can still be in Christ. The "in Christ" part of you doesn't change—no matter your situation—because He doesn't change. As the writer of Hebrews assures us: "Jesus Christ is the same yesterday, today, and forever" (Hebrews 13:8, TLB).

Jesus' response to (and about) John is pretty amazing:

This is the one about whom it is written, 'BEHOLD, I SEND MY MESSENGER AHEAD OF YOU, WHO WILL PREPARE YOUR WAY BEFORE YOU.' Truly I say to you, among those born of women there has not arisen anyone greater than John the Baptist! (Matthew 11:10-11)

John was in the worst position he had ever been in. And Jesus said that this did not change what He thought about him. Jesus was saying, *When your exclamation-mark life changes to a question-mark life, I am still who I AM and I do not change my exclamation-mark feelings about you. Just because you doubt Me doesn't mean I doubt My love for you and what I think of you.*

Even in your worst state, you are still the greatest to God. Jesus gave the highest statement of John after John gave Him the lowest statement. John asked, "Who are You really?" And Jesus responded that no one has been born greater than John. That's pretty amazing, right?

So if your Sunday exclamation point got punched in the gut on Monday, straighten up and remember that God is still the same.

TAKING MY 18,000 REAL SERIOUSLY

Today's Reading: Matthew 12

While I am writing today's devotional, a television show about Jack Ryan, the fictional CIA analyst, is trending online. Some knew him as Harrison Ford; for others, he was Chris Pine; and for us old folks, we knew him as Alec Baldwin. Jack Ryan is Tom Clancy's creation. And those actors portrayed him in the movie versions of Clancy's thriller books, such as *Hunt for Red October, Patriot Games, Clear and Present Danger, The Sum of All Fears, Without Remorse*. His works are always very thick, about five hundred to seven hundred pages long. There are a half million to three-quarter million words in an average Tom Clancy novel.

How long would it take you to say as many words as he writes in one of his books? According to researchers, people open their mouths an average of seven hundred times in a day. In those seven hundred times, you will use an average of eighteen thousand words a day. Those eighteen thousands words translate to about fifty-four printed pages. That means that in one year, an average person would fill . . . sixty-six books of eight hundred pages each. Every year you write with your words sixty-six volumes that are larger than those Tom Clancy novels.

That's a lot of words! And what makes it even more impressive is that each of those words matter.

Why do those eighteen thousand words each day matter? We find the answer in the Old Testament book of Proverbs: "Death and life are in the power of the tongue" (18:21). Another version says it like this: "Words kill, words give life; they're either poison or fruit—you choose" (MSG).

That's why we take our eighteen thousand really seriously.

So here's the question: What is your life-and-death ratio on your eighteen thousand?

Is it that big of a deal? Let's see what Jesus said about it in today's reading:

For the mouth speaks out of that which fills the heart. The good man brings out of *his* good treasure what is good; and the evil man brings out of *his* evil treasure what is evil. But I tell you that every careless out of *his* evil treasure what is evil. But I tell you that every careless word that people speak, they shall give an accounting for it in the day of Judgment. For by your words you will be justified, and by your words you will be condemned. [Matthew 12:34-37]

You and I will be held accountable for every careless word we speak, so yes, we definitely need to take our eighteen thousand seriously. It's a scary thought, isn't it? God thinks our words are so important and can make such a difference in someone's life that he holds us accountable for them.

Proverbs 12:25 tells us, "Anxiety in a man's heart weighs it down, But a good word makes it glad." So here's a challenge for you: give someone a good word today.

Text it, say it, write it. But choose your words to bring life.

Recently my family and I were traveling. As we sat together on the long flight, I watched my youngest daughter write a five-sentence note of thanks to the flight attendant. My daughter wanted to give life with her words.

One good word can change anxiety into gladness. Your words have that capability. Do something useful with your eighteen thousand today.

WHY IS IT HARD FOR ME TO READ THE BIBLE?

Today's Reading: Matthew 13

Every day as you read one chapter of the New Testament, the goal is more than just experiencing a feeling of accomplishment but to grow and become more like Christ. Sometimes when you struggle to find time for God's Word, it isn't because you're busy, it is because you're experiencing spiritual warfare!

This book is a supernatural book and changes people's lives. That's why it's hard to read the Bible. Jesus explained about this in today's Scripture reading. In Matthew 13, Jesus told seven parables, or Kingdom stories. The most famous parable in this chapter is called the sower and the seed. Jesus used the surroundings of the people, more specifically the agricultural fields, to explain the battle that goes on to stop the Word of God from taking root in people's lives and changing them.

> Behold, the sower went out to sow; and as he sowed, some *seed*s fell beside the road, and the birds came and ate them up. Others fell on the rocky places, where they did not have much soil; and immediately they sprang up, because they had no depth of soil. But when the sun had risen, they were scorched; and because they had no root, they withered away. Others fell among the thorns, and the thorns came up and choked them out. And others fell on the good soil and yielded a crop, some a hundredfold, some sixty, and some thirty. He who has ears let him hear. (Matthew 13:3-9)

His big point was this: Satan sees what God's Word can do in people's lives and so he will do whatever he can to stop it from producing in you.

The seed being planted in the story is the Bible, God's Word, and it faces challenges to take root and produce.

Challenge #1: the devil. That is the seed on the roadside. The moment you read the Bible or listen to a sermon, Satan waits to steal that Word because it is powerful. Sin will keep you from the Bible or the Bible will keep you from sin.

Challenge #2: difficulties. That is the seed that takes root but does not go deep. The way you win against difficulties is through depth. Go deep in God. Go deep in His Word.

Challenge #3: distractions. Jesus said the weeds that choke the seeds are the worries of the world and deceitfulness of riches. If you're too busy to read the Bible, you're too busy.

And yet there are those who will get through these hurdles and produce fruit with their lives. Jesus called them seeds that grow in good soil and produce a good crop—a good God-honoring life.

The devil will challenge every word and chapter you read in the Bible, because he knows what it can do. When you signed up for this 260 Journey, you also signed up for a battle. But it's a winnable battle!

If you want to win at it, start treating your Bible like you treat your cell phone. Ever wonder what would happen if we did that?

- What if we carried it around in our purses or pockets?
- What if we scrolled through it several times a day?
- What if we turned back to get it if we forgot it?
- What if we used it to receive messages from the text?
- What if we treated it as though we couldn't live without it?
- What if we gave it to kids as gifts?
- What if we used it when we traveled?
- What if we used it in case of emergency?

And something even better: unlike our cell phones, we don't have to worry about our Bible being disconnected, because Jesus already paid the bill.

The best protection against Satan's lies is to know God's truth. The next time you find yourself struggling to read the Bible, remember who's behind that struggle and then remember that you were meant for the good soil.

WHEN SOMEONE I LOVE DIES

Today's Reading: Matthew 14

As he awaited his death as a prisoner in a Nazi concentration camp, the famed theologian, pastor, and Christian martyr, Dietrich Bonhoeffer, wrote a letter about losing people we love. He wrote, in part:

> There is nothing that can replace the absence of someone dear to us, and one should not even attempt to do so. One must simply hold out and endure it. At first that sounds very hard, but at the same time it is also a great comfort. For to the extent the emptiness truly remains unfilled one remains connected to the other person through it. It is wrong to say that God fills the emptiness. God in no way fills it but much more leaves it precisely unfilled and thus helps us preserve - even in pain - the authentic relationship. Furthermore, the more beautiful and full the remembrances, the more difficult the separation. But gratitude transforms the torment of memory into silent joy. One bears what was lovely in the past not as a thorn but as a precious gift deep within, a hidden treasure of which one can always be certain.[17]

I love this statement: "Gratitude transforms the torment of memory into silent joy." Gratitude helps us deal with loss. Jesus showed us one other way to deal with the grief that accompanies the loss of people we love—compassion.

In today's reading we see that Jesus faced loss:

> When Jesus heard *about John*, He withdrew from there in a boat to a secluded place by Himself; and when the people heard of *this*, they followed Him on foot from the cities. When He went ashore, He saw a large crowd, and felt compassion for them and healed their sick. (Matthew 14:13-14)

John the Baptist was Jesus' cousin. John was murdered because of a crazed and convicted adulterer and a robot of a dancing daughter. She danced before Herod, who became so intoxicated with this sensual dance, he offered her whatever she wanted. The little girl went to her mom for her advice on what to ask for. Her mother hated John because he had confronted and condemned her for sleeping with the king. She told her daughter to demand John's head on a platter. Can you be more vindictive than that?

So Herod gave the order and had John the Baptist beheaded.

When Jesus heard the news, He withdrew out of grief and sorrow. He went to a lonely place by Himself. He wanted to be alone. Tragic death paralyzes.

The big problem for Jesus was that though He wanted to be alone to grieve and process His loss, the multitudes wanted His healing. When they realized where He had gone, they followed Him.

Now consider this . . . when He saw them, He felt compassion for them. He did not say, "Hey, I need some time alone. Let's do this next Thursday." Even in His deep grief, He felt something when He saw them and their needs.

This is instructive to us. This is one of the great ways to overcome our grief when we have lost a loved one. Our tendency leads us toward loneliness: "I just want to be alone," "Give me some private time," "I don't want to see anyone or talk to anyone," "Just leave me alone."

Jesus was alone, but He shows us that compassion trumps grief.

The way out of the grief funk is not through a season of loneliness but through ministering to others. When you start to tend to others' needs, God heals you and takes care of you. The passage says, "He healed their sick." We would say, "I need healing."

Among all the "professional Christian counseling" and "grief counselors," I've never heard them tell us in the midst of our grief to "go help others."

Seclusion does not fix you. It's dangerous to be left alone with your thoughts when you suffer great loss. It is in giving that you receive.

FIGHTING TO GET MY ANSWER

Today's Reading: Matthew 15

Abraham Lincoln famously stated, "I have been driven many times to my knees by the overwhelming conviction that I had absolutely no other place to go."[18] In today's reading, we find a woman who had absolutely no other place to go but on her knees in front of the Son of God. This has to be the craziest story on prayer in the entire New Testament. Sometimes it's a fight to get an answer to prayer and prayer can seem like a wrestling match. In fact Paul used one of the Greek words for prayer when he wrote in Colossians 4:12 (CSB): "Epaphras, who is one of you, a servant of Christ Jesus, sends you greetings. He is always wrestling for you in his prayers."

Wrestling in prayer for you. The Greek word is *agonizomai*. What does that sound like? Agonizing. That is what we see in today's story.

They call her "The Syrophoenician Woman."

> Jesus . . . withdrew into the district of Tyre and Sidon. And a Canaanite woman from that region came out and *began* to cry out, saying, "Have mercy on me, Lord, Son of David; my daughter is cruelly demon-possessed." But He did not answer her a word. And His disciples came and implored Him, saying, "Send her away, because she keeps shouting at us." But He answered and said, "I was sent only to the lost sheep of the house of Israel." But she came and began to bow down before Him, saying, "Lord, help me!" And He answered and said, "It is not good to take the children's bread and throw it to the dogs." But she said, "Yes, Lord; but even the dogs feed on the crumbs which fall from their masters' table." Then Jesus said to her, "O woman, your faith is great; it shall be done for you as you wish." And her daughter was healed at once. (Matthew 15:21-28)

This woman participated in a wrestling match to get her demon-possessed daughter healed. The end of the story was that she received what she asked for. The journey there, though, is worth discussing.

This Gentile woman came to Jesus and faced three big hurdles to get her answer—three hurdles we too must wrestle through if we want to experience a breakthrough in our prayers, especially when we're involved in a wrestling match for someone else's deliverance.

An old preacher friend used to say that we must "pray the price."

And this woman did.

The first hurdle she had to overcome is *receiving silence*. When she begged God for an answer, "He did not answer her a word" [verse 23].

Can we pray when we feel like nothing is being heard or responded to? This woman was crying and getting nothing. This is one of the battles we face in prayer. We're doing all the talking but not hearing anything back.

Do we stop?

Do we give up?

I think it's a test. As Rick Warren says, "The teacher is always silent when the test is given."[19] God wants to know how serious we are.

The second hurdle is *being overlooked for others*.

Jesus told his disciples, "I was sent only to the lost sheep of the house of Israel" [verse 24]. He spoke but not to her. She had to overhear what Jesus said. She did not even get a direct word. She was listening to Jesus explain and speak to others.

Others are getting God but not you. Can you get over the hurdle when God does for others before He does for you?

Still she did not stop.

The third hurdle is getting a *standard answer but not the answer*.

Jesus told her, "It's not good to take the children's bread and give it to the dogs" [verse 26]. These seem like harsh words but they were simply standard lines. The children's bread is what God gave to Israel. Dogs is what Israel called all non-Jews. She was listening to standard lines.

Instead of being offended, she fought through the standard answers everyone hears. Still she didn't give up. She told Him, essentially, "All this is good but I need my daughter healed."

And Jesus' response? "'O woman, your faith is great; it shall be done for you as you wish.' And her daughter was healed at once" [verse 28].

Prayer is wrestling. And to get your answer, you have to fight on when you receive silence.

You have to fight on when everyone else is getting an answer and you are being overlooked.

You have to fight on when you receive only standard answers.

You fight on. Just as the woman did, you don't give up, you don't stop praying. Keep wrestling!

SOME DAYS SIMON, SOME DAYS PETER, AND SOME DAYS SATAN

Today's Reading: Matthew 16

Poor Alexander. He was having a terrible, horrible, no good, very bad day. Maybe you've read about his day?

From the moment he woke up, one terrible thing after another horrible thing happened to him. From finding gum in his hair to tripping over his skateboard to dropping his sweater in the sink while the water was running. And when his brothers found wonderful prizes in their cereal boxes, Alexander found . . . nothing.

On his way to school, he was squished in the center seat, and at school his teacher picked on him. After school he had a dentist appointment and the dentist found Alexander had a cavity.

And on and on it went—one catastrophe after another. Alexander decides he wants to move to Australia, where they probably never have bad days—but his mom tells him they do have bad days there too. What a terrible, horrible, no good, very bad day Alexander had.

Alexander had a bad day. Australians have a bad day. And what's not hard to believe is that Christians do too. We have no promises from God that once you and I become a Christian, all our days are always going to be great. But somehow we forget that when we have bad days!

In today's reading, we see a disciple who had a great day—and then he had terrible, horrible, no good, very bad day. Or to put it another way, he had a Simon day, a Peter day, and a Satan day—all in one day.

You already read this chapter, but let's take another look at Matthew 16:

"Who do you say that I am?" Simon Peter answered, "You are the Christ, the Son of the living God." And Jesus said to him, "Blessed are you, Simon Barjona, because flesh and blood did not reveal *this* to you, but My Father who is in heaven. I also say to you that you are Peter, and upon this rock I will build My church; and the gates of Hades will not overpower it. (verses 15-18)

Wow! Jesus changed Simon's name based on his revelation of Jesus. None of the other disciples had this happen.

But then Peter had his name changed again. This is where it becomes the terrible, horrible, no good, very bad day:

> Jesus began to show His disciples that He must go to Jerusalem, and suffer many things from the elders and chief priests and scribes, and be killed, and be raised up on the third day. Peter took Him aside and began to rebuke Him, saying, "God forbid it, Lord! This shall never happen to You." But He turned and said to Peter, "Get behind Me, Satan! You are a stumbling block to Me; for you are not setting your mind on God's interests, but man's." (verses 21-23)

What a change—from Simon to Peter to Satan. Have you ever feel like that? You're going along having a Simon day (ordinary), and something happens in which you move to a Peter day (revelation that God is awesome), and then all of a sudden you get smacked with a Satan day (get behind Me).

In all of those days, though, you are loved by God. Your worst day does not make you any less accepted by God. The prodigal son covered in mud never stopped being a son, did he? He was still loved by his father. Jesus didn't stop loving Peter, did He? No. And the same is true of you.

Author Brennan Manning does a good job of giving us a glimpse into the revolutionary love of God: "His love is never, never, never based on our performance, never conditioned by our moods—of elation or depression. The furious love of God knows no shadow of alteration or change. It is always reliable. And always tender."

I read those words while traveling from Queens to Brooklyn on the F Train, and I started crying.

The revolutionary thinking that God loves me as I am and not as I should be requires radical rethinking and profound emotional readjustment. Our religion never begins with what we do for God. It always starts with what God has done for us, the great and wondrous things that God dreamed of and achieved for us in Christ Jesus.

What makes Jesus amazing is that He absolutely knows you and me and every evil and wicked thought and not only accepts us but furiously loves us— even when we mess up.

Your behavior does not dictate His behavior. He is who He is. He doesn't change based on who you are. Your actions don't control His character. Second

Timothy 2:13 tells us, "If we are unfaithful, he remains faithful, for he cannot deny who he is" (NLT).

I love this verse! He cannot deny who He is. God is absolutely consistent. He can't be anything but who He is. Your bad day does not change God.

Regardless of how your day will go today or if it already went, there is one unchanging thought to carry with you:

We change, we get moody . . . but God is always the same, which means no matter what kind of day you're having, He loves you.

Day 17

A PRIVATE "WHY"

Today's Reading: Matthew 17

If you had a chance to ask God a "why?" question, what would you ask him? *Why did this bad thing happen to me? Why did my mom pass away?*

How about a personal failure question? That's what we find in Matthew 17! The disciples failed at something they were empowered to do and did not know why they'd failed.

The disciples had tried to heal a young man and were unable. So the man brought his son to Jesus. Let's pick up the story:

> "Lord, have mercy on my son, for he is a lunatic and is very ill; for he often falls into the fire and often into the water. I brought him to your disciples, and they could not cure him." And Jesus answered and said, "You unbelieving and perverted generation, how long shall I be with you? How long shall I put up with you? Bring him here to me." And Jesus rebuked him, and the demon came out of him, and the boy was cured at once.
>
> Then the disciples came to Jesus privately and said, "Why could we not drive it out?" And He said to them, "Because of the littleness of your faith; for truly I say to you, if you have faith the size of a mustard seed, you will say to this mountain, 'Move from here to there,' and it will move; and nothing will be impossible to you. But this kind does not go out except by prayer and fasting." (verses 15-21)

Verse 19 highlights the private *why*—"Why couldn't we drive the demon out?"

I love that the disciples asked this question. People don't do this today when they finish a task. It's rare to find someone asking for critique to get better, but these disciples did. We live in a culture that will blame others but not inspect ourselves.

Jesus' answer is astounding and multi-layered:
* The big issue Jesus says is: faith.
* The problem is the size of it: it's little.

• Because of that: failure.

Jesus refers to mustard-seed faith: if the mustard seed is little and that's all you need to get big stuff moving, then you're not in the ballpark of "little faith." Your faith is smaller than little, it's microscopic because nothing got changed.

And then he tells you what can get you microscopic faith kick-started and moving toward little: prayer and fasting.

Faith is not a concept about God. Faith is like a lens on how big we see God. When Jesus spoke about prayer and fasting as His follow-up to their little faith failure, He said that prayer and fasting will help get the God lenses on.

How? It's about connecting fasting to prayer. Does fasting make God big? Not really.

Fasting is not a hunger strike to get God's attention. Fasting *creates space* for God. To make a meal during this time period was not going to Whole Foods or Costco, it was an all-day affair from killing an animal and cooking it. Fasting meant creating space to pray, space for God.

When someone fasts they are giving God more time, and when you get more time with God, trust me, God gets bigger. That's why I believe you can fast from many different types of things and not just food—social media, television, certain activities—to create space for prayer.

How do you deal with demons? Not by deliverance classes and learning crazy ways to deal with the dark world. Create more space for God by fasting. When you do that, God gets bigger. When God gets bigger, faith starts getting bigger. And when faith gets bigger, then mountains (and demons) start moving.

The way you get a grain of faith is by praying and fasting. A private "why" did not help only the disciples. What great insight for us to have when we need some movement on things that won't budge.

An Incredible Promise of His Presence

Today's Reading: Matthew 18

When I was working toward my undergrad degree in corporate finance, the students would say cash is king. When I was doing my graduate work in theology, the students would say context is king.

So many Bible verses get their punch from context, not from a denominational bent. One of those punchy passages is in Matthew 18. I couldn't tell you how many prayer meetings I have attended where not many people showed up and the pastor said, "All I know is that Jesus said where two or three are gathered together there I am in that place."

I have this sneaky suspicion that Jesus was not giving us a sentence we can use when we have bad attendance—where we just quote Matthew 18:20, and everyone is content and off the hook.

Let's be honest, the Bible is full of people who met God by themselves and not with two or three people.

But context is king. This verse ends Jesus' huge thought on fixing a broken relationship. Listen to the verses connected with it:

> If your brother sins, go and show him his fault in private; if he listens to you, you have won your brother. But if he does not listen *to you*, take one or two more with you, so that BY THE MOUTH OF TWO OR THREE WITNESSES EVERY FACT MAY BE CONFIRMED. If he refuses to listen to them, tell it to the church . . . For where two or three have gathered together in My name, I am there in their midst. (Matthew 18:15-17, 20)

Two important thoughts:

1. It's interesting that Jesus used the word *church* only twice in the entire Bible. One was in the chapter before that the gates of hell can't prevail against His church. And second, when dealing with broken relationships. Devils and broken relationships . . . think about that—two of the church's biggest enemies.

2. In the powerful context of two or three being gathered, I believe Jesus was saying more than encouraging us when there's bad attendance. He was saying, "When you choose to fix a relationship in My house, and do it the right

way, I want you to know that when you get the parties in the room, My presence plans on being there." What an incredible promise.

The Bible reminds us over and over that we not only need God in our lives, we need people to be part of our lives as well. God wired us that way and designed life in such a way that life works better with people rather than in isolation. Relational isolation is especially dangerous. Just because it's difficult doesn't mean we give up on community.

To be certain, important and vital relationships, though they bring joy to our lives, can also have the potential of bring pain and conflict. Conflict in and of itself is not bad, but *unresolved* conflict is. Unresolved conflict creates a toxic environment.

I think that's why Peter responds to Jesus' words with this question: "Lord, how often shall my brother sin against me and I forgive him? Up to seven times?" (verse 21).

Jesus didn't let him off the hook. He told him, "I do not say to you, up to seven times, but up to seventy times seven" (verse 22).

Remember this math equation that Jesus brought up, seventy times seven?

It has to do with forgiveness. It's connected to how often should I forgive my brother. Sounds like everyone has an account of 490 offenses with each other. I think C. S. Lewis gave the best insight on this idea: "We need to forgive our brother seventy times seven not only for 490 offenses but for one offense."

To forgive for the moment is not difficult. But to go on forgiving, to forgive the same offense again every time it recurs to the memory—there's the real tussle.

We forgive . . . and a week later some chain of thought carries us back to the original offense, and we discover the old resentment blazing away again. And we forgive again.

Wow, what an insight! Seventy times seven is not forgiving 490 different offenses but forgiving one offense 490 times. Forgiving over and over when our mind is plagued.

When the two or three whom Jesus is talking about try to work out an issue between them, Jesus says in essence, "Plan on Me being in attendance, because this is really important." Jesus is not only committed to your relationship with Him, He is committed to healthy relationships with the others who are in your life, even if takes 490 times to get it right and resolved inside and out.

DO YOU KNOW SOMEONE WHO NEEDS TO BE SAVED?

Today's Reading: Matthew 19

J. C. Ryle wrote, "The highest form of selfishness is a man content to go to heaven alone."[20] I don't ever want to be content to go to heaven alone. I want to take as many as I can with me. But I have some hard cases in my relationship circle that need a miracle. I bet you do too. If you know someone who needs to be saved, fortunately, today's reading in Matthew 19 gives us hope.

Listen to what Jesus said about God: "With people this is impossible, but with God all things are possible" (verse 26).

With God all things are possible. *All* things! This is a powerful promise, because of what this verse is connected to. It is a response to a question, which makes this amazing verse even more amazing. It follows after Jesus personally invited a very rich young and powerful man known as the rich young ruler to follow Him. But the man refused. Let's look at the story in context:

> Jesus said to him, "If you wish to be complete, go *and* sell your possessions and give to the poor, and you will have treasure in heaven; and come, follow me." But when the young man heard this statement, he went away grieving; for he was one who owned much property. And Jesus said to His disciples, "Truly I say to you, it is hard for a rich man to enter the kingdom of heaven." (verses 21-23)

And then came the question: "When the disciples heard this, they were very astonished and said, 'Then who can be saved?'" (verse 25).

They were probably thinking of others who needed to follow Jesus, and asked this profound question. Our question will be more like this: "Will my mother, my father, my family ever get saved?" And the answer to that question is . . .

With God all things are possible!

Who do you want to be saved? Who have you been praying for? Over their name declare: "With God all things are possible."

Those words are for your unsaved loved ones every time you think there is no way. That is the context that gives hope for us who have people we really want to become Christians. Think of the hardest case and the most helpless condition and then announce to hell and Satan, "With God all things are possible!"

Corrie ten Boom said it like this: "If all things are possible with God, then all things are possible to him who believes in Him."[21]

If God is all you have, then you have all you need.

GOD'S GENEROSITY GOES BEYOND WHAT'S FAIR

Today's Reading: Matthew 20

Inevitably when someone well known dies, I get asked, "Do you think that person is in heaven?" Before I respond, I always think of John Newton, the eighteenth-century former slave ship captain who became an abolitionist and clergyman. He said, "If I ever reach heaven I expect to find three wonders there: first, to meet some I had not thought to see there; second, to miss some I had expected to see there; and third, the greatest wonder of all, to find myself there."[22]

With that thought in mind, I tell the person a story:

"Let's say you knew a guy named Rudy who was from the worst part of town. Rudy grew up with no father and no discipline in the home, and from an early age he got in trouble with the law. As a kid, he stole candy; by the time he was a teenager, he'd worked up to stealing cars. Into his early adulthood, he broke into people's homes. During one break-in, he discovered the residents at home and he killed them. He got convicted and sentenced to death. You also knew the people he killed, so you attended the execution. He saw him enter the room, then walk behind a curtain for his execution. Question: Does that thief who killed those people go to heaven?"

The person always responds, "Of course not. I knew him till the end. He didn't repent."

But then I add a twist and change the scenario.

"Okay," I tell the person. "On that day three executions were scheduled simultaneously in that room. Rudy and one other man were thieves. The third was a deranged man who claimed He was God. Just before Rudy died, he had a conversation with the so-called deranged man, in which he heard something about paradise and he accepted the man at His word. Did he go to heaven?"

The person typically knows the "right" answer: that Rudy went to heaven. But I can see the confusion and frustration on the person's face, especially because of the sins Rudy committed. Inevitably, the person is grappling with the fairness of it all.

Surely he can't be in heaven, the person thinks. *He was a thief and a murderer. How is that fair?*

And yet this twist in the story is not made up. It happened at Calvary. A life of sin and selfishness was altered in seconds—all because the thief talked to the Middle Man.

Jesus is our middle man—the one whose sacrifice made a way for us to go to heaven. No matter who the person is or what they have done, on the day they die, they enter heaven and walk on streets of gold.

Before that scene at Calvary even happened, Jesus prepared us for the reality of salvation with this parable, what we call a little story with a big meaning, which comes from today's reading, Matthew 20:1–16 (NIV).

Jesus compared the kingdom of heaven to a vineyard owner who hired workers early in the morning and agreed to pay them a certain amount of money, a denarius, for their day's wages.

Around midmorning, the vineyard owner caught sight of some others who were loitering in the marketplace, so he offered them work and set wages to tend to his vineyard. He rounded up more workers at noon, at midafternoon, and in the early evening, offering the same work for a set wage.

At quitting time, the owner directed his foreman to summon the workers, starting with the last group, and to pay them their wages. Each group received a denarius. By the time the foreman summoned the first group who had worked all day, they believed they should receive more wages because they had worked longer. And yet the foreman handed each person a denarius.

The men in the first group complained to the owner, saying it wasn't fair that the last group of men, who only worked a brief time, received the same amount they received. "We worked harder and longer. We dealt with the heat of the day! How is this fair?"

But the owner explained that he wasn't being unfair. They had agreed to work for the set amount. "I want to give the one who was hired last the same as I gave you. Don't I have the right to do what I want with my own money? Or are you envious because I am generous?"

Jesus ended his parable by saying, "So the last will be first, and the first will be last" (Matthew 20:1-16).

I was born again at a very young age, so I am part of that first group of workers Jesus talked about. And one day my payment will be heaven and eternal life.

Others are part of the last group, what I call the eleventh-hour person.

They won't work as long as I and others in the earlier groups have worked. But here's their payment: heaven and eternal life. They will receive that payment even if they repent of their sins and accept Jesus mere moments before they take their final breath. They receive exactly the same payment.

How is that fair? You may think. You've worked hard, lived a good life, followed all the rules, so how is it fair that some guy who lived a terrible life gets the same reward when he seeks forgiveness within moments of his death?

Jesus explains that the reward is given because God is generous.

So if you are wondering about the eternal destination of a friend whom you knew to be hardened toward God for all of his life, wait to pass that judgment. You don't know what happened in the eleventh hour, you don't know if the Holy Spirit got through to him. Remember that a thief got into heaven in the eleventh hour. Your friend may have that same experience. All because of God's amazing generosity.

TWO HURDLES AWAY FROM MOVING A MOUNTAIN

Today's Reading: Matthew 21

Theologian John Calvin said, "To know God as the Master and Bestower of all good things, who invites us to request them of Him, and still not go to Him and ask of Him—this would be of as little profit as for a man to neglect a treasure, buried and hidden in the earth, after it had been pointed out to him and he had the map."

Jesus gave us a map and it's called prayer. Right after Jesus spoke to a fig tree because it had no fruit, the "marveling" disciples asked, "How?" How did Jesus speak to that thing that was not producing fruit? And then Jesus revealed two treasure map verses:

> Jesus answered and said to them, "Truly I say to you, if you have faith and do not doubt, you will not only do what was done to the fig tree, but even if you say to this mountain, 'Be taken up and cast into the sea,' it will happen. And all things you ask in prayer, believing, you will receive. (Matthew 21:21-22)

All things you ask in prayer, believing . . . you will receive. There are only two hurdles to get over in order to get to receive: (1) you must ask and (2) you must believe. They seem simple but they are challenges we all face.

Hurdle #1: Asking

Statistics suggest the average Christian spends three to seven minutes a day in prayer. Our asking is limited today. If "asking" is what gets us to receive, we are not even asking very well.

C. S. Lewis may have captured the enemy's plan for the Christian in his *Screwtape Letters*, a fictional letter of instruction to the demon Wormwood: "Interfere at any price and in any fashion when people start to pray, for real prayer is lethal to our cause."[23]

F. B. Meyer said it like this: "The greatest tragedy of life is not unanswered prayer, but unoffered prayer."[24] Let's make a commitment to fight busyness and get to prayer.

Hurdle #2: Believing

There is a difference between believing someone and believing in someone. The first one deals with existence. The second deals with character and who they are.

To have faith in God is to believe He is and who He said He is.

Suppose you tell a friend you have faith in her. What does that mean? It means two things. First, you are sure the person you are talking to actually exists. And second, you are convinced she is trustworthy; you can believe what she says and trust in her character. Believing in prayer is believing who God said He is. Faith honors God and God honors faith. Faith cashes God's checks. Faith in God will not get you everything you want, but it *will* get you everything God wants you to have.

CHANGE STARTS WITH LOVE

Today's Reading: Matthew 22

The Bible never says you have to believe with all your heart, even though it says you must believe in your heart. But when it comes to loving God—that must be done with all the heart.

I think God leaves room for growing faith and doubts that come with belief. But when it comes to love, we can make a choice immediately. Love is our greatest weapon against sin.

Nineteenth-century Scottish theologian Thomas Chalmers wrote, "The only way to dispossess the heart of an old affection is through the expulsive power of a new one—the expulsive power of a new affection."

How do you get rid of an old boyfriend? Get a bigger boyfriend. Jesus is the bigger boyfriend.

So when Jesus was asked about the greatest commandment, He did not start with, "Thou shall not . . ." or "Thou shall . . ." Jesus started with love. "Jesus declared, "LOVE THE Lord YOUR God WITH ALL YOUR HEART AND WITH ALL YOUR SOUL AND WITH ALL YOUR MIND" [Matthew 22:37].

If you get loving God right, loving your neighbor is easy—because it all starts with God and loving Him.

So many people want to change today. Change must have a starting point. To change a life without first addressing the core becomes futile. To educate and to try to reprogram without dealing with the love issue is a dead end. Why?

What you love you will do. What you love you will sacrifice for. What you love you will make time for. If you love your boyfriend, you will sacrifice all to be with him. If you love baseball, you will find a way to play year round or watch year round. If you love your spouse, you will sacrifice to please him or her. Change starts with love. Change starts with asking the question, "What do I love most?" And the answer could startle us.

Jesus said, "LOVE THE Lord YOUR God WITH ALL YOUR HEART AND WITH ALL YOU SOUL AND WITH ALL YOUR MIND." Everything self-corrects from there. To pursue Christianity without love does not last long. So pray each day that you will love God with all your heart, soul, and mind. Because when you love, the other stuff naturally follows.

Start with love today. To try to change stuff without loving God is not change, it is conformity and it won't last long. A friend of C. S. Lewis asked him, "Is it easy to love God?" Lewis answered, "It is easy to those who do it."[25] Christianity is not easy for those who don't love God but love church, love being moral, love the atmosphere. When you fall deeply in love, you want to please the Beloved. And that's when real change will occur.

HYPOCRITE!

Today's Reading: Matthew 23

Today's reading is an intense chapter. It's about hypocrites and religion—hypocrites in religion. In fact, Jesus said, "Woe to you hypocrites and religious people" eight times! (See verses 13-16, 23, 25, 27, and 29) The word *woe* is an expression of how dreadful and how awful this is—to take something as powerful as God and pretend.

This is the argument of so many people who don't want to go to church or be a Christian: "The church is full of hypocrites! That is why I don't believe, that is why I don't go to church." To put it another way: Christians say they have Jesus, but we don't see much of Him in their lives. If Jesus is in them, then He must be hiding.

In his autobiography Mahatma Gandhi wrote that during his student days he read the Gospels seriously and considered converting to Christianity. He believed that in the teachings of Jesus he could find the solution to the caste system that was dividing the people of India. So one Sunday he decided to attend services at a nearby church and talk to the minister about becoming a Christian. When he entered the sanctuary, however, the usher refused to give him a seat and suggested that he worship with his own people. Gandhi left the church and never returned. "If Christians have caste differences also," he said, "I might as well remain a Hindu." Later Gandhi admitted, "I like your Christ; I do not like your Christians. Your Christians are so unlike your Christ."[26] In his prejudice that usher not only betrayed Jesus, he also turned away a person from trusting Jesus as Savior.

What exactly is a hypocrite? A hypocrite is someone who does not practice what he believes. He can talk the talk but he doesn't walk the walk. Lifestyle doesn't equal his profession. Mouth and action are inconsistent.

And yet, let's consider a couple things:

1. If there are hypocrites, then there must be genuine Christians. Counterfeit always implies a genuine. Christ said there would be hypocrites in the church. He called them wheat and tares growing together (see Matthew 13:24-30).

2. There is a difference between sinner and hypocrite. Hypocrisy is just one

of many sins that all of us have committed. Full of it, no; in it, yes. Better to say the church is full of sinners.

The answer to the hypocrite problem? Look at the Savior! You don't start by looking at the church, you start by looking at Jesus—and Jesus is not a hypocrite.

Since Christianity depends on Jesus, it is incorrect to try to invalidate the Christian faith by pointing to horrible things many have done in the name of Christianity. If this is your argument then be consistent with it.

What do hospitals do? Make sick people well. So if sick people are in the hospital, is it full of hypocrites? You have mistaken what the church really is. It's not a museum or a hall of fame, it is a hospital with a lot of sick people getting better . . . and you are looking at one of them.

So what is a Christian? A Christian is not a perfect person but is someone who is a continually growing work in progress. When you get saved you don't receive maturity all at once, you are not a theologian, and you do not have it all together. You got born again because you don't have it all together.

Christianity is Christ. We are not perfect—but He is. When you take your eyes off of Him, you will see our issues. The church is like Noah's ark: the stench on the inside would be unbearable if it weren't for the storm on the outside. Many times we stink and the world is stormy.

I love what Ruth Graham made her family put on her gravestone long before she was bedridden and passed away. She was driving one day and entered into a construction zone on the highway. When she reached the end, the sign said, "End of construction. Thank you for your patience."[27] That was it! That is what she wanted chiseled onto her headstone long before she needed it.

And this is true of all of us as we grow to be like Jesus. We are all one big construction zone—but one day we will reach the end of the construction and then: "We will be like Him, because we will see Him just as He is" (1 John 3:2). There's no hypocrisy in that.

John Newton, author of the famous hymn "Amazing Grace" said it best: "I am not what I ought to be, I am not what I want to be, I am not what I hope to be in another world; but still I am not what I once used to be, and by the grace of God I am what I am."[28]

Day 24

THE DAY THE CURTAINS COME DOWN

Today's Reading: Matthew 24

"When the Author steps on the stage the play is over."[29] This is how C. S. Lewis spoke about the ending of planet Earth. We would call that the second coming of Jesus. This is where we are in today's reading. This chapter is very sobering; it's all about the last days just before the Author steps on the stage.

In the 260 chapters of the New Testament, there are 318 references to the second coming of Christ. To break that down even more: one out of every thirty verses in the New Testament speaks about the second coming; twenty-three of the twenty-seven New Testament books refer to the second coming of Jesus. For every prophecy in the Bible concerning Christ's first coming, there are eight that look forward to His second! Matthew 24 and 25 devote a lot of space to it.

The second coming of Jesus is going to be the most dramatic happening in human history. It will terminate human history and will usher in eternity. In a moment God will say to human history, "Curtains!" And down the curtains will go.

What's interesting is that Matthew 24 and 25 are Jesus' final words before His crucifixion. What stands out to me is something He stated five times in chapter 24—that no one knows when the second coming will happen:

- "Of that day and hour no one knows, not even the angels of heaven, nor the Son, but the Father alone." (Matthew 24:36)
- "They did not understand until the flood came and took them all away; so will the coming of the Son of Man be." (Matthew 24:39)
- "Therefore be on the alert, for you do not know which day your Lord is coming." (Matthew 24:42)
- "You also must be ready; for the Son of Man is coming at an hour when you do not think *He will*." (Matthew 24:44)
- "The master of that slave will come on a day when he does not expect *him* and at an hour which he does not know." (Matthew 24:50)

Five times in this chapter Jesus tells us that the time cannot be known.

Augustine said, "The last days is hidden so that every day would be regarded."[30]

Somebody asked John Wesley, "Supposing that you knew you were to die at twelve o'clock to-morrow night, how would you spend the intervening time?"

"How, madam?" Wesley told her. "Why, just as I intend to spend it now. I should preach this evening at Gloucester, and again at five tomorrow morning; after that, I should ride to Tewkesbury, preach in the afternoon, and meet the societies in the evening. I should then repair to friend Martin's house, who expects to entertain me, converse and pray with the family as usual, retire to my room at ten o'clock, commend myself to my heavenly Father, lie down to rest, and wake up in glory."[31] It did not matter whether his home going would be by death or rapture. He would not change anything. It did not make any difference to him.

How about you?

Jesus said, "They will see the SON OF MAN COMING ON THE CLOUDS OF THE SKY with power and great glory. And He will send forth His angels with A GREAT TRUMPET and THEY WILL GATHER TOGETHER His elect from the four winds, from one end of the sky to the other" (Matthew 24:30-33).

In *The Rapture*, Dr. Tim LaHaye vividly imagined what the unexpected suddenness of the rapture will be like: When Christ calls His living saints to be with Him, millions of people will suddenly vanish from the earth. An unsaved person who happens to be in the company of a believer will know immediately that his friend has vanished. There will certainly be worldwide recognition of the fact, for when more than one-half of a billion people suddenly depart this earth, leaving their earthly belongings behind, pandemonium and confusion will certainly reign for a time.

A million conversations will end midsentence. A million phones will suddenly go dead. A woman will reach for a man's hand in the dark and no one will be there. A man will turn with a laugh to slap a colleague on the back and his hand will move through empty air. A basketball player will make a length-of-the-floor pass to a teammate streaking down the court and find there is no one there to receive it. A mother will pull back the covers in a bassinet, smelling the sweet baby smell one moment but suddenly kissing empty space and looking into empty blankets.

So what is our job before this happens? Oswald J Smith tells us: "We talk of the second coming, while half the world has never heard of the first."[32] Let's tell the world why Jesus came the first time.

THREE STORIES THAT REMIND ME OF FOREVER

Today's Reading: Matthew 25

Leonard Ravenhill, one of my spiritual fathers, said: "Many pastors criticize me for taking the Gospel so seriously. But do they really think that on Judgment Day, Christ will chastise me, saying, 'Leonard, you took Me too seriously'?"[33]

This chapter makes us take eternity seriously. Jesus starts right away in verse one with, "God's kingdom is like . . ." and then He tells three stories.

This chapter is made up of three parables on the kingdom of heaven. It is very simple to outline. In His first parable, He tells of the silly, or foolish, virgins. Then He tells about the parable of the talents. Finally He shares the parable of the sheep and goats at the throne.

We can see similarities among the three. First, there are winners and losers. Everyone does not go to heaven. There is consequence for living a selfish life and there is reward for living a life sold out to Jesus. In parable 1, He called the winners the ready and the wise. In parable 2, He called them the faithful. And in parable #3, He called them the blessed ("of My Father") or the righteous. The wise, the faithful, and the righteous. The losers were called the foolish, the wicked, and the accursed ones.

Second, no one is born a loser but a chooser. That means they all had opportunities to be on the right side, filled with oil, a prospering talent, or doing the right thing with the poor, imprisoned, and sick. Things were presented to them that would determine what they would do with their life.

Third, each of the losing groups had explanations, excuses, and desires to get freebies and not play by the rules. The coming of the Lord will be a time of separation, a time of evaluation, and a time of commendation.

Time of separation: all of them were virgins and looked alike.

Time of evaluation: we are held responsible for what we are given.

Time of commendation: everything we do for God does not go unnoticed.

Finally, the end result of the silly virgins, the one-talent man, and the goats was final. Finally is final. It is called "the door is shut," outer darkness, going away into eternal punishment—a place for the devil and his angels.

Let me give you one quick lesson from each of the three:

Parable 1's lesson: What is on the inside is not looked after. Though the outside resembles everyone else, it is the inside that makes all the difference.

Parable 2's lesson: What we are given must produce.

Parable 3's lesson: Jesus does not look like any of the pictures. Is He black, white, Hispanic? Jewish? None of the above. He is naked, a convict, and one who is hungry and thirsty.

Leonard Ravenhill said, "If Jesus had preached the same message that ministers preach today, He would never have been crucified."[34] And this is one of those sobering messages Jesus preached.

HOW CAN YOU BE THAT FAR OFF?

Today's Reading: Matthew 26

Every time I get a new Bible, I write the same thing in each one before I start reading. I put it right on the flyleaf. It is a five-hundred-year-old poem a prison convict wrote: "There was a man, and they called him mad; the more he gave, the more he had."[35] That prison convict was John Bunyan.

The more he gave, the more he had.

It doesn't make sense. It seems like a contradiction.

The English language does this. We have words and phrases in English that seem to make no sense and at times, appear contradictory. Consider a few:

- A ship carries cargo, and a car carries shipments.
- You park on a driveway but you drive on a parkway.
- Your nose runs and your feet smell.
- The person who invests all your money is called a broker.
- And why do doctors call what they do practice? Shouldn't they be good at it by now?

Then some words are way off in their descriptions of an item. We see this an example in today's reading. Jesus and His disciples saw the same event at the same time . . . but their definitions of it were so far apart that it feels contradictory. Let's look at the story.

Jesus now proceeded to Bethany, to the home of Simon the leper. While he was eating, a woman came in with a bottle of very expensive perfume and poured it over his head. The disciples were indignant. "What a waste of good money," they said. "Why, she could have sold it for a fortune and given it to the poor." Jesus knew what they were thinking and said, "Why are you criticizing her? For she has done a good thing to me. You will always have the poor among you, but you won't always have me. She has poured this perfume on me to prepare my body for burial. And she will always be remembered for this deed. The story of what she has done will be told throughout the whole world, wherever the Good News is preached." (Matthew 26:6-13, TLB)

Here is the contradiction:
- The disciples' interpretation of this woman's act: "What a waste" (verse 8).
- Jesus' interpretation: "a good thing" (verse 10).

These perspectives were based on this woman's extravagant gift. Listen to the words of comparison. Two views of the same deed: *waste* and *good*. These are really far apart. How could someone who had been with Jesus for three years be that far off on something like this? What's worse is that I can see myself in those disciples. How can I be with Jesus for almost four decades and still misinterpret and misdefine so badly?

This woman took Jesus seriously and became the center of attention just days before the crucifixion. What did Jesus see in this act that the disciples did not? What made it beautiful and significant?

It had the extravagance of God on it.

It was extravagant—it spared no expense; it showed a lack of restraint in using resources; it was elaborate. This woman's act looked a lot like what God does.

Think about creation. When God created He was extravagant. He was not stingy. He could have created one star but decided that was not enough for the space, so He loaded the heavens with hundreds of billions of them.

Everything he created is with extravagance. He spoke and ten million insects were created, ten million species. Not one hundred, not one thousand. There are 2,500 variations of *ants* (most in my home) and three hundred thousand species of beetles. Extravagance.

He created more than ten thousand species of birds. Five billion birds live in the United States alone! Then He got extravagant with their personalities. Some can fly up to five hundred miles nonstop. Mallard ducks fly 60 mph; eagles, 100 mph; falcons, 180 mph. Some he created to navigate by the stars.

He created more than 28,000 species of fish.

This was God breaking His alabaster box for the world to see beauty. Everywhere you look at the world around you, you can't miss God.

I wonder if that is why Jesus praised this woman. He saw that her act was just like what the Father does and it caught His attention.

Mother Teresa told a story that showcases God's extravagance toward us.

A nun once said to me, "Mother Teresa, you are spoiling the poor people by giving them free things. They are losing their human dignity." . . .

I said calmly, "No one spoils us as much as God himself. See the wonderful gifts he has given to us freely. . . . All of you have no glasses yet you all can see. If God were to take money for your sight, what would happen? Continually we are breathing and living on oxygen that we do not pay for. What would happen if God were to say, 'If you work four hours you will get sunshine for two hours?' How many of us would survive then? . . . There are many congregations that spoil the rich; it is good to have one congregation in the name of the poor, to spoil the poor."[36]

Jesus saw extravagance in this gift. Jesus saw Himself in this gift.

It was giving the best with nothing left.

In that time, it was common to offer small amounts of fragrant ointment to refresh the dinner guests. But Mary went beyond custom and what was common. She poured the whole vial on Jesus' head as if she were inaugurating a King to His office or, as Jesus would say later, preparing a body for burial.

The story as Mark told it put a dollar amount on it:

Some were indignantly remarking to one another, "Why has this perfume been wasted? For this perfume might have been sold for over three hundred denarii, and the money given to the poor." [Mark 14:4-5]

Three hundred denarii was one year's wages.

When was the last time you gave to God and nothing was left? Not just money . . . but in worship, in serving, in sacrifice, in a conviction that could cost you friends, reputation, and maybe a job?

I think she got overwhelmed with Jesus and thought, *Everything. He gets everything because He deserves all.*

God gave it all when He gave His Son and . . . in just a few days from this anointing, Jesus was about to give His everything—His life. I think Jesus saw the character of God in this gift.

When I read this story, I think of the prayer of Jim Elliot, the 1960s martyr who prayed, "Forgive me for being so ordinary while claiming to know so extraordinary a God."[37]

This woman got it right. An extraordinary God deserves an extraordinary gift.

Let's not give too ordinary.

THE TEARFUL EYE OR THE BROKEN NECK

Today's Reading: Matthew 27

If ever a man had a chance to become a saint it should have been Judas. Judas Iscariot, the one who betrayed Jesus.

For more than two years, he lived with Jesus. He listened to His words, watched His miracles, and yet this man deliberately planned to betray Him. No one in history had a better chance than Judas. The rich young ruler only met Jesus once, and yet Judas was with Him every day.

Judas ruined for all time the name he bore. No woman in history ever thinks of naming her child "Judas"; yet Judas was an honorable name at one time. There was Judas Maccabeus—who bravely fought to defend the Jewish land and religion more than a hundred years before Jesus was born. Even one of Jesus' brothers bore the name Judas. And now forever that name is associated with betrayal.

When Jesus said, "One of you will betray me." No one said, "Is it Judas?"

Jesus always has a double effect but He never allows neutrality. Just as fire can soften wax or harden clay, to be with Jesus is either a blessing or a curse. The presence of Jesus changed fickle Peter into a rock and exposed Judas's greed.

The sin of Judas was a sin against repeated warnings. The more I think about Judas, the more I see how many times he heard Jesus speak about the perils of money. Judas heard, "You cannot serve God and mammon." He heard, "What does it profit a man to gain the whole world but lose his soul." Judas heard the parable of the man who filled his barns but did not prepare his soul and was called a fool. I believe Jesus calling him "friend" in Matthew 26:50 was a last-ditch effort to win Judas back before the deal went through in the garden of Gethsemane.

There is a butterfly hidden within the confines of an ugly caterpillar. But not all caterpillars become butterflies. Scientists tell us that sometimes flies thrust the bodies of the caterpillar with a tiny egg. The egg hatches into a grub, which feeds upon the butterfly, forming elements in the makeup of a caterpillar. The caterpillar does not even know it happens. It goes right on living and eating, but the grub has destroyed its capacity to advance. The glorious winged creature, which might have been, is now gone and it never becomes the butterfly.

Judas had a grub inside him that made him a lover of money more than a lover of God. When he saw the woman break the alabaster box and pour the costly perfume upon the Jesus' head, his first thought, *It might have been sold*.

Listen to the end of his betrayal while Jesus was being tried and led to the cross. Here is what was happening with Judas:

> When Judas, who had betrayed him, saw that Jesus was condemned, he was seized with remorse and returned the thirty pieces of silver to the chief priests and the elders. "I have sinned," he said, "for I have betrayed innocent blood."
>
> "What is that to us?" they replied. "That's your responsibility."
>
> So Judas threw the money into the temple and left. Then he went away and hanged himself. (Matthew 27:3-5, NIV)

I thought hard about this: Peter and Judas. One was a denier and the other a betrayer.

After he denied: Peter went out and wept bitterly. After he betrayed: Judas went out and hanged himself. Each of these men had a chapter in their life where sin ruled them. Both failed but their stories ended differently. Should not have Peter's story ended up like Judas's? Which is the better end—the disciple with the tearful eye or the disciple with the broken neck?

Why would failure bring suicide? And why would failure bring repentance? One disciple after failure became a swinging corpse on a tree and the other became a preacher on the day of Pentecost.

Why did the Master choose a man like Judas? The better question is why did He ever choose someone like me? He did not choose him or us for what we were—certainly not for what he became—but for what he, and we, might become.

We are going to sin. We are going to mess up. There have probably been times when I have sold Him for far less than thirty pieces of silver. Sold Him for a temporary thrill. But here I am by the grace of God. And there have been times I have denied Him. I have been ashamed to speak up like Peter and cowered into silence. Why am I still here? Why am I not swinging? Why am I not preaching like Peter? Instead of trying to figure out the end of Peter and Judas's differences, we must make sure our end is gripping to the mercy of God.

THE FIRST WORDS OF THE RESURRECTED JESUS

Today's Reading: Matthew 28

What does famed NFL player Barry Sanders and resurrected Jesus have in common? I am not trying to be disrespectful, but I do have a point.

Barry Sanders is considered one of the greatest NFL running backs of all time. He holds many of the coveted NFL records. Two things make Barry iconic in the sport's world. First, his elusiveness. Barry's runs were choreographed like a ballet. Though it was impressive to watch, what stood out more than anything about Barry's plays was what happened after he scored a touchdown. In a time in sports where every tackle, sack, hit, and first down was celebrated like winning a Nobel Peace prize, Barry was a non-conformist and contrarian. He wouldn't dance, jump into the stands, point to heaven, or find a hidden marker in the goal post. Every time without fail, he simply handed the ball to the ref. In his biography, people took the words of famed football coach Vince Lombardi to describe this action and said, "When you get to the end zone, act like you have been there before."[38] **Barry had been there, a lot. No need to act like a kid seeing Walt Disney World for the first time.**

So what does Barry Sanders and resurrected Jesus have in common?

We have come to the end of our first New Testament book (Matthew) and in today's reading, we're studying about the greatest event in world history, the resurrection of Jesus. He has accomplished His mission. Jesus has died for the sins of the world and resurrected from the dead after three days. He crushed death, hell, and Satan and crossed the goal line. He scored, to stay with our NFL comparison. Did Jesus shout over His accomplishment? Did He thump His chest? Did He jump into the crowd of disciples like a Lambeau leap?

This has to be one of my favorite moments of the resurrected Jesus. It took me by surprise and stunned me. Jesus flipped the ball to the ref. He acted like, *This is what I do. No need to get all crazy*.

Ready for this? These were the first words of the resurrected, I-just-beat-up-hell-and-the-devil Jesus:

The women ran from the tomb, badly frightened, but also filled with joy, and rushed to find the disciples to give them the angel's message. And as they were running, suddenly Jesus was there in front of them! "Good morning!" he said. And they fell to the ground before him, holding his feet and worshiping him. (Matthew 28:8-9, TLB)

Good morning? That's what you say after you did all that? Thank God I'm not Jesus. My first resurrection appearance line would be something like: "Ha! Told you! Look at me now. You didn't think I could do it. *Bam*, done!"

Not Jesus. He offered a ball flip, and a simple, "Good morning." He said it like it was just another day at the job and time to go back to work. Unbelievable!

Only people who are secure and know who they are do something like this.

Some of the older translations say that Jesus said, "All hail," which literally means "Good morning." I don't like *all hail*; it sounds like "Caesar" should come next. Sounds formal. I like, "Good morning." Sounds like He's saying, *Yeah, it's just another thing I do: kill devils and death and get people to heaven.*

That is Jesus. "Good morning," the ball flip, tells us a lot about Jesus. It tells us when you are the real thing, you don't have to tell people. It shows every time you cross the goal line.

If you are a praying man, a prophetic woman, a pastor, an evangelist, a godly person, or someone who hears from God, all you have to tell people is, "Good morning." They will know. Jesus did not come out saying, "I am resurrected!" What happened and who He was spoke for itself. In the passage we see that after Jesus said, "Good morning," the people surrounding Him worshiped Him. That's all it took. That's all that was needed. "Good morning," and they worshiped.

When you have to tell people to respect you, honor you, clap for you, it means you are doing things that don't call for that response. Jesus scored. Flipped the ball and simply said, "Good morning." It's enough.

Day 29

DEMON PRAYERS AND FEVER PRAYERS

Today's Reading: Mark 1

Today's reading showcases the cool way Jesus began His ministry. Who Jesus healed, what He healed, and where He healed it makes this amazing. Take a look at this passage:

> [The people] were amazed at [Jesus'] teaching; for He was teaching them as *one* having authority, and not as the scribes. Just then there was a man in their synagogue with an unclean spirit; and he cried out, saying, "What business do we have with each other, Jesus of Nazareth? Have You come to destroy us? I know who You are—the Holy One of God!" And Jesus rebuked him, saying, "Be quiet, and come out of him!" Throwing him into convulsions, the unclean spirit cried out with a loud voice and came out of him. They were all amazed, so that they debated among themselves, saying, "What is this? A new teaching with authority! He commands even the unclean spirits, and they obey Him." Immediately the news about Him spread everywhere into all the surrounding district of Galilee. [Mark 1:22-28]

First, a demon showed up in the synagogue. While Jesus was teaching, a demon tried to take center stage from Jesus. Verse 22 says when Jesus taught them, they were amazed. Then when the demon showed up, Jesus rebuked it and it came out of the man. And again "they were all amazed" [verse 27]. These two words for *amazed* were different, though. The amazement the people felt over Jesus' teaching was something like "blowing their minds." They were in awe and wonder. But the second amazement the people felt was different—and Mark used a different word to convey it. That word adds something to the first. It adds the physical and the emotional aspect to it. The second word means to be in fear and trembling.

When Jesus teaches us, we respond by shaking our heads in amazement. When Jesus heals and delivers us, we shake on the ground in fear and trembling awe. This was a huge miracle in the synagogue in front of non-followers getting an introduction to the powerful ministry of the Son of God.

Then after the prayer to get rid of the demon, Jesus prayed again. I call it the fever prayer.

> Now Simon's mother-in-law was lying sick with a fever; and immediately they spoke to Jesus about her. And He came to her and raised her up, taking her by the hand, and the fever left her, and she waited on them. (Mark 1:30-31)

I love the phrase *they spoke to Jesus about her*. That's really important. That is the best scriptural definition for "intercession." It is a form of prayer that prays for others not for ourselves. What is intercession? It's when we speak to Jesus about others.

Quick side note—this kind of praying also heals the church of gossip. We don't speak to other people about someone, we speak to Jesus about that person.

This fever prayer is so encouraging. The demon prayer was in the church. The fever prayer was in the home. That's where I need the most answers to prayer.

I think Jesus was showing us something about Himself. Fever prayers are just as important to Him as demon prayers. I love what Paul says in Philippians about our prayers. "Don't worry about anything; instead, pray about everything; tell God your needs, and don't forget to thank him for his answers" (Philippians 4:6, TLB).

Pray about everything—demons and fevers. There's nothing to small or insignificant to pray about. Too often we don't want to take something to God, because we feel as though He would say, "Do you know how busy I am—and you're asking for that?"

Here's the truth: God tells us to pray about *everything*. God created us and He is interested in every aspect of our lives. He wants to know what's on our minds. If it's bothering us, He wants us to tell Him about it.

Ask God today for big stuff *and* for little stuff. Pray for a scholarship to cover this year at university, pray for cancer to be healed, pray for that prodigal daughter to come back to Jesus. But it's also okay to pray for no traffic, pray for the grocery store not to run out of a certain item, pray that an article of clothing is on sale. Pray demon prayers and pray fever prayers. And then be amazed!

Day 30

FOUR OF A KIND BEATS A FULL HOUSE

Today's Reading: Mark 2

I've never played poker in my life. I'm not saying that to sound righteous or religious, I'm just saying it . . . That being said, I had to google if four of a kind beat a full house. It does. That's our story today.

I want to show you this concept in Mark 2 in which two things are competing. In one verse we find a full house and in another verse we find four of a kind. (And remember, four of a kind always beat a full house.)

> When He had come back to Capernaum several days afterward, it was heard that He was at home. And many were gathered together, so that there was no longer room, not even near the door; and He was speaking the word to them. (Mark 2:1-2)

There is the full house. The full house didn't do anything for a paralyzed man. The full house sat listening to Jesus but that did not fix the paralysis. The four of a kind was about to show up in verse 3. A paralyzed man did not need people just sitting there. He needed someone to get him to Jesus.

Mr. Rogers, an ordained minister and the famous host of one of the first children shows on television back in the 1970s once said, "When I was a child and my mother and I would read about such events in the newspapers or see them in newsreels, she used to tell me, 'Always look for the helpers. There's always someone who is trying to help.'"[39]

I want to be one of the "helpers." Don't you? One of the four of a kind.

> They came, bringing to Him a paralytic, carried by four men. Being unable to get to Him because of the crowd, they removed the roof above Him; and when they had dug an opening, they let down the pallet on which the paralytic was lying. And Jesus seeing their faith said to the paralytic, "Son, your sins are forgiven." (Mark 2:3-5)

Do you have friends who will get you to Jesus? If not, then you need new friends. They may be able to get you to a golf course, get you to a sports game, get you to a concert, or get you to a club or bar. But do you have anyone who gets you to Jesus? These four got the sick man to Jesus.

There are times you are meant to bear another's stretcher and not just sit and hear the Word. You must not only carry your Bible to church, you may need to carry your brother or sister also at times to the Lord. Our problem here in Mark 2 is we have a full house but only four people who were carrying the stretcher. Not many left the full house to help another. How did they do it? When doors are shut, they went higher!

The four of a kind could not get through the door. So they had to take it up higher, literally to the roof. There is a good principle we need to learn from the actions of these four men: when it seems like the door is shut, go higher.

Problems are surmountable from above. You can't solve everything by walking through a door of a doctor's office or a church. You have to take some things higher.

Going up higher means getting it to Jesus. It's prayer! As Watchman Nee said, "Our prayers lay the track down on which God's power can come. Like a mighty locomotive, His power is irresistible, but it cannot reach us without rails."

These men didn't quit when they saw the full house. They carried him to the roof, removed the shingles, and dug, and then they had to connect ropes to lower him down.

Jesus did not see roof busters but He saw their faith (verse 5). Always remember—when you go higher, you get more than you asked for.

That's the twist in the story. They went through all this work to get a paralyzed man in front of Jesus and Jesus did not say, "Be healed!" or "Rise up and walk!" He said, "Your sins are forgiven." Had I done all that work, His words would have taken the air out of me. I would have wanted my buddy to walk. I might have thought, *I didn't do all this for an inside work, but for an outside thing*.

You can't have Jesus for only what *you* want. If you want Jesus, you get all of Him. He is not some buffet line that you pick and choose and say, "I'll take the Sermon on the Mount and healing when I am sick, but not the holiness and hell stuff. Tithing? Yuck. Love your neighbor. Okay, but only if they are lovable."

Had Jesus just said, "Take up your pallet and walk," everyone would have been happy. But it's all or nothing with Jesus. That is why I don't think He told the man to arise first but focused on forgiveness first.

I'm no gambler, but I'd take four of a kind over a full house—with all of Jesus—any day.

Day 31

JESUS PULLS A WEBSTER

Today's Reading: Mark 3

When you want to know the definition of a word, you look in the one trusted place that settles all doubt—the dictionary. When you think of the dictionary, you think of one name—Webster. But do you know who this Webster is?

Noah Webster was a devout Christian. His word speller was grounded in Scripture, and his first lesson began, "Be not anxious for your life, what ye shall eat, or what ye shall drink; nor for your body, what ye shall put on; for your heavenly Father knoweth that ye have need of these things."[40]

His 1828 American dictionary contained the greatest number of biblical definitions given in any reference volume. Webster considered education "useless without the Bible." He claimed to have learned twenty different languages in finding definitions for which a particular word was used. From the preface to the 1828 edition of Webster's *American Dictionary of the English language*:

> In my view, the Christian religion is the most important and one of the first things in which all children, under a free government ought to be instructed. No truth is more evident to my mind than that the Christian religion must be the basis of any government intended to secure the rights and privileges of a free people.

In fact, Noah Webster wrote the first paraphrase of the Bible called the common Bible in 1833. Webster molded the King James Version to correct grammar, replaced words that were no longer used, and did away with words and phrases that could be seen as offensive.

When you are looking up a word, read the whole definition. You may just stumble into something amazing about the what it means and where it came from.

That happened to me. Noah Webster redefined the word *enthusiasm* for me. Here is his second definition for the word: "belief in special revelations from the Holy Spirit." The noun *enthusiasm* comes from the Greek word *enthousiasmos*, from *enthous*, meaning "possessed by a God, inspired."[41]

The famous 1828 version said: "special divine communications from the Supreme Being, or familiar intercourse with him."

Special revelations from the Holy Spirit!

Seriously? That's incredible.

That redefined *enthusiasm* for how I think about the word. I get enthusiastic to preach, to go to church, to be a dad and a husband. I get inspired by God and receive special communications from Him to do these things.

Redefinitions were needed when Jesus came to earth. Jesus went all Noah Webster from the outset of His ministry and brought an adjustment to a very important concept in today's reading of Mark 3.

In Mark 3:32, a crowd was sitting around Him. They told Him, "Behold, Your mother and Your brothers are outside looking for You."

Here are the words Jesus wanted to redefine: "Answering them, He said, "Who are My mother and my brothers?" Looking about at those who were sitting around Him, He said, "Behold My mother and My brothers!" (verses 33-34).

Here comes the redefinition: "For whoever does the will of God, he is My brother and sister and mother" (verse 35).

Did you see how He redefined terms?

"Who is My mother?" And, "Who is my brother?"

When Jesus came, He redefined things by putting them in their true light. He did that on the sermon on the mount when He redefined adultery. It's not just in the bed but in the head (see Matthew 5:27-28).

Jesus asks these questions: Who is my real family? Who is related to me?

We hear all the time that blood is thicker than water. But Jesus took it even further by saying that spirit is thicker than blood.

Jesus redefined blood relationships for us. He said the ones whom we are closest to are not the ones who have the same father and mother but the ones who "do the will of God."

Remember this important thing: whose definition really counts?

In *Renaissance*, Os Guinness wrote something that made me think redefinitions and how the crowd wants us to be stuck and not look up how Jesus defines something: "For the followers of Jesus, the voice of the people must never be taken as the voice of God."[42]

We live under the pressure that numbers (the crowd) are truth and they tell the truth and they make the truth. And so we give numbers and majority huge value. We are counting opinions instead of weighing them.

It tells you externals but never the heart of something. They can tell you what men spend on Valentine's Day cards but never if he loves his wife as Christ loves the church.

They can tell you about church membership and frequency of attendance but never gage those who are on fire in their love for God.

One hundred million tweets and "likes" still never add up to truth, wisdom, or what is right and good. The bandwagon is replacing the Bible—popularity rather than principle—horizontal pressure over vertical authority.

"Thus says the Lord" should always trump 51 percent. That's something to get enthusiastic about. That's something to redefine. That's what Jesus did.

TWO STORMS STORIES

Today's Reading: Mark 4

I want to tell you two stories about storms, Jesus, and a bunch of guys (the twelve disciples) in a boat. Both storms had winds and fear. But their endings were different.

We encounter the first storm in today's reading. Let's read about it together:

> On that day, when evening came, He said to them, "Let us go over to the other side." Leaving the crowd, they took Him along with them in the boat, just as He was; and other boats were with Him. And there arose a fierce gale of wind, and the waves were breaking over the boat so much that the boat was already filling up. Jesus Himself was in the stern, asleep on the cushion; and they woke Him and said to Him, "Teacher, do You not care that we are perishing?" (Mark 4:35-41)

"Do you not care?" is a huge indictment on God's character, and it plays into this "no faith" issue. So keep these two phrases in mind: *Do You not care* and *Do you have no faith*.

Let's continue reading:

> He got up and rebuked the wind and said to the sea, "Hush, be still." And the wind died down and it became perfectly calm. And He said to them, "Why are you afraid? Do you still have no faith?" They became very much afraid and said to one another, "Who then is this, that even the wind and the sea obey Him?" (Mark 4:39-41)

Their "no faith" was revealed in this statement, "Who is this man?"

Faith is connected to knowing who this Man is. Think of the important progression.

A storm arises, as it does in life, and fear comes—fear of tomorrow, fear of going to the doctor or waiting for a call from the doctor, fear of being single, fear of not being pregnant, fear of getting laid off. These are all called storms.

If storms produce fear and distrust, then we have a faith issue. When storms drive us to fear, faith has been punctured and is leaking somewhere.

This storm ends with a question mark. It ends with questioning Who God is.

Faith is a journey, and that's what these disciples were on. They ended their first Jesus boat ride with, "Who is this Man?" The question mark.

If storms produce fear, then we have a faith problem. And if we have a faith problem, then it's a God issue. What does that mean?

Knowing God increases faith. Always remember that if you want faith to increase, find out more about the character of God. As someone once said, "Feed your faith and your fears will starve to death."

Faith is based on who God is. That's how you increase in faith. The disciples did not get an increase of faith from the last storm, just more questions.

Now let's dip back into Matthew for our second storm story:

He made the disciples get into the boat and go ahead of Him to the other side, while He sent the crowds away. After He had sent the crowds away, He went up on the mountain by Himself to pray; and when it was evening, He was there alone. But the boat was already a long distance from the land, battered by the waves; for the wind was contrary. And in the fourth watch of the night He came to them, walking on the sea. When the disciples saw Him walking on the sea, they were terrified, and said, "It is a ghost!" And they cried out in fear. But immediately Jesus spoke to them, saying, "Take courage, it is I; do not be afraid."

When they got into the boat, the wind stopped. And those who were in the boat worshiped Him, saying, "You are certainly God's Son!" (Matthew 14:22-33)

They worshiped him. They recognized who Jesus was: "You are certainly God's Son!"

Remember our first boat story ended with a question. This one still ended with worship.

If storms make me a better worshiper, then so be it. I would just rather do it with music on Sunday. But that does not always happen. God wants your and my tests to end with praise not questions.

Andráe Crouch put it this way: "If I'd never had a problem, I wouldn't know God could solve them."[43]

There is a difference between praise and worship. Praise means telling others about how good God is; telling others what God has done. Worship means telling God Who He is.

If you know Who He is then you can know what He can do. And no storm has enough power to stand up to that.

THE MAN WHO LIVED IN A CEMETERY

Today's Reading: Mark 5

Wow, today's reading is filled with action, miracles, and healing. It's nonstop from verse 1 to verse 43. Mark 5 starts with a town demoniac who lived in a graveyard who acts as the welcoming committee for Jesus and the disciples and ends in a house where a dead twelve-year-old girl's body is laid out and a bunch of laughing people who think Jesus is out of His mind. In this chapter Jesus casts out a legion of demons, heals a woman of a twelve-year disease that doctors had no cure for, and raises from the dead a young whose body would soon be in a coffin for her burial. Go Jesus!

Let's pause and consider the first miracle of the man who lived in a cemetery. Read that section with me, will you?

> When [Jesus] got out of the boat, immediately a man from the tombs with an unclean spirit met Him, and he had his dwelling among the tombs. And no one was able to bind him anymore, even with a chain; because he had often been bound with shackles and chains, and the chains had been torn apart by him and the shackles broken in pieces, and no one was strong enough to subdue him. Constantly, night and day, he was screaming among the tombs and in the mountains, and gashing himself with stones. Seeing Jesus from a distance, he ran up and bowed down before Him. (Mark 5:2-6)

I have had people ask me, "Can a Christian be demon possessed?" The answer to that question is based on your definition of Christian.

Paul tells us in Colossians 3:3 says that when you become a Christian, "your life is hidden with Christ in God." That means demons can't find you to live in you. They can't find the door to enter your soul and spirit; your life is hidden in Christ. That is my definition of a believer in relation to the demonic world.

The man was demon possessed, and the demon in this man had a name or a descriptive name: Legion.

He was asking him, "What is your name?" And he said to Him, "My name is Legion; for we are many." (Mark 5:9)

Legion. This is not really a name but a description of what was going on internally in this man and the magnitude of the dark forces in his soul.

Legion was the term given for a battalion or squadron in the Roman army. It usually had 5,400 soldiers and 120 horsemen. This man was possessed by an army.

But something huge happened to start this man's healing, something that gives us hope for people no matter how messed up they are. It's all in verse 6: "Seeing Jesus from a distance, he ran up and bowed down before him."

A man with 5,400 demons still has the ability to get to Jesus. He is able to run to Him and bow before Him. No matter how much demonic control is going on, we can see that God doesn't let the demons control a life who wants help and freedom.

Look what happens next. *The Message* says it like this:

Everyone wanted to see what had happened. They came up to Jesus and saw the madman sitting there wearing decent clothes and making sense, no longer a walking madhouse of a man. (Mark 5:14-15)

Why would Satan launch that kind of attack against this man?
He would be a mouthpiece of God.
He isn't just delivered.
He is about to be a preacher.
If Satan does not stop this man, ten cities are about to be changed.
But Jesus said no. "Go home to your friends," he told him, "and tell them what wonderful things God has done for you; and how merciful he has been."

So the man started off to visit the Ten Towns of that region and began to tell everyone about the great things Jesus had done for him; and they were awestruck by his story. (Mark 5:19-20, TLB)

A. W. Tozer said, "I'm not afraid of the devil. The devil can handle me—he's got judo I never heard of. But he can't handle the One to whom I'm joined; he can't handle the One to whom I'm united; he can't handle the One [who lives in me]."[44]

No one is unsavable. No one is unchangeable. No one is too far gone. No one has too many problems. Not with Jesus around! Even if they have 5,400 addictions, we can be freed because of Jesus, who can command that stronghold to flee.

If you know someone who is far from God, who is really messed up, who is so out there that you have no idea if they would ever come back to their senses, let this story put faith in you.

Day 34

LIMITING JESUS

Today's Reading: Mark 6

No one would disagree that Jesus had all the potential to heal anyone, anywhere, anytime. Can you imagine having the person who could heal you, your child, your family, or your marriage right in your town and nothing happens?

How is that possible?

By limiting Jesus.

We have only two times in the Gospels that Jesus was shocked and both have to deal with the issue of faith.

The words *wonder* or *marveled* in the gospels mean to be shocked. The first time it occurs is in Matthew when He was shocked at the great faith of a Roman centurion for a servant who was paralyzed. The centurion said to Jesus, "Just say the word and my servant will be healed" (Matthew 8:8). The centurion's faith shocked Jesus:

> When Jesus heard *this*, He marveled and said to those who were following, "Truly I say to you, I have not found such great faith with anyone in Israel." (Matthew 8:10)

The second time Jesus was shocked is in today's reading in Mark 6. But this is a different kind of shock. This is a shock that happens in a negative way in his hometown. Let's read it together:

> He could do no miracle there except that He laid His hands on a few sick people and healed them. And He wondered at their unbelief. (Mark 6:5-6)

The unbelief was not from a Roman pagan but from the people who saw Jesus as a boy and grew up with Him. The people who knew Him best trusted Him least. The people who were around Him most, missed who He was and received only a few things when the potential for everything was in their little town.

When Jesus was shocked, it was either no faith or great faith and this incident was no faith, unbelief. What makes this story crazy is what it's on the heels of.

In chapter 5 He had just raised a dead girl, set a demoniac free of some 5,400 demons, and healed a woman who had suffered from an incurable condition for twelve years. Then in chapter 6, He went into Nazareth, His hometown, and "could do no miracle" except for healing a few sick people. And here is what's insane—all these miracles were within walking distance. They happened around Capernaum, and then Jesus walked to Nazareth. The people of Nazareth had Jesus but not His miracles.

Can that happen? You have Jesus but nothing miraculous?

Nazareth was located in the hills of Galilee and had a population of around two hundred people. So the presence of Jesus could literally have changed this town.

How did they limit Jesus?

How can we stop Jesus from doing what He does best—changing lives? We see in Mark 6 that it is through unbelief. What is unbelief?

Unbelief cannot be little faith. The disciples had that, got rebuked, but still had Jesus calm the sea in Mark 4.

What is the difference between unbelief and little faith?

It seems that little faith is seeing our bad and big circumstances as bigger than Jesus. I think unbelief is different; it is doubting the one's character who can bring the miracle.

When Jesus taught the people, they challenged who He is because of their limited knowledge:

When the sabbath came, He began to teach in the synagogue; and the many listeners were astonished, saying, "Where did this man *get* these things, and what is *this* wisdom given to Him, and such miracles as these performed by His hands? Is not this the carpenter, the son of Mary, and brother of James and Joses and Judas and Simon? Are not His sisters here with us?" [Mark 6:2-3]

Little faith—what Jesus sometimes labeled as doubt—is when you question what you believe, or if you believe it, or why you believe it.

That's okay. God is still there. Miracles can still happen with doubt present and questions swirling in your mind. But nothing happens when there is unbelief.

Unbelief is the refusal to believe. There is no doubt, there are no questions. You have come to your conclusion.

The people of Nazareth had unbelief: Jesus was the carpenter's son,

Mary's boy. Nothing more. They left no room to be wrong. They decided that they already knew, and what they knew couldn't be wrong. Well, the Nazareth people were not just wrong, they were limited, and therefore Jesus was limited. This was the carpenter's son and also God's Son. He made things out of wood and made a universe out of nothing. He came from a virgin's womb but also came down from heaven as Immanuel.

But they chose not to believe.

After viewing the works in a renowned art museum, a man said to the guard, "I don't see any great value in this artwork."

"Sir," the guard answered, "the paintings are not what's on trial here. The visitors are."

That's so true. If you look at a Rembrandt or a Monet, and you say, "I don't see anything good about that," it simply shows your ignorance concerning art.

That's the Nazareth problem. The people said, "We don't see anything special about Jesus. He's just the carpenter, and we know His mother, brothers, and sisters."

Jesus wasn't on trial in Nazareth. The Nazarites were and they failed. Let's be careful not to make the same mistake. Always remember He is much more that you can ever imagine.

Let's not limit Jesus in our churches, in our cities, or in our homes.

Let Jesus, be Jesus!

Putting the Word of God in a Wheelchair

Today's Reading: Mark 7

In today's reading, Jesus makes a statement to religious people that we have to put the spotlight on. Jesus speaks to the Pharisees and Scribes these cutting words of their relationship to the Bible, God's Word. Let's read it from The Passion Translation:

> "You abandon God's commandments just to keep men's rituals, such as ceremonially washing utensils, cups, and other things."
>
> Then he added, "How skillful you've become in rejecting God's law in order to maintain your man-made set of rules. For example, Moses taught us: 'Honor your father and your mother,' and, 'Whoever insults or mistreats his father or mother must be put to death.'
>
> "But your made-up rules allow a person to say to his parents, 'I've decided to take the support you were counting on from me and make it my holy offering to God, and that will be your blessing instead.' How convenient! The rules you teach exempt him from providing for his aged parents. Do you really think God will honor your traditions passed down to others, making up these rules that nullify God's Word? And you're doing many other things like that." (Mark 7:8-13)

The New American Standard Bible says, "*Thus* invalidating the Word of God by your tradition" (verse 13).

Wow! Invalidating the Word of God. Nothing could be more horrible.

Taking something as powerful as God's Word and making it invalid. That word is so vivid and so appropriate. An invalid is a person who is disabled by an injury, illness, or disease. They cannot do what they were designed to do because of their handicap.

Jesus told them they had just put the Word of God in a wheelchair. Instead of it walking on its own, they crippled it and did it by their traditions.

That's what had happened to these religious people. They studied the Bible and did not do what it said. Instead, they made it confirm their lifestyle.

E. Paul Hovey said it like this: "Men do not reject the Bible because it contradicts itself, but because it contradicts them."[45] The Bible contradicted them so they made it say what they wanted it to say, "thus invalidating the Word of God by their tradition."

This verse is so important. Jesus was cautioning the religious from interpreting the Bible through their religion. They saw things with their experience instead of letting the Bible interpret the Bible.

Now before we get really ticked at the Pharisees, this is happening to us today. Consider the last part of Jesus' statement, "by your tradition." Let's take out the word *tradition* and fill in the blank.

Ways people can invalidate the Word of God:

It is invalid . . .

* by their denomination. They will interpret passages denominationally (such as water baptism).
* by their soap box. They will interpret passages from their soapbox (such as political leanings).
* by conspiracy. They will interpret passages from their conspiracy (such as end times).
* by experience. They will interpret passages from their experience (such as Jesus visitations).
* by their pain. God is a horrible Father based on their natural father.
* by their ethnicity. Seeing passages a minority standpoint and cause instead of for what they say.
* by their parents.
* by their upbringing in church.
* by their pastor.
* by their seminary.

As Søren Kierkegaard said, "The Bible is very easy to understand. But we Christians are a bunch of scheming swindlers. We pretend to be unable to understand it because we know very well that the minute we understand, we are obliged to act accordingly."[46]

The story that has always intrigued me is from Jack Deere's *Surprised by the Voice of the Spirit*. Jack Deere was a seminary professor at Dallas Theological Seminary. Both they and he held to a very strong cessationist theology, which basically says that the gifts of the New Testament are no longer needed or in existence. One of the simplest things that changed Jack Deere was this thought: *If I gave a new convert a Bible and put him in a room and told him to read the*

Bible, I can't see him coming out saying, "That was such power in the New Testament, too bad we don't have access to that power today. Too bad the gifts are no longer available for us." He said that was impossible. He realized that by simply reading the Scriptures, you can't end up as a cessationist. You end up as a continuationist, someone who believes the spiritual gifts given in the early church continue on today.

Jack Deere realized that entire generations are being influenced by men's interpretation of the Bible and theology, and he wanted to be influenced by what the Bible is really saying.

One of the liveliest debates I had in seminary was with a great theology teacher whom I highly respected. He said that those that know Greek can read the Bible better than those who don't. I countered, "So just to be clear, are you saying an unsaved Greek scholar has a better chance of understanding the Scriptures than I do, who is in my fourth semester of Greek and who loves Jesus? He said, "Absolutely." Nothing could be further from the truth. He was influenced by his Greek and ancient language.

Make a commitment not to allow your "traditions" to put your faith in a wheelchair.

I Don't Want to Be Known As 409

Today's Reading: Mark 8

Today's reading opens with a familiar story. But if we examine it closely, we will notice something really puzzling and even humorous.

We've all heard the saying, "Experience is the best teacher," but it is simply not true. Experience is not the best teacher; it never has been and never will be. Maturity doesn't always come with time. Sometimes age brings nothing more than wrinkles and gray hair. And though experience is not the best teacher, *evaluated* experience *is* the best teacher.

Someone once said, "Experience teaches only the teachable." And when that happens, maturity happens. But maturity is not a gift. As author Aldous Huxley reminds us, "Experience is not what happens to you, it is what you do with what happens to you." This is important for us to remember as we dig into today's reading:

> In those days, when there was again a large crowd and they had nothing to eat, Jesus called His disciples and said to them, "I feel compassion for the people because they have remained with Me now three days and have nothing to eat. If I send them away hungry to their homes, they will faint on the way; and some of them have come from a great distance." And His disciples answered Him, "Where will anyone be able to find enough bread here in this desolate place to satisfy these people?" [Mark 8:1-4]

This story probably sounds familiar to you. Either you've heard it before or you've recently read something similar before—such as two chapters ago:

> *The people* saw them going, and many recognized them and ran there together on foot from all the cities, and got there ahead of them. When Jesus went ashore, He saw a large crowd, and He felt compassion for them because they were like sheep without a shepherd; and He began to teach them many things. When it was already quite late, His disciples came to Him and said, "This place is desolate and it is already

quite late; send them away so that they may go into the surrounding countryside and villages and buy themselves something to eat." But He answered them, "You give them *something* to eat!" And they said to Him, "Shall we go and spend two hundred denarii on bread and give them *something* to eat?" And He said to them, "How many loaves do you have? Go look!" And when they found out, they said, "Five, and two fish." (Mark 6:33-38)

Think about this. Two chapters ago this same scenario took place. Jesus fed five thousand men (not counting women and children) in Mark 6 with five loaves and two fish. And in chapter 8, we have the same situation with four thousand people (verse 9) and seven loaves (verse 6). So in Mark 8, we have less people, more food, and the same Jesus—and they still didn't get it.

After the miracle of watching five thousand men being fed on a little boy's lunch, His disciples still asked Jesus this humorous but very sad question: "Where will anyone be able to find enough bread here in this desolate place to satisfy these people?" (verse 4).

Let's switch gears for a moment. A popular cleaner on the market—one you may already use—is call Formula 409®. What you probably aren't familiar with, though, is that the name is actually a tribute to the tenacity of two young Detroit scientists whose goal was to formulate the greatest grease-cutting, dirt-destroying, bacteria-cutting cleaner on the planet. The thing is, creating the ultimate cleaner doesn't just happen on the first try. And it didn't happen on the 101st or the 301st either. It wasn't until batch number 409 that they were finally satisfied. And the name stuck: Formula 409.

I don't want it to take 409 times to get a lesson from Jesus. I want Him to call me 1 or 2. I'll even take 3 or 4—but not 409. The disciples couldn't put it together that the same Jesus was present for both miracles. Jesus who turns little to a lot was present for them—and is present for us.

When you find yourself stuck with no way out, go backward into your mind and think. When you do that, you will end up with a moment that God got you out, God came through, God multiplied the little into a lot.

Don't get stuck and forget.

Don't get spiritual amnesia.

Don't start over like this is the first time.

And for heaven's sake, don't be 409.

If He did it before, He can do it again!

Day 37

SEIZED STATEMENTS

Today's Reading: Mark 9

If there was anything you ever wanted to tell people, it would be what happened to three disciples on a mountain in Mark 9:2-7. The conversation might go like this . . .

"Guess who I saw today? Moses. Oh yeah, and Elijah. And guess whose voice I heard? *Audible* voice? God's! Yep, God Himself. I know what He sounds like now."

These are the ultimate bragging rights. Seeing two celebrity Old Testament guys and hearing God's audible voice? It doesn't get better than that.

And Jesus messed the whole thing up. He messed it all up when He said . . . "You can't say anything till after the resurrection."

What?

It was about to become a really good day for the disciples, and Jesus tapped the breaks and put a pause on it.

Listen closely. There is a huge challenge here for all of us. Just because you saw something and hear it from God doesn't mean you share it immediately. We are all guilty of saying things too quickly that we heard from God.

Let's speculate for a moment: what could have happened if they would have told that story when they came down?

The truth is whatever might have happened wouldn't have been what Jesus wanted for a good reason. The truth is that some things need to marinate before they are spoken. I think there are many things I read in the Bible that I was called to sit on before speaking them—for the following reasons:

- to grow in me
- to protect me from pride
- to give me more clarity on it
- to determine the best place and the best way to share it

And the best place or best way are not always immediately. Waiting develops self-control and turns it to God to say, *I trust Your timing*.

In this transfiguration scene, we do know whether this event occurred around AD 29 or AD 30, which means they may have had to keep their mouths shut for more than a year. Though Mark tells the story, Peter does too in 2 Peter 1:17-18:

> I was there on the holy mountain when he shone out with honor given him by God his Father; I heard that glorious, majestic voice calling down from heaven, saying, "This is my much-loved Son; I am well pleased with him." (TLB)

Peter finally got his time. He was finally able to tell it. And are you ready for this? That 2 Peter passage was written in AD 67, which would be almost forty years later. We have no record that he said anything before that.

One final thought: what are you supposed to do when God says to pause on speaking? Don't say anything. Let's read it together:

> As they were coming down from the mountain, He gave them orders not to relate to anyone what they had seen, until the Son of Man rose from the dead. They seized upon that statement, discussing with one another what rising from the dead meant. (Mark 9:9-10)

The Bible says when Jesus gave them the command, "they seized upon that statement." That is such a good phrase for us to learn in this journey. As you read the New Testament, you will seize upon a verse or seize a story.

Seize. This is such a strong word. To seize a statement means to take forcibly possession of something. You make it your own. They did that with something they did not understand fully. So practically, what do you do when one of these New Testament passages seize you? You do what the disciples did:

First, in verse 9 it says they "discussed it with one another." They got others' perspective from experience, study, and their own wrestling with a passage. For you and me, this means we need to read books, ask our pastor, discuss with our friends. We can't simply trust our viewpoint.

And second, verse 11 says, "They asked Him." Don't forget this: the author of the Bible is still alive and He knows what He wrote. There comes a time when you have to go to God in prayer and simply ask Him. In answer, He may speak to your heart (revelation) or He may guide you to other passages. The best interpretation of the Bible is the Bible. Let God interpret God.

So be quiet, ask God, and then listen to how He responds.

Day 38

JESUS GETS A TEST

Today's Reading: Mark 10

Today's reading is a tough one. Jesus gets a test . . . a test about marriage and divorce.

Before we dive into this chapter, listen to these poignant words from Augustine, which apply to what we're studying today: "If you believe what you like in the Gospel, and reject what you don't like, it is not the Gospel you believe, but yourself."

Now let's read about Jesus' test: "*Some* Pharisees came up to Jesus, testing Him, and *began* to question Him whether it was lawful for a man to divorce a wife" (Mark 10:2).

There are some hot-potato issues in the church—and one of those is about divorce and remarriage. Not only is this controversial today in the body of Christ, it was also in the first century when Jesus was here on the earth.

It's important to note that not every question is from an honest heart. Not every questioner is asking to get a truthful answer. Some people ask to see if you agree with them. That is why the divorce question here is not for the religious people to learn the truth, to discover insight or wisdom, but to see if Jesus agrees with them. They already had their opinions and now they want to test Jesus.

To test assumes two things: (1) you are the teacher; (2) you already know the answer, so you're seeing if your student knows the answer. Then you grade them on their answer. Think of the audacity—they are testing the omniscient God to see if He knows, not the right answer, but *their* answer.

That is really the issue today. When was the last time you asked Jesus a question about your struggling marriage? When was the last time you sought direction and theological wisdom from Him?

So many times we will go to a book, a pastor—someone who has already decided for us. But what about this issue? Have you ever asked Jesus: Should I divorce?

Most never ask Jesus if we should, instead we ask for help once it's already decided. Then we ask for Him to bless our already decided-upon plans.

If this is what you do, then this is the painful truth: you are testing Jesus just as these religious people did.

So how did Jesus respond?

First, we need to see it from a biblical basis and not a culture or society basis. With all the divorce that is happening today, people try to adjust Jesus' words to fit our epidemic of marriages falling apart. It's like our government that can't stop drugs so they legalize it to make that the best answer. But that is not an answer to a problem.

So if half of the marriages in the church end in divorce, as some statistics suggest, do we have to adjust Jesus' words based on the twenty-first-century marriage problem? I don't think so. Some have cited successful remarriages as their reason that divorce can't be wrong. They argue, "So and so got remarried and look at them after twenty-five years. It must be okay."

But we must be careful that we don't adjust Scripture to fit our beliefs or wants. Instead we must take Jesus' words as they stand:

> He answered and said to them, "What did Moses command you?" They said, "Moses permitted *a man* TO WRITE A CERTIFICATE OF DIVORCE AND SEND *her* AWAY." But Jesus said to them, "Because of your hardness of heart he wrote you this commandment. But from the beginning of creation, *God* MADE THEM MALE AND FEMALE. FOR THIS REASON A MAN SHALL LEAVE HIS FATHER AND MOTHER, AND THE TWO SHALL BECOME ONE FLESH; so they are no longer two, but one flesh. What therefore God has joined together, let no man separate." (Mark 10:3-11)

Here's my summary based on Jesus' words: Divorce was instituted by Moses. The motive for divorce was that our hearts are hard. Therefore, the reason for divorce was because we have hard hearts. Every marriage, no matter the struggle or the sin or the offense, can have a miracle ending with God if our hearts are soft.

God's intention from the beginning of creation was for two to become one flesh—and what God has joined together, *no one* should separate.

I heard a counselor once say to a young woman contemplating marriage: "Do not accept a man's proposal until you have successfully worked through at least one significant disagreement. Better yet, make it a heated argument that leaves one of you preferably in tears. If you have never been in the thick of a serious conflict with that person, you don't really know their heart. And marriage needs a soft heart to face hard situations."

So let me try to make this applicable. Divorce *is* an option—but it occurs because of a person becoming hard hearted.

Just look at the statistics on divorce and remarriage. Statistics have shown that in the United States, 50 percent of first marriages end in divorce. The number raises to 67 percent of second marriage, and 73 percent of third marriages. Why do the percentages go up each time a person gets married? Because they very likely have not addressed the hardness issue.

So now the question is . . . where is your heart today? Are you working toward a soft and tender heart? Or have you allowed your heart to become hardened?

Someone said it like this: "How do you fix your troubled marriage? You don't need a change of partners, but a change *in* partners."

We are only halfway through our scene with Jesus, though. When the disciples hear Jesus' response to the Pharisees, they ask for more insight. Notice verse 10: "In the house the disciples *began* questioning Him about this again." They are not testing Him, but genuinely questioning Him. They wanted answers. That was the difference between them and the religious leaders.

As you read Jesus' response, think about what that means for you in your marriage, if you are married, or if someday you want to pursue marriage. Ask Jesus what He means, just as the disciples did.

Day 39

What Stops Mountains from Ending up in the Ocean?

Today's Reading: Mark 11

Sometime ago, Dave Hagler, who works as an umpire in a recreational baseball league, was pulled over for driving too fast in the snow in Boulder, Colorado. He tried to talk the officer out of giving him a ticket by telling him how worried he was about insurance and how he's normally a very safe driver, and so on. The officer said that if he didn't like receiving the ticket, he could take the matter to court.

At the first game in the next baseball season, Dave was umpiring behind the plate when the first batter approached. And can you believe it, it was the policeman. As the officer was about to step into the batter's box, they recognized each other and offered a long pause.

Finally the officer asked, "So how did the thing with the ticket go?"

Dave said, "You'd better swing at everything."

Someone once said, "'I can forgive, but I cannot forget,' is only another way of saying, 'I cannot forgive.'"

I think Dave couldn't let it go. And all of that affected a recreational softball game.

Unforgiveness is underestimated. Marilyn Hickey tells us that a person who lives in unforgiveness does three things:

1. Curses the offense.
2. Nurses the offense.
3. Rehearses the offense.[47]

In today's reading, we focus on unforgiveness—and Jesus tells us there is a lot at stake when someone won't forgive. It's bigger than a softball game; instead, it infects the most powerful weapon we are given on this planet: prayer. Listen to what Jesus instructs us about prayer and unforgiveness:

Whenever you stand praying, forgive, if you have anything against anyone, so that your Father who is in heaven will also forgive you your transgressions. But if you do not forgive, neither will your Father who is in heaven forgive your transgressions." (Mark 11:25-26)

Today's Scripture mentions one of these problems that breaks the communication line. It's similar to a circuit breaker in a house. A circuit breaker in your house is an electrical device that interrupts the flow of electricity from one site to the other. Prayer circuit breakers are things in our lives that interrupt or hinder our communication with God. So when prayer is not working, something broke the circuit.

There are two commanding moments in this chapter on the power and importance of prayer. In verse 17, Jesus says that His house should be called a house of prayer. I think this is really missing today. While today, His house is a house of worship, preaching, teaching, serving, but not many believers have placed the importance on prayer on their church.

Jesus also tells us in verses 22-24 the power of prayer:

Jesus answered saying to them, "Have faith in God. Truly I say to you, whoever says to this mountain, 'Be taken up and cast into the sea,' and does not doubt in his heart, but believes that what he says is going to happen, it will be *granted* him. Therefore I say to you, all things for which you pray and ask, believe that you have received them, and they will be *granted* you."

One little thing can hinder mountains being put into the ocean—and that is unforgiveness. Jesus said all things for which we pray, we must believe we have received them and they will be granted—except when we don't forgive our spouse for disrespecting us yesterday. Or a friend for breaking a confidence. Or a supervisor for yelling at us in a staff meeting, which embarrassed us.

The bigger question is this: is unforgiveness really worth it?

If my not forgiving people stops me from seeing God answer my prayer and short circuits my prayer, I need to let my unforgiveness go. There's too much at stake.

Don't try to ask big when unforgiveness is big in you. Every time you want to hold on to an offense, just think, *If I do this, I get no mountains in the ocean.*

Norman Vincent Peale related how that, as a boy, he once bought a large cigar that he began to smoke. He was feeling bold until he saw his father approach him on the street. He tried to hide the cigar behind his back. Searching desperately for something to say, he made a certain request of his father. "My father's voice wasn't harsh when he answered; it was simply firm. 'Norman,' he said, 'one of the first lessons you should learn is this: never make a petition and at the same time try to hide a smoldering disobedience behind your back.'"[48]

Next time you go to God in prayer and you realize you are harboring something that you need to forgive, do it quickly and get those mountains thrown into oceans. Nothing is worse than asking our Father for something with the glaring disobedience of unforgiveness holding on.

WHEN THE RENTERS THINK
THEY ARE THE OWNERS

Today's Reading: Mark 12

Today's reading starts with a parable, a little story with a big meaning. Jesus tells it in nine verses but the actual story covers almost three thousand years. It is God telling His story from the beginning to ending with His Son coming to earth.

As we read this passage together, remember that Mark 11:27 says Jesus is in the Jerusalem temple telling this story to chief priests, scribes, and elders.

[Jesus] began to speak to them in parables: "A man PLANTED A VINEYARD AND PUT A WALL AROUND IT, AND DUG A VAT UNDER THE WINE PRESS AND BUILT A TOWER, and rented it out to vine-growers and went on a journey. At the *harvest* time he sent a slave to the vine-growers, in order to receive some of the produce of the vineyard from the vine-growers. They took him, and beat him and sent him away empty-handed. Again he sent them another slave, and they wounded him in the head, and treated him shamefully. And he sent another, and that one they killed; and *so with* many others, beating some and killing others. He had one more *to send*, a beloved son; he sent him last *of all* to them, saying, 'They will respect my son.' But those vine-growers said to one another, 'This is the heir; come, let us kill him, and the inheritance will be ours!' They took him, and killed him and threw him out of the vineyard. What will the owner of the vineyard do? He will come and destroy the vine-growers, and will give the vineyard to others. [Mark 12:1-9]

Verse 6 is the fast forward to the present of this story—the vineyard owner (the father) had one more to send, his beloved son, believing they would respect him. Yet the story ends with them killing the owner's son.

Who do you think Jesus is speaking about?

It is His own bio.

In fact, to make sure there is no misunderstanding, Jesus tells these religious Old Testament experts that this story is connected with the Scriptures they know so well as He quotes from Psalm 118:

> Have you not even read this Scripture: "THE STONE WHICH THE BUILDERS REJECTED, THIS BECAME THE CHIEF CORNER *stone*; THIS CAME ABOUT FROM THE LORD, AND IT IS MARVELOUS IN OUR EYES"? (Mark 12:10-11)

Jesus reminds us in the story that this is God's planet and we are just stewards of it.

I don't know if you have ever rented a house, a piece of property, an apartment that belonged to you and the renters forgot that it isn't their property? From the way they treated it and even becoming lax in their rent payments, they assumed the role of owner.

I am always reminded of the old 1901 hymn, "This Is My Father's World":

> This is my Father's world:
> O let me ne'er forget
> That though the wrong seems oft so strong,
> God is the Ruler yet.
> This is my Father's world:
> Why should my heart be sad?
> The Lord is King: let the heavens ring!
> God reigns, let the earth be glad![49]

We are the renters. God is the owner. This is our Father's world, we are stewards of it.

It's always dangerous when the renters act as though they are the owners—and it is especially dangerous when the owner is God. It's easy for us to forget and act like we're owners with our money and tithing when we give God our 10 percent. But it all belongs to God. We get to steward the other 90 percent. The same thing is true of our lives, which the apostle Paul reminds us in 1 Corinthians 6:19-20 (NIV): "You are not your own; you were bought at a price. Therefore honor God with your bodies."

When some women begin to announce that their bodies are their own—"my body, my choice"—regarding abortion practices and laws, nothing could be further from the truth. The renters are acting like owners. Those ladies and legislators are all bought with a price.

In order to say those kinds of words . . . you have to kill the Son.

One fundamental problem is that they did—but He rose again! The renters are still renters. We have to honor the Son.

Years ago, I heard an amazing story about a wealthy man who had one son, whom he loved dearly. He was a lover of art and he taught his son to love fine art. Because he was wealthy, he and his son amassed a valuable private collection of priceless works of art.

When he was old enough, the son joined the marines and was deployed to Vietnam, where he was killed in action. The father's heart was broken.

Several years later, when the wealthy man died, his estate planned to auction off his works of art, which were estimated to be worth in the millions of dollars were to be auctioned off. The day of the auction, with art dealers crowding in waiting to bid on the Van Goghs and the Monets, the lawyer announced that before any of the valuable art could be auctioned, the deceased had left specific instructions that the portrait of his son must be auctioned off first.

"Get on with it," the impatient art dealers complained. "Get that picture out of the way so we can bid on the real art!"

The auctioneer held up the painting. "Who'll you give me one hundred dollars for the picture of the son?" No one replied. Finally, a friend of the son's who was also a soldier said, "I'll give you twenty dollars for it."

"Twenty once," the auctioneer said, looking around the room. "Twenty twice. Sold for twenty dollars."

At that moment, the rich man's attorney stepped forward again and announced, "Ladies and gentlemen, there will no more bidding. My client left secret and specific instructions that whoever bought the painting of his son would receive all the other works of art at no additional charge. . . . To quote the words in his last will and testament, he wrote, 'Whoever chooses my son, gets it all.' This concludes the auction."

Whoever chooses God's Son gets it all.

As Romans 10:11 (TLB) reminds us: "The Scriptures tell us that no one who believes in Christ will ever be disappointed."

Not church.

Not religion.

Not a denomination.

Only the Son.

Day 41

THE BEST WAY TO STUDY END TIMES

Today's Reading: Mark 13

It seems that in Jesus' ministry, when something significant was going to happen, He took with Him the same three guys: Peter, James, and John. It is as if their names roll off your tongue. Those names just sound right together.

Those three men saw and heard things the other nine close disciples missed out on. When Jesus went to the Mount of Transfiguration, for instance, He took with Him Peter, James, and John. When He went into a room to raise a little girl from the dead, He went in with Peter, James, and John. In the garden of Gethsemane, when Jesus hit His agony moment and moved from the twelve, He asked those three to move with Him.

And then something crazy happened . . . someone broke through the clique: "As He was sitting on the Mount of Olives opposite the temple, Peter and James and John *and Andrew* were questioning Him privately" (Mark 13:3, emphasis added).

Somehow Andrew broke through and got entrance into the private club. It may be late but he made it. And the four of them—Peter, James, John, and . . . Andrew—all asked Jesus privately about the end times. The four received an eschatology lesson. Move aside Jack Van Impe and Tim LaHaye! And in giving them this lesson, He taught us as well.

Marty Duren gave five good pitfalls to avoid when talking about the coming of Jesus:

1. Making every news item a sign of the end times.

2. Playing "Name the Antichrist": in the 1970s and '80s, this was huge. People claimed Henry Kissinger, Ronald Reagan, the pope, even some secret guy in the Middle East were being raised up as the Antichrist.

3. Neglecting the original audience. This is important; some of the things Jesus said was for the AD 70 destruction of Jerusalem by Titus and not for "you" and the twenty-first century.

4. Setting dates for the coming of Jesus. As C. S. Lewis said, "Precisely because we cannot predict the moment, we must be ready at all moments."[50]

5. Overemphasizing an American role: people have gone so far as to say that "eagle's wings" in the Bible is the American mascot. Please. God sees every nation as a drop in the bucket (see Isaiah 40:15-17).[51]

So how do we deal with Bible prophecy like this Olivet discourse that Jesus gave in a private discussion not to three men but to four? We need to hear about the end times and the rapture and the judgment to come, but we must do it the right way. It was so important, Mark dedicated this whole chapter to their private conversation. The book of Daniel, the book of Revelation, and the Olivet discourses from Mark 13 are important but should be approached carefully.

If you want to understand the second coming and interpret things correctly, then be a student of the first coming. We see how God thinks when He sent His Son the first time. Read the Old Testament prophecies and images and see how this worked in the first coming. God is consistent. There are more than three hundred prophesies of times and places and events when Jesus came the first time. Learn the way God predicts the future. If you are not a student of the first coming, you will embellish Bible verses for the second coming.

And finally, I like what Charles H. Spurgeon said, which we can apply to contemplating end times. It is really what the four disciples did in their conversation with Jesus. Spurgeon said that prayer is the best way to open up the Scriptures.

Brethren in the ministry, you who are teachers in the Sunday school and all of you who are learners in the college of Christ Jesus, I pray you remember that prayer is your best means of study—like Daniel you shall understand the dream and the interpretation when you have sought God. And like John you shall see the seven seals of the precious Truth of God unloosed after you have wept much. "Yes, if you cry after knowledge and lift up your voice for understanding: if you seek her as silver and search for her as for hid treasures: then shall you understand the fear of the Lord and find the knowledge of God." (Prov 2:3-6)

Stones are not broken except by an earnest use of the hammer. And the stone-breaker usually goes down on his knees. Use the hammer of diligence and let the knees of prayer be exercised, too, and there is not a stony doctrine in Revelation which is useful for you to understand which will not fly into shivers under the exercise of prayer and faith. Martin Luther said it best "To have prayed well is to have studied well." You may force your way through anything with the leverage of prayers.[52]

You want to know about end times? Study the first coming and the Scriptures and pray, seeking God's wisdom.

WHAT WERE YOU THINKING AT #1?

Today's Reading: Mark 14

A man who felt convicted for lying on his last tax return wrote this letter to the IRS:

> Dear IRS: Enclosed you will find a check for $150. I cheated on my income tax return last year and have not been able to sleep ever since. If I still have trouble sleeping, I will send you the rest.

His problem: he is waiting for more sleepless nights to bring closure. He is not fixing it on the first go around. That first sleepless night should have been a signal.

In today's reading we see the important of handling things in first go around. And it has to do with Peter and a crowing rooster.

Let me read to you about this dreadful Thursday night:

> Jesus said to them, "You will all fall away, because it is written, 'I WILL STRIKE DOWN THE SHEPHERD, AND THE SHEEP SHALL BE SCATTERED.' But after I have been raised, I will go ahead of you to Galilee." But Peter said to Him, "Even though all may fall away, yet I will not." And Jesus said to him, "Truly I say to you, that this very night, before a rooster crows twice, you yourself will deny me three times." But *Peter* kept saying insistently, "Even if I have to die with You, I will not deny You!" And they all were saying the same thing also. [Mark 14:27-31]

And between verses 66-71 we read that Peter denied Jesus three times. One of them being with him cursing and swearing to make sure the people knew he was *not* a disciple.

And then the fulfillment of what Jesus said to Peter came to him: "Immediately a rooster crowed a second time. And Peter remembered how Jesus had made the remark to him, 'Before a rooster crows twice, you will deny Me three times.' And he began to weep" (verse 72).

Prominent American Methodist minister Halford Luccock said: "In Christian experience, great living begins in tears. It is God's starting point. When Peter broke down and wept, all pride, of which he had much, and all self-sufficiency and self-trust dropped away from him."[53]

Listen to Jesus' warning again in verse 30—"Before a rooster crows twice." Then in verse 72, after Peter's third denial, it says, "A rooster crowed a second time" and at that second crowing, Peter began to weep because he remembered what Jesus had said.

Sometimes we don't take seriously the Word of God until it is finally fulfilled. That is a dangerous way to live.

I had a rooster that lived next to me in Detroit, right in the heart of the inner city. It was the craziest thing. My neighbors had chickens and a rooster that perched in a tree. That rooster would crow every morning at 5 a.m. and every morning, one of my roommates would say, "Oh, Jesus, don't let me deny You today."

Amazing how that rooster reminded him of that story. That rooster's crow made Peter recall every word of the Master. No sooner had he completed his third denial then the rooster crowed. So my question to Peter: What were you thinking at rooster crow #1?

We read about #2, which was after the full denial. But what about the first crow? What went through Peter's mind?

Obviously he did not heed it. It does not seem that it slowed him down. We don't have a verse that shows Peter thinking, *Hmm, this can't be a coincidence. . . . The Rabbi said something along these lines . . . that I would deny Him and that the signal would be a rooster's crow.*

But nothing. No brake lights for Peter. This was not some new convert. This was a disciple trained by Jesus Himself.

It just goes to show the power of fear, sin, and compromise. As James S. Stewart said in *The Strong Name*:

It might seem natural to suppose that every time a man sins he would know a little more about sin, its nature and its methods. Actually the exact reverse is true. Every time he sins he is making himself less capable of realizing what sin is, less likely to recognize that he is, in fact, a sinner; for the ugly thing (and this, I feel sure, has never been sufficiently grasped), for the really diabolical thing about sin is that it perverts human judgment.[54]

Hence every time any of us sins, we are making it not more but *less* probable for us to appreciate what sin is, and therefore not more but less likely that we shall feel there is anything to be forgiven. Every time I reject some voice in conscience, I am making it certain that next time that voice is going to speak not more but less imperiously and convincingly.

I think crow #1 was the shout from God to say, *Put on the brakes. God's Word is true. Stop here and don't go any further!*

To hear crow #1 is the canon ball over the bow of the boat. It shouts that God is right!

Listen to him. No one jumps to #2 without first receiving a #1 warning.

There are nine words in the Greek language for *sin*. But the one that always catches my attention is the *trespass*. Have you ever violated a "no trespassing" sign? You have to do a lot to get by it. You have to climb through barbed wire. Climb over a fence. Go by the blaring sign.

Trespass means you have to *really* work to sin. God is active in wanting to warn and protect you.

Though you may not be as fortunate as I was to live next to a rooster in Detroit, it does not mean you don't get the same effect. Let me give you a rooster crow that you will be sure not to miss: It is the conviction of the Holy Spirit.

A conviction does not stop you from doing anything, it just keeps you from enjoying it. I love this young boy's definition of conviction: "Something that makes you tell your mother before your sister does."

The Holy Spirit begins to bring a feeling inside of us that something is not right. This is a crow #1 protection. Before a failure turns into a fall, He will convict us.

The old churches built in America some hundreds of years ago were built with the steeple that had weather cocks on them. They were put there to remind the people that even Peter, the first among the apostles, fell into the deep grievous sin of pride and denied his Lord.

I wonder what church members and boards would say today if a pastor put the rooster back on the church so folks would not backslide. We might hear . . .

"That's so negative!"

"Why remind us of failure and sin?"

"You are so judgmental!"

But I would be thinking, *God is always right, listen to Him.*

CAN YOU IMAGINE IF YOUR DAD CARRIED JESUS' CROSS?

Today's Reading: Mark 15

Today we come to the darkest day in human history: the crucifixion of Jesus. Calvary shows how far people will go in sin—and how far God will go for our salvation (God always goes a step further, loving us). Every step that Jesus took to the cross said, *I love you* to every person in history.

As we study the crucifixion, we need to look at something that happened on the way to the cross, which has huge significance:

> After they had mocked Him, they took the purple robe off Him and put His own garments on Him. And they led Him out to crucify Him. They pressed into service a passer-by coming from the country, Simon of Cyrene (the father of Alexander and Rufus), to bear His cross. (Mark 15:20-21)

The Bible not only tells us the name of the man who carried Jesus' cross, Simon of Cyrene, it also tells us the names of his children. We know this about Simon: he was a father of two boys, Alexander and Rufus, and also it was not his plan or desire to carry the cross of Jesus. The Bible says in verse 21 that they pressed him into service. Simon wasn't even a spectator, he was just a "passer-by," whom they had to force to carry the cross.

Can you imagine the family story if your dad carried Jesus' cross? I come from a storytelling family and this would have been the story around our dinner table (where we told most of our stories with very loud Italian emotion and hands flying everywhere).

Seriously, though, can you imagine if one of those stories from your dad was, "Did I ever tell you the time when I was in Jerusalem, minding my own business, and a Roman soldier pulled me out of the crowd?"

As a father, I want to live such a godly life in front of my children that I will not have to say to them, "Don't do what I did." I want to say to them, "Live how I lived." I want them to imitate me.

I wonder if that's what Simon told Rufus? Do you know the father-and-son relationship between Simon and Rufus? Do you know these two biblical names?

In Romans 16:13, most historians and commentators believe that the Rufus mentioned there was the son of a cross carrier. And not just *a* cross carrier, but *the* cross carrier: "Greet Rufus, a choice man in the Lord, also his mother and mine."

Rufus was the son of Simon of Cyrene, the man who was called out of the crowd to carry the cross of Jesus. And that family's introduction to faith in Jesus could have very well started on the day the dad carried Jesus' actual cross.[55]

Can you imagine Rufus hearing the story from his father about that day of the redemption of the planet? It was Simon not only being in the right place at the right time, but being willing to do the right thing when called upon.

Cross carrying is not out of style. It's still on our agenda. But not one time only. Luke 9:23 tells us something about taking up a cross: "[Jesus] was saying to *them* all, 'If anyone wishes to come after Me, he must deny himself, and take up his cross daily and follow Me."

It isn't one-and-done, like Simon's literal experience. It's daily, right in your home, on your campus, at your job. So what does taking up your cross look like?

What Simon did was interrupt his plans and his life at whatever expense for Jesus.

Each day Jesus will interrupt us. It could be that He's leading us to apologize, to complement, to encourage, to correct. It could be in generosity, giving to the poor, stopping and praying with someone. Taking up our cross is when our plans are interrupted by God to do whatever He needs us to do.

It could be as simple as wanting to watch Netflix or FOX news or CNN or ESPN, and God interrupts you and says, *My plan is for you to be with your family or be in the Word of God*. That can happen, that's the cross, interrupting what you want to do, and doing what God is wanting you to do.

Taking up your cross daily is when Jesus calls upon you to do something for Him. No one cheered for Simon that day, except heaven.

Just as Rufus knew his father carried the cross, I want my children to know that when I was called on to carry the cross, I did it each day.

Theologian A. W. Tozer explains the results of a cross-carrying person: "There are three marks of one who is crucified. One, he is facing in only one direction. Two, he can never turn back. And three, he no longer has any plans of his own."[56]

I hope that what can always be said of you and me.

THE BIG ROCK STORY SOUNDS LIKE A BIG BANG STORY

Today's Reading: Mark 16

Today's reading brings us to Mark's account of resurrection morning. Mark's description of resurrection morning is priceless. My favorite moment is in verses 3-4:

> They were saying to one another, "Who will roll away the stone for us from the entrance of the tomb?" Looking up, they saw that the stone had been rolled away, although it was extremely large.

They were saying to each other, "Who will roll away the stone?" And verse 4 gives us insight to the why of their question: "Looking up, they saw that the stone had been rolled away." That means their heads were down as they asked the question. If they would have come with their heads up, they would have seen it was done already. They were asking for something already accomplished.

I think this lesson is significant. Looking up may already give you your answer. One of those wrong-look questions goes like this: "I wish God existed and He was easily proven."

Look up is what I want to say!

David says God's creation is always talking to us about the One who created it. It's pouring out speech to the planet. Look up, it's talking, it's saying something: "The heavens are telling of the glory of God; And their expanse is declaring the work of His hands. Day to day pours forth speech, And night to night reveals knowledge" (Psalm 19:1-2).

The Message says it like this: "God's glory is on tour in the skies, God-craft on exhibit across the horizon. Madame Day holds classes every morning, Professor Night lectures each evening. Their words aren't heard, their voices aren't recorded, but their silence fills the earth: unspoken truth is spoken everywhere" (Psalm 19:1-4).

Why is this important? Because people are looking in the wrong places and ending up with the wrong conclusions about God's existence.

Romans 1:20 tells us, "Since the creation of the world His invisible attributes, His eternal power and divine nature, have been clearly seen, being understood through what has been made, so that they are without excuse." Paul is saying that God's creation clearly shows God. We don't need a "made by God" stamp underneath every rock.

His workmanship is so clear that God says there is no excuse for anyone not to believe. The issue is not that it's seeable, but that humans refuse to look and believe.

Let's look at Romans 1:19 out of *The Message*: "The basic reality of God is plain enough. Open your eyes and there it is!"

Sounds a lot like a big rock story. The big rock story is like the Big Bang story.

If you don't look correctly, you end up with the wrong conclusions. When you see creation you end up with a big God not a big bang. The science community is divided on this and not slanted. Many would make you think that there are only a few crazy creationist scientists and all the others figured it out. It's not that way in science. Scientists are looking up and seeing a big God.

When you look up, you may see more than you bargained for. This is how Isaiah explains it:

Lift up your eyes on high and see who has created these stars, the One who leads forth their host by number, He calls them all by name; because of the greatness of His might and the strength of *His* power, not one of *them* is missing. Why do you say, O Jacob, and assert, O Israel, "My way is hidden from the Lord, and the justice due me escapes the notice of my God"? Do you not know? Have you not heard?

The Everlasting God, the Lord, the Creator of the ends of the earth does not become weary or tired. His understanding is inscrutable. He gives strength to the weary, and to *him* who lacks might He increases power. Though youths grow weary and tired, and vigorous young men stumble badly, yet those who wait for the Lord will gain new strength; they will mount up *with* wings like eagles, they will run and not get tired, they will walk and not become weary. (Isaiah 40:26-31)

Isaiah says that if we lift up our eyes, we may see something pretty cool about God. The women at Jesus' tomb lifted up their eyes and saw that God is stronger than death and He doesn't lie, He rose from the dead.

Lift up your eyes when you pray for something. God may have already done it for you.

Day 45

You Never Know What Could Happen if You just Show Up

Today's Reading: Luke 1

Change is hard for those who have been doing the same thing for a long time. We see that truth in today's reading about an older couple who are about to have their world turned upside down—all because they prayed something when they were young and it didn't get answered until they were old.

It's the story of Elizabeth and Zacharias, cast members in God's story. They were about to discover their why in life. Let's read this passage from Luke 1:5-7:

> In the days of Herod, king of Judea, there was a priest named Zacharias, of the division of Abijah; and he had a wife from the daughters of Aaron, and her name was Elizabeth. They were both righteous in the sight of God, walking blamelessly in all the commandments and requirements of the Lord. But they had no child, because Elizabeth was barren, and they were both advanced in years.

That's just a kind way of saying they were old, although we don't know how old. And yet notice something ageless that happened to Zechariah—he was faithful. And faithfulness is always rewarded by God. Let's read the passage together—and notice how boring it is on how he was led to the spot where God showed up.

> Now it happened that while he was performing his priestly service before God in the *appointed* order of his division, according to the custom of the priestly office, he was chosen by lot to enter the temple of the Lord and burn incense.
>
> And the whole multitude of the people were in prayer outside at the hour of the incense offering. And an angel of the Lord appeared to him, standing to the right of the altar of incense. Zacharias was troubled when he saw *the angel*, and fear gripped him. But the angel

said to him, "Do not be afraid, Zacharias, for your petition has been heard, and your wife Elizabeth will bear you a son, and you will give him the name John. [Luke 1:8-13]

Don't take faithfulness lightly. God sees it as rewardable and promotable. This is amazing to me and nothing seems spiritual about this, but his name was on the list. It didn't magically appear there; he was scheduled to do the priestly service.

He wasn't led by the Holy Spirit. He didn't feel it. That day he just showed up, and guess what? God showed up too—with his destiny.

Who knows what will happen if you look at the schedule and realize this week it's your turn—and maybe something will happen to you as it did to Zacharias. The children's department put you on the schedule. A leader said you are on ushering or greeting this Sunday. Here is a thought, look at the calendar and go, believing that maybe if you show up, God will show up.

Zacharias showed up and God did show up. Don't ever take it lightly that you showing up every Sunday simply because it's on the list.

The longest standing ovation in sport's history was twenty-two minutes for Cal Ripken Jr. of the Baltimore Orioles when he beat Lou Gehrig's record for most consecutive games played in Major League Baseball. He just showed up every day for 2,632 games without taking a day off.[57] Cal Ripken is in the hall of fame because he showed up.

What you think is routine and redundant, God calls faithful. As Hudson Taylor said, "A little thing is a little thing, but faithfulness in a little thing is a big thing."[58]

Why did this happen when it happened? Because God's timing is perfect.

Here is what the angel told him: "Do not be afraid, Zacharias, for your petition has been heard, and your wife Elizabeth will bear you a son, and you will give him the name John" (verse 13).

After the word *heard*, we find a comma. Sometimes that is not simply a place for us to catch our breath and pause. Sometimes it means there is a pause in the conversation. I think it's the latter.

I think Zacharias forgot what he and Elizabeth had prayed for. It reads like the angel said, "Your prayer has been heard." Silence . . . "Elizabeth will bear you a son."

They prayed the prayer when they were young is the implication. For Elizabeth and Zacharias, the answer to their prayer was slow in coming . . . really slow.

"Your petition has been heard. You will bear a son and you will call him John." God couldn't answer their original prayer at the time they prayed, since Jesus was not born yet. The life of Jesus needed the life of John the Baptist. They were going to bring fulfillment to what Isaiah talked about. We see this from Matthew 3:3: "For this is the one referred to by Isaiah the prophet when he said, 'THE VOICE OF ONE CRYING IN THE WILDERNESS, "MAKE READY THE WAY OF THE LORD, MAKE HIS PATHS STRAIGHT!"'"

God was sending His Son. John the Baptist was needed to prepare the way. And it was the perfect time to answer the prayer of the older couple. And it all happened because Zecharias showed up, because his name was on the volunteer list that day. Go Zacharias. Go church volunteers!

LOSING JESUS

Today's Reading: Luke 2

One of my favorite quotes about moms comes from the old 1960s' comedian Milton Berle: "If evolution really works, how come mothers only have two hands?"

With all a mother has to do, it is no surprise when a child gets accidentally left behind in the rush and frenzy of trying to get someplace. Have you ever done that? My wife and I have . . . or should I say, I have. I think each of my children have called me while I was driving in my car to tell me I left them at church.

Have you ever lost a child in a store? In our family when I was growing up, we had a special whistle that my mom had. When we were lost we just listened for that whistle. Every mother has experienced losing a child at one time or another. Don't be discouraged; even the best mother ever messed up. Ready for this? Mary, the mother of Jesus, lost Him.

That's our study today as we dive into Luke 2.

It can be embarrassing to lose a child. But what if your child is Jesus—and you lost Him? Then it's cataclysmic. Let's read the story:

Now His parents went to Jerusalem every year at the Feast of the Passover. And when He became twelve, they went up *there* according to the custom of the Feast; and as they were returning, after spending the full number of days, the boy Jesus stayed behind in Jerusalem. But His parents were unaware of it, but supposed Him to be in the caravan, and went a day's journey; and they *began* looking for Him among their relatives and acquaintances. When they did not find Him, they returned to Jerusalem looking for Him. Then, after three days they found Him in the temple, sitting in the midst of the teachers, both listening to them and asking them questions. And all who heard Him were amazed at His understanding and His answers. When they saw Him, they were astonished; and His mother said to Him, "Son, why have You treated us this way? Behold, Your father and I have been anxiously looking for You." And He said to them, "Why is it that you were looking for Me? Did you not know that I had to be in My Father's *house*?" (Luke 2:41-49)

I love Mary and think she is an amazing woman. This story tells me why Mary could not be sinless, though. You can't be sinless and lose God.

Let's get a couple of lessons from our story. Mary and Joseph made two big mistakes in this situation:

1. They supposed Him to be in the caravan;
2. They looked for Him among their relatives.

Let's consider the first mistake: they assumed Jesus was there without checking. They "supposed Him to be in the caravan." How many times have we supposed something? We suppose because we are in a church that Jesus is there; or we suppose because someone says they are saved that Jesus is there in their heart. We can't suppose anything. The question is: "Is He there or is He not there?" How do I know if Jesus is with you? Because wherever Jesus is, change happens. Not change on your weekend when you come to church, but an everyday change!

How long has your journey gone on and you have not stopped even to ask yourself, *Is Jesus with me?* Or how long has it been until you realized that Jesus is not there with you? Thank God it took Mary and Joseph only a day to figure out that He wasn't with them; many go on for years.

Their second mistake was that they assumed, *If He is with the family, He is with me.*

This is really dangerous. They looked for Him among their relatives, but they looked in the wrong place. We do that too. We look for Jesus in a church, a denomination, even on a day of the week. How often have we even thought, *My mom is religious, so I am religious too.* Your mom may have Jesus, but that doesn't mean you do. The place you look for Jesus is in your own heart. God only comes where we invite Him into our lives. He is not there automatically. As John 1:12-13 (niv) tells us: "Yet to all who did receive him, to those who believed in his name, he gave the right to become children of God—children born not of natural descent, nor of human decision or a husband's will, but born of God."

When it was all said and done, it took Mary and Joseph four days to finally find Jesus:

> When they did not find Him, they returned to Jerusalem looking for Him. Then, after three days they found Him in the temple, sitting in the midst of the teachers, both listening to them and asking them questions. (Luke 2:45-46)

As Tim Keller reminds us:

Every religious founder of every major religion says, "I'm a prophet who has come to show you the way to God." But of all the major religions of the world, only Christianity has a founder who has the audacity to say "I *am* God, and I have come to find *you*." Do you realize how different that is?[59]

If Jesus is not with us, let's find Him today. Or let's get it straight that He is not lost, we are.

John the Baptist's Water Baptism Instructional Class

Today's Reading: Luke 3

Today I want to take you to a water baptism class. I believe that water baptism displays the difference between the casual Christian and a serious follower of Jesus, because it is clear in the Bible that it is a next step after being born again. As Max Lucado says, "Baptism separates the tire kickers from the car buyers."

Water Baptism does not mark an arrival but a beginning. Let me tell you four things that are important about water baptism:

1. It's Scriptural

Water baptism was Jesus' idea not the church's. In Matthew 28:19-20, we read that Jesus connected water baptism to discipleship. Water baptism is done when a person is born again. You never read of an unbaptized believer anywhere in the Bible. Water baptism is done after second birth, not the first birth. There is not one single verse in the Bible that says you become a Christian when your body touches the water.

2. Historically, It's Public

You are going public with your faith. When you get water baptized, you get advertised. It is a public declaration to show everyone whom you are following. You will see places in Scripture that say, "There was much water."

They would do this outside in a lake or a river. Wherever it took place, it was for everyone to see what had happened to that person. The same is true for you. The city, your family, your coworkers, heaven, and hell now know you have taken the second step of discipleship with your walk with Jesus.

3. It's Symbolic

When we get married, we say, "With this ring, I thee wed." Though we make that statement, we know that putting the ring on the finger is not what makes us married. The same is true with water baptism. There is no magic water. It's not the water that does anything; it is our step of obedience that is the big deal.

To make it anything more than a symbol is dangerous, it's like worshiping our wedding bands.

To cling to a symbol is what many try to do, though. And they miss what God is trying to show us. What is the symbol? It is a symbol of death, burial, and resurrection.

4. Practically, It's a Next Obedience Step

Can we go to heaven dry and unbaptized? Of course we can. Anyone who says differently forgot a story about a thief on the cross who did not have the time or the tank to be baptized (see Luke 23:39-43).

You express love by obedience. Love is not just a feeling. Love is a controlling passion to do something for the one we love. The apostle John told us, "If you love me, show it by doing what I've told you" (John 14:15, MSG).

What makes Luke 3 crazy is how different John the Baptist's baptismal class is:

> [John] *began* saying to the crowds who were going out to be baptized by him, "You brood of vipers, who warned you to flee from the wrath to come? Therefore bear fruits in keeping with repentance, and do not begin to say to yourselves, 'We have Abraham for our father,' for I say to you that from these stones God is able to raise up children to Abraham. Indeed the axe is already laid at the root of the trees; so every tree that does not bear good fruit is cut down and thrown into the fire." (Luke 3:7-9)

I don't know if I would start my water baptism class with calling the people "snakes." My class would start off with something like this, "I am so glad you are here."

After John called them snakes, he told them that an axe was resting on the root of their hearts waiting to chop it down if they have not repented and fruit has not come from their lives.

It's incredible what happens next: the people ask, "What shall we do?"

They got it!

I remember Leonard Ravenhill once telling me that when God is moving with repentance, we don't have to tell people what to do, because they will ask us what to do before we tell them.

That's what the people did with John the Baptist. What's interesting is that in verses 11-14, we see he gave direction to three different groups of people:

The first group were the multitudes. He told this group to learn to be givers, to share their blessings (verse 11).

The second group were the tax collectors. He told them not to be like everyone else; to be different and to act like believers in their jobs. He wanted them to use their jobs as an arena for them to show off God's power in their lives, that they should be different—no matter how others act (verses 12-13).

The third group were the Roman soldiers. He told them to stop abusing their authority, build relationships, and be content with their wages (verse 14).

Then something amazing happened: the people got baptized that day—the multitudes, the tax collectors, and the soldiers. Not only did they get baptized, verse 21 tells us that Jesus also got baptized.

They got baptized with Jesus! What a powerful lesson for you today: you never know what will happen when you do what God wants you to do.

SATAN QUOTES THE BIBLE

Today's Reading: Luke 4

In today's reading we actually get to read one of the most amazing chapters of a different book—Psalm 91. Psalm 91 starts off with these familiar words:

> He who dwells in the shelter of the Most High will abide in the shadow of the Almighty. I will say to the LORD, "My refuge and my fortress, my God, in whom I trust!" [Verses 1-2]

And then Psalm 91 ends with these powerful words from God:

> "He will call upon Me, and I will answer him; I will be with him in trouble; I will rescue him and honor him. "With a long life I will satisfy him and let him see My salvation." [Verses 15-16]

It is an entire psalm of God's protection on His children. Sandwiched in between these verses is specific protection from God's angels, His army:

> He will give His angels charge concerning you, to guard you in all your ways. They will bear you up in their hands, that you do not strike your foot against a stone. [Verses 11-12]

We find this psalm quoted in Luke 4, but what makes this crazy is the one who quotes it. Ready for this? Satan, the devil himself quotes the Bible—to Jesus, God Himself.

As we read today, Jesus is in the wilderness with the devil and He is fighting against the three temptations Satan throws at Him by quoting Scripture. Three times Jesus says, "It is written" to the devil. For the second temptation, Satan takes Jesus to the top of the temple and tempts Jesus to jump off the pinnacle and then complicates the temptation by quoting Psalm 91:

> The devil led him to Jerusalem and had him stand on the highest point of the temple. "If you are the Son of God," he said, "throw yourself down from here. For it is written: 'He will command his angels concerning

you to guard you carefully; they will lift you up in their hands, so that you will not strike your foot against a stone.'" (Verses 9-11, NIV)

A crazy temptation gets muddied when the devil quotes the Bible, which makes it seem justified. Satan says, "It is written" just as Jesus said it. The devil knows the Bible and that the devil quotes and uses and manipulates it is a very scary thought.

People don't realize that nothing is off limits for Satan. His attacks are not always to tempt us with obvious things, like porn, alcohol, or drugs. He can use the Bible to try to get people to do things in the name of God, without God being anywhere near it.

Just because you have a Bible verse to back up your thoughts and actions may not mean that verse came from God. Could the devil have spoken a verse to you?

He did to Jesus. Listen closely. How do you think cults get started. With just one verse that Satan manipulates and tempts people to believe. Where do cults gets their beginning? With a Satanic interpretation of a Bible verse. Satan's interpretation of Psalm 91 was that God wanted Jesus to jump off the highest point of the temple to show that God wouldn't let Him fall, that His angels would catch Him. Nothing could be more of an abuse to a passage of Scripture than what Satan told Jesus.

He tried to get Jesus to do something based upon an isolated Scripture that wasn't interpreted in light of the whole Bible.

Did you get that? It is not that the Bible is in contradiction, it is that our interpretations contradict the Bible. And the misinterpretation comes when we define a verse without understanding its context, when we define a verse isolated from the entire Bible's intent.

Some years ago I was sitting with a young man in a Detroit diner who was convinced that Billy Graham and I were both going to hell if we were not baptized with a certain formula that his group said we had to be baptized with. For him salvation was built on a baptism formula instead of on the blood shed at Calvary. His religious group took a Bible passage and instead of adding all the other verses together, they jumped off into thin air. The very thing Jesus did not do.

Remember the issue in the wilderness temptation: It isn't the Bible that contradicts itself, but our wrong interpretations that contradict the Bible.

Bible interpretation must be done with a number of things in view:

- Historical context
- Original languages
- Context
- Rest of the Bible (seeing the whole not just the one passage)

There are people who will take passages and find themselves jumping into thin air and will find no angels to catch their fall.

So here is what Jesus does in this scene: He interprets the Word with the Word. Many times we interpret the Word with books. The Bible interprets the Bible.

So what does all this mean to you and me?

First, nothing is off limits to Satan. He will use holy things and pervert them. The Bible is not out of bounds; Satan is no respecter of persons. Think about it, he quoted God's Word to *Jesus*, not to some new convert. He will pervert passages and preachers and churches. Nothing is safe when the devil is around.

Second, we must live by the whole Bible not a verse. People have have done crazy things based on one verse and have failed to enrich themselves and others.

Satan can use an "out of context" Bible verse to get us to do something out of God's will. Out of context is out of God's will. Be prepared and be alert to the devil's schemes.

Day 49

I Want My Own Fish Story

Today's Reading: Luke 5

I have a prayer I pray that a pastor friend from Alabama taught me. It goes like this: "Lord, the answer is yes even before You ask."

I want to be able to say yes to the Lord at all times. I want you to be able to do that too, so let me talk to you about fishing and your *yes, Lord* agreement.

I don't really fish. I *have* been fishing but I am by no means a fisherman nor do I enjoy it.

You always hear of people telling their fish story where the fish seems to get bigger and bigger the more they tell it. In actuality they caught Nemo, but over time they hooked Jaws.

Today's reading shows us a great fish story. This one is Peter's:

> Now it happened that while the crowd was pressing around Him and listening to the word of God, He was standing by the lake of Gennesaret; and He saw two boats lying at the edge of the lake; but the fishermen had gotten out of them and were washing their nets. And He got into one of the boats, which was Simon's, and asked him to put out a little way from the land. And He sat down and *began* teaching the people from the boat. When He had finished speaking, He said to Simon, "Put out into the deep water and let down your nets for a catch." Simon answered and said, "Master, we worked hard all night and caught nothing, but I will do as You say and let down the nets." When they had done this, they enclosed a great quantity of fish, and their nets began to break; so they signaled to their partners in the other boat for them to come and help them. And they came and filled both of the boats, so that they began to sink. But when Simon Peter saw that, he fell down at Jesus' feet, saying, "Go away from me Lord, for I am a sinful man!" For amazement had seized him and all his companions because of the catch of fish which they had taken. (Luke 5:1-9)

Don't miss those first few words, because they are significant.
Jesus saw two boats (verse 2).

He got into one boat (verse 3).

He saw two, He got into one. This leaves me with the question, had I been there, would it have been my boat He got into?

Why is that important? It's important because that's the boat the miracle came from. That's the boat that had the big fish story attached to it. That's the boat that caught so many fish that the net broke.

But something else happened. Verse 7 says when the fishermen saw that the net was breaking, "they signaled to their partners in the other boat." That's boat number 2 of the story—the boat that wasn't chosen. Peter received the miracle; the other boat received the overflow.

The other boat didn't have Jesus preach from it.

The other boat didn't have Jesus challenge them to go out deeper.

The other boat didn't hear fishing commands from a carpenter.

The other boat got to participate with the fish.

The other boat did not get a fish story but they got to tell another man's fish story.

The more I thought about it, the more I realized . . .

I want God to choose me.

I want God to pick my boat.

I want God to pick my family.

I'm tired of telling other people's fish stories. I'm tired of getting to experience other people's obedience.

It's time for me to go out deeper.

It's time for me to hear from God for myself.

It's time for me to let the carpenter tell the experienced man, "You don't know everything, do what I say."

It's time for me to get my own fish story.

Tired of secondhand fish stories? There are always two boats ready! It's time for you to say, "Yes, Lord! Use my boat, Jesus!"

Day 50

A Christian's Retaliation Response

Today's Reading: Luke 6

I know there is a lot of folklore that goes with the masterpiece of the Lord's Supper painting by Leonardo Da Vinci. Whether this is true or not, I love this story I read recently about the painting.

When Leonardo Da Vinci was working on this famous Last Supper painting, he became angry with one of his assistants, berating the man without mercy. After banishing his assistant from his studio, he went back to work. As an act of revenge, he used the person's face who had offended him for the face of Judas.

He continued his work until he tried to paint the face of Jesus, and he couldn't do it. No matter how hard he tried, he was unable to paint Christ's. So he stopped painting, went to his assistant and asked his forgiveness. Only when the man forgave him and they reconciled was Da Vinci able to return to the table of the Last Supper and paint Jesus.

When Leonardo showed mercy and pardon to his assistant, Jesus became a lot clearer. This is where we land in today's reading. Jesus becomes clearer to us and the world around us based on how we respond to people who hurt us or take advantage of us. In fact, when we read this chapter, we recognize that it's about Christian retaliation.

Listen to Jesus' words from Luke's Sermon on the Mount:

> I say to you who hear, love your enemies, do good to those who hate you, bless those who curse you, pray for those who mistreat you. Whoever hits you on the cheek, offer him the other also; and whoever takes away your coat, do not withhold your shirt from him either. Give to everyone who asks of you, and whoever takes away what is yours, do not demand it back. Treat others the same way you want them to treat you. (Luke 6:27-31)

Here is the Christian retaliation: Do good to those who hate you. Pray for those who mistreat you. Notice I didn't say to post about it on social media. We are to pray, not post.

If a person hits you on one side, offer the other side. If they steal, give them something else they didn't ask for. Give to everyone who asks of you and don't demand back.

This seems unnatural to do—and it is. It's supernatural. This is where the face of Jesus shows up clearer for you, on you, and for others.

A number of years ago, Dr. David H. Fink, a psychiatrist for the veterans' administration, wrote a book titled, *Release from Nervous Tension*. In his book, he outlined his research into the causes of mental and emotional disturbances in people's lives.

From more than ten thousand case studies, he discovered a common trait among all his patients who suffered from severe tension. They were habitual fault-finders, constant critics of people and things around them. Those who were free from tension and anxiety were the least critical. His conclusions were that the habit of fault-finding is a prelude or mark of the nervous, or the mentally unbalanced. Those who wish to retain good emotional and mental health should learn to free themselves from a negative and critical attitude.[60]

Thank you, Dr. Fink, but Jesus already mapped this out for us two thousand years earlier in His Sermon on the Mount. Instead of Jesus coming from a case-study standpoint, He came from the Creator standpoint. He already knew what was best for the people He created. So Jesus said, "Here's how you respond to the craziness of people's actions and reactions . . . instead of being critical and negative, do the supernatural."

And here is the result: when we do that, we get what we give and we will get more of it.

> If we show love, we will get a lot more back.
> If we show mercy, we will get it overflowing back.
> If we show pardon, we will be forgiven many times over.

Jesus was telling us to let someone off the hook today. You may "have them" and have a screenshot of a text they sent, for example. You have a smoking gun. But how about showing mercy and pardoning them? Your goal every day is not to convict and find evidence on how bad people are to you. Instead, Jesus wants your goal to be to pardon when you have the evidence to convict.

Here is the rest of Jesus' words to those who retaliate this way:

> Love your enemies, and do good, and lend, expecting nothing in return;
> and your reward will be great, and you will be sons of the most high;
> for He Himself is kind to ungrateful and evil *men*. (Luke 6:35)

Did you catch that? Your reward will be great when you retaliate God's way. What kind of reward was Jesus referring to? He tells us in verse 38:

Give, and it will be given to you. They will pour into your lap a good measure—pressed down, shaken together, and running over. For by your standard of measure it will be measured to you in return.

I have heard this verse in regards to money. If this is how you've interpreted this verse, I hate to break this to you, but there are no dollar signs around this verse. Instead read the prior ten verses to see what verse 38 means:
- It has to do with what you give to people who hurt you
- It's a new level of relating to people
- It's Christian retaliation

Over the years, leaders have preached that the "give" in verse 38 is money, but not according to Jesus. There are enough verses on money in the Bible that we don't need to make square pieces fit into round holes. Jesus is not talking about giving money but giving pardon and mercy to people.

In New Testament times, men wore their outer garment in such a way as to have a pocket on the front, which was used for holding wheat that had been purchased. They would buy a pocket full of wheat and pour it into the pocket and press and shake it down so as much as possible would fit in. If the purchaser received so much wheat that even after doing all that pressing and shaking it still overflowed outside of his garment, he was considered to be especially blessed.

Jesus was saying that when you show mercy, pardon, love, and generosity to those who deserve the opposite, you are about to get a whole bunch of mercy, pardon, love, and generosity coming your way.

Retaliate the right way—the Jesus way—and you'll find the rewards are amazing.

I could have saved Dr. Fink the time and government money he spent in studying those ten thousand cases and just had him study the Sermon on the Mount in Luke 6.

What Do I Do with All These Tears?

Today's Reading: Luke 7

Today we land on Luke 7. In the last story of the chapter (verses 36-50), Jesus is in a house with a number of a religious people and a prostitute comes in and washes His feet with her hair. This is how pastor and author Chuck Swindoll explains it in a chapter titled "Jesus at His Best":

> While families gather for dinner and close their door for the night, her workday begins. With saffron scarves and lavender veils, dangling earrings and a dab of perfume, she dresses herself for show. . . . [she] survives by her looks . . . and looks she'll get. A leer. A scowl. A wink. A sneer. All sorts of looks, except one . . . love.
>
> She is a prostitute. How many times has her heart ached to be wanted for more than one night? To be valued instead of evaluated? To be prized instead of priced? Her scarlet letter will never rub clean. This day though, she will meet what she's hardly dared to hope for. For she will meet love. She will meet kindness. She will meet Jesus.[61]

Into this refined religious party comes a woman, a prostitute, unclean and out of place. She has taken a risk:

> Now one of the Pharisees was requesting Him to dine with him, and He entered the Pharisee's house and reclined *at the table*. And there was a woman in the city who was a sinner; and when she learned that He was reclining *at the table* in the Pharisee's house, she brought an alabaster vial of perfume, and standing behind Him at His feet, weeping, she began to wet His feet with her tears, and kept wiping them with the hair of her head, and kissing His feet and anointing them with the perfume. (Luke 7:36-38)

The thirty years I ministered in Detroit, our church worked with many prostitutes. We saw the hurt and brokenness and longing to be whole again.

They all wanted freedom but were afraid. Many were scared to leave the business because of retaliation by their pimp. That is this woman in Luke 7.

While men were looking at her, I too want us to look at her. Let's look at three parts of her body—for all the right reasons.

1. Her Back

The best seats at this kind of party were at the table and reserved for the host and his friends. This woman did not have a shot at getting near Jesus. While these kind of parties can have bystanders, they must stand with their backs against the wall as observers. This woman was one of them. Her back was on the wall. She must have thought about what happened earlier in her town, that a funeral was interrupted when Jesus resurrected the body. And now she is close to Him. If he raised someone from the dead, he must certainly be able to free her from her life and her choices. She has a decision to make: does she take her back off the wall and give Jesus a chance.

She chooses well—she takes her back off the wall.

2. Her Hair

Today if we want to know if someone is married, we look at their left ring finger. This wasn't the case in the first century. It was their hair. If a person's hair was *up*, they were available. If their hair was let *down*, they were married, taken. Every prostitute had their hair up but on this day, she found her man and let down her hair so she could wash His feet with it.[62] She became a taken woman.

3. Her Eyes

Or more specifically her tears. How much can a person really cry? Enough to wash Jesus' feet? They say a good cry is 1 to 2 cc's.[63] This is not nearly enough to wash Jesus' feet. But that is not what happened. She did not put her eyes on His feet, she broke open her tear bottle. In *Strange Scriptures that Perplex the Western Mind*, Barbara Bowen said that every person had in their possession a tear bottle and they would actually bottle their tears from painful situations.[64] I saw these bottles when I went to Israel. Think about what this woman did—she held in her hand all those painful moments where she cried and did not know who was able to handle this pain. Who could she get to give her pain and tears to? She found Him. She broken open that bottle and put her pain at His feet.

She had a choice either to try to manage those tears herself or pour it on the feet of Jesus. Why His feet? Hebrews 2:8 tells us that "You have put all things in subjection under his feet." All things go to the feet of Jesus. She took her back off the wall. Let down her hair and broke open that tear bottle. And that day she found forgiveness.

One person said this about tears: "Tears are prayers too. They travel to God when we can't speak." This woman found the feet of Jesus. That's where her tears belonged and that's where your and my tears belong. It's too much for us to manage our own tear bottles, so let's break them open in the presence of Jesus.

LIVING A HIGH-DEF LIFE

Today's Reading: Luke 8

A friend of mine said, "You're only as sick as your secrets." Christianity is not something that works well with secrets.

In fact, in today's reading we come to an amazing chapter packed with teaching, healing, and miracles, and tucked away in this long chapter is one thing that Jesus taught that particularly stands out to me:

Nothing is hidden that will not become evident, nor *anything* secret that will not be known and come to light. (Luke 8:17)

Or as *The Message* paraphrase puts it:

We're not keeping secrets; we're telling them. We're not hiding things; we're bringing *everything* out into the open.[65]

Freedom happens when everything is out in the open.

For us older folks . . . we remember growing up with television sets the size of a couch. A little white dot signified the television was warming up. We didn't have cable; we called it "rabbit ears"—an antenna that sat on top of the set, and if you were tech savvy you put aluminum foil on the antenna to get "better" reception. And because there was no remote, just a loose knob to change channels, when the knob fell off and someone lost it—as always seemed to happen in my house—we had to change channels with pliers.

Televisions have changed. Everything is HD, 4k. You can see everything. Every drop of sweat, every wrinkle in the skin, the spit coming out of a mouth—it's all there in high definition.

And in today's reading, Jesus is challenging us to living a life in high def. Though it is not easy, it is the best way. Something liberates others when people go high def.

Living in high def, we have no secrets. Why is living high def the right way? Because . . .

- Secrets don't work with God
- Secrets always get exposed or get confessed (exposed by others or confessed by you)

The bigger why is because sin grows in the dark. High def puts light on it and stunts its growth. When you put the light on something, you take the legs out from something growing bigger. You expose the lies that incubate in darkness.

Let me challenge you with something: apologizers get exposed, confessors go high def. They tell the secrets before anyone else can. They build trust from vulnerability not by portraying invincibility.

I have learned this in my marriage and in any healthy relationship. When do I know there is growth in any relationship? When I confess my wrong before my spouse or friend confronts my wrong. I confess before I am confronted. I am convicted before they can get offended. That is a huge win and huge progress. This is putting light on secrets. This is living in hi def.

Jesus warned us that all secrets are going to go public. As a Christian, I choose to make sure I have no secrets in my life, in my Christian walk, and in my marriage. It's so much easier to be real then to pretend. It takes a lot of work pretending.

I remember Jack Hayford, former pastor of Church on the Way saying, "The holier a man is, the more real he is." I want to be a real Christian.

A group of new Christians went high def and this is what happened: "Many of those who believed now came and openly confessed what they had done" (Acts 19:18, NIV).

That's high def, 4k. What did it do when they went honest?

A number who had practiced sorcery brought their scrolls together and burned them publicly.... In this way the word of the Lord spread widely and grew in power. (Acts 19:19-20, NIV)

Transparency and confession do more than bring healing: they start a revolution. Openly confessed . . . affects a number of people in the occult to change.

I'm too exhausted pretending. I don't have that kind of energy to be impressive, but I do have just enough to be real. You too?

"Jesus, You Promised and Then I Can't— I Don't Understand"

Today's Reading: Luke 9

Can we have a promise from Jesus that doesn't work for us? Can Jesus tell us what we are to do and then we can't do it?

That's the situation we find in today's reading. In Luke 9, we are filled with faith and expectation from the very first verses and then just forty verses later, we are overcome with failure in what we were told to do.

"Jesus, You promised, and now I can't. I don't understand." Let's read so we see how both confusing and revelatory this is for us today:

> He called the twelve together, and gave them power and authority over all the demons and to heal diseases. And He sent them out to proclaim the kingdom of God and to perform healing. (Luke 9:1-2)

Sent out by Jesus and given power and authority over all the demons. This is an exciting day. Then it all goes south. What Jesus tells them to do, commissions and equips them to do doesn't happen:

> A man from the crowd shouted, saying, "Teacher, I beg You to look at my son, for he is my only *boy*, and a spirit seizes him, and he suddenly screams, and it throws him into a convulsion with foaming *at the mouth*; and only with difficulty does it leave him, mauling him *as it leaves*. I begged Your disciples to cast it out, and they could not." (Luke 9:38-40)

Verse 40 appears like an explosion.

"I begged your disciples to cast it out, and they could not."

What?

In verse 1, Jesus gives them authority over all demons. And by verse 40, they can not get rid of one.

What went wrong?

In order to understand what happened, we have to understand what discipleship is all about. It's hard to isolate the Luke 9 failure without adding a discipleship journey of seeing the demonic world crushed by the kingdom of God. So let me give you the thirty-thousand-foot view of discipleship.

Here are the three levels of discipleship:

1. Watch me as I do it
2. I help you as we do it
3. I watch you as you do it

Here are examples of each:

1. Watch me as I do it

Soon afterwards, He *began* going around from one city and village to another, proclaiming and preaching the kingdom of God. The twelve were with Him, and *also* some women who had been healed of evil spirits and sicknesses: Mary who was called Magdalene, from whom seven demons had gone out. [Luke 8:1-2]

In Luke 9, Jesus commissions the Twelve to do what He has already been doing and what they have seen Him doing. *Watch me as I do it.* He doesn't just tell them something, He shows them something.

Notice the important phrase: *the twelve were with Him.*

Discipleship is more presence then information. Discipleship is more with Him than heard Him. We think discipleship is to sit in a classroom or a Bible study and get information. Discipleship calls for a bodily presence from the discipler and not just information.

Discipleship is leading by example. It is not telling people to do what you yourself have not and will not do. Jesus tells them to preach the kingdom and to cast out demons and He models it for them. *Watch me as I do it.*

2. I help you as we do it

Luke 9 is so important on the discipleship journey. Where the disciples fumble the ball on this, Jesus picks it up and delivers the boy. But more is happening.

This is the tweaking stage. Luke 9 is the humility moment for them to realize, *I'm called but I can't get too far from the Teacher.*

These are teaching moments. Something both strange and familiar happens after the fumble. What they do next when they can't cast it out is a learning moment for all: they get critical of others instead of examining themselves.

A few verses later after their failure, they see others casting out demons with success and the Twelve don't like that. Jesus is about to help them. Here we see two crazy verses thrown into the narrative, but these verses are so important to discipleship:

> John answered and said, "Master, we saw someone casting out demons in Your name; and we tried to prevent him because he does not follow along with us." But Jesus said to him, "Do not hinder *him*; for he who is not against you is for you." (Luke 9:49-50)

These other guys are successful but the disciples aren't. Therefore, their thinking goes, *Let's prevent them. Let's get critical of their success because that is supposed to be us.*

This is an ego deal. A pride moment.

We're much closer to Jesus then they are, so why do they cast out demons? So ridiculous.

Jesus is teaching them two things. He is helping them as they do it together. First, we must celebrate kingdom success in others and stop criticizing because they don't follow along with our certain group. And second, we must question ourselves and not others when we face failure. Something the disciples don't do here. They look at and get angry with others getting the job done. Jesus needs to help them.

3. I watch you as you do it and celebrate

We're moving into tomorrow's reading, but look let's look at Luke 10:

> The seventy returned with joy, saying, "Lord, even the demons are subject to us in Your name." And He said to them, "I was watching Satan fall from heaven like lightning. Behold, I have given you authority to tread on serpents and scorpions, and over all the power of the enemy, and nothing will injure you. Nevertheless do not rejoice in this, that the spirits are subject to you, but rejoice that your names are recorded in heaven."
>
> At that very time He rejoiced greatly in the Holy Spirit.
> (Luke 10:17-21)

Jesus is so joyful that His disciples are getting it. It says that, "He rejoiced greatly." The word actually means that He jumped up and gushed out with excitement.

I believe that Jesus still gets happy when we do what we were intended to do for Him.

Don't isolate a failing moment on your journey. These are just parts of the journey, not the whole. As Abraham Lincoln said: "My great concern is not whether you have failed, but whether you are content with your failure."[66]

Always remember: failure isn't final until you quit. Luke 9 is real and real failure but not final. It's just part of your discipleship journey.

Helping People I Hate

Today's Reading: Luke 10

A Politician finds their opponent on the side of the road with their car broken down, do they stop and help her? If a die-hard Yankees fan sees a Boston Red Sox fan at a check-out at a local store and he is short money, does the Yankees fan help him?

More serious: if a racial justice advocate sees an adversary standing at a stop light with a legitimate sign that says that person needs food or assistance, do they keep on driving?

This is not crazy talk, this is Jesus talk. And this is exactly what happens in Luke 10 where we come to one of the most intriguing parables Jesus ever told.

These crazy contrasts are what the story of the good Samaritan asks and answers. But instead of Democrats and Republicans or sports rivals, He uses two people groups who disdained each other:

Just then a religion scholar stood up with a question to test Jesus. "Teacher, what do I need to do to get eternal life?"

He answered, "What's written in God's Law? How do you interpret it?"

He said, "That you love the Lord your God with all your passion and prayer and muscle and intelligence—and that you love your neighbor as well as you do yourself."

"Good answer!" said Jesus. "Do it and you'll live."

Looking for a loophole, he asked, "And just how would you define 'neighbor'?"

Jesus answered by telling a story. "There was once a man traveling from Jerusalem to Jericho. On the way he was attacked by robbers. They took his clothes, beat him up, and went off leaving him half-dead. Luckily, a priest was on his way down the same road, but when he saw him he angled across to the other side. Then a Levite religious man showed up; he also avoided the injured man.

"A Samaritan traveling the road came on him. When he saw the man's condition, his heart went out to him. He gave him first aid, disinfecting and bandaging his wounds. Then he lifted him onto his donkey, led him to an inn, and made him comfortable. In the morning he took out two silver coins and gave them to the innkeeper, saying, 'Take good care of him. If it costs any more, put it on my bill—I'll pay you on my way back.'

"What do you think? Which of the three became a neighbor to the man attacked by robbers?"

"The one who treated him kindly," the religion scholar responded.

Jesus said, "Go and do the same." (Luke 10:25-37, MSG)

This story is explosive because of the characters involved. The Jews and the Samaritans hated each other. And so Jesus asked the question: which of the men was a real neighbor?

For me, I have been part of helping a lot of people in very needy inner cities. Let me confess . . . the ones I hate helping are ungrateful people.

We bring them food, their response is, "That's not enough" or "I don't like that kind of meat" or "I wanted Sprite not Coke." It's frustrating enough to make me not want to help them, because I want to only help the people who say, "Thank you."

But Jesus does not give me that option. Jesus says, "You can't pick and choose who you will help."

As Brennan Manning reminds us, "The litmus test of our love for God is our love of neighbor."[67] The apostle John puts it this way: "If anyone says 'I love God,' but keeps on hating his brother, he is a liar; for if he doesn't love his brother who is right there in front of him, how can he love God whom he has never seen?" (1 John 4:20, TLB).

What does that mean? It means that I love God as much as the person I dislike the most.

In our story, we have an injured Jew, and no Jews help him. He is the victim of a crime. And two religious people pass by—a priest and a Levite—and they do nothing. And the one who finally does something is the Jew's archenemy.

The priest found an angle.

The Levite avoided.

The Samaritan saw someone, felt something, and acted.

That's called compassion.

Jesus isn't separating the men from the boys, Jesus is separating the real Christian from the merely religious.

We take three philosophies from the good Samaritan story:

1. The robber's philosophy was, *What you have is mine, and I will take it.*

2. The priest and Levite had the philosophy, *What is mine is mine, and I will keep it.*

3. The Samaritan's philosophy was, *What is mine is yours, and I will share it.*

In 1973 two researchers at Princeton, John M. Darley and C. Daniel Batson, told a group of theology students that they were to go across campus to deliver a sermon on the topic of the Good Samaritan. As part of the research, some of these students were told that they were late and needed to hurry up. Along their route across campus, Darley and Baston had hired an actor to play the role of a victim who was coughing and suffering. They discovered that 90 percent of the "late" Princeton Theology Seminary students ignored the needs of the suffering person in their hurry to get across campus.

"Indeed," the study reports, "on several occasions, a seminary student going to give his talk on the parable of the Good Samaritan literally stepped over the victim as he hurried on his way!"[68]

The lawyer's question, "Who is my neighbor?" is not answered. Instead, Jesus answers the larger question, "To whom must I become a neighbor?" The answer: anyone in need.

The Good Samaritan has lived in memory for centuries without a name. I think that is because any name can be inserted. It's not, "Well, that's Mother Teresa." It's left open for you to insert a name.

In one of his sermons, Martin Luther King Jr. said, "I imagine that the first question which the priest and the Levite asked was: 'If I stop to help this man, what will happen to me?' But by the very nature of his concern, the Good Samaritan reversed the question: 'If I do not stop to help this man, what will happen to him?'"[69]

Are you willing to insert your name in the blank of the story?

Do you want to know how to be a good Samaritan?

Do you want to know how to put your name in the blank?

First, keep your eyes open on your daily journeys. People need help everywhere. Jesus told the man and tells us, "Go and do the same."

Second, you can't be a Samaritan without the oil, time, and money. I see help coming three ways: oil for the wound; time to help; money for the hotel.

It costs to be a good Samaritan.

It costs to do God's will.

It's a cost . . . but it's worth it.

I AM NOT GOING TO HAVE ANOTHER UNUSED GIFT

Today's Reading: Luke 11

When it comes to giving a gift today, one of the most popular gifts, which doesn't require much thought or effort is a gift card.

According to the National Retail Federation, about 59 percent of shoppers will purchase a gift card for friends and family.[70] According to estimates, the typical American home has an average of $300 in unused or "unredeemed" gift cards in their house right now.[71] These cards are often misplaced, accidentally thrown out, or only partially redeemed. Over a period of seven years in America, $41 billion in gift cards went unused.[72] Forty-one *billion* dollars! *Unused!*

Someone was given a gift and that person never cashed it in. I am one of those people. I have a lot of gift cards that I have not used. While that's a terrible waste, there's a worse thing we can do—and that's when we do this to God's gifts and leave them unused.

God is a good gift giver.

In fact, the greatest gift God has ever given to us is the gift of the Holy Spirit, but for too many of us we never tap into the gifts and the anointing and the power that comes from the Holy Spirit. And what makes it the most terrible is how easy it is to cash in on this gift.

That's where we land today in our reader. Luke 11 is a great chapter on prayer. I want us to see an aspect of prayer in regards to the Holy Spirit that we often miss.

Let's read together what Jesus said about prayer and the Holy Spirit:

Everyone who asks, receives; and he who seeks, finds; and to him who knocks, it will be opened. Now suppose one of you fathers is asked by his son for a fish; he will not give him a snake instead of a fish, will he? Or *if* he is asked for an egg, he will not give him a scorpion, will he? If you then, being evil, know how to give good gifts to your children, how much more will *your* heavenly Father give the Holy Spirit to those who ask Him?" [Luke 11:10-13]

Two important thoughts from Jesus.

First, notice that Jesus uses fish and eggs. This is deliberate. Why is that important? Jesus did not say, "What if a son asked a father for steak and shrimp" or "What if a son asked a dad for lamb chops." Why? Those foods are luxury foods. They were not the everyday food for the common man. Fish and eggs are what everyone ate practically every day in that first-century geography. What Jesus was saying was that the Holy Spirit is not some luxury whom we need occasionally; the Holy Spirit is Someone we need every day. He is not a gift for Sundays; He is a gift for every day. We must not relegate Him to an occasional moment. You and I need the presence of the Holy Spirit with us every moment of every day.

Second, Jesus reminds us how simple it is to cash in on God's gift of the Holy Spirit. Ready for this? "How much more will your heavenly Father give the Holy Spirit to those who ask Him?" Ask. That's it. Don't let the religious tell you it's more complicated.

God gives a gift and makes that gift accessible. Why is the gift accessible? Because it isn't a luxury but a necessity.

It's an everyday ask.

Every day ask God for you to be filled with the Holy Spirit.

The last thing I want is to have another unused gift that is available but not enjoyed.

Let's start today. *Fill me, God, with the Holy Spirit.* Cashing in is as simple as asking.

MY, MY, MY, MY

Today's Reading: Luke 12

A. W. Tozer, the famous Christian writer, said that there are seven ways to really know ourselves and know what our character is like. He called them rules for self discovery. They are:

1. What we want most
2. What we think about most
3. What we laugh at
4. What we do with our leisure time
5. The company we enjoy
6. Who and what we admire
7. How we use our money[73]

How we use our money . . . Number 7 is a big one.

That's where we land in today's reading. Jesus tells a story in Luke 12 about someone we call the rich fool who messed up on number 7: He spent it on himself.

Remember, God entrusted us with His money not to hoard for ourselves but to make a difference. When we think bigger and not longer, when we think *me* and not others, we fail the test at number 7.

Calvin Coolidge, our thirtieth US president said it like this: "No person was ever honored for what he received. Honor has been the reward for what he gave."[74] This Luke 12 man missed that lesson. Let's read the story and see where the number 7 part got really messed up.

> [Jesus] told them a parable, saying, "The land of a rich man was very productive. And he began reasoning to himself, saying, 'What shall I do, since I have no place to store my crops?' Then he said, 'This is what I will do: I will tear down my barns and build larger ones, and there I will store all my grain and my goods. And I will say to my soul, "Soul, you have many goods laid up for many years to come; take your ease, eat, drink *and* be merry."' But God said to him, 'You fool! This very night your soul is required of you; and *now* who will own what you have

prepared?' So is the man who stores up treasure for himself, and is not rich toward God." [Luke 12:16-21]

The number one reason people get upset when money is mentioned in church is that they think it's "my" money. (This was the rich fool's issue.) They have mistaken themselves for God and think it's theirs. But as famed missionary stateman, J. Oswald Sanders, reminds us, "The basic question is not how much of our money we should give to God, but how much of God's money we should keep for ourselves."[75]

Wow. Ponder that. That's a new way of thinking about the offering this Sunday.

God called this man a fool for one reason—because the man kept using one word over and over.

The rich fool said . . . *my* barns . . . *my* grain . . . *my* goods . . . *my* soul.

My, my, my, my

Always remember, no one is an owner—we are stewards. It is not . . . my children . . . my health . . . my house . . . my life . . . my soul . . . my education . . . my business . . . my company . . . my future. Once you live a my, my, my, my life, you realize how short that kind of life is. There is no future in a my, my, my, my life.

God told the man, "You messed up." Jesus said he had "treasure for himself" but he was not rich toward God. How do we become rich toward God? The answer to our greed is that we give your greed away—that's how we become rich toward God. When we give our money away, we take a hammer to our stingy heart. As John Wesley famously said, "Earn all you can, save all you can, give all you can."[76]

It's impossible to be selfish and happy at the same time. Happiness comes from giving not getting. Mother Teresa said, "One of the greatest diseases is to be nobody to anybody."[77]

My, my, my, my is nobody to anybody.

It isn't a sin to possess money, but it is a sin when what you possess possesses you. Is getting rich wrong? Of course not. In the Bible, many heroes of the faith, such as Abraham and David, were rich. Money can be a great vehicle for changing people's lives. But if it is not used correctly, it can adversely change yours, just as it did this man in Luke 12.

The rich fool made three mistakes:

1. He mistook his body for his soul. His body had the stuff but his soul was starving.

2. He mistook time for eternity. He acted as if his future were in his own hands. His soul would be demanded of him that night; it was a word that was used when a debt or loan was due and it was payday.

3. He mistook himself for God. Six times the man used the pronoun *I*, and if you add the number of times he used the other personal pronouns, the total comes to eleven.

It's all a matter of what you do with what God has given you.

Day 57

How to Face Tragic Death

Today's Reading: Luke 13

There are more than 7 billion people on earth. Nearly sixty million of them will die this year.[78] That is approximately 153,000 people dying every day, 6,400 people dying every hour, 107 people dying every minute, two people dying every second.[79] Not a great thought to start your day.

Death is unavoidable and undeniable, and you will one day become one of these statistics. Statistics tell us that one out of one will die. I know that is hard to believe, but it is true.

We try to sanitize the topic of death. Years ago people would die in their homes; today they die in hospitals or nursing homes. We try to keep death far from us. We think out of sight is out of mind. We don't even let our pets die; we put them to sleep.

We use nice phraseology to deal with death. We say, "He is no longer with us," "She is resting," or "He has passed away." None of this changes the definiteness of death.

They now call funeral homes eternal management care centers.[80] Funeral home directors don't want to be called undertakers or morticians, they call themselves death managers.[81] People don't care about what you call death as long as they can avoid it.

The great American poet W. H. Auden (the great American Poet) said, "Death is the sound of distant thunder at a picnic."[82] No matter what your picnic is, you still hear the thunder. People will try to avoid death and listening to that distant thunder through any means they can.

There is this crazy thing called Cryonics in which scientists will put your legally-dead body after death in liquid nitrogen and hope one day through technology they will discover a way to wake the person up. The fee can be as high as $200,000 or more for whole body cryopreservation and $80,00 for a "neuro," or head only option.[83]

There is something about our mortality and death we don't want to talk about. You can take vitamins and drink green tea but we all will face death. You may live longer doing this stuff, but no one will know at your funeral whether you ate tofu or Twinkies.

Speaking about death is hard. But processing tragic death is even harder.

Jesus deals with this topic and how we are to process it in today's reading. The opening scene of Luke 13 is intense. People come to Jesus with a tragic death story and then Jesus intensifies it:

> Some of those present informed Jesus that Pilate had slaughtered some Galilean Jews while they were offering sacrifices at the temple, mixing their blood with the sacrifices they were offering.
>
> Jesus turned and asked the crowd, "Do you believe that the slaughtered Galileans were the worst sinners of all the Galileans? No, they weren't! So listen to me. Unless you all repent, you will perish as they did." (Luke 13:1-3, TPT)

Jesus doesn't stop there, but then tells more tragedy to make His point:

> Or what about the eighteen who perished when the tower of Siloam fell upon them? Do you really think that they were more guilty than all of the others in Jerusalem? No, they weren't. But unless you repent, you will all eternally perish, just as they did. (Luke 13:4-5, TPT)

"Why did these people die?" the people ask Jesus, and Jesus responds by telling that they are asking the wrong question. Basically He tells them, "There is a better question you should be asking and here it is: why haven't you died yet?"

Jesus essentially says, "Do you think they died because they were great sinners and deserved it? Of course not, but keep this in mind all of you are going to perish one day, a great thing to do while your breathing is to repent."

Instead of processing why they died, we need to process if we are prepared to die.

Always remember, the Bible is not like a newspaper; it doesn't have new stuff in it every day. It is always the same, because it's the truth. And truth has no expiration date.

Jesus is telling us the issue is not why were these babies aborted, but why haven't we been aborted. The issue is not why my friend died in a highway head-on collision with a drunk driver but why haven't I? The issue is not figuring out if someone bad got cancer and deserved it, but why haven't I?

The people were asking the wrong question. And too often we ask that same wrong question. That is the question Jesus is asking us to skip and to fast forward to something more important.

There are very few death scenes in the Bible because the Bible is concerned with how you live *now*. Consider this story:

A little girl whose baby brother had just died asked her mother where baby had gone.

"To be with Jesus," replied the mother. A few days later while talking to a friend, the mother said, "I am so grieved to have lost my baby."

The little girl heard her, and remembering what her mother had told her, looked into her face and asked, "Mother, is a thing lost when you know where it is?"

"No, of course not."

"Well then, how can the baby be lost when he has gone to be with Jesus?"

That's the part you have to settle while you are alive. It's not tragic if we know where they are. We have to settle on where *we* are going.

Until you are ready to deal with the question of your eternity then you are not prepared to deal with your death. Here is a way to explain it: Have you ever worked on a jigsaw puzzle? What do you do before you start putting pieces together? You start with the picture on the box in front of you. With the focus, you are able to make the crazy pieces make sense and as you connect them, you can see the big picture alongside the little pieces. If you don't have the right box top in front of you while you are living, then life is confusing. The pieces don't fit together.

Eternity is confusing, and how to get to heaven is confusing.

You need the correct box top in front of you. The way not to see life and tragedy as confusing is to see it from an eternal perspective. It is to set the box top in front of you—to put the Bible and Jesus in front of you and define the little pieces with the big picture, God's picture.

EXCUSES! EXCUSES! EXCUSES!

Today's Reading: Luke 14

You've been invited to a big party. Not just a party but God's party. And it lasts a really long time . . . for eternity. In order to understand how this party works, Jesus told a parable. And what makes this parable amazing is when and where He told it.

I come from a family in which dinner table talk was the norm. Dinner would last a long time not because eating took long but because the conversation did. And here in Luke 14, this dinner conversation started in verse 1 and ended at verse 24—and the topics were intense. The conversation started with healing and proceeded all the way to the big party.

At our dinner table I learned the art of debate and how to defend your point of view over anything from politics to theology. Nothing was off limits. We are Italians, so the conversations would get loud and emotional, but always ended with dessert and coffee.

This Luke 14 dinner conversation with Jesus didn't end with cheesecake and coffee, but did end with an intense talk about God's final party in heaven and why people will miss it.

In New Testament times, two invitations were usually given to a party or banquet. The first was given well in advance so that people could RSVP. Then when everything was ready for the party to begin, the host sent servants with a second invitation to tell everybody to "come, for everything is now ready." You'd think that receiving such a wonderful invitation and news would cause people to stop whatever they were engaged in and go to the party, but that is not what Jesus said happened in this parable:

> He said to him, "A man was giving a big dinner, and he invited many; and at the dinner hour he sent his slave to say to those who had been invited, 'Come; for everything is ready now.' But they all alike began to make excuses. The first one said to him, 'I have bought a piece of land and I need to go out and look at it; please consider me excused.' Another one said, 'I have bought five yoke of oxen, and I am going to try them out; please consider me excused.' Another one said, 'I have

married a wife, and for that reason I cannot come.' And the slave came *back* and reported this to his master. Then the head of the household became angry and said to his slave, 'Go out at once into the streets and lanes of the city and bring in here the poor and crippled and blind and lame.' And the slave said, 'Master, what you commanded has been done, and still there is room.' And the master said to the slave, 'Go out into the highways and along the hedges, and compel them to come in, so that my house may be filled. For I tell you, none of those men who were invited shall taste of my dinner.'" (Luke 14:16-24)

This invitation came at a time that something would have to be interrupted . . . something great would have to be chosen over something good. We have to choose the lasting over the temporal, the great over the good if we want to go to the party.

In the parable, Jesus said that some chose not to come because the party interfered with their business, possessions, and relationships. In each case the excuses were legitimate but not sufficient.

Legitimate but not sufficient. The point is—if you miss God's party, it isn't because you were not invited. It's because you chose to make other things a priority over responding to Him.

The people who were invited all began to make excuses. The definition of excuse: that which makes (an offense or a crime) seem less serious or something used to justify a fault.

There are countless websites for excuses for sleeping in class, sleeping at work, and missing school and work. The following are actual notes that parents wrote to schools so their children could be excused for their absence:
- Please excuse Lisa for being absent. She was sick and I had her shot.
- Dear school: Please excuse John being absent on Jan. 28, 29, 30, 31, 32, and also 33.
- Please excuse Jennifer for missing school yesterday. We forgot to get the Sunday paper off the porch, and when we found it Monday, we thought it was Sunday.

I heard about four college freshmen who hung out together and were always intent on having more fun than studying. These guys were always late to a certain class, because they knew the professor was a pushover. They had a multitude of excuses why their assignments weren't finished on time or why they hadn't shown up for class. When it came time for the final exam, they were late. About the time everyone else was finishing, they showed up giggling and told the professor their car had a flat tire, so they wanted to take a make-up test later.

"No problem," the professor said. "Have a seat in the four corners of the classroom. I'll prepare a special final exam just for you guys, and I'll make it easier—it will only have one question. And since you guys haven't turned in all your assignments, I'll give you another chance. If all four of you answer this question correctly, you'll all get an 'A,' but if any of you miss it, you'll fail the class." He took a moment to write the question in four exam bluebooks.

The four guys were grinning when he handed them their books, but their smiles disappeared when they opened the test. The single question on the final exam was, "Which tire was flat?"

As the professor stood between them, they realized they were done for. They each tossed their exam books in the trashcan as they walked out. Their excuses had caught up to them!

Jesus said that when the second invitation was sent, "they all alike began to make excuses" (verse 18).

The first excuse: "I need to go and look at my new property." The field would be there the next day. We make desires our needs. And when we do that, our desires start to control decisions and this will always be a train wreck. The desire to be known, to be wanted, and to be loved. Our need is for God who will meet all our desires. We should have gone to the party.

The second excuse was that he'd just bought five oxen. He had something new and the novelty was exciting. Some people hear the call to serve God and be part of a church, and they want to—until something shiny and new excites them. They get a new friendship, a new hobby, a second home. God always plays second fiddle to them. That means we're there unless something new invites our attention.

Finally, the third excuse, that the man just got married. At times human affections can keep us from turning our love upon the Lord. This is not about putting marriage in a wrong priority. This is about being careful that we are not involved in relationships that keep us from making the right God decisions in our lives. That runs the gamut. I have watched affection make men and women compromise morals and standards, making unwise future decisions and marrying too fast without getting wisdom. Affection for people is important *in second place*. When people take the first priority over God choices, life is about to get real hard.

When it was all said and done . . . desires, novelty, and affection took the place over a God invitation.

God is throwing a big party and it's going to happen really soon. I want to see you there—no excuses.

THE FATHER IS MORE PRODIGAL THAN THE SON

Today's Reading: Luke 15

Today's reading contains one of the most incredible stories ever told. We call it the story of the prodigal son. Let's read it together:

[Jesus] said, "A man had two sons. The younger of them said to his father, 'Father, give me the share of the estate that falls to me.' So he divided his wealth between them. And not many days later, the younger son gathered everything together and went on a journey into a distant country, and there he squandered his estate with loose living. Now when he had spent everything, a severe famine occurred in that country, and he began to be impoverished. So he went and hired himself out to one of the citizens of that country, and he sent him into his fields to feed swine. And he would have gladly filled his stomach with the pods that the swine were eating, and no one was giving *anything* to him. But when he came to his senses, he said, 'How many of my father's hired men have more than enough bread, but I am dying here with hunger! I will get up and go to my father, and will say to him, "Father, I have sinned against heaven, and in your sight; I am no longer worthy to be called your son; make me as one of your hired men."' So he got up and came to his father. But while he was still a long way off, his father saw him and felt compassion *for him*, and ran and embraced him and kissed him. And the son said to him, 'Father, I have sinned against heaven and in your sight; I am no longer worthy to be called your son.' But the father said to his slaves, 'Quickly bring out the best robe and put it on him, and put a ring on his hand and sandals on his feet; and bring the fattened calf, kill it, and let us eat and celebrate; for this son of mine was dead and has come to life again; he was lost and has been found.' And they began to celebrate. [Luke 15:11-24]

When it comes to the word *father*, some people cringe. Today that name can evoke all kinds of images—from absentee, abusive, uncaring, never saying "I love you" or "I'm proud of you." Jesus enters an environment in which He is about to redefine the image of *father*, just as it needs help today.

In Middle Eastern culture,[84] to ask for the inheritance while the father is still alive is to wish him dead. A traditional Middle Eastern father can only respond one way. He is expected to refuse and then drive the boy out of the house with verbal and physical blows.

But something strange happens . . . .

The father's granting the request makes clear that the character of the father in the parable is not modeled after a traditional Middle Eastern patriarch. Though in the previous two parables that Jesus tells—the shepherd in his search for the sheep and the woman in her search for the coin—the people do not do anything out of the ordinary beyond what anyone in their place would do. But the actions of the father in the third story are unique, marvelous, divine actions that have not been done by any earthly father in the past. On three different occasions the father in this parable clearly violates the traditional expectations of a Middle Eastern father. This is the first of them. An awareness of the redefinition of the word *father* takes place.

You are about to see that the father is more prodigal than the son. I'll explain shortly.

In the parable the reader learns that the son "gathered all he had," which the New English Bible rightly translates, he "turned the whole of his share into cash."

This is demonstrated by the fact that the prodigal completes all transactions in "not many days." He just wants the money for the inheritance.

The son got all that he wanted (gathered everything).

He got to spend it on whatever he wanted (loose living).

He got to go where he wanted (distant country).

And do it with whomever he wanted.

And when it was all done, he ended up with nothing.

You knew this when it came to pod eating. Can't get lower than this.

That's when something happens to this boy. He comes to himself:

When he came to his senses, he said, "How many of my father's hired men have more than enough bread, but I am dying here with hunger!" (Luke 15:17)

Now enters the dad—the prodigal father. Did you catch what I called him?

The focus is so much on the prodigal son when it should be on the prodigal father.

What does *prodigal* mean? We think prodigal means sinful and that bad living that's associated with it. But *prodigal* is a neutral word. You can attach it to any noun, and the noun determines if it's positive or negative.

It means to lavish, to go all out, extreme generosity. In the story the father is just as prodigal. This is the challenge for us who have prodigals. We must be just as prodigal as them. We have to be prodigal with grace, forgiveness, and love and lavish it on them.

Then the father does something unusual—he runs. He is getting prodigal *big time*.

Eastern gentlemen do not run in public. People of prominence did not and do not run in public.

Why does the father run? To protect him against others. He does not want him meeting the city first; he wants his son to meet open arms first.

Why does he run? To protect him from the comments of others. He is sending a signal to the community—a signal of forgiveness.

And then it gets crazier. He starts giving the son really significant things. The first is to order the servants to dress the prodigal. He doesn't tell his son to go and get cleaned up. Rather he instructs the servants to dress him with the best robe and sandals. "Quickly bring out best robe and put it on him" (verse 22). This can only mean, *I don't want anyone else to see him in these rags!*

The son never stops being a son while covered in mud. That's an important message for you to remember. God loves you as you are—not as you should be. God loves you without caution, regret, boundary, limit, or breaking point. When the prodigal son comes back home, he doesn't just get a ring, a robe, and shoes. The greatest thing he gets back is his father.

Day 60

HELL IS A REAL PLACE

Today's Reading: Luke16

What if you could hear from someone who had died, and they could tell you what's on the other side? That's what a story in today's reading is. It's a story that will stop you in your tracks. It's the story of eternity. It's the story of what's beyond. More specifically, it's a story about hell, realized too late.

> There was a rich man, and he habitually dressed in purple and fine linen, joyously living in splendor every day. And a poor man named Lazarus was laid at his gate, covered with sores, and longing to be fed with the crumbs which were falling from the rich man's table; besides, even the dogs were coming and licking his sores. Now the poor man died and was carried away by the angels to Abraham's bosom; and the rich man also died and was buried. In Hades he lifted up his eyes, being in torment, and saw Abraham far away and Lazarus in his bosom. And he cried out and said, "Father Abraham, have mercy on me, and send Lazarus so that he may dip the tip of his finger in water and cool off my tongue, for I am in agony in this flame." But Abraham said, "Child, remember that during your life you received your good things, and likewise Lazarus bad things; but now he is being comforted here, and you are in agony. And besides all this, between us and you there is a great chasm fixed, so that those who wish to come over from here to you will not be able, and that none may cross over from there to us." And he said, "Then I beg you, father, that you send him to my father's house— for I have five brothers—in order that he may warn them, so that they will not also come to this place of torment." But Abraham said, "They have Moses and the prophets; let them hear them." But he said, "No, father Abraham, but if someone goes to them from the dead, they will repent!" But he said to him, "If they do not listen to Moses and the prophets, they will not be persuaded even if someone rises from the dead." [Luke 16:19-31]

I have heard and read stories of people telling their beyond-death stories—some who visited heaven and some who visited hell. I'm not saying their stories aren't true or false, we just don't know. But we do know that this story is true because of who told it: Jesus, who always tells the truth. Jesus told this story different from a parable. Parables had no names of people, whereas this story did. And his name was Lazarus.

Here is a big question: what is the length of every man's life? Forever, everlasting. Once born, the existence of man becomes as everlasting as the existence of God. His length on earth may be seventy or eighty years, which the Bible calls a vapor (see James 4:14). But your departed friends still exist right now. Remember that the poor man died but so did the rich man.

When the rich man and the poor man were born, they were both born without Christ; but when the rich man and the poor man died, Lazarus had Christ and the rich man had nothing. The rich man in fact had everything but God. The beggar had nothing but God.

And once you enter eternity, your destiny is fixed and cannot be changed. It was too late for the rich man.

I see some *too lates* here in this story.

1. He saw heaven too late. He who never thirsts for God here will thirst for Him immediately after he dies. He who never longs for a savior on earth will long for one in hell. The rich man was contented without a savior in this life, but as soon as he was in hell, he realized his need and his first cry was, "I thirst." But the problem was that he thirsted for heaven and water too late!

2. He prayed too late. This was hell's prayer meeting. The rich man not only saw what he never saw on earth, but his very first act in hell was to do what he never did on earth: he prayed . . . but he prayed too late because he prayed in hell.

He got thirsty too late and prayed too late. And when he did pray, he prayed to the wrong person: "He cried out and said, 'Father Abraham, have mercy on me, and send Lazarus, that he may dip the tip of his finger in water and cool off my tongue; for I am in agony in this flame.'" (verse 24).

He prayed to father Abraham. This prayer could never have been answered. Even if this prayer was offered up on earth, it could have never been answered. This is the only instance in Scripture of a man praying to a saint, and it bore no fruit and got no answer.

If only this man could have felt the need on earth that he was feeling in hell and cried to Jesus on earth instead of Abraham in hell, God would have given him salvation.

Here's what is scary about hell. The rich man had all five senses in hell.

He opened his eyes: he recognized Lazarus when he lifted his eyes.

He opened his mouth: he cried to Abraham.

He knew what water was and craved a drop of it.

He had feelings because he said he was being tormented.

He knew what was tormenting him—flames.

He remembered his father's house and his brothers.

There was no lapse of time between the rich man's death and him being in the flames of hell. Just as the believer dies and is in the presence of the Lord, I believe that the sinner goes immediately into the flames of hell.

Some think these are hard words to hear. It may be hard but it's important. I think Billy Graham said it best: "If we had more hell in the pulpit, we would have less hell in the pew."[85]

As Thomas Hobbes once said, "Hell is truth seen too late."

If you are alive today, it's not too late.

Day 61

GETTING MORE THAN YOU ASKED FOR

Today's Reading: Luke 17

My goal today is to put you in a special category, which not many are in. My goal is to move you to the 10 percent category, because if I can get you there, I can get you some extra help on what God has already done for you.

How many want more miracles happening in their lives?

They can have that. And it is as simple as saying, "Thank You, God."

Our 260 Journey leads us to Luke 17, where we read about an amazing miracle and then an even more amazing response. Someone got more than what they asked for.

> While He was on the way to Jerusalem, He was passing between Samaria and Galilee. As He entered a village, ten leprous men who stood at a distance met Him; and they raised their voices, saying, "Jesus, Master have mercy on us!" When He saw them, He said to them, "Go and show yourselves to the priests." And as they were going, they were cleansed. Now one of them, when he saw that he had been healed, turned back, glorifying God with a loud voice, and he fell on his face at His feet, giving thanks to Him. And he was a Samaritan. Then Jesus answered and said, "Were there not ten cleansed? But the nine—where are they? Was no one found who returned to give glory to God, except this foreigner?" And He said to him, "Stand up and go; your faith has made you well." (Luke 17:11-19)

Let's read the last part from *The Message*: "One of them, when he realized that he was healed, turned around and came back, shouting his gratitude, glorifying God. He kneeled at Jesus' feet, so grateful. He couldn't thank him enough" (verses 15-16).

One leper said "thank you" and something happened: he got more than he asked for.

Being grateful will separate you from the group. Not many people say thanks. From the cashier at Walgreens to the drive-through worker at Dairy

Queen to the supervisor at work—all the way to God Himself. The leper went from receiving healing to getting one more thing by just saying, "Thank You, Jesus." Something happened physically and spiritually to him.

Ten lepers were healed—nine went on their way (90 percent); one returned with thanksgiving (10 percent). Which group are you in?

We are quick to pray but slow to praise. I want to help you get to that elite 10 percent. As we move you from the majority to the powerful minority, keep these words and phrases from our verses in mind:

Realized

Shouting gratitude

Healed and saved

Realized

The realization is the wake-up call. God deserves your gratitude. One day you *realize* that what you received is not by accident and not by your own doing.

Jesus asked, "Where are the nine?" (MSG). God was asking what He already knew the answer to. He says about us: *Where are the nine whom I have given life to, provision to, healing to, a house to, breath to, health to, a vacation to, a job to, a child to? They have thanked everyone but Me today?*

In *Life Together*, theologian and pastor Dietrich Bonhoeffer wrote: "Only he who gives thanks for little things receives big things. We prevent God from giving us the great spiritual gifts He has in store for us, because we do not give thanks for daily gifts."[86]

If you want to be part of the 10 percent, wake up to the realization that God deserves your thanks.

Shouting gratitude

Go big with your thank yous. Author Glady Bronwyn Stern said, "Silent gratitude isn't much use to anyone."[87] True gratitude is vocal and focused. Luke says that the leper was "glorifying God with a loud voice." You realize not only who it came from, but you want *others* to know who the *who* is.

Gratitude goes the extra mile. Consider what this leper did:

He turned around.

He came back.

He shouted.

He kneeled at His feet.

Poet George Herbert says it best: "Thou who hast given so much to me, give me one more thing—a grateful heart!"[88]

Healed and saved

"Thank You" gets God's attention. And it makes God want to do more.

The leper was "healed and saved." Nine got healed on the outside; one got healed both on the outside *and* on the inside. One "thank you" got him a lot extra.

Gratitude opens the door for you to get more than you asked for.

As Steven Furtick once said: "You can't be grateful for something you feel entitled to."[89] So let's stop today and enter the elite 10 percent and thank God for all He has done.

IT SHOULD BE EASY TO PICK OUT WHO GOD LIKES BEST . . . OR MAYBE NOT

Today's Reading: Luke 18

In today's reading, Jesus tells a story on prayer. But I think through the story, He wants us to pick the guy we think God likes best so He can teach us a lesson. Sometimes we assume that God likes who we like and what we like. It should be easy to pick out who God likes best:

> He told his next story to some who were complacently pleased with themselves over their moral performance and looked down their noses at the common people: "Two men went up to the Temple to pray, one a Pharisee, the other a tax man. The Pharisee posed and prayed like this: 'Oh, God, I thank you that I am not like other people—robbers, crooks, adulterers, or, heaven forbid, like this tax man. I fast twice a week and tithe on all my income.'
>
> "Meanwhile the tax man, slumped in the shadows, his face in his hands, not daring to look up, said, 'God, give mercy. Forgive me, a sinner.'"
>
> Jesus commented, "This tax man, not the other, went home made right with God. If you walk around with your nose in the air, you're going to end up flat on your face, but if you're content to be simply yourself, you will become more than yourself." (Luke 18:9-14, MSG)

The two guys were a Pharisee and a tax man. Really, it's the story of the church guy and the street guy. The church guy basically says: "I haven't done bad stuff and I have done all the good stuff." The street guy says: "I have done all the bad stuff; I am a sinner."

They are both seemingly doing the same thing at the present—praying. But for prayer to be prayer, God has to hear it. Verse 11 (NASB) says, "The Pharisee stood and was praying this to himself." God wasn't listening. I love how Danish philosopher Søren Kierkegaard sums it up: "It is so much easier to become a Christian when you aren't one than to become one when you assume you already are."[90]

If my wife and I have a disagreement and I am in the wrong, I have two ways to try to fix it:

The first way is that I do a lot of good things (self-righteously) for her. I give her gifts, do the dishes and laundry. I am being a good boy now. I am making myself acceptable to her. I keep doing stuff until the guilt is gone. That's the first guy who prayed. He is trying to make himself right before God—to show how good and righteous he is. But the problem with this is that the offense is never addressed and fixed. It's still on the account.

Or I can pursue the second way. The atmosphere is thick. What needs to happen? I need to offer an apology. I ask her for forgiveness. Why do I want her forgiveness? Because it puts the relationship back in order. Happy home, good meals, good conversation. I want to be forgiven so things can be happy between us. Things can be set right because the thing that separated us is now addressed and the relationship can be restored. Forgiveness is the way to remove the obstacles so we can talk with each other.

The second way to find yourself back in relationship is by saying you are sorry. That is the heart of the gospel.

The only way to become a Christian is to understand that forgiveness is the starting point not good deeds.

You are not raised into being right with God. You can't make yourself likable to God. But you can come to God and say that you are sorry for the things you have done against Him.

Two men went to the temple and both prayed. But they didn't leave with the same thing. One left right with God. The other left in the same condition as when he walked in.

I remember the story of a lawyer and a doctor sitting in the same church service and both heard the same message. The doctor made a decision to be born again that day. The lawyer did not. Like the Pharisee and the tax collector, one left with God and the other left exactly the same way. It took the lawyer three weeks to make that born-again decision of saying to God, "I'm sorry." The lawyer said to the doctor, "How did you do it faster than me? I could have died and gone to hell." The doctor said: "While I pleaded guilty, you were pleading your case."

That's Luke 18 and the two guys who prayed one day. I thought it would be easy to see who God liked best—but it's the worst guy, because he asked for mercy.

DESPERATE TIMES CALL FOR DESPERATE MEASURES

Today's Reading: Luke 19

Today's reading contains the story of a crazy conversion of a rich man. But in order to get its full picture, we have to read something from the previous chapter about a crazy miracle healing of a blind man.

Luke 18:35 says, "As Jesus was approaching Jericho . . ." (Remember *Jericho*, because we'll come back to that.) "As Jesus was approaching Jericho, a blind man was sitting by the road begging." The blind man's name is Bartimaeus. Everyone tells him not to ask Jesus to do anything for him, but he doesn't listen to their admonitions and calls out to Jesus to be healed. And the last verse of chapter 18 says: "Immediately he regained his sight and began following Him, glorifying God" (verse 43).

Remember that the chapter divisions were placed in the Bible around the 13th century.[91] I think this is a running story, so let's connect the two stories and continue reading in Luke 19: "He entered Jericho . . ." (verse 1). Jesus was approaching Jericho and now He entered the city. Let's keep reading:

> There was a man called by the name of Zaccheus; he was a chief tax collector and he was rich. Zaccheus was trying to see who Jesus was, and was unable because of the crowd, for he was small in stature. So he ran on ahead and climbed up into a sycamore tree in order to see Him, for He was about to pass through that way. When Jesus came to the place, He looked up and said to him, "Zaccheus, hurry and come down, for today I must stay at your house." And he hurried and came down and received Him gladly. When they saw it, they all *began* to grumble, saying, "He has gone to be the guest of a man who is a sinner." Zaccheus stopped and said to the Lord, "Behold, Lord, half of my possessions I will give to the poor, and if I have defrauded anyone of anything, I will give back four times as much." And Jesus said to him, "Today salvation has come to this house, because he, too, is a son of Abraham. For the Son of Man has come to seek and to save that which was lost." (Verses 2-10)

The great American evangelist D. L. Moody wrote something interesting about these two stories:

Pardon me, if I now draw a little on my imagination. Bartimaeus gets into Jericho [with Jesus], and he says, "I will go and see my wife, and tell her about it." A young convert always wants to talk to his friends about salvation. Away he goes down to the street, and there he meets a man who passes him, goes on a few yards, and then turns round and says, "Bartimeus, is that you?"

"Yes."

"Well, I thought it was, but I could not believe my eyes. How have you got your sight?"

"Oh, I just met Jesus of Nazareth outside the city, and asked Him to have mercy on me."

"Jesus of Nazareth! What, is He in this part of the country?"

"Yes. He is right here in Jericho. . . ."

"I should like to see Him," says the man, and away he runs down the street; but he cannot catch a glimpse of Him, even though he stands on tiptoe, being little of stature, and on account of the great throng around Him. . . . [So] he climbs up into a sycamore tree.

"If I can get on to that branch, hanging right over the highway, He cannot pass without my getting a good look at Him."

That must have been a very strange sight to see the rich man climbing up a tree like a boy, and hiding among the leaves, where he thought nobody would see him, to get a glimpse of the passing stranger![92]

He was small . . . there was a tree . . . and he was desperate. And when you are desperate, you will do whatever it takes to get what you want.

A little boy told his father, "I want a new bike."

The father said, "In this house we pray and ask God for the things we want and need."

That night the little boy prayed, "Dear God, I need a new bike."

The next morning the little boy woke up and ran to the garage, but he found no bike. The little boy prayed the same prayer for three nights with no results. On the fourth day, while playing at his Grandma's house, he found a small statue of Mary. He carefully wrapped the statue in tissue paper and put the statue in a shoe box. That night he prayed, "Dear God, if you ever want to see your mother again . . ."

Desperate times call for desperate measures. Whether you are kidnapping Jesus' mom or a rich guy climbing a tree.

The key verse of the conversion is verse 5: "When Jesus came to the place, He looked up and said to him, 'Zaccheus, hurry and come down, for today I must stay at your house.'"

These phrases are packed with power.

He looked up

Jesus noticed the man.

There is a Shepherd bringing home His sheep. As they come in at night, He counts them all. I can see Jesus the Great Shepherd counting, "One, two . . ." When He gets to the last one, He has only counted 99. One is missing. He does not say, "I'll let that one stay out to let him learn his lesson. I will see what happens by morning." No, the Shepherd goes out and hunts the one that is lost and when He find it He lays it on his shoulder and carries it home.

The sheep does not find the Shepherd; it's the Shepherd who finds the sheep. It was the Shepherd who rejoiced, not the sheep.

People talk of finding Christ, but really it's the opposite. Jesus looked up and saw the man.

He said, "Zaccheus"

It looked as though Jesus was walking right by, but He stopped and said, "Zaccheus."

Zaccheus must have wondered, *Who told Him my name?*

Ah! Jesus knew him. He always knew him. Sinner, Christ knows all about you. He knows your name.

Hurry and come down, for today

Proverbs 27:1 says, "Do not boast about tomorrow, for you know not what a day may bring forth." C. H. Spurgeon said it like this:

If you were sick, would you send for your physician tomorrow? If your house were on fire, would you call "fire!" Tomorrow? If you were robbed in the street on your road home, would you cry "Stop! Thief!" Tomorrow? No. But man is foolish in the things that concern his soul. Unless divine and infinite love shall teach him to number his days, he will still go on boasting of tomorrows until his soul has been destroyed by them. The great mischief of most men is that they procrastinate. It is not that they resolve to be damned, but that they resolve to be saved *tomorrow*. It is not that they reject Christ forever, but that they reject Christ *today*. They might as well reject him forever, as continue perpetually to reject him *now* . . . the road to hell is paved with good intentions. Oh, you that lingers, pull up the paving stones and hurl them at the devil's head. He is ruining you; he is decoying you to your destruction.

Tomorrow, tomorrow, tomorrow! Alas, tomorrow never comes! It is in no calendar except the almanac of fools.[93]

And finally, something crazy happened at this man's conversion, which made it real: "Zaccheus stopped and said to the Lord, 'Behold, Lord, half of my possessions I will give to the poor, and if I have defrauded anyone of anything, I will give back four times as much'" (verse 8).

You know it's a conversion when it reaches a person's wallet. No offering was asked for. No money requested. When something happens in the heart, something happens on the outside.

That's Zaccheus. That's Luke 19.

Taking a Page from Jesus' Method in Hostile Environments

Today's Reading: Luke 20

Not everyone who asks you a question wants an answer or wants the truth. Listen to one of the most profound questions ever asked. It was a question someone asked of Jesus, and the one who asked it never stopped to hear the answer: "Pilate said to Him, 'What is truth?' And when he had said this, he went out again to the Jews . . ." (John 18:38).

Pilate asked the question and did not even give the One who is called "the truth" a moment to answer. I don't know if he was really interested. Many times people ask questions not for the answer, but to see what side you have taken. Their question is for exposure not for truth.

In today's reading, that is what Jesus faced three times. The religious were asking questions not to know the answer but to see what "side" He was on.

Today in this hostile culture we are in, we face the same thing in our workplaces, college campuses, even the local coffee shops. Maybe we can take a page out of Jesus' book, from His methods of dialoguing in a hostile environment.

Let's look at two of the three situations. Notice what was asked and then notice how Jesus responded:

> On one of the days while He was teaching the people in the temple and preaching the gospel, the chief priests and the scribes with the elders confronted *Him*, and they spoke, saying to Him, "Tell us by what authority You are doing these things, or who is the one who gave You this authority?" Jesus answered and said to them, "I will also ask you a question, and you tell Me: Was the baptism of John from heaven or from men?" (Luke 20:1-4)

> They watched Him, and sent spies who pretended to be righteous, in order that they might catch Him in some statement, so that they *could* deliver Him to the rule and the authority of the governor. They

questioned Him, saying, "Teacher, we know that you speak and teach correctly, and you are not partial to any, but teach the way of God in truth. Is it lawful for us to pay taxes to Caesar, or not?" But He detected their trickery and said to them, "Show Me a denarius. Whose likeness and inscription does it have?" (Luke 20:20-24)

Jesus did the same thing with every ill-intented question. Remember, none of these religious people were asking Jesus to hear the answer but to discover what side He was on. Or as apologist Ravi Zacharias explains that every question comes with an assumption.[94] That is why C. S. Lewis said, "Nothing is so self-defeating than a question that has not been fully understood."[95]

Let's take a page from Jesus. What did He do in each situation? Jesus asked questions to the questioner. He questioned the question. Many ask questions but never have been questioned themselves.

I have seen preachers on television being asked these kinds of questions—from hosts on the *Today* show to Oprah to reporters on CNN and Fox News. Every time they are asked a question as Jesus was, they answer it and get in trouble. Instead of doing what Jesus did, some of these pastors wrongly assessed that these people wanted an answer, which wasn't true. They wanted to know their side, so the attack could commence.

Answer the question when people want an answer. Question the question when people want to fight.

Jesus would not let them catch Him, but His questions put them on the defensive. One of the most explosive question Christians are asked today: What is your view of same-sex marriage? Let's take a page from Jesus: What question can we ask in return that would turn the tables?

Maybe something like this: Do you believe in God? Do you think this is something important enough that He has something to say about it? Would you believe in God even if He contradicts what you think? So where would you find out what God thinks?

Someone said, "Most people dismiss the Bible not because it contradicts itself but because it contradicts them."

The next time someone asks you a question, take a page out of Jesus' playbook and ask a question in return.

Day 65

NO NOISE OFFERINGS

Today's Reading: Luke 21

When I begin to think about what Jesus can see, I am amazed. Consider these:

- Jesus sees the past. In John 1, He tells Nathaniel the day he was under a fig tree.
- Jesus sees the future. He prophesies in John 21 about Peter's death.
- Jesus sees into the heavenly realm and the spiritual battle that goes on when sickness is being conquered. He says in Luke 10 that He saw Satan falling like lightning as the disciples were doing their calling.
- Jesus sees into the minds of people. In Mark 2 when the religious leaders are thinking that He cannot forgive sin and Jesus questions their thoughts.

With all these amazing things that Jesus sees, would He be interested in the scribble on a church tithing envelope? I think He *is* interested and He *does* look at what we give. Consider this opening story in Luke 21.

> He looked up and saw the rich putting their gifts into the treasury. And He saw a poor widow putting in two small copper coins. And He said, "Truly I say to you, this poor widow put in more than all *of them*; for they all out of their surplus put into the offering; but she out of her poverty put in all that she had to live on." (Luke 21:1-4)

We get worried too much about what the government can see and what they know about us that we forget something really important. That God is omniscient. And He knows everything that is going on in our lives.

He sees it all. *Omniscience* is a theological word to describe one of the attributes of God. It means that He is all knowing. That He knows everything about you and me—not just what we do but why we do it.

A few years ago, I was sitting in a meeting next to a very talented graphic designer for a major Christian organization. He told me, "When we are designing something, we always tell ourselves that when people do something, there is the good reason and there is the real reason. Our company always tries to figure out the real reason."

I was reading the story about the American industrialist, Henry Ford, who was asked to donate money for a new medical facility's construction in Ireland:

> The billionaire pledged to donate $5,000. The next day in the newspaper, the headline read, "Henry Ford contributes $50,000 to the local hospital." The irate Ford was on the phone immediately to complain to the fund-raiser that he had been misunderstood. The fund-raiser replied that they would print a retraction in the paper the following day the headline to read, "Henry Ford reduces his donation by $45,000 to the hospital." Realizing the poor publicity that would result, the industrialist agreed to the $50,000 contribution.[96]

Real reason? Saving face.

Jesus knows the real reason—all the time. This is Jesus' last time in the temple before the crucifixion and His last message to the people. And His last message in the temple is on giving.

Understand this about the offering time at church: He is not just there, He is watching. He knows not only who is giving but what they gave.

He saw the woman drop in her two small copper coins. And the offering that caught His attention was a "no noise" offering.

Let me explain. First remember this: she put in a *lepta*. It was less than a penny. It was the smallest currency in Palestine. Jesus has to be very close to see someone drop in two pennies. In fact their nickname was "small change."[97]

At that time the bigger denominations of money, the heavier the money. Literally heavier. The heavier the cash, the louder it was.

Why is loud important? So people could hear your offering make a sound and clap and cheer for you when it hit the brass offering buckets.

The treasury where they placed their offerings consisted of thirteen brass treasure chests called trumpets because they were shaped like inverted horns, narrow at the top and enlarged at the bottom. The rich's coins on the brass trumpets caused oohing and aahing.

But then when a widow passed by and put in her thin ones, there was no noise from the trumpets. The widow received no noise from the trumpets but she did get noise from God! Jesus stood up and cheered her offering.

John Calvin got it right when he said that there is a message here for the poor and for the rich:

To the poor: you can always give. Those in poverty can be greedy like anyone else. You don't need stuff to be greedy. Yet this poor widow gave everything. I have watched just as much greed with little as I have with much.

To the rich: amount is not the issue, sacrifice is. God can do great things with tiny offerings that are a big sacrifice. Don't be deceived by amounts. They deceive us but not Jesus.

What do you need to remember about giving?

First, only one person that day saw correctly what this woman gave and He was the only one who mattered. Who knew that Jesus was going to be in the audience that day during the offering?

If we knew Jesus was going to be at our church on Sunday, would our worship or our giving be any different?

Well, here it is: Revelation 2:1 tells us that He is always in His church walking among us: "The One who holds the seven stars in His right hand, the One who walks among the seven golden lampstands."

Also, what Jesus hears and sees is not what everyone else hears and sees. The people did not hear anything. Or if they did, they heard the clanging of the copper. But Jesus heard "all"—all that she had. She did not give copper, she gave it all. I wish we had the rest of the story.

But I guarantee there is one. Because I know God, and He always responds to this kind of giving. This is one of those stories that, when I get to heaven, I want to find out about. "What happened to the widow who now had nothing in her possession after she gave all in the offering?"

Guaranteed she has a story to tell. God will always give you a story when you give it all to Him.

Day 66

Plotting Satan and Praying Christ

Today's Reading: Luke 22

In today's reading we are entering into Luke's telling of the Passion Week. While Jesus is with His disciples in the garden of Gethsemane, He speaks some remarkable words to Peter, which will be important to all of us, because it is what Jesus does right now for every one of His children.

At the Last Supper, right after Jesus says that one of the Twelve will betray Him, He then says these words to Peter:

> Simon, Simon, Satan has asked to sift all of you as wheat. But I have prayed for you, Simon, that your faith may not fail. And when you have turned back, strengthen your brothers. [Luke 22:31-32, NIV]

Simon, Simon.

Just like when you heard your parents use your full name when you were a kid—this is what it means when Jesus repeats Peter's name twice. This is the full name with the middle name—and that means trouble. What makes this interesting is Jesus goes back to the name, Simon, which He'd changed to Peter.

Remember the story from Matthew 16:15-18, when Peter said to Jesus, "You are the Christ, the Son of the living God." And Jesus said, "Blessed are you, Simon Barjona, because flesh and blood did not reveal *this* to you, but My Father who is in heaven. I also say to you that you are Peter, and upon this rock I will build My church."

Now Jesus goes back to the old name and says it twice. Peter is not necessarily in trouble, but is about to experience trouble . . . Satanic trouble.

Jesus says, "Satan has asked."

Satan is God's Satan. He is not an independent agent who can take your life without God's permission. He is not an independent entity who does what he wants. We see that in the book of Job when Satan had to get permission to attack Job.

Try to imagine the picture Jesus gives Simon Peter: Satan is on one side trying to take Peter and to sift him like wheat. And on the other side, Jesus is praying for him. "Satan has asked to sift all of you . . . I have prayed for you." At the same time that Satan is asking for Peter, Jesus is interceding for him. That changes everything! That alters the whole case! There may be failure, defection, cowardly denial, and compromise, but there can never be ultimate ruin. Why? The praying Christ.

We think our spiritual lives are all about what we do—our prayer lives, our consistency in Bible reading—and our successes in those things secure us. But nothing could be further from the truth.

The plotting of Satan is no match for the praying Christ.

It isn't your prayers that secure your place with Him in eternity—it's Jesus' prayers that secure you.

I don't think we can mention the praying Christ without referencing His post-resurrection heaven ministry. Listen to it: "He is able to save fully from now throughout eternity, everyone who comes to God through him, because he lives to pray continually for them" (Hebrews 7:25, TPT).

Satan does not get his way with you. Because you have a Savior who neither sleeps nor slumbers (Psalm 121:4) and is continually praying for you.

Peter doesn't just get a praying Christ; we get a praying Christ. A person must get past the love of Christ for us, the cross of Christ that values us, and the prayers of Christ before he or she can make their bed in hell.

I love this story. Little Johnny would wake up every night, because he would hear a bump. But the sound was him as he fell out of bed in his sleep. This happened five nights in a row, until finally Johnny said to his father, "Daddy, I'm so tired of falling out of the bed. Can you fix it?" His father said, "Son, it is really simple. You never got far enough in."

The reason you keep falling out of Jesus is because you never got far enough in. You got in church, now it's time to get in Christ. In Christ, you have a praying Christ.

Satan doesn't just want Peter, Satan wants you. Let the words of the Scottish preacher Robert Murray M'Cheyne give you encouragement and empower you to walk in victory: "If I could hear Christ praying for me in the next room, I would not fear a million enemies. Yet distance makes no difference [to him]. He is praying for me."[98] And He is praying for you too.

JUST BREATHE

Today's Reading: Luke 23

Today we come to the last solemn minutes of Jesus' life on the cross. It is His final comment from the cross that catches my attention. It is a prayer but goes further than up. That prayer goes wide.

Let's read Jesus' final words before He breathed His last breath:

> Jesus called out with a loud voice, "Father, into your hands I commit my spirit." When he had said this, he breathed his last. The centurion, seeing what had happened, praised God and said, "Surely this was a righteous man." (Luke 23:46-47, NIV)

What a scene! Jesus was dying and this was His final sentence on earth before He was the resurrected Lord. He said, "Father, into your hands I commit my spirit." Then He simply breathed His last.

Here is the incredible part—that when the centurion saw what had happened, he began praising God and saying that Jesus was a righteous man. A centurion who beat and dragged the Son of God to calvary, witnessed Jesus' cry and final breath and, with praise, declared who Jesus was!

Søren Kierkegaard said something remarkable: "The gospel is seldom heard but it is overheard."[99] Jesus wasn't even talking to the centurion; He was talking to His Father. Yet this man overheard and something changed in him.

It gets crazier in Mark's account. I think it is the same centurion, but Mark adds a bit of a twist: "When the centurion, who was standing right in front of Him, saw the way He breathed His last, he said, 'Truly this man was the Son of God!'" (Mark 15:39).

What? Breathing. Just His breathing. Just the way He breathed. And the man's response to breathing was, "Truly this man was the Son of God."

St. Francis of Assisi said, "Preach the gospel at all times and when necessary use words." Jesus didn't use words in Mark's account. He just breathed. What was happening? Did the centurion get saved by simply observing Jesus' breath? I don't think so. Let me explain.

Breathing is what we do every day and in every moment. And people watch the way we do life every day and in every moment. The simple things we do, such as breathing, we do them without thought. But there are other things we do that people watch: the way we raise our children, the way we speak to them; the way we treat people in retail; how we handle our finances; how we have a good work ethic; how we don't get an attitude when we drive or when we work behind a counter or desk; when we come to work on time and don't leave till the job is done; how we finish tasks.

I call that breathing. The stuff we do—that we do the right way.

The centurion did not get saved from Jesus' one breath but by watching Jesus until the moment He died. It was the way Jesus responded to the abuse. Listen to how Peter described those moments on the cross, which gave breathing power:

> If you endure suffering even when you have done right, God will bless you for it. It was to this that God called you, for Christ himself suffered for you and left you an example, so that you would follow in his steps. He committed no sin, and no one ever heard a lie come from his lips. When he was insulted, he did not answer back with an insult; when he suffered, he did not threaten, but placed his hopes in God, the righteous judge. (1 Peter 2:20-23, GNT)

The centurion did not just see breathing, he saw more—he saw no lies coming from Him. When Jesus was insulted, He did not answer back. When He was beaten, He did not threaten back. He placed His hope in God.

Everything added up to the centurion's realization that "truly this man was the Son of God." After seeing Him breath during the pain, the suffering, and the false accusations, and then watching Him breathe that final breath was the icing on the cake.

When you live the way Jesus lived, then the simplest thing—like breathing—can change someone's life.

We think it is a gospel-preaching moment or a church service or a powerful verse that draws people to get saved. We forget that if that happens, it was because they saw a lot of breathing before that.

Keep inviting people to church, keep sharing life with them, keep telling them about the love of Jesus. But don't forget that when someone responds to Jesus, it wasn't the breathing of one moment but the breathing that took place every day.

That's what the famous African missionary, Dr. Albert Schweitzer, remembered when he stepped off a train in Chicago during the height of racial discrimination. He'd attained some renown and had won a Nobel peace prize, so, the story goes, when he arrived at the station, the city officials greeted him with handshakes and the key to the city and reporters questioned him about his long trip from Africa. As he took it all in, he finally noticed something over his shoulder and excused himself from the crowd.

Everyone watched as he maneuvered back to the train to help an older black woman who was struggling with her luggage. When he got back to the group, one of the reporters said, "That's the first time I ever saw a walking sermon."[100]

Albert Schweitzer was just breathing. Doing what he did every day.

May we have the same said about you and me.

A Fire Seven Miles Outside of Jerusalem

Today's Reading: Luke 24

It's resurrection morning for Jesus. All of the Gospels highlight Jesus' post-resurrection conversations with His disciples and followers, but only Luke highlights a conversation that happened seven miles outside of Jerusalem. To put it another way, a fire started seven miles outside of Jerusalem.

No building burst into flames.

No property was damaged.

No one was trapped.

No life was lost.

But two hearts caught on fire in a conversation with the resurrected Jesus. As someone once said, "Get on fire for God and men will come watch you burn."

Fire needs no advertisement. When people hear the fire engines, people look for smoke. And seven miles outside of Jerusalem on a road heading toward Emmaus two hearts caught fire.

Let's look at the story.

> Two of them were going that very day to a village named Emmaus, which was about seven miles from Jerusalem. And they were talking with each other about all these things which had taken place. While they were talking and discussing, Jesus Himself approached and *began* traveling with them. But their eyes were prevented from recognizing Him. And He said to them, "What are these words that you are exchanging with one another as you are walking?" . . . And they said to Him, "The things about Jesus the Nazarene, who was a prophet mighty in deed and word in the sight of God and all the people, and how the chief priests and our rulers delivered Him to the sentence of death, and crucified Him. But we were hoping that it was He who was going to redeem Israel. Indeed, besides all this, it is the third day since these things happened." . . .
>
> He said to them, "O foolish men and slow of heart to believe in all that the prophets have spoken! Was it not necessary for the Christ

to suffer these things and to enter into His glory?" Then beginning with Moses and with all the prophets, He explained to them the things concerning Himself in all the Scriptures. . . .

They urged him, saying, "Stay with us, for it is *getting* toward evening, and the day is now nearly over." So He went in to stay with them. When He had reclined *at the table* with them, He took the bread and blessed it, and breaking it, He began giving it to them. Then their eyes were opened and they recognized Him; and He vanished from their sight. They said to one another, "Were not our hearts burning within us while He was speaking to us on the road, while He was explaining the Scriptures to us?" And they got up that very hour and returned to Jerusalem, and found gathered together the eleven and those who were with them, saying, "The Lord has really risen and has appeared to Simon." (Luke 24:13-17, 19-21, 25-27, 29-34)

I have been reading a sermon a day for almost thirty years. It's a practice I picked up when I started pastoring. One of my favorite preachers is the great Baptist, Vance Havner. In one of his sermons based on this story, Havner gives four characteristics that happen to someone who has a genuine experience with God.

First, their experience is based on the Scriptures. As Luke 24:27 tells us, "He explained to them the things concerning Himself in all the Scriptures." Men who part company with the Old Testament also part company with Jesus. Moses wrote Genesis. Jesus promoted Genesis.

Second, it stirs their hearts. Luke 24:32: They said to one another, "Were not our hearts burning within us while He was speaking to us on the road, while He was explaining the Scriptures to us?" A genuine experience with God has its foundation in the Bible, not in our feelings, although that does not mean our feelings aren't affected. We are not saved because we feel saved, but being saved makes us happy. As Havner said, "There was never a real revival that did not produce heartburn and hallelujahs."[101]

Third, Jesus shows up at their house: "They urged Him, saying, 'Stay with us, for it is *getting* toward evening, and the day is now nearly over.' So He went in to stay with them. When He had reclined *at the table* with them, He took the bread and blessed *it*, and breaking *it*, He *began* giving *it* to them" (Luke 24:29-30). Men stop at the Bible or they stop at feelings. If it's real, it goes home with you. A genuine experience with God affects your home life, not your church life.

Fourth, it sends them back out to tell others. Read how the two men responded after Jesus disappeared: "They got up that very hour and returned to Jerusalem, and found gathered together the eleven and those who were with them, saying, 'The Lord has really risen and has appeared to Simon.' They *began* to relate their experiences on the road and how He was recognized by them in the breaking of the bread" (Luke 24:33-35).

And as they told the story, He showed up again: "While they were telling these things, He Himself stood in their midst and said to them, 'Peace be to you'" (Luke 24:36).

What a great grid for a genuine experience with Jesus:
- Scripture based
- Heart stirring
- Home-life affected
- Can't stop talking about it

People need to experience Jesus, not church. As Havner said, "Sunday-morning Christianity is the greatest hindrance to true revival."[102]

I think it was all God's plan that those two men's hearts burned seven miles outside of Jerusalem. Not in the temple, not in a church, not in the mecca of Judaism and birthplace of Christianity. But seven miles outside a fire burned, meaning God can set us on fire anywhere.

THE FIRST 10:00 A.M. SERVICE

Today's Reading: John 1

I am excited that today on our 260 Journey we begin a journey through the Gospel of John. This is the most unique Gospel, because it doesn't start out like the other three Gospels. It takes us to the beginning . . . the *real* beginning. Listen to its opening verse: "In the beginning was the Word, and the Word was with God, and the Word was God" (John 1:1).

That sounds very much like Genesis 1:1 at creation: "In the beginning God created the heavens and the earth."

Here's what's even crazier: the "In the beginning" of John takes place before the "In the beginning" of Genesis.

What does that mean?

This puts Jesus in a unique category as the only person who ever lived before He was born. As one theologian said, "Jesus is the invisible God and God is the visible Jesus." And that visible Jesus was about to embark on a three-year ministry that would change the planet forever.

French Emperor Napoleon Bonaparte said it with the greatest clarity: "I know men, and I tell you that Jesus Christ is not a man. Superficial minds see a resemblance between Christ and the founders of empires and the Gods of other religions. That resemblance does not exist. There is between Christianity and every other religion the distance of infinity."[103]

Let's start this journey through John by reading verses 37-39 and see one of the most amazing venues Jesus ever taught in: "The two disciples heard him speak, and they followed Jesus" (verse 37). It's good to stop here and take note that the "him" in this verse is John the Baptist. We would think it should have been that John spoke and they followed John. But this is epic: "They heard him [John] speak and followed Jesus." John, you rock. You challenge me.

The challenge and the proof of any true minister and ministry is that people here us speak and they follow Jesus, not us, our church, our denomination.

That is why distinctives about denominations are so bogus. Distinctives about what day we worship on, what we call Jesus, our water baptism formula, our theology about the gifts. It's so anti New Testament. They make the organization distinct not Jesus.

Can people hear me speak and not follow my church or my denomination? Can people hear an Assembly of God pastor speak and not follow Pentecostalism or a Baptist preacher preach and not follow Calvinism? This is a challenge to twenty-first-century preaching. Thank you, John the Baptist for modeling what we should be doing.

Here is where it gets good: Jesus' first 10:00 a.m. service. It's a service unlike any other in history. It's in an unexpected place but it's in the best place:

> Jesus turned and saw them following, and said to them, "What do you seek?" They said to Him, "Rabbi (which translated means Teacher), where are You staying?" He said to them, "Come, and you will see." So they came and saw where He was staying; and they stayed with Him that day, for it was about the tenth hour. (verses 38-39)

They asked Jesus, "Where are You staying?" Or, "Where is Your home?" And Jesus responded, "Come and you will see." "Come to My home," they came, and they had the first home group. The first Christian 10:00 a.m. service would take place where Jesus resided.

There is something about teaching and learning in a home. They went that day to where Jesus was staying and had no idea how that 10:00 a.m. service would impact their "forever."

The home of Jesus. Wow! It's one thing to learn from a pulpit and in a pew, it's another level to learn from a classroom and a lecture. But the playing field changes when you learn in a home—and it beats all other venues.

Jesus' first place of teaching wasn't the synagogue, it was the home. When the home is involved, you are inviting people up close for them to see if what you have is real. Anyone can put on a show on Sundays for an hour and a half. When you have a whiteboard and pulpit, you are inviting them into your academic life and knowledge. But the home is different—it points to relationships.

I think from the get go, Jesus was saying that this relationship was not for the weekends but for every day.

One of my favorite preachers from the past, G. Campbell Morgan, said this: "If you cannot be a Christian where you are, you cannot be a Christian anywhere. It is not place, but grace."[104]

And the home—not the church—needs to be the first place we are Christian.

Home means to these disciples:

• They see faith worked out
• They see vulnerability

- They see up close
- They see life, not words

David had a word for all of us in Psalm 101:2 that tackles this very topic: "I'm doing the very best I can, and I'm doing it at home, where it counts" (MSG).

The disciples could hear a sermon on the mount—and that's good. But when it's a sermon in the home—that's epic!

BAD STUFF IS ALWAYS TRYING TO MAKE ITS WAY BACK IN MY LIFE

Today's Reading: John 2

Today our 260 Journey takes us to John 2. If we are not paying attention, we may feel as if we are at the end of the Gospel and not at the beginning. Let me explain why this can be confusing by reading something Jesus did in this chapter:

> The Passover of the Jews was near, and Jesus went up to Jerusalem. And He found in the temple those who were selling oxen and sheep and doves, and the money changers seated *at their tables*. And He made a scourge of cords, and drove *them* all out of the temple, with the sheep and the oxen; and He poured out the coins of the money changers and overturned their tables; and to those who were selling the doves He said, "Take these things away; stop making My Father's house a place of business." (John 2:13-16)

Anything seem odd to you?

What Jesus did here is in all three Synoptic Gospels—Matthew, Mark, and Luke. But here is what makes this scene stand out: it isn't the same thing.

Think about this, Jesus cleared the temple of the money changers and those buying and selling. He made a scourge and then declared, "My Father's house shall be called a house of prayer." This happens in Matthew 21, Mark 11, and Luke 19—all on Jesus' triumphant entry into Jerusalem, which we call Palm Sunday.

But this is totally different. This is not Palm Sunday. This is the beginning of His ministry. This is John 2, not John 19.

Wow! This is huge. This is Jesus clearing the temple at the beginning of His ministry where the other Gospels record Jesus clearing the temple at the end of His ministry.

What He cleaned out, three years later came back in.

Why? Junk is always trying to make its way back into the temple. That's not just true for this New Testament temple but for another temple. In this same chapter, in verse 19, Jesus said, "Destroy this temple, and in three days I will raise it up"—and then it goes on to say, "He was speaking of the temple of His body" (verse 21).

In other words: *I am now the temple that sin and money changers are looking to get back into.*

This is so true. Stuff that was driven out of my life years ago is always trying to find its way back in years later; just like those money changers were.

In *I Surrender*, Patrick Morley wrote that the church's integrity problem is in the misconception "that we can add Christ to our lives, but not subtract sin. It is a change in belief without a change in behavior. . . . It is revival without reformation, without repentance."[105]

Jesus would not let something into the temple that did not belong. I need God to come into my life each day and make a clean sweep of my personal temple, because junk always wants to come back. The same is true of you. As C. S. Lewis reminds us, "We have a strange illusion that mere time cancels sin. . . . But mere time does nothing either to the fact or to the guilt of a sin."[106]

How do we keep sin out? The Holy Spirit's conviction is the scourge to make us aware, and repentance drives the money changers out. Conviction and repentance get the money changers out of our temples that are trying to get back in like old times.

Repentance is best defined by a little girl who said, "It's to be sorry enough to quit."

The great American evangelist, Billy Sunday, spoke about the fight against sin being a fight he would wage until he died: "Listen, I'm against sin. I'll kick it as long as I've got a foot, I'll fight it as long as I've got a fist, I'll butt it as long as I've got a head, and I'll bite it as long as I've got a tooth. And when I'm old, fistless, footless, and toothless, I'll gum it till I go home to glory and it goes home to perdition."[107]

Fight sin. Let Jesus clean house. Each day you wake up, ask Jesus to go through the temple and expose anything in your life that should not be there.

DON'T MAKE IT HARDER THAN IT IS

Today's Reading: John 3

There are a few chapters in our 260 Journey where you just pause, exhale, and know you are seeing beauty and majesty. John 3 is one of those chapters.

Plato said, "Whoever tells the stories shapes society." Do we have a story to tell or what? We have *the* story—the gospel story. *God's* story.

John 3:16 is God's story stuffed into one verse. And Jesus tells it in twenty-five words—because that's all He needed.

If we could choose one verse of the 31,102 verses of the Bible, this one verse sums up the gospel. The word *gospel* means Good News.

So here's God's story: "For God so loved the world, that He gave His only begotten Son, that whoever believes in Him shall not perish, but have eternal life."

This is the most wonderful sentence ever written. It begins with God, who has no beginning, and concludes with life that has no ending.

Let's break down the verse:

God . . . the greatest lover
so loved . . . the greatest degree
the world . . . the greatest number
that He gave . . . the greatest act
His only begotten Son . . . the greatest gift
that whoever . . . the greatest invitation
believes . . . the greatest simplicity
in Him . . . the greatest person
shall not perish . . . the greatest deliverance

but . . . the greatest difference
have . . . the greatest certainty
everlasting life . . . the greatest possession

How did John 3:16 come to be? It was spoken to one man, Nicodemus, one night. (The original Nick at Night.)

Nicodemus was a religious man, and it seemed something was bothering him. Religion wasn't enough.

What's interesting is that some of the greatest verses in the Bible from Jesus' lips happen through one-on-one conversations, not in sermons.

While Nicodemus did not ask a question to be answered, Jesus answered the question he meant to ask. He did not realize the conversation would be turned from religion to regeneration. To make sure we understand what Jesus was emphasizing that night to Nicodemus, let's read a few verses surrounding this one so we can get a sense of the context:

> So that whoever believes will in Him have eternal life. For God so loved the world, that He gave His only begotten Son, that whoever believes in Him shall not perish, but have eternal life. For God did not send the Son into the world to judge the world, but that the world might be saved through Him. He who believes in Him is not judged; he who does not believe has been judged already, because he has not believed in the name of the only begotten Son of God. (John 3:15-18)

If I were to say to my children: "Dinner is great, but now it's time to clean up. When you clean up, Mom and Dad are happy, because cleaning up means you respect our words, and when you clean up you do your part." What is the key phrase? *Clean up.*

Jesus did the same thing. You have to pay attention to see it in these verses. Jesus' key word: *believe.*

Belief is crucial, because it is the hinge upon which the door to heaven turns. Jesus used variations of *belief* five times. If you were to speak three sentences, and you included one verb five times, I would get the feeling you were stressing a highly critical point. And indeed, He was.

John 3:16 begins with God and His love, and it ends in heaven. But the one variable in the equation is this word, *believes.*

Believe is at the fork in the road of perish and eternal life.

God's love gave us Christ, who died, giving us our only access to heaven. Therefore, salvation is not in question. It is there for the taking. The only thing in question is our response. Will we believe?

Pastor J. C. Ryle put it succinctly: "Salvation . . . does not turn on the point, 'Did Christ die for me?' but on the point, 'Do I believe in Christ?'"[108]

Think about it in this way. When the word finally came over the telegraph in New York City in 1912 that Titanic had sunk, despite all the rich and famous on the ship, the list had only two columns—lost and saved.

Don't miss the important word, *believe*.

Not baptize. Believe.

Not communion. Believe.

Not join a group. Not pick one of nine thousand denominations to attend. Believe, believe, believe.

The story goes that a man had a dream. He stood at the gate of heaven and confronted Peter. "What does it take to get into heaven?"

"One thousand points," Peter said.

"Okay," the man said. "I have been faithful in church attendance all my life."

"That's one point," said Peter.

The man could not believe it. "I was a deacon in my church for more than twenty years."

"That's another point."

Getting very anxious, the man said, "I did many good things to help people."

"That's another point."

In great despair the man said, "If all I can get is three points for a long life in the church and doing good works, I guess I'm just going to have to throw myself on the mercy of God and the love of Christ displayed on the cross, and believe that Jesus paid for my sins on the cross."

Peter smiled. "That's a thousand points. Come on in."

Today I want you to get your thousand points. Throw yourself on the mercy of God and stop trying to pay for something that's impossible to accomplish. Simply believe that Jesus did what you could not do for yourself.

Here is the obvious: Jesus said eternal life comes through "belief." Don't make it more difficult than it is.

Day 72

TWO TRUTHS FOR FREEDOM

Today's Reading: John 4

The average American is exposed to between four thousand and ten thousand commercial messages every day.[109] But it's truth that is a rarity. We have opinions but not truth.

One of my friends put it this way: "Everyone is entitled to their own opinion, but not everyone is entitled to their own truth."

Truth is universal. It isn't limited to individuals, geography, or ethnicity.

We see this in today's reading of John 4, in which Jesus has such an important one-on-one conversation with a Samaritan woman. In this conversation Jesus will tell the truth, the difficult truth, but the liberating truth. In fact, He will share two truths that will set this woman—and an entire city—free. For as He said in John 8:32 (TLB), "You will know the truth, and the truth will set you free." That means we need truth in order to have freedom.

And as He shared two truths with the Samaritan woman, He shares those same truths with us: (1) the truth about God; and (2) the truth about ourselves. It's the second truth that we usually miss.

After this immoral woman met Jesus at a well and realized this is not just some Jew but this was the Messiah (truth about God), she went back to her city. Listen to her words: "The woman left her waterpot, and went into the city and said to the men, 'Come, see a man who told me all the things that I *have* done'" (John 4:28-29).

What a message. She did not say, "Come see the Messiah." She did not even say, "Come see a man who told me all my good points and increased my self esteem."

She said, "Come see a man who told me the truth about me. He told me my faults, my sins, and revealed to me my past."

And Jesus did. He told her that she was immoral and living in immorality.

This Samaritan woman was saying, "Come see a man who has told me two truths—the truth about Himself and the truth about me." We need truth to be free; we need to understand and embrace these two truths to experience freedom.

We live in a society that grossly overexaggerates ourselves, but Jesus doesn't do that. Remember the truth about this woman:

He said, "Go call your husband and then come back."
"I have no husband," she said.
"That's nicely put: 'I have no husband.' You've had five husbands, and the man you're living with now isn't even your husband. (John 4:16-18, MSG)

In *Finding God*, Larry Crabb wrote: "Feeling better has become more important to us than finding God."[110] You can't feel better unless you find God, let's be clear. Listen to the Samaritans' response when they heard this woman's raw words: "From that city many of the Samaritans believed in Him because of the word of the woman who testified, 'He told me all the things that I *have* done" (John 4:39). She was telling the city, "Today I am free because of two truths: I met a man who told me all things (truth about God) and all things that I have done (truth about me)." In other words, she was saying, "And after He exposed my dark past, He still wanted me and loves me. This is not a normal man. He is different!"

When we come to Jesus, we will hear the truth about ourselves, but we will also hear the truth about Him. And despite the revelation of our real selves and our messed-up lives, we discover that He loves us and wants us. That's two big truths.

Plato said, "We can easily forgive a child who is afraid of the dark. The real tragedy of life is when men are afraid of the light." When you come to Jesus, you come to the light. Don't be afraid. The true "you" will come to light, but so will the true God. And He is amazing.

Day 73

You Don't Need Bubbles Anymore

Today's Reading: John 5

Today we land on John 5, an up-close view to a phenomenon of miracle healing waters called the waters of Bethesda. When the waters moved, the first in the pool got healed. Here's the first part of the story:

> After these things there was a feast of the Jews, and Jesus went up to Jerusalem. Now there is in Jerusalem by the sheep *gate* a pool, which is called in Hebrew Bethesda, having five porticoes. In these lay a multitude of those who were sick, blind, lame, and withered, [waiting for the moving of the waters; for an angel of the Lord went down at certain seasons into the pool and stirred up the water; whoever then first, after the stirring up of the water, stepped in was made well from whatever disease with which he was afflicted.] A man was there who had been ill for thirty-eight years. (John 5:1-4)

Methodist preacher Halford Luccock made this profound observation about this chapter:

> Here were a group of invalids depending for their on some external commotion. They put all their trust in "bubbles." Society is very much like a boiling spring. It has its periodic fashions and crazes. . . . The surface of the pool of life is disturbed; it bubbles. [And we say,] "Lo, here! This is the thing which will put me on my feet. . . . The man at the pool was saved not by the coming of an external disturbance but by the advent of a Person [Jesus].[111]

I love that. It wasn't bubbles but Jesus who healed him. Here is the rest of the story:

> When Jesus saw him lying there, and knew that he had already been a long time *in that condition*, He said to him, "Do you wish to get well?" The sick man answered Him, "Sir, I have no man to put me into the

pool when the water is stirred up, but while I am coming, another steps down before me." Jesus said to him, "Get up, pick up your pallet and walk." Immediately the man became well, and picked up his pallet and *began* to walk. Afterward Jesus found him in the temple and said to him, "Behold, you have become well; do not sin anymore, so that nothing worse happens to you." (John 5:6-9, 14)

Jesus said three things to this man, and regarding those things I want to say something:

Do you wish to get well?
Get up, pick up your pallet and walk.
Do not sin anymore, so that nothing worse happens to you.

First, Jesus said, "Do you wish to get well?" Seems an odd thing to say to a man who has been there for thirty-eight years, doesn't it? I think people learn to survive and adjust with something they have had for thirty-eight years.

That's why Jesus asked him the question, "Do you wish to get well?"

Notice this man's answer: "Sir, I have no man to put me into the pool when the water is stirred up, but while I am coming, another steps down before me" (verse 7). This man blamed other people for his lack of healing. Either someone did not help him in first, or the problem was that there were faster sick people. There is something dangerous to think that our lack of freedom, healing, or success is because others are not doing their jobs.

Second, Jesus said to him, "Get up, pick up your pallet and walk." He was about to show this man that it wasn't others but now he could do something about it. To get a command from Jesus and not obey is like one who says he believes in education and never goes to school. Destiny is not a matter of chance but choice. No one is born a winner or loser but a chooser.

Jesus told him essentially, "Choose to do what I tell you, and you will walk. Don't make excuses; do something." Like Corrie Ten Boom said, "Don't bother to give God instructions; just report for duty."[112]

Third, Jesus went to the newly healed man after he was walking and said, "Behold, you have become well; do not sin anymore, so that nothing worse happens to you" (verse 14).

I love the order of Jesus. Jesus touched this man physically and then dealt with him spiritually. To have a walking man whose heart is not right is useless. I would rather be lame and go to heaven than be a track star and go to hell.

These were the same words Jesus spoke to the woman caught in adultery: "Jesus said to her, 'Woman, where are they? Did no one condemn you? She said, 'No one, Lord.' And Jesus said, 'I do not condemn you, either. Go. From now on sin no more.'" (John 8:10-11).

No need to blame others when Jesus is here. No need to wait for others when Jesus gives you a choice for healing and walking. And finally, no need to live an old way when Jesus' new way is so much better than waiting for bubbles.

Day 74

YOU SHOULD HAVE STOPPED AT THE FISH

Today's Reading: John 6

The Christian life is a journey, not an arrival. As part of that journey, we all have to do hard but noble stuff at some point:
- tell someone about Jesus
- say no to something we used to say yes to
- end a toxic relationship
- decide to tithe

As Oswald Chambers said, "If we are going to live as disciples of Jesus, we have to remember that all noble things are difficult. The Christian life is gloriously difficult, but the difficulty of it does not make us faint and cave in, it rouses us up to overcome."[113] Sometimes the hardest thing and the right thing are the same thing. Don't miss out on something amazing because it's difficult. We are ordinary people who know an extraordinary God!

Talk about doing the hard thing: In October 1912, Theodore Roosevelt was campaigning for the presidency and on a stop in Milwaukee, Wisconsin, a man shot him point-blank with a .32-caliber pistol. Though the bullet lodged in his chest, Roosevelt refused to cancel his campaign rally. "The bullet is in me now, so that I cannot make a very long speech, but I will try my best," Roosevelt told the crowd. In fact, Roosevelt spoke for eighty-four minutes![114] That's doing the difficult thing!

In today's reading, John 6 helps us get ready for the hard thing that God sometimes calls us to. It's the story of the loaves and fishes. It's not a story simply about a miracle. It's a test for the disciples! It's them being challenged with a hard thing. Let's read it:

After these things Jesus went away to the other side of the Sea of Galilee (or Tiberias). A large crowd followed Him, because they saw the signs which He was performing on those who were sick. Then Jesus went up on the mountain, and there He sat down with His disciples. Now the Passover, the feast of the Jews, was near. Therefore Jesus, lifting up His eyes and seeing that a large crowd was coming to Him, said to Philip, "Where are we to buy bread, so that these may eat?" This He was saying to test him, for He Himself knew what He was intending to do. (John 6:1-6)

This story wasn't just about feeding people, it was also about testing the disciples with a one-question test: "Where shall we buy bread for all these people to eat?"

That's it.

It was "fill in the blank." (I hated those tests because you had no chance to guess, like you could on the multiple-choice tests.)

If Jesus would have said something like . . .

"Where shall we buy bread for all these people?":

A. Costco

B. Sam's

C. a and b

D. Me!

I think I could have gotten this one right.

Philip started filling in his test paper: "Two hundred denarii worth of bread is not sufficient for them, for everyone to receive a little."

Wrong!

Then it was Andrew's turn: "There is a lad here who has five barley loaves and two fish, but what are these for so many people?" (verse 9).

When Andrew started his answer with, "There is a lad here who has five loaves and two fish," I want to shout, "Stop right there! You got it. Don't say anything else." If he would have ended his sentence there, he would have been a hero. But he threw in, "But what are these for so many people?"

He should have stopped at the fish.

When he continued to talk, he magnified the crowd and lessened God. He was minimizing the material God had to work with. From the beginning, God has never had much to work with. But that's what happens when our problems get big: God gets little.

Andrew was so close to the answer. In fact, he got the answer right, but then messed it up with the conjunction *but*.

When you are faced with a huge need, just tell God all the stuff you've got and what He has to work with. Tell God what you've got—then stop there!

"I've got two mad people in a marriage. That's it, God."

"I've got a job that doesn't pay much and a lot of bills. That's all, God."

"I've got a rebellious child who won't listen."

Just tell God what you've got to work with, then say, "The rest is up to you, Lord."

Let's look at how Jesus responded:

Jesus said, "Have the people sit down." Now there was much grass in the place. So the men sat down, in number about five thousand. Jesus then took the loaves, and having given thanks, He distributed to those who were seated; likewise also of the fish as much as they wanted. (verses 10-11)

Don't tell God their value or whether something is enough. He made the world from nothing. God doesn't need your commentary. The only word that should go after *but* is *God*. And God's got it from there.

Now You Know the Rest of the Story

Today's Reading: John 7

Not many young people would know the radio show or his iconic voice, but some years ago, 21 million Americans would tune in on their radios to hear from the most listened-to voice in America. They would hold their breath in suspense as the storyteller recounted a true story with a surprise ending. It was called The Rest of the Story, a real life mystery Paul Harvey would share. After he revealed the shocking ending, he would say, "Now you know . . ." pause . . . "the rest of the story." And then close with his signature broadcast ending, "Good day."

We just hit our Paul-Harvey moment in our 260 Journey. And we find it in a parenthetical statement within a verse of John 7. The parentheses tell us the rest of the story.

Question: what do you think of when I mention the name Nicodemus?

His claim to fame was a one-on-one night conversation with Jesus and in the midst of that interaction in John 3, we hear Jesus say the most amazing sentence ever spoken in human history: "For God so loved the world, that He gave His only begotten Son, that whoever believes in Him shall not perish, but have eternal life" (verse 16).

Thank you, Nicodemus, for having the guts to talk to Jesus. That statement Jesus gave you has probably led more people to Jesus than any other Bible verse.

But Nicodemus is more than just that scene. People can easily be caricatured for one thing and known by only one event in their life. Nicodemus seems to get stuck in John 3 and his story goes no further. What is amazing is that Jesus' "born again" talk never seems to come to a conclusion and we never know if it "took" with Nicodemus. Did the religious leader gain a second birth and become a follower of Jesus?

In our reading today in John 7, though, if you blink, you will miss the rest of Nicodemus's story. It sheds light on the most famous New Testament chapter without a conclusion. Here is the amazing parentheses of John 7 and the anticipated conclusion of the iconic John 3 meeting: "Nicodemus *(he who came to Him before, being one of them)* said . . ." (verse 50, emphasis added).

Did you see it? *He who came to Him . . .*

That is John 3, the born-again-talk evening.

Then verse 50 continues, "before being one of them."

That's it. He is one of them. One of who? The disciples, a follower of Jesus.

Nicodemus heard the words of Jesus that night and took them to heart. Nicodemus was born again. Did it happen that night? Did it happen in John 3? We don't know. We don't have those facts. But it happened! We know that conversation changed that man.

I sometimes miss the parentheses in people's lives. I have talked to people on planes and in coffee shops and in parks about Jesus and never saw anything happen. But that doesn't mean they don't have those parentheses. Just because it doesn't happen in your chapter doesn't mean it hasn't happened at all. Who knew? And who knows if your talk with someone about Jesus touched someone. We find out about Nicodemus four chapters later, though you may not find out for four years. But always remember, God's Word never returns void.

All I know is that Jesus shared with Nicodemus about the new birth. It changed his life. And John 7:50 says in those parentheses the results of the conversation—"he who came to Him before being one of them"—gives us all the results of that special night in John 3. Nicodemus became a follower.

Do I dare say it?

Should I say it?

Forgive me, Mr Harvey. Now you know . . . the rest of that John 3 story. Good day.

TRYING TO DECLAW THE LION

Today's Reading: John 8

In *Christian Letters to a Post-Christian World*, renowned English writer, Dorothy Sayers, aimed some powerful words at religious people who have watered down the Son of God and made Jesus accommodating:

> The people who hanged Christ never accused Him of being a bore; on the contrary, they thought Him too dynamic to be safe. It has been left for later generations to muffle up that shattering personality and surround Him with the atmosphere of tedium. We have very efficiently pared the claws of the Lion of Judah, certified Him "meek and mild," and recommended Him as a fitting household pet for pale curates and pious old ladies.[115]

As we have seen throughout our 260 Journey so far, Jesus is anything but those things. Four times in today's reading, Jesus refers to Himself by using a common Old Testament title used only for God: I Am (see verses 12, 24, 28, and 58). That's why this chapter opens with the religious wanting to stone a woman caught in adultery and end with them wanting to stone Jesus. Look at the ending of the chapter with me:

> The Jews said to Him, "You are not yet fifty years old, and have You seen Abraham?" Jesus said to them, "Truly, truly, I say to you, before Abraham was born, I am." Therefore they picked up stones to throw at Him, but Jesus hid Himself and went out of the temple. (John 8:57-59)

By Jesus using that phrase for Himself, He clearly meant for them to understand that He was saying that He was God. And the religious were not having it—thus the stones. They needed the stones to "declaw" the Lion of Judah and make Him a manageable kitty cat, as Sayers said.

Consider this revelation U2's lead singer Bono offered: "Religion can be the enemy of God. It's often what happens when God . . . has left the building."[116]

Or to say it another way . . . religion is what is left when God leaves the room. That is the truth!

Many years ago, a woman entered a Häagen-Dazs store in Kansas City to buy an ice-cream cone. After she'd ordered she turned and found herself staring directly into the face of Paul Newman, the famous actor who was in town filming *Mr. & Mrs. Bridge*. He smiled and said hello. His blue eyes were even bluer in person, which made her knees buckle. She finished paying and quickly walked out of the store. When she'd regained her composure, however, she realized she didn't have her cone, so she turned to go back in and met Newman who was coming out.

"Are you looking for your ice cream?" he asked her.

Unable to utter a word, she simply nodded.

"You put it in your purse with your change."[117]

When was the last time the presence of God made you forget what was going on around you? Made you forget the dishes? Made you forget the ballgame? Made you forget the bank account? Made you forget . . . where you put your ice-cream cone?

Christian writer Donald McCullough writes on how cavalier we treat the privilege of standing in God's presence Sunday after Sunday: "Reverence and awe have often been replaced by the yawn of familiarity. The consuming fire has been domesticated into a candle flame, adding a bit of religious atmosphere, perhaps, but no heat, no blinding light, no power for purification."[118]

Author Annie Dillard echoes the sentiment:

Does anyone have the foggiest idea what sort of power we so blithely invoke? Or, as I suspect, does no one believe a word of it? The churches are children playing on the floor with their chemistry sets, mixing up a batch of TNT to kill a Sunday morning. It is madness to wear ladies' straw hats and velvet hats to church; we should all be wearing crash helmets. Ushers should issue life preservers and signal flares; they should latch us to our pews. For the sleeping god may wake some day and take offense, or the waking god may draw us out to where we can never return.[119]

And in John 8 when the religious heard this man speak about Himself by using the Old Testament term for being God—I Am—four times, no one thought of strapping in and putting on a crash helmet because they were talking to God.

They just decided to try to stone Him. But that didn't work, so they crucified Him. Crucified the Great I Am.

We must be careful that we do not try to do the same. As Charles Spurgeon once remarked, "Nobody can do so much damage to the church of God as the man who is within its walls, but not within its life."[120] May that not be you and me.

Day 77

I Once Was Blind but Now I See

Today's Reading: John 9

"Amazing Grace"—considered to be one of the greatest hymns of all time, sung by Christians and non-Christians alike. It transcends religious boundaries. The hymn's popularity would have surprised its composer, John Newton. For the circumstances that inspired him to write the hymn more than two hundred years ago were amazing.

Newton was just a boy when he set sail as a sailor on his father's ship. As he grew older, his life became one filled with debauchery. His duties on the ship included capturing West Africans and taking them to the West Indies to be sold as slaves. Slavery's unspeakable horrors did not seem to bother Newton and he soon worked his way to becoming the captain of his own slave ship.

But in 1748, after many years transferring slaves, while voyaging from Africa to England, God's grace intervened. An awful storm arose, so furious that the waves threatened to capsize the ship. Unable to control the situation, Newton went to his cabin and searched for a book to take his mind off his fear. He picked up Thomas à Kempis's *The Imitation of Christ,* a classic Christian devotional. Though the ocean and the storm eventually calmed, the experience changed him.

Even still Newton continued serving as captain of his slave ship for several more years. He tried to justify his continued work by improving the conditions on the ship and even by offering religious services for his crew. But over time he finally realized that there was nothing he could do to justify what was so clearly abhorrent to God. He left the slave trade and became a powerful abolitionist. He also became an ordained minister as well as a prolific songwriter, penning hundreds of hymns, including "Amazing Grace."[121]

One of the lines from that hymn comes from today's story in John 9. It is the healing of a blind man—much like John Newton's spiritual blindness—except this man was healed physically and spiritually. And all of John 9 is devoted to his story. The climax of this blind man's experience happened when he responded to the religious leaders who were trying to get him to discredit Jesus—the One who had just opened his eyes with a miracle. The man's response was memorable and hymn worthy: "Whether He is a sinner, I do not know; one thing I do know, that though I was blind, now I see" (verse 25).

Those are not Newton's words but words fresh from the lips of a miracle man.

I love the two words in this response: "*One thing* I do know." *One thing* means he was focused.

It doesn't occur much in the Bible but when it does, it removes the peripheral and puts what matters in the crosshairs. *One thing* . . . those are highly potent and targeted words.

Here are a few other *one things* in the Bible:

David's one thing . . .
Here's the one thing I crave from God, the one thing I seek above all else: I want the privilege of living with him every moment in his house, finding the sweet loveliness of his face, filled with awe, delighting in his glory and grace. I want to live my life so close to him that he takes pleasure in my every prayer. (Psalm 27:4, TPT)

Mary's one thing . . .
The Lord answered her, "Martha, my beloved Martha. Why are you upset and troubled, pulled away by all these many distractions? Are they really that important? **Mary has discovered the one thing most important by choosing to sit at my feet. She is undistracted, and I won't take this privilege from her.**" (Luke 10:41-42, TPT)

Paul's one thing . . .
I am still not all I should be, but I am bringing all my energies to bear on this one thing: Forgetting the past and looking forward to what lies ahead, I strain to reach the end of the race and receive the prize for which God is calling us up to heaven because of what Christ Jesus did for us. (Philippians 3:13-14, TLB)

David, Mary, and Paul are *one thing* people. And now the John 9 blind man joins the *one thing* team.

And the blind man's one thing is simple: talk is cheap. He essentially was saying to the religious of his day: *If your theological debates on the person of Jesus don't set people free, I'm going with the guy you are arguing about. While you use your mouth, I get to use my eyes. If all your talking does not open up blind eyes, then I'm not interested.*

While men are parsing words and discussing concepts, I want to think like this blind man—that if Jesus is opening eyes, that's good enough for me. He may not do it like I'm used to, but if people see, then His way is best. I'm not sure about spit and mud, but who can argue with open eyes.

Here is one thing for me and the other religious guys of John 9: just shut up and praise God. Unless your debates on theology help blind eyes see again, I'll go with the unorthodox spit and mud while you try to continue on with your orthodoxy debates.

Not long before John Newton died at the age of eighty-two, he said, "My memory is nearly gone, but I remember two things: that I am a great sinner and that Christ is a great Savior!"[122]

That's a good thing to remember if you have to remember something. That's one thing more than one thing, but those are a pretty good two things to remember.

Day 78

SHEEP NEED A SHEPHERD

Today's Reading: John 10

Jesus is called *Shepherd* three times in the New Testament. And each time, a special adjective is put in front of the word to show His role in their lives.

In John 10:11, Jesus is called the *Good* Shepherd, with the emphasis of laying down His life for the sheep.

In Hebrews 13:20, Jesus is called the *Great* Shepherd, with the emphasis on His resurrection and how He accomplishes His purposes through His sheep.

And in 1 Peter 5:4, He is called the *Chief* Shepherd, which stresses His second coming and His reward to the under-shepherds.

As the Good Shepherd, He dies for the sheep. As the Great Shepherd, He rises from the dead. As the Chief Shepherd, He returns to reward His people.

Today we're studying the Good Shepherd. Before I tell you about the Good Shepherd, though, we have to realize our role as sheep. That is how the Bible describes all of us: "We're all like sheep who've wandered off and gotten lost. We've all done our own thing, gone our own way" (Isaiah 53:6, MSG).

Notice the emphasis on the word *all*. That means all of us are included, no one excluded. We are *all* sheep. While *sheep* is not a flattering term, it is appropriate.

Have you ever noticed that no colleges or universities use sheep as their mascot? They always choose something vicious, majestic, or strong. The Louisiana State University Tigers, University of Michigan Wolverines, or Kentucky Wildcats. No one uses sheep. Alabama Sheep, UCLA Sheep? Doesn't even sound right. Why? Because of who sheep are.

Sheep are easily frightened; they are defenseless and they are highly dependent. They need guidance and protection. It may not be complimentary to be a sheep, but it is comforting to know we have a Good Shepherd, and that changes everything.

Listen to Jesus' words: "I am the good shepherd; the good shepherd lays down His life for the sheep" (John 10:11).

John 10 is about the relationship between the Good Shepherd and the needy sheep. Sheep have no chance unless they have a shepherd, and not just a shepherd but a Good Shepherd.

Always remember, we never graduate from being a sheep the older we get in Jesus. We always need the Shepherd. We *always* need Him!

The chief enemy of the sheep is the wolf. Sheep have no defense mechanism except for the shepherd. And here is what is so important: sheep are only as strong as the shepherd. If the shepherd fails, they fail.

The wolf scatters the sheep. Why? So he can isolate them away from the shepherd. If he can get them away from the shepherd, then he can devour them. He scatters, isolates, and then has the helpless, defenseless sheep to himself.

Here's how Jesus put it:

I am the Good Shepherd. The Good Shepherd puts the sheep before himself, sacrifices himself if necessary. A hired man is not a real shepherd. The sheep mean nothing to him. He sees a wolf come and runs for it, leaving the sheep to be ravaged and scattered by the wolf. He's only in it for the money. The sheep don't matter to him.

I am the Good Shepherd. I know my own sheep and my own sheep know me. (John 10:11-14, msg)

Sheep are known by their shepherd. They are known in two ways: sheep know their name and they know the voice of their shepherd who calls it.

So as sheep, we have one job: stay close to the Shepherd and when we do, we are within ear shot of His voice. He is our protection. He is our provider.

An Australian man was arrested and charged with stealing a sheep. He adamantly denied the accusation, claiming it was one of his own that had been missing for days. When the case went to court, the judge heard the arguments, but was unsure how to decide the matter. Finally he asked that the sheep be brought into the courtroom. He ordered that the accuser go outside the room and call the animal. The sheep's only response was to raise its head and look frightened. The judge then told the defendant to go to the courtyard and call the sheep. When the accused man did so, the sheep ran toward the door and that voice. He recognized the familiar sound of his master. "His sheep knows him," the judge said, and dismissed the case.[123]

Our Shepherd calls us each day. Let's follow His voice.

NOT TILL IT STINKS

Today's Reading: John 11

Has God ever been confusing to you? Have you ever asked Him, "What are You doing? I don't understand?"

Our 260 Journey brings us to John 11 and to one of those moments. It's the story of Lazarus—a man who went from health to sickness and from sickness to death. And here is where the confusion starts. This all happened with Jesus close enough to prevent his death but doesn't.

What makes it confusing are two things Jesus does from the outset.

Let's read the story:

> A certain man was sick, Lazarus of Bethany, the village of Mary and her sister Martha. It was the Mary who anointed the Lord with ointment, and wiped His feet with her hair, whose brother Lazarus was sick. So the sisters sent *word* to Him, saying, "Lord, behold, he whom You love is sick." But when Jesus heard *this*, He said, "This sickness is not to end in death, but for the glory of God, so that the Son of God may be glorified by it." Now Jesus loved Martha and her sister and Lazarus. So when He heard that he was sick, He then stayed two days *longer* in the place where He was. (John 11:1-6)

Here is where Jesus becomes confusing: we are told very clearly that Lazarus is sick and Jesus loves him. There is something in us that thinks if Jesus loves us then we have a "get out of jail" free card from pain. Nothing could be further from the truth.

C. S. Lewis was once asked, "Why do the righteous suffer?" To which he replied, "They're the only ones who can handle it."[124]

The second confusing moment with Jesus happens when He hears about the sickness. If you love someone, and they are in desperate need, you rush to them. Not Jesus. The Bible says when He heard Lazarus was sick, He stayed where He was for two days longer. What? Seriously? No movement, Jesus?

It frustrates us when Jesus moves too slow. We want Jesus' hand but we don't want His calendar.

I always remember in one of my frustration moments how an old church mother in Detroit reminded me of the old adage, "He may not come when you want Him, but He's always right on time." And in John 11, Jesus is going to be right on time. What is on time? Four days later and not till Lazarus stinks.

Why? Jesus says that it's so His glory can be seen. Glory is what makes God famous and stand out.

Let me take you to the tomb and why Jesus waited:

> Jesus, again being deeply moved within, came to the tomb. Now it was a cave, and a stone was lying against it. Jesus said, "Remove the stone." Martha, the sister of the deceased, said to Him, "Lord, by this time there will be a stench, for he has been *dead* four days."
> (John 11:38-39)

It would have been easier for Jesus to come to sick Lazarus not to stinky-and-dead Lazarus. And here is where I want you to see as the confusion starts to get clarity:

> When He had said these things, He cried out with a loud voice, "Lazarus, come forth." The man who had died came forth, bound hand and foot with wrappings, and his face was wrapped around with a cloth. Jesus said to them, "Unbind him, and let him go." Therefore many of the Jews who came to Mary, and saw what He had done, believed in Him.
> (John 11:43-45)

When Jesus doesn't come when you call Him, something bigger is about to happen.

What was Jesus showing them? A resurrection is better than a healing. His message to Mary and Martha was this: *If I heal your brother, three people will feel good. If I resurrect your brother, many will believe.* We learn from this story too that there is a divine strategy in unanswered prayer.

The account of Jesus not healing Lazarus is proof that unanswered prayer may well mean that God has something better in mind for us than we ourselves had. There are times that God waits till something stinks before He shows up. Because Lazarus was resurrected instead of being healed, many saw the glory of God and believed.

Our prayers are for our well-being when God sees bigger. That day a dead man was resurrected instead of a sick man healed so a bunch of people could be resurrected.

So when your prayer is not immediately answered and you are dealing with delay, don't doubt that He loves you. He may just be saying, "It just doesn't stink yet."

Day 80

PARADOXICAL CHRISTIANS

Today's Reading: John 12

A paradox is a statement that contradicts itself. It goes something like this:

"Deep down, I know you are shallow."

"One thing I know—that I know nothing."

"I am nobody."

"He's a wise fool."

It's putting opposite words in a sentence together that don't seem to work.

These are silly paradoxes that have no bearing on anything of eternal importance. But in today's reading, we run right into a very strange paradox that has great eternal consequences. Consider this statement with its contradiction:

> Many even of the rulers believed in Him, but because of the Pharisees they were not confessing *Him*, for fear that they would be put out of the synagogue; for they loved the approval of men rather than the approval of God. (John 12:42-43)

This is a serious paradox: "Many even of the rulers believed in Him, but . . . they were not confessing Him."

Is that even possible? Believing without confessing. Can you be a paradoxical saint? When I was reading John 12, I was excited to see that the rulers believed in Him. People of influence realizing that this was the Messiah. But my excitement was short lived when I hit the paradox, separated by a comma.

Confessing is a big part of belief, or should I say, it's a big partner with belief. Listen to how Paul put it:

> If you confess with your mouth Jesus *as* Lord, and believe in your heart that God raised Him from the dead, you will be saved; for with

the heart a person believes, resulting in righteousness, and with the mouth he confesses, resulting in salvation. (Romans 10:9-10)

Believe and confess are a big part of salvation. Think of these important words from Jesus, recorded in Matthew 10:32-33: "Everyone who confesses Me before men, I will also confess him before My Father who is in heaven. But whoever denies Me before men, I will also deny Him before My Father who is in heaven."

These rulers decided to rewrite the script. This paradox seems serious. And verse 43 gives us the eye-opening "why" behind the paradox: they loved the approval of men rather than the approval of God.

Has wanting to please people silenced you from going public about your belief in God? When you know that people in your circle are Jesus antagonistic or church haters, do you keep quiet to please them? Do you shut your mouth on truth so as not to rock the boat? Does their open mouth contradict my belief keep my mouth shut?

If these are true of us, we are paradoxical believers. And we know the source of it. It is a love issue—and it exposes what we love most. Do we love the approval of people or the approval of God? The answer to this question will determine if we will be paradoxical, or in other words, a believer but not a confessor.

It's dangerous to believe without confessing, because it exposes something about us. Can that really happen? It did happen and the result was catastrophic. Ready for this? James 2:19 tells us that "you can believe all you want that there is one true God, that's wonderful! But even the demons know this and tremble with fear before him, yet they're unchanged—*they remain demons*" (TPT).

We can have the right belief in God and still be unchanged. Our belief should not lead us to church only, but on a journey to love God with all our hearts, minds, and souls. I think the lack of confessing is from loving the wrong thing. They loved the approval of men rather than the approval of God.

When I recognize that I have a problem going public about my relationship with God, it's at that point that I don't pray for boldness but for God to help me to love Him more.

Love goes public. Love shouts it out. When I fell in love with my now-wife, Cindy, I wanted everyone to know who I discovered. Way before smart phones with thousands of pictures, we used to carry an actual photo of the one we loved. I wanted people to see her, but how would I get a photo? One day I saw a photo of her in a newspaper from a deal she made for a bank and I cut it out. I carried that black-and-white newspaper clipping folded up in my wallet everywhere. And when people asked me if I had a picture, I would tell them, "Do I have a picture? Look at this." And I would proceed to unfold it. I was confessing because I was in love.

Love tells!

When there is no telling, we may have a love issue. Or it may be that we love the wrong thing.

When we believe in Jesus, we start a journey of love not a journey of knowledge.

C.S. Lewis tells us an old author who asked, "Is it easy to love God?"

"It is easy," the other man replied, "to those who do it."[125]

Christianity is not easy for those who love church, love being moral, love the atmosphere. When you fall deeply in love, you want to please the one you are in love with. Love makes confession easy.

FOUR SHOULDN'T FOLLOW THREE

Today's Reading: John 13

I know in mathematics 4 always follows 3. But I have to tell you that there is one place in the Bible that 4 should not follow 3. And it's only because it does not make sense. Or let me say it another way, my 4 and Jesus' 4 are totally different.

In today's reading, we come upon two verses that seem disconnected to the human mind, but not to Jesus. Listen to how powerful John 13:3: "Jesus knew that the Father had put him in complete charge of everything, that he came from God and was on his way back to God" (MSG).

Listen to the sure facts in this verse that Jesus knew:

- "The father had put him in complete charge of everything"
- "He came from God"
- "He was on his way back to God."

These are three big statements. So what should follow these incredible words? If I were in complete charge of everything, my 4 would look something like this . . . "lightning bolts came out of Him." Or maybe Jesus levitating off the ground and saying, "I told you I was God. I am in charge now!"

That's what 4 should look like. That's what I would have done. Not Jesus. Here is what happens next. Here is Jesus' 4:

He got up from the supper table, set aside his robe, and put on an apron. Then he poured water into a basin and began to wash the feet of the disciples, drying them with his apron. (John 13:4-5, MSG)

The transition does not even make sense in my mind. In my selfish, prideful heart, I don't understand how this 4 follows the previous three. But when you know what Jesus knows, you do something spectacular, something that blows our minds. Guess what? That's exactly what He did.

Jesus washed the disciples' feet. His knowledge, His position, and His relationship with the Father in heaven made Him the ultimate servant and greatest example of humility. This has to be the greatest model for us: that the more we know, the more secure we become. And the more secure we become, the more we serve.

The insecure won't serve. They are busy proving to others what they should know about them. They are in charge, they are the boss, they are the parent, they are the supervisor, they are the pastor. Those who keep telling you what to know don't really know themselves.

I probably would have taken those three "knowing" statements from verse 3 and not served but gotten servants. But Jesus served. That is how messed up my thinking is.

Let me throw one more crazy transition in this whole mix. He took that whole teaching moment and said to them in verse 14, "If I then, the Lord and the Teacher, washed your feet, you also ought to wash . . ." Fill in the blank. Think of what is normal, or since we are dealing with Jesus, what is abnormal to our way of thinking?

Here is what makes sense to me: "If I then, the Lord and the Teacher, washed your feet . . . you ought to wash My feet."

That is not what Jesus said. He said, "If I then, the Lord and the Teacher, washed your feet, you also ought to wash one another's feet."

This is another crazy 4 after 3 conundrum.

He wasn't washing feet to get His feet washed. I know there are times that I have done stuff to others hoping to get the same back from them. Not Jesus.

I invited you over for dinner, therefore you should invite me over. I let you borrow my car; therefore you should let me borrow your car. I complimented your hair, you should compliment mine. I invited you to speak at my church, you should invite me to speak at your church.

Do you see how unlike Jesus this is? He washed feet to get them to wash others' feet not His.

Jesus is amazing. I have such a long way to go. My 4 after 3 and Jesus' 4 after 3 are so far apart. I need to learn more about Jesus' 4. You too?

Day 82

One Comes After Thirty-Eight

Today's Reading: John 14

I remember listening to one of my daughters as she was learning to count. When she got to the number eleven, what came next seemed normal to her. Unfortunately, it was wrong: eleventeen, twelveteen, thirteen . . . Why not? Seems logical.

In today's reading, we see that Jesus had one of those logical moments. It happens in yesterday's reading: John 13:38. Jesus' eleventeen moment follows verse 38. It isn't supposed to, but it does: one comes after thirty-eight.

John 14:1-6 is a popular passage for funerals. In fact, I have read it many times at funerals:

> "Do not let your heart be troubled; believe in God, believe also in Me. In My Father's house are many dwelling places; if it were not so, I would have told you; for I go to prepare a place for you. If I go and prepare a place for you, I will come again and receive you to Myself, that where I am, *there* you may be also. And you know the way where I am going." Thomas said to Him, "Lord, we do not know where You are going, how do we know the way?" Jesus said to him, "I am the way, and the truth, and the life; no one comes to the Father but through Me." (John 14:1-6)

As heavenly as these words are, they were not given for a funeral, they were given to help an arrogant and self-assured disciple named Peter, who was very much alive.

Always remember that the chapter and verse numbers in the Bible were never there when written. They were not added into a printed Bible until around the 1500s by Robert Stephens in the Geneva Bible.[126] That's why I am not a fan when people try to take the verse number or chapter number and make it part of the message of the text. It just is not there. So if that's true, Jesus was right, verse 1 comes after verse 38 since there are no chapter divisions.

When Jesus spoke these words in John 14, it was in response to and directly after these final words in John 13: "Jesus answered, 'Will you lay down your life for Me? Truly, truly, I say to you, a rooster will not crow until you deny me three times" (verse 38).

Here is what I love: instead of Jesus leaving it there and letting Peter know that he was about to blow it big time, Jesus gives hope.

Peter says, "I will lay down my life for you."

Jesus says, "You will deny Me three times."

We all know who's telling the truth.

The iconic Golden Gate Bridge was completed in 1937 and was, at the time, the longest suspension bridge ever built. It was also very deadly work. "At the time, the industry standard was that for every million dollars spent, there would be a loss of life," says the bridge's spokeswoman, Mary Currie. The bridge's estimated cost? Thirty-five million dollars. But the structural engineer, Joseph Strauss, concerned for the workers' safety—as almost two dozen men died in the first half of construction—insisted on placing a safety net under the bridge to catch any workers who accidentally fell. It was a novel idea at the time and cost $130,000. After the net was put in place, no one else died.[127] The safety net made the difference.

In John 14, we see that Peter is about to get his $130,000 safety net when he falls. Jesus essentially tells Peter, "What you say will not happen; what I say will . . . but there is more." Here's the safety net: *You won't lose when you fall, you win when you fail. Peter, you will deny Me and not keep your word, but I will keep My word.*

What is that word? "I go to prepare a place for you. If I go and prepare a place for you, I will come again and receive you to Myself, that where I am, *there* you may be also."

This is not heaven, this is restoration. The prepared place was not in the clouds but on a beach in John 21. Jesus was telling Peter that when he walks away from Jesus, he will still have a place. Jesus will receive him and they will be together.

God knows every failure and fall . . . and He has a net. Peter was falling into grace.

Charles Spurgeon said this about God's grace: "Grace puts its hand on their boasting mouth, and shuts it once for all."[128]

No more boasting Peter. I think if Peter was counting, he too would say one comes after thirty-eight. The same is true for us, and I am so glad.

WILL YOU ACCEPT THE CHALLENGE?

Today's Reading: John 15

Today's reading is a challenge. It's a second step that Jesus gives to those who choose to follow Him.

During Jesus' life, He constantly said to those who were ready to start a journey with God to "follow Me." And for those who accepted the challenge, he gave them a revolutionary second step: "Abide in Me."

Listen to these challenging words of this new kind of relationship with God:

Abide in Me, and I in you. As the branch cannot bear fruit of itself unless it abides in the vine, so neither *can* you unless you abide in Me. I am the vine, you are the branches; he who abides in Me and I in him, he bears much fruit, for apart from Me you can do nothing. (John 15:4-5)

What does it mean to abide? The word *abide* simply means to spend time. Or more specifically, to *abide* means to give God time (because relationships need time to grow). It isn't just "come to church" but "come to Me." God wants time with you.

The day you followed Jesus, you got a taste of God. The day you accept the challenge for what is next, you get a shower (you go from drinking water from a straw to drinking water from a fire hydrant).

You got on the king's property, now it's time to enjoy the king's palace. All of us are given the same amount of time. Those who are successful use it wisely—they abide.

American businessman, Jim Rohn, said it like this, "There are only three colors, ten numbers, and seven notes; it's what we do with them that's important."[129]

What keeps us from abiding?

The cost: time.

The cry: "I don't have any more time."

The challenge: It isn't adding but subtracting.

Louie Giglio, one of the most amazing pastors in the Atlanta area, said,

"Whatever you say yes to in life means less for something already there. Make sure your yes is worth the less."[130]

Here is the bad news: time flies.

Here is the good news: you're the pilot.

Direct your life correctly.

In John 15, Jesus connected abiding to four amazing benefits. If you take the challenge and choose to go on a journey of abiding, just as you did to follow Jesus, look for these four things to happen:

1. *Joy*: "These things I have spoken to you so that My joy may be in you, and *that* your joy may be made full" (John 15:11). Talk about standing out in your arena of life. Joy is attractive because it's rare today.

2. *Obedience*: "If you keep My commandments, you will abide in My love; just as I have kept My Father's commandments and abide in His love" (John 15:10). Abiding makes obedience easy and joyful.

3. *Answered prayer*: "If you abide in Me, and My words abide in you, ask whatever you wish, and it will be done for you" (John 15:7). The thought of praying and seeing it answered is worth the price. I pray, God answers—because of abiding.

The more I'm with God . . . that's abiding.

The more I talk with Him . . . that's prayer.

The more prayer gets answered . . . that's exciting.

As Louis Lallemant [131]said, "A man of prayer will do more in one year than another will do in his whole life."

4. *I'm productive . . . bearing fruit*: "Abide in Me, and I in you. As the branch cannot bear fruit of itself unless it abides in the vine, so neither *can* you unless you abide in Me" (John 15:4). Producing fruit is what a branch is meant to do. Without fruit, it's just a stick.

"Bearing fruit" in verse 4 means doing what you are meant to do. Branches bear fruit, but not all branches—only the ones connected to the vine. You can't be connected with God without being effective for God.

Many of us chose salvation, that is we accepted Jesus' call to "follow Me." Now it's time for us to accept Jesus' second challenge to "abide in Me." Abiding is not just time with God in heaven, abiding is time with God here on earth.

Day 84

THE WARNING SIGN OR THE HOSPITAL

Today's Reading: John 16

In *The Grace Awakening*, author and pastor Charles Swindoll used an imaginative illustration for how best we can live: imagine driving on a treacherous mountain road with a cliff on both sides. As you approach a hairpin turn, you must decide which is better: a state-of-the-art hospital with the best doctors in the world at the bottom of the mountain or a giant yellow warning sign before the curve telling you, "Danger! Curve Ahead. Drive slowly"? The answer is obvious: a warning sign.[132]

In John 16, we find Jesus giving His followers a life of warning signs so they don't end up at the bottom of the mountain in the hospital. The warning sign is called conviction and it's a ministry of the Holy Spirit. Read with me what Jesus says about it:

> I tell you the truth, it is to your advantage that I go away; for if I do not go away, the Helper will not come to you; but if I go, I will send Him to you. And He, when He comes, will convict the world concerning sin and righteousness and judgment; concerning sin, because they do not believe in Me; and concerning righteousness, because I go to the Father and you no longer see Me; and concerning judgment, because the ruler of this world has been judged. (John 16:7-11)

When He comes, He will convict.

What is conviction?

It is an inner warning, a big yellow sign that says, "Slow down! This may not be right."

Conviction of the Holy Spirit is the opposite of peace; it's a disturbance in the soul that can be silenced only by stepping on the brake when coming to the turn. The conviction of the Holy Spirit is what saves us from crashing and burning and needing the hospital at the bottom of the mountain.

The hospital at the bottom of the hill can be a counselor's office, a pastor's office, etc. I'm not saying those hospitals can't fix the damage inflicted, but think of the pain that people could have avoided had they yielded to the Spirit's conviction.

Most of the times the conviction comes when we are entering into a compromise, an area of sin, a place that will hurt our spiritual lives. People will confuse conviction and condemnation.

Conviction is the feeling that what I was *doing* was wrong, and with God's help, I can change. Condemnation is the feeling that *I* am wrong and I can never measure up. There is no hope of change in condemnation.

Conviction is the work of the Holy Spirit. Condemnation is the work of man. Conviction is so you could look like Jesus. Condemnation is because you don't look like another person.

Conviction is from God. Conviction is the warning sign on the hairpin turns.

Our job is to yield, like in this story:

During the Great Awakening—a time of revival throughout our country— Jonathan Edwards was leading a prayer meeting in which eight hundred men were in attendance. In the midst of the meeting, a woman sent in a note asking them to pray for her husband. She described him as unloving, prideful, and difficult. Edwards read the message aloud the men, thinking that perhaps the woman's husband was present. Then he boldly asked if the man whom he had described would raise his hand, so the whole group could pray for him. Three hundred men raised their hands.[133]

Really, three hundred men yielded to the yellow sign to avoid the hospital. All because they yielded. May we do the same.

Day 85

LIFT UP YOUR EYES IN PRAYER

Today's Reading: John 17

John 17 is holy ground. If I were God's editor, I never would have allowed this chapter in the Bible. It's sacred, it's other world, it's uncomfortable . . . it's the prayer closet of Jesus. This is a very solemn chapter, what we call the high priestly prayer of Jesus.

I have thousands of books in my library on so many topics. But to my amazement, I've seen only two authors ever venture to take on one of the most incredible chapters, prayers, and words ever penned to mankind and write on them. I am not sure if the two men who did had a lapse of judgment or a leading of the Holy Spirit.

John 17 lets us eavesdrop on what Jesus was praying before He was taken to die on Calvary *and* we are allowed to hear Him. We are given what seems to be a glimpse into the holy of holies where the Son is talking to the Father.

The Lord's prayer is *very* powerful. But it is one thing to be taught something and another to see it modeled. Luke 6 is the teaching; John 17 is the modeling. Prayer is better exemplified than taught.

And in this chapter we are allowed to see how Jesus prayed. I think we can all agree that if anyone knows how to pray, it is Jesus. If there is anyone who is going to have His prayers answered, it is Jesus. The right way to pray is Jesus' way of praying. If He did not want to be heard, it would not have been recorded. If this prayer was not meant for us to look at, He would not have had His disciples hear it. Since they heard it, and since they recorded it, there must be something for us to learn from it.

As I growing up on Long Island, New York, I had the wonderful opportunity to overhear my Russian grandmother pray. She was a great prayer warrior. Many times I would come home from school in the afternoon and hear my grandmother praying in Russian, because she never learned English. She would be in our living room crying and praying in a language I did not know. Sometimes I would listen, but most of the time I would feel as if I should not be there.

There is something powerful about a person pouring out themselves in prayer to God. There is something uncomfortable about listening to someone's private prayer time. I could not stand there for more than a few minutes before I would have to leave her and God alone. If I felt this way about my grandmother, how much more would I feel about opening the door to John 17 and listening to the private prayer of Jesus and His Father. There is something in me that says I should not be there. I should read the Bible up to John 16 and then go quickly to John 18. But there is something in me that wants to open the door and listen to Jesus. There is something in me that says I should be there and I should listen very carefully.

Let's open the prayer closet of the second member of the Trinity, the Son of God, the Savior of the world, Jesus, and hear Him pray.

This is the very first verse: "Jesus spoke these things; and lifting up His eyes to heaven, He said, 'Father, the hour has come; glorify Your Son, that the Son may glorify You.'"

I will take the risk that this would not be incorporated as a biblical absolute but as a challenge of focus the next time we pray, that we use John 17 as our model in our prayer time. It says that when Jesus prayed, He lifted up His eyes. This was not just His prayer posture, it was a Jewish posture. No Jew would ever pray as we do today. The first thing we often hear before we pray in a church service is, "Let's bow our heads." The words out of our mouths when praying over a meal is, "Let's bow our heads." A Jew would never look down when talking to Jehovah. They would see this as dishonoring. A Jew would always lift their eyes.

On a natural level, there is a difference between a person you see with their head bowed down and a head that is lifted up. A bowed head carries with it dejection, self-consciousness, fear of making eye contact. It carries no good thing with it. But a person who walks and talks with head up and eyes lifted seems to have a confidence and certainty to them and their words.

The next time you pray, go John 17 in your prayer time. Lift up your eyes to heaven and realize that you have a living Father who hears you. And if you want to make it even crazier, lift up your eyes and read out loud the prayer of Jesus in John 17.

What Kind of Pilate/Pilot Are You?

Today's Reading: John 18

I remember a few years ago flying out of a large midwestern city in the middle of bad storms. Planes were still taking off, but passengers were feeling uneasy. I have to tell you, as I waited at my gate, I wasn't feeling it either, and fear started to hit me.

Then I saw our pilot come to our gate. He was this old, wrinkle-faced man. His uniform bore a lot of gold bars on his coat sleeve, and his bags, covered with stickers, were beat up and falling apart. Did seeing him help the situation and my fear? You bet it did!

What did beat-up bags, gray hair, and a wrinkly face represent? Experience. No doubt he had been in this situation before and up in the air a lot. I did not want to see some wide-eyed young man who was excited about his first flight as he pulled his new bags to the gate. I wanted the old pilot captaining my plane. His experience quelled my fear.

Consider this: what would you think if the pilot got on the loud speaker and said, "This is your pilot, and I am so excited today because this is my first flight. I've never been in the air before but I got all A's on my flight school tests." I don't know about you, but I would be looking for the exit door. To be a good pilot, you can just be book smart. You need something called flight hours. You have to be in the air, not just studying for tests on the ground. You need experience.

There was another Pilate in the Bible who knew some stuff, but did not have the experience of flight hours. And we meet him in today's reading at the bogus trial of Jesus.

Jesus was standing before Pilate, and Pilate asked Him a question. Pay special attention to Jesus' epic response:

> Pilate entered again into the Praetorium, and summoned Jesus and said to Him, "Are you the King of the Jews?" Jesus answered, "Are you saying this on your own initiative, or did others tell you about Me?" (John 18:33-34)

Jesus' question to Pilate's question was rhetorical. No answer was expected, because we know the answer. Jesus' question was: are you saying this on your own initiative, or did others tell you about me?

What Jesus was saying was, "Are you just repeating information, or have you experienced what you are saying?" *Do you just have ground school or did you get in some flight time?*

When Pilate asked Jesus about being King of the Jews, he did not know Jesus as King, he was simply repeating something he'd heard. He had no flight time with this King.

What kind of Pilate are you? Did you just hear this and are saying what you heard, or do you know Jesus as King? Have you experienced Jesus as King? Jesus was challenging not only Pilate, He is challenging all of us. Just because we say the right things doesn't mean we have experienced the right things. Christianity is not just knowing the right stuff but experiencing a relationship with God personally as our King.

A marriage license doesn't guarantee intimacy and a healthy marriage. You can have a document that says you are married and have no relationship with your spouse. The same is true with the Word of God. You can read the Bible, but that does not guarantee experience. Just because you know the Word of God doesn't mean you know the God of this Word. Knowing this book is not based on education, but on a relationship with its Author.

Pilate said the right words but it got him nowhere. So as you go on the 260 Journey, may you go further than the Pilate of John 18 and become like the pilot who flew my plane out of Gate 34A. One was just repeating what he heard, the other had the experience.

What kind of Pilate are you?

YOU CAN'T HIDE ONE HUNDRED POUNDS

Today's Reading: John 19

One hundred pounds is a lot of extra weight to carry with you. It is noticeable when you put it on and it's noticeable when you shed it. Our story today is one hundred pounds put on and it's noticeable, because you can't hide one hundred pounds.

Let me tell you about a person whose name you will recognize. Nicodemus. And he picked up one hundred pounds on his Jesus journey. Nicodemus has a three-verse bio journey through the Gospel of John.

What do you think when I mention his name? For me, my first thought goes to John 3:16. He was the one to whom Jesus personally shared that amazing verse. Thanks to Nicodemus going to Jesus at night, we got the verse that has probably led more people to Jesus than any other Bible verse: "God so loved the world, that He gave His only begotten Son, that whoever believes in Him shall not perish, but have eternal life."

Thank you, Nicodemus, but there is so much more.

People can easily be known by one thing in their life and no one goes any further with them. It could be something they say, do, a crime they commit, a public sin they are known for, a heroic act. This can work both ways, good and bad. Something bad that someone has done can be remembered and all the good that they try to do is overshadowed by that one moment. Their character gets judged by that one thing.

Oswald Chambers, the great Christian devotional writer, said this about character:

> Character is the whole trend of a man's life, not isolated acts here and there. . . . Character is the sum total of a man's actions. You cannot judge a man by the good things he does at times; you must take all the times together, and if in the greatest number of times he does bad things, he is a bad character, in spite of the noble things he does intermittently."[134]
>
> A man's character is what he does habitually. A man's character cannot be summed up by what he does in spots, but only by what he is

in the main trend of his existence. . . . Character is that which steadily prevails, not something that occasionally manifests itself.[135]

Now back to the man I want us to see a little further with—Nicodemus—and that his new Jesus journey gets more rooted as the Gospel goes on.

Nicodemus' next verse happens in John 7:50, as we looked at earlier: "Nicodemus (he who came to Him before, being one of them)."

The parentheses are so important. "He who came to Him" is a reference to John 3, "before being one of them." Nicodemus becomes a follower of Jesus after talking with Jesus that night. His interview, Nic at night, is what changed his life. In John 7, Nicodemus seems to be defending Jesus to the other pharisaical leaders. Though he is a slow witness, at least he is opening his mouth.

And then we see his final passage on how far he has come. It's in John 19—and this is where the hundred pounds comes in: "Nicodemus, who had first come to Him by night, also came, bringing a mixture of myrrh and aloes, about a hundred pounds *weight*" (verse 39).

By the time we reach John 19, Nicodemus is unashamed and unafraid. He really is one of them, meaning a disciple of Jesus. Think about this: while everyone leaves Jesus at the crucifixion, not only does Nicodemus show up, he shows up with a lot of extra weight. Weight that he can't hide. He does not flee and run and deny. He brings, get this, *one hundred pounds* of burial ingredients (myrrh and aloes). One hundred pounds he has to drag to the sight of the cross and then on to the grave. Everyone knows he is doing this for Jesus.

That tells me that he is unashamed. The people know who it is for and what it is for. He is very clearly aligning himself with Jesus on Good Friday. The ruler of the Jews and the spokesman for the Pharisees put on a hundred pounds for Jesus.

I love the process that happens in people's lives. We want everything to happen instantly, but God has different growth patterns for different people. Give them their space, and they will get there.

Here's what I love about this John 19 story: it's that he dragged a hundred pounds of stuff to the burial site. He wasn't preaching and giving these glorious words like, "Jesus, I will never deny you." He just lived it out. It is life and not words that impact. We have great speakers for Christianity but not everyone who can speak is living it. Let's spend more time living than speaking.

Remember, the preachers were all gone at the cross, but Nic was there. Nic and a hundred pounds. He was all in when it counted most. Follow his example. Live it.

A Sunday-Night Message from Jesus

Today's Reading: John 20

What if Jesus showed up to your Sunday night service today? I know we talk about Resurrection morning, but not many talk about what happened that night. Resurrection night was a huge event for the disciples. I'm afraid if Jesus showed up to one of our twenty-first-century Sunday evening church services, He wouldn't find many there. And Jesus had an important Sunday-night message for the church.

Today we have landed in our 260 journey on John 20. It's Resurrection day— but not the morning. It's the evening. Let's read the passage:

> When it was evening on that day, the first *day* of the week, and when the doors were shut where the disciples were, for fear of the Jews, Jesus came and stood in their midst and said to them, "Peace be with you." (verse 19)

The Sunday evening church service is slowly fading out of church life. I grew up in a time when Sunday night service was "the" service to go to. There would be less traditional hymns and more choruses. There were water baptisms, altar calls for the baptism of the Holy Spirit, and as a child, the best was that there was always the possibility of an "after glow." Us "old timers" know that to mean eating after church in the fellowship hall.

Since I grew up in the church, I can tell you that I have been water baptized on a Sunday night, filled with the Holy Spirit on a Sunday night, seen great gospel bands and Christian movies on a Sunday night, and most importantly in my youth, eaten good cake and punch.

Traditionally, Sunday night service was a little more casual for the members. But it was a night that allowed more freedom and had a greater expectation for "the spirit to move." Unfortunately, today the Sunday night service is becoming an extinct species. Let me say, I am not saying there is something magical about Sunday night, I am just talking about what I experienced. And I'm also talking about the time Jesus chose to give really important directions to His disciples.

Many of us pastors dread the Sunday night service when the morning service is a holiday service, such as Mother's Day and Easter. Most people have no motivation to get back to church those nights, especially after eating a big meal and meeting with family. Thank God the resurrection of Jesus did not take place in our time . . . or Jesus would have had to accomplish everything in the morning service, because no one would have been at the night service.

And yet Resurrection night was just as important as Resurrection morning. It's in the evening that Jesus offered a three- point message, and every point was the same:

Point 1: Peace *be* with you (verse 19)

Point 2: Peace *be* with you (verse 21)

Point 3: Peace *be* with you (verse 26)

Jesus comes to the house of the disciples, closed doors and all. Looks a little like our churches on Sunday night. But this is Jesus, so He walks through the walls. The doors are shut, yet Jesus gets in. The risen Christ does not know the barricades of locked doors or locked hearts. The risen Christ is not limited by our closed windows or closed minds.

I've always appreciated the suggestion of C. S. Lewis, that the risen Jesus could walk through walls because he is *more real* than them—in the same way that an airplane can move through the clouds that look so solid.[136]

What was so significant about Resurrection evening? Each of the three times He stated "Peace be with you" was important. The first "Peace *be* with you" was a challenge to bring Christianity outside the walls of our meeting places. The disciples were afraid, and Jesus told them, in essence, *Don't meet in your little clique. There is a whole world out there that needs to know I am alive, so go in peace.*

The second time Jesus says "Peace *be* with you" in verse 21, comes with a breathing of the Holy Spirit on them. He was essentially saying, "Not only am I sending you out beyond these walls, I will not send you alone. You will have the Holy Spirit going with you, so you can go in peace." When we go outside our religious walls, we go with His presence.

And finally, the third "Peace *be* with you" in verse 26 is pretty special. This one came eight days later. Let's read it: "After eight days His disciples were again inside, and Thomas with them. Jesus came, the doors having been shut, and stood in their midst and said, "Peace *be* with you."

Jesus' statement came eight days later for one man, Thomas. Verse 24 tells us that for point 1 and 2, "Thomas, one of the twelve, called Didymus, was not with them." So Jesus came eight days later to say the same words. Why? Because one guy needed to hear it.

Just when you think, *I blew it, I messed up, I missed God*, Jesus shows up again. Jesus died for the world, but most importantly, Jesus died for me and Thomas and you. I think Jesus offered a point 3 for one guy.

Resurrection night doesn't even get any props, but it should. Because we need to hear Jesus' words: "Peace be with you."

DROPPING THE LIGHT BULB

Today's Reading: John 21

We know that Thomas Edison invented the light bulb in 1879. Back then they didn't have mass production, so each bulb had to be created separately. He and his colleagues worked twenty-four painstaking and meticulous hours straight to put just one together. The story goes that when Edison was finished with that light bulb, he gave it to a young boy to deliver up the stairs to another part of Edison's workshop. The boy nervously carried it—step by step cautiously watching his hands, terrified of dropping this treasure. But when he got to the top of the stairs, the poor boy dropped it.

It took the team of men another twenty-four hours to create the second light bulb. Tired and ready for a break, Edison needed it carried up the stairs. Guess who he asked to deliver it? He gave it to the same young boy who dropped the first one. This time he made it to the top.[137]

Jesus had a light bulb and Jesus had a clumsy kid. The light bulb would be the church and the kid's name was Peter.

Peter's stair drop? Peter denied Jesus three times at Jesus' most critical moment of his life. And after the resurrection, Jesus found Peter to give him the light bulb—right after his failure. That's where we land in today's reading.

God is amazing—not only because He forgives us after failure, but also because God *trusts* us after failure. As Psalm 130:3-4 [MSG] says, "If you, GOD, kept records on wrongdoings, who would stand a chance? As it turns out, forgiveness is your habit, and that's why you're worshiped."

In John 21, Peter and Jesus met the first time after Peter dropped the light bulb. And Jesus wanted to see where Peter was in his failure. In other words, He was looking at Peter with an eye toward what Abraham Lincoln said: "My great concern is not whether you have failed, but whether you are content with your failure."[138] Jesus was making sure Peter was not content.

Failure is part of life, everyone experiences it. Getting up from failure, though? Not everyone does. Yet failure isn't final until you quit. Let's look in on the scene:

After these things Jesus manifested Himself again to the disciples at the Sea of Tiberias, and He manifested *Himself* in this way. Simon Peter, and Thomas called Didymus, and Nathanael of Cana in Galilee, and the *sons* of Zebedee, and two others of His disciples were together. Simon Peter said to them, "I am going fishing." They said to him, "We will also come with you." They went out and got into the boat; and that night they caught nothing. (John 21:1-3)

The craziest phrase is in the first verse: *After these things*. What things? The things in John 20.

"After these things . . ." (verse 1) and "Simon Peter said, 'I'm going fishing . . .'" (verse 3). That's your response, Peter, to the resurrection and to what you just saw?

Remember what Peter saw:

• An empty tomb, which he entered.
• Mary overcome with emotion and clinging to Jesus.
• Jesus walking through walls.
• Being commissioned to tell the whole world.
• Doubting Thomas becoming believing Thomas

Shouldn't the next phrase after 21:1's "After these things" be something like:

• Peter preached.
• Peter went to church.
• Peter worshiped.

You would think, but nope. Peter saw the resurrected Jesus and got his tackle box. He was told he would be a "fisher of men," but he went back to being a "fisher of fish." Why? Because Peter forgot. The emotions, the feelings of God, fear, and excitement wore off.

To Peter, the event of the resurrection was done and now it was Monday. He was thinking, *It was a good run. We did the Jesus thing for three years and now it's time to get back to normal life.*

After September 11, 2001, many churches were full, but soon the fear and the horror of it all wore off and life went on and it was back to fishing. Peter was part of an event, but during that event he had no encounter with Jesus personally.

Events don't change us. A personal encounter with Jesus changes us. Peter experienced a resurrection event but never had a resurrection encounter.

To say "I'm going fishing" was a huge statement. Fishing to us is a hobby. Fishing to Peter was his old way of life. *I'm going fishing* were strong words for Peter.

Peter was very persuasive, for seven of the eleven went with him—and three of those were not even fisherman. Life does go on if it's an event. But life can never be the same if the resurrection is an encounter. Here comes the encounter for Peter:

> When the day was now breaking, Jesus stood on the beach; yet the disciples did not know that it was Jesus. So Jesus said to them, "Children, you do not have any fish, do you?" They answered Him, "No." And He said to them, "Cast the net on the right-hand side of the boat and you will find a *catch*." So they cast, and then they were not able to haul it in because of the great number of fish. Therefore that disciple whom Jesus loved said to Peter, "It is the Lord." So when Simon Peter heard that it was the Lord, he put his outer garment on (for he was stripped *for work*), and threw himself into the sea. But the other disciples came in the little boat, for they were not far from the land, but about one hundred yards away, dragging the net full of fish.
>
> Jesus said to them, "Come *and* have breakfast." None of the disciples ventured to question Him, "Who are you?" Knowing that it was the Lord. Jesus came and took the bread and gave *it* to them, and the fish likewise. This is now the third time that Jesus was manifested to the disciples, after He was raised from the dead.
>
> So when they had finished breakfast, Jesus said to Simon Peter, "Simon, *son* of John, do you love Me more than these?" (John 21:4-15)

After breakfast, Peter had an encounter. Because forgiveness happens in encounters not in events. As pastor Robert Schuller said: "Failure doesn't mean you are a failure. It just means you haven't succeeded yet."[139]

Peter was about to get the light bulb again.

Your failure is not final. God wants to get that light bulb in your hands again.

How Your Problems Can Be the Fulfillment of Your Dream

Today's Reading: Acts 1

Pastor R.T. Kendall recalls words his mother told him once about an old saint who had great influence on his mother's life—and consequently on his. She said, "I have served the Lord for so long now that I can hardly tell the difference between a blessing and a trial."[140]

She understood something important: that what you call a problem can really be an answer to prayer. What you think is an interruption is a catapult to your calling and dream.

Today in our 260 journey, we turn to the book of Acts. Acts 1 is about to give you a dream—and then I want you to see how it is accomplished.

Jesus said in Acts 1:8: "You will receive power when the Holy Spirit has come upon you; and you shall be My witnesses both in Jerusalem, and in all Judea and Samaria, and even to the remotest part of the earth."

Jesus said that He would release the disciples as witnesses first in Jerusalem, then in Judea and Samaria, and then to the outermost parts of the earth. Jerusalem happens immediately in Acts 2. Let's cover how part 2 of the plan is accomplished. Always remember, God is creative. And in Acts 8, God uses a strange element to cooperate with His blueprint: Philip is in Samaria and a whole city is being turned upside down.

How did they get there and how did it happen? Let's take a look with the goal that you and I will get a whole new appreciation for the tough stuff we face, or as my friend tells me, to "dignify your trial":

> Saul was in hearty agreement with putting [Stephen] to death. And on that day a great persecution began against the church in Jerusalem, and they were all scattered throughout the regions of Judea and Samaria. . . . Those who had been scattered went about preaching the word. Philip went down to the city of Samaria and *began* proclaiming Christ to them. [Acts 8:1, 4-5]

How is the promise fulfilled? Through persecution—or more specifically, great persecution. Believers headed to Judea and Samaria. How does God get the ball rolling to these two places? He uses attack and persecution against the church to scatter them.

What seems so bad? Scattering and persecution is literally God's agent to fulfill the mission. Here is the end of the story: "So the church throughout all Judea and Galilee and Samaria enjoyed peace, being built up; and going on in the fear of the Lord and in the comfort of the Holy Spirit, it continued to increase" (Acts 9:31).

So a promise (Acts 1:8) was fulfilled by trouble (Acts 8:1-6).

This is similar to another biblical character who suffered trials in order to fulfill God's plan.

Joseph was closer to his dream in jail than he was in Potiphar's home. He was closer as a slave to the dream he had than at home as Daddy's favorite boy. As William Secker said, "If Joseph had not been Egypt's prisoner, he had never been Egypt's governor."[141]

Call it what you want, but all the stuff you are going through—false accusations, betrayals, being fired for no reason—all that trouble may be the catalyst to God doing something great in your life. Or as some anonymous person reminds us, "Sometimes good things fall apart, so better things can fall together."

How Do You Face the Worst Times?

Today's Reading: Acts 2

The church was entering a time that would prove to be the most difficult to be a Christian. Believers would die or be persecuted for following Jesus. The persecution started in the first century and continued for three centuries under the orders of Roman emperors Nero to Diocletian who ordered some of the most horrific things done to Christians.[142] Jesus knew this difficult time lay ahead for His followers so He wanted to make sure they were prepared.

One of the greatest movies is *Gladiator*. One of the deleted scenes on the DVD depicts Russell Crowe, a once-powerful Roman general who had been forced to become a common gladiator, in the bowels of the Colosseum viewing the Christians being fed to the lions. It was accurately portrayed that he would view the Christians' persecution before the gladiators would go into the fight. Why? To fill the stomachs of the lions so they would be more playful with the gladiators during the games.

Why did the Romans kill the early Christians? Not for worshiping Jesus but for not worshiping and acknowledging all the other gods in the roman empire, because they clung to Jesus as the way, the truth, and the life. The first-century government hated the Christians not because they were Christians but because they didn't say all the other religions were legit. We call that pluralism—all religions are equal.

So at the beginning of Acts, with the creation of the early church, Jesus was equipping them with something for the worst times Christianity would face. He was also equipping us. How does God get His people ready for this type of environment? He gives a gift—the gift of the Holy Spirit, as we read in today's chapter:

When the day of Pentecost had come, they were all together in one place. And suddenly there came from heaven a noise like a violent rushing wind, and it filled the whole house where they were sitting. And there appeared to them tongues as of fire distributing themselves, and they rested on each one of them. And they were all filled with the

Holy Spirit and began to speak with other tongues, as the Spirit was giving them utterance. [Acts 2:1-4]

This is not a denominational thing. This is not a Pentecostal thing. This is a Jesus thing.

I have been fortunate that I was raised by great Christian parents and had godly grandparents. From a young age I was saved and filled with the Holy Spirit. When I was a pastor for thirty years in Detroit, someone once told me that they could do a better job on those streets because they have experienced that world and I haven't. They had a life of addiction that I did not have and so they could speak to the people on the street better than I could. That did not seem right to me—the best way to be effective in ministering to the world is to experience the world? I don't think so.

This is the reason for Acts 2. The best way to face the world is *not* to experience it and see that sin is not fulfilling. God doesn't say taste and see the world is no good; God goes the other way: taste and see that the *Lord* is good. Jesus didn't tell Peter to get high, Martha to experience sex outside of marriage, James to get drunk, John to go to prison and kill someone so they could all really minister to people. He said an experience with God is what we need to tell people about God's kingdom and living a Holy-Spirit-filled life. Jesus knew that our power was in experiencing God, not in experiencing sin. Sin takes away, God fills and gives.

So when you are filled with the Holy Spirit, He wants to give you a power to face what is ahead and equip you to share the Good News unafraid.

If Jesus said that the best thing for us was for Him to leave so He could send the Holy Spirit, then it is best. And He will help us through the hardest times.

We need another Pentecost. We need this fire. We need the Holy Spirit.

The founder of the Salvation Army, William Booth, wrote a song called "Send the Fire." Consider his first verse:

Thou Christ of burning, cleansing flame, send the fire!
Thy blood-bought gift today we claim, send the fire!
Look down and see this waiting host, give us the promised Holy Ghost;
We want another Pentecost, send the fire!

3 P.M. CHRISTIANS

Today's Reading: Acts 3

When a big event is over and life starts up again, how do we cope? How does that look? Or how do we look?

After an inspiring Sunday church service, Monday will be there. Mondy is always coming. There will be no lights, no band, no greeters at the door, no hugging . . . because it's Monday and we have a job and a schedule to keep.

The biggest event in church history after the cross and resurrection is the day the Holy Spirit fell upon the church—called the day of Pentecost, the birthday of the church, which we read about in Acts 2. Fire touched them, the church was started, and people were changed.

And what came after, which we read about in Acts 3, is monumental. It is a great guide for us on how to look at Mondays:

> Now Peter and John were going up to the temple at the ninth *hour*, the hour of prayer. And a man who had been lame from his mother's womb was being carried along, whom they used to set down every day at the gate of the temple which is called Beautiful, in order to beg alms of those who were entering the temple. When he saw Peter and John about to go into the temple, he *began* asking to receive alms. But Peter, along with John, fixed his gaze on him and said, "Look at us!" And he began to give them his attention, expecting to receive something from them. But Peter said, "I do not possess silver and gold, but what I do have I give to you: In the name of Jesus Christ the Nazarene—walk!" And seizing him by the right hand, he raised him up; and immediately his feet and his ankles were strengthened. With a leap he stood upright and began to walk; and he entered the temple with them, walking and leaping and praising God. (Acts 3:1-8)

Look at verse 1 again: "Now Peter and John were going up to the temple at the ninth *hour*, the hour of prayer." After the most powerful move of God in the church, the church went back on schedule.

The ninth hour is 3 p.m., the normal hour of prayer in the Jewish culture. God put them back on schedule. They started attending the normal prayer meeting. That is insightful. They became 3 p.m. Christians.

What is a 3 p.m. Christian? It is a Christian who was touched by the Holy Spirit in a special setting but now takes that new touch and brings it into their everyday environment and schedule. They are new people in the same old place. A 3 p.m. Christian comes to the same places with a different heart and different perspective. God doesn't change places, He changes the person.

Acts 3 determines if Acts 2 is real. Real life determines if the experience and change are real. Monday behavior is a great test of Sunday inspiration.

What happened to the disciples? One thing that was very noticeable was that the ordinary started to look extraordinary. They received new eyes. That lame man wasn't new, he had been placed there every day from the time he was a kid. They passed that guy, but today he looked different. He looked like a candidate for a miracle.

One of the best tests for us is that we will notice people: when God touches us, then we love people—not just God—better. It isn't a true work of God if we don't treat people better. The ordinary and the common should start looking different—from the people in Starbucks to our spouses, our kids to our bosses to our coworkers.

God didn't change you for church. God changed you for life—everyday life, Monday life. He changed you to be a 3 p.m. Christian.

Day 93

THE "CAN'T HELP IT" CONDITION

Today's Reading: Acts 4

Today's reading in Acts 4 is connected to a miracle story in Acts 3. In Acts 3, Peter and John prayed for a man they had seen every day at the temple, but this time they saw him with a fresh power from the Holy Spirit, which they received in Acts 2. Because of that they were able to see this lame man walk. Peter and John told the people that Jesus did this miracle.

That's where we pick up our story in Acts 4. The people who saw the miracle and heard their story became Christians—5,000 of them! But there was another group listening who did not believe:

> As they were speaking to the people, the priests and the captain of the temple *guard* and the Sadducees came up to them, being greatly disturbed because they were teaching the people and proclaiming in Jesus the resurrection from the dead. And they laid hands on them and put them in jail until the next day, for it was already evening. (Acts 4:1-3)

The miracle and the message landed Peter and John in jail. And after questioning them, this is what happened:

> When they had summoned them, they commanded them not to speak or teach at all in the name of Jesus. But Peter and John answered and said to them, "Whether it is right in the sight of God to give heed to you rather than to God, you be the judge; for we cannot stop speaking about what we have seen and heard." (Acts 4:18-20)

The authorities told Peter and John not to speak or teach at all in the name of Jesus. Let me say this about the Christian and our government. Talking about Romans 13, pastor John R. W. Stott says that "we are to submit right up to the point where obedience to the state would entail disobedience to God."[143] At that point our Christian duty is to disobey the state in order to obey God. If the state misuses its God-given authority either to command what God forbids or to forbid what God commands, we have to say no to the state in order to say yes to Christ. As John Calvin said, "Obedience to man must not become disobedience to God."[144]

And that is where this story lands us. The Jewish authorities told Peter and John they could no longer speak in the name of Jesus, which has to be a no to the state to say yes to Christ. So Peter told the authorities that would be impossible for them. They didn't have the ability not to not, and Peter said, "We cannot stop."

Dr. E. V. Hill, one of the great Baptist preachers preached on this moment when Peter challenged the "no speaking" rule of the courts:

> Peter spoke up and said, "You'll have to judge whether or not we should obey you or obey God. But as for us, we have a condition, and it's contagious and it's called 'can't-help-it.' We couldn't stop if we wanted to. We could not stop in spite of your threats. We are not spectators; we are participators. No matter how you have threatened us and forbidden us to preach by this name, we will continue to do it, because we can't help it. This isn't something we can cut on and off. . . .
>
> "We were with Jesus when He turned the water to wine. We were right there with Him when He hollered to Lazarus to come forth. . . . We were there when He gave sight to the blind. Don't tell us to shut up; we've got evidence." They said that on that basis they were going to keep on preaching Jesus. "We can't help it."[145]

You and I need that "can't help it" condition too. We all do.

It May Look Exactly the Same but Be Drastically Different

Today's Reading: Acts 5

Ananias and Sapphira are well known in church history. For those unfamiliar with their catastrophic ending, listen closely as we discuss Acts 5. They are a couple who sold some real estate, brought a portion of the money for the offering at church, and was called out by Peter and judged by God on the spot.

Listen to the scariest offering section of a church service ever:

> But a man named Ananias, with his wife Sapphira, sold a piece of property, and kept back *some* of the price for himself, with his wife's full knowledge, and bringing a portion of it, he laid it at the apostles' feet. But Peter said, "Ananias, why has Satan filled your heart to lie to the Holy Spirit and to keep back *some* of the price of the land? While it remained *unsold*, did it not remain your own? And after it was sold, was it not under your control? Why is it that you have conceived this deed in your heart? You have not lied to men but to God." And as he heard these words, Ananias fell down and breathed his last; and great fear came over all who heard of it. The young men got up and covered him up, and after carrying him out, they buried him. (Acts 5:1-6)

After Ananias's death, the same thing happened to his wife. We must guard against our services being fireplaces and fireworks and not fire from heaven. God is not a fireplace who simply warms you and makes you feel comfortable while at the same time you still stay a distance from the hearth. The fireplace is contained and controlled. Meeting Him in the church service is not fireworks either. It is not just a show with "oohs" and "aahs" and then everyone goes home in the same condition they came. Both of these create an illusion of fire but is not the real thing. We must have a place where fire from heaven falls.

That was the early church, and this was definitely Acts 5 where the fire fell in the offering time.

Why the harsh penalty for not giving the amount they were supposed to give in the offering? I think it's connected to the word *but*, the first word of chapter 5. It connects it to chapter 4 and the last few verses. That day during the offering another person gave and was called out for good reasons, and his name was Barnabas. The story makes sense if we read the ending of Acts 4:

> Joseph, a Levite of Cyprian birth, who was also called Barnabas by the apostles (which translated means Son of Encouragement), and who owned a tract of land, sold it and brought the money and laid it at the apostles' feet. (Acts 4:36-37)

Barnabas sold property and brought all the money to the offering that day. Then the contrast. I believe Ananias and Sapphira saw what Barnabas had done and decided to put on a show instead of being genuine. They acted like Barnabas but had hypocrisy in their hearts. God could not allow in this newborn church such craziness, and He exposed it.

On the outside, Barnabas and Ananias looked the same: both sold property, both brought money, both laid it at the apostles' feet. But both were not the same. God knew their hearts.

Something may look exactly the same but be drastically different. And God gave Peter discernment to know that difference immediately.

I have to tell you that to read this on paper is scary. What if you were an outsider and reading about this in the *Jerusalem Times* under a headline that read "People Who Lie Die"? I would be scared about that church.

Yet here is what is amazing: people want the real thing. They don't want the fireplace or the fireworks, they want the real fire of God. And when we read the Bible, God's fire will lead us through a wilderness and baptize us just like in Acts 2. But that same fire will kill people, like Aaron's sons in Leviticus and Ananias and Sapphira. Either way it's real.

So here is what happened after the two deaths during the offering: "All the more believers in the Lord, multitudes of men and women, were constantly added to *their number*" (Acts 5:14).

Instead of it being called some cult thing, the unbelievers knew it was the real thing. It seems the world always knows whether it's real or phony. And just when we think that a public discipline of a member happens, that the verse would say, "A lot of people left the church, and everyone in town stayed away," just the opposite happened. Verse 11 says that "great fear came over the whole church, and over all who heard of these things." I bet it did!

I can imagine how big the next offering was. And then multitudes were getting saved. That to me shows that when God is in the mix, people know it's real. Whether it's a sign or wonder of healing or sign or wonder of God taking someone's life for hypocrisy. We need more of the real thing today.

THE REASON IT'S A REQUIREMENT: BECAUSE IT WILL BE NEEDED FOR A WEAPON

Today's Reading: Acts 6

God sees beyond anything we can ever see. That's why the Bible is quick to point out to us in Isaiah 55:8 that His thoughts are not our thoughts and His ways are higher than our ways. That's important for us to remember as look at today's reading in Acts 6, because this is where the early church starts to get organized. It's all brand new for them, as there has never been a church before.

I heard it said before: "If you find a path with no obstacles, it probably doesn't go anywhere." Well, the church had obstacles . . . and they were going somewhere. They were on a path to change the world.

Growth means life. But growth also means more people, and where there are more people, there are more problems. This is exactly what we find in Acts 6:1: "At this time while the disciples were increasing *in number*, a complaint arose on the part of the Hellenistic *Jews* against the *native* Hebrews, because their widows were being overlooked in the daily serving *of food*."

I have heard people say that we need a church today like the early church. I know they don't mean exactly what they are saying. They want the presence of the Holy Spirit but they forget that the early church had problems too. By Acts 5 and 6, the church already had people lying about the offering and dying and really upset widows who were not getting any food and being overlooked, and the implication was racism. The upset widows were Hellenistic and the widows who had food were Jewish. That's the early church. They had their problems, but they also had leadership responsible to deal with it well.

That is our focus in today's reading—how they dealt with this issue. The disciples knew this problem was not simply telling the people to start feeding the Hellenistic widows, it was also a great lesson on leadership and delegation: *do what only you can do and not what others can contribute.* So in response to this issue, they decided to choose the first deacons of the church. And this point is key: remember that His ways are higher than our ways. People need to be fed and served:

The twelve summoned the congregation of the disciples and said, "It is not desirable for us to neglect the word of God in order to serve tables. Therefore, brethren, select from among you seven men of good reputation, full of the Spirit and of wisdom, whom we may put in charge of this task. But we will devote ourselves to prayer and to the ministry of the word." [Acts 6:2-4]

Pick people who have a good reputation, full of the Spirit and wisdom.

God has higher ways. It would have been easy to look for those who had been in the restaurant business, worked as a waiter or maître de, or a race relations person. I'm thinking of the issue at hand and trying to connect the issue with experience. But God's ways are higher.

God says we need to be Spirit filled and we need wisdom and a good reputation. Why? Because God is higher and He sees further down the road and knows what we need. Because the requirements will be a weapon we can use later on.

Why these requirements?

It seems that the enemy knew that the Twelve were willing to die for their faith in God, so he had to attack the next level of leaders, which he did. It didn't take long for these deacons to come under attack just as the twelve apostles had:

The word of God kept on spreading; and the number of the disciples continued to increase greatly in Jerusalem, and a great many of the priests were becoming obedient to the faith. And Stephen, full of grace and power, was performing great wonders and signs among the people. But some men from what was called the Synagogue of the Freedmen, *including* both Cyrenians and Alexandrians, and some from Cilicia and Asia, rose up and argued with Stephen. But they were unable to cope with the wisdom and the Spirit with which he was speaking. Then they secretly induced men to say, "We have heard him speak blasphemous words against Moses and *against* God." [Acts 6:7-11]

The deacons's three requirements would become their three weapons to fight the enemy's attacks.

The widow issue was fixed. The church was still growing and even a great many priests were becoming born again. And that made the religious institution really upset, so they attacked the next level of leadership, and Stephen was in the crosshairs of their attack.

And this is amazing. When the religious leaders rose up to fight them, they were unable to cope with Stephen's wisdom and the Spirit. Sound familiar from the verse 2 requirements?

We are still not done! They hired people to spread lies about Stephen (verse 11). But they had a problem with that: Stephen had a good reputation. That means all three requirements became weapons to fight their attacks.

When you see God giving prerequisites to a task, whether that be in pastoring, lay leadership, or even in marriage, it is because God sees further, and what you think is going to be a bother is going to be useful in the future. When God says not to marry an unbeliever (a prerequisite for a successful Christian marriage), but you are dead-set on marrying that person, you just lost your weapon for marriage. Marriage is hard enough, but to have two different worldviews for life and children? That's almost impossible.

And by the way, when the devil thought only the apostles were willing to die for their faith, he got that way wrong! Stephen was all in and willing to lay his life on the line. As we'll read tomorrow in Acts 7, Stephen died for Jesus. The first Christian martyr was a deacon.

It's really easy to find people who know the truth. It's really hard to find people who will stand up for the truth. No matter the cost.

You can't skip steps with God. When God gives a requirement, it's for a weapon. What you think is cumbersome is really armor.

Day 96

WHERE DO ALIENS COME FROM?

Today's Reading: Acts 7

One of my favorite books by C. S. Lewis is called *God in the Dock: Essays on Theology and Ethics.* In it, he includes a chapter called "Cross Examination," which is a question and answer time with Professor Lewis. One of the questions: Do you think there will be widespread travel in space? His response: "I look forward with horror to contact with the other inhabited planets, if there are such. We would only transport to them all of our sin and our acquisitiveness. . . . I can't bear to think of it."[146]

Of alien life, George Bernard Shaw noted, "The longer I live, the more I am inclined to the belief that this earth is used by other planets as its lunatic asylum."[147]

But my favorite is Rick Warren's statement: "If UFO aliens are so smart, why do they kidnap the dumbest people on earth?"[148]

Today we're talking about aliens, but let me tell you about the aliens I am referring to. They aren't from Mars or Venus, they're from right here in Acts 7. The word *alien* has become familiar today with all the debate surrounding our southern borders and the wall. But that's the word I want us to see here in Acts 7.

It is from a sermon that Stephen preached. This sermon is the second longest sermon in the New Testament, next to the Sermon on the Mount. Stephen will not end his sermon with music, an altar call, or a challenge. This sermon will end with his listeners being so angry that they stone him to death.

The longest part of his sermon speaks about Moses and the alien issue. I want to show you how God's man and God's deliverer became an alien before he became a deliverer. Stephen recounted, "At this remark, MOSES FLED AND BECAME AN ALIEN IN THE LAND OF MIDIAN, where he became the father of two sons" (Acts 7:29).

Think of that: *a remark* changed Moses' life. The remark was, "Are you going to kill me like you killed that Egyptian yesterday?" (Acts 7:28, MSG). The back story is that Moses started to feel his calling rise up when he saw an Egyptian abuse a Jewish slave. He killed the Egyptian and expected his people to celebrate. Instead they criticized. And then someone made the remark, which made Moses flee and become an alien.

Our words have life and death to them. As Proverbs 18:21 reminds us:

"Death and life are in the power of the tongue." *The Message* says it like this: "Words kill, words give life; they're either poison or fruit—you choose."

What have you heard that has lodged in your soul? What word have you heard that changed what you are and where you are today? And who spoke those words to you? Has someone said something to you that has changed you into something you never wanted to be?

Someone can be one crazy comment away from becoming an alien.

It happened to Moses: "At this remark, Moses fled and became an alien." Twenty-four words changed royalty into a fugitive and alien at forty years old. A remark took him from the palace and put him in the desert. The words brought fear and put him on the run.

Have you ever heard life-altering words?

You will never be anything.

You're stupid.

You aren't even my real child.

You were a mistake.

You are just like your father.

I hate you.

I wish I never had you.

People's hearts are so fragile and people's words are so careless. And when fragile and careless intersect, you get aliens. People becoming something they never intended to become.

The opposite happens when life words are spoken.

I love you.

I'm proud of you.

I was thinking of you.

I'm praying for you.

Those are life words.

Some of these words you have never heard, I have never heard, our youth have never heard, but we can change that today. When life words are spoken, huge life comes to them.

There is a place in Sydney, Australia, called the gap. You don't buy clothes there for your teenager. You go there if you want to commit suicide. It's a rocky cliff where people jump off. Don and Moya Ritchie live next to the gap, and for almost fifty years, the Ritchies saved an estimated 160 people from certain death. Every morning as soon as Don woke up, he would look out their window to see if anyone was standing all alone too close to the edge. If he sensed someone contemplating suicide, he approached them and asked if there was something he could do to help them, hoping for an opportunity to "sell them" on life.[149]

"Be [kind]," says Rev. John Watson, "for every man is fighting a hard battle."[150] How can we help people with heavy hearts today? We can speak life. Proverbs 12:25 tells us that "anxiety in a man's heart weighs it down, but a good word makes it glad." Give someone a life word today. Text it. Say it. Write it. You don't know what it will mean to them.

BE CAREFUL OF PLAYING WITH FIRE

Today's Reading: Acts 8

All of us, as children, heard the warning about playing with fire. The combination of youth and fire can be destructive. This is true naturally and spiritually.

In today's reading, we learn about a great revival that came to a city called Samaria. The city faced two kinds of fire, and thank God, the right one came:

> When the apostles in Jerusalem heard that Samaria had received the word of God, they sent them Peter and John, who came down and prayed for them that they might receive the Holy Spirit. For He had not yet fallen upon any of them; they had simply been baptized in the name of the Lord Jesus. Then they *began* laying their hands on them, and they were receiving the Holy Spirit. [Acts 8:14-17]

Philip went to Samaria and preached. When those in the Jerusalem church heard how well the Good News was received there, they sent reinforcements—Peter and John—to help him. After Samaria received the Word of God, Peter and John prayed that the fire of heaven would come upon them, as it did them at Pentecost. They laid hands on the Samaritans, who received that Pentecostal fire, the baptism of the Holy Spirit. There is something special about this moment, but to understand it, we have to go back to Luke 9 and read about two disciples who were playing with fire:

> When the days were approaching for His ascension, He was determined to go to Jerusalem; and He sent messengers on ahead of Him, and they went and entered a village of the Samaritans to make arrangements for Him. But they did not receive Him, because He was traveling toward Jerusalem. When His disciples James and John saw *this*, they said, "Lord, do You want us to command fire to come down from heaven and consume them?" But He turned and rebuked them, and said, "You do not know what kind of spirit you are of; for the Son of Man did not come to destroy men's lives, but to save them." [Luke 9:51-56]

The disciples were dealing with racist hearts. The Samaritans were half-breeds to the Jews. They were part Assyrian and part Jewish—a result of the Jews' Assyrian captivity. They were a mixed race whom the Jewish people considered impure.

Jesus rebuked them and their racist spirits. He told them that the Son of Man did not come to destroy lives but to save them.

Thank God for His rebukes and His corrections upon our lives. Can you imagine what would have happened if those disciples actually called fire down in Luke 9? We would not be reading Acts 8. There would be no Samaria. Wrong fire, boys! God was wanting to send another fire but not the one they wanted. This is very important—the two boys who wanted to call down judgment fire, or Elijah fire, as it says in the KJV, were James and John. And when Jesus rebuked them, it set them back on course.

Sometimes it takes encouragement to get us on the right path, sometimes teaching, sometimes rebuke—but always combined with patience. The Bible says it like this: "We urge you, brethren, admonish the unruly, encourage the fainthearted, help the weak, be patient with everyone" (1 Thessalonians 5:14).

Jesus' patience paid off.

Do you remember who was sent to the Samaria of Acts 8?

Peter and here it is . . . John. The man who was playing with judgment fire. Jesus was patient with him, and two years after Jesus' rebuke, John returned to the same city. This time he did get to call down fire, the right kind of fire—Pentecostal, Holy-Spirit-baptism fire. And instead of a people being judged, they were filled with God.

Thank you, God, for your rebukes.

Thank you, John, that you listened.

And now the right fire came to Samaria.

How a Really Bad Man Becomes the Greatest Christian

Today's Reading: Acts 9

Today we read about the incredible conversion story of the greatest Christian who ever lived, the apostle Paul. We find his story in Acts 9. Before his conversion, Paul was murdering and persecuting young Christians. But he was about to be changed forever:

> Saul, still breathing threats and murder against the disciples of the Lord, went to the high priest, and asked for letters from him to the synagogues at Damascus, so that if he found any belonging to the Way, both men and women, he might bring them bound to Jerusalem. As he was traveling, it happened that he was approaching Damascus, and suddenly a light from heaven flashed around him; and he fell to the ground and heard a voice saying to him, "Saul, Saul, why are you persecuting Me?" And he said, "Who are You, Lord?" And He *said*, "I am Jesus whom you are persecuting, but get up and enter the city, and it will be told you what you must do." The men who traveled with him stood speechless, hearing the voice but seeing no one. Saul got up from the ground, and though his eyes were open, he could see nothing; and leading him by the hand, they brought him into Damascus. And he was three days without sight, and neither ate nor drank.
>
> Now there was a disciple at Damascus named Ananias; and the Lord said to him in a vision, "Ananias." And he said, "Here I am, Lord." And the Lord *said* to him, "Get up and go to the street called Straight, and inquire at the house of Judas for a man from Tarsus named Saul, for he is praying." (Acts 9:1-11)

I am amazed at how in one day a man goes from breathing threats and murder against the baby church in Acts and in ten verses we find him praying. How does this happen?

It is nothing but the power of God's voice and God's Word. One word from

God can change anyone. I am still amazed at the power of God's Word. He does not speak much but enough. We are so wordy, and God is so precise.

This man was such a tough case that even the disciples took some time to believe that a change happened. As a side note: I love the dialogue between Ananias and the Lord in verses 10 through 17. God wanted him to lay hands upon the new convert Saul, but Ananias was apprehensive because he was aware of Saul's reputation. He dialogues with the Lord and tells him about Saul (verses 13-14), as though the omniscient God had never heard of him before. God responded to him with a "Go" in verse 15.

God can change even the worst of sinners. As D. Martyn Lloyd-Jones said, "A Christian is the result of the operation of God; nothing less, nothing else. No man can make himself a Christian. God alone makes Christians."[151]

Someone once said, "God has no grandchildren." Do you know what that means? You cannot be a Christian because of your parents. You must experience God for yourself. And Saul did. And now the murderer was on the path to being the key writer of the New Testament.

The Damascus Road is the conversion site of the apostle Paul. It gives hope to people who want to see friends and family born again but they seem so far away. Paul's conversion shows us that when people seem furthest from God, they may be closer than we think to being born again. Paul was hunting Christians in verse 2 and praying like the Christians he wanted to kill by verse 11.

I am so thankful there is nothing we do that God can't forgive. Paul was killing Christians. I wonder if that's why no New Testament writer wrote more on God's grace than the apostle Paul. He was that horrific person, yet he experienced God's grace. Paul learned what Christian writer Jerry Bridges wrote: "Your worst days are never so bad that you are beyond the *reach* of God's grace. And your best days are never so good that you are beyond the *need* of God's grace."[152]

It's not just any old grace. It's amazing grace—how sweet the sound.

Day 99

HOW AN ITALIAN MET A JEW

Today's Reading: Acts 10

I'm excited about today's chapter. Acts 10 is one of my favorite chapters in the New Testament. It gives the thirty-thousand-foot view of why we pray. And it does this by telling a story of two separate guys, an Italian and a Jew, and how their worlds intersected through prayer.

It reminds me of something I've often heard said: "The more I pray, the more coincidences happen." Coincidence is just another name for the providence of God and the activity of God in our daily lives, connecting and intersecting situations that had no way of being connected.

Peter and Cornelius were about to have that intersection. They are more than thirty miles apart, and God was set to bring their two worlds together. There is also a wider gap between their ethnicity, Gentile and Jew, and God brought that together also.

Let's read first about the Italian:

There was a man at Caesarea named Cornelius, a centurion of what was called the Italian cohort, a devout man and one who feared God with all his household, and gave many alms to the *Jewish* people and prayed to God continually. About the ninth hour of the day he clearly saw in a vision an angel of God who had *just* come in and said to him, "Cornelius!" And fixing his gaze on him and being much alarmed, he said, "What is it, Lord?" And he said to him, "Your prayers and alms have ascended as a memorial before God. Now dispatch *some* men to Joppa and send for a man *named* Simon, who is also called Peter; he is staying with a tanner *named* Simon, whose house is by the sea." [Acts 10:1-6]

If Cornelius didn't pray, then how would he know about Simon, also called Peter, in a city called Joppa, staying with another Simon, who has a leather business near the sea? Oh my goodness, incredible instructions from prayer.

This is why I pray. There are things you will never know if you don't pray. I've heard it said, "When I work, I work. But when I pray, God works."

God was working in Acts 10.

Listen closely: those who don't pray are boring. You miss the exciting extras God adds to your life. Prayerlessness is a boring existence for a Christian.

George Mueller, the nineteenth-century pastor who housed and cared for orphans in Bristol, England, believed that four hours' worth of work and one hour of prayer could accomplish much more than five hours of work.[153] Prayer is the work, which opens up and intersects worlds that never would have come together. Just as it did here in Acts 10.

When I pray, three things happen:

- I go places I never would have gone.
- I meet people I never would have met.
- And I go through doors I never would have gotten through.

Prayer brought together an Italian and a Jew who had nothing in common in their own minds, but there was a bigger purpose in God's mind.

Prayer widens the boundaries beyond your zip code, geography, and relationships.

Now here's the intersection: while Cornelius prayed and sent his men to get Peter . . . "on the next day, as they were on their way and approaching the city, Peter went up on the housetop about the sixth hour to pray" (verse 9).

While Peter is praying, men were coming to see him. Peter received a vision, and the voice of God as a knock on the door from these men happened: "While Peter was reflecting on the vision, the Spirit said to him, 'Behold, three men are looking for you. But get up, go downstairs and accompany them without misgivings, for I have sent them myself'" (verses 19-20).

Those were Cornelius's guys.

Two men's prayer lives brought an intersection that would never have happened. And God brought the Italian and the Jew together. That's what prayer does, and that's why we pray.

Peter went with the men to Cornelius's house and preached to them. And "while Peter was still speaking these words, the Holy Spirit fell upon all those who were listening to the message" (verse 44).

This is off the charts! It was the Gentiles' Pentecost, in which men and women were filled with the Holy Spirit and baptized in water. And a few verses later (verse 47), Peter said that this was just like what happened to them in Acts 2.

All of this happened because two men prayed.

This is why we pray.

Who knows who we will meet today?

Who knows what door we will see opened?

Who knows where God will send us?

Louis Lallemant, a seventeenth-century monk couldn't have said better the importance of why we pray: "A man of prayer will do more in one year than another will do in his whole life."[154]

ONE OF THREE

Today's Reading: Acts 11

In today's reading we see a word that we use all the time but it's used for the first time in the entire Bible. In fact, the word is used only three times in the entire New Testament. It is the word *Christian*.

That sounds impossible, but it's true. Pastor Sam Pascoe once said, "Christianity started out in Palestine as a fellowship; it moved to Greece and became a philosophy; it moved to Italy and became an institution; it moved to Europe and became a culture; it came to America and became an enterprise."[155]

It's time to see how the Bible uses the word *Christian*. The Bible is very careful with this word, and I think so we must be. Let's build a description of a Christian with the three passages, starting with Acts 11: "He left for Tarsus to look for Saul; and when he had found him, he brought him to Antioch. And for an entire year they met with the church and taught considerable numbers; and the disciples were first called Christians in Antioch" (verses 25-26).

The "he" in this verse is Barnabas, Paul's mentor. The two men went to Antioch for an entire year. And it was in that city where *Christian* was first used.

Let's build our description on this economy of words.

First, a Christian is a reminder. I love that the church did not make up this word about themselves and get T-shirts made. The word, which means, "little Christ," was a derogatory slang word made up by unbelievers. They were in essence saying that the believers reminded them of the man with the thorns on the cross whom was crucified a year before. A real Christian looks like Jesus, not like a church, a religion, a denomination, or a culture. Hopefully when an unbeliever sees us, they see Him.

The second time this word is used is in Acts 26:28. Paul was talking to a king who was not a Christian. Paul was not just dispensing knowledge and information but was trying to persuade and change: "Agrippa *replied* to Paul, 'In a short time you will persuade me to become a Christian.'"

The second thing we need to understand about a Christian is that a Christian is a persuader. Christianity is not just right for me and you; it's right for the planet. We are not inviting people to a place but to a person.

Finally, we leave the book of Acts to find the last use of the word. It's in 1

Peter 4:16: "If *anyone suffers* as a Christian, he is not to be ashamed, but is to glorify God in this name."

A Christian is a reminder, a Christian is a persuader, and a Christian is a sufferer.

What does that mean? It's suffering for doing the right thing. There will be times when a Christian will not get an award for doing the right thing, will not get cheers for doing the right thing, and will not get a plaque for doing the right thing. Instead that Christian will get laughed at, mocked, reprimanded, fired, and even sued for living like Jesus. There will be moments when your only audience will be an audience of one—God Himself. But that is enough motivation for doing what's right.

Christians are considered by many to be crazy, and, as A. W. Tozer suggests, with good reason: "A real Christian is an odd number anyway. He feels supreme love for One whom he has never seen, talks familiarly every day to Someone he cannot see, expects to go to heaven on the virtue of Another, empties himself in order to be full, admits he is wrong so he can be declared right, goes down in order to get up, is strongest when he is weakest, richest when he is poorest. . . . He dies so he can live, forsakes in order to have, gives away so he can keep, sees the invisible, hears the inaudible and knows that which passeth knowledge."[156]

May that be true of you and me always.

What If Someone's Future Was in the Hands of Your Prayer Life?

Today's Reading: Acts 12

Today we come to a challenging passage of Scripture. We are about to see two men in prison, yet those same men's lives have a different outcome. And it *seems* there is something that happened that changed one of these men's future. Let's read the story:

> About that time Herod the king laid hands on some who belonged to the church in order to mistreat them. And he had James the brother of John put to death with a sword. When he saw that it pleased the Jews, he proceeded to arrest Peter also. Now it was during the days of Unleavened Bread. When he had seized him, he put him in prison, delivering him to four squads of soldiers to guard him, intending after the Passover to bring him out before the people. (Acts 12:1-5)

Herod arrested two key figures in the first church: James and Peter. Both were imprisoned. James was put to death by the sword, and Peter was about to face the same outcome . . . but Peter was miraculously delivered. Something seemed to change Peter's meeting with the executioner: "Peter was kept in the prison, but prayer for him was being made fervently by the church to God" (verse 5).

Read that verse again: "But prayer for him was being made fervently by the church to God."

Could it be that God was showing us the power of prayer? James got a sword; Peter got an angel:

> On the very night when Herod was about to bring him forward, Peter was sleeping between two soldiers, bound with two chains, and guards in front of the door were watching over the prison. And behold, an angel of the Lord suddenly appeared and a light shone in the cell; and he struck Peter's side and woke him up, saying, "Get up quickly." And his chains fell off his hands. (Acts 12:6-7)

I have to say this about the angelic visit in prison. Take a look this sentence: "He struck Peter's side and woke him up." Talk about the peace of God. If I knew I was going to die the next day, I would not be in such a deep sleep that an angel would need to strike me on the side and yell, "Get up."

Why did Peter have the peace of God? Because he knew the promise of God.

This is really important. Back in John 21, Jesus made Peter a promise about his death:

> "Truly, truly, I say to you, when you were younger, you used to gird yourself and walk wherever you wished; but when you grow old, you will stretch out your hands and someone else will gird you, and bring you where you do not wish to *go*." Now this He said, signifying by what kind of death he would glorify God. And when He had spoken this, He said to him, "Follow Me!" (John 21:18-19)

He was telling Peter that he would not die young but as an old man who can't even dress himself.

Peter knew a promise that Jesus made over him twelve years before. So Peter could go to sleep, because he believed God would get him out.

And God *did*. Puritan writer Thomas Watson said that "the angel fetched Peter out of prison, but it was prayer that fetched the angel."[157]

Could the difference be that God is showing us that prayer is intercession? That prayer gets people out of a death sentence. One gets killed, the other gets delivered. And the thing separating their fates was a praying church.

Peter was going to be killed, but prayer trumped Herod's intentions. My prayer, our church's prayer, can be a matter of life and death.

If Peter's life depended on your prayer life or on your church's prayer life . . . would he have had a chance? Or would he have faced the same fate as his companion?

A Christian lady lived next door to an atheist. Every day she prayed, and the atheist could hear her. Many times, he would harass her and say, "Why do you pray all the time? Don't you know there is no God?"

But still she kept on praying.

One day she ran out of groceries. As usual, she was praying, and the atheist could hear her. As she prayed, she explained her situation to the Lord, thanking Him for what He was going to do.

The atheist was so annoyed with her praying, that he decided to get her.

He went to the store, bought groceries, dropped them off on her front porch, rang the doorbell, and hid in the bushes. When she opened the door and saw the groceries, she began to praise the Lord!

The atheist jumped out of the bushes. "You old crazy lady. God didn't buy you those groceries. *I* bought those groceries!"

His announcement started her shouting and praising God all the more. "I knew the Lord would provide me with some groceries, but I didn't know he was going make the devil pay for them!"[158]

Can your prayer life get someone out of jail?

Day 102

YOU NEVER KNOW WHAT CAN HAPPEN WHEN YOU WORSHIP

Today's Reading: Acts 13

In her children's novel, *The Candymakers*, Wendy Mass wrote, "If nothing ever changed, there'd be no butterflies." Well, in today's reading we see that the butterfly is about to come out, because a change is coming.

Can you imagine having Sunday school teachers in your home church named Paul and Barnabas? I mean *the* Paul and Barnabas. The church in Antioch did. Acts 13 tells us this and then tells us what happened during their worship service. And it's the butterfly moment:

> There were at Antioch, in the church that was *there*, prophets and teachers: Barnabas, and Simeon who was called Niger, and Lucius of Cyrene, and Manaen who had been brought up with Herod the tetrarch, and Saul. While they were ministering to the Lord and fasting, the Holy Spirit said, "Set apart for Me Barnabas and Saul for the work to which I have called them." Then, when they had fasted and prayed and laid their hands on them, they sent them away. So, being sent out by the Holy Spirit . . . ." [Acts 13:1-4]

Paul had been saved in AD 34—Acts 9. In Acts 13, it was AD 48—fourteen years later. It had been fourteen years since Paul's conversion. Antioch was a six-year-old church, which we saw had been started in Acts 11, where the followers of Jesus were first called Christians. Paul was teaching there but had not been released into full-time ministry yet until the music started one Sunday in the service. Let's read verse 2 again, this time in a different translation: "While they were worshiping the Lord and fasting, the Holy Spirit said, 'Set apart for me Barnabas and Saul for the work to which I have called them'" (NIV).

You have to worship. It's a command. Not only because God deserves it, but because it positions us for God to talk to us and even guide us. And on this day in Antioch, God tapped Paul and Barnabas on the shoulders and said that it was time for them to change locations and ministries.

You may have thought you are just singing when the music starts at your church, but so much more can happen. When you worship you are positioning yourself to hear God's voice.

The songs were playing and God said it was time for a change in the Antioch staff team. Whatever their role was at the Antioch church, it would have been cool to go to Barnabas and Paul's church. But their church was soon about to have a staff shake up.

Just when it seems like you have the perfect leadership team, God may say, "Change." That doesn't seem too cool to do to your dream team, but in this case, we know the end of the story and we know it was the right move, because this was the beginning of Paul's missionary journeys and the spread of the gospel around the world.

Remember, God's will is more important than any of our preferences. His Kingdom is more important than personalities and our comfortability. When it's a God thing, there may be sadness but there is never harm to God's work. God will not change the landscape to harm one place and bless another. God will not change something to kill ministries, but will raise up others to do the work of the ministry that did not have a chance before. Abrupt vacancy sometimes means we got comfortable with the same people doing the same thing for a long time and God wants others developed.

Don't think any person is off limits to God. Don't put any boundaries around a singer. A musician. A pastor. A leader or faithful worker. As Corrie ten Boom reminds us: "Hold everything in your hands lightly, otherwise it hurts when God pries your fingers open."[159]

That's exactly what was about to happen to Paul and the church at Antioch. They were both holding their hands lightly when God tapped them on the shoulder during the worship service.

Next time you stand and sing at church and you feel a tap, it may not be the person behind you. I'm just saying.

Day 103

A Strange Response to a Miracle

Today's Reading: Acts 14

C. S. Lewis wrote, "Miracles in fact are a retelling in small letters of the very same story which is written across the whole world in letters too large for some of us to see."[160] Lewis was saying that a miracle was retelling the big story that God exists and God is good. Seeing a miracle should help us to see the big letters. Unfortunately, as we find in today's reading, Lystra missed it.

Acts 14 is about a man being able to walk for the first time. It's a miracle! But the chapter shows us more: it shows how the people who *can* walk are lame. They are crippled in their worldview. The people in Lystra saw a miracle and end up worshiping the guys who performed it:

> While they were at Lystra, Paul and Barnabas came upon a man with crippled feet. He had been that way from birth, so he had never walked. He was sitting and listening as Paul preached. Looking straight at him, Paul realized he had faith to be healed. So Paul called to him in a loud voice, "Stand up!" And the man jumped to his feet and started walking.
> When the crowd saw what Paul had done, they shouted in their local dialect, "These men are gods in human form!" They decided that Barnabas was the Greek god Zeus and that Paul was Hermes.
> (Acts 14:8-12, NLT)

A man walks who had never walked. God healed him. And when the town saw it, they responded with a wrong conclusion—that Paul and Barnabas must be gods. And they decided, "Let's praise these guys."

So Paul had to speak to their false conclusion:

> Friends, why are you doing this? We are merely human beings—just like you! We have come to bring you the Good News that you should turn from these worthless things and turn to the living God, who made heaven and earth, the sea, and everything in them. In the past he permitted all the nations to go their own ways, but he never left

them without evidence of himself and his goodness. For instance, he sends you rain and good crops and gives you food and joyful hearts." (Acts 14:15-17, NLT)

Verse 17 is so important. Paul was explaining the reason Lystra blew it when the man was healed: God had left them evidence of His existence and His goodness. When it rains, it's because God is good. When they had good crops, that was from a good God.

Émile Cammaerts was right in these profound words: "The first effect of not believing in God is to believe in anything."[161] Because the people of Lystra *missed God's evidence*, they had to come up with their own gods—and this day it was Paul and Barnabas.

Paul's words are not just important for Lystra to know but for our world to know. This is so important: we see something amazing happen and we praise people and leave God out of the mix. People know how to blame God for the bad but they don't know how to praise God for the good. That was Lystra, and that's happening today.

Some years ago, I was flying home only to have my flight canceled because of a weather-related issue. Huge thunderstorms grounded all the flights. The other passengers and I would have to wait until the storm passed, which looked to be the next morning. When I asked the gate agent if the airline would cover the expenses of my night in a hotel, her response was, "We only cover that when it's mechanical. When it's an act of God, you are on your own."

I laughed when I realized what she'd said. She was saying God exists! But He exists only when bad stuff happens, and the airline isn't responsible for His storms. When the good stuff happens, though, the airline did it. When storms happen, passengers have to pay. Insurance companies and airlines call storm-related damages acts of God. But they forget that the sunshine is from God too.

In 1970, the Apollo 13 mission was almost a catastrophe. Apollo 13 was the third mission NASA was sending to the moon, but after an oxygen tank explosion onboard en route, they had to abort the mission. This is where the famous "Houston, we've had a problem . . ." line occurred. Many people only know about the event from watching the iconic movie Tom Hanks starred in and Ron Howard directed. The part the movie did not show us was that the president of the United States, Richard Nixon, came on television and asked the nation to pray for the astronauts' safe return.

And this is what happened: the capsule landed in the Pacific Ocean and was put on an aircraft carrier. And when the astronauts were safely aboard the carrier . . . don't miss this . . . the president praised American space technology for the return of our astronauts. He asked us to pray, and when God answered that prayer, he praised human skill and technology. He should have just called NASA Zeus and Hermes.

It was just a few years later that Watergate occurred and that president resigned in disgrace.

God is good all the time. And all the time, *God* is good.

THE BEST OF MEN ARE STILL MEN AT BEST

Today's Reading: Acts 15

I'll always be thankful for my friend and mentor, R. T. Kendall, who during a critical time in my life quoted these words from an unknown source: "Always remember that the best of men are still men at best." We all have our faults and flaws, even the greatest Christian leaders. In today's reading, we will see how true these words are.

First let me tell you a revival story from the First Great Awakening in the 1700s that shook two continents. The awakening was spreading from England to a nation soon to form (the United States of America). What God did during that time became the DNA for the language used in our foundational documents, the Declaration of Independence and the Constitution.

Though the revival was great, it was not without controversy. Two great preachers and close friends, John Wesley and George Whitefield, who played significant spiritual roles during that time often found themselves in sharp disagreement with each other. Both men led countless thousands to faith in Christ, but they were at odds theologically.

Whitefield had traveled to the American colonies and when he returned to England, the men had a heated confrontation. Wesley wrote of the event: "He told me that he and I preached two different gospels; and therefore he would not only not join with or give me the right hand of fellowship, but was resolved publicly to preach against me and my brother [Charles], wheresoever he preached at all."[162]

The best of men are still men at best.

Before Whitefield came to the end of his life, he asked Wesley to preach his funeral sermon. Wesley agreed, and while there, a woman approached and asked, "Dear Mr. Wesley, do you expect to see dear Mr. Whitefield in heaven?"

After a lengthy pause, Wesley responded solemnly, "No, Madam."

"Ah, I was afraid you would say so," she said.

"But," Wesley continued, "do not misunderstand me. . . . George Whitefield will stand so near the throne that one like me will never get a glimpse of him!"[163]

Just like the first Great Awakening, the first missionary journey of the church to take the gospel beyond Jerusalem had problems between its leaders:

After some days Paul said to Barnabas, "Let us return and visit the brethren in every city in which we proclaimed the word of the Lord, *and see* how they are." Barnabas wanted to take John, called Mark, along with them also. But Paul kept insisting that they should not take him along who had deserted them in Pamphylia and had not gone with them to the work. And there occurred such a sharp disagreement that they separated from one another, and Barnabas took Mark with him and sailed away to Cyprus. But Paul chose Silas and left, being committed by the brethren to the grace of the Lord. (Acts 15:36-40)

The greatest Christian of his time (Paul) and the greatest encourager of his time (Barnabas) had a sharp disagreement.

The best of men are still men at best.

I heard someone say it like this: "The church is like Noah's ark. The stench on the inside would be unbearable if it weren't for the storm on the outside." Many times we stink, but the world is really stormy. Paul and Barnabas only traveled together on one of the three missionary journeys because of this fight. The sharp disagreement between them was based upon whether to take the young disciple John Mark with them. Earlier, the young man seemed to have gotten scared and deserted the dynamic duo. Paul thought John Mark's actions should get him fired, but Barnabas wanted to give him a second chance.

When things are emotional, people tend to become illogical. The disagreement over John Mark became emotional and illogical. Sharp disagreement implies the emotional; separating and going different ways is illogical.

When we read how this disagreement ended, it's good for us to consider some questions: Who do you have in your life who will tell you the truth? Who can disagree with you without the situation becoming disagreeable and defensive? Can your spouse, best friend, family member challenge your opinion—spiritually, politically, racially, socially—without it turning into a shouting match?

Here's the truth: when you are shouting over a differing opinion, it isn't the opinion that is revealing, it's the yeller being revealed.

Two quick thoughts to use for the times someone disagrees with you:

First, get the second side of everything. Job 11:6 says that "sound wisdom has two sides." You are not able to see everything and you are not able to know everything. Go in trying to find the truth not trying to be right.

Second, surround yourself with wise people, those who feed your soul, not your ego, those who won't be afraid to disagree with you, who will force you to practice getting the second side. As Proverbs 27:17 says, "As iron sharpens iron, so a friend sharpens a friend" [NLT]. Prominent 1920s attorney Dudley Field Malone said it this way, "I have never in my life learned anything from any man who agreed with me."[164]

I am happy the Bible records the argument of the apostle and the encourager, but not so happy about their separation. In the end, God used Paul and Silas on the other two missionary journeys, however, I wish we would have seen a resolution instead of a separation between the two. But it really is true . . . the best of men are still men at best.

A PAINFUL NO CAN LEAD TO AN INCREDIBLE YES

Today's Reading: Acts 16

Welcome to one of the most important New Testament chapters, Acts 16. This chapter is the reason we meet for church, and it all started with God saying no to the apostle Paul.

Let me tell you that my "no" story changed the direction of my life. In the summer of 1983, I had the opportunity to go on two mission trips. The first was to Jamaica and the other to Detroit. Without praying, I said yes to Jamaica. I thought the sun, beach, and sand was the best place to minister. Then I did something that changed everything—I prayed and asked God what He wanted me to do. God said no to Jamaica and yes to Detroit. If left to me, I was heading to the Caribbean; if left to God, I was heading to one of the most impoverished inner cities in the country. Didn't make sense . . . yet.

That summer mission's trip changed my life. What I thought would be two months between semesters at university, ended up becoming thirty years of my life and a call to ministry. And it all started with hearing no to Jamaica.

That is not only my story, that is Paul's story in Acts 16. God was doing great things in Asia, and Paul was on his second missionary journey. While he was starting to make plans for his "Jamaica," he heard God's no twice:

They passed through the Phrygian and Galatian region, having been forbidden by the Holy Spirit to speak the word in Asia; and after they came to Mysia, they were trying to go into Bithynia, and the Spirit of Jesus did not permit them. [Acts 16:6-7]

Two no's, then the yes from God:

Passing by Mysia, they came down to Troas. A vision appeared to Paul in the night: a man of Macedonia was standing and appealing to him, and saying, "Come over to Macedonia and help us." When he had seen the vision, immediately we sought to go into Macedonia, concluding

that God had called us to preach the gospel to them.
(Acts 16:8-10)

Two thoughts for us to remember:
1. God is a father and fathers say no.
2. No is not rejection but protection.

Remember, Satan always says yes.

Sometimes you have to hear some no's before you get a yes. If you have never heard no from God, then your relationship with Him is suspect and you're probably not talking to Him.

When He does say no, it means He has something bigger and better for you.

For Paul, that bigger and better was that God had a global strategy for the church, one He mapped out way back in Acts 1:8: "You will receive power when the Holy Spirit has come upon you; and you shall be My witnesses both in Jerusalem, and in all Judea and Samaria, and even to the remotest part of the earth."

Jerusalem was covered in Acts 2 on the day of Pentecost. Acts 8 moved the gospel into Judea and Samaria through the great persecution: "On that day a great persecution began against the church in Jerusalem, and they were all scattered throughout the regions of Judea and Samaria, except the apostles. . . . Therefore, those who had been scattered went about preaching the word" (Acts 8:1, 4).

Part 3 of the Acts 1:8 strategy had yet to be fulfilled—until we hit chapter 16. This was the gospel going to Europe and eventually around the world. If Paul didn't listen to God and did what was comfortable by staying in Asia, then your church and my church wouldn't exist today. It was so much easier to stay in Asia, but God had something bigger in mind, and so God said no.

Thank You, God, for saying no to us, and especially to the apostle Paul.

Day 106

Sixty Miles' Worth of Jealousy

Today's Reading: Acts 17

Quaker minister and advocate of religious freedom, who also founded Pennsylvania, wrote about the dangers of jealousy:

> Jealousy is a kind of civil war in the soul, where judgment and imagination are at perpetual jars [odds]. . . . Nothing stands safe in its way: nature, interest, religion, must yield to its fury. It violates contracts, dissolves society, breaks wedlock, betrays friends and neighbors. Nobody is good, and everyone is either doing or designing a mischief. It has a venom that . . . bites.[165]

On our 260 journey today we find Paul ensnared in the consequences of jealousy. Paul had just finished preaching in Thessalonica and he left to preach in Berea—and jealousy was about to enter the picture:

> The brethren immediately sent Paul and Silas away by night to Berea, and when they arrived, they went into the synagogue of the Jews. Now these were more noble-minded than those in Thessalonica, for they received the word with great eagerness, examining the Scriptures daily *to see* whether these things were so. Therefore many of them believed, along with a number of prominent Greek women and men. (Acts 17:10-12)

His trip from Thessalonica to Berea was a sixty-mile journey. Sixty miles to walk and preach the gospel. While he was there, he was seeing success. It says that "many of them believed."

But then another group made the sixty-mile walk. Not only does love and mission make you walk sixty miles, hate, jealousy, and anger will make you walk that far too. The Jews of Thessalonica were walking after them to mess up Paul's journey. They hated Paul in Thessalonica. They were so jealous of him that they wanted to make his life miserable sixty miles from their hometown: "When the Jews of Thessalonica found out that the word of God had been proclaimed by Paul in Berea also, they came there as well, agitating and stirring up the crowds" (verse 13).

This all started in their hometown, which we read about in verses 5-7:

The Jews, becoming jealous and taking along some wicked men from the market place, formed a mob and set the city in an uproar; and attacking the house of Jason, they were seeking to bring them out to the people. When they did not find them, they *began* dragging Jason and some brethren before the city authorities, shouting, "These men who have upset the world have come here also."

Instead of letting it go and saying, "At least they are out of our city," their jealousy made them walk sixty miles. It takes about forty-five minutes to walk three miles if you're walking at a brisk pace (you do the math) . . . that's at least fifteen hours of walking.

They couldn't let it go. They couldn't be happy that Paul and Silas were out of their town. They had to go and wreak havoc in the other city for them. That is the power of jealousy.

There is a distinction between jealousy and envy. To envy, or covet, is to want something that belongs to another person. The tenth commandment says, "You shall not covet your neighbor's house; you shall not covet your neighbor's wife or his male servant or his female servant or his ox or his donkey or anything that belongs to your neighbor" (Exodus 20:17). In contrast, jealousy is the fear that something we possess will be taken away by another person. Although jealousy can apply to our jobs, our possessions, or our reputations, the word more often refers to anxiety that comes when we are afraid the affections of a loved one might be lost to a rival. We fear that our mates, or perhaps our children, will be lured away by some other person who, when compared to us, seems to be more attractive, capable, and successful.

Jealousy is a form of hatred built upon insecurity and fear.

What were they afraid of? They were losing their influence to the gospel and they projected it on Paul. It was really Jesus, but Paul was the spokesperson, so their insecurity and fear made them go after Paul.

The story is told of a great English preacher, F. B. Meyer, and his struggle with jealousy when another great English preacher, G. Campbell Morgan, returned to England after being in America. Meyer admitted to some friends, "It was easy to pray for the success of Campbell Morgan when he was in America. But when he came back to England and took a church near mine, it was something different. The old Adam in me was inclined to jealousy, but I got my heel upon his head, and whether I felt right toward my friend, I determined to act right."[166]

F. B. Meyer's jealousy is that insecurity that said, *You are close, now I don't want you to do so well. Do well in America but not around the corner.*

As R. T. Kendall wrote in Jealousy, "It takes minimal grace to weep with those who weep; it takes a lot of grace to rejoice with those who rejoice."[167] That second part—rejoicing with those who rejoice—reveals the heart. Rejoicing with those who rejoice is saying they got blessed and you didn't, and that you're okay with that.

Can you and I be joyful when other people are blessed by God? That is a sure sign of jealousy being defeated. Those sixty-mile walkers did not like all those people believing. Instead of rejoicing that lives were being changed, they saw it as Judaism no longer holding the leading voice in their lives because Jesus was.

Let's make it a point today to rejoice with someone. How do we rejoice someone? By loving them. The presence of jealousy means the absence of love.

Paul reminds us in the love chapter: "Love is *large and* incredibly patient. Love is gentle and consistently kind to all. It refuses to be jealous *when blessing comes to someone else*" (1 Corinthians 13:4, TPT).

That's love . . . when you refuse to be jealous.

WHAT DIFFERENCE CAN THE INFILLING OF THE HOLY SPIRIT REALLY MAKE? PART 1

Today's Reading: Acts 18

I had a discussion with a friend who believed the gifts of the Spirit were only for the first century and not for today, that the gifts ceased. That is called "cessation" theology. He keyed in on one gift he said he had a hard time with, and that was what "you Pentecostals call the filling of the Holy Spirit, speaking in tongues. It's the last and least of all the gifts and you make a big deal about it."

I responded, "Let's assume that Paul's list of the gifts in 1 Corinthians 12 *is* written in order of importance." (That's why people say tongues is the least of the gifts, because it's last in the list.) "Even the least gift of God is a great gift from God. Don't ever minimize a gift that God gives because He chose to make it number 9 on your list. I'll take God's number nine over any man's number one. A low gift from God is still a great gift. There is no one who can't be better having a gift from God, even if it is speaking in tongues. Don't minimize God's gift."

This is precisely what happened in the city of Ephesus, which we read about in Acts 18. This is a powerful lesson that actually goes into tomorrow's reading as well.

Ephesus was the number-one city in Asia Minor. It was known for having the greatest marketplace in the world—it really was the world's shopping capital. It was one of the locations for the ancient Olympic festivals, in which people from everywhere would come to see the best athletes in the world compete. It was also the home for some of the most notorious criminals. The temple of Artemis (Diana), which was one of the seven wonders of the world, was an asylum for any criminal.[168] If you committed a crime and if you made it there, you were guaranteed safe haven and off limits to authorities. (So Ephesus had the richest shopping, the greatest athletes, and the most deplorable criminals all there.)

The temple also was a seller of magic charms and superstition items. They had the famous "Ephesian letters." If you carried these papers, you were guaranteed safety for you and your traveling companions. They would also be good luck for your business or believed to get someone to love you—like a love potion. People would come from all over the world to buy little magic charms of Diana. The Goddess Diana was ugly—she was half-animal and half-human. And that temple was full of prostitutes.

Ephesus had all of this—and they had a new church. This church was so important that Timothy pastored it, John the apostle pastored it, and Paul stayed in Ephesus longer than in any other city. But for our purposes, I want you to meet their first pastor, Apollos:

> A Jew named Apollos, an Alexandrian by birth, an eloquent man, came to Ephesus; and he was mighty in the Scriptures. This man had been instructed in the way of the Lord; and being fervent in spirit, he was speaking and teaching accurately the things concerning Jesus, being acquainted only with the baptism of John; and he began to speak out boldly in the synagogue. But when Priscilla and Aquila heard him, they took him aside and explained to him the way of God more accurately. (Acts 18:24-26)

Apollos had the resume for pastoring any church in America. Everyone would have wanted Pastor Apollos. Consider his resume: he was eloquent—people loved to listen to him; he was mighty in the Scriptures—there was no false doctrine; he was fervent in spirit—this is amazing to have an educated man who is fervent in spirit. Usually education dulls the passion.

He was speaking and teaching accurately the things concerning Jesus. He was speaking out boldly in the synagogues. He was unafraid of popular opinion in that city. And finally, Apollos powerfully refuted the Jews in public showing them Jesus was the Christ through the Scriptures.

Apollos was eloquent, mighty in the Scriptures, educated, fervent in spirit, taught the Bible accurately, and proclaimed boldly outside the church. Who wouldn't want this man to be their pastor? That's if you just wanted a church service or a church but not a change in the city. These are great things but not enough for where they were located. This was Ephesus and it needed more. It needed someone with a gift from God. It needed a leader filled with the Holy Spirit.

How do we know that? When Paul left Ephesus, he left a husband-and-wife team, Aquila and Priscilla, there to attend the church services. They listened to an Apollos Sunday sermon, and "when Priscilla and Aquila heard him, they took him aside and explained to him the way of God more accurately" (verse 26).

The "more accurately' goes along with verse 25—that he had been "acquainted only with the baptism of John." The baptism of John is water baptism. So they explained another baptism, one without water but full of fire, a baptism of the Holy Spirit.

A correctable educated man is very rare, but Apollos was. He listened to the visiting couple, and here's the result of his encounter with Priscilla and Aquila: "When he wanted to go across to Achaia, the brethren encouraged him and wrote to the disciples to welcome him; and when he had arrived, he greatly helped those who had believed through grace, for he powerfully refuted the Jews in public, demonstrating by the Scriptures that Jesus was the Christ" (verses 27-28).

They encouraged Apollos to go Achaia, and he became a help to that city. But Ephesus needed help, big time help—and help was on the way. Same city, same church, but a different man—and this time, one filled with the fire of God, one filled with the Holy Spirit.

In Acts 19, we'll see that the apostle Paul came to Ephesus. And something happened not only in church but in the entire city.

What difference can the infilling of the Holy Spirit really make? That's Acts 19.

Day 108

What Difference Can the Infilling of the Holy Spirit Really Make? Part 2

Today's Reading: Acts 19

In Acts 18 we were introduced to the first pastor of the Church of Ephesus, Apollos. This pastor had everything going on: he was eloquent, mighty in the Scriptures, fervent in spirit, committed to Bible accuracy, and spoke boldly in public about Jesus.

Paul's traveling companions, Aquila and Priscilla, heard him preach and noticed something missing in this impressive resume. They took him aside and helped him understand a baptism beyond John's water, which he knew instinctively. They were going to introduce him to the Holy Spirit's baptism.

With his long impressive resume, did that Holy Spirit baptism really make that much of a difference? Can the infilling of the Holy Spirit really add any more to what Pastor Apollos was doing in Ephesus? You be the judge. Not by your theological bent, but by Acts 19.

Our cities don't need another church with Sunday services, our cities need people filled with the Spirit who brings change to lives every day of the week. You can have great church services and yet your city goes on being unchanged. That's what we see in Ephesus. Acts 18 and 19 are an incredible contrast. In Acts 18 we have a preacher with an education, and in Acts 19 we have a preacher with an education and filled with the Spirit.

Apollos leaves. Paul comes. Ephesus is still there, but something is about to happen beyond the Sunday service:

> It happened that while Apollos was at Corinth, Paul passed through the upper country and came to Ephesus, and found some disciples. He said to them, "Did you receive the Holy Spirit when you believed?" And they *said* to him, "No, we have not even heard whether there is a Holy Spirit." And he said, "Into what then were you baptized?" And they said, "Into John's baptism." Paul said, "John baptized with the baptism of repentance, telling the people to believe in Him who was coming

after him, that is, in Jesus." When they heard this, they were baptized in the name of the Lord Jesus. And when Paul had laid his hands upon them, the Holy Spirit came on them, and they *began* speaking with tongues and prophesying. (Acts 19:1-6)

For the next two years, Paul taught and preached. Miracles also came to Ephesus:

God was performing extraordinary miracles by the hands of Paul, so that handkerchiefs or aprons were even carried from his body to the sick, and the diseases left them and the evil spirits went out. But also some of the Jewish exorcists, who went from place to place, attempted to name over those who had the evil spirits the name of the Lord Jesus, saying, "I adjure you by Jesus whom Paul preaches." Seven sons of one Sceva, a Jewish chief priest, were doing this. And the evil spirit answered and said to them, "I recognize Jesus, and I know about Paul, but who are you?" And the man, in whom was the evil spirit, leaped on them and subdued all of them and overpowered them, so that they fled out of that house naked and wounded. This became known to all, both Jews and Greeks, who lived in Ephesus; and fear fell upon them all and the name of the Lord Jesus was being magnified. Many also of those who had believed kept coming, confessing and disclosing their practices. And many of those who practiced magic brought their books together and *began* burning them in the sight of everyone; and they counted up the price of them and found it fifty thousand pieces of silver. So the word of the Lord was growing mightily and prevailing. (verses 11-20)

Let me recap:
• People baptized in the Holy Spirit and prophesying (verses 2-6)
• Extraordinary miracles happen (verse 11)
• Handkerchiefs and aprons healing the sick and evil spirits (verse 12)
• Sons of Sceva—"Jesus I know, Paul I know, but who are you?" (verse 14)
• False preachers exposed (verse 17)
• Jesus being magnified (verse 17)
• Conviction and confession of occult practices (verse 18)
• Occult books burned (verse 19)
• The word of God growing and prevailing (verse 20)
This is what being filled with the Holy Spirit can do. As Andrew Murray said,

"Men ought to seek . . . with their whole heart . . . to be filled with the Spirit of God. . . . Without being filled with the Spirit, it is utterly impossible that an individual Christian or a church can ever live or work as God desires."[169]

Which chapter do you live in? What kind of church do you have? Does your Christianity thrive in church but not in your city? Is it an Acts 18 church or an Acts 19 church? One has good services, the other changes a city. So you be the judge, but it seems the difference between Acts 18 and Acts 19 is the baptism of the Holy Spirit. And when that happens, Ephesus is changed. Without it, you get to do church.

So here's the question: Will you pastor a church or change a city?

A document, a denomination, or a diploma can give someone a pulpit, but it cannot give them the power to change a city. Only the power and infilling of the Spirit can.

Corrie ten Boom once said, "Trying to do the Lord's work in your own strength is the most confusing, exhausting, and tedious of all work. But when you are filled with the Holy Spirit, then the ministry of Jesus just flows out of you."[170]

That's the difference between Acts 18 and Acts 19.

Day 109

NODDING

Today's Reading: Acts 20

Nodding off. We have all done it. In church, a board meeting, a lecture, a conference, while someone is talking, in school on all levels.

I have nodded off while praying and while others are praying.

My favorite nodding-off story is from one of my dear friends in Michigan. While he was at university, his friend always slept in one of their large lecture classes, so he decided to play a trick. Right in the middle of the lecture, he nudged his sleeping friend and told him the professor wanted him to close the class in prayer. And in the middle of the lecture, his friend stood and began praying, thanking God for the class. The professor stopped, the students bowed their heads, and class was over.

The worst seems to be nodding off in church. Why do people fall asleep in church? Pastor and author Chuck Swindoll said that people sleep in church for five reasons:

First, because of *tradition*: when we were youngsters and churches still had pews, we associated sermons with our moms' laps and we were allowed to sleep on them.

Second are *physical factors*: the church is stuffy, poorly lit, hot, not ventilated.

Third are *personal factors*: occasionally we don't get enough of sleep or we are on medication that makes us drowsy.

Fourth is *indifference*: our lack of interest in spiritual things. We can get preoccupied; we start texting folks or scrolling through our social media or newsfeeds.

Fifth is because of a *boring preacher*: poorly organized, rambling, unpassionate, not saying anything. It happens, and it happens too much in our pulpits.[171]

As the great eighteenth-century preacher George Whitefield said, "To preach more than half an hour, a man should be an angel himself or have angels for hearers."[172]

We get a nodding-off story in today's reading. And how embarrassing that

Luke recorded this story for every generation to read across the world and across history? Can you imagine people reading your nodding-off story? This is the only time you're mentioned in the Bible and this is the story you get? I might have registered a complaint!

But then again, I am thankful it's there.

> On the first day of the week, when we were gathered together to break bread, Paul *began* talking to them, intending to leave the next day, and he prolonged his message until midnight. There were many lamps in the upper room where we were gathered together. And there was a young man named Eutychus sitting on the window sill, sinking into a deep sleep; and as Paul kept on talking, he was overcome by sleep and fell down from the third floor and was picked up dead. But Paul went down and fell upon him, and after embracing him, he said, "Do not be troubled, for his life is in him." When he had gone back up and had broken the bread and eaten, he talked with them a long while until daybreak, and then left. They took away the boy alive, and were greatly comforted. (Acts 20:7-12)

I love that this nodding-off story is in the Bible.

Do you know that many of the Puritan preachers of the past would preach for two to three hours? Some actually appointed a person to walk around during the sermon with a giant pole (fishing-like) with a string and a wooden ball to hit people on the head who were nodding off.[173] Can you imagine that being a ministry in your church? For some reason I think people would sign up for the wrong reasons.

This is really important that we have a glimpse and *not* a model of what a New Testament, early-church service looked like. First day of the week, breaking bread, and a long-winded preacher.

Paul preached well into the midnight hour. It's late, so we need to go easy on the kid, Eutychus. He nodded off during the preaching, fell out of the window, died, Paul prayed and resurrected him . . . and then this is classic . . . they ate more and Paul preached more. Amazing!

I love that Eutychus wasn't chastised for sleeping during the apostle Paul's sermon, and I love the resurrection moment after he died. This tells me that if you put yourself in the right place even with the wrong disposition, you are going to get something valuable even if you fall asleep.

Even if you go to church Sunday and nod off, still go! You are going to get something—it could even be a resurrection moment.

Everything worked against poor Eutychus: the preacher was long-winded, it was the middle of the night, he'd just eaten, and he was sitting on a window sill. This was an accident waiting to happen.

You could say the same thing with updated language: the kids were up late, I had to work Saturday, I'm exhausted, the weather is horrible outside . . . Still show up, even being tired, because God will show up.

God still has something for you, even if you nod off.

Day 110

A Story with a Big Gap

Today's Reading: Acts 21

In order to talk about Acts 21 today, I have to tell you a story with a big gap. Technology has made the world a neighborhood. Because of technology, people get famous real fast today. If you have a smart phone, you have a camera. And with social media, you have an audience. And if enough people watch it, you can be viral.

Did you know that 42 percent of the world population is twenty-four years old and younger?[174] If that's true, then technology is their life. All that being possible, remember that viral doesn't last long. It's fake fame. They call it your "fifteen minutes of fame."

The authentic has longevity to it. It's the difference between buying a ten-dollar, knock-off Rolex watch on the streets and the authentic ten thousand dollar one in a high-end jewelry store. Which one lasts longer? The authentic has longevity.

I want to show you someone who lasted a long time because he was authentic. His name was Philip, and his story starts in Acts 6 and goes through Acts 8. Let me tell you his quick viral story and then a huge gap.

He became the first deacon in the church. Then he led an all-city revival in Samaria. He also led to the Lord a number-one occult leader named Simon. Then he got into a conversation with an angel, and the angel sent him to talk to an Ethiopian, who many believe is responsible for the gospel going to Africa. Philip led him to Christ and baptized him. And for his finale . . . after Philip baptized him, he vanished!

Two men went into the water, and only one, the Ethiopian, came out: "When they came up out of the water, the Spirit of the Lord snatched Philip away; and the eunuch no longer saw him" [Acts 8:39]. That seems to be the last time we see Philip.

The book of Acts spans thirty-two years, from AD 30 to AD 62. Acts 6 (Philip's introduction) happened in AD 31. That was when he became a deacon. By the time we reach Acts 21, our chapter for today's reading, it was AD 59. And something crazy happened in AD 59. Philip showed up again!

He reappeared after twenty-eight years: "On the next day we left and came to Caesarea, and entering the house of Philip the evangelist, who was one of the seven, we stayed with him. Now this man had four virgin daughters who were prophetesses" (Acts 21:8-9).

That's the Acts 6–8 Philip. Today we are reading about the twenty-eight-years-later Philip. If it's real, it lasts.

I see three key words in those Acts 21 verses that make him a legacy and a legend: *balance, current, priority.*

Balance: His home life was just as important as his church life. The passage says that Paul was "entering the house of Philip." Philip was thirty years older and his home was a refuge for Paul on his journey. I love that when Paul needed a home to go to in Caesarea, he could go to Philip's. Philip wasn't some bitter, retired pastor who got burned by the ministry or the church. He was not divorced and living with his third wife.

Current: Philip was not just about what God had done in his life, but about what God was still doing. He was called "Philip the evangelist." He was not Philip the deacon or the baptizer. That was chapters 6–8 Philip, this is chapter 21 Philip. If he had the same old names, then it would have been the same old stories.

If anyone would have had old stories, it would have been Philip: "Yeah, I was the first deacon . . ." Every time Philip saw a water baptism in his church, he would have said, "That's great, but let me tell you about what happened at my water baptism thirty years ago." But that wasn't Philip. He was current!

We need to stop with what we *did* and tell what we are we doing *now* for Jesus. We need to be current with the people in our lives. We must never make Christianity ancient when Jesus is alive and active right now!

Priority: good stuff does not come without work. I see good stuff when I read about Philip's children. Two words stand out: *virgin* and *prophetesses.* Those are big words because they describe moral purity and calling. Those two things don't happen on accident. Someone took time with those four girls for them to be virgins and prophetesses.

Philip wasn't just ministering to widows in Acts 6 and to an Ethiopian in Acts 8. He was influencing his daughters in Acts 21. That is a lesson for all of us.

I find it interesting that the book of Acts is not called the book of Truths. It isn't about knowing stuff; it's about doing stuff. Knowledge of the Bible does not guarantee application or action of Bible verses. To know does not mean we will necessarily do.

How do we make an impact after three decades? We pursue balance, stay current, and have strong priorities.

That's why we are reading about Philip in Acts 21. It is a challenge for all of us. It's a challenge for me with my four children. I hope it is for you today too.

Day 111

THE POWER OF YOUR PERSONAL STORY

Today's Reading: Acts 22

The apostle Paul met Jesus on the road to Damascus in Acts 9. That was AD 34. It was an amazing story of Paul encountering the resurrected Jesus. Our chapter today is Acts 22, and we find here, thirteen chapters later, that Paul is telling his story from chapter 9. This was in AD 59, twenty-five years after his conversion, he is still telling about his encounter with Jesus with a freshness and a conviction as though it had happened just the day before.

Paul's story is not in a church after a powerful worship service. He is telling his story in Jerusalem to a hostile mob. Their hostility is in chapter 21, when they beat him and have him in chains. But Paul wants to speak, which is what we read in chapter 22. This is what Paul says to the hostiles:

"It happened that as I was on my way, approaching Damascus about noontime, a very bright light suddenly flashed from heaven all around me, and I fell to the ground and heard a voice saying to me, 'Saul, Saul, why are you persecuting Me?' And I answered, 'Who are You, Lord?' And He said to me, 'I am Jesus the Nazarene, whom you are persecuting.' And those who were with me saw the light, to be sure, but did not understand the voice of the One who was speaking to me. And I said, 'What shall I do, Lord?' And the Lord said to me, 'Get up and go on into Damascus, and there you will be told of all that has been appointed for you to do.' But since I could not see because of the brightness of that light, I was led by the hand by those who were with me and came into Damascus." (verses 6-11)

There's an old saying, "A man who has an argument is always at the mercy of a man who has an experience." Paul had an experience that he is willing to die for. It's so important to him, in fact, that he tells that story three times in the book of Acts. The last time he tells it is in Acts 26, which is AD 62, twenty-eight years after his conversion.

Your story of you and God is powerful. It's not old though you may be. It is important and people need to hear it. And you need to tell it. When you don't know what to say when you are engaged in a talk about religion with someone, tell them your story. Ask them, "Can I tell you my personal story that changed me forever?" Paul did that, and his audience was a tough crowd.

But also, your story never gets old. Tell it even if it's thirty years old. You may be older but God is the same. It's still effective. It seems there is no expiration date on telling it. That's what we see with the apostle Paul.

One of my spiritual heroes and ministry partners is ex-gang member Nicky Cruz. His story is told in *The Cross and the Switchblade*. Nicky was part of the notorious New York City gang, the Mau Maus. David Wilkerson went to New York City in 1958 and won Nicky to the Lord.

I've had the privilege to preach with Nicky around the world, and each time he will tell his conversion story, much as Paul did, with the same passion and conviction. No matter how many years pass since Nicky's story, it's powerful every time. His story has literally brought tens of thousands to Christ.

Don't underestimate the power of your testimony. It's funny, Paul never referred to his Epistles when he talked to people. He never said, "I wrote this letter that one day will be part of the Bible, so you should listen." He told his story. Before you quote the Bible, you may be able to lessen the gap for people by telling them what changed your life.

When you tell your story, as Paul did, you are using one of the weapons God gave us to conquer the devil. Listen to it in the book of Revelation: "They defeated him by the blood of the Lamb and by their testimony" (Revelation 12:11, TLB).

You may think, my story is not that great. It may not be as dramatic as Nicky's or Paul's, but it's still powerful. Consider what Louie Giglio said about testimonies:

> People say all the time "I don't have a good testimony" because they think their story has to involve some dramatic story of change from "bad" to "good." But Jesus didn't come to save people this way. Sin doesn't make us bad, it makes us dead. Jesus came to save by bringing the dead to life. And that's an amazing testimony.[175]

That means, *you too* have an amazing testimony. Share it.

LOSING IT: CHRISTIAN CURSING

Today's Reading: Acts 23

My father used to use a phrase when we were about to get spanked when we were kids—*The bag is getting full.* It meant that a bunch of things we did were adding up, and he couldn't take anymore. Have you ever just got so full that you could not take anymore and you lose it? Words come flying out. Maybe even a profanity or two. Things are said that if somebody heard you, they wouldn't know you're a Christian.

In *Slaying the Giants in Your Life*, David Jeremiah writes on anger:

Road rage, parking rage, air rage, boat rage, surf rage, fishing rage, river rage, pedestrian rage, pavement rage, jogger rage, biker rage, trucker rage, cell phone rage, shopping rage, grocery cart rage, and checkout line rage. I'm told there's such a thing as pew rage. . . . What makes anger so elusive and so incredibly dangerous is that it flares suddenly, powerfully, and irrationally. It takes no counsel of the future. It takes no consideration of personal safety.[176]

This kind of stuff would seem like it would hit new converts. And it does. Can it hit mature Christians? It does. The bag can get full, and we lose it. Can it hit super Christians? Big time believers? How about Paul the apostle? Absolutely. We have a time in Acts when Paul lost it, Christian cursing. Read it for yourself:

Paul, looking intently at the Council, said, "Brethren, I have lived my life with a perfectly good conscience before God up to this day." The high priest Ananias commanded those standing beside him to strike him on the mouth. Then Paul said to him, "God is going to strike you, you whitewashed wall! Do you sit to try me according to the Law, and in violation of the Law order me to be struck?" But the bystanders said, "Do you revile God's high priest?" And Paul said, "I was not aware, brethren, that he was high priest; for it is written, 'YOU SHALL NOT SPEAK EVIL OF A RULER OF YOUR PEOPLE.'" (Acts 23:1-5)

It may not read as bad as it sounds. It *was* bad. Paul got slapped in the face for saying that his conscience was clear before God. It seemed to have a sense of sarcasm in it as he stood before the Council. And then after he was struck in the mouth, Paul lost it. He called Ananias a "whitewashed wall" and then stared him down, saying, "Do you sit to try me . . . and . . . order me to be struck?"

When you call someone a "whitewashed wall," you are saying that person may dress well and look good on the outside but something stinks on the inside. Everyone in Paul's presence knew what it meant. It was a common insult; a curse word to call someone, if that would make sense.

He was saying to them, "You stink!" Or, "This stinks!"

Let me tell you about Paul's week before we get hard on him. It's not to excuse him but to show you that we all can lose it when our bags get full. To explain better, let me use Charles Swindoll's words from his Acts commentary:

> Let me give you a little reminder of the kind of week that the apostle Paul has just had before entering into the situation of chapter 23 of Acts. So far this week he has been beaten by a mob (21:27-32), bound in chains (21:33), had his death demanded by a group of zealous Jews (22:1-22) and then came within a hairsbreadth of being scourged (22:23-29). Now he wants to know for certain why he has been accused by the Jews. . . . Having little sleep, food, or physical care, he stands weary and bruised before the highest Jewish court, the Sanhedrin.[177]

All that added up to this moment. The bag got full, and a flood came out of Paul. Controlling himself no longer, he suddenly poured out a scalding stream of contempt directed at his accusers and judges. In effect, Paul called the judge a stinking hypocrite. This was more flesh than spirit. Correction, it was all flesh and no spirit.

He realized his mistake when a bystander rebuked him. Paul had not been part of this council for some twenty years and would not have known who the high priest was at the present time. Whatever the reason, the damage was done. In a heated moment, Paul said the wrong thing to the wrong person and lost his opportunity to receive a fair trial—but more importantly, he blew his opportunity to explain the gospel.

Now he had nothing but a red mark on his face and was sent back to jail, left with only himself and his condemning thoughts. Imagine Paul in his cell, thinking, *I had a once-in-a-lifetime chance to preach the gospel to the highest Jewish court in the land and I blew it. How stupid it was it to lose my temper. Surely God put me there to touch the Jewish elite, and all I could do was curse them out.*

That night . . . in a prison cell . . . no angel. He didn't deserve one. That is why God is a God of mercy.

Who showed up? The Lord. Paul did not need an angel, he needed a Friend:

On the night *immediately* following, the Lord stood at his side and said, "Take courage; for as you have solemnly witnessed to My cause at Jerusalem, so you must witness at Rome also." (Acts 23:11)

God said nothing about the failure. Instead He spoke to him about the future. When Paul lost it, God continued to stand at his side. Now that is one incredible God. He stands closest when we blow it most.

Have you ever felt like your tongue cost you an opportunity? You don't have plans to lose it, but you know it can happen.

Though our actions can be unpredictable, I am thankful for a God who is very predictable: He is merciful and kind. He is gracious and loving.

Notice one amazing thing about that night. Jesus said to Paul, "So you must witness at Rome also." He gave him encouragement so Paul would know that God sees future for him. I love these words from Brennan Manning: "God not only loves me as I am, but also knows me as I am. Because of this I don't need to apply spiritual cosmetics to make myself presentable to Him."[178]

God loves you unconditionally, as you are and not as you should be, because nobody is as they should be.

A SERMON THAT MADE A KING TELL THE PREACHER TO STOP

Today's Reading: Acts 24

Recently I read a quote about being good stewards of our time and made me sit back and really think about what I do with the time God has given me:

Each new day brings us 24 hours, 1440 minutes, 86,400 seconds, each moment a precious gift from God . . . each calling for us to be good stewards, mindful that one day we must give an account for how we spent the time God loaned us, how effectively we "bought up" the opportunities He provided.[179]

William Penn once said, "Time is what we want most, but what, alas! we use worst."[180]

Acts 24 is about a man who did not use time effectively. The man, Felix, was a king, and he heard a three-point sermon preached by one of the best, the apostle Paul. It was a sermon that made a king tell the preacher to stop:

Some days later Felix arrived with Drusilla, his wife who was a Jewess, and sent for Paul and heard him *speak* about faith in Christ Jesus. But as he was discussing righteousness, self-control and the judgment to come, Felix became frightened and said, "Go away for the present, and when I find time I will summon you." At the same time too, he was hoping that money would be given him by Paul; therefore he also used to send for him quite often and converse with him. But after two years had passed, Felix was succeeded by Porcius Festus. (Acts 24:24-27)

Listen to an old Methodist preacher, Halford Luccock, and what he makes of Felix's mistake:

There is a unique characteristic about time which we overlook: We can lose time, but we can never find it. We have to make it. Felix found lots of moments for what he wanted to do—to satisfy his curiosity about

Paul and open the way for a bribe. We read that he would send for him "pretty frequently" (Acts 24:26), but he found no moments to face the big issue squarely and render a judgment. Such moments are never found. They must be made."[181]

And what we conclude from the passage is that Felix never found time to deal with the most important issue of his life—eternity. Here is how it reads in *The Message*, and it's raw:

As Paul continued to insist on right relations with God and his people, about a life of moral discipline and the coming Judgment, Felix felt things getting a little too close for comfort and dismissed him. "That's enough for today. I'll call you back when it's convenient." (Acts 24:25)

To say, "I don't have time," is like saying, "I don't want to" or "I'm not interested." I read something that is only too true: "Time is a strange commodity. You can't save it, borrow it, loan it, leave it, or take it. You can only do two things with it—use it or lose it."[182]

Felix lost it.

AW Tozer said it like this: "When you kill time, remember that it has no resurrection."[183]

Felix heard a sermon that keyed in on righteousness, self-control, and the judgment to come. And he got frightened. I know that feeling. It happened to me. I was twelve years old and picked up a comic book at a youth camp, called *The Late Great Planet Earth*. It was the kid version of the book by the same name by Hal Lindsey, that dealt with the end times and the judgement to come. I was struck with such conviction and fear that I was not ready for the rapture that I sought out my counselor to get things right with God.

What I learned was this, when you don't do something about the conviction of the soul, the intensity does not get stronger. The opposite happens and it lessens. The more we ignore the voice of God toward obedience, the more difficult it is to act.

When God speaks, respond. When you feel convicted about something, *do* something. Felix got convicted and all he did for two years was listen to Paul but would not respond. It seems he never felt that way again, and by verse 27 he was out and another king came in.

Make use of time wisely, especially if it is dealing with your soul and eternity. As Mother Teresa allegedly said, "Yesterday is gone. Tomorrow has not yet come. We have only today. Let us begin."[184] Amen.

Day 114

OVERRATED

Today's Reading: Acts 25

There are two ways to view yourself—from a photo or in a mirror. Photos are how we wished we looked. Mirrors are how we really look. One is fantasy, the other reality. We can fix our hair and our make-up for a photograph. But when we look into a mirror, that is the real us staring back. Until we see and acknowledge our real selves, we never understand our need for God. In other words, if our lives are constantly about over-inflating ourselves, we undervalue our need for a Savior.

In today's reading, we find a very overrated moment. It's men seeing their photo and not looking into the mirror.

Paul was on trial and about to go to Rome, but not without some overrated people showing up to see the "little man" who was changing the region with the message of Jesus. Look at this one verse in particular. The contrast of people is amazing: "On the next day when Agrippa came together with Bernice amid great pomp, and entered the auditorium accompanied by the commanders and the prominent men of the city, at the command of Festus, Paul was brought in" (Acts 25:23).

In this scene, we have the king of Judea, Agrippa, his wife, Bernice, and Festus, the procurator of Judea. There were the commanders and the prominent men of the city all in this one verse. But there was one other person there also.

In the midst of all this pomp, there was also one man in chains who was changing the world—the apostle Paul. All of those other people looked at their photos and decided how great they were. Paul looked into a mirror and realized what a great sinner he was. And the latter man changed a planet.

It says they came "amid great pomp." An interesting tidbit: *Pomp* is the Greek word *phantasia*, from which we get *fantasy*. The photo was fantasy.

In the Daily Study Bible, William Barclay described the fantasy like this:

There is no more dramatic scene in all the New Testament. It was with splendour that Agrippa and Bernice had come. They would have worn their purple robes of royalty and the gold circlet of the crown on their brows. Doubtless Festus had donned the scarlet robe which a governor wore on state occasions. Close at hand there must have stood Agrippa's court, and also in attendance were the most influential figures of the Jews. Close by Festus there would stand the captains in command of the five cohorts which were stationed at Caesarea; and in the background there would be a solid formation of the tall Roman legionaries on ceremonial guard. Into such a scene came Paul, the little Jewish tent-maker, with his hands in chains; and yet, from the moment he speaks, it is Paul who holds the stage.[185]

Think of the contrast of having a tentmaker in chains and a king in purple, and people forgetting that the man in chains was really the man in authority in that room.

This story made me think about Mother Teresa's speech at the Washington DC prayer breakfast on February 3, 1994. Three thousand people attended the event, mostly DC officials. The president and first lady, Bill and Hillary Clinton, were there, along with the vice president and second lady, Al and Tipper Gore.

Mother Teresa stood to speak, and the room's atmosphere became intensely uncomfortable when she started by saying, "I feel that the greatest destroyer of peace today is abortion, because Jesus said, 'If you receive a little child, you receive me.' So every abortion is the denial of receiving Jesus, the neglect of receiving Jesus."

Journalist Peggy Noonan recounted the scene:

Silence. Cool deep silence in the cool round cavern for just about 1.3 seconds. And then applause started on the right hand side of the room, and spread, and deepened, and now the room was swept with people applauding, and they would not stop for what I believe was for five or six minutes.

But not everyone applauded. The president and the first lady, seated within a few feet of Mother Teresa on the dais, were not applauding. Nor were the vice president and Mrs. Gore. They looked like seated statues at Madame Tussaud's. They glistened in the lights and moved not a muscle, looking at the speaker in a determinedly semi-pleasant way.[186]

Mother Teresa was not part of the Washington elite, but she had a message. She didn't talk about airy, politically correct issues that everyone could get behind. Instead, she dug in and spoke of God-honoring ways to combat abortion. "It was all so unhappily unadorned, explicit, impolitic," Noonan continues. "Mother Teresa seemed neither to notice nor to care. She finished her speech to a standing ovation and left as she had entered, silently, through a parted curtain, in a flash of blue and white. . . . She could do this, of course, because she had a natural and unknown authority."[187]

I love that story and the images it evokes. It looks like Acts 25 between three thousand Agrippas and a little apostle named Paul. Imagine it, a tiny slightly slumped-over woman standing on a box to allow her to be seen over the lectern and addressing some of the most powerful men and women in the world. And packed into that aging frame was enough authority to lay low anyone who dared raise a finger in opposition. You tell me who was the most powerful person in that banquet hall that day? And you tell me who was overrated?

Such is the power of truth when spoken with authority. It silences all the critics.

Day 115

SOMETHING WE NEVER HEARD BEFORE

Today's Reading: Acts 26

In today's reading, the apostle Paul is about to make his defense before king Agrippa before leaving for Rome. It is so powerful that at the end of his speech, the king says to Paul, "In a short time you will persuade me to become a Christian."

What was so powerful about this speech Paul made? He told his conversion experience (this is the third time he tells it in Acts). Always remember that something may be old to you, but it may be new for someone else. D. L. Moody, the great American evangelist in the nineteenth century, was never afraid to tell people about Jesus wherever he was. He had a reputation for it. One day Moody intercepted a man who was hurrying toward a train and asked the stranger, "Are you saved?" The man told him, "That is none of your business." Moody replied, "That is just my business," to which the stranger said, "Then you must be Moody."[188] He was an amazing storyteller who could make the gospel more understandable to his listeners. After one meeting in which he preached, a woman approached him and said, "Moody, I've heard those stories you told, they were repeats." To which Moody replied, "The people need to hear those stories, and I must tell them."[189] And that is what Paul did before the king. He retold his story.

But this time we get something we have never heard before. It is as if Paul's memory was jarred the more he told his conversion story:

> While so engaged as I was journeying to Damascus with the authority and commission of the chief priests, at midday, O King, I saw on the way a light from heaven, brighter than the sun, shining all around me and those who were journeying with me. And when we had all fallen to the ground, I heard a voice saying to me in the Hebrew dialect, "Saul, Saul, why are you persecuting Me? It is hard for you to kick against the goads." (Acts 26:12-14)

Did you hear it? Every time he told his story, it always had Saul. "Saul, why are you persecuting me?" But this time he added the second part, "It is hard for you to kick against the goads."

These are red-letter words, which means Jesus was talking. That is why we have to take note of the addition to Paul's story. The risen Christ told Paul that it was hard for him to kick against the spikes or goads. When a young ox was first yoked, it tried to kick its way out of the yoke. If it was yoked to a one-handed plough, the ploughman held in his hand a long stick with a sharpened end, which he held close to the ox's heels so that every time it kicked, it was caught by the spike. The sharp end would urge the ox in the right direction, but if it wanted to do its own thing, the small pain of being guided was traded for the big pain of being stabbed in the heel for not listening. It was the pain of disobedience.

It seems that Paul was making an important point. He was saying that God was pricking his conscience, and every time he refused and fought against it, it just got harder for him. Many believe that when Paul witnessed Stephen's stoning in Acts 8, that act started the pricking of his conscience. He saw Stephen's face look like an angel. He saw Stephen forgive the men who were forgiving him. He saw Stephen commit himself into the arms of Jesus. To see all this and not turn to Jesus was nothing but kicking against the goads.

When God is trying to get our attention and we keep on going our own way, we join the goad-kicking club. The pain of disobedience is way more costly than the pain of obeying. Every time God asks us to draw closer to Him in obedience, it is our chance either to say yes and all Him to guide us to our destination or to say no and have Jesus discipline us to our intended destination.

This is really important. With God, He is going to get you to your intended destination. So you can do it the easy way or the hard way.

What was Paul's destination? "I am sending you to them to open their eyes and turn them from darkness to light, and from the power of Satan to God, so that they may receive forgiveness of sins and a place among those who are sanctified by faith in me" (Acts 26:17-18, NIV).

God said you chose the sharp goads but we still got there.

It's nice to get where God wants us to be. It's better to do it without getting the sharp end of a goad. It's so much easier to listen to the voice of God than to be stubborn.

Day 116

THE DAY THE CONVICT BECAME A CAPTAIN

Today's Reading: Acts 27

Today, we take a boat ride on some rough waters in Acts 27. This boat has 276 on board, most of them prisoners. The apostle Paul is below deck in shackles and on his way to Rome. At one point the most famous prisoner on the boat tells the professional seafarers, "I wouldn't go that direction." And his advice is rejected vehemently:

> Paul *began* to admonish them, and said to them, "Men, I perceive that the voyage will certainly be with damage and great loss, not only of the cargo and the ship, but also of our lives." But the centurion was more persuaded by the pilot and the captain of the ship than by what was being said by Paul. (Acts 27:9-11)

Paul's warning is that if they continue on this journey, they will experience damage and great loss. They probably hear him and think, *What does a religious man know about sailing?*

They do not listen to the Christian and this is what happens:

> Before very long there rushed down from the land a violent wind, called Euraquilo; and when the ship was caught *in it* and could not face the wind, we gave way to *it* and let ourselves be driven along. . . . The next day as we were being violently storm-tossed, they began to jettison the cargo; and on the third day they threw the ship's tackle overboard with their own hands. Since neither sun nor stars appeared for many days, and no small storm was assailing *us*, from then on all hope of our being saved was gradually abandoned. When they had gone a long time without food, then Paul stood up in their midst. (Acts 27:14-21)

At some point, some Einstein on the crew goes, "Where is the guy who told us not to go on this journey? Maybe we should listen to him?"

They pull the prisoner up on deck. Now they want to hear from Paul. They have an awakening.

That is what an awakening is in our country—it's when people want to hear from God again and not the professionals: not the politicians, not the news reporters, not Hollywood celebrities or athletes. They says, "Let's hear what God has to say."

The sailors are at that place of desperation and want to hear from Paul. This is what he tells them:

Men, you ought to have followed my advice and not to have set sail from Crete and incurred this damage and loss. *Yet* now I urge you to keep up your courage, for there will be no loss of life among you, but *only* of the ship. For this very night an angel of the God to whom I belong and whom I serve stood before me, saying, "Do not be afraid, Paul; you must stand before Caesar; and behold, God has granted you all those who are sailing with you." Therefore, keep up your courage, men, for I believe God that it will turn out exactly as I have been told. But we must run aground on a certain island. [Acts 27:21-26]

When Paul says, "An angel of . . . God . . . stood before me," that means God gave Paul a word for the ship. The captive is now the captain! The one they put in the bowel of the ship is now being listened to. Wait till you hear the answer for their survival: in verse 44, Paul tells them that when the ship breaks up, they are to grab hold of a plank and float to shore.

Holding on to a piece of wood is going to get you through your storm. I have a sneaky suspicion you may have caught where I'm going with this. The only chance for America and the impending storm we will face is still a piece of wood—a two-thousand-year-old piece of wood on which the Son of God died, the cross.

And there's enough wood for everybody. Paul is speaking to his enemies. Paul is helping those survive who made him a prisoner. All 276 make it to shore during a terrible storm. The storm allows the captive to become captain. And he guides the ship and those on board to safety. How does Paul get this?

It is like two men who are on a beach gazing out at sea. One man says, "I see a ship." The friend replies that he doesn't see anything. The first man persists in saying he sees a ship. The friend says, "Well, I have 20/20 vision and I don't see anything." To which the first man says, "Yes, but I have binoculars. And there *is* a ship."

The godly have binoculars. They know what is coming.

Many times the world won't listen to the church until the storm comes and until hope is lost. And then we listen as we stand up with the Word from God. The world won't listen to us sitting in our church seats. But they were listening to Paul while drenched in water, on deck of a boat being battered by a storm.

God has a way of using storms to bring us to places in our lives and in our hearts that we would not have gone to on our own. It's called providence. God using circumstances and directing our steps. When hope is lost in our society, there is wood that can get us to safety. Grab a plank. It is the cross of Jesus.

Forty-Three-Mile Friends

Today's Reading: Acts 28

In today's reading we look at the last chapter of Acts, chapter 28. And we are going to discover real friends today—forty-three-mile friends.

When talking about friendship, John Churton Collins said, "In prosperity our friends know us; in adversity we know our friends."[190] In Acts 28 Paul is in adversity. He is in Rome where he will meet death. But something happens that can be overlooked. Acts 28:15 shows an extraordinary act of friendship: "The brethren, when they heard about us, came from there as far as the Market of Appius and Three Inns to meet us; and when Paul saw them, he thanked God and took courage."

Let me give you some timelines: Acts 21–23 took place in AD 59; Acts 24–28 took place in AD 62. We are dealing with a very tough three years of prison for the apostle Paul, who has been defending himself against the angry mobs and has faced an unexpected amount of tragedies and also miracles before he lands in the final place he will live, Rome.

Let me take you through his journey and show you how important Acts 28:15 is in Paul's life. It all starts getting crazy in Acts 21. Paul will never again be free from chains after Acts 21:30. He ends up on an island from a shipwreck. While building a fire, a snake bites him, and yet God protects him. But because God heals him from the bite, everyone thinks he is a god. He ends up staying on the island for three months until he finally gets to Rome . . . and Acts 28:15 shows up. People who love Paul and care about him come to see him. They take an important journey to get there.

Let me explain. Apii or Appius is forty-three Roman miles (roughly thirty-nine-and-a-half contemporary miles) from Rome.[191] That means Christians walked forty-three miles to be with Paul, forty-three miles to encourage the apostle.

I love that Luke, the writer of Acts, uses the Greek word that translates *to meet us*. This Greek word is of people going to meet a general or a king or a conqueror. They go to meet Paul as one of God's generals.

This is so important to Paul. He thanks God and takes courage. It lifts his heart and spirit, because he realizes he isn't alone. The body of Christ is there to encourage him.

Christians are never alone. You have a family called the church. Every time someone makes a sacrifice to call you, and you are encouraged, you have forty-three-mile friends. Every time you are visited in the hospital, you have forty-three-mile friends. When someone sends you a Bible verse or someone prays for you, you have a forty-three-mile friend. If you ever have someone give you a hug when you are down in the dumps, you have a forty-three-mile friend.

To be a forty-three-mile friend like these no-name-people who encourage Paul, that costs time. If they walked a quick pace and made a mile every 20 minutes, that adds up to about 14-15 hours of walking, just to encourage Paul. And it's sacrificial. It takes time out of their schedules and lives.

It's such a quick part of the Scripture—so quick that we glance over Appius to Rome without ever giving it a thought, but it's important and telling about those Christians. They were forty-three-mile friends.

I have forty-three-mile friends in my life who have made journeys to encourage me when I did not know if I had the strength to go on. Think about your friends. Your real friends, not your "friends" on social media. A court in Florida recently made a decision on the legal definition of "friendship." It was based on this question: "Are your friends on Facebook actually your friends?" According to an appeals court, legally, Facebook friends aren't necessarily your friends. The court dove into this question because of a judge who may have been required to recuse herself from a case—because an attorney involved in that case was friends with the judge on Facebook. However, the court ruled that a recusal was not necessary, because they said Facebook friends are not really friends.[192]

Thank God someone is getting it right. Just because you follow someone, just because you like someone, just because you friend someone doesn't mean you have a friend.

Real friends go forty-three miles and not just hit "follow" or "friend."

What About the People Who Have Never Heard the Gospel? Will They Go to Hell?

Today's Reading: Romans 1

"What about the people in other countries who have never heard the gospel? Will they go to hell?" That was the question one of our worship band members asked me. I was finishing up a late meeting at the church, and he was finishing up practice. We met each other in the lobby and he dropped that question on me. More specifically, he said, "We preach the gospel here, but what about for all the other countries around the world? How will they know what we know?"

Today's reading in Romans 1 is where I began with this young man's legit and important question.

I wish I were a universalist and an annihilationist, but I can't be, based on what the Bible teaches. A universalist says everyone goes to heaven no matter how they interpret God. All of humanity will be in heaven. And an annihilationist says there is only heaven and no hell. Those who are evil simply cease to exist. They remove the final judgment. I wish I were both, then the answer to a question like this is easy. However, the Bible does address this question. Here in the book of Romans is where we start.

This is how I explained the difference between the band member in the local church, and the tribesman in a remote part of the Amazon or a nomad in the Sahara who have never heard the Good News. It's all in two verses: one about God; one about humanity.

Let's start with humanity: "That which is known about God is evident within them; for God made it evident to them. For since the creation of the world His invisible attributes, His eternal power and divine nature, have been clearly seen, being understood through what has been made, so that they are without excuse" (Romans 1:19-20). Paul says God has two witnesses on the planet: one is internal and the other is external. Both creation and conscious speak about God—we see this very clearly in this Romans passage. It is the evidence of God "without" and "within." In other words, what is inside us and what is outside of us.

German philosopher Emmanuel Kant spoke of believing in God because of two realities that converted him—"the starry heavens above and the moral law of God within."[193]

In addressing the evidence "without," a story about Sir Isaac Newton and his atheist friend serves as a wonderful example. Newton's friend did not believe in God, but preferred to take the position that the universe just happened. One day the friend was visiting Newton and Newton showed him a model of the solar system. The sun, the planets, and the moons were all in place. The sizes of the spheres were in proportion, and the planets and the satellites revolved around the sun at their relative speeds. The friend admired the model. "It's intriguing," he said. "Who made it?"

"Nobody," said Newton. "It just happened."[194]

Newton was saying that in order to have a design in the universe, we need a designer of the universe. A big bang didn't do it, but a big God did.

The "within" argument is the moral law. The distinguishing between right and wrong is innate within humanity. This was the whole premise of C. S. Lewis's conversion and his must-read book, *Mere Christianity*.

What is not clear is how much information the person gets within and without? If a person has only these two witnesses, though, I do know that it is enough to be judged by and not have any excuses.

For all of us in the west, I believe we will be judged more severely than the person in an Indian remote village, because we have had the gospel made clear to us almost our entire lives.

That is the verse about humanity. Now the verse about God: "Shall not the Judge of all the earth do right?" (Genesis 18:25, AMP).

This verse is so powerful. Abraham said this about God. God will do what is right with what He has given humanity to believe.

From conscious and creation will they know Jesus, was God in the flesh, came from a virgin, died for the sins of humanity on the cross, rose from the dead, and ascended to the right hand of God the Father? That I don't know. It doesn't seem so. But whatever they get will be enough for them to be judged by and they will be without excuse.

Day 119

WHY THE PREACHER GOT RUN OUT OF TOWN

Today's Reading: Romans 2

Haddon Robinson tells the story during the American frontier days, there was a settlement in the West whose citizens were engaged in the lumber business. As the town grew, the people wanted a church, so they built a building and called a minister.

One afternoon the preacher spotted some of his parishioners dragging logs, which had floated down the river from another village upstream, onto the bank. The owner's stamp was marked on the end of each log. To his shock and dismay, the minister saw his members pulling in the logs and sawing off the ends where the owner's stamps appeared.

The following Sunday he preached on the commandment "Thou shall not steal." At the close of the service, people lined up and offered enthusiastic congratulations: "Wonderful message, Pastor." "Mighty fine preaching." "Keep up the good work." It wasn't the response he expected, so the following Sunday, he preached on the same commandment, but gave it a different ending: "Yes, thou shall not steal," he said. "But thou shall also not cut off the end of thy neighbor's logs." When he got through, the congregation ran him out of town.[195] While the church shouted amen to "thou shalt not steal," they gave the pastor a one-way ticket when the "thou" became "you."

Romans 2 is about to get close to the heart of us all. Like that old west pastor, the apostle Paul is about to address us cutting off the end of the logs with the owner's stamps on them:

> You have no excuse, everyone of you who passes judgment, for in that which you judge another, you condemn yourself; for you who judge practice the same things. And we know that the judgment of God rightly falls upon those who practice such things. But do you suppose this, O man, when you pass judgment on those who practice such things and do the same *yourself*, that you will escape the judgment of God? [Romans 2:1-4]

Later on, Paul says: "You, therefore, who teach another, do you not teach yourself? You who preach that one shall not steal, do you steal? You who say that one should not commit adultery, do you commit adultery?" (Romans 2:21-22).

The apostle Paul is challenging us to be careful about condemning others for what we do ourselves. That is what that congregation was doing who ran their pastor out of town. They cheered about not stealing but were doing it themselves. They loved the sermon on others stealing but not about their own stealing.

It's like the saying I heard recently, "We are very good lawyers for our own mistakes and very good judges for the mistakes of others."[196]

Paul's challenge is for us to look no further than our own lives. Because the church in Rome sees the sin issue as what others do but not what they do, Paul has to get them—and us—to practice some self-introspection.

When you speak as Paul did, people will cry out, "You're judging me!" Always remember this: correction is called judgment by those who don't want to change their behavior. When someone says, "You are judging me," they are using a smoke screen to keep them from having to change.

Challenging people's immoral lifestyle is not popular today. Rick Warren diagnoses why it's a problem in our country. Consider these profound words: "Our culture has accepted two huge lies: The first is that if you disagree with someone's lifestyle, you must fear or hate them. The second is that to love someone means you agree with everything they believe or do. Both are nonsense. You don't have to compromise convictions to be compassionate."[197]

Verse 4 is what blows me away in Romans 2. Paul says essentially, "What's incredible about God is that you will see His goodness on your life while you are living a duality of life, and yet God is still there." Paul is saying that we must not misinterpret the goodness of God as the approval of God on our actions. God's goodness is to get us to turn from our wicked ways to Him.

Here is the verse in the Contemporary English Version: "You surely don't think much of God's wonderful goodness or of his patience and willingness to put up with you. Don't you know that the reason God is good to you is because he wants you to turn to him?"

As someone once said, "Truth is like surgery. It hurts but it cures. Lies are like painkillers. It gives instant relief but has side effects for a long time." Not only does our society need an injection of truth, but you and I need it too. We need it to start with you and me.

THE PLACE WHERE SIN SHOWS UP MOST

Today's Reading: Romans 3

Rabbi Joseph Telushkin has lectured throughout the United States on the positive and negative impact of words. He often asks audiences if they can go twenty-four hours without saying any unkind words about, or to, another person. Within each audience only a few people raise their hands. He tells them,

> All of you who can't answer yes . . . must recognize how serious a problem you have. Because if I asked you to go for twenty-four hours without drinking liquor, and you said, "I can't do that," I'd tell you, "Then you must recognize that you're an alcoholic." And if I asked you to go for twenty-four hours without smoking a cigarette, or drinking coffee, and you said, "That's impossible," that would mean that you're addicted to nicotine or caffeine. Similarly, if you can't go for twenty-four hours without saying unkind words about or to others, then you've lost control over your tongue."[198]

We have a tongue issue because we have a heart issue. And every person's heart is faced with a serious issue called *sin*. It isn't until the heart is changed that our words will change. And the only one who can change our heart and fix the sin issue is God.

Romans 3 reminds us that all of humanity has a sin issue that needs to be fixed: "We have already made the charge the Jews and Gentiles alike are all under the power of sin. As it is written: 'There is no one righteous, not even one'" (verses 9-10, NIV).

No one is righteous . . . not even one. Regarding sin in the world, Reinhold Niebuhr said something profound: "Most of the evil in this world does not come from evil people. It comes from people who consider themselves good."[199] We are all sinners. No one is good.

A British newspaper editor once asked G. K. Chesterton, "What's wrong with the world?" Without missing a beat Chesterton replied simply, "I am."[200] Chesterton realized that sin is devastating to the individual and to humanity. How devastating?

Charles Finney was right when he said: "Sin is the most expensive thing in the universe. . . . If it is forgiven sin, it cost God his only Son. . . . If it is unforgiven sin, it cost the sinner his soul and an eternity in hell."[201]

But this is the incredible part. Right after Paul reminds us that we are all under sin, and that no one is excluded from this pronouncement, he makes a huge revelation and shows us where sin shows up consistently. You have to pay attention to see it. Remember Paul has just said in verse 10 that "there is none righteous, no not one."

Now he says in verses 11-15:

There is no one who understands; there is no one who seeks God. All have turned away, they have together become worthless; there is no one who does good, not even one. "Their throats are open graves; their tongues practice deceit." "The poison of vipers is on their lips. Their mouths are full of cursing and bitterness." "Their feet are swift to shed blood." (NIV)

The apostle Paul lists five different parts of the body that are the most common vehicles of sin: throats, tongues, lips, mouths, and feet. Ready for this? Four of the five body parts relate to the tongue.

Wow! That small member of our body is the biggest dispenser of our sin nature. Our mouths can be used to destroy lives. Adolf Hitler's manifesto was *Mein Kampf*. Someone once calculated every word in that book and said for every word, Hitler killed 320 lives. They calculated that 60 million people died in World War II, and that book has 187,000 words in it.[202] His words killed millions of people.

Whatever is in your heart will find its way to the place where sin shows up most. That's why we need God in our hearts and sin out of our hearts. A. W. Tozer said it like this: "What's closest to your heart is what you talk about and if God is close to your heart, you'll talk about Him."[203]

We need God in our hearts today.

Day 121

STEP IN STEPS

Today's Reading: Romans 4

Romans 4 is just as much a faith chapter as is Hebrews 11, which gets called the hall of faith. Romans 4 gives us a ground level look of the steps of faith of the father of faith, Abraham. Paul shows us a specific situation Abraham had to walk out in faith and how he did it. And then Paul encourages us to "follow in the steps of the faith of our father Abraham" (verse 12).

Let me take you to the dead of winter in the Midwest. Overnight a foot of snow has fallen, and today, you have to trudge through that snow as you walk to the train or bus. In that much snow, you don't step in fresh snow, you step in steps—the footprints of people who went before you. They left a track that makes it a bit easier for you to negotiate the terrain. The easiest way to walk then is to put your feet where feet have been. Step in their steps and it makes the journey easier. So let's look for those steps that Abraham already laid for us, and step in his steps.

Let's first refresh our memories about the story that underlies Abraham's steps of faith. God promised Abraham and Sarah, his wife, a baby. The problem: he was one hundred years old and she was ninety. I'm not a doctor, but I think this is a problem . . . unless you have an even bigger God involved in the situation. And Abraham did.

What steps did Abraham leave for us to walk in?

First, faith doesn't ignore the raw and discouraging facts that are staring us in the face. Real faith is able to look at what really exists. This is the kind of faith Abraham had: "Without becoming weak in faith he contemplated his own body, now as good as dead since he was about a hundred years old, and the deadness of Sarah's womb" (Romans 4:19).

Abraham contemplated. That means he looked at the facts carefully and with great deliberation, looking at every possibility, leaving nothing out. Here is what Abraham knew to be the facts: In regards to himself, at one hundred years old, his body was as good as dead. Regarding his wife, Sarah, at ninety years old, her womb was dead.

Smith Wigglesworth once said, "I am not moved by what I see. I am moved only by what I believe."[204] Faith looks at the situation and faces it. And Abraham's situation looked impossible.

Second, faith finds good footing in God's Word. I have a Bible that puts in capital letters any Old Testament passage quoted in the New Testament. In verses 17 and 18, that happens twice. It is Abraham going back to what God told him. The two times the capital letters are used are God speaking to Abraham:

> [As it is written, "A FATHER OF MANY NATIONS I HAVE MADE YOU"] in the presence of Him whom he believed, even God, who gives life to the dead and calls into being that which does not exist. In hope against hope he believed, so that he might become a father of many nations according to that which had been spoken, "SO SHALL YOUR DESCENDANTS BE."

As it was written about Abraham, "A father of many nations I have made you." That is future. But in the present, he was father of no one.

You can be honest about what the situation looks like. But you then must find yourself speaking more about what God says to your situation in the Word of God. Staying close to God's Word will help you speak into future instead of complaining about your present circumstances. Fill your mouth with what He promised, His Word.

Finally, the God you believe in will determine your faith level. There is a biblical phrase used many times about Abraham: "Abraham believed God." It is used all over the Bible—from Genesis to Romans, Galatians to James. But what makes the phrase valid is that there is another phrase associated with Abraham in the Bible just like this one. It's in 2 Chronicles, Isaiah, and James. And I think it has something to do with the first phrase. The second phrase determined his faith level. It is *friend of God*. Friend of God makes belief in God easy.

Abraham could say, "Regardless of what circumstances I am facing, my Friend is with me." The God Abraham believed in was his Friend. He trusted his Friend.

That's why when you connect Abraham's raw circumstances with his faith in his Friend, you get these verses that *The Passion Translation* makes come alive:

> In spite of being nearly one hundred years old when the promise of having a son was made, his faith was so strong that it could not be undermined by the fact that he and Sarah were incapable of conceiving

a child. He never stopped believing God's promise, for he was made strong in his faith *to father a child*. And because he was mighty in faith and convinced that God had all the power needed to fulfill his promises, Abraham glorified God! (Romans 4:19-20, TPT)

Edna Butterfield tells one of my favorite stories of what faith is. Her husband, Ron, works with teenage children who have severe learning disabilities. And Ron started looking at his students' capabilities rather than their limitations, so he got them to play chess, restore furniture, and repair electrical appliances. Most important, he taught them to believe in themselves. Young Bobby was one of those boys. And he soon proved how well he had learned that last lesson of belief. One day he brought in a broken toaster to repair. He carried the toaster tucked under one arm and a half-loaf of bread under the other.[205]

That's faith.

The broken toaster of Romans 4—that's the age of Abraham and Sarah.

The loaf of bread of Romans 4—that's painting the baby's room blue, because it's going to be a boy, and they will name that little loaf of bread . . . Isaac.

A PRAISE THAT DOESN'T HAPPEN IN CHURCH

Today's Reading: Romans 5

In today's reading, we land on Romans 5 and see a different kind of praise. A praise that I don't think is done in church. It's a new praise for your repertoire.

We have so much to praise God for. In Romans 5:1-2, Paul reminds us of the greatest thing to thank God for: "Having been justified by faith, we have peace with God through our Lord Jesus Christ, through whom also we have obtained our introduction by faith into this grace in which we stand; and we exult in hope of the glory of God" (Romans 5:1-2).

The Message takes that last phase, *exult in hope of the glory of God*, and paraphrases it this way: "standing tall and shouting our praise." We praise God that we have peace with God through Jesus. That last part is really important: "through our Lord Jesus Christ." Not through our promises or our good deeds, but through what Jesus has done on the cross. We don't get anything from God unless it is through Jesus Christ.

In June 2006, Warren Buffett, the world's second-richest man at the time, announced that he would donate 85 percent of his forty-four-billion-dollar fortune to five charitable foundations. Commenting on this extreme level of generosity, Buffett said: "There is more than one way to get to heaven, but this is a great way."[206]

Sorry, Warren, that just isn't true. You may know a lot about investments, but you don't know much about heaven. Religion says: *If I change, God will love me.* The gospel says: *God's love changes people.* This is something we should praise God about.

But it isn't this praise that I struggle with. My problem is with the second praise:

Having been justified by faith, we have peace with God through our Lord Jesus Christ, through whom also we have obtained our introduction by faith into this grace in which we stand; and we exult in hope of the glory of God. And not only this, but we also exult in our tribulations, knowing that tribulation brings about perseverance; and perseverance, proven character; and proven character, hope. (Romans 5:1-4)

Or as *The Message* says: "We continue to shout our praise even when we're hemmed in with troubles, because we know how troubles can develop passionate patience in us." Are you kidding me? I can praise Him for grace and peace—but not for tribulations. *Exult* in our tribulations?

How can I exalt when things are falling apart?

How can I worship when I'm crying on the inside?

How can I dance when I am hurting?

But this is what I have learned. First, praise has nothing to do with music. Music may help, but we don't need it to praise God. This praise goes deeper than a melody line. When we praise God in trials, it means we know something *beyond* the music. We see a little further than the present.

What do we see? That something is on the other side of our painful situations, for "tribulation brings about . . ." something that could not come from music. Paul says that proven character is on the other side. Perseverance is on the other side. Hope is on the other side.

That means the music in our church doesn't have to be that good to praise Him. We can praise God for the other side of our painful tribulation.

Romans 5:1-2 praise happens every Sunday. It's the Romans 5:3-4 praise at which I need to get better.

Perhaps you've heard the saying, "There are two times to praise the Lord: when you feel like it, and when you don't." Basically when we praise we are saying what David said in Psalm 34:1: "I will bless the LORD at all times; His praise shall continually be in my mouth."

Let's add Romans 5:3-4 praise to our repertoire this Sunday—and every day. Even in our tribulations, we can exult God.

THERE'S A NEW KING ON THE THRONE

Today's Reading: Romans 6

There is probably no better chapter in the New Testament that deals with the relationship of the Christian and sin than Romans 6. And that relationship is . . . there is no relationship. You have victory because sin is no longer in charge. There's a new King on the throne of your heart.

C. H. Spurgeon was right when he said, "Sin murdered Christ; will you be a friend to it? Sin pierced the heart of the Incarnate God; can you love it?"[207] We can't be a friend to sin. We have a new friend and our new friend is now our King:

> Do not let sin reign in your mortal body so that you obey its lusts, and do not go on presenting the members of your body to sin *as* instruments of unrighteousness; but present yourselves to God as those alive from the dead, and your members *as* instruments of righteousness to God. For sin shall not be master over you, for you are not under law but under grace. (Romans 6:12-14)

"Do not let sin reign in your mortal body" (verse 12). The word *reign* is a word for a king or royalty who is in charge of a nation and has the throne. Paul was saying that when you got saved, sin was dethroned from the throne of your heart, and now King Jesus sits as the sole authority and He has no rivals. There may be fighters but no rivals. There may be a coup here and there, but no one ultimately defeats this new King.

Sin may be present and sin may fight, but sin will never again be king of your heart. Just because sin fights doesn't mean it is in charge. Always remember that.

Our sin leaves us in a knot, and we need God's help to unties it. And that's what happens at salvation. He unravels sin and gives us new life. He undoes the knot of sin. And yet humanity tries to redefine the very thing that Christ died for and set us free from.

• Man calls it an accident; God calls it an abomination.
• Man calls it a blunder; God calls it blindness.

- Man calls it a defect; God calls it a disease.
- Man calls it a chance; God calls it a choice.
- Man calls it an error; God calls it an enmity.
- Man calls it a fascination; God calls it a fatality.
- Man calls it an infirmity; God calls it an iniquity.
- Man calls it a luxury; God calls it a leprosy.
- Man calls it a liberty; God calls it lawlessness.
- Man calls it a trifle; God calls it a tragedy.
- Man calls it a mistake; God calls it a madness.
- Man calls it a weakness; God calls it willfulness.

Paul goes on to say in verse 13: "Do not go on presenting the members of your body to sin *as* instruments of unrighteousness; but present yourselves to God as those alive from the dead, and your members *as* instruments of righteousness to God."

This verse is important for our understanding of the new King in our hearts. Paul tells us three important things:

1. We surrender to a person. We do not surrender to an idea, a denomination, a church, Protestantism, or Catholicism. It says, "present yourselves to God." No church can fight off sin as King Jesus can.

2. We surrender for a purpose. Paul said, "as instruments" not as ornaments. There is a purpose in our surrender, it leads to something—righteousness. What are the instruments? The members of our bodies. We surrender our minds, our hands, our creativity, our eyes—all to the King.

3. We surrender at a price. Don't miss the part that says "as those alive from the dead." There is something costly here. Jesus paid the price for our resurrection. As Ravi Zacharias said:

"Jesus Christ did not come to make bad people good, but to make dead people alive."[208] We were dead and King Jesus gave us new life. Something sin never did. In fact, listen to what R. C. Sproul reminds us about sin: "I have committed many sins in my life. Not one of my sins has ever made me happy."[209]

But our new King brings joy to us and tells us sin is not in charge any more. *The Message* translation captures well the concept of sin being rendered powerless when Jesus comes into our lives:

You must not give sin a vote in the way you conduct your lives. Don't give it the time of day. Don't even run little errands that are connected with that old way of life. Throw yourselves wholeheartedly and full-time—remember, you've been raised from the dead!—into God's way of doing things. Sin can't tell you how to live. After all, you're not living under that old tyranny any longer. You're living in the freedom of God. [Romans 6:12-14]

Wow! Sin doesn't get a vote and sin can't tell us how to live. There's a new King on the throne.

Day 124

THE INFECTION IN ALL OF US

Today's Reading: Romans 7

The Nuremberg war-crime trials were trials of some of the most wicked men who ever lived. These men were responsible for the deaths of six million Jews during the Holocaust. One of those men was Adolf Eichmann, who killed millions of people in the concentration camps during World War II.

Holocaust survivor Yehiel Dinur witnessed Eichmann's trial. He entered the courtroom and stared at Eichmann behind a bullet-proof glass. The courtroom was hushed as victims confronted their butcher. Dinur began to sob and collapsed onto the floor. Many assumed he was overcome by anger or bitterness. But Dinur later explained to Mike Wallace on *60 Minutes* that he had been overtaken by a horrific realization: "I was afraid about myself," he said. "I saw that I am capable to do this I am . . . exactly like he [Eichmann]."

Wallace concluded the segment with these thoughts: "How was it possible for a man to act as Eichmann acted? "Was he a monster? A madman? Or was he perhaps something even more terrifying: Was he normal?" He closed by telling his viewers that "Eichman is in all of us."[210]

In a moment of chilling clarity, Yehiel Dinur saw beneath the skin. We are not morally neutral. We've often heard the question, "Why do good people do bad things?" The more appropriate question is, "Why do bad people do good things?" As Augustine said: "My sin was all the more incurable because I did not think myself a sinner."[211]

This is what Romans 7 is all about. It's about an infection that's in all of us, and it's called sin. And Paul makes it personal, by starting with himself (see verses 9, 11, 13-14, 17). He reminds us that the great apostle is a great sinner.

Sin is the potential evil in all of us. No one has sinned in such a way that others couldn't also sin. We are all infected by the devastating disease called sin.

Listen to how Paul speaks of this disease:

I'm a mystery to myself, for I want to do what is right, but end up doing what my moral instincts condemn. And if my behavior is not in line with my desire, my conscience still confirms the excellence of the law. And now I realize that it is no longer my true self doing it, but the unwelcome intruder of sin in my humanity. For I know that nothing good lives within the flesh of my fallen humanity. The longings to do what is right are within me, but will-power is not enough to accomplish it. My lofty desires to do what is good are dashed when I do the things I want to avoid. So if my behavior contradicts my desires to do good, I must conclude that it's not my true identity doing it, but the unwelcome intruder of sin *hindering me from being who I really am.* (Romans 7:15-20, TPT)

Listen to verse 18 again: "I know that nothing good lives within." This is a huge statement. Why? If *Paul* reached this conclusion, we *all* must reach that conclusion.

Have you reached that conclusion about yourself? Have you ever, without hesitation or reservation, put yourself before God and said, "I do here and now solemnly believe and attest and vow and declare that in me no good thing dwells"?

This is what holds people back from being born again. They still hold on to the idea that we are all basically good people. Think about it. Why would God have to send His Son Jesus to die the awful death on the cross if you and I are basically good and our goodness is what will get us to heaven? If that idea is true, then God is guilty of the worst case of child abuse in human history. It's illogical.

Someone once said, "God formed man, sin deformed him, education informs him, religion may reform him, but only Jesus Christ can transform him." The transformation starts with the acknowledgment that "no good thing dwells within me." Sin deceives us by making us think that we are good and that our goodness impresses God.

Let me tell you what "religion" is. It's humans exhausting themselves to impress God enough that God will invite them to His house in heaven to live forever. It's the believe that we can influence God.

Watchman Nee tells a story of watching a man drown while an expert swimmer who had all the ability to save the man watched from the dock without moving. When it looked as though the man was going down for the last time, the swimmer jumped in to save him. The swimmer explained his motive to Nee, saying that going earlier would have drowned them both. "A drowning man cannot be saved until he is utterly exhausted and ceases to make the slightest effort to save himself,"[212] he said.

When we give up, then God takes over. He is waiting till we are at the end of our strength and we realize we cannot defeat the sin inside of us by sheer will power.

Here is how Romans 7 ends. The word *I* is all over this chapter until Paul lets out a final cry from penultimate verse: "What an agonizing situation I am in! So who has the power to rescue this miserable man from the unwelcome intruder of sin and death?" (verse 24, TPT).

And then no more I's. The rescuer jumps in the water to save the drowning man who's going under. Paul closes out the chapter by showing us who can rescue us: "The answer, thank God, is that Jesus Christ can and does" (verse 25, MSG).

Day 125

BAD NEWS, GOOD NEWS

Today's Reading: Romans 8

Anybody ever ask you, "I have good news and I have bad news, which do you want to hear first?" I always say, "The bad news first." Because I want to finish on a high note. So that's what we're going to do today as we open Romans 8. Bad news and then the good news:

> In the same way the Spirit also helps our weakness; for we do not know how to pray as we should, but the Spirit Himself intercedes for *us* with groanings too deep for words. (Romans 8:26)

Here's the bad news, which Paul tells: we don't know how to pray. The greatest Christian on the planet admits he does not know how to pray right—that's why he said "we." He included himself.

Those whom you think are amazing at prayer, all those intercessors . . . they don't know how to pray. None of us do. Not your pastor, professor, church mother, older Christian.

But we have good news. The good news comes right after the bad news in this verse: we have help in the Holy Spirit: "The Spirit Himself intercedes for us."

How does He do that? Let's jump over to Ephesians 3:20: "To Him who is able to do far more abundantly beyond all that we ask or think, according to the power that works within us." God takes our ask and makes it better and bigger than we can ever articulate in prayer.

What a relief! We don't have to be eloquent. We just have to ask and God will take that request, that groan, that plea and make it bigger than what we just said.

Paul is saying to us, *Say something, say anything, and God will get it right for you, because He goes beyond our ask.* He takes our ask and goes further. God takes what we say and puts power to it. That takes the pressure off of you and me. We can be saved for ten minutes and still be powerful at prayer. Because it isn't you, and it isn't me. It's God.

Hymnwriter William Cowper's words are true: "Satan trembles when he sees the weakest saint upon his knees."[213]

Why? It's true that we don't know how to pray. But it's also true that we have the best help to pray. With that understanding, Brennan Manning's words are an important truth for us to remember: "The only way to fail in prayer is to not show up."[214]

God is committed to taking my simple, silly prayer words and adding power to them. The power depends on whose hands it's in. I read a poem by an unknown author that fits our purposes here perfectly. I've changed up a few bits to make it more contemporary.

A basketball in my hands is worth about $19.
A basketball in Keven Durant's hands is worth about $75 million.
It depends whose hands it's in.

A baseball in my hands is worth about $6.
A baseball in Mike Trout's or Aaron Judge's hands is worth $19 million.
It depends whose hands it's in.

A tennis racket is useless in my hands.
A tennis racket in Serena Williams's hands is a French Open or Wimbledon Championship.
It depends whose hands it's in.

A rod in my hands will keep away a wild animal.
A rod in Moses' hands will part the mighty sea.
It depends whose hands it's in.

A slingshot in my hands is a kid's toy.
A slingshot in David's hand is a mighty weapon.
It depends whose hands it's in.

Two fish and five loaves of bread in my hands is a couple of fish sandwiches.
Two fish and five loaves of bread in God's hands will feed thousands.
It depends whose hands it's in.

Nails in my hands might produce a birdhouse.

Nails in Jesus Christ's hands will produce salvation for the entire world.

It depends whose hands it's in.

Your prayer is in good hands; it's in God's hands. That makes the bad news not that bad because the good news is really good.

IT'S NOT SUPPOSED TO HAPPEN LIKE THAT

Today's reading: Romans 9

We now enter three of the most difficult chapters of the entire New Testament, Romans 9–11. We are venturing into, what we call in theology, election, predestination, and the Sovereignty of God. There is no way we can discuss with clarity all of these important words in detail in our brief time together, but we can at least introduce them. As we start today in Romans 9, let's be challenged by the verses ahead. First, we need to brush up on our Old Testament stories to figure out what Paul is talking about.

Paul starts with the Genesis story of Rebekah and Isaac's children, Jacob and Esau, and something God did after they were born. That something had nothing to do with the children but with God's character:

> There was Rebekah also, when she had conceived *twins* by one man, our father Isaac; for though *the twins* were not yet born and had not done anything good or bad, so that God's purpose according to *His* choice would stand, not because of works but because of Him who calls, it was said to her, "THE OLDER WILL SERVE THE YOUNGER." Just as it is written, "JACOB I LOVED, BUT ESAU I HATED." What shall we say then? There is no injustice with God, is there? May it never be! [Romans 9:10-14]

Remember the story of Jacob and Esau, the twins. Esau is the older and Jacob is the younger. Who is older is important. Why? The book of Genesis is a window into what cultures were like before the revelation of the Bible. One thing we see early on is the widespread practice of primogeniture—that's when the eldest son inherited all the family's wealth. That is how they ensured the family kept its status and place in society.

The second or third son got nothing, or very little. And here is what I want you to see on the sovereignty of God.

Pause for a moment first. What is the sovereignty of God? The sovereignty of God is God exercising His prerogative to do whatever He pleases with His creation because He created everything. He can do this because it belongs to Him. God does it by virtue of ownership.

For example, if you came into my home and said, "I don't like the way you decorated this room. You should put furniture here against the wall."

My response would be, "When you start buying the furniture you want to move and paying the mortgage, then we can consider your opinions and viewpoints. Right now your views mean nothing, because I am the owner." God is in charge of this planet, so He can do whatever He wants.

Daniel 4:35 puts it this way: "He does as he pleases" (NIV). That's sovereignty.

Why doesn't that bother me? Because God is all wise, all loving, all powerful. I can trust His sovereignty. I don't trust any man's sovereignty, because they don't have the character and nature to wield that kind of power. As Charles Spurgeon says, "Cheer up, Christian! Things are not left to chance: no blind fate rules the world. God hath purposes, and those purposes are fulfilled. God hath plans, and those plans are wise, and never can be dislocated."[215] Or Corrie ten Boom puts it simply, "God doesn't have problems, only plans. There never is any panic in heaven."[216]

So back to our verse: God chose not the oldest son to carry out His plans but the younger one. That is countercultural. We should be saying, "The God of Abraham, Isaac, and Esau," not Jacob. Culture is not in charge of God.

Throughout the Bible, when God chose someone to work through, He chose whomever He wanted, and in this case Paul reminds us that He chose the younger sibling in Genesis. Think for a moment of who else God chose.

He chose Abel over Cain.

He chose Isaac over Ishmael.

He chose David over all eleven of his older brothers.

Time after time He chose not the oldest, not the one the world expected and rewarded. Never the one from Jerusalem, as it were, but always the one from Nazareth.

Then Paul finishes the sovereignty of God thought with these verses:

So, what does all this mean? Are we saying that God is unfair? Of course not! He had every right to say to Moses: "I will be merciful to whomever I choose and I will show compassion to whomever I wish." Again, this proves that God's choice doesn't depend on how badly someone wants it or tries to earn it, but it depends on God's kindness and mercy. (Romans 9:14-16, TPT)

Let me close with these powerful words from David Qaoud:

"The sovereignty of God is a sweet pillow that you can lay your head at night. It is a beautiful truth not only that God is in control over all, but is also working everything out—the good and the bad—for your good, and his glory. This sweet doctrine is medicine for the soul that you can take in any season of life."[217]

Don't Change the Price of the Tickets— That's Ticket Scalping

Today's Reading: Romans 10

Today's chapter contains one of the most well-known passages that brings people to salvation.

Recently I was rereading *Mere Christianity* by C. S. Lewis. It's even better the second time. Lewis reminds us of the greatness of salvation. Consider his words:

Christ offers something for nothing: He even offers everything for nothing. In a sense, the whole Christian life consists in accepting that very remarkable offer. But the difficulty is to reach the point of recognising that all we have done and can do is nothing.[218]

That is how amazing salvation is. And it was Jesus' mission—why He came. Salvation is for humanity. Andy Stanley said it like this: "We are not *mistakers* in need of *correction*. We are sinners in need of a Savior. We need more than a second chance. We need a second birth."[219]

Let's read what Paul says about salvation, the second birth: "If you confess with your mouth Jesus *as* Lord, and believe in your heart that God raised Him from the dead, you will be saved" (Romans 10:9-10).

This is so simple, that's what makes this incredible. The old Baptist pastor from Dallas, W. A. Criswell, said every time someone was speaking about salvation in the Bible, they could describe how to be saved in one sentence.[220] Romans 10 is no exception. Here it is: Confess with your mouth Jesus is Lord and believe in your heart that God has raised Him from the dead, and you will be saved.

It doesn't get simpler and clearer than that.

This is the ticket price into the stadium. This is the ticket to eternity, to heaven. There are people who will try to change the ticket price. That's called ticket scalping.

These ticket scalpers will say, "You have to be water baptized." It doesn't say that.

"You have to speak in tongues." It doesn't say that.

"You have to take communion." It doesn't say that.

The thief on the cross could never have gotten to heaven if he let people change the ticket price.

Some say you have to stop doing certain things before you can become a Christian. That's not what this verse says. You don't get good and come to Jesus. You come to Jesus and He makes you good. Some people then cry, "What about their bad habits? They can't become a Christian if they're cursing, smoking, gambling." They sure can. We can't change the ticket price.

Remember this: "God loves you just the way you are, and because He loves you the way you are, He refuses to leave you the way you are."[221] That means God wants to get us in His family, baggage and everything, and then He will deal with the junk that hurts and hinders our lives. But the ticket in to salvation is simple.

Confess with your mouth Jesus as Lord. "Lord" means He is the boss. He is in charge. He has veto power in your life. If you come to a point where what you believe and think is different from what God thinks, then God wins if He is Lord.

And second, you must believe in your heart that God has raised Jesus from the dead. Paul is careful that this is not just saying the right words, but that you also believe it to the core of your being. So you are saying the words because you believe them in your heart.

That's how we get to heaven. Some may say, "I'm not sure this is the way." Will Houghton said, "If you decide you want to go to heaven then you have to go God's way because it is God's heaven."[222]

Listen closely, if you wanted to come to my house, I think I can give you the best directions to my house. Because it's my house. Heaven is God's home. And God knows how to get to His home. He knows the best directions. If you want to go to heaven, let God give you the directions. And God did, and they are simple.

Day 128

HIGH JUMPING OR POLE VAULTING

Today's Reading: Romans 11

There is a fundamental difference between a pole vaulter and a high jumper. A high jumper runs as fast as he can and leap as high as he can, and if he is good, he can get about seven-and-a-half feet. If he wants the world record, he aims for eight feet. His human effort and strength can only take him so far. The pole vaulter is different. He has to run too, but he does not trust his own two legs. He carries a pole and sticks that pole into a hole in the ground. He puts all of his trust in that pole not only to hold him but to raise him higher than what he could do on his own. He will go three times higher than the high jumper. The world record for a pole vaulter is more than twenty feet.

You can try to leap on your own and do Christian high jumping, but you will only get so high. But when you run and then lean all of your weight on Jesus and His Word, He takes you higher and higher over things you could never get over on your own. That's what we learn in Romans 11.

This chapter opens with a story about Elijah who got caught high jumping when he should have been pole vaulting. He was depending on his own strength and insight instead of on God's. Read how Paul tells the story in which Elijah is speaking at a tough time in his ministry:

> "Lord, THEY HAVE KILLED YOUR PROPHETS, THEY HAVE TORN DOWN YOUR ALTARS, AND I ALONE AM LEFT, AND THEY ARE SEEKING MY LIFE." But what is the divine response to him? "I HAVE KEPT for Myself SEVEN THOUSAND MEN WHO HAVE NOT BOWED THE KNEE TO BAAL." [Romans 11:3-4]

I love how Paul frames Elijah's story of negativity. Elijah tells the Lord, "THEY HAVE KILLED YOUR PROPHETS, TORN DOWN YOUR ALTARS, AND I ALONE AM LEFT."

What are the Lord's strong words, the divine response?

This is an important question we always need to ask over our tough situations. When we ask that, we go from high jumping to pole vaulting.

"What is the divine response?" Or, "What does God have to say about this?"

Is there something in God's Word we can hold on to?

God says to Elijah that what Elijah is seeing is not the reality of the situation: *There is not one person but seven thousand who have not bowed their knees. That means, Elijah, there are people just as committed as you, others who are no nonsense and no compromise. You are not alone. When you look with your natural eyes (high jumping), you are the only one. When you ask Me for the divine response (pole vaulting), I know a lot of people who are sold out to Me.*

God was telling Elijah the high jumper that he was 6,999 off! That's what happens when we try to assess situations with fear and anxiety and with what we perceive. We will always be 6,999 off.

We have a pole that takes us higher. It's the divine response. It is God's opinion of our situations.

I love this story about a woman who tracked her spiritual pole-vaulting legacy. D. L. Moody told of an old Christian woman who habitually wrote two letters in the margins of her Bible—a "T" and a "P," which stood for "Tried and Proven."[223]

This woman received the divine response for every trial. She received a pole vault.

Hopefully Elijah received a T & P when he realized that God knew more people than he did, and that Elijah was not alone.

Always ask for the divine response, you will go higher.

THE TWENTY-SEVEN-QUESTION EXHORTATION TEST

Today's Reading: Romans 12

Romans 12:9-21 is some of the most powerful exhortations of the New Testament. I use the word *exhort* because it's the right word to use with these verses. Exhort is a passionate urging to do something. Passion does not leave a lot of room for wordiness. Passionate words spill out of you because it *has* to come out of you. Paul starts the passionate pleas, and it seems he can't stop once he starts.

Each verse is packed with two or three exhortations that cut to the heart and that are so countercultural. Right after the challenge for us to use our gifts of prophecy, serving, teaching, exhorting, giving, leading, and mercy, he goes into this long stretch of challenge for all of us. Though the gifts are limited to the gifted person, what comes next is about character traits to pursue and should be present in all of us:

> *Let* love *be* without hypocrisy. Abhor what is evil; cling to what is good. *Be* devoted to one another in brotherly love; give preference to one another in honor; not lagging behind in diligence, fervent in spirit, serving the Lord; rejoicing in hope, persevering in tribulation, devoted to prayer, contributing to the needs of the saints, practicing hospitality. Bless those who persecute you; bless and do not curse. Rejoice with those who rejoice, and weep with those who weep. Be of the same mind toward one another; do not be haughty in mind, but associate with the lowly. Do not be wise in your own estimation. Never pay back evil for evil to anyone. Respect what is right in the sight of all men. If possible, so far as it depends on you, be at peace with all men. Never take your own revenge, beloved, but leave room for the wrath *of* God, for it is written, "VENGEANCE IS MINE, I WILL REPAY," says the Lord. "BUT IF YOUR ENEMY IS HUNGRY, FEED HIM, AND IF HE IS THIRSTY, GIVE HIM A DRINK; FOR IN SO DOING YOU WILL HEAP BURNING COALS ON HIS HEAD." Do not be overcome by evil, but overcome evil with good. (Romans 12:9-21)

Wow! Twenty-seven challenges he rattles off like a drill sergeant. You can't even catch your breath and examine how you are doing with "persevering in tribulations" before "be devoted in prayer" hits you in the face. We could combine a few of these character traits and make it twenty-five. So what if we made it a twenty-five-question test in which you rate how you're doing on each one? Let's say each one was worth four points, which adds up to one hundred points total. What would your grade be? I'm afraid of my grade on the character test.

The Christian devotional writer Oswald Chambers gives us insight into what character really is:

> Character is the whole trend of a man's life, not isolated acts here and there. . . . Character is the sum total of a man's actions. You cannot judge a man by the good things he does at times; you must take all the times together and if in the greater number of times he does bad things, he is a bad character; in spite of the noble things he does intermittently.[224]

One of the first-century Greek philosophers, Plutarch, summarizes those words like this: "Character is simply long habit continued."[225]

I know this will sound redundant, but I think it's worth it to list Paul's exhortations:

Love without hypocrisy
Abhor what is evil
Cling to what is good
Be devoted to one another in brotherly love
Give preference to one another in honor
Not lagging behind in diligence
Fervent in spirit
Serving the Lord
Rejoicing in hope
Persevering in tribulation
Devoted in prayer
Contributing to the needs of the saints
Practicing hospitality
Bless those who persecute you
Bless and curse not

Rejoice with those who rejoice

Weep with those who weep

Be of the same mind toward one another

Do not be haughty in mind

Associate with the lowly

Do not be wise in your own estimate

Never pay back evil for evil to anyone

Respect what is right in the sight of all men

Be at peace with all men (so far as it depends on you)

Never take your own revenge

Do not be overcome by evil

Overcome evil with good

These twenty-seven character traits are so important in our life, especially in a society that promotes gift over character. If you get someone with a high gift and low character, you are in for a train wreck.

In talking about the difference a strong and good character makes, the legendary Dallas Cowboys coach, Tom Landry, said:

> I've seen the difference character makes in individual football players. Give me a choice between an outstanding athlete with poor character and a lesser athlete of good character; and I'll choose the latter every time. The athlete with good character will often perform to his fullest potential and be a successful football player; while the outstanding athlete with poor character will usually fail to play up to his potential and often won't even achieve average performance.[226]

To stay in the sports arena, I'll leave you with the great UCLA basketball coach John Wooden's words to encourage you: "Ability will get you to the top - but it takes character to keep you there."[227]

REPLACING CONSEQUENCE WITH MOTIVATION

Today's Reading: Romans 13

In *No Bad Dogs*, British dog trainer Barbara Woodhouse claims that dogs understand love better than we do. She writes,

> In a dog's mind, a master or a mistress to love . . . is an absolute necessity. . . . Thousands of dogs appear to love their owners, they welcome them home with enthusiastic wagging of the tail and jumping up, they follow them about their houses happily and, to the normal person seeing the dog, the affection is true and deep. But to the experienced dog trainer this outward show is not enough. The true test of love takes place when the dog has got the opportunity to go out on its own as soon as the door is left open by mistake and it goes off and often doesn't return home for hours. That dog loves only its home comforts. . . . True love in dogs is apparent when a door is left open and the dog still stays happily within earshot of its owner. [228]

The real test of our love for God isn't seen in our activity or even in our theological purity. It's found when we have an opportunity to wander away, to leave His presence, and we choose instead to stay close to Him.

This is what makes our chapter today so powerful. It's about love. That when we love, we do the right thing. Let's read it together:

> Owe nothing to anyone except to love one another; for he who loves his neighbor has fulfilled the law. For this, "YOU SHALL NOT COMMIT ADULTERY, YOU SHALL NOT MURDER, YOU SHALL NOT STEAL, YOU SHALL NOT COVET," and if there is any other commandment, it is summed up in this saying, "YOU SHALL LOVE YOUR NEIGHBOR AS YOURSELF." Love does no wrong to a neighbor; therefore love is the fulfillment of the law. (Romans 13:8-10)

Verse 9 is the "You shall not" commandments. And then Paul gives the groundbreaking thought that Jesus talked about: you shall love your neighbor. Paul is saying that you won't do the "you shall nots" when you love your neighbor. Love makes you do what's right.

This is so powerful. Paul starts with four negative commands:

You shall not commit adultery.

You shall not murder.

You shall not steal.

You shall not covet.

And then Paul says to love your neighbor. He says when you love your neighbor, you will not steal, covet, commit adultery, or murder. That is not only powerful, it makes sense.

Religion wants to legislate the "you shall nots." Jesus wants to empower you to love. Remember in the gospels, Jesus condensed the 613 Old Testament commands into two commandments: Love God and love your neighbor. It's so much easier to remember.

But He had a reason for doing this. He was speaking to motive. When the motive is love, it automatically takes care of the things we should not do.

Think about this in the relationship between a husband and a wife. The greatest protection against adultery in a marriage is "you shall not commit adultery" or there will be consequences. The greatest motivation to not commit adultery is by pursuing the first command husbands have for their wives: husbands love your wife as Christ loves the church. Not "don't commit adultery." So the best way to start making a healthy marriage is for husbands to pray each day, "Lord, help me to love my wife as Christ loves the church."

If you start with a "don't" in any relationship, then you have to give the consequence to prevent the behavior—for a spouse who commits adultery, the consequences are hell with God and divorce with a spouse. But that is such a poor motivation to do what's right. When you have a disobedience problem, it's a love problem. If you say, "I can't stop sinning," then start loving God. When you love God, you are fighting sin.

How do you fix the love issue? The best way to love God is to know God. And the best way to know God is by reading His Word. And love will grow.

My Faith Is Personal but It Isn't Private

Today's Reading: Romans 14

Romans 14 is about personal convictions not a private faith. Nowhere does the Bible give anyone the right to a private faith, though it is a personal faith. Because not everyone is at the same place in their walk with God. And when we don't take notice of where people are in the Christian walk, then the strong can become a stumbling block to the weak. Paul says it like this: "Forget about deciding what's right for each other. Here's what you need to be concerned about: that you don't get in the way of someone else, making life more difficult than it already is" (Romans 14:13, MSG).

Making life more difficult for newer Christians—that is a horrible thought.

How does that happen? It happens when the lines of personal and private faith get blurred, landing us with legalism. Imposing our standards on others. When we do that we get in the way of people's growth in Christ.

Let me explain the origin of legalism and how important Romans 14 is to keeping it out of our lives. Legalism originates when Christians make a personal conviction into a corporate conviction. When you believe what God demands of you is what He is demanding of everyone.

Now there are extracurriculars that God will call His servants to that He doesn't intend for everyone. But be very careful of imposing those extracurriculars on those around you. Your convictions are not meant for everyone.

Throughout my ministry I have seen that the greater the anointing, the greater those kinds of personal convictions happen. The wider the influence, the more intense those personal convictions are for a person.

As you listen to the Holy Spirit, He may be speaking to you personally. If that's the case, don't expand any larger than the personal dimensions. Once you expand your convictions to everyone, then your relationship has turned religious, and religion always sours and goes rogue into legalism.

Just because God tells you to get up and pray at 5 a.m. does not mean everyone has to. Just because you fast once a week doesn't mean everyone else in your house has to go hungry. I have seen this with what people wear, with bringing Jewish elements into the church. Be careful.

If God has something to say specifically to others, let Him say it. He is very well capable of speaking. He did speak a universe into existence, so I do think He can tell someone, *You're watching too much television*.

Romans 14 helps us with this. In fact, an old friend helped me understand this chapter better by categorizing a few things. There are biblical absolutes, community standards, and personal convictions.

Biblical absolutes are for all people, all times, and all places (things like homosexuality, adultery, lying). These are things we cannot do or we will die spiritually. They are fixed, unchanging, no matter the culture, era, or circumstance. And these are clearly in the Bible for us.

Community standards are for some people, for some situations, for some times. I've heard it said, "If it was sin then, then it is sin now." Have you ever heard that? It really depends upon what you are talking about, though. There are things that don't impact salvation but impact your growth. There were times in the church decades ago when a woman could not wear black pantyhose or red shoes without being labeled a sinner. It used to be a sin to have a radio or television or to read the comics on Sundays. There is a difference between that which impacts salvation and that which impacts growth—and those things have to be differentiated. People confuse biblical absolutes with community standards. They say, "If you don't do these things, you will go to hell." Well, you will not go to hell, but you won't grow.

Acts 15:1 has a key phrase to notice: "Some men came down from Judea and *began* teaching the brethren, 'Unless you are circumcised according to the custom of Moses, you cannot be saved.'" Did you see it? *You cannot be saved.* They imposed a community standard as a biblical absolute.

Finally, personal convictions are for you. They are custom-made from God for your personal life. Your personal conviction is not every person's conviction. Do not make a personal conviction into a community standard. It is immature for people to say that because it's wrong for them, then it is wrong for everybody.

Paul helps us in Romans 14 by encouraging us to ask three questions in regards to our personal faith and the things we do. It's a great grid for our walk with God, especially when something we do could be misunderstood.

We must ask ourselves, does what I do . . .

Glorify God? (verses 5-8)

Edify? (verses 13-16)

Bring peace? (verse 19)

If it doesn't, Paul says the reward for doing it just isn't worth it.

I want a life that will glorify God and help others. It isn't simply about me. I don't want my actions to be a stumbling block to anyone's faith.

The best description of the church was made by one of the church's first enemies in the first century named Celsus. His was the oldest literary attack on Christianity, from about AD 178, of which any details have survived. We get it from Origen's reply, Contra Celsum, Celsus wrote, "The root of Christianity is its excessive valuation of the human soul, and the absurd idea that God takes an interest in man."[229]

Exactly right, Celsus! And that's why Romans 14 is so important—because people are important even if I have to cease and desist something that may be right for me but a stumbling block for them. I will do it. Because we excessively value the human soul.

Day 132

WHY THE 929 IS LEGIT

Today's Reading: Romans 15

In today's reading the apostle Paul is about to tell us how legit the Old Testament is. We are going to be given a reason why we should think larger than 260. The New Testament has 260 chapters that we are reading through together. But we don't have to stop there! The Bible has 929 other chapters that also have purpose. As Paul tells us, "Everything that was written in the past was written to teach us, so that through the endurance taught in the Scriptures and the encouragement they provide we might have hope" (Romans 15:4, NIV).

The "everything was written in the past" is defined as the Old Testament narrative—the Old Testament stories. The 929 chapters beyond the 260.

But Paul is saying these are not "just" stories. These are "our stories." Paul is telling us to take notice of people's stories in those 929 chapters. There is wisdom and instruction in them for our lives. Since we know not every story in those chapters end with "they lived happily ever after," we need them as reminders and warnings not to let their stories become our stories.

Always remember, we don't have to experience something to gain wisdom and understanding. That saying, "Experience is the best teacher"? That isn't completely true. I don't need to get on drugs or get a DUI to know that those things are bad for me. Instead *evaluated* experience is the best teacher. And many times our best evaluating comes by observing and learning about what others have gone through.

Paul is telling us that the stories in the Old Testament are not just stories to read, they are stories to heed. The Old Testament gives us what others experienced and asks us to evaluate and to receive from them wisdom for personal growth and instruction and to avoid failures and even train wrecks. Christian author, the late R. C. Sproul got to the real problem of why we don't make those stories our stories:

> Here, then, is the real problem of our negligence. We fail in our duty to study God's Word not so much because it is difficult to understand, not so much because it is dull and boring, but because it is work. Our problem is not a lack of intelligence or a lack of passion. Our problem is that we are lazy.[230]

We can find stories for every circumstance we may face. There are Old Testament stories of adultery and immorality, of losing a child, a wife, a friend. There is the story of going bankrupt. There are stories of betrayal, false accusations, and getting through them. There are stories of standing strong against temptation and saying no to sexual immorality, as well as stories of those who gave into sexual temptation and the consequences that followed. We find stories of how to be an amazing witness in a very difficult, ungodly environment. We get to see people's decisions from beginning to end. All there so we can learn. Paul is saying that we need to read the 929, that they are there for us to take note of, to learn from, to value.

You have a bad neighbor situation? There is help in the Old Testament for how to handle that. Proverbs 16:7 says, "When a man's ways are pleasing to the LORD, he makes even his enemies to be at peace with him." How do you fix the bad-neighbor situation? Please God now and make it His responsibility.

Some people say, "I just wait to hear the voice of God speak to me." He did speak to you—in the Scriptures. If you have not been faithful with what is clear, why would He continue to speak?

You've doing well by taking the 260 journey, but remember also the 929. Each time you read an Old Testament story, say to yourself, "These are stories for me. The 929 is legit."

Day 133

TURN THE MIC BACK ON— SAYING AMEN TWICE

Today's Reading: Romans 16

Occasionally on Sundays after I'd finished the sermon, we'd completed the last song, and I'd said the final amen, I'd realize I forgot to announce something to the congregation. I'd have to tell our sound technician to turn the mic back on so I could tell the people what I forgot.

I'm in good company. Even Paul forgot something in Romans and had to essentially tell the sound technician to turn his mic back on.

Today's reading of our final chapter in Romans is one of Paul's most overlooked and undervalued. They are words spoken after the microphone is turned off.

Look with me at Romans 15:33. It seems like a great ending prayer for this amazing Epistle. Paul usually ends his Epistles with short doxologies. Here he writes, "Now the God of peace be with you all. Amen." "Amen" means it's over, time to go, time to eat.

Then Paul stops everyone and says, "Wait, wait, wait! I forgot something. Turn the mic back on. I missed a huge announcement!"

And then in one of the most amazing chapters that doesn't get its props, Paul goes on for the next twenty-seven verses before he gives his second amen. Here's the second doxology, the second closing: "To the only wise God, through Jesus Christ, be the glory forever. Amen" (Romans 16:27).

Between those two amens Paul mentions thirty-three names! Go back through today's reading and count them all. He starts with "our sister Phoebe who is a servant of the church which is at Cenchrea" (verse 1) and spends twenty-four verses listing people who wants to recognize. Thirty-three names of people who helped him in ministry. Thirty-three names who made Paul's ministry possible. He's recognizing them with a "there's no way we do what we do without these people."

One of the greatest coaches of any sports franchise or university has to be John Wooden of UCLA. He coached his teams to ten national championships in twelve years. He had an 800-winning percentage. He is an icon. In *A Game Plan for Life: The Power of Mentoring*, he wrote

When one of my players scored, he knew he was supposed to point to the teammate who had passed him the ball or made the block that allowed that basket to happen. It wasn't about deflecting praise, but about sharing it with everyone who was working hard as a part of the team.[231]

Today many athletes thump their chests while the team has to follow them around as they carry on without giving any recognition to anyone who helped them get there. When was the last time you saw a defensive end sack a quarterback and then turn around and point to every defensive lineman who made the hole so he can get in? Never! He stands in the middle of the field as if it were his talent alone that gave him that moment and forgot to point to all the players who made it happen for him.

Wooden said his dad taught him, "There is nothing you know that you haven't learned from someone else. . . . He . . . was reminding us to always be thankful for each lesson an individual offers, wittingly or unwittingly, because those lessons become a kind of borrowed experience."[232]

I found this short course in human relations from an unknown, but very wise, author:

> The six most important words: *I admit I made a mistake*
> The five most important words: *You did a good job*
> The four most important words: *What do you think?*
> The three most important words: *I love you*
> The two most important words: *Thank you*
> The one most important word: *We*
> The least important word: *I*

After Ronald Reagan became the fortieth president, he put a plaque on his desk to remind him of an important piece of wisdom: "There is no limit to how far a person may go as long as he doesn't care who gets the credit."[233]

Romans 16 is best known for its pointing fingers instead of thumping chests. No doubt behind every one of these names there is a hidden story. Time wouldn't allow us to trace their individual stories. Whatever their stories may have been, those people influenced and helped Paul in his work, and Paul knew it. That's why he turned the mic back on and gave well-deserved shout outs to otherwise-would-be-considered no names.

Paul portrayed a good model, which even Albert Einstein followed: "A hundred times a day I remind myself that my inner and outer life are based on the labors of other men, living and dead, and that I must exert myself in order to give in the same measure as I have received."[234]

Here's a challenge for you today. Thank someone for their investment and help in your life. Thank a parent, a pastor, a professor, or a friend. Send them a text, an email, or call and thank them. Listen to Coach Wooden and don't come down the court thumping your chest. Remember that a bunch of other people helped you to be where you are today. Paul had at least thirty-three of them. I had a lot more than thirty-three. How many do you have?

It's All About Who Owns It

Today's Reading: 1 Corinthians 1

Sotheby's in New York City had an auction some years ago and sold some of the belongings of iconic people. Winston Churchill's desk, C. S. Lewis's pipe, and one sheet of Johan Sebastian Bach's music all auctioned that day. Here are three items and their final auction prices that caught my attention.

Napoleon's toothbrush sold for $21,000.

Jackie Kennedy Onassis's fake pearl necklace went for $215,000.

John F. Kennedy's wood golf clubs sold at $772,500.[235]

These items are not worth that price on their own. Think about it. A used toothbrush, wooden golf clubs, and fake pearls. They have no intrinsic value. So what makes these items valuable? And why did they sell for so much money? Who they belonged to.

Since they belonged to someone important, famous, or significant, their price skyrocketed.

In today's reading, the apostle Paul reminds us of our value. Listen to this verse: "In everything you were enriched in Him, in all speech and all knowledge" (1 Corinthians 1:5).

Two words from this verse are important: *everything* and *enriched*.

First, Jesus touches all areas of our lives. Paul says God has an effect on *everything*. Nothing is left out and nothing is off limits to God. So when Jesus comes in, every area gets affected. Religion asks for a day a week, while a relationship with Jesus wants every day. Why everyday? Because He wants everything.

Second, *enriched* is a money word, a financial word. It means to add value to something and make it pricey. God added value to your life. The day you became a Christian, your value skyrocketed because He started improving every area of your life. He started cleaning up the mind, the heart, the speech, the priorities—as Paul said, "In everything."

But what really makes you valuable is not that you are different, it's Who you belong to. You belong to God. That's better than JKF, Jackie O, and Napoleon. These owners were a president, a first lady, and an army general. But your Owner is the Maker of the universe. And since you belong to Him, your value has skyrocketed. Which means at auction, your worth is off the charts.

And all of this from being in Him. *In Him* is such an important phrase. And it is considered one of Paul's most incredible and most quoted phrases in describing a Christian.

Donald Coggan, the Archbishop of Canterbury, drew attention to the 164 occurrences of "in Christ" in Paul's writing. Listen to his defining of this phrase:

> It is a strange phrase. We can scarcely find a parallel use to it in ordinary life. If, let us say, an intimate friend of Churchill who had spent many years with him and then had given a decade to the writing of his life were talking to us about that great man, he might sum up his relationship to him in a wide variety of ways. He might say that he feared him or admired him or revered him or even loved him. But he never would say, "I am a man in Churchill." It would never occur to him to use that phrase. But Paul was above everything else, "a man in Christ."[236]

The part that I love about *in him* in verse 5 is that because Paul is in Christ, his speech changed, all speech. If Christianity is a heart thing, then it is a speech thing. When you read 1 Corinthians, Paul can't stop talking about Jesus. Just look at the first nine verses. I will help you by emphasizing a few words so you can see a pattern.

> Paul, called as an apostle of *Jesus Christ* by the will of God, and Sosthenes our brother, to the church of God which is at Corinth, to those who have been sanctified in *Christ Jesus*, saints by calling, with all who in every place call on the name of our *Lord Jesus Christ*, their *Lord* and ours: Grace to you and peace from God our Father and the *Lord Jesus Christ*. I thank my God always concerning you for the grace of God which was given you in *Christ Jesus*, that in everything you were enriched in Him, in all speech and all knowledge, even as the testimony concerning *Christ* was confirmed in you, so that you are not lacking in any gift, awaiting eagerly the revelation of our *Lord Jesus Christ*, who will also confirm you to the end, blameless in the day of our *Lord Jesus Christ*. God is faithful, through whom you were called into fellowship with His Son, *Jesus Christ* our Lord. Now I exhort you, brethren, by the name of our *Lord Jesus Christ*." (1 Corinthians 1:1-10, emphasis added)

Jesus is in nine out of ten of the first verses. I think Paul's speech has been affected by Jesus. He can't stop talking about Him. That's what happens when Jesus is in the heart, He changes your conversation.

LET'S BE REAL

Today's Reading: 1 Corinthians 2

A friend of mine was just voted in as the new president of a Bible school in the Midwest. When I think of that school, I think of one of the most embarrassing things I did to appear impressive: I lied as I preached to them. I was supposed to speak to students who wanted to start a church, and because we'd just started ours in a very difficult spot in Detroit, they wanted me to talk about it. I not only wanted to speak about it, I wanted to be impressive. I rounded up the numbers—not so bad that they would be suspect, but enough that I would look awesome. As I was speaking, God told me, *You just lied. Repent.* I mentally responded, *Absolutely. When I get back to the hotel.* But God said that I needed to fess up right there. *I can only anoint truth*, He said. *When you embellish, then your story no longer has Me in it.*

God cannot be part of anything that is not truthful.

I went through all of this just so I could look impressive. How inauthentic I was being!

One of the most amazing stories about authenticity is about former first lady Betty Ford. While her husband, Gerald, was president, she admitted that she was addicted to prescription drugs and that she was an alcoholic. That took a lot of courage to be that transparent—especially being the first lady of the United States. But as a result of her honesty, she got help and then was able to start helping many other people through her Betty Ford Center. All because she said no to be inauthentic.

I like this anonymous seventeenth-century nun's prayer:

Lord, thou knowest me better than I know myself that I am growing older and will some day be old. Keep me from the fatal habit of thinking I must say something on every subject and on every occasion. Release me from craving to straighten out everybody's affairs. Make me thoughtful but not moody; helpful but not bossy. With my vast store of wisdom it seems a pity not to use it all, but Thou knowest, Lord, that I want a few friends at the end.

Keep my mind free from the recital of endless details; give me wings to get to the point. Seal my lips on my aches and pains. They are increasing and love of rehearsing them is becoming sweeter as the years go by. I dare not ask for grace enough to enjoy the tales of others' pains, but help me to endure them with patience. I dare not ask for improved memory, but for a growing humility and a lessening cocksureness when my memory seems to clash with the memories of others. Teach me the glorious lesson that occasionally I may be mistaken. Keep me reasonably sweet; I do not want to be a saint— some of them are so hard to live with—but a sour old person is one of the crowning works of the devil. Give me the ability to see good things in unexpected places and talents in unexpected people. And give me, O Lord, the grace to tell them so.

Amen.[237]

No one lived a better Christian life than the apostle Paul. He was authentic. He was real. I love Paul's honesty to the Corinthians. He was not trying to impress them. He was redirecting them to the One they should be impressed with:

You'll remember, friends, that when I first came to you to let you in on God's master stroke, I didn't try to impress you with polished speeches and the latest philosophy. I deliberately kept it plain and simple: first Jesus and who he is; then Jesus and what he did—Jesus crucified. I was unsure of how to go about this, and felt totally inadequate—I was scared to death, if you want the truth of it—and so nothing I said could have impressed you or anyone else. But the Message came through anyway. God's Spirit and God's power did it, which made it clear that your life of faith is a response to God's power, not to some fancy mental or emotional footwork by me or anyone else. (1 Corinthians 2:1-5, MSG)

Paul was saying, "I was telling you the truth about me so you would fall in love not with your pastor but with your Savior."

Make sure they are impressed with the Savior not the one talking about the Savior. As A. J. Gossip is attributed as saying, "You can't come across clever and have Jesus wonderful at the same time."[238] Sobering words from a nineteenth-century preacher for those who teach God's Word.

The humility of Paul is mind-boggling. Listen to what he says in these three verses:

"I am the least of the apostles."

(1 Corinthians 15:9; written AD 54)

"I am the very least of all the saints."

(Ephesians 3:8; written AD 62)

"I am the foremost of sinners."

(1 Timothy 1:15; written AD 63)

He moves from apostles to saints to sinners. And the only time he is the top of the list is for the sinner's part. Paul gets more and more honest about himself as he gets older. We pretend more as adults. Paul went the opposite way.

A. W. Tozer put it this way; "A Pharisee is hard on others and easy on himself, but a spiritual man is easy on others and hard on himself."[239]

When you come vulnerable, you take away people's ammunition against you. They are not saying anything about you that you haven't already said about yourself.

IT'S AMAZING WHAT HAPPENS WHEN WE WORK TOGETHER

Today's Reading: 1 Corinthians 3

In an old Peanuts cartoon, Lucy demanded that her brother, Linus, change television channels, and then threatened him with her fist if he didn't.

"What makes you think you can walk right in here and take over?" asked Linus.

"These five fingers," said Lucy. "Individually they are nothing, but when I curl them together like this into a single unit, they form a weapon that is terrible to behold."

"What channel do you want?" sighed Linus. Turning away, he looked at his fingers and said, "Why can't you guys get organized like that?"

Just as Lucy's fingers working together to form a fist can get Linus to change a channel, the body of Christ working together can get a soul bound for hell to heaven. In today's chapter, the apostle Paul speaks to the power of team work.

When Herman Edwards was coaching the NFL Kansas City Chiefs, in regards to teamwork, he insightfully challenged the Chiefs: "The players that play on this football team will play for the name on the side of the helmet and not the name on the back of the jersey."[240]

The name we play for is God. And here is what we are to remember as we work together:

> When one says, "I am of Paul," and another, "I am of Apollos," are you not *mere* men? What then is Apollos? And what is Paul? Servants through whom you believed, even as the Lord gave *opportunity* to each one. I planted, Apollos watered, but God was causing the growth. So then neither the one who plants nor the one who waters is anything, but God who causes the growth. Now he who plants and he who waters are one; but each will receive his own reward according to his own labor. For we are God's fellow workers; you are God's field, God's building. (1 Corinthians 3:4-9)

Paul and Apollos were the names on the backs of the jerseys. Let me give you five words that come to mind especially when I read verse 8: "He who plants and he who waters are one; but each will receive his own reward according to his own labor."

1. *Teamwork*. Each member surrenders a high profile. For those who have an ego, this is difficult. We all fight this. Don't believe it? When you see a group photo, who do you look for first? Yourself! When one member is determined to stand out, then the whole team loses. What causes disunity in the church? A bruised ego. In order for a team to be a team, its members must each be willing to have a low profile. Teamwork means we surrender. We surrender identity, surrender independence, surrender inflexibility, surrender indifference, surrender inequality, surrender self-interest.

2. *Talent*. Planting and watering are metaphors that refer to a specific gift of ministry people have. The point is that none of us has them all and when you add up everything all of us doing together, our jobs equal *one work*.

3. *Test*. This is the willingness to become one, to go unnoticed and unrecognized. If Paul had said, "I have planted and God gave the increase," there would be room for self-importance. How humbling it is that God uses more than one person in a person's conversion! There is not one of us who owes their conversion and growth to just one person. The test is the willingness to let Jesus be wonderful.

4. *Time*. What does "each will receive his own reward" mean? This refers to the future. This may disappoint you. We all want to be paid now. It says "will receive," which is future tense. If we keep a low profile now, we get high pay then.

Do you only get involved in church activities that are working? Or something that gets immediate results and is high on the radar? Then you want your reward now.

5. *Treasure*. There is a prize at the end of this. And it's worth it. What Paul is talking about here are people. Lives being transformed. When the body of Christ works together, amazing things can happen. When one waters and one plants, a miracle takes place—the miracle of changed lives.

That's what happens when we work together: lives are changed and God is glorified.

Keith Green, one of my favorite Christian artists from the 1970s and 80s wrote a song called "Oh Lord, You're Beautiful." In it, he sings, "When I'm doing well, help me to never seek a crown, for my reward is giving glory to You."[241]

That's the end of working together. When we are doing well, our reward is giving glory to our beautiful Lord.

One Out of **86,400**

Today's Reading: 1 Corinthians 4

Children do not always appreciate what parents do for them. They have short memories. Their concern is not what Mom and Dad did for them yesterday, but what are Mom and Dad doing for them today, right now. The past is meaningless and so is the future. They live for the present. Whereas those who are mature are deeply appreciative for past, present, and future.

Thanksgiving is the language of heaven, and we need to learn it here before we get to heaven. Just as we, who are parents are committed to teaching our children to say "Thank you," God also is committed to teaching His children gratitude.

Many of us don't think too often about gratitude. Author William A. Ward convicts us when he said, "God gave you a gift of 86,400 seconds today. Have you used one to say 'thank you?'" One out of 86,400 to say thanks, to show gratitude. That's .00001 percent.

Remember the days before Kindles and Ibooks when we used to have to go to libraries to get a book? I remember having to read newspapers on microfiche film and going through card catalogues to locate where the books where on the shelves. My family and I still use the library, and we always seem to have overdue books because my children can't find them to return them. Most of us who frequent libraries have brought back overdue books and paid the few pennies' fine. It's irritating, of course, but it's what we get for being so forgetful. When I read this story about fines, though, our family's fines didn't seem nearly so terrible.

George Szamuely borrowed books from the New York University library but never returned them. In fact, he'd horded more than five hundred books! That's taking overdue books to a new level. Police finally called on him to get him to pay his fine and return the books. The fine exceeded $31,000! He couldn't pay it, So George was hauled into court, where he faced grand larceny charges, meaning possible jail time. The forty-four-year-old was charged with possession of stolen property.[242] It's kind of a funny story, and yet it's also irritatingly sad. How can a man let so many books be overdue and neglect to return them?

I think worse than overdue books are overdue *thank you*'s to God.

I am in arrears in gratitude to God. Steven Furtick once said, "You can't be grateful for something you feel entitled to."[243] And the truth is, you're not entitled to anything, because it's all a gift from God. First Corinthians 4:7 is one simple sentence that sums up the motive of our gratitude: "What have you that was not given to you?" (AMPC).

Meister Eckhart said, "The most important prayer in the world is just two words long: *Thank you*."[244] I owe a lot of those to God today. I'm betting you do too. How about we pause today and give God one of out 86,400 with a "thank you"?

Day 138

WHEN HURT COMES FROM UNEXPECTED PEOPLE

Today's Reading: 1 Corinthians 5

These verses are going to be tough today. It's about hurt. At some point we are all going to be hurt, that's life. But what makes hurt confusing and difficult is when it comes from unexpected people and places. And when we are hurt, those are the times we want to isolate and self protect. This is dangerous and unsafe for our hearts.

Listen to what C. S. Lewis said about hurt and isolation:

> To love at all is to be vulnerable. Love anything, and your heart will certainly be wrung and possibly be broken. If you want to make sure of keeping it intact, you must give your heart to no one, not even to an animal. Wrap it carefully round with hobbies and little luxuries; avoid all entanglements; lock it up safe in the casket coffin of your selfishness. But in that casket—safe, dark, motionless, airless—it will change. It will not be broken; it will become unbreakable, impenetrable, irredeemable.[245]

Today in 1 Corinthians 5, Paul speaks to something that has affected all of us—hurt. But not just any kind of hurt, hurt that happens from Christian on Christian. It's when the source of our problem comes from a place and person we would expect better and more from. This is what Paul says about when this happens within the church:

> I *am* saying that you shouldn't act as if everything is just fine when one of your Christian companions is promiscuous or crooked, is flip with God or rude to friends, gets drunk or becomes greedy and predatory. You can't just go along with this, treating it as acceptable behavior. I'm not responsible for what the *outsiders* do, but don't we have some responsibility for those within our community of believers? (1 Corinthians 5:11-12, MSG)

Another version says verse 11 like this: "I am writing to you that you must not associate with anyone who claims to be a brother or sister but is sexually immoral or greedy, an idolater or slanderer, a drunkard or swindler. Do not even eat with such people" (NIV).

Forgiveness is never optional for us as Christians. Forgiveness is a mandate. When someone offends us, we must forgive. Why? Because God has forgiven you and me. As Paul tells us in Ephesians 4:32: "Forgiv[e] each other, just as God in Christ also has forgiven you."

But this is very important. I used to think that once I forgive someone for their offense, afterward we go out to eat and forget all about the offense. But Paul says something very insightful: if brothers or sisters in the church have dangerous flesh patterns, we are not even to eat with them. This is deep. We can forgive, but we must exercise caution of proximity, it seems.

It is important to define the difference of forgiving and giving. You can give forgiveness without giving proximity. We must offer forgiveness completely without reservation. Giving is caution that we exercise based upon the other person's repentance and flesh patterns. Because there may be flesh patterns that are unhealthy for our souls and could be damaging.

I can love you and forgive you without giving you access into my life, because of your destructive habits. That's what Paul is saying. He is reminding us that even though it's called the church, there are a lot of people still under construction.

The little saying is so true:

To dwell above with saints we love,
That will be grace and glory.
To live below with saints we know;
Well, that's another story![246]

It is biblically acceptable to distance ourselves from certain believers who are abusive and are toxic to our souls. Remember forgiveness is not an option. But proximity is. It takes one to forgive but two to reconcile. Forgiveness and reconciliation are different. Reconciliation starts with repentance. And forgiveness starts with you and me. Always remember that the pain of hurt is never wasted.

Day 139

JUST BECAUSE YOU CAN DOESN'T MEAN YOU SHOULD

Today's Reading: 1 Corinthians 6

Columbia researcher Sheena Iyengar has found that the average person makes about 70 decisions every day.[247] That's 25,500 decisions a year. Over 70 years, that's 1,788,500 decisions. The twentieth-century philosopher, Albert Camus once said, "Life is a sum of all your choices."[248] You put all of those 1,788,500 choices together, and that's who you are. As Stephen Covey said: "I am not a product of my circumstances. I am a product of my decisions."[249]

Job opportunity

Ministry position

Dating

Marriage

Investments

One person insightfully said: "Many people today want filet mignon results but make hot dog decisions. It doesn't work that way!" I want to help you with your filet-mignon results and give you filet-mignon decision-making skills from the apostle Paul. In fact if we take one verse in 1 Corinthians 6 and add one more verse from 1 Corinthians 10, I think we can take from Paul a good decision-making grid for our daily lives. In these two verses, Paul gives us three questions you and I are to impose on our choices each day. And they all start with "all things are lawful":

All things are lawful for me, but not all things are profitable. All things are lawful for me, but I will not be mastered by anything. (1 Corinthians 6:12)

All things are lawful, but not all things are profitable. All things are lawful, but not all things edify. (1 Corinthians 10:23)

Another way to say "all things are lawful" is to follow how *The Message* describes it: "Just because something is technically legal doesn't mean that it's spiritually appropriate" (1 Corinthians 6:12). What Paul is saying to us is just because we can doesn't mean we should.

These are not things that "send you to hell" but they can be things that cause hell in your life if you aren't careful.

Scrutinize your decisions with these Pauline questions. Impose questions on things that will take up your most precious resource—time.

First question: All things are lawful, but is this thing profitable?

That word, *profitable*, meant a traveling companion. Does it travel well with my travel partner Jesus? Can Jesus and this new decision go well together? Or will there be tension in the house?

Second question: All things are lawful, but will it control me?

One version of this verse says: "Even if I am allowed to do them, I'll refuse to if I think they might get such a grip on me that I can't easily stop when I want to" (TLB).

One test of being controlled or mastered by something: Do you get angry when people ask you to stop? Or when people challenge you on it?

This can be a great question to impose on anything as simple as . . .

Social media

Video games

Sports activities

Fantasy football to watching football every Saturday

Old friends and relationships

The list goes on. All these things are lawful, but is this thing profitable? Will it control me and master me—or get a "grip on me that I can't easily stop when I want to"?

The third question to ask is from 1 Corinthians 10:23: All things are lawful, but will it edify others?

Say this with me, "It's not all about me." The word *edify* is from the word *edifice*. It's a building word. It's about helping people build their lives. If you say, "I don't care what other people think about what I say or do," you're clinging to a belief that is unbiblical. You and I have to care, because we are responsible for their growth. We don't live by people's opinions but we do live to help them grow.

One Christmas someone became upset because I put a Christmas tree up in the church and they thought it was a druid idol. So I took it down. I am not going to fight over a Christmas tree, but I *will* fight over the truth of the Bible. I will yield on preference but not on biblical conviction.

Let's sum up the decision grid Paul gives us: All things are lawful, but . . . can Jesus hang out with this choice? Is something hanging on that won't let go? Am I hanging someone up by my choices?

The great Russian author Dostoyevski reminds us why these three questions are important for us: "The second half of a man's life is made up of the habits he acquired during the first half."[250]

Let's get some good first-half habits.

Day 140

SINGLE PEOPLE, THIS CHAPTER IS FOR YOU

Today's Reading: 1 Corinthians 7

The second most-important decision we can make is deciding with whom we want to spend the rest of our lives in marriage. The first is with whom we want to spend eternity. Because these decisions are important, God guides us through His Word to help us.

Good news. If you're single, today's chapter is especially for you. What makes this chapter so important is that it doesn't tell us what kind of person to look for, but what kind of person we are to be while we wait. God takes this season of waiting seriously and wants you to do that too. And He knows we have questions during this season:

Will I be alone forever?

I am so lonely, is there something wrong with me?

Why does everyone else seem to have someone and I don't?

What's crazy is that the early church had questions on the same topics. Paul provides answers here in 1 Corinthians 7. Look at these words in verse 1: "Now, getting down to the questions you asked in your letter to me" (MSG).

Because of that verse we know chapter 7 will provide answers to their questions. I find it hilarious that their first question is the sex question: "First," Paul continues in verse 1 (MSG), "Is it a good thing to have sexual relations?"

Paul's answer comes in verse 2: "Certainly—but only within a certain context" (MSG).

Here is a huge point for us to be clear on, especially in today's culture: sex has a context. Listen closely to the rest of verse 2: "It's good for a man to have a wife, and for a woman to have a husband. Sexual drives are strong, but marriage is strong enough to contain them and provide for a balanced and fulfilling sexual life in a world of sexual disorder" (MSG).

Lust is often compared to fire. In the New Testament the apostle Paul encourages men to get married if they're burning with lust or desire. The fire analogy is throughout the Bible.

Fire is incredibly powerful, not to mention fun and useful. The problem is, it's also difficult to contain and enormously destructive if it isn't kept where it belongs. Sex is like that. Wonderful and powerful, but it will destroy everything in its path if it's used out of place.

Fire in a fireplace? Awesome! Fire in your garage? Big problem! This context is God's design. God designed sex to be expressed in the correct context. That context is within the covenant of marriage. You can choose to express yourself outside of those parameters and covenant, but you can't choose the outcome and the consequences when you do.

Here is Paul's sex-out-of-context verse: "This is the will of God, your sanctification; *that is*, that you abstain from sexual immorality" (1 Thessalonians 4:3). Let me be clear: sexual immorality is having sex with someone you have not married. If you are doing that right now, if you are living with them right now, it is not God's will. It is immorality. It is sin.

"I love them" does not change the parameters of what the Bible says. Marry them then, because you love what Jesus says more. If you love that person, sex is not the next step, marriage is.

Every couple I meet with for premarital counseling, I always ask this one question, "Have you had sex?" Why? Premarital sex sabotages the relationship. This is going to get people mad but it needs to be said very clearly. This shows whether they love them or not: the chapter that defines real Bible love is 1 Corinthians 13, and the first characteristic of love is patience.

Why is this important? Listen to what Paul said in the chapter from yesterday's reading:

Since we want to become spiritually one with the Master, we must not pursue the kind of sex that avoids commitment and intimacy, leaving us more lonely than ever—the kind of sex that can never "become one." There is a sense in which sexual sins are different from all others. In sexual sin we violate the sacredness of our own bodies, these bodies that were made for God-given and God-modeled love, for "becoming one" with another. Or didn't you realize that your body is a sacred place, the place of the Holy Spirit? Don't you see that you can't live however you please, squandering what God paid such a high price for? The physical part of you is not some piece of property belonging to the spiritual part of you. God owns the whole works. So let people see God in and through your body. (1 Corinthians 6:17-20, MSG)

Sex is not just physical, it's connected to the soul. It cuts deep and it scars the soul. Sexual sin is not unforgivable, but it can make life unbearable. Sex is like glue. You shouldn't apply it until you're absolutely sure you're ready to stick two things together permanently. Apply it too soon, and you'll have a mess and you will realize too late the mistake you made.

This is difficult, I know. But in the midst of that we need to remember that singleness is a gift, not a curse. The gift of singleness is that you get time and less distractions to focus on becoming a better you. You can become the person God wants you to be so you can be ready for the second most-important relationship you will ever have.

Couples generally don't have relationship problems. They have problems they bring to the relationship. The better you that you bring, the fewer problems you bring with you:

> When you're unmarried, you're free to concentrate on simply pleasing the master. Marriage involves you in all the nuts and bolts of domestic life and in wanting to please your spouse, leading to so many more demands on your attention. The time and energy that married people spend on caring for and nurturing each other, the unmarried can spend in becoming whole and holy instruments of God. I'm trying to be helpful and make it as easy as possible for you, not make things harder. All I want is for you to be able to develop a way of life in which you can spend plenty of time together with the master without a lot of distractions. (1 Corinthians 7:32-35, MSG)

You have to deal with the right questions. When you look in the Bible for "how do I find the right person?" It isn't there. But once you ask, "How do I become the right person?" The Bible comes alive. If you are as intentional about becoming the right person as you are about meeting the right person, you will position yourself to bypass a boatload of unnecessary pain, regret, and wasted time. Spend your energy becoming the right person, not looking for the right person.

Day 141

OTHERS BEFORE ME, THAT'S MATURITY

Today's Reading: 1 Corinthians 8

People see Christian maturity as *I don't mess up a lot like I used to*. I see it differently. Maturity is when you see others before you see yourself. That's what 1 Corinthians 8 is about. It's an encouragement to live the Christian life wider and bigger. And by that, Paul means that our decisions and lives are to help others grow. How I parent, how I treat my wife, what I do with my free time, what I listen to, and what I watch is not just about me, but it's to be an example to others. As A. W. Tozer said, "There are rare Christians whose very presence incites others to be better Christians. I want to be that rare Christian."[251]

At our church we have four services every Sunday, each with the same message. One of our elders had a conversation with me one Sunday when I wasn't preaching but was at each service since I was participating. His words both encouraged and inspired me. At our 5 p.m. service, he said to me, "I can't believe the way you listened to that sermon. Wasn't this the fourth time you heard it today?"

"Yes," I said.

"You looked like you never heard it before," he said. "You sat on the edge of your seat and took notes as if this were the first time you ever heard that sermon."

What I learned from that interaction: (1) people are watching our lives; (2) we can inspire others unknowingly by our decisions.

I chose to take notes.

I chose to be excited four times.

I chose to sit on the edge of my seat and put myself in the posture of a learner.

I just forgot that it could be an example for someone else.

I realized that a good example is more powerful than a good sermon.

In 1 Corinthians 8 Paul is showing this same principle but from a different standpoint—but still with the power of influencing others. He speaks about the freedom that Christians have, though we must be careful if our freedom trips up someone newer and weaker in the faith. The challenge Paul gives us is that it isn't for them to step it up; it's for me to take a step back and a step down for their benefit." Here's what he says:

> Christ gave up his life for that person. Wouldn't you at least be willing to give up going to dinner for him—because, as you say, it doesn't really make any difference? But it *does* make a difference if you hurt your friend terribly, risking his eternal ruin! When you hurt your friend, you hurt Christ. A free meal here and there isn't worth it at the cost of even one of these "weak ones." So, never go to these idol-tainted meals if there's any chance it will trip up one of your brothers or sisters. (1 Corinthians 8:11-13, MSG)

We must care for their growth by adjusting ourselves for their sakes. If a nice hotel that we stay at has a casino and if that trips up anyone who has stumbled with gambling, then guess what? We don't stay there. For their sake. This could be with the music we listen to or a movie with a certain rating we watch. If it affects a weaker or younger Christian, we stop—for their sake.

Why? Because maturity in the Christian life is putting others first. It's living a life that is not just about ourselves but about seeing and being concerned for others.

Young Christians are called children in the Bible. James Baldwin said something profound about elders and children that can apply to parenting and even in the church: "Children have never been very good at listening to their elders, but they have never failed to imitate them."[252] Paul is preaching that example in 1 Corinthians 8. He wants us to realize that it's others before ourselves, which is a sign of maturity.

I remember as a teenager in church someone telling me, "Tim, do you know what joy stands for? Jesus first, others second, you last."

That still holds true today. If you want joy . . . put others before yourself.

Day 142

I'm Living to Win

Today's Reading: 1 Corinthians 9

George Washington Carver once said, "When you can do the common things of life in an uncommon way, you'll command the attention of the world."[253] The apostle Paul lived for God in an uncommon way. He commanded the attention of the world with how he lived for Christ. He made the Christian life a pursuit of doing it the best he could:

> You've all been to the stadium and seen the athletes race. Everyone runs; one wins. Run to win. All good athletes train hard. They do it for a gold medal that tarnishes and fades. You're after one that's gold eternally. I don't know about you, but I'm running hard for the finish line. I'm giving it everything I've got. No sloppy living for me! I'm staying alert and in top condition. I'm not going to get caught napping, telling everyone else all about it and then missing out myself.
> (1 Corinthians 9:24-27, msg)

We live in a sports infested society, just as they did in the first century. Paul speaks sports to get our attention and he gets it. The image Paul uses is of the Greek games. The Greeks dated their calendars based on those games. The Jews dated their calendars by what they thought the creation date was. The Romans dated theirs by when they thought Rome was founded. And we date ours by the life of Christ.

Because sports were important to the Greeks, those calendars were based on their sports games. And so to get our attention and to help us better grasp about the Christian life, he uses a sports image.

I want my goal to be what Paul is speaking about, which is not just to get to heaven but to win on the way there. In order to help us do that, he chooses two sports that are the most grueling in their training: boxing and running. They both require treacherous workouts in order to be good and to compete. And they both require even more sacrifice to win. To win at Christianity Paul puts everything on the table. He says that Christ and that relationship is worth giving up anything else. Everything else is a distant second.

Look at what Paul puts on the table in the preceding verses: he would give up certain eating habits (verse 4), getting married (verse 5), and even a salary (verse 6-7). Think about it. To be a world-class athlete, they are also willing to give up certain foods, committed relationships, and even a career to pursue their passion. So was Paul—but for a greater reason that sports. The end he is reaching toward is eternal. He says:

> You've all been to the stadium and seen the athletes race. Everyone runs; one wins. Run to win. All good athletes train hard. They do it for a gold medal that tarnishes and fades. You're after one that's gold eternally. (1 Corinthians 9:24-25, MSG)

The power and strength of anything is determined by what we are willing to sacrifice for it.

Is it worth giving things up for?

Is it worth dying for?

Only fanatics make a difference. Those who follow the status quo won't even make a dent. Baptist preacher Harry A. Ironside said: "No sacrifice should be too great for Him who gave Himself for us."[254]

Notice how many times Paul says "that I may win" in verses 19-24:

> For though I am free from all *men*, I have made myself a slave to all, so that I may win more. To the Jews I became as a Jew, so that I might win Jews; to those who are under the Law, as under the Law though not being myself under the Law, so that I might win those who are under the Law; to those who are without law, as without law, though not being without the law of God but under the law of Christ, so that I might win those who are without law. To the weak I became weak, that I might win the weak; I have become all things to all men, so that I may by all means save some. I do all things for the sake of the gospel, so that I may become a fellow partaker of it. Do you not know that those who run in a race all run, but *only* one receives the prize? Run in such a way that you may win. (1 Corinthians 9:19-24)

Six times in six verses. Winning was on his mind. And you can't win unless you sacrifice. He was in it to win it!

When it's all said and done, in five years, even in one year, no one is going to care who won the NBA finals, Wimbledon, the Super Bowl, the World series, or the NCAA men's basketball final four. Those athletes hold up their trophies that no one will care about even the following week. That winning has an expiration date. Ours doesn't.

Jim Elliot was a missionary in the 1960s who not only knew that concept but lived it. Jim put these words in his journal: "He is no fool who gives what he cannot keep to gain that which he cannot lose."[255] Later, he wrote, "'We are the sheep of His pasture. Enter into His gates with thanksgiving and into His courts with praise.' And what are sheep doing going into into the gate? What is their purpose inside those courts? . . . Those sheep were headed for the [sacrificial] *altar*."[256] He gave up his life trying to reach a group of South American Indians with the gospel, and they eventually killed him. He sacrificed. He was in it to win it.

Don't just be a Christian. Don't just do Christian. Win. Give it all.

Day 143

REFLECTING ON THE PAST IS NOT THE SAME AS LIVING IN THE PAST

Today's Reading: 1 Corinthians 10

We are always warned about dwelling in the past. Especially the bad past. Dwelling is one thing; forgetting is entirely another. Why? As George Santayana, a former philosophy professor at Harvard, said, "Those who cannot remember the past are condemned to repeat it."[257]

We have a responsibility to look to the past when it will guide our steps into a successful future. The past is not meant to be cement to hold us hostage to our mistakes and blunders, but it should help us reflect when we need the past to make a wise future decision. Reflecting on the past is not the same as living in the past. Certain parts of all of our pasts can either keep us stuck and condemned or reflective and wiser. It's up to us how we use it.

This is the truth the apostle Paul is bringing to the light for the Corinthians in chapter 10. Listen as he reflects on the Israelites' blunders while they were in the desert:

> These things occurred as examples to keep us from setting our hearts on evil things as they did. Do not be idolaters, as some of them were; as it is written: "The people sat down to eat and drink and got up to indulge in revelry." We should not commit sexual immorality, as some of them did—and in one day twenty-three thousand of them died. We should not test Christ, as some of them did—and were killed by snakes. And do not grumble, as some of them did—and were killed by the destroying angel. These things happened to them as examples and were written down as warnings for us, on whom the culmination of the ages has come. (1 Corinthians 10:6-13, NIV)

I don't have to sin to understand sin better. I can evaluate others' experiences to help me come to a wise conclusion. And Paul is asking us to use a scenario from almost two thousand years earlier. Paul is asking the Corinthians and us to evaluate their bad decisions so we can make good decisions.

Paul starts the section by reminding us that these are not just Old Testament stories we are reading but "these things occurred as examples" to keep us from doing the same things. That means when we read the Old Testament, we read those stories not simply with a historical mindset but as present-day students imposing the question to the text, "What is this saying to me? How can this story help me?"

Look at the four things he warns us against.

1. Do not be idolaters. We probably should pause on this word *idolatry*. When we hear it, we immediately think of an ugly statue that people bow to and claim to be over them. Twenty-first-century idolatry still exists. The statues are less conspicuous. They may have an apple on them and we can carry them in our hands. They can be a little box on top of the television that will not let us stop playing. They can be a person, a sport, a casino, or something in a glass. Idolatry is whatever has the power over you. So Paul tells us not to be idolators.

2. Do not commit sexual immorality. That means having sex outside of marriage.

3. Do not test the Lord. What does that mean? It means when we go into tough seasons with no regard of God's faithfulness and deliverance before. We test God when we go into a difficult moment with no recollection or memory of what He did before to help us. This is an affront to God.

4. Do not grumble. No complaining.

Then Paul reminds us again in verse 11: "These things happened to them as examples and were written down as warnings for us" (NIV). He starts in verse 6 with the words, *these things happened as examples*, and bookends the passage with those same words in verse 11. Paul is saying that we need to pay attention to these markers, reminders, reflective materials for us to live in the future. The challenge is for us to read them that way.

Paul ends with this exhortation: "No temptation has overtaken you but such as is common to man; and God is faithful, who will not allow you to be tempted beyond what you are able, but with the temptation will provide the way of escape also, so that you will be able to endure it" (1 Corinthians 10:13).

Keeping all the past in mind, here is how we get out of the difficult present: endure and exit. It's two ways through hell. There's always an exit for us and there's always strength too. Satan's job in those times is to blind our eyes and create a narrative like this . . . "No one has ever gone through this. You're the only one, so God must hate you" or "This is so intense, there's no way out and this will finally crush you." Neither is true.

It will never be too much to handle. No one can say, "There's no way to overcome this."

God is faithful to provide the way. He will offer us escape or endurance.

Paul tells us in 2 Corinthians 4 that Satan blinds eyes. In temptation, in the casino, in the arms of a lover, at a website, around a bottle, he blinds people so they don't see their family, our future, and God Himself. And Paul says that those people in the desert went blind and forgot that God provided a way out and strength to make it through.

Paul connects three important words with every trial and temptation. Don't miss them.

God is faithful.

Theologian Wayne Grudem explains about God's faithfulness: "God's faithfulness means that God will always do what he has said and fulfill what he has promised."[258]

Whenever I think about God's faithfulness, my mind goes back to this hymn I sang so many times growing up in the church:

> Great is Thy faithfulness, O God my Father,
> There is no shadow of turning with Thee;
> Thou changest not, Thy compassions, they fail not
> As Thou hast been Thou forever wilt be.
> Great is Thy faithfulness! Great is Thy faithfulness!
> Morning by morning new mercies I see;
> All I have needed Thy hand hath provided—
> Great is Thy faithfulness, Lord, unto me![259]

Day 144

THE SYMBOL IS TO REMIND US

Today's Reading: 1 Corinthians 11

Depending on which generation you are from will determine which historical tragedy you will remember as an American.

On Sunday morning, December 7, 1941, Japanese war planes bombed Pearl Harbor. Eighteen battleships were sunk or destroyed. Two hundred airplanes were put out of commission. And the servicemen who were either killed or wounded numbered 3,581. America's war cry as she entered World War II was, "Remember Pearl Harbor."

I grew up when that changed to "Remember 9/11." That was the day— September 11, 2001, when the towers fell.

The world does not need so much as to be informed as it needs to be reminded. The Bible tells us again and again to "remember." That is what Communion is. And that is what Paul is challenging us to do in 1 Corinthians 11. Some churches participate in Communion every week, some do it once a month, and some churches a few times a year.

Communion is a mini drama of salvation, using the props of bread and wine. Here's what Paul says about Communion in verse 26: "Whenever you eat this bread and drink this cup, you are retelling the story, proclaiming our Lord's death until he comes" (TPT).

Here's how it reads in *The Message* translation: "What you must solemnly realize is that every time you eat this bread and every time you drink this cup, you reenact in your words and actions the death of the Master. You will be drawn back to this meal again and again until the Master returns. You must never let familiarity breed contempt."

Communion is one way we can express our love for Jesus, because it is a way we can say to Him, "We remember what you did for us." Whenever we participate at the Lord's table, we too have a battle cry: "Remember Jesus Christ." Remember the cross.

And to help us remember, we get the bread and wine props.

Props are important reminders. When we get married, an important prop is part of the wedding ceremony. When we get the prop, we say, "With this *ring* I thee wed." When we say those words, we don't mean that the ring or putting the ring on the finger is what makes us married. It's a prop to remind us, and to show everyone around us, the commitment we have made. That's what the sacraments of the church are. Props to remind us.

To make it anything more than a symbol is dangerous. It's like loving our wedding band, when we need to love our spouse.

To cling to a symbol is what many try to do and they miss what God was trying to show us. What was God reminding us of with the bread and the cup?

The bread means God came. We say the bread is His body—that God in person. In his first epistle, John says that this Jesus came in bodily form: we touched Him, we saw Him, we heard Him. He did not write a message in the sky for us. He did not shout it audibly. He came to tell us that God loves us. God came in person for us.

The cup reminds us that God cares. The blood means God cares. The cup of juice reminds us that it should have been us paying for our sins, but God cares so much for you and me that He took our place. He cares and He died for you and me on the cross. The juice means God cares and took our place.

Did you know that some astronauts had Communion on the moon? On July 20, 1969, two human beings changed history by walking on the surface of the moon. But what happened before Edwin "Buzz" Aldrin and Neil Armstrong exited the Lunar Module is perhaps even more amazing. We know that Neil Armstrong was the first man to walk on the moon, but Buzz Aldrin took Communion on the surface of the moon. Some months after his return, he wrote about it in *Guideposts*.

Aldrin knew he would soon be doing something unprecedented in human history and he felt he should mark the occasion somehow, so he took Communion elements with him out of the earth's orbit and on to the surface of the moon. He and Armstrong had been on the lunar surface only a few minutes when Aldrin made a public statement: "This is the LM pilot. I would like to request a few moments of silence. I would like to invite each person listening in, wherever and whomever he may be, to contemplate for a moment the events of the past few hours and to give thanks in his own individual way." He ended radio communication and there, on the silent surface of the moon, 250,000 miles from home, he read a verse and took Communion. Here is his account of what happened:

In the radio blackout I opened the little plastic packages which contained bread and wine. I poured the wine into the chalice our church had given me. In the one-sixth gravity of the moon the wine curled slowly and gracefully up the side of the cup. It was interesting to think that the very first liquid ever poured on the moon, and the first food eaten there, were communion elements. As so, just before I partook of the elements, I read the words which I had chosen to indicate our trust that as man probes into space we are in fact acting in Christ. . . . I read: "I am the vine, you are the branches. Whoever remains in me, and I in him, will bear much fruit; for you can do nothing without me." John 15:5 (TEV)[260]

"And of course," says Eric Metaxas, writing about the event, "it's interesting to think that some of the first words spoken on the moon were the words of Jesus Christ, who made the Earth and the moon."[261] So whether we take Communion on the moon or in our home or in our church, it has one purpose: to remind us that God came and God cares.

Day 145

EVERYONE IS GIFTED

Today's Reading: 1 Corinthians 12

An incredible phenomenon occurs every winter in the sky. It isn't with constellations but with migrating geese.

When geese migrate, they can be seen flying in a V-shaped formation. To us on the ground, it is a thing of beauty. But to the geese, it is essential for survival. Science has recently learned that the flock actually travels up to 71 percent faster and easier by maintaining this pattern.

At certain intervals relative to the strength of the wind, the lead bird who is doing the most work by breaking the force of the wind will drop off and fly at the end of the formation. The flapping wings create an uplift of air, and the effect is greater at the rear of the formation. So the geese take turns uplifting one another. By cooperating and working together, the geese achieve long migrations that otherwise would be exceedingly difficult for even the strongest.[262]

In 1 Corinthians 12, we see Paul's V-formation for the church. It's one of the significant chapters of the New Testament for the church, because it is in in this chapter that he teaches us how to fly. This is the chapter on the gifts of the Spirit.

Spiritual gifts are tools to build with, not toys to play with, or weapons to fight with. Paul tells us something we all need to hear—that every believer has a gift: "A spiritual gift is given to each of us so we can help each other" (verse 7, NLT). They are gifts of the Holy Spirit—not our gifts. He owns them. You might say they are on loan to us.

How do we find what our spiritual gift is?

Practically speaking, here are a few simple questions to ask yourself to begin that journey:

- What do I find joy in doing?
- What do I do that tires me but never burns me out?
- What are some things I do that others are helped by and encouraged with?

After you ask yourself those questions, ask your spiritual leadership what they see as a dominate gift in you.

In the New Testament, we have three gifts chapters— Romans 12, 1 Corinthians 12, and Ephesians 4. God's purposes are designed around these gifts.

The job of every believer is to identify and employ their gift for a specific reason. As 1 Peter 4:10 tells us, "God has given each of you a gift from his great variety of spiritual gifts. Use them well to serve one another" (NLT). It seems that every time the Bible reminds us that we are all gifted by God, it reminds us why! "Use them to well to serve one another," Peter says. And Paul says in 1 Corinthians 12, "so we can help each other."

When we identify our gift, we have just found our place in the geese flight plan. We are part of the V to move the church forward. And we all must do our part.

Why does part of my body fall asleep? Because I sit on my foot and then it falls asleep. If it is doing what it's supposed to do, then it isn't sleeping. When a church is asleep, it is because people are not doing using the gifts they have been given. In order to be effective, we must know where we belong in the body and then participate.

Let me say one important thing about understanding gifts. To pursue gifts without the development of character is to sabotage the platform that the gift provides. Gifts can get you a position. Character is what keeps the position.

Don't separate the gifts of the Spirit from the fruit of the Spirit. We need both gifts and fruit in the church. The gifts provide a power far beyond natural abilities. By the fruit of the Spirit, the life of Christ is manifested. And by the gifts of the Spirit, the ministry of Christ is continued.

Spiritual maturity is not measured by the gift but by the presence of Christlike fruit. The fruit keeps the gift in check. We must be careful not to let the gifts replace the fruit as standards of spirituality. Jesus said you will know Christians by their gifts? No. You will know Christians by their *fruit*.

I wonder if the Holy Spirit was being strategic to put the greatest fruit of the Spirit—love—(in 1 Corinthians 13) right next to the gifts chapter? I think God was trying to tell us something. We will talk about that tomorrow.

A. T. Pierson, a Bible teacher from an earlier era, said,

Every one has some gift—therefore all should be encouraged. No one has all the gifts—therefore all should be humble. All gifts are for the one body—therefore all should be harmonious. All gifts are from the Lord—therefore all should be contented. All gifts are mutually helpful and needful—therefore all should be studiously faithful. All gifts promote the health and strength of the whole body—therefore none can be safely parted with. All gifts depend on His fulness for power—therefore we should keep in close touch with Him.[263]

We are all part of the church's V-formation. We need you to use your gift to help others.

DEFINITIONS ARE IMPORTANT

Today's Reading: 1 Corinthians 13

Definitions are important; it gives us a starting point. Definitions guide us and direct how to view things. Some new definitions for words you may already know:

- Calories: the tiny creatures that live in your closet and sew your clothes a little tighter every night.
- Study: the act of texting, eating, and watching Youtube with an open textbook nearby.
- Latte: Italian for, *You paid too much for that coffee.*
- Vegetarian: a Latin phase from centuries ago; it's original meaning is a really bad hunter.
- Tomorrow: the best time to do everything you had planned to do today.
- Feet: a device used for finding Legos in the dark.
- Love: giving someone the last piece of cake no matter how much you want it.[264]

Now let's get ready to define the most powerful word on the planet. That word *love* is the most important word in the human language and yet it's hard for us to define.

People say . . . I love my family. I love my wife. I love my job. I love my church. I love my dog. I love my Harley. I love your hair, your nails, that dress. I love pizza. Here's a "love" letter that I'm not sure about:

> Dearest Jimmy,
>
> No words could ever express the great unhappiness I've felt since breaking our engagement. Please say you'll take me back. No one could ever take your place in my heart, so please forgive me. I love you. I love you. I love you!
>
> Yours forever,
> Marie
> P.S. Congratulations on winning the state lottery.

How would you define love? There are so many love definitions out there. Remember, definitions guide and direct us; they are our starting points. If our definition is wrong, the longer we go with it, the further off course we will get. And that will affect our relationships with people and with God.

A group of four to eight year olds were asked, "What does love mean?" These were their answers:

- When someone loves you, the way they say your name is different. You just know that your name is safe in their mouth. (Billy, age 4)
- Love is what makes you smile when you're tired. (Terri, age 4)
- Love is when a girl puts on perfume and a boy puts on shaving cologne and they go out and smell each other. (Karl, age 5)
- Love is when you go out to eat and give somebody most of your French fries without making them give you any of theirs. (Chrissy, age 6)
- When my grandmother got arthritis, she couldn't bend over and paint her toenails anymore. So my grandfather does it for her all the time, even when his hands got arthritis too. That's love. (Rebecca, age 8)[265]

These are cute, but we don't need cute, we need accurate. The Bible doesn't disappoint, it defines love for us. It gives us a whole chapter—1 Corinthians 13:

Love is patient, love is kind *and* is not jealous; love does not brag *and* is not arrogant, does not act unbecomingly; it does not seek its own, is not provoked, does not take into account a wrong *suffered*, does not rejoice in unrighteousness, but rejoices with the truth; bears all things, believes all things, hopes all things, endures all things. Love never fails; but if *there are gifts of* prophecy, they will be done away; *if there* are tongues, they will cease; if *there is* knowledge, it will be done away. For we know in part and we prophesy in part; but when the perfect comes, the partial will be done away. When I was a child, I used to speak like a child, think like a child, reason like a child; when I became a man, I did away with childish things. (Verses 4-11)

Let's pause at the last part: *When I was a child*. I think it's important that Paul puts this here. Why? It's a call to put away childish ways you look at love. It's a call to retire your high-school letter jacket and act like an adult in relationships and define love the right way. That's the context. It's real love up against childish speaking, thinking, and reasoning.

Paul gives us the grown-up version of what love really is: "Love is patient, love is kind. It does not envy, it does not boast, it is not proud. It does not dishonor others, it is not self-seeking, it is not easily angered, it keeps no record of wrongs. Love does not delight in evil but rejoices with the truth. It always protects, always trusts, always hopes, always perseveres. Love never fails" (verses 4-8, NIV).

There is a lot here for what love is. That's why when you say "I love you," it is a big deal—especially if it's the Bible's definition. Thomas à Kempis was right when he said, "Whoever loves much, does much."[266]

The word Paul uses for love is *agape*. In *Your Father Loves You*, J. I. Packer points out that "the Greek word *agape* (love) seems to have been virtually a Christian invention—a new word for a new thing. . . . It is almost nonexistent before the New Testament. Agape draws its meaning directly from the revelation of God in Christ."[267] Agape is not an emotional word or affection. It has a much deeper motivation. Agape operates by choice rather than feeling. It is natural to love those who love us, but it is supernatural agape to love those who hate us. C. S. Lewis explained it this way: "Love is not affectionate feeling, but a steady wish for the loved person's ultimate good as far as it can be obtained."[268] That's agape. That's love.

How to Take Your Singing & Praying to a New Level

Today's Reading: 1 Corinthians 14

An article in a Detroit newspaper, titled "Remedy for a Prune Face," said, "Ladies, do you want to stay young? Then join a church choir. Women who sing stay younger-looking. A singer's cheek muscles are so well developed by exercise that her face will not wrinkle nearly as soon as a nonsinger!"[269]

Singing makes you look good. And that's biblical. Psalm 33:1 says, "Praise is becoming to the upright." The Detroit newspaper article was confirming what the psalmist claimed: that you look good when you praise God.

So let me help our praise. In 1 Corinthians 14, our singing and praying are about to get expanded. Paul is going to show us how to take our singing and praying to a new level. Here it is: "What's the solution? The answer is simple enough. Do both. I should be spiritually free and expressive as I pray, but I should also be thoughtful and mindful as I pray. I should sing with my spirit, and sing with my mind" (verse 15, MSG).

Here is how the Living Bible says it: "Well, then, what shall I do? I will do both. I will pray in unknown tongues and also in ordinary language that everyone understands. I will sing in unknown tongues and also in ordinary language so that I can understand the praise I am giving."

It's easy to get stuck in ordinary language. Paul tells us to go to another level—to pray and sing in the spirit. Is this Pentecostal? No, this is 1 Corinthians 14. Paul encourages us to sing and pray two ways—to pray with the spirit and pray with the mind. I believe the simple way of putting this is in English (*the mind*) and in tongues (*with the spirit*). Sometimes we sing what's on the screen and sometimes we sing from what is filling our hearts. To sing in the spirit is to sing in tongues; we go off script.

Paul is saying the same about prayer. Sometimes it's in English and sometimes in tongues. How do we know this "with the spirit" is tongues? Look at the next verse: "Otherwise if you bless in the spirit *only*, how will the one who fills the place of the ungifted say the "Amen" at your giving of thanks, since he does not know what you are saying?"

When you pray or sing in the spirit, as verse 16 tells us, people do not know what we are saying. Why? Because we are praying and singing to God. When we are praying and singing in the spirit, what is happening? It's just a new level, a new way of saying, "Thank You." As verse 17 shows us: "For you are giving thanks well enough."

The story goes that Niccolo Paganini (1782–1840), an amazingly gifted violinist, willed his violin to city of Genoa, Italy, on one condition: that no one would ever play it. What he failed to understand was that when the wood on the instrument was handled and used, the violin would wear only slightly. But unused, it would decay. Today Paganini's lovely violin has today become worm-eaten and useless.[270]

We are given a gift by the Spirit to be used not simply to discuss the theological implications. Use it!

If the Bible gives me the option to expand my singing and praying to a new level, I'm all in. Mind is what I am comfortable with, but spirit and mind together give me another tool, another weapon, but also takes it out of my control and now under the control of the Spirit. This is important because this is something that is part of Paul's life.

He tells us in verse 18: "I speak in tongues more than you all."

Jackie Pullinger has made an enormous impact in Hong Kong. She is the author of *Chasing the Dragon*, in which she tells the story of how she went to the walled city of Kowloon in Hong Kong to minister to the Triad gang members. Because of who and where she was, Jackie says she committed herself to praying in the spirit every day for fifteen minutes—by the clock. After about six weeks of this, she found new power in her evangelism, and people were much more open to receiving Christ.[271]

Remember, Paul is not giving you a denominational slant but a new level of singing and praying, which makes us more powerful.

MY CHILDREN DO NOT LEAVE FOR SCHOOL WITHOUT HEARING THESE WORDS

Today's Reading: 1 Corinthians 15

A woman asked her pastor when she should start training her child in spiritual things. "Should I start at six?"

"No," he said. "That's too late."

"At three years old?"

"Still too late."

"Then when should I?" she asked.

"With the grandparents."

That means my mom and dad for me and for my children. It's about generational influence.

In today's chapter we will see how important relationships are.

The other day I called my mom and thanked her for doing a devotional with me every morning when I was growing up. She already read the *Daily Bread* devotion with its corresponding Scripture prayed the verse over me.

Today as a parent, guess who never lets their kids leave the house without praying? Me! Where do you think I learned that?

Every morning before my four children leave for school, I pray over them. I would encourage you to do this as well. For your children. Your grandchildren. Your nieces and nephews.

My children never leave the house without me praying these three things: First, I pray to make them great students like Daniel.

Daniel 1:20 says, "In every matter of wisdom and understanding about which the king questioned them, he found them ten times better than all the magicians and enchanters in his whole kingdom [NIV]."

So I pray, "Make them ten times better, God. Give them a great ability to learn. Your Word says in Daniel 1:17 that God gave these four youths great ability to learn, that they soon mastered all the literature and science of the time and that You gave to Daniel special ability in understanding the meanings of dreams and visions."

Second, I pray to make them great Christians (that God would give them great convictions and great boldness for the things of God), like Joseph and Esther who stood for God in the public arena (See Genesis 41 and Esther 5).

Third, I pray for God to give them good, honoring friendships. And then I pray 1 Corinthians 15:33 over them: "Do not be misled: Bad company corrupts good character [NIV]." My children can quote this verse and do it with a tiredness in their voices because they have heard it literally hundreds of times.

I also add a companion verse to it, which I discovered recently: "The righteous choose their friends carefully" (Proverbs 12:26, NIV).

There is a difference between authority and influence. As Erwin McManus explains in *Seizing Your Divine Moment*: "Influence is always more powerful than authority. Authority can shape what a person does, but influence shapes who a person becomes." McManus says to look in the middle of the word *influence* and what do you see? *Flu*. "People who are influential pass on what they have like the flu. If you don't want what they've got, stay away from them because they'll sneeze all over you." People with influence are contagious. How does the flu get passed on? "Human contact, but proximity still endangers your contamination. . . . And through our character we pass on attitudes, values, and other life-shaping virtues. . . . Character is the resource from which our influence draws. Relationships are the venue through which influence travels. Influence is defined as 'a power affecting a person, thing or course of events' especially one that operates without any direct or apparent effort."[272]

Here is what I think I have learned about influence with raising children. Children are influenced on four levels at different ages/stages.

Stage 1: From birth to twelve, parents are the most powerful voices in their lives.

Stage 2: When they hit their teens, from ages thirteen to nineteen, peers become the more powerful influence. This is where, as parents, we need to be cognizant of who they hang with. We still have some control of who they are with. We want to be *the* house where they all want to hang out, so we have more influence.

Stage 3: Once they graduate high school, ages twenty to twenty-nine, their professors and heroes become the overwhelming influence on them. They start imitating and admiring and wanting to be like a musician, an athlete, a writer, etc. A professor becomes a new voice of authority to them. (Quick note: when choosing a college, my advice is to remember that the subjects are the same, so get them connected to school that is connected to a great church.)

Stage four: Finally, things come full circle back to parents. By age thirty, most kids realize their parents are pretty wise. As Mark Twain is claimed to have remarked, "As one boy said, 'I was thinking all these horrible thoughts about my parents when suddenly it hit me, if they're all that bad, how come I'm so wonderful?'"

Day 149

THE RAPTURE AND SUNDAY'S OFFERING . . . ANY CONNECTION?

Today's Reading: 1 Corinthians 16

Seriously, a connection between the rapture and the offering at church? It's not my idea but the apostle Paul's. And there is a big-time connection.

As we discussed previously, the chapters and verses of the Bible were not divided until much later. Sometimes when you connect the last verse of a chapter with the first verse of the next chapter, you will discover a cool connection and collaboration. That it is a single thought and we unintentionally removed some of its energy and poignancy when we separated them into chapters. One of my favorites in this vein is when 1 Corinthians 15 ends with this crescendo of praise:

> I tell you a mystery; we will not all sleep, but we will all be changed, in a moment, in the twinkling of an eye, at the last trumpet; for the trumpet will sound, and the dead will be raised imperishable, and we will be changed. For this perishable must put on the imperishable, and this mortal must put on immortality. But when this perishable will have put on the imperishable, and this mortal will have put on immortality, then will come about the saying that is written, "DEATH IS SWALLOWED UP IN VICTORY. O DEATH, WHERE IS YOUR VICTORY? O DEATH, WHERE IS YOUR STING?" The sting of death is sin, and the power of sin is the law; but thanks be to God, who gives us the victory through our Lord Jesus Christ. Therefore, my beloved brethren, be steadfast, immovable, always abounding in the work of the Lord, knowing that your toil is not *in* vain in the Lord. (1 Corinthians 15:51-58)

How powerful are these verses? Heaven, our earthly bodies, the rapture, twinkling of an eye, where is death's sting, death is swallowed up, thanks be to God who gives us the victory, so we need to remain "steadfast, immovable, always abounding in the work of the Lord."

Without skipping a beat—remember no chapter divisions in the original letter—see what Paul does: "Now concerning the collection for the saints" (1 Corinthians 16:1).

Wow, what a switch. From the rapture to the offering. Paul, are you serious? Let us down a little gentler. You just had us shouting, now you have us groaning as we reach for our wallets. To the average person, it would seem a downer to go from the rapture to the offering, but not so with Paul.

There is no transition, no segue, no bridge. He does a Left Behind series talk and then jumps right to "It's time for the collection." The rapture and the collection can be mentioned together because they are both important to God. It's important to get the saints home to heaven. And it's important to get money for the work of the ministry on earth.

We would think they have no connection, but not to the Holy Spirit.

Giving and the rapture, if it's in the Bible, it's important no matter where their placements are. Let's read the rest of the passage and make a few comments to help us today.

> Now, concerning the collection I want you to take for God's holy believers *in Jerusalem who are in need*, I want you to follow the same instructions I gave the churches of Galatia. Every Sunday, each of you make a generous offering by taking a portion of whatever God has blessed you with and place it in safekeeping. (1 Corinthians 16:1-2, TPT)

Two documents reveal a lot about us: our schedules and our bank accounts. They show how we use our most precious resources—time and money.

According to a Barna poll, only 3 percent of those who attend church actually title consistently.[273] This info is telling us something important about the church: church members are changing from stewards to consumers.

When you go to a doctor for your annual check-up, he or she will often poke, prod, and press various places, all the while asking, "Does this hurt? How about this?" If you cry out in pain, there's something wrong, and the doctor will say, "We'd better do some more tests. It isn't supposed to hurt there!" So it is when pastors preach on finances. I'm going to start pushing. Why? Because tithing is important to God.

Sixteen of the thirty-eight parables Jesus told concerned how to handle money and possessions. In the Gospels, an amazing one out of ten verses (288 in all) deal directly with the subject of money. The Bible offers five hundred verses on prayer, less than five hundred verses on faith, but more than two thousand verses on money and possessions. The Bible does not shy away from money, and neither should we.

My Brooklyn NYPD Italian father—the son of an immigrant and a man who went through the Great Depression as a kid—taught me to do three things with every check I receive:

1. Pay God: tithing;
2. Pay yourself: savings;
3. Pay your bills: integrity and wisdom.

With all of us struggling, I often hear people say, "I need money, and you said 'Pay' in all three things. How? How do I get money?" The answer is going to surprise you.

Need money? Need financial assistance? You may not like this, but here we go . . .

We don't get it by dropping hints of our need with people. That is covert manipulation. We don't really get financial assistance by simply praying. Jesus says it very plainly: we receive by giving. Why do we want to bypass that simplicity? Some pray for money without any giving. That's impossible. It would contradict what Jesus says. Jesus does not say, "Pray, and it will be given." He says, "Give, and it will be given":

> Give, and it will be given you. They will pour into your lap a good measure—pressed down, shaken together, *and* running over. For by your standard of measure it will be measured to you in return. (Luke 6:38)

Jesus put the return amount you get back in your hands: "For by your standard of measure it will be measure to you in return." No giver has ever gone broke. In fact, it's the contrary.

Not pray and get.

Not tell others and get.

But *give*, and it will be given to you.

No better way to put this into action than giving to God, or we call tithing. Which is consistent, joyful, thoughtful giving to God's church.

Tithing is a thank-you note to God who is our Provider. What Paul writes in 1 Corinthians 16 is just to give us the mechanism for giving—every Sunday, be generous because God has blessed us with something to give.

I want us to be in the rapture and go to heaven, and I want us to be generous with our offerings on earth. Thanks, Paul, for the reminder.

How Can I Help You?

Today's Reading: 2 Corinthians 1

There is a fine line between gossip and intercession. Intercession is when you talk to God about other people. Gossip is when you talk to people about people—and they can only listen but never be a solution. My dear friend R. T. Kendall says these profound words: "Remember this rule of thumb: if people gossip *to* you, they will also gossip *about* you."[274]

Gossip and intercession are so closely associated, it's just an issue of who you go to about other people. The Corinthians choose intercession and not gossip. Intercession is so important. They are about to show us what prayer for people can do for them.

Charles Bent wrote, "Intercessory prayer might be defined as loving our neighbour on our knees."[275] The Corinthian church loves Paul and loves him on their knees. Listen to these words:

> As you labor together with us through prayer. *Because there are so many interceding for us*, our deliverance will cause even more people to give thanks to God. What a gracious gift of mercy surrounds us because of your prayers! (2 Corinthians 1:11, TPT)

Or if you want a real punch to this verse, read it out of *The Message*:

> You and your prayers are part of the rescue operation—I don't want you in the dark about that either. I can see your faces even now, lifted in praise for God's deliverance of us, a rescue in which your prayers played such a crucial part.

Every time you pray for someone, you are helping them. Intercession is so much better than gossip. Choose to talk to the right person about the information you have about people. The Corinthian church did and amazing things happened. *The Message* says it best: "You and your prayers are part of the rescue operation." You get to be connected to people through your prayer life and be on a rescue mission for them.

When your prayer life is weak, so is your helping. People we love and their deliverance from a situation could very well be connected to your prayer life. Your greatest contribution to the people you love is to develop a prayer life on their behalf.

Here's an important lesson I have learned: when I pray for people, I don't gossip about them.

Let me be practical for a moment. Be deliberate in asking people if you can pray for them and then really pray for them. Don't just tell them, "I'll be praying for you." Actually do it. Write it down. Get a notebook and label it "INTERCESSION."

Here's a thought for you at church. Go one more step in your greetings and your hellos in church. We have so much surface, "Hey, how you doing?" and responses like "Great," "Good," and "Praise the Lord." Make it a point if you hear of a need, pray for them right then and there. You don't need to have an answer for their situation, but you can be part of the solution with prayer. Ask them, "Can we pray right now about that?" If you are having lunch with them, pray for their request while you pray for the meal.

Think of Paul's words to these Corinthians: "You and your prayers are part of the rescue operation—I don't want you in the dark about that either. I can see your faces even now, lifted in praise for God's deliverance of us, a rescue in which your prayers played such a crucial part."

Can you imagine one of the members of the Corinthian church having this on their next job application: "Name a big project you helped create and worked on that had success." And they write, "I helped the apostle Paul with his second missionary journey." Did they go with him?

No, they just prayed for him and he said they played a crucial role. And then they hand the interviewer Paul's "reference" letter.

We don't think prayer counts. But according to the Bible, it counts. Big time. We need to have a high view of prayer. Prayer is participating in someone's life. Prayer makes me part of your adventures. And you part of mine.

One of my favorite quotes on intercession is by Walter Wink. In fact, it's one of the five prayer quotes I try to say every day before I pray. And this one is always a good reminder about 2 Corinthians 1:11. It's simple but powerful: "History belongs to the intercessors."[276]

Make history today. Pray for someone today.

I Need Someone with Skin on

Today's Reading: 2 Corinthians 2

Frightened by the storm's thunder and lightning, little Gabby cried out for her parents. Her father entered her room and held her securely in his arms. He explained that she didn't need to be afraid, since God would take care of her, because He loved her greatly. "Daddy, I know God will take care of me and He loves me," she said. "But right now, Daddy, I just need someone with skin on to love me."[277]

God wants us to be His skin to express His love to people. Second Corinthians 2 is a plea for skin. It's the challenge for the people of God to show the forgiveness of God:

> If anyone has caused grief, he has not so much grieved me as he has grieved all of you to some extent—not to put it too severely. The punishment inflicted on him by the majority is sufficient. Now instead, you ought to forgive and comfort him, so that he will not be overwhelmed by excessive sorrow. I urge you, therefore, to reaffirm your love for him. (2 Corinthians 2:5-8, NIV)

Many times we know that God forgives us. But the hard thing is feeling the forgiveness from others. We need forgiveness with skin on. God is not the only One who is called upon to pronounce forgiveness, we are too. And not just forgiveness but the part that puts the skin on the forgiveness. That's in verse 7. We are called to do what Jesus did: He forgave and then gave us the comforter. And here Paul asks us to forgive. That's the concept we do in our hearts toward an offense. And then the crazy part is that Paul says add comfort to our forgiveness.

The word *comfort* here is the same word used in the Gospel of John for the Holy Spirit when Jesus said, "I will send the Comforter." The word means someone to walk alongside us. Paul isn't just encouraging us to forgive, but also to close the distance with the person who caused the offense.

Paul is speaking about an offense that was caused to him and the church here in this chapter. An offense that has caused him sorrow.

Perhaps you remember the cartoon strip, *Calvin and Hobbes*. Calvin is a little boy with an overactive imagination and a stuffed tiger, Hobbes, who comes to life as his imaginary friend. In one cartoon strip, Calvin turns to Hobbes and says, "I feel bad I called Susie names and hurt her feelings. I'm sorry I did that." Hobbes replies, "Maybe you should apologize to her." Calvin thinks about it for a moment and then responds, "I keep hoping there's a less obvious solution."[278]

Many believe the offense Paul is speaking about is one he first addressed in 1 Corinthians 5. There was a scandal in the church where an incestuous relationship was taking place. A man was living inappropriately with his stepmother. Second Corinthians 2 is the continuation of dealing with the brother who is starting to be broken and repentant over his sin.

There is a difference between forgiveness and probation. Probation says to the offender, *I forgive you, but I don't trust you. I forgive you but I'm watching you*. When we say, in essence, "I will forgive, but I will not forget," that is just another way of saying, "I will not forgive." The comfort Paul speaks about is a deathblow to this probational way of thinking.

Martin Luther King Dr. summarized the kind of forgiveness Paul is talking about: "Forgiveness is not an occasional act; it is a constant attitude."[279] Because we are dealing with broken people who mess up. As Lewis Smedes said, "Gandhi was right: if we all live by 'an eye for an eye' the whole world will be blind. The only way out is forgiveness."[280]

Why is forgiveness and comfort so important? Because unforgiveness unlocks the door for satanic activity:

> One whom you forgive anything, I *forgive* also; for indeed what I have forgiven, if I have forgiven anything, *I did it* for your sakes in the presence of Christ, so that no advantage would be taken of us by Satan, for we are not ignorant of his schemes. (2 Corinthians 2:10-11)

When we fail to provide forgiveness, we welcome the devil. Do you want to know what spiritual warfare is? It's fighting to forgive. This is a warning to us: this phrase, *advantage would be taken of us by Satan*, is one of the strongest warnings in the New Testament. It means direct involvement by the devil himself. That means we have a double problem: unforgiveness and demonic activity.

The devil takes "advantage," gets more than he deserves, in the situation. Satan always wants more of you and me, and unforgiveness gives him that.

C. S. Lewis was telling the truth when he said, "Everyone says forgiveness is a lovely idea, until they have something to forgive."[281] Second Corinthians 2 takes the lovely idea of forgiveness and makes it alive with people really forgiving and adding proximity and reaffirming love to the one who needs it.

It's skin on forgiveness.

Day 152

WHAT ARE WE SUPPOSED TO LOOK LIKE?

Today's Reading: 2 Corinthians 3

Today's chapter is so important because it is a challenge for the church and for us and how we are supposed to look. As we keep attending church every Sunday, going to small groups, listening to preaching, what is the end game? Where is all of this heading? What's the win? Maybe a better question is, "How do I know I am winning and on the right track?" In 2 Corinthians 3, Paul give us "the win":

> But we all, with unveiled face, beholding as in a mirror the glory of the Lord, are being transformed into the same image from glory to glory, just as from the Lord, the Spirit. [2 Corinthians 3:18]

When you read the entire chapter, Paul recounts the story of Moses from thousands of years ago and what would happen to him every time he went on the mountain and talked with God. His countenance would change and radiate after being in God's presence, and everyone saw it. But after some time away from the presence of God, the brightness would fade. Paul then explains that this new covenant brings something very special that the old covenant didn't: change without the fading.

Paul is giving us the win. Let's unpack this concept.

There are two really important thoughts here. First, there are the words, *But we all with unveiled faces*. This is huge. When Moses came down from the mountain, Moses' face would shine from talking with God and he would put a veil over his face. Here is where the problem lies: some think he put on the veil because his face was so shiny and people couldn't look at it. But that doesn't seem to be the reason according to verse 13: "And [we] *are* not like Moses, *who* used to put a veil over his face so that the sons of Israel would not look intently at the end of what was fading away."

He would put the veil on his face to cover the fading not to cover the brightness. This distinction is important. It seems he wanted the children of Israel to think more was there than what really was. The veil was not to protect them from the brightness but to try to impress them that it was still there. The veil was to impress not to protect.

This is where Paul drops the new covenant bomb. He tells us that we all have unveiled faces. He's saying, don't try to hide behind something as if you've got something going on when you don't. We have to be real to be changed. Stop pretending to be shiny when you are not. Then God can do something that lasts.

That's the next part: "But we all, with unveiled face, beholding as in a mirror the glory of the Lord, are being transformed into the same image from glory to glory, just as from the Lord, the Spirit" [verse 18]. Like Moses speaking to God and being changed, as we behold the glory of the Lord, it happens to us. What is the glory of the Lord?

Hebrews 1:3 says that Jesus is the glory of the Lord. And as we see Jesus, we are being transformed into the same image. The more we see Jesus in His Word, in His people, in His church . . . change is happening to us. Beholding is transforming. And the transforming is into the same image. That means we start looking like Jesus in our ways, attitudes, and actions.

That's the difference between Moses and us. We don't need a veil to hide fading, because it's a transformation that has lasting effect.

Our end goal, our win is not to look like our church, our denomination, or our pastor. It is to look like Jesus. Anything else fades and we need to pull out the veil. And each day we see Jesus, we become more like Him.

Day 153

THE INSIDE DETERMINES
OUR RESPONSES TO THE OUTSIDE

Today's Reading: 2 Corinthians 4

Today's chapter challenges us to remember that what's on the inside determines our responses and reactions to outside forces. Listen to Paul's outside issues that he has been facing: "*We are* afflicted in every way, but not crushed; perplexed, but not despairing; persecuted, but not forsaken; struck down, but not destroyed" (2 Corinthians 4:8-9).

Wow! There is a lot of outside stuff trying to take out Paul. There is affliction, perplexities, persecution, and people attempting to strike him down. I like the way *The Living Bible* paraphrases it:

> We are pressed on every side by troubles, but not crushed and broken.
> We are perplexed because we don't know why things happen as they
> do, but we don't give up and quit. We are hunted down, but God never
> abandons us. We get knocked down, but we get up again and keep
> going.

Based on these outside forces, Paul needs a miracle to stay alive. Pastor Rick Joyner once said, "Most Christians long to see miracles, but they don't want to be put in a position where they will need one."[282]

How in the world can Paul survive this? How can the apostle live through verses 8 and 9? He can face 8 and 9 because of verse 7: "We are like common clay jars that carry this glorious treasure within, so that the extraordinary overflow of power will be seen as God's, not ours" (TPT).

We have a silly container housing an awesome treasure. God is in us! The Holy Spirit dwelling in us is the treasure. Never mistake packaging as the treasure. We are the clay pot, the Styrofoam cup, the brown paper bag with something of infinite value in us.

We contain it but we are not it. We are not the source, just the delivery system. Because of the treasure, no matter what we face, the treasure on the inside makes it possible to handle whatever happens on the outside.

Whenever there is something valuable, we put it in a museum behind indestructible glass in a beautiful building. But when God has a treasure, where does He put it? He puts it in a common clay jar, because it isn't about the jar but about the treasure *in* the jar.

If you didn't do this in high-school science class, you can Youtube it. If you take a paper cup and put it over a hot flame, what happens? The cup burns up. But (and here is where it gets really cool and very much 2 Corinthians 4:7-ish) if you put water in a paper cup and put it over the same fire, the cup will not burn. Did you get that? The cup with the water in it does not burn up. Why? Because what is in the cup changes the dynamics of the cup.

Scientifically speaking, the water can only reach a temperature of 212 degrees Fahrenheit before it turns to steam. Since the water is in constant contact with the paper cup, the paper cannot get any hotter than 212 degrees. However, in order for the cup itself to burn, it must reach a kindling point, which happens to be higher than 212 degrees. The water maintains the temperature of the paper at a constant 212.

Or to make it really simple, the contents of the cup (the water) take on the heat and protect the outer cup from the heat. The treasure within disperses the heat.

When I am perplexed when I don't know how to decide or when I have been embarrassed, I may think I am out of resources, but I'm not out of God. All the verses say "not." Why is the not in these verses? All because we have a treasure in this earthen vessel.

We must never confuse the contents and the container. It is not that our vessel is some indestructible vessel; it is the treasure that changes our dynamic. We can't make it in life without that treasure in us. The outside forces win.

What's on the inside determines the power of the outside elements, and if God is on the inside, then "if God is 'in me,' then nothing can be against me."

Day 154

CONTROLLED BY SOMEONE ELSE

Today's Reading: 2 Corinthians 5

One of the pieces of advice I give to expecting fathers is what happens the moment about the moment they leave the hospital with their first child. I tell them that while they're still in the hospital, their baby will have around-the-clock care from professionals. Nurses and doctors will watch over that newborn, changing their diaper, and meeting every need. They are always just a button away from coming into the wife's room. The moment the new parents steps outside that hospital door, they're on their own. It's scary. And the place it starts is in the car. They put that little bundle of joy in the car seat for the first time and start driving. But Dad's driving is now controlled by what's in the backseat.

When my wife, Cindy, and I took our firstborn home from the hospital, I drove in a place that I had never been in for the first time—the slow lane. The speed limit was fifty-five but I have to tell you, I don't think I ever hit that speed. All because I was being controlled by someone else, my newborn son.

The apostle Paul tells us the same thing about his life. He is a man under another person's control: "For the love of Christ controls us" (2 Corinthians 5:14).

Why does Paul preach? His answer is that the love of Christ makes him do it. Paul is a helpless man. Paul is not deciding to do anything on his own. He cannot help himself.

Paul says that the "love of Christ controls us;" not "love for Christ" but Christ's love for us. This is an important distinction. It should be our priority that we understand the love of God. Why does temptation and fear and lust often control us? Because we do not understand the love of Christ. To have a revelation of His love for us is to be controlled by that love. When we realize how much Christ loves us, something in that revelation says there is nothing greater that is in charge of our actions.

The word *control* is an important word. The King James Version uses the word *constraineth*.

I have a set of commentaries in my library that have always been helpful in interpreting words. Since the New Testament was written in Greek, it's profitable that we occasionally expand on a word. *Control* is an important word for us to unpack. William Barclay's New Testament commentary does this brilliantly. He says that the word *control*, which Paul uses in this verse, was used in four different ways in the first century when Paul decided to use it.

First, it was an instrument that pushed on the side of an animal to keep it from moving so the farmer could administer medication. It controlled the animal from moving away from something that would make it healthier.

Second, it forced a ship to stay straight as it is sailing through a narrow channel. If the ship was to go off course just a little it can be devastating. The control of that steering wheel kept the vessel straight ahead, because straight meant safety. It was keeping on course.

Third, it meant to be so completely occupied with business that the person has no time for anything extracurricular. Their life and schedule was controlled by their commitment to their job.

Fourth, it was a word used for a prisoner who was in the control of the prison. It meant their schedule was dictated, their meals arranged, and their future determined and under the prison's control.[283]

To Paul being controlled by the love of Christ means . . . keeping still to receive medicine for health; being kept from diverting off course; being so preoccupied with his job that very little else interests him; being a prisoner, in which his life is dictated by Christ's schedule not his own. That's how strong "control" is to Paul.

To put all of those definitions together, I think the New English Bible captures verse 14 well: "Christ's love leaves us no choice."

When Hudson Taylor, the man responsible for taking the gospel to China, interviewed candidates for the mission field, he would always ask about their motivations for service. One person told him, "I want to [be a foreign missionary] because Christ has commanded us to go into all the world and preach the gospel to every creature." Another said, "I want to go because millions are perishing without Christ."

After Taylor listened to the men give a number of different answers, he said, "All of these motives, however good, will fail you in times of testings, trials, tribulations, and possible death. There is but one motive that will sustain you in trial and testing; namely, the love of Christ."[284]

That's what controlled Paul—the love of Christ.

Day 155

GETTING STUCK WITH THE WRONG PERSON

Today's Reading: 2 Corinthians 6

In today's chapter, Paul introduces us to a very important word, *yoke*. Listen to what Paul warns about it:

> Do not be yoked together with unbelievers. For what do righteousness and wickedness have in common? Or what fellowship can light have with darkness? What harmony is there between Christ and Belial? Or what does a believer have in common with an unbeliever? What agreement is there between the temple of God and idols? For we are the temple of the living God. (2 Corinthians 6:14-16, TNIV)

This principle was familiar in this agricultural culture. Listen to what the Old Testament said about a yoke: "You shall not plow with an ox and a donkey together" (Deuteronomy 22:10).

A yoke is a crossbar with two U-shaped pieces that encircle the necks of a pair of work animals that force them to work together as a team. It was essential to put together in it two of the same animals in size and species, like two oxen or two donkeys. You could not yoke two different animals like an ox and a donkey, because they were not like-minded and had different strengths. Both animals had to be the same so they could drive forward as one.

In today's passage, Paul switches to putting different things inside the yoke—the believer and the unbeliever, because this is important for a successful future. Another way to define a yoke is it means to be stuck together for the journey. You are in a relationship through a device that says you can't go where you want any longer.

Paul warns against being yoked with an unbeliever, someone who has not made Jesus Christ the Lord of their life. What kind of relationship could Paul be referring to? I believe this is true in dating and marriage. Yoked together has the idea of a long-term relationship, one that can't be easily exited from—it can be in business, marriage, investment, partnerships. And Paul is warning us that to be unequally yoked with someone who does not let the Word of God have the final say in their life is a train wreck waiting to happen.

Paul adds four questions to this argument:

What do you have in common?

What harmony can there be?

Is there any agreement between you?

What kind of fellowship?

These are the four key words of being yoked to the unbeliever.

Let's be practical for a moment. Remember we are dealing with believers in Jesus and unbelievers getting stuck in a long-term relationship, which cannot be terminated easily. In a dating relationship, the believer wants to wait to have sex in the context of marriage, while the unbeliever does not see a reason to wait. In a business deal, the believer may have ethical standards based on doing things with honesty and integrity, whereas an unbeliever sees the bottom line as the reason for doing something regardless of what they have to do to make money. In a marriage, how does a believer and an unbeliever raise their children? There is a conflict of values.

Paul is in no way saying we aren't to have contact with people who don't believe in Jesus. He is speaking specifically to the yoke—to a relationship in which you are stuck together, going somewhere together, but you have two different types of species in the yoke—one who says, "Jesus is Lord," while the other says, "I am in charge of me."

We live with people who don't believe in the resurrected Jesus, go to school with them, see them at our children's events, sit with them at football games. Those are not yokes. Having lunch, getting ice cream, doing dinner with a couple who are not Christians—that isn't a yoke.

When I do things with unbelievers, I am not thinking fellowship, I am thinking ministry. I am thinking I want them to know about the greatest Person in the universe who loves them so much. It may take some time to introduce Jesus, but when the focus is ministry and not fellowship, then I look for opportunities. It's about distinguishing between fellowship and ministry.

My job with unbelievers is not to be yoked with unbelievers, but I want to find a way to get them ready for heaven. As J. C. Ryle said, "The highest form of selfishness is that of the man who is content to go to heaven alone."[285] Let's take a bunch of people with us today. But until they become believers, let's not yoke ourselves with them.

DOING 360S

Today's Reading: 2 Corinthians 7

A man wrote to the IRS, "I haven't been able to sleep because last year on my income tax report, I deliberately misrepresented my income. I am enclosing a check for $150, if I still can't sleep, I'll send you the rest."[286]

If we are going to repent of dishonesty and do the right thing then let's do it all the way—not like this fellow in his IRS letter. Today's chapter reminds us what real repentance is. In *A Long Obedience in the Same Direction*, Eugene Peterson wrote, "Repentance is not an emotion. It is not feeling sorry for your sins. It is a decision."[287] True repentance is not just feeling bad about what we have done, it's about getting it fixed. Repentance is best defined by a little girl who said: "It's to be sorry enough to quit."

The word *repentance* is so important because it means a change of mind, a 180-degree turn from something. It carries the idea that you are heading one way, a change comes, and you turn around and head in the right direction.

The problem has been that God's people have been doing 360s most of their Christian lives. Remember what a 360 is? As a teen you go in the parking lot with your month-old driver's license and step on the gas with the steering wheel turned. And your car goes around in circles, burning rubber. There is movement but no forward movement.

False repentance is a life of 360s. We need to break the cycle. We are good at the sorry part, it's the quitting part that comes hard and comes with a price. I think victory over sin has been far from some of us because we have misdefined repentance. We have put crying and feeling horrible in the definition. The apostle Paul seems to define repentance a different way. Listen to his profound words on repentance in 2 Corinthians 7:9-11:

> I now rejoice, not that you were made sorrowful, but that you were made sorrowful to *the point* of repentance; for you were made sorrowful according to *the will* of God, so that you might not suffer loss in anything through us. For the sorrow that is according to *the will* of God produces a repentance without regret, *leading* to salvation, but the sorrow of the world produces death.

He lists seven things that describe repentance. None of them include feeling bad or tears; they're all about 180 decisions:

> Godly sorrow brings repentance that leads to salvation and leaves no regret, but worldly sorrow brings death. See what this godly sorrow has produced in you: what earnestness, what eagerness to clear yourselves, what indignation, what alarm, what longing, what concern, what readiness to see justice done. (2 Corinthians 7:10-11, NIV)

Paul says true repentance has earnestness, eagerness to clear yourself, indignation, an alarm, longing, concern, and readiness for justice to be done. These are all important things to stop the 360s so we can have 180s. Paul says when it is real repentance, certain attitudes attach to your feeling badly. The IRS letter guy felt a $150 bad but not enough bad to do what's right.

Paul says when we repent, we pull out of the 360 by indignation, hating what we have done. Hating the sin that got us there. Longing to make things right, that's the readiness of justice. The willingness to do whatever it takes to make it right with the IRS, our spouse, our children, whomever. In fake repentance, we just wants to say, "I said I'm sorry. Can't we just move on?" In real repentance, we say, "Tell me what I have to do to win over your heart and trust again?"

Paul says it produces an alarm in us. It's a wake-up call of the sin in us that is longing to be in control. The King James Version uses the phrase, *what carefulness*. Real repentance makes us careful not to put ourselves, our marriages, our families in any compromising position that could take us into a 360 spin.

In *I Surrender*, Patrick Morley writes that the church's integrity problem is in the misconception "that we can add Christ to our lives, but not subtract sin. It is a change in belief without a change in behavior. . . . It is revival without reformation, without repentance."[288]

When we remove repentance from our Christian life, we add 360 cycles. Let me remind you of someone who has been in a 360 spin for a long time. Her name is Lucy.

Several years ago, the *Peanuts* comic strip had Lucy and Charlie Brown practicing football. Lucy held the ball for Charlie's placekicking, and then Charlie would kick the ball. But every time Lucy held the ball, Charlie kick with all his might. At the precise point of no return, Lucy would pick up the ball, and Charlie's momentum, unchecked by the ball, which was no longer in place, would cause him to fall flat on his back.

This comic strip opened with Lucy holding the ball, but Charlie Brown refusing to kick. Lucy begged him to kick the ball. But Charlie Brown said, "Every time I try to kick the ball, you remove it and I fall on my back."

They went back and forth for the longest time, and finally Lucy broke down in tears and admitted, "Charlie Brown, I have been so terrible to you over the years, picking up the football like I have. I have played so many cruel tricks on you, but I've seen the error of my ways! I've seen the hurt look in your eyes when I've deceived you. I've been wrong, so wrong. Won't you give a poor penitent girl another chance?"

Charlie Brown was moved by her display of grief. "Of course, I'll give you another chance." He stepped back as she held the ball, and he ran with all his might toward it. At the last moment, Lucy picked up the ball, and Charlie Brown fell flat on his back. Lucy's last words were, "Recognizing your faults and actually changing your ways are two different things, Charlie Brown!"[289]

Wow! The Peanuts gang is telling us exactly what 2 Corinthians 7 is telling us. I hope Lucy gets out of the 360.

I Think We Messed Up This Giving Thing

Today's Reading: 2 Corinthians 8

Today's chapter may hurt as we unpack it because it deals with money, generosity, and giving. Listen to these powerful words:

> We want you to know about the grace that God has given the Macedonian churches. In the midst of a very severe trial, their overflowing joy and their extreme poverty welled up in rich generosity. For I testify that they gave as much as they were able, and even beyond their ability. Entirely on their own, they urgently pleaded with us for the privilege of sharing in this service to the Lord's people. And they exceeded our expectations: They gave themselves first of all to the Lord, and then by the will of God also to us. (2 Corinthians 8:1-5, NIV)

What makes this so cool is who was doing the giving. The Macedonian church. Remember this Macedonian church? It was the first church in Europe. This church was only eight years old and it was birthing other churches and giving. The events of Acts 16 took place around AD 49, when this church started, and despite its own struggles, it was helping other believers and other churches to start.

How they gave is an example to all of us. I see three elements in their generosity, which is a challenge to us all.

First, their economic position did not determine whether they would be givers or not. Paul says in "their extreme poverty." Giving is not for the rich, giving is for the believer. Never say, "I don't have anything to give." That is just not true, especially for the Macedonian church. We must all give to learn how to be givers wherever we are financially; just as we must all pray to learn how to pray.

Giving is learned by doing not by reading about it or watching others. The wealthy John D. Rockefeller Sr. said, "I never would have been able to tithe the first million dollars I ever made if I had not tithed my first salary, which was

$1.50 per week."[290] This silly piece of prose is packed with truth: "It's not what you do with the million if fortune should ere be your lot, but what are you doing at present with the dollar and quarter you got."[291]

Second, obedience is never convenient. There is never an easy time to obey. The Macedonians gave "in the midst of a very severe trial." They were not only battling extreme poverty but spiritual battles. Things were hitting them from all sides but still they gave. Although Paul did not mention the details of their severe trials or the cause of their poverty, his letters to the Christian communities in this province confirm these hardships.

If you are looking for an easy time to give, it won't come. Bills arrive, expenses happen. You must give despite or in spite of. That is the trust moment.

Martyn Lloyd-Jones told a story about a farmer who went into the house one day to tell his wife and family some good news. "the cow just gave birth to twin calves, one red and one white," he said. "We must dedicate one of these calves to the Lord. We will bring them up together, and when the time comes, we will sell one and keep the proceeds and we will sell the other and give the proceeds to the Lord's work."

His wife asked him which he was going to dedicate to the Lord.

"There's no need to bother about that now," he replied. "We'll treat them both in the same way and when the time comes, we'll do as I say."

A few days later one of the calves died. The man entered the kitchen looking unhappy. "I have bad news," he said. "The Lord's calf is dead."[292]

It's always the Lord's calf that dies. Never ours.

Third, though they gave during extreme poverty and severe trial, Paul said they gave with overflowing joy. The hard part of giving is getting out of the starting block. Once you have done it, a joy comes on you—because you have just done a Kingdom thing. God honors givers.

One of the parts I think brought joy was giving two ways—what they could do and what they had to trust God to help them do. Look at verse 3: "I testify that they gave as much as they were able, and even beyond their ability" (NIV). The "beyond ability" giving crosses from the discipline of giving to the joy of giving. One is by sweat, hard work, and discipline that they "gave as much as they were able." That is getting your paycheck and writing your tithe check. The other giving is by faith—they gave "beyond their ability." That is a step of faith. And that brings overflowing joy.

The pastor stood before the congregation. "I have bad news, good news, and more bad news." The congregation grew quiet. "The bad news is: the church needs a new roof!" The congregation groaned. "The good news is: we have enough money for the new roof." A sigh of relief rippled through the gathered group. "The bad news is: it's still in your pockets."[293]

Based on the Macedonian-2 Corinthians 8-model, that should be the good news! We have money to give, let us go Macedonian on the need. That's why verse 4 says, they (those giving) begged for the opportunity to give. It wasn't the preacher begging but the givers begging for the opportunity. Wow, we really messed up this giving thing.

ARE YOU A THERMOSTAT
OR A THERMOMETER?

Today's Reading: 2 Corinthians 9

Some people are thermostats and some are thermometers. Thermometers just register the temperature of the room, while the thermostat controls the temperature of the room. This is not just for hot and cold but for hot and cold attitudes. The people who are thermostats try to control a room with their attitudes. If they are happy, we all get to be happy. If they are quiet and sad, no one gets to be exuberant and laugh. The thermostat just dictated how the room will be. This is both good and bad. Good with good attitudes. Bad with bad attitudes. Second Corinthians 9 is a good attitude from the Corinthian Christians. It's so good that the apostle Paul boasts about therm. Listen to what Paul says about the Corinthian thermostat:

> I keep boasting to the churches of Macedonia about your passion to give, telling them that the believers of Corinth have been preparing to give for a year. Your enthusiasm is contagious—it has stirred many of them to do likewise. (2 Corinthians 9:2, TPT)

Their good contagious attitude showed itself through generosity and giving. The Corinthians enthusiasm to give was a thermostat and started an epidemic of giving among other Christians. They seemed to follow what Sir Winston Churchill said: "We make a living by what we get, but we make a life by what we give."[294] The Corinthians not only made a life, but made a life worth emulating and imitating.

I love Paul's phrase, *Your enthusiasm is contagious*. I want to be a good thermostat. I want to live a life worth imitating. I want my giving to inspire people. I want my life to inspire other people. I want my love for Jesus to inspire other people.

Do you?

Paul tells the Corinthians how wide their influence has been on other Christians. He tells them that their generosity didn't just meet a need, but inspired people to be better. The dividends on their gift far exceeded their expectations of simply meeting a need. The result? Paul says much more happened to the church than having a need met.

> So two good things happened as a result of your gifts—those in need are helped, and they overflow with thanks to God. Those you help will be glad not only because of your generous gifts to themselves and to others, but they will praise God for this proof that your deeds are as good as your doctrine. And they will pray for you with deep fervor and feeling because of the wonderful grace of God shown through you.
> (2 Corinthians 9:12-14, TLB)

J. L. Kraft (the head of Kraft Cheese Corporation) said this about giving to God's work: "The only investments I have ever made which have paid constantly increasing dividends is the money I have given to the Lord."[295] The apostle Paul is about to tell us about those increasing dividends. Paul says your gift inspires people toward gratitude and praise. There are some times in which praise can come through an offering not just an instrument.

He also says, their gift was proof that their "deeds are as good as [their] doctrine." That is powerful. Their generosity fleshes out what they believe. It's one thing to say we believe a doctrine but a whole other thing to live it out. Generosity is the proof. Donald Miller says it like this: "What I believe is not what I say I believe; what I believe is what I do."[296]

And finally, their generosity got them on the prayer list. Verse 14 says, "They will pray for you with deep fervor and feeling because of the wonderful grace of God shown through you." Generosity made people praise, gave them proof, and inspired them to pray.

Praise, proof, and prayer. All from a generous offering.

Why is it so hard to give away money? Why is it difficult not only to tithe but to be available to be generous when we hear of a need? It's because Satan has found a way to block praise, proof, and prayer from coming our way by stopping generosity.

The famed psychiatrist Karl Menninger said, "Generous people are rarely mentally ill."[297] He's right! They know the rewards of generosity—the rewards for them and others. As we mentioned earlier, but it's a good reminder, Jim Eliot said it best, "He is no fool who gives what he cannot keep to gain what he cannot lose."[298]

What a great gain for those generous Corinthian givers. Help us, Lord, to inspire people like that.

I Wrote Someone a Prescription the Other Day

Today's Reading: 2 Corinthians 10

I wrote someone a prescription the other day. Don't get nervous and don't report me just yet. The condition the person had was *deilia* (day-lea).

Ever heard of it? A lot of people I talk to and counsel with face deilia and are in desperate need of a prescription. There are times I've even have had this condition myself.

For this person, I prescribed three: *sophronismos* (you may not recognize this, but it is very powerful), *dunamis*, and *agape*.

These are not chemicals, these are Greek words.

Deilia is the Greek word for fear. Fear can be debilitating. And the Bible clearly gives the prescription for us in 2 Timothy 1:7: "God has not given us a spirit of fear, but of power and of love and of a sound mind" (NKJV).

We live a culture of fear today. We have names of fear for everything. Consider just a few:

Peladophobia: fear of baldness and bald people

Gamophobia: fear of marriage

Levophobia: fear of objects on the left side of the body

Aphenphosmphobia: fear of being touched

Hippopotomonstrosesquippedaliophobia: fear of long words

Euphobia: fear of hearing good news

Syngenesophobia: fear of relatives

Fear is so paralyzing to people today because there are so many things to be afraid of. Fear can make us do things that are not even sensible. In fact, fear can kill someone.

I had a person tell me one time that she and her family wanted to come to our church, but because it was located in the inner city, they were too afraid. They actually came to the church building one Sunday, and while parking, faced the fear that someone would rob them. They drove all the way there and fear made them turnaround. "Was that the Lord speaking to me and protecting me?" My response was absolutely not!

God is a Father. He does not lead us by fear, because we are His children. He leads us by wisdom and by speaking to us. Fear is not a way God guides us. I gave her the 2 Timothy 1:7 prescription of fighting fear with love, power, and a sound mind.

So what does all of this have to do with 2 Corinthians 10? Here it is: we don't fight the spiritual with the natural. If we are faced with a spiritual enemy, we need a spiritual weapon. At times I've been afraid of getting cancer, because my father died of it. That isn't a fear we break with barley green, wheat grass, and essential oils. That helps but fear is a spirit. And that spirit wants to control us. Once we are cancer free, we will face some other thing to be afraid of.

We have to fight spiritual enemies with spiritual weapons. That is today's challenge. Listen to what the apostle Paul tells us about fighting:

> Although we live in the natural realm, we don't wage a military campaign employing human weapons, *using manipulation to achieve our aims.* Instead, our spiritual weapons are energized with divine power to effectively dismantle the defenses *behind which people hide.* We can demolish every deceptive fantasy that opposes God and break through every arrogant attitude that is raised up in defiance of the true knowledge of God. We capture, like prisoners of war, every thought and insist that it bow in obedience to the Anointed One.
> (2 Corinthians 10:3-5, TPT)

So let's go back to our fear story. Because there are other prescriptions we can give from the Bible. Remember, God has not given us a spirit of fear. Fear is a supernatural enemy and needs a supernatural prescription to fight it. So here's another prescription. What is our weapon against the spirit of fear?

> The Spirit you received does not make you slaves, so that you live in fear again; rather, the Spirit you received brought about your adoption to sonship. And by him we cry, "*Abba*, Father." The Spirit himself testifies with our spirit that we are God's children. Now if we are children, then we are heirs—heirs of God and co-heirs with Christ, if indeed we share in his sufferings in order that we may also share in his glory.
> (Romans 8:15-17, NIV)

This is incredible. Paul tells us that we don't have to live in fear again—of cancer, of being robbed in the inner city, of . . . Why? Because we have been adopted by God. He's our Father and He cares for His children.

Paul says the spirit of fear is seeking to blind us and hide the fact that we have a heavenly Father who sees us and protects us. Every time we let fear control us, then we are blinded to our adoption papers. And instead of crying, "Abba Father," we cry to other people. We take away the relationship of God as our Father and make Him smaller in our eyes.

A plane was en route to Boston and because of bad weather, the plane was being battered around profusely. Everybody onboard was in a panic, wondering if they would even reach Boston because of such forceful turbulence. Everyone, that is, except for one lady who sat quietly knitting a sweater. One of the passengers by her noticed how calm she was, so he leaned over to her to ask her how she could be so peaceful at a time like this.

"Young man, I am on my way to visit my son in Boston, but I have another son who died and went to heaven. It doesn't matter which one of them I visit. My Father knows which son I will see today."[299]

This woman realized that her Father was greater than any turbulence threatening a plane. That's using a spiritual weapon to fight a spiritual enemy.

THE UNCOMPLICATED CHRISTIAN LIFE

Today's Reading: 2 Corinthians 11

Click on google.com and you'll find a predominantly white screen with less than forty words on it. That's it. Compare it to other search engines where the user is confronted with hundreds of words. More than 75 percent of all web searches are done on Google.[300] They are simple, so they appeal.

As we look at today's chapter, we find that Paul is calling us to go "Google" with our Christianity: "I am afraid that, as the serpent deceived Eve by his craftiness, your minds will be led astray from the simplicity and purity of *devotion* to Christ" (2 Corinthians 11:3).

I love that word *simplicity*. The goal of Satan is to lead you from that. Simple is in, complex is out. Paul is telling us that Satan is a complicator of things. His goal is to move you from simplicity to complexity. And the most important thing Satan wants to complicate is how to become a Christian. And yet Christianity is very Google-ish. Consider Romans 10:9, which has only twenty-six words: "that if you confess with your mouth Jesus as Lord, and believe in your heart that God raised Him from the dead, you will be saved."

Religions want to add to the big twenty-six. Carry a briefcase, go on a mission trip, die as a martyr, cut your hair, wear this dress, don't eat this, the list goes on and on.

Confess Jesus with your mouth and believe God raised Him from the dead and you will be saved. Add anything else to those twenty-six Google-ish words and you have been led astray from simplicity, as Eve was. God makes it simple for us.

I love the name of Jesus. So simple. Maybe not to us today, but back then, definitely. It was one of the most common names of the first century. It was like someone naming their child John or Scott or Joe. God did not give Jesus some space-age name—Moonstruck, Alphaman, or Zorg. God picked a common name and then gave Jesus a job as a carpenter. A common occupation of that time. Not something as spectacular as technology director for Jerusalem. It was simply a job to build stuff like a table out of wood. He wasn't creating things as He did in Genesis, but He was building tables like we do. God is simple, Satan is complicated.

Jesus boiled down 613 commandments to two. Why? That's what Jesus does. He doesn't complicate life, He uncomplicates it.

Sin complicates your life. Have sex outside the boundaries of the covenant of marriage and watch how life gets complicated for you. God is really simple. Satan complicates.

Finally, think how simple the playlist of heaven is. Today in churches around the world, think of all the songs people are singing, and all the lyrics we have to put on the screen. Now think of heaven and the angels. They are singing one song with three words: *Holy, holy, holy.*

Why do the angels sing the same song? Wouldn't you think that after four millennia some angels would say, "Okay we got it. We don't even need words on the screen any more. *Holy, holy, holy.* Can't we do some Elevation or Hillsong music?" Why do they sing the same song? My simple take is that every time the angels look at Jesus, they cover their eyes when they see Him, and I think they forget the words, so that all they can say over and over is, "Holy, holy, holy."

The closer you get to the living God, the simpler things become. God helps simplify things, and Satan complicates things.

Let's get Google with our Christianity.

SURPRISED BY THE RED LETTERS WHEN I WASN'T EXPECTING THEM

Today's Reading: 2 Corinthians 12

In today's chapter we see a set of red letters, which come alive in a place that we don't expect. Do you know what I mean when say red letters? For those of us who grew up in the church when KJV was just about our only option of Bible translation, we know that all of Jesus' words were in red letters to distinguish them from all other letters. We knew those red letters were all in Matthew, Mark, Luke, John, and the very beginning of Acts. Those were the books of the Bible that covered when Jesus was on the earth. But red letters in 2 Corinthians 12?

Paul needed an answer to his prayer, and he got red letters:

Because of the surpassing greatness of the revelations, for this reason, to keep me from exalting myself, there was given me a thorn in the flesh, a messenger of Satan to torment me—to keep me from exalting myself! Concerning this I implored the Lord three times that it might leave me. And He has said to me, *"My grace is sufficient for you, for power is perfected in weakness."* Most gladly, therefore, I will rather boast about my weaknesses, so that the power of Christ may dwell in me. Therefore I am well content with weaknesses, with insults, with distresses, with persecutions, with difficulties, for Christ's sake; for when I am weak, then I am strong. (2 Corinthians 12:7-10, emphasis added)

Paul said he was given a thorn in the flesh. No one knows exactly what the thorn was. Many have speculated everything from a physical handicap of eye sight to epilepsy. But as men fight over what the thorn was, it's easy to miss the big point of Paul's prayer. He asked God three times to take away the thorn. And out of nowhere come red letters!

Jesus responds to Paul's prayer to remove his thorn. His response, though, is not what Paul expected. To me it was a yes-or-no question. Jesus answered better. Jesus said to Paul, "My grace is sufficient for you."

To divorce these words from their context is an unpardonable atrocity. It is one of the most touching pieces of Pauline autobiography in the New Testament. It was from the ascended, throne-sitting, righthand of God—Jesus. And it was given to a pain-racked, baffled, questioning, no-answer-to-prayer apostle. These words turned him around in an instant.

Read the beginning of what Paul said: thorn in the flesh; messenger of Satan to keep me from exalting myself; entreated the Lord three times for it to leave; nothing happened.

Then Jesus spoke—the red letters. "And He has said to me . . ." The "He" was Jesus.

And right after the red letters, the change came to Paul.

He went from "I got a thorn in the flesh, and God won't answer my prayer about it" to "Not only can I handle the thorn, but because Jesus spoke to me, I can handle a lot more." And Paul added to the thorn list more issues:

Most gladly, therefore, I will rather boast about my weaknesses, so that the power of Christ may dwell in me. Therefore I am well content with weaknesses, with insults, with distresses, with persecutions, with difficulties, for Christ's sake; for when I am weak, then I am strong. (verses 9-10)

One word from Jesus and Paul was able to take on five more challenges.

Jesus may not say what you want, but He always says what you need. Paul was looking for a thorn answer and received a grace supply.

Jesus did not say, "I will remove the thorn." But He did say, "I will give you a great grace, which is better than a thorn being removed."

Did you get that? Sufficient grace with a thorn is better than no grace without a thorn.

CLEAR YOUR DESK AND TAKE OUT A PIECE OF PAPER

Today's Reading: 2 Corinthians 13

Charles Schwab's CEO, Walt Bettinger, opened the vault to the Schwab test he uses for potential high-level hires. He told the *New York Times* that we can discover a person's character by the ways they respond during times of great pressure and distress. So before each new hire, to test out the job candidate to see how they react when things don't go according to plan, Bettinger takes the potential employee out for a breakfast interview. What the candidate doesn't know is that beforehand, they arrive, Bettinger asks the restaurant staff to purposefully mess up the order in exchange for a substantial tip.

His "wrong order" test helps him see how prospective hires deal with adversity. "Are they upset, are they frustrated, or are they understanding? Life is like that, and business is like that," he said. "It's just another way to look inside their heart rather than their head."

In the same interview with the *Times*, Bettinger shared one of his own biggest failures. After spending hours studying for a final college exam, he went to class ready to figure out calculations. Instead the professor handed to each student a blank sheet of paper.

"The professor said, 'I've taught you everything I can teach you about business in the last ten weeks," Bettinger recalled. "But the most important message, the most important question, is this: What's the name of the lady who cleans this building?"

Bettinger had no idea. He failed the exam, got a B in the class, and ruined his 4.0 average. But it taught him an important lesson on recognizing individuals "who do the real work."

"That had a powerful impact," he said. "Her name was Dottie, and I didn't know Dottie. I'd seen her, but I'd never taken the time to ask her name."

Since then, he admits he's "tried to know every Dottie I've worked with."[301]

That failure in college became an important reminder of what truly matters in life.

Two tests that people never saw coming. The wrong-order test and the name-of-the-lady test.

We encounter a very important we-never-saw-it-coming test in today's chapter. The apostle Paul goes all "Charles Schwab" on the church people. It's sobering. After coming to the end of 2 Corinthians, we are almost blindsided by the "clear your desk and take out a piece of paper" announcement—which means a test is coming:

Test yourselves *to see* if you are in the faith; examine yourselves! Or do you not recognize this about yourselves, that Jesus Christ is in you— unless indeed you fail the test? But I trust that you will realize that we ourselves do not fail the test. (2 Corinthians 13:5-6)

I hate tests. But this is one I can't take lightly. This is not for a science or an English grade. This is about eternity. So now the big questions: How do we test ourselves? How do we ensure we don't fail this test?

Paul tells us it's a test to recognize if Jesus is in you. D Martyn Lloyd Jones said:

"A Christian is the result of the operation of God, nothing less, nothing else. No man can make himself a Christian; God alone makes Christians."[302] So how do we examine ourselves to see if we are in the faith?

Since God does the birthing, we should have His birthmarks. God gave us some birthmarks if we have been born again. Birthmarks that looks like His family likeness. We find those in 1 John. The apostle John uses the phrase *born of God* over and over, giving us the birthmark. If we are born of God, then we have the life of God and we pass the test.

Let me give you a few of those birthmarks, which can help us on the "see if you are in the faith" test. Look at this verse from 1 John: "No one who is born of God will continue to sin, because God's seed remains in them; they cannot go on sinning, because they have been born of God" (1 John 3:9, NIV).

Christians are not sinless, but we will sin less and less, because we are born of God. Here's another: "Dear friends, let us love one another, for love comes from God. Everyone who loves has been born of God" (1 John 4:7, NIV). A love for people comes to those born of God.

Here's one more from 1 John: "Everyone born of God overcomes the world. This is the victory that has overcome the world, even our faith" (1 John 5:4, NIV). When you are born of God, your mind starts to renew and you don't think about things and assess things as you used to.

Before someone is born again, the Bible says, "we are dead," dead in trespasses and sins. The way we see if someone is not dead is to check their pulse. Is that vital organ, called the heart, showing a pulse? The heart must be beating. These passages from 1 John help us know if the heart is beating. As Soren Kierkegaard said, "It is so much easier to become a Christian when you aren't one than to become one when you assume you already are."[303]

Paul's see-if-you're-in-the-faith test is serious and reminds us not to assume anything.

What's Supposed to Happen When You Tell Your Story

Today's Reading: Galatians 1

A biography always ends with a person, their story, and what *they* did. A testimony is different. A testimony ends with what *God* did. God is the star of a testimony. A person is the star of a biography.

The old saints used to say, "No test? Then no testimony." The test is what gives us the testimony and the story. I grew up always hearing the word *testimony*. We don't hear that anymore. It's a forgotten form of storytelling that needs to be reintroduced. We used to call it "testimony services" in my church when I was growing up. It was in those services we got to hear people's stories.

The basic plot line to a testimony is this: "It's bad, really bad. I was at the end of my rope. Jesus stepped in. And this is what He did. He rescued me."

I grew up in a storytelling family. We would have incredible Christian heroes sit around our table at home and share their stories with us. And if I wasn't there, I would hear the stories from my parents. I heard how Pennsylvania country preacher David Wilkerson started Teen Challenge in New York City. How converted gang member Nicky Cruz went from killing people to preaching to them. How Sonny Argonzoni, a notorious New York drug addict, got saved and started a movement of churches worldwide called Victory Outreach. How my dad witnessed miracles when he was evangelist Kathryn Khulman's bodyguard when she was in town and he was off duty with the NYPD. My parents told me about the healings they saw through the ministry of Smith Wigglesworth when he would come to their church, Glad Tidings, in lower Manhattan. I got to hear stories from Paul Yonggi Cho, pastor of the million-member church in Seoul, South Korea, as he sat at our dinner table.

All these stories would inform and inflame. That's what a testimony does. It sets us on fire and helps us realize how amazing God is.

We're missing these stories today, especially for our youth. Eugene Peterson calls it "historical amnesia" and has this to say about it:

Another characteristic of the adolescent that has spread into the larger population is the absence of historical sense. The adolescent, of course, has no history. He or she has a childhood, but no accumulation of experience that transcends personal details and produces a sense of history. His world is highly personal and extremely empirical.

As a consequence, the teenager is incredibly gullible. . . . They may know the facts of history and read historical novels by the dozen, but they don't feel history in their bones. It is not *their* history. The result is that they begin every problem from scratch. There is no feeling of being part of a living tradition that already has some answers worked out and some procedures worth repeating.[304]

I'm so happy my parents connected me to the stories of God's people. It helped me see a much bigger picture than my own small world.

In today's chapter Paul tells his testimony. And he also shares how people realized that what happened to him couldn't have happened unless God stepped in. That this was nothing short of a miracle:

The only thing they heard about me was this: "Our former enemy, who once brutally persecuted us, is now preaching the good news of the faith that he was once obsessed with destroying!" *Because of the transformation that took place in my life*, they praised God even more! (Galatians 1:23-24, TPT)

Shannon L. Alder once said, "God can deliver you so well that some people won't believe your testimony."[305]

Someone said it like this:

God formed man.
Sin deformed him.
Education informs him.
Religion may reform him.
But only Jesus Christ can transform him.

Paul made it to the final "only Jesus Christ can transform him" part. Most people tell their story and stop at the education part. Transformation happens with Jesus not from a university degree.

This is Paul's testimony: "Our former enemy, who once brutally persecuted us, is now preaching the good news of the faith that he was once obsessed with destroying!" Or to put it another way, Paul was saying, "The people I was persecuting are now on my team. The religion I made fun of has changed my life."

What a story Paul had. And when he told his story, people were drawn to God not to Paul. That is the mark of a powerful testimony. We hear crazy stuff and realize only God could have gotten them out.

There is something powerful when people tell their stories. In fact, the Bible says that these stories have devil-defeating ability. Listen to Revelation 12:11: "They overcame him by the blood of the Lamb, and by the word of their testimony" (KJV). The "him" they overcame is Satan. The apostle John is saying something profoundly powerful—that your testimony is right up there with the blood of Jesus in defeating the devil. That will make you think twice about what God has done in you and for you.

Tell your story. The Kingdom wins, people glorify God, and the devil is defeated.

How a Really Good Man Ends up Very Bad

Today's Reading: Galatians 2

Barnabas was not even his real name; it was a nickname given to him by the people in the early church. His real name was Joseph. In Acts 4 we read that Joseph was so positive in his conversations that people nicknamed him Barnabas, because everything he said made them feel great.

His journey starts in Acts 4, and the last verse we get about him is in Galatians 2, today's chapter. This is Barnabas's journey on how a really good man ended up pretty bad. Strap in for a jolting journey.

I remember reading something interesting about the first Olympics in Greece. The ancient Greeks, the originator of the Olympic games, had a twist to some of their running events. The runners were all given torches before the race, which they had to pass on in a relay. The runner who won the race was not the man who crossed the line in the shortest time but the man who crossed it in the least time with his torch still burning.[306]

That sounds about right for every Christian. We want to make sure we are not just doing "stuff" but doing things with a heart on fire for God.

Let's check out Barnabas's torch. His journey is all through Acts. He was the encourager in Acts 4. By Acts 9, we can see why he is called "encourager," because his gift was exactly what the apostle needed at his conversation. Paul, who had been bringing havoc to the early Christians through imprisonment and death, had a vision of Jesus on the road to Damascus and became a Christian. There is a big problem, though: no one trusts Paul. They think it's a ploy to kill more Christians. Enter Barnabas:

Listen to these verses in Acts 9:

Upon arrival in Jerusalem he tried to meet with the believers, but they were all afraid of him. They thought he was faking! Then Barnabas brought him to the apostles and told them how Paul had seen the Lord on the way to Damascus, what the Lord had said to him, and all about his powerful preaching in the name of Jesus. Then they accepted him. (Acts 9:26-28, TLB)

If it weren't for Barnabas, Paul could have chucked it all and said forget this Christian thing if this is the way His people act. Truth be told, if there were no Barnabas, there may not have been a Paul. Barnabas played a key role in the church and in Paul's growth and ministry.

Barnabas and Paul even go on the very first missionary journey together to share the gospel. Then in Acts 15, the torch seemed to have a gust of wind come against it. A very big disagreement happened between disciple and discipler, Paul and Barnabas, right before the second missionary journey. It was over whether they should take a young man named John Mark. These words in Acts 15 are important to note before we head to Galatians 2:

> There occurred such a sharp disagreement that they separated from one another, and Barnabas took Mark with him and sailed away to Cyprus. But Paul chose Silas and left. (verses 39-40)

And then that's it. No more mention of Barnabas until Galatians 2. It's been six years after this disagreement. Now we read the last verse in the Bible about Barnabas, and we find out where the torch is:

> When Peter came to Antioch, I had to oppose him to his face, for what he did was very wrong. When he first arrived, he ate with the Gentile believers, who were not circumcised. But afterward, when some friends of James came, Peter wouldn't eat with the Gentiles anymore. He was afraid of criticism from these people who insisted on the necessity of circumcision. As a result, other Jewish believers followed Peter's hypocrisy, and even Barnabas was led astray by their hypocrisy. (Galatians 2:11-13, NLT)

Barnabas, the encourager. Barnabas, the visionary. Now Barnabas, the hypocrite.

Paul's ministry partner, Paul's first mentor, Paul's copastor and co-missionary became a hypocrite.

That word *hypocrite* is such an ugly word. It's a Greek word that means actor on a stage. You start acting instead of being who you really are.

How does that happen? And how did it happen to Barnabas? The first verse about Barnabas, the encourager, was in Acts 4, around AD 30. The last verse about Barnabas, the hypocrite, was in Galatians 2, around AD 54. That's twenty-four years later. Barnabas was finishing his race as a hypocrite with the torch going out.

Barnabas, no longer on the mission field, was back and had found a group of people bitter just like him. He was with people who fueled his fleshly flame and not the spiritual flame. If you are with people who let you talk about your offense that you have with others and they don't challenge you to fix it, then you are with the wrong group.

Barnabas went to be with a group of people just as dysfunctional as he was.

So here's the question: how does a really good man end really bad?

And the question for us: can this happen to me?

I don't think I am out of bounds to think Barnabas's choice stemmed ultimately from the disagreement he had with Paul in Acts 15. Something got in Barnabas's heart when it happened and he didn't fix it by resolving it. What's dangerous about these kinds of issues is that what doesn't seem to be a problem at first, over time can become toxic.

Which tells me something important: time doesn't fix all wounds. A wound unfixed over time corrodes the heart. It is an awful doctor; it mistreats and deceives its patients. It isn't time but forgiveness that heals the wounds.

I think God may be showing us through Paul and Barnabas's relationship not to take disagreements lightly. Unresolved conflict has a way of blowing out our fire. As Rick Warren said, "It's always more rewarding to resolve a conflict than to dissolve the relationship."[307] We can't finish well with unforgiveness.

Barnabas' journey should have ended in Acts on three missionary journeys with Paul and spreading the gospel. Instead a good man ended his journey by telling his people his side of the disagreement. Barnabas was supposed to finish with the torch burning, declaring the Good News.

One of my mentors and friends, Winkie Pratney, was insightful when he said, "There are a lot of happy young sinners, but you don't see happy old sinners. Sin does not age well."[308]

Boy, that's the truth. Sin does not age well.

Acts 15 to Galatians 2 was six years. This disagreement sat in Barnabas's heart for six years. The sin didn't age well.

How Did the Old Testament People Become Christians?

Today's Reading: Galatians 3

The letter to the Galatians is a call back to reintroducing the simplicity of the gospel message. It's so simple that the formula has not been changed for five thousand years. And Galatians 3 tells us something epic and answers a question I have been asked many times: how did the Old Testament people become believers or Christians?

How did those in Genesis through Malachi have a relationship with God?

This may surprise you, but there's no better New Testament letter to answer this than the book of Galatians. Paul says this:

> Even so Abraham BELIEVED GOD, AND IT WAS RECKONED TO HIM AS RIGHTEOUSNESS. Therefore, be sure that it is those who are of faith who are sons of Abraham. The Scripture, foreseeing that God would justify the Gentiles by faith, preached the gospel beforehand to Abraham, *saying*, "ALL THE NATIONS WILL BE BLESSED IN YOU." So then those who are of faith are blessed with Abraham, the believer. (Galatians 3:6-9)

These words are incredible. Paul associates so many New Testament salvation words with Abraham: Abraham believed; reckoned to him as righteous; God preached the gospel to Abraham; and finally called the believer.

Wow! This sounds like a Christian from the book of Acts not someone from 2000 BC, from the book of Genesis. Abraham the believer is a great name for the Old Testament patriarch.

How did an Old Testament person become a Christian? Simple. The same way we do. They were called upon to believe God—just as the book of Romans tells us that belief in God makes us righteous, or reckoned.

I love that word. *Reckoned* is a word Paul uses for the result of belief. The word means to impute. To make it even simpler, it is to put into an account. It's like watching a spy movie and the characters are electronically sending huge sums of money to a Cayman island account. This is what happens to those who believe in God: God sends righteousness to your account. Righteousness is not from stringing together a bunch of obedient successes and good days in being a Christian. Righteousness is imputed, reckoned, sent to our account, like to a Cayman island offshore account. It's something huge . . . righteousness.

All because we do one thing: believe in God.

That's the gospel of the New Testament and that was the gospel of the Old Testament, which Abraham had preached to him.

Jonathan Whitfield was preaching to coal miners in England, and he asked a man, "What do you believe?"

"Well, I believe the same as the church," the man said.

"And what does the church believe?"

"Well, they believe the same as me."

Seeing he was getting nowhere, Whitfield said, "And what is it that you both believe?"

"Well, I suppose the same thing."[309]

That's elusive belief. The question we should ask is, what did Abraham believe? I think Hebrews 11:6 tells us: "Without faith it is impossible to please *Him*, for he who comes to God must believe that He is and *that* He is a rewarder of those who seek Him." The writer of Hebrews says that we must believe that He is. That means Abraham believed all that God disclosed about Himself. That God is exactly who He said He is.

Why is that important?

First, it's not making up things about God's character but believing what He reveals. And for Abraham, it started with "God is one, not many," like the polytheistic cultures he was surrounded by. Abraham did what Martin Luther King Jr. expressed: "Take the first step in faith. You don't have to see the whole staircase, just take the first step."[310]

Apologist Ravi Zacharias said: "We have a right to believe whatever we want, but not everything we believe is right."[311] As time progressed all the way to the book of Galatians, it still holds true that we must believe that He is. God has shown us a lot more. He has shown more of Himself through His Son Jesus. Belief is based on God disclosing Himself, revealing Himself, and the pinnacle of God's self-revelation is in the person of Jesus.

Everything starts to make sense when you believe God. C. S. Lewis said it best: "I believe in Christianity as I believe that the Sun has risen, not only because I see it but because by it, I see everything else."[312]

So how did Old Testament saints become Christians? The same way we do. Abraham believed God is. We do the same. We must believe God is. The only difference is that to believe that He is became so much clearer in God's Son Jesus.

Day 166

RIGHT ON TIME

Today's Reading: Galatians 4

In his autobiography, Buck O'Neil tells what it was like being a black man who played professional baseball before African-Americans were allowed to play in the all-white major leagues. By the time the color barrier was broken in 1947, O'Neil was considered too old to play in the big leagues, as were most of his teammates. Many of his friends grew bitter about their missed opportunities. O'Neil writes:

> At a reunion of Negro league players in Ashland, Kentucky, a reporter from *Sports Illustrated* asked me if I had any regrets, coming along as I did before Jackie Robinson integrated the major leagues. And this is what I told him . . . "Waste no tears for me. I didn't come along too early—I was right on time."[313]

That was the title of his autobiography, *I Was Right on Time*.

And that's what today's chapter is about, perfect timing. God's timing couldn't have been any better than when Jesus came to earth. The apostle Paul confirms that:

> When the right time came, the time God decided on, he sent his Son, born of a woman, born as a Jew, to buy freedom for us who were slaves to the law so that he could adopt us as his very own sons.
> (Galatians 4:4-5, TLB)

Here is where it gets really amazing. Why couldn't God have timed it any better? Let's answer the why by looking at history.

When we look at history, the coming of Jesus was perfect for two reasons. Centuries earlier, Alexander the Great had conquered most of the known world, which didn't just bring Greek culture to the world, it also unified the planet with one language, Greek. That's why the New Testament is written in Greek.

After the demise of the Greeks, the Roman Empire picked up where Alexander left off and the Romans started expanding but doing something that would make the Good News of Jesus expand also. The Romans opened the way for expansion over three continents through roads and safe sea travel. They brought order to intercountry travel. One language and a world that was able to be traveled in. That's a good time for Jesus to come.

But it gets crazier. This is why God is right on time.

I was recently reading apologist Dinesh D'Souza's book *What's So Great About God*. In it he quotes statistician Erik Kreps. Think of Erik's numbers and think of our Galatians verse for today: "When the right time came . . . he sent his Son."

Now buckle your seat belts.

The Population Reference Bureau estimates that the number of people who have ever been born in human history is approximately 105 billion. Of this number, about 2 percent were born . . . before the birth of Christ. "So, in a sense," Erik Kreps notes, "God's timing couldn't have been more perfect. If he'd come earlier in human history, how reliable would the records of his relationship with man be? But he showed up just before the exponential explosion in the world's population . . . only 2 percent of humanity had previously been born, so 98 percent of us have walked the earth since the redemption.[314]

God is so smart. His timing is impeccable. That is one, big, great reason that God knew the right time to send His Son. When most of the world would be born after Jesus died. Someone said, "Stress makes you believe that everything has to happen right now. Faith reassures you that everything will happen in God's timing."[315]

God's whole plan was the adoption of humanity. We see this in Galatians 4:5: "God sent him to buy freedom for us who were slaves to the law, so that he could adopt us as his very own children" [NLT].

There is something special about being adopted as opposed to being born. Olympic skater Scott Hamilton was adopted as a child and often teased for it. "You aren't the real son of your parents," they'd said and laugh. Hamilton took their mocking as long as he could, until finally he told them, "My parents chose me, but your parents were stuck with you!"[316]

He came at the right time to adopt everyone He could.

Day 167

I Win by Walking

Today's Reading: Galatians 5

Karl Wallenda, the great tightrope walker, fell to his death in 1978 from a seventy-five-foot high wire in downtown San Juan, Puerto Rico. Here's what his wife, Helen, said about the fall:

> All Karl thought about for three straight months prior to it was falling. It was the first time he'd ever thought about that, and it seemed to me that he put all his energies into not falling rather than walking the tightrope.[317]

He was virtually destined to fall.

As Christians we are commanded to walk in the Spirit. We are not commanded not to fall. Those who pursue not falling end up like Wallenda. Those who think about falling and failure never really walk. Galatians 5 teaches us how to walk and not fall. Today, with God's help, we will walk with God.

The apostle Paul gives us these fighting words: "But I say, walk by the Spirit, and you will not carry out the desire of the flesh Galatians" (5:16). The opening word of this verse, *But*, is a response word. It's a response to having healthy relationships and not hurting people.

Here is the verse before it: "But if you continue to criticize and come against each other over minor issues, you're acting like wild beasts trying to destroy one another!" (verse 15, TPT). Paul is saying, *Do you want to not fall into criticism and hurting one another?*

He didn't say "bind the devil" or be free from a critical spirit or even "just stop it." He said that we can win if we walk.

Just like Wallenda. Walk!

Walk in the Spirit.

A father and son arrived in a small western town looking for an uncle whom they had never seen. Suddenly, the father, pointing across the square to a man who was walking away from them, exclaimed, "There goes my uncle!"

"How do you know when you have not seen him before?" his son asked.

"Son, I know him because he walks exactly like my father."[318]

If we walk in the Spirit, the world should know us by our walk. The apostle Paul said walking is a weapon. It's how we fight. When we walk by the Spirit, we will not carry out the desires of the flesh.

What is the flesh? That is our old sinful nature that is always popping up. In fact, we find a whole list of those fleshly desires in verses 19-21:

Now the deeds of the flesh are evident, which are: immorality, impurity, sensuality, idolatry, sorcery, enmities, strife, jealousy, outbursts of anger, disputes, dissensions, factions, envying, drunkenness, carousing, and things like these, of which I forewarn you, just as I have forewarned you, that those who practice such things will not inherit the kingdom of God. (Galatians 5:19-21)

To try to fight each one of them would take a lifetime, and even at that, winning seems impossible. So Paul says, "Here's how you fight. If you walk by the Spirit, you will not fulfill those fleshly desires."

This is important: he did not say they won't come and attack you. People think that once you become a Christian, you won't have evil thoughts any more. Paul says, that's not true, you will get the desire, but you don't have to fulfill the crazy thought. Because walking in the Spirit is now your focus.

It's not a run or a jog but a walk. Even a child can walk. But for the Christian, that walk is valuable. Why?

A Christian can commit any sin a non-Christian can commit but he can't commit it without a fight. Because when we walk in the Spirit, God is helping us to keep moving forward. We need the Holy Spirit to walk.

Every time you choose to go to church, you are walking in the Spirit.

Every time you choose your family over yourself, you are walking in the Spirit.

Every time you choose to spend time in the Bible, you are walking in the Spirit.

Every time you choose to be kind, to be generous, you are walking in the Spirit.

Walking is your weapon. Walking is how you win. Just keep moving forward.

The best story about winning with walking is the children of Israel. When they left Egypt after four hundred years of slavery, they came to the Red Sea. The Egyptians decided they wanted them back. They wanted the old relationship with them, just as our desires of the flesh want us back. So they hunted them down. The children of Israel had the Egyptians behind them and the Red Sea in front of them. What did God tell them to do? He did *not* tell them to fight the Egyptians, to fight the past, to fight the old enemy.

God told them to walk . . . walk in unchartered territory. He wanted them to walk through the Red Sea. God split the sea in half and the children of Israel walked through on dry ground. When they got to the other side, the Egyptians tried to follow them, and God closed the water on top of them. They beat the Egyptians by just walking forward.

Your past will try to come after you, but you can outwalk it every time when you walk in the Spirit.

The story is told about a little boy who was flying a kite. It was a windy day, and the kite kept going higher and higher. Finally it got so high that it was out of sight. A man passed by and saw the little boy holding onto the string. The man could not see the kite, and he asked the boy, "How do you even know you have a kite up there?" The boy replied, "Because I can feel it."[319] Although we cannot see the Holy Spirit, we should be able to sense His work in our lives changing us and helping us to walk each day.

WE ARE FAMILY

Today's Reading: Galatians 6

Hu Jen-chuan was two years old when he fell from a table and went into a coma. When he woke after six days, he was unable to talk or move. Like any parent, his mother, Liu Kuei-lan, was terrible distressed. Yet her distress was multiplied by the fact that she could not afford to place him in medical care or any type of rehab. Instead she has cared for him herself, and for the past thirty years, she has carried her son on her back. As she's grown older and more frail, she has fallen and fractured bones while carrying her grown son who weighs 180 pounds. Yet she continues to carry him. When asked how this sixty-five-year-old, ninety-five pound woman can do it, her reply is simple: "He ain't heavy, he's family."[320]

Galatians 6 is about us remembering that very thing: they ain't heavy, they're family. Paul ends the book of Galatians with us learning how to carry one another, or another way he puts it, bearing one another's burdens:

> Brethren, even if anyone is caught in any trespass, you who are spiritual, restore such a one in a spirit of gentleness; *each one* looking to yourself, so that you too will not be tempted. Bear one another's burdens, and thereby fulfill the law of Christ. For if anyone thinks he is something when he is nothing, he deceives himself. (Galatians 6:1-5)

Galatians 6 is the antithesis of Galatians 5. In chapter 5 people are devouring, criticizing, and destroying each other. But in chapter 6, Paul challenges the church to help carry one another. That is what the body of Christ does.

Keep this in mind: the sign of a healthy body is its ability to heal itself. The church is called the body of Christ, and when it is healthy, the church has healing components within itself. That's what Paul sees when he reminds us to carry each other's troubles or burdens.

Our privacy, though, can become our downfall. When we are afraid to come clean and be vulnerable that we need help with our marriages, our thought lives, our finances, our children, we are only deceiving ourselves and setting ourselves up for failure.

Verse 3 is a warning to those who try to appear stronger than they really are: "For if anyone thinks he is something when he is nothing, he deceives himself."

The Christian life isn't meant to be done alone. Only weak people think they are strong enough to do the Christian life alone. If you try to make yourself look like a superhero, a super-Christian, your life expectancy will not be very long.

The New Testament puts this phrase throughout its pages: *one another*. It shows we need each other. Listen to a few of them:

- Build up one another (Romans 14:19)
- Accept one another (Romans 15:7)
- Care for one another (1 Corinthians 12:25)
- Serve one another (Galatians 5:13)
- Bear one another's burdens (Galatians 6:2)
- Be kind to one another (Ephesians 4:32)
- Comfort one another (1 Thessalonians 4:18)
- Encourage one another (1 Thessalonians 5:11; Hebrews 3:13)

There are things we go through that need the help of other people. This means that in relationships, we find weight bearers to help us carry what we could not and cannot carry by ourselves. God makes it that way so that we *can't* do Christianity by ourselves.

When you are not in a church and connected to the body of Christ, you make the Christian life something it was never meant to be. It's like what happened during the 1976 Special Olympics in Spokane, Washington. As the competitors began their race after the gun sounded, only a few yards into the race, one of the children fell and began to cry. Several other athletes stopped running and came back to their fallen comrade. The children lifted him together, and arm in arm, they ran over the finish line—together.[321] For a fleeting moment these children showed us what the Kingdom of God is like.

Here's the Passion Translation of Galatians 6:2-3: "*Love empowers us* to fulfill the law of the Anointed One as we carry each other's troubles. If you think you are too important to stoop down to help another, you are living in deception." Those athletes with special needs show us what that looks like. They stooped to help the fallen.

If we keep running when someone has fallen, I think we are in more need than the fallen comrade. Let's always remember, they ain't heavy, they're family.

THE ONLY PERSON HYPERBOLE BELONGS TO

Today's Reading: Ephesians 1

Today people use a lot of hyperbole. From their social-media posts to their arguments with their families, people say words like *every*, *never*, and *always* to "prove" their points.

Hyperbole is exaggerated statements. It sounds like this:

You never pick up your dirty laundry.
Every time we talk you never listen.
You do this to me every time.
You always make us late.
This is all impossible.

Why can't we make those hyperbole statements?

Listen closely. We can't because no one on the planet can ever be that consistent. There is only *one* who can be that consistent, and that is God Himself. God never lies. God is always faithful. And in Ephesians 1, Paul associates another word of hyperbole with God: "Blessed *be* the God and Father of our Lord Jesus Christ, who has blessed us with every spiritual blessing in the heavenly places in Christ" (verse 3).

Every spiritual blessing. Wow! The word *every* is what makes this verse and the ones following amazing. *Every* spiritual blessing belongs to you. Paul is saying, *What else do you need when you've got all you need!*

Every is a strong word. It's hyperbole, and it's all God.

Every spiritual blessing means, *nothing* is missing for you and me to win in this Christian life. It means that since God says it, we can trust it. And *every* can be fulfilled only by a consistent God.

What Paul shares next shows us how incredible God is—how much He loves us and cares for us. After Paul goes all hyperbole about God, He tells us why we have received every spiritual blessing:

Just as He chose us in Him before the foundation of the world, that we would be holy and blameless before Him. In love He predestined us to adoption as sons through Jesus Christ to Himself, according to the kind intention of His will, to the praise of the glory of His grace, which He freely bestowed on us in the Beloved. In Him we have redemption through His blood, the forgiveness of our trespasses, according to the riches of His grace which He lavished on us. . . . In Him also we have obtained an inheritance, having been predestined according to His purpose who works all things after the counsel of His will, to the end that we who were the first to hope in Christ would be to the praise of His glory. In Him, you also, after listening to the message of truth, the gospel of your salvation—having also believed, you were sealed in Him with the Holy Spirit of promise, who is given as a pledge of our inheritance, with a view to the redemption of *God's own* possession, to the praise of His glory. (Ephesians 1:4-8, 10-14)

He has blessed us *how*?

Here are some of God's amazing blessings in Paul's list:

He chose us before the foundation of the world. To be chosen is to have God already have us in mind before we were even born.

He predestined us to adoption. He is our Father. What an amazing thing to know in a fatherless society. We have a Father when we get saved.

In Him we have redemption through His blood, the forgiveness of our trespasses, according to the riches of His grace which He lavished on us. What do you think about when you think of *lavish*? I think of a rich father who keeps giving to his children. God our Father never stops giving to us; He is a lavish God. It means giving to overflowing.

You were sealed in Him with the Holy Spirit of promise. You were given the Holy Spirit the moment you became God's property. The Holy Spirit in you is a seal and a pledge that you are going to heaven and you belong to God. When people in the first century wanted to claim something they had purchased, they would put their family seal on it. God's seal is the Holy Spirit.

God *is* all that. He is amazing. That's why it's okay to go all hyperbole with God, because He can be that. Our God is a 100-percent kind of God. This is no hyperbole—He leaves nothing undone or unattended. Remember, nothing in this life is that consistent. Even if we can be 99.9 percent accurate, the result can still be catastrophic.

If 99.9 percent is good enough, then . . .

- 2 million documents will be lost by the IRS this year.
- 22,000 checks will be deducted from the wrong bank accounts in the next sixty minutes.
- 12 babies will be given to the wrong parents each day.
- 268,500 defective tires will be shipped this year.
- 14,208 defective personal computers will be shipped this year.
- 2,488,200 books will be shipped in the next twelve months with the wrong cover.
- 2 plane landings daily at O'Hare International airport in Chicago will be unsafe.
- 18,322 pieces of mail will be mishandled in the next hour.
- 20,000 incorrect drug prescriptions will be written in the next twelve months.
- 114,500 mismatched pairs of shoes will be shipped this year.
- 107 incorrect medical procedures will be performed by the end of the day today.[322]

The God we serve is 100 percent. *Every, never, always* is who He is.

I think that's why Paul starts us off in verse 3 with praise and then proceeds to tell us how amazing God is. *The Living Bible* says verse 3 like this: "How we praise God, the Father of our Lord Jesus Christ, who has blessed us with every blessing in heaven because we belong to Christ."

We praise God because He is worthy.

NOT THE ABSENCE BUT THE PRESENCE

Today's Reading: Ephesians 2

I love the bummer sticker that says, "No Jesus, no peace. Know Jesus, know peace."

Ephesians 2 reminds us what real peace is and the source of it. "Peace is not the absence of problems but the presence of God in the midst of our problems."[323] Paul tells us that in verses 13-17:

> Now in Christ Jesus you who formerly were far off have been brought near by the blood of Christ. For He Himself is our peace who made both *groups into* one and broke down the barrier of the dividing wall, by abolishing in His flesh the enmity, *which is* the Law of commandments *contained* in ordinances, so that in Himself He might make the two into one new man, *thus* establishing peace, and might reconcile them both in one body to God through the cross, by it having put to death the enmity. AND HE CAME AND PREACHED PEACE TO YOU WHO WERE FAR AWAY, AND PEACE TO THOSE WHO WERE NEAR.

Three times Paul mentions "peace" in those verses:

1. "He Himself is our peace." That's the Source. He is.

2. "He came . . . establishing peace." That was His mission. Peace between humans and God.

3. "He came and preached peace." We are the recipients.

When Jesus came and preached peace, these are the recipients: "To you who were far away and peace to those who were near." This is really important that Paul uses these two phrases: *those who were far* and *those who were near*. They are good reminders that whether you were far or near, you still needed Jesus to bring you to God.

Some people are born far from God. They were not raised in a Christian home. Some were from a country very antagonistic to the gospel. They needed Jesus to die for their sins to bring reconciliation between them and God. We see that clearly. They were far from God.

The part we sometimes forget is that you could have been born in the church pew or in the choir loft, like I almost was, and hear about Jesus in your childhood and throughout your life, but make no mistake, no matter how close you think you were to Jesus, you still need Jesus' death on the cross to get you to God. The close are not close enough regardless of how close you think you are.

The far and the near can be best explained by a contest that's prize is one million dollars to anyone who can swim from Los Angeles to Hawaii. Let's say several great swimmers—the best swimmers in the world—enter to win the money. Obviously we all know that all those swimmers will ultimately fail. But each one will try really hard. Some will get farther than others. Regardless how far you get, though, you will not make it to Hawaii, because you can't make it to Hawaii on your own swim stroke. Some are far away from Honolulu, and some closer to it. Remember, it doesn't matter how far you swim, you can't make that swim. That distance needs outside help—a boat, a plane.

The distance from here to heaven is even farther than Honolulu and LA. No matter how hard you try, you do not have the capability to make it to heaven on your own; you need outside help. Enter Jesus. The far and the near all fail but He came to get both groups to God. As Brennan Manning said, "The gospel declares that no matter how dutiful or prayerful we are, we can't save ourselves. What Jesus did was sufficient."[324]

In the article, "Perfection Required for Acceptance at Stanford University," Brian Kohout wrote:

> Stanford University ranks as <u>one of the toughest schools to give an acceptance letter</u>. The university recently updated their admission standards and stated that only five percent of applying students are accepted. In 2017, 42,497 students applied, and 2,140 were accepted.
>
> On their website, they give students realistic answers for the question "What is the academic standard to be accepted?" An ACT score of 33 or higher will put you into the top 50 percent of applicants, however the average score for accepted students is 35. The perfect score is 36.
>
> Accepted students will also need an average SAT score of 1520 (out of 1600), an average GPA of 4.18 (out of 4.0), plus a robust "resume" of extracurricular activities, leadership qualities, references, and recommendations. Of course new students also have to pay for Stanford at $60,000 per year.[325]

Thank God He doesn't have the requirements of Stanford. The far don't have a shot and the near aren't close enough. Because Jesus came, we all have the opportunity to get in—regardless of where we live, what we have done, and who we know. The far need Jesus and the near need Jesus. Just remember, the one place that matters to be accepted is not Harvard, Yale, or Stanford. It's heaven. And Jesus has made that happen.

NOT THE BAD BUT THE GOOD

Today's Reading: Ephesians 3

I knew her for more than a decade. When she finally accepted Jesus into her life, I asked her, "How did it happen? We talked about Jesus a lot, but why did you finally commit your life to Him? And then you just stopped living a lifestyle you knew was destructive. How did all this happen?"

She looked at me and smiled. "You never told me what I was doing was wrong. You told me how right Jesus is. You just kept talking about Jesus." She was saying in essence that Jesus was so attractive, why would she want anyone or anything else?

That is Paul's message in Ephesians 3:

This is my life work: helping people understand and respond to this Message. It came as a sheer gift to me, a real surprise, God handling all the details. When it came to presenting the Message to people who had no background in God's way, I was the least qualified of any of the available Christians. God saw to it that I was equipped, but you can be sure that it had nothing to do with my natural abilities. And so here I am, preaching and writing about things that are way over my head, the inexhaustible riches and generosity of Christ. (Ephesians 3:7-8, MSG)

Paul wants to talk about Jesus—"the inexhaustible riches and generosity of Christ." The New American Standard Bible calls it "the unfathomable riches of Christ." Too often we want to talk about other things. Author D. Martyn Lloyd-Jones says: "A great danger confronting us all at the present time is to keep on talking about Christianity instead of talking about the Lord Jesus Christ."[326] Paul said talk about Jesus.

Christianity has never been about encountering the right church but the right Person. I know sin is awful. But sin really speaks for itself through its consequences. Our culture may not call it sin, but they know consequences for wrong actions. We live in a society and a time that has misinterpreted and misrepresented Jesus. Why make the bulk of our preaching and sharing be about how awful something is (when people already know), when they don't realize how wonderful Jesus is?

I want people to see the real Jesus and know about the real Jesus, not the twenty-first-century Jesus, not the Western Jesus, not the denominational Jesus, and not the religious Jesus. Famed Christian writer Dorothy Sayers talked about the real Jesus:

> The people who hanged Christ never . . . accused Him of being a bore— on the contrary; they thought Him too dynamic to be safe. It has been left for later generations to muffle up. . . . We have very efficiently pared the claws of the Lion of Judah, certified Him "meek and mild," and recommended Him as a fitting household pet for pale curates and pious old ladies.[327]

Let's consider some of the impressive record Jesus inspired. I read recently about someone who took Jesus and stacked Him against the greatest painters, musicians, and philosophers of the world. These are the results:

- Socrates taught for forty years, Plato for fifty, Aristotle for forty, and Jesus for only three. Yet the influence of Christ's three-year ministry infinitely transcends the impact left by the combined 130 years of teaching from these men who were among the greatest philosophers of all antiquity.
- Jesus painted no pictures; yet some of Raphael, Michelangelo, and Leonardo da Vinci's finest paintings received their inspiration from Him.
- Jesus wrote no poetry; but Dante, Milton, and scores of the world's greatest poets were inspired by Him.
- Jesus composed no music; still Haydn, Handel, Beethoven, Bach, and Mendelssohn reached their highest perfection of melody in the hymns, symphonies, and oratorios they composed in His praise.
- Every sphere of human greatness has been enriched by the humble Carpenter of Nazareth. His unique contribution to the race of humans is the salvation of the soul! Philosophy could not accomplish that. Nor art. Nor literature. Nor music. Only Jesus Christ can break the enslaving chains of sin and Satan. He alone can speak peace to the human heart, strengthen the weak, and give life to those who are spiritually dead.[328]

C. S. Lewis is considered one of the most influential authors of the twentieth century. The way he went from atheism to a relationship with Christ is what Paul is reminding us of in Ephesians 3. Lewis was able to put aside the contemporary and the religious Jesus and come to terms with the real Jesus. That's why his words from *Mere Christianity* are so important to us and help us remember the real Jesus:

> I am trying here to prevent anyone saying the really foolish thing that people often say about him: "I'm ready to accept Jesus as a great moral teacher, but I don't accept His claim to be God." That is the one thing we must not say. A man who was merely a man and said the sort of things Jesus said would not be a great moral teacher. He would either be a lunatic—on a level with the man who says he is a poached egg—or else he would be the Devil of Hell. You must make your choice. Either this man was, and is, the Son of God: or else a madman or something worse. You can shut Him up for a fool, you can spit at Him and kill Him as a demon; or you can fall at His feet and call Him Lord and God. But let us not come with any patronizing nonsense about His being a great human teacher. He has not left that open to us. He did not intend to.[329]

Let's heed Paul's plea to remember who Jesus is—and share those "inexhaustible riches and generosity of Christ" with others.

DOING IT JUST LIKE GOD DOES

Today's Reading: Ephesians 4

I love these words from Corrie ten Boom: "When we confess our sins . . . God casts them into the deepest ocean, gone forever. . . . God then places a sign out there that says NO FISHING ALLOWED."[330] She is giving a unique way to describe Isaiah 43:25, which tells us something so important about God's forgiveness. God says in that verse "I will not remember your sins." That's incredible when we think about God's forgiveness of our sin.

Today in Ephesians 4, we are going to see that incredible forgiveness, that is bestowed on us, take one giant leap forward in a direction that will blow you away. Think about this. God sees the people who have cursed Him and blasphemed His name but yet have been forgiven of their sins. He never says to them, "Oh yeah, you're the guy who said this about me" or "I remember you, you committed that sin." Not once does God bring up our past. He chooses to never remember what we did.

Clara Barton, the founder of the American Red Cross, was reminded one day of a vicious deed someone had done to her years before. But she acted as though she had never heard of the incident. "Don't you remember it?" her friend asked. "No," came Barton's reply. "I distinctly remember forgetting it."[331]

God remembers our sin no more. That's forgiveness. Think of the biggest sinner you know and what God's forgiveness looks like for them. God never turns down anyone who asks to be forgiven and He never places limits on what He will forgive. How amazing is that kind of forgiveness?

Now get ready Ephesians 4. I want you to think of the biggest sin committed against you. Someone and something that hurt you to the core. What has been the hardest thing for you to forgive? Have you ever turned down someone's request to be forgiven? Now we take God's forgiveness to a crazy place. Paul tells us, "Be kind to one another, tender-hearted, forgiving each other, just as God in Christ also has forgiven you" (Ephesians 4:32).

Did you catch that? Forgive each other *just as God has forgiven you*. I know, I know, you are already thinking of the crazy list.

But it was adultery.

It was sexual abuse.

That man hit me every day.

She betrayed my confidence.

He raped me.

She stole thousands of dollars and put my family at risk.

They fired me.

These are big deals. I am not minimizing these offenses. But I don't want you to minimize what this verse says either. Augustine said something powerful. Ponder these words: "If you believe what you like in the gospels, and reject what you don't like, it is not the gospel you believe, but yourself."[332]

Here is what Paul is saying—and it's revolutionary: if God would forgive the offense, then you must forgive it. This is not a suggestion. This is the way a Christian is supposed to live. Keep in mind that Ephesians 5:1, the verse that follows Ephesians 4:32, says, "Imitate God." Or *The Message* says it like this: "Watch what God does, and then you do it."

C. S. Lewis reminds us of the why: "To be a Christian means to forgive the inexcusable because God has forgiven the inexcusable in you."[333] When it comes to imitating God, we would love to imitate some of His attributes that would make us big-time important: His sovereignty, so no one bosses us around; His power, so we are in control; His healing so we can be adored; His teaching, so we can be stand outs; His holiness, so we can be admired. But imitate His forgiveness? Seriously?

But as Andy Stanley tells us, "In the shadow of my hurt, forgiveness feels like a decision to reward my enemy. But in the shadow of the cross, forgiveness is merely a gift from one undeserving soul to another."[334]

In 1948, a group of communists led the Yŏsu Rebellion in Korea. Taking over one city, they grabbed Pastor Son Yang-Wŏn's two sons, Matthew and John, and executed them. Before they died, the boys called on the persecutors to have faith in Jesus. Later when the communists were driven out, Chy Soon, a young man of the village, was identified as the man who fired the murderous shots that had killed the pastor's sons. Chy Soon was convicted and sentenced to be executed. But the Pastor requested that the charges be dropped and that the boy be released to him as his adopted son. "I thank God that He has given me the love to seek to convert and adopt the enemy that has murdered my boys," he said.[335] The young man was adopted and accepted Jesus. Did this young man have a choice? Can you respond to that demonstration of forgiveness any other way but to except Jesus?

All because someone forgave him as God forgives.

I am forgiven to be a forgiver.

I am forgiven to be an imitator of God.

I am forgiven to forgive as God forgives.

Our reason to forgive is not because the person is forgivable or the offense is forgivable. We are to forgive because we have been forgiven. And because we are to imitate God in forgiveness. Forgiveness is not just *for us* but must come *through us*.

It's Not Just for Sundays

Today's Reading: Ephesians 5

In today's chapter Paul reminds us of something that will take our Christianity to another level.

When we become Christians, we don't simply get church, we get God. And God is not limited to Sundays for a few hours. Religion wants a few hours on Sunday. A relationship with Jesus is God every day. That's what today's revolutionary verse out of Ephesians 5 is about. And it breaks away from denominationalism norms.

This is pneumatology gone rogue. Pneumatology is the study of the Holy Spirit—something we keep bound in church or restricted to the classroom. But today Paul is telling us to break free of those boundaries. Listen to Ephesians 5:18 from the Contemporary English Version: "Don't destroy yourself by getting drunk, but let the Spirit fill your life."

Devotional writer Oswald Chambers said this about the Holy Spirit: "The Spirit is the first power we practically experience, but the last power we come to understand."[336] I want to help you understand His power today. We don't do this often, but it's worth taking a little journey into the Greek.

First, the verb *fill* is in the imperative mode. That means it is a command. It isn't an option for certain Christians; we all need to be filled. Since this is a command, are we free to disobey any commands of God? This is as strong as, "Thou shalt not kill." *Thou shalt not kill* and *be filled with the Spirit* are in the same category. Do you negotiate with the kill command? Of course not. Don't do it with this one either.

Second, the tense of the verb is present. Present tense in the imperative mode always represents action going on. It is not filling for preaching and doing stuff in the church but for the believer's life every day in every task, moment by moment.

Now get ready for the really revolutionary part. After Paul says to be filled with the Spirit, he tells wives to submit to their husbands, and husbands to love their wives as Christ loves the church. He then tells children to obey their parents, parents to bring up their children in the instruction of the Lord, and workers to work as unto God. Remember, the original New Testament had no chapter or verse divisions, so from talking about being filled with the Spirit, Paul moves right into marriage, parenting, children, and working.

How can we be a great . . . wife or husband? son or parent? worker on the job? We need to be filled with the Holy Spirit. The filling of the Holy Spirit is not for Sundays, it is for every day. We need the Holy Spirit in our homes, our marriages, our parenting, and our jobs.

Third, the verb is in the *plural*, which teaches us that this command is addressed not only to the preacher and the deacon but to *every* Christian. As A. W. Tozer reminds us, "The Spirit-filled life is not a special, deluxe edition of Christianity. It is part and parcel of the total plan of God for His people."[337]

Fourth, the verb is in the passive voice. This grammatical classification represents the subject of the verb as inactive but being acted upon. This teaches us that the filling with the Spirit is not the work of man but of God. That means it's easy. It is not a difficult command, because it is not you doing it but you receiving it.

All this being true, we realize how important those words are to be filled with the Holy Spirit. Some have said that the most accurate interpretation of that verse is "Be being filled with the Holy Spirit" or "Keep being filled with the Holy Spirit."

The great American evangelist of the nineteenth century, D. L. Moody, was once asked why he urged Christians to be filled constantly with the Holy Spirit. He said, "I need a continual infilling because I leak!"[338]

A friend of mine was asked if he believed in the "second blessing"—the baptism of the Holy Spirit. He said, "Of course I do! And in the third, fourth, fifth blessing, and so on." He believed in "be being filled" because he leaks. We all leak.

WE HAVE LOST BECAUSE WE FORGOT HOW TO FIGHT

Today's Reading: Ephesians 6

Men will argue over which is the greatest "man movie" of all time. The movie "winners" range from certain Westerns to mob movies to the historical heroic tales of *Braveheart*, *300*, and my favorite, *Gladiator*. Ridley Scott's *Gladiator* is set during a time of both Roman world domination and Roman persecution of a group who seem to beat Rome without weapons, the early Christians. Russell Crowe plays Maximus, the Roman army general. In a scene when he is in the arena fighting for his life with other gladiators, he tells these men: "Whatever comes out of these gates, we've got a better chance of survival if we work together. If we stay together we survive." And they did. Maximus gave them the key to winning the fight.

In today's chapter, Paul gives us a key to winning the spiritual fight. Ephesians 6 is called the spiritual warfare chapter. It speaks about the armor of the Christian by associating it with the armor of the Roman soldiers.

Ephesians is called a prison epistle, because Paul wrote it while in prison. During that time, if someone was in prison, he was chained to a Roman soldier 24/7. Many believe Paul, writing under the inspiration of the Holy Spirit, was looking at the guard he was chained to and was giving the Christian a picture of his weapons in a bigger and different fight.

In Ephesians 6, Paul gives us two contrasts in the fight that we need to focus on. First, Paul tells us that people are not our fight, the government is not our fight, Democrats and Republicans are not our battle. It's much deeper and bigger than that:

We wrestle not against flesh and blood, but against principalities, against powers, against the rulers of the darkness of this world, against spiritual wickedness in high places. (Verse 12, KJV)

If you want to get really raw, listen to this verse in the Passion Translation:

Your hand-to-hand combat is not with human beings, but with the highest principalities and authorities operating in rebellion under the heavenly realms. For they are a powerful class of demon-gods and evil spirits that hold this dark world in bondage.

The apostle is warning us not to fight people but to realize we are fighting in another realm, the spiritual realm. That's the first contrast—natural versus spiritual.

The second contrast, which we often overlook, comes when we read verses 12 and 13 together. In verse 12, Paul says that "we wrestle not," and then in verse 13 he says, "put on the whole armor of God." Then he proceeds to go through each of the Roman soldiers' equipment and associates each piece with a spiritual weapon we have. The sword the soldier carries represents the Word of God, the sword of the Spirit. The shield protects the Roman against fiery darts, but for us it is a shield of faith to protect us from the enemy's missiles.

The contrast comes between "we wrestle not" and "put on the whole armor of God." For wrestlers in the first century, the men would oil up their bodies, enter a ring, and fight until one was actually killed. It was one man against one man. The apostle Paul is saying, though, that if we are Christians, we are not wrestlers, we are soldiers. That means we are not in the Christian life by ourselves. We have soldiers side by side.

One of the great things the Roman army used to do when going into battle was to lock arms with each other, which would show strength and unity in the hand-to-hand combat. We often lose because we wrestle instead of being a soldier.

Recently a number of Christian leaders, authors, and musicians have gone public, announcing that they are abandoning their faith. They have denounced everything from the books they have written to the songs they've composed. They have come to the conclusion that God does not exist. Let me tell you that their tragic declarations show that they have faced their faith as individual wrestlers, not as soldiers, and they did not lean on other soldiers. You can't win when you wrestle by yourself. One of my dear friends said, "Only weak people think they are strong enough to do the Christian life alone." These leaders who abandoned their faith were doing the Christian life alone.

Have you ever seen a redwood tree up close? They can stand upwards of three-hundred-feet tall (almost the length of a football field), and have roots that stretch only five feet under the ground and still remain unmovable. Their roots are shallow but because they can't go deep. But they do something else: they never grow alone. They know they can't wrestle so they have to be soldiers. That's why Redwoods grow in bunches. Their roots can intertwine with one another and be strengthened by one another. With that height and those shallow roots, what keeps them from blowing over and uprooting in wind storms? They are all connected to one another. A storm can't blow just one over, it has to be strong enough to blow them all over.[339]

Those tragic Christian leaders did not connect roots with anyone and they lost their faith and got blown over. They didn't reveal that God doesn't exist. The only thing they revealed is that their root systems did not exist and that they'd tried to wrestle instead of soldier.

Let me remind you of Maximus's words from *Gladiator*: "Whatever comes out of these gates, we've got a better chance of survival if we work together. If we stay together we survive."

Those are not just Maximus's words, that is God's Word in Ephesians 6.

You Never Know How Your Prayer Is Going to Be Answered

Today's Reading: Philippians 1

H. B. Charles Jr. said these poignant words about answered prayer: "It may seem God did not answer prayer when the real issue may be that we did not like the answer."[340] Today's chapter discusses answered prayer in the apostle Paul's life. If you don't look closely, you can easily miss his prayer and his answer.

Always remember that our job is to pray and not forecast the answer on how we think it should be answered. We leave that to God to figure out. Let's look together to see what Paul was praying throughout his life and how the answer came in Philippians 1. Paul had a great desire to preach the gospel in Rome and made it a matter of prayer. Listen to some of these passages that reveal his heart:

> Now after these things were finished, Paul purposed in the Spirit to go to Jerusalem after he had passed through Macedonia and Achaia, saying, "After I have been there, I must also see Rome." [Acts 19:21]

He wrote to the church in Rome and told them of his desire and prayer:

> Always in my prayers making request, if perhaps now at last by the will of God I may succeed in coming to you.... So, for my part, I am eager to preach the gospel to you also who are in Rome. [Romans 1:10, 15]

Paul had no idea how that prayer would be answered. But that wasn't his problem, that was God's problem. Philippians 1 tells us God did answer that prayer. How did it happen? Rome never became his fourth missionary journey on his itinerary, because he got arrested and put in jail. Can you imagine Paul saying, "I wanted to go to Rome and preach the gospel, and now I can't go." And then he was sent to Rome for his trial.

He wanted to go as a preacher but he went as a prisoner. He made it to

Rome but he was in chains. He was eager to preach the gospel there, but because of his circumstances, that seemed like a bust—at least in Paul's mind. Remember, we pray and let God figure out the answer.

But then it happened. Paul's prison sentence became the platform. The trial was his answer. God came through:

> I want you to know, brothers and sisters, that what has happened to me has actually served to advance the gospel. As a result, it has become clear throughout the whole palace guard and to everyone else that I am in chains for Christ. And because of my chains, most of the brothers and sisters have become confident in the Lord and dare all the more to proclaim the gospel without fear. (Philippians 1:12-14, NIV)

The palace guards were the handpicked bodyguards of the Emperor Nero. Paul was saying that as a prisoner he was chained to a Roman soldier, which meant the gospel had been penetrating the handpicked bodyguards of the emperor. The gospel was going through the most guarded place in the world and was advancing. It was going through a place that was very anti-Christ. Nero persecuted the Christians so harshly and inhumanly, that God decided to bring the Good News through Nero's front door and into the palace.

Listen to Paul's words again: "What has happened to me has actually served to advance the gospel." His prayer was answered and even better than he prayed. He was not only advancing the gospel, it made its way right into the elite army. The message was getting to the palace guards. Paul in Rome as a preacher; he was limited, because he was there as a prisoner; yet he was in a place he could never have gotten into—Caesar's palace. And he got to preach in that high-security place for two years!

Paul was in Rome, the imperial city, capital of the world, the seat of the government, and right in the imperial palace—and so was the gospel of Jesus, because God answered Paul's prayer better than Paul could ever have imagined. That's why these words resonate even more on this palace answer from Ephesians:

> Glory be to God, who by his mighty power at work within us is able to do far more than we would ever dare to ask or even dream of—infinitely beyond our highest prayers, desires, thoughts, or hopes. (Ephesians 3:20, TLB)

What was defined as an imprisonment was really an answer to prayer. It was beyond the prayer and desires Paul had back in Acts. Sometimes we stop short in our prayers, thinking God did not answer, when the real truth is, He may not have answered it the way we wanted.

One day I was listening to an interview with Luis Palau, considered by many to be the Billy Graham of South America. Luis said in his life he has seen God answer prayer five different ways. Remember these, because you will need them one day, so you can see imprisonment as an answer as Paul did.

God answers, "Yes, I thought you'd never ask." We often tell everybody except the Lord that we need this, or we want that. Secondly, "No, I love you too much." That's a good answer to prayer. Many times the Lord answers, "No, buddy. I know better, and I love you too much to give you that one." Number three, "Yes, but not yet." Timing. Number four, "Yes, and here's more." That's the one I really like. The Lord not only answers your prayer, but he throws in some extras. Then [fifth:] "Yes, but differently from what you thought."[341]

Five ways God answers prayer
1. Yes. I never thought you'd ask.
2. No. I love you too much.
3. Yes, but not yet. The timing is not right.
4. Yes. And here's more.
5. Yes. But differently than you thought.

HEROES AND CELEBRITIES

Today's Reading: Philippians 2

We live in a time when it is more popular to be a celebrity than a hero. Numbers of followers or views have replaced the one who risks their life for others. Media has given us celebrities, where danger and risk give us heroes. The gap is much wider between fame and greatness. Heroism is linked to honor and bravery, while celebrities just have links. We have big names today but not big persons.

The scary part of all this celebrity worship is that we are seeing celebrities and not heroes rise in the church. We must be careful that we don't allow pastors to become the center of the story. Jesus is. We have to make sure the "stars" aren't outshining the Son.

Philippians 2 reminds us of who is the center of attraction. The apostle Paul gives us the Hero of the greatest story ever told:

> God exalted him and multiplied his greatness! He has now been given the greatest of all names! The authority of the name of Jesus causes every knee to bow in reverence! Everything and everyone will one day submit to this name—in the heavenly realm, in the earthly realm, and in the demonic realm. And every tongue will proclaim in every language: "Jesus Christ is Lord Yahweh," bringing glory and honor to God, his Father! (Philippians 2:9-11, TPT)

Paul not only wants us to remember this, he also wants to remind us of what the Father thinks of His Son. Paul tells us that God put Jesus on the pedestal. And we must always remember it's all about the Son. As Augustine said, "Christ is not valued at all unless He is valued above all."[342]

Don't get it mixed up. It's not what church you go to, it isn't who your pastor is, it isn't whether your ministry is on television. It's whether or not you chose the Son! Anything before that means you have chosen celebrity over Hero. Hero Jesus. That's the name that gets you it all. That's the name that gets you to heaven. Jesus is the name that changes your life.

I have had people tell me, "I tried Jesus and it just didn't work."

"Wait one second," I tell them. "You may have tried *church*. You may have tried religion, or a denomination. But you *didn't* try Jesus. It's impossible to say, 'I tried Jesus and it just didn't work.'"

Why? Romans 10:11 answers that for us: "The Scriptures tell us that no one who believes in Christ will ever be disappointed" (TLB). Can you name one true follower of Jesus who was on his deathbed and said, "Jesus is a liar. I regret ever following Him"?

Jesus is not a hobby. He is not a Sunday thing.

The words Paul uses in Philippians 2 to describe Jesus is really important. He seemingly hijacks a verse from Isaiah 45, which speaks about Jehovah God, and he inserts it into his chapter to describe Jesus in Philippians 2:10: "At the name of JESUS EVERY KNEE WILL BOW, of those who are in heaven and on earth and under the earth."

And now Jesus is being bowed to and declared to be Jehovah. Let me make it even simpler. Listen to Isaiah 45:21-23:

> Is it not I, the LORD? And there is no other God besides Me, a righteous God and a Savior; there is none except Me. Turn to Me and be saved, all the ends of the earth; for I am God, and there is no other. . . . To Me every knee will bow, every tongue will swear *allegiance*.

God says in Isaiah that every knee will bow and every tongue confess to Him. Now in Philippians 2, every knee will bow and every tongue will confess to Jesus. It not only tells me about the deity of Jesus and that Jesus is God, it also reminds me that Jesus is the Hero of our story. Whenever I am tempted to follow a celebrity or try to be one, I need to remember Philippians 2. If we want to be reminded of our part of the story, remember the words of Robert Capon.

> Jesus came to raise the dead. The only qualification for the gift of the Gospel is to be dead. You don't have to be smart. . . . You don't have to be good. You don't have to be wise. You don't have to be wonderful. You don't have to be anything. . . . You just have to be dead. That's it.[343]

DECLARING BANKRUPTCY

Today's Reading: Philippians 3

We mentioned this powerful Kierkegaard quote in an earlier day's reading, but it bears repeating, because it fits the apostle Paul. Kierkegaard said, "It is so much easier to become a Christian when you aren't one than to become one when you assume you already are."[344]

This statement seems to fit clearly with Paul's evaluation of himself pre- and post-conversion in today's reading. His assessment may shock you because it seems somewhat reversed. Here is how the apostle thought of himself before meeting Jesus in Acts 9 on the road to Damascus. As a reminder, in Acts 9, he was on his way to imprison and kill Christians:

> It's true that *I once relied on all that I had become*. I had a reason to boast and impress people with my accomplishments—more than others—for my pedigree was impeccable. I was born a true Hebrew of the heritage of Israel as the son of a Jewish man from the tribe of Benjamin. I was circumcised eight days after my birth and *was raised in the strict tradition of Orthodox Judaism*, living a separated and devout life as a Pharisee. And concerning the righteousness of the Torah, no one surpassed me; I was without a peer. Furthermore, as a fiery defender of the truth, I persecuted the messianic believers with religious zeal. (Philippians 3:4-6, TPT)

Verse 6 in the New American Standard Bible says that "as to the righteousness which is in the Law, [he was] found blameless." *Found blameless?* He was killing Christians, but he said he was innocent of any wrongdoing. One of the strongest deceptions of sin is that we exaggerate our goodness and importance and we become dismissive of our behavior. That's exactly the lie of being a Pharisee.

The New Testament will use this word, the *flesh*. It does not mean human skin. It means *human effort*. It deals with human energy to make our humanity acceptable and exceptional, especially to God. In the Bible, God is clear that human effort, the flesh, cannot make God like us any more than He does already.

Here's the part that Paul found as a hurdle to trusting his life to God—

his flesh. Paul was saying, *I had good flesh, or my flesh was making me look exceptional*. That's why Paul said if anyone could have bragged or boasted on how well he was doing it was Paul. This is what happens to a lot of moral people—they believe they are good and don't see their need for a Savior.

In *A Grief Observed*, C. S. Lewis profoundly observed, "All [of us are] equally bankrupt, but some have not yet declared."[345] Lewis was telling us that whether our flesh is good or bad, we are all bankrupt and need God. That's our starting place with God—acknowledging, "I am bankrupt."

Now I want you to see the difference of pre-conversion Paul and post-conversion Paul. He encounters the resurrected Jesus and has a new assessment after declaring bankruptcy with God:

> I'm not saying that I have this all together, that I have it made. But I am well on my way, reaching out for Christ, who has so wondrously reached out for me. Friends, don't get me wrong: By no means do I count myself an expert in all of this, but I've got my eye on the goal, where God is beckoning us onward—to Jesus. I'm off and running, and I'm not turning back. (Philippians 3:12-14, MSG)

Before he was blameless and innocent. Now he recognizes he doesn't have it all together anymore and is not even close. When we think about it, we would think the opposite should happen. Before we become a Christian, we feel like we don't have it all together and after we become a Christian, we are something. And Paul shows us the opposite happened to him.

As C. S. Lewis wrote, "History . . . [is] the long terrible story of man trying to find something other than God which will make him happy."[346] You will never find that happiness even when you are doing your best without God, because you will realize something is missing and something is hollow inside. The best man, the apostle Paul, got it. I hope you get it today.

SHAPE YOUR WORRIES INTO PRAYERS

Today's Reading: Philippians 4

Did you know Amazon keeps track of your highlights? When Kindle readers mark sentences, the online retailer notes it so that everyone can see a faint dotted line on their e-reader that tells them someone underlined the sentence or passage. Readers can also see how many other people underlined that same passage.

Recently Amazon released a list of the most popular passages in some of its bestselling books, such as *The Hunger Games*, the Harry Potter series, and classics like *Pride and Prejudice*. Amazon also included the Bible in this list. Guess what the most highlighted passage in the Holy Bible was around the world? I covered the answer to see if I could guess correctly. I was certain it had to be one of three passages: John 3:16, Psalm 23, or the Lord's Prayer in Matthew 6:9-13. But no, it was one that's striking a deep chord in today's worried world, and it comes from today's chapter:

> Do not be anxious about anything, but in every situation, by prayer and petition, with thanksgiving, present your requests to God. And the peace of God, which transcends all understanding, will guard your hearts and your minds in Christ Jesus. (Philippians 4:6-7, NIV)

Kindle readers throughout the whole world highlighted this Bible passage on their Kindle more than any other verse. Here's the passage from *The Message*:

> Don't fret or worry. Instead of worrying, pray. Let petitions and praises shape your worries into prayers, letting God know your concerns. Before you know it, a sense of God's wholeness, everything coming together for good, will come and settle you down. It's wonderful what happens when Christ displaces worry at the center of your life.

I love that part—"Instead of worrying, pray. Let petitions and praises shape your worries into prayers." As author Tiffany Berry once said, "If you're going to worry, there's no need to pray, and if you're going to pray, there's no need to worry."[347]

We live in a worried world. And anxiety can get the best of us. *In the Me I Want to Be*, pastor John Ortberg offers insight on how to respond to anxiety:

> Psychiatrist Edward Hallowell says it like this: *Never worry alone.* When anxiety grabs my mind, it is self-perpetuating. Worrisome thoughts reproduce faster than rabbits, so one of the most powerful ways to stop the spiral of worry is simply to disclose my worry to a friend.[348]

In today's chapter, Paul tells us who our best friend is to disclose our worry to: God Himself. As Donald J. Morgan says, "Every evening I turn my troubles over to God—He's going to be up all night anyway."[349] According to the apostle Paul, we choose to shape worries into prayers and that in essence is disclosing it to our Friend.

I had someone once talk to me about their week. This person said, "I have sighed more than I breathed." Wow, I have been there. Those are weeks weighed down with worry and not peace. When we're in those kinds of weeks, as the saying goes, "It's not the load that breaks you down, it's the way you carry it."[350] Philippians 4 gives us a way to carry the load—by shaping our worries into prayers.

When was the last time you meditated on a Bible verse? Some people get weird definitions of what "meditation" is. Let me explain it like the Puritan writers of the past explained it. They said you know how to meditate if you know how to worry, as worry is simply negative meditation. When you worry, you think about the problem all day long.

When you meditate in a positive way, you take a Bible verse and turn it over in your mind all day long. This is one of those verses I would attempt to meditate on. Write it down and put it in your car so you can see it as your drive. Tape it on your bathroom mirror so that as you get ready for work in the morning, those are the first words you see. Tape it to the refrigerator door, the most used door in the home, so you can keep it always before you. And whisper to yourself all day long, "I am shaping my worries into prayer."

It goes something like this: The washer is broken, and it will cost you $400, out of an already tight budget, to get it fixed. *I will shape my worries into prayer*, you remind yourself. So you pray, "God, You've got this. I'm grateful for the clothes on my back. And I would like to have clean clothes on my back. You can provide in ways I can't even imagine. I give You this setback."

Or it goes like this: You hear through the grapevine that your company is going to lay off employees. You have worked there for the past ten years. In your mind, you are fearful that you are not going to make the cut. You remind yourself, *I will shape my worries into prayer.* And you pray, "God, my future is in Your hands. You have always been faithful to me and my family, and I believe You will be faithful with whatever happens. I don't have the energy or the emotional capacity to stress over this, so I let You take it off my heart and mind and let You carry it."

An average person's anxiety is focused on:

40 percent: things that will never happen

30 percent: things about the past that can't be changed

12 percent: things about criticism by others, mostly untrue

10 percent: health, which gets worse with stress

8 percent: real problems that will be faced[351]

The lead character, Van Wilder, in the movie of the same name makes an insightful observation, "Worrying is like a rocking chair: it gives you something to do, but doesn't get you anywhere."[352]

Shape your worries into prayers.

Day 179

FIRST THINGS FIRST

Today's Reading: Colossians 1

C. S. Lewis once said, "Put first things first and we get second things thrown in: put second things first and we lose *both* first and second things."[353] Lewis is reminding us that even if good second things get first, we end up with nothing. If church is first, your denomination is first, worship music is first—those good but must be second.

In today's chapter, Paul makes it really clear that Jesus is first and Jesus is everything. Paul is telling us what is at the heart of Christianity.

What do lollipops, truffles, and the Christian life all have in common? It's what's at the center that counts![354] If you get to the middle of your lollipop or truffle and discover nothing, then there is nothing but disappointment.

This may be obvious, you can't have the word *Christianity* without *Christ*. Otherwise, it's just *ianity*. Like that makes sense. You can't be a *Christian* without Christ, then the word is just *ian*. It doesn't make sense. And if the chewy-centered Tootsie Pop or truffle of the church, the Christian life, the Bible, prayer is not *Christ*, then it's nothing but a farce and failure.

Here is the center for Paul—and I'm replacing the pronouns with the name of Jesus, so it's very clear:

> *Jesus* rescued us from the domain of darkness, and transferred us to the kingdom of [God's] beloved *Jesus*, in *Jesus* we have redemption, the forgiveness of sins. *Jesus* is the image of the invisible God, *Jesus* is the firstborn of all creation. For by *Jesus* all things were created, *both* in the heavens and on earth, visible and invisible, whether thrones or dominions or rulers or authorities—all things have been created through *Jesus* and for *Jesus*. *Jesus* is before all things, and in *Jesus* all things hold together. *Jesus* is also head of the body, the church; and *Jesus* is the beginning, the firstborn from the dead, so that *Jesus* Himself will come to have first place in everything. For it was the Father's good pleasure for all the fullness to dwell in *Jesus* and through *Jesus* to reconcile all things to *Jesus*, having made peace through the blood of *Jesus'* cross. [Colossians 1:13-20, author changes in italics]

Jesus first and Jesus everywhere.

The word to describe this is *preeminence*. That big word means Jesus is first and everything. That's what Paul is telling us in Colossians 1: Jesus is the center, not the circumference. My favorite part of Paul's praise is in verse 18 where he states "that He would have first place in everything." There is no place Jesus is not first and preeminent.

Consider these words from Charles Spurgeon: "I believe there will be more in Heaven than in hell. If anyone asks me why I think so, I answer, because Christ, in everything, is to 'have the pre-eminence,' and I cannot conceive how He could have the pre-eminence if there are to be more in the dominions of Satan than in Paradise."[355]

That is so good. There will be more in heaven than in hell. Why? Because He must be preeminent.

You are familiar, no doubt, with one of the most famous paintings ever done by any artist: "The Last Supper" by Leonardo da Vinci, that classic portrayal of Christ and the twelve apostles at the table. Many stories have sprung up over the centuries about the painting. Many students of art history believe that the painting, when first created, was different from the version we now see. They believe that initially, an exquisite lace border race the outside length of the tablecloth. Upon completion, when da Vinci invited a group of art students to view his masterpiece, they were impressed by the delicate design of that lacework and praised its exquisite design. Upon seeing the reaction of these young men, the artist grabbed a paint brush and proceeded to paint over the lace. "Now, you fools, look at the face of Christ!"[356]

da Vinci said it. The apostle Paul is doing the same.

Day 180

WATCH OUT FOR SAWDUST

Today's Reading: Colossians 2

Charles Spurgeon told of an event that took place in ancient Rome. A severe famine had struck the North African colonies, so Emperor Nero sent ships to the stricken area. When the starving people saw the ships arriving, they shouted with joy. But Spurgeon recounted the tragic end of the story. When the ships sailed into port, the North Africans discovered they were full of sawdust to lay on the floor of the circuses Rome was exporting to the colonies. The people yearned for sustenance; they received sawdust.[357]

Unlike what was exported from Rome, I'm happy to say that in the book of Colossians we are about to find the arrival of something that *will* fill our hearts and souls—Jesus. The book of Colossians is a vessel bringing Christ back to His rightful and proper place *and* it's a book that fights religions that want to export sawdust and a circus!

The apostle Paul said to be very careful of people wanting to distract you from the main attraction. Consider his warning:

Watch out for people who try to dazzle you with big words and intellectual double-talk. They want to drag you off into endless arguments that never amount to anything. They spread their ideas through the empty traditions of human beings and the empty superstitions of spirit beings. But that's not the way of Christ. Everything of God gets expressed in him, so you can see and hear him clearly. You don't need a telescope, a microscope, or a horoscope to realize the fullness of Christ, and the emptiness of the universe without him. When you come to him, that fullness comes together for you, too. His power extends over everything. . . .

So don't put up with anyone pressuring you in details of diet, worship services, or holy days. All those things are mere shadows cast before what was to come; the substance is Christ. Don't tolerate people who try to run your life, ordering you to bow and scrape, insisting that you join their obsession with angels and that you seek out visions. They're a lot of hot air, that's all they are. They're completely out of touch with the source of life, Christ, who puts us together in one piece, whose very breath and blood flow through us. (Colossians 2:8-10, 16-19, MSG)

When you have a lot of people, you have a lot of opinions. And you can have a lot of opinions, but not have a lot of truth. Everyone is entitled to their own opinion, but not everyone is entitled to their own truth. There is a difference between truth and opinion. The problem comes when you think your opinion is truth.

We have to define what is opinion and what is truth. We must hold on to truth for dear life and hold onto personal opinion very lightly. Truth is that which is *true* for all times, all people, and all places. It can't be American truth. It can't be Democrat or Republican truth. Truth is truth. Opinions are for our personal world and always have an expiration date. Opinions don't last forever. But truth doesn't expire; it has no expiration date.

Author and pastor Charles Caleb Colton once said, "The greatest friend of truth is time, her greatest enemy is prejudice, and her constant companion humility."[358] What is catastrophic is when we think our opinion is truth and we are unwilling to listen to those who see it differently.

The apostle Paul is telling the church to grasp on to truth and not opinion. Colossians is a fighting book, and Paul is telling us to fight against syncretism. Syncretism is when we combine Christianity with so called "cool stuff from other religions." In Colossians, Paul was fighting against this because the believers were trying to get two things synched with Christianity—ceremonies and philosophy, or more specifically, Jewish ritualism and eastern mysticism.

This is not just a first-century issue and problem. It is also a twenty-first-century problem. We see people trying to import sawdust into Christianity. Whenever we need Jesus plus something else, it's sawdust. If we need Jesus plus a special book or to be part of a certain group of people or to wear a certain outfit, it's a boat of sawdust for the circus.

Tullian Tchividjian wrote a book that's title says it all: *Jesus + Nothing = Everything*.[359] Paul is fighting for the second part of the equation. Paul is telling us to stop inserting something where nothing belongs. If we do, it's religion and religious, but not Jesus.

Day 181

GOD'S UMPIRE

Today's Reading: Colossians 3

Every spring and summer, fields all over the United States are filled with athletes playing baseball. In the major leagues, the Bigs, the best players in the world come together in the thirty stadiums. They draw great attention and praise. But those games wouldn't happen or go well without the people on the field dressed in black jackets. They look different from any other person on the field. They are called the umpires.

No matter how good the players are—how fast they can pitch, how far they can hit or throw . . . the emotions of the game can cloud their decisions. And they need those umpires to keep order. Umpires decide the course and calls of the game. Who is safe and who is out. Which pitches are balls and which are strikes.

The baseball diamond needs a neutral party who sees the situation clearly and makes the correct call—not the call the fans or the players want, but the *right* call. They cannot be impaired by emotion, peer pressure, or even popular opinion. They must be moved by justice and the right thing.

Baseball isn't the only thing that needs an umpire. We need an umpire for the same reason. Emotions can cloud all our decisions. We want to do the right thing, but we have so many forces fighting against us. When peer pressure comes, and the voices from the outside try to get you to move into chaos, you too have an umpire to make a call. The apostle Paul tells the Colossian believers who are being inundated with outside religious opinions and additions to walk very carefully and keep Christ in focus. He says, "Let the peace of Christ keep you in tune with each other, in step with each other. None of this going off and doing your own thing. And cultivate thankfulness" (Colossians 3:15, MSG).

Think about this phrase, *Let the peace of God rule in your hearts.* The peace of God is your umpire. The key word is *rule.* In *Sparkling Gems from the Greek,* Rick Renner discusses this word:

I especially want you to notice the word "rule" in this verse. It is from the Greek word *brabeuo,* which in ancient times was used to describe the *umpire* or *referee* who moderated and judged the athletic competitions that were so popular in the ancient world.

Paul uses this word to tell us that the peace of God can work like an umpire or referee in our hearts, minds, and emotions.[360]

Peace must guide us to each place and in each decision. Colossians 3:15 could be translated: "Let the peace of God call the shots in your life"; "Let the peace of God be the umpire in your life and actions"; "Let the peace of God act as referee in your emotions and your decisions."

If we have no peace over something, then we are *out* at first base, and we need to get off the field. If we have peace over a decision, the umpire has told us that we are *safe* and we get to stay and continue on. Peace is the guiding principle for the believer—the umpire that tells us what's right so that chaos doesn't ensue.

Ever say about a decision, "I feel funny about this" or "Something doesn't feel right about going here or doing this"? That means you don't feel peace.

Don't over rule the umpire. Peace is God's mechanism to help you make good decisions today and stay on the field. As Curtis Hutson said, "When the believer is faced with a decision regarding a questionable matter, he should never proceed unless he has complete peace about it."[361] A host of emotions comes to us because life throws so many things at us. And nothing can blur our decision making like emotions.

Look at Paul tells us after the peace verse. It's brilliant: "Let the Word of Christ—the Message—have the run of the house. Give it plenty of room in your lives. Instruct and direct one another using good common sense" (verse 16, MSG). Paul is saying that the best place to start with wanting to know the right call is the Bible. If you want the peace of Christ, start with the Word of God. You can always bet on a *safe* from the umpire if the Word of God supports the next steps.

Peace is the umpire. The Word of God is the playbook the umpire work out of.

Day 182

ONLY A NAME NOW

Today's Reading: Colossians 4

Colossians 4 contains only 406 words. And of those 406 words, one in particular is big. It tells a story all by itself. But in order to grasp its importance, we need to call in two Bible verses. The one word is a name, and it's in verse 14: *Demas*.

Paul was finishing up an Epistle unlike any other he had written. We call it a polemic letter; it's a written debate. Maybe a better way to put it is that he issued fighting words. The church in Colossae was under attack, and Paul had to write a fighting letter, not to them but toward those trying to add anything outside to Christianity.

In chapter 1, he challenged them to be grounded in truth, and there is no better truth to be grounded in than the Person of Jesus. In chapter 2, he put on the boxing gloves and challenged those who were trying to get the new Christians to add special days, rituals, and visions to their newly found salvation. Paul told them to have nothing to do with that. In chapter 3, Paul told them what Christianity really is. Paul closed out chapter 4 by mentioning some important people who had been part of spreading the truth of Jesus. He brought up eleven names, and with almost all of them, he included something of their contribution:

There was "Tychicus, our beloved brother and faithful servant and fellow bond-servant in the Lord," who would "encourage your hearts" [Colossians 4:7-8]. There was "Onesimus, *our* faithful and beloved brother, who [was] one of your *number*" [verse 9]. Justus, who "proved to be an encouragement to me" [verse 11]. "Epaphras, who [was] . . . always laboring earnestly for you in his prayers, that you may stand perfect and fully assured in all the will of God" [verse 12]. And Nympha, the woman who had church in her house [verse 15]. Luke, "the beloved physician" [verse 14]. Name after name included with it information. And then there was "*also* Demas" [verse 14]. Demas was surrounded by eleven people who had godly contributions connected to their names, from praying to encouraging to providing their home for church services. He had nothing attached to his name.

Why is this something we must take notice of? Because two years earlier,

Paul wrote another letter called Philemon, and mentioned Demas in that letter. And in that letter, Demas got an attachment: "Epaphras, my fellow prisoner in Christ Jesus, greets you, *as do* Mark, Aristarchus, Demas, Luke, my fellow workers" [Philemon 1:23-24]. Demas was considered one of Paul's fellow workers. Two years later in AD 62, when Paul wrote Colossians, "fellow worker" was removed from his name and it was just Demas.

Demas gets one more verse in the New Testament and it comes all the way at the end of Paul's ministry, in AD 67. In fact, it's in the last letter he wrote, 2 Timothy. Paul wrote, "Demas, having loved this present world, has deserted me" [4:10]. Five years after the Colossians passage, we learn that Demas deserted Paul. *The Message* says that Demas "left me here" because he was "chasing fads." How did one of Paul's workers go rogue? How did he turn from loving Jesus to loving this present world?

I think the three-verse progression may explain it. In Philemon, Demas was called "my fellow worker," along with Luke and Mark. Other translations calls them "coworkers" (MSG) and "companions in this ministry" (TPT).

Then something happened two years later, in which "worker" was disconnected from Demas's name. He was no longer a coworker. He was no longer a companion. He was just a name in the church, but not a contributor anymore. It seems Demas vacated his job of serving.

I think that was the set up. That was the thing that turned his heart. It didn't take long for Demas to exit when he was no longer invested.

When we get to the end of Paul's ministry, the Contemporary English Version says that "Demas loves the things of this world so much that he left me." What happened? What caused this desertion? I think the Colossians verse tells his story—not by words but by the omission of words.

It's just a name now. Just a body in a pew, with no investment in serving anyone.

I read an amazing study that looked at what differentiated those who rescued Holocaust survivors and those in the same city in the Netherlands who did nothing to help them. Rescuers and non-rescuers alike were people from the same backgrounds, occupations, educations—all who faced the same decision: would they help and hide the Jews?

Samuel and Pearl Oliner, the sociologists who did the research found an interesting bit of information in the Holocaust rescuers: it was in how their parents disciplined them as children. When they were disciplined, their parents placed the emphasis not on their consequences but on what their behavior did to others, how their consequences affected those around them. Instead of parents teaching them what to do and what not to do, the parents taught them values and how to make decisions from values, especially seeing others as part of the consequences to their decisions. It was the emphasis on moral values instead of specific rules that made the difference in who acted as a rescuer versus who didn't.[362]

To make it simple, we don't live for ourselves, we live to make a difference in people's lives. I wish Demas would have learned that lesson. I wonder if Colossians' Demas would have opened his home to one of the Jews who were being hunted by the Nazis? Would you?

THE GREATEST TRUTH I KNOW

Today's Reading: 1 Thessalonians 1

Some time ago I was flying on a 10 p.m. flight. Earlier that day I'd preached four messages. I was exhausted. I noticed the man sitting next to me was reading *Heaven Is for Real*.

This is good. He is a Christian, I thought. *I can go to sleep because we are both going to heaven.*

He saw my Bible, which I'd pulled out to read, and began talking to me—a lot. Come to find out, he was part of a cult. I prayed the strangest prayer that flight: "God, I am *so tired*. Please don't use me. Find someone else. But I do ask that You don't let this kid die and go to hell." I felt terrible praying that way, but I simply didn't have the energy to engage him in conversation.

As disappointing as I know I must have been to God, the amazing thing is that I was still secure in God's love for me. His love did not decrease one ounce because of my poor tired attitude. He loved me exactly same when I prayed that lame prayer as when I preached for Him.

One of the saddest things that happens in Christianity is that we overemphasize what we do for God rather than what God has done for us. I used to think God loved me only when I was doing good. But 1 Thessalonians reminds me of the truth.

Paul starts chapter 1 with a thunderbolt. In fact, I consider it the greatest truth I know, and it's all in verse 4: "My dear friends, God loves you" (CEV). God *loves* you! Those words change everything *and* cost everything.

I came from a background in Christianity where the emphasis was on how much we love God and not on how much God loves us. In fact, I thought my actions determined how much God loves me.

But there is not one thing you and I can do to make God love us any more than He does right now. We believe this in theory but we don't live this way. We think God loves us more when we are at our spiritual best. Here is good news: God loves us the same when we are at our worst on planes praying *Don't use me* prayers.

William Coffin reminds us: "God's love doesn't seek value, it creates value. It is not because we have value that we are loved, but because we are loved that we have value."[363] Every religion in the world is based on what *we* do. The stars in those other religions is anyone who dies a martyr, carries a briefcase, rides a bike, or gives up years on the mission field. In Christianity, however, it's all about what *God* has done.

One of my favorite authors, Brennan Manning, said: "My deepest awareness of myself is that I am deeply loved by Jesus Christ and I have done nothing to earn it or deserve it."[364] That's the scandal and that's the deal of the century. So if those words, *God loves you,* are difficult to accept, let me help you today.

There is no greater place to deal with doubts of God's love than at the only place that settles the question—and that's at the cross. In the man Jesus, the invisible God became visible and audible. God can't *not* love us. The cross is the proof of His love—love that He demonstrated at Calvary. The well-known saying goes like this: *I asked God how much He loves me, and He said this much. And He held His hands wide to his side and died for me.*

When you look at the cross, you see what price you are worth to God. God loves you just as you are and not as you should be. He died for you at your worst. He did not wait for you to change in order to die for you. Isn't it staggering to think you are worth the death of someone and most of all, God? That is what puts a large gulf between Christianity and other religions, such as Islam. Islam asks you to die for Allah, but Christianity has God dying for you.

Brennan Manning tells an amazing story in *Souvenirs of Solitude*:

More than a hundred years ago the atheist philosopher Friedrich Nietzsche reproached a group of Christians: "Yuck, you make me sick!" When their spokesman asked why, he answered, "Because you redeemed don't look like you're redeemed. You're as fearful, guilt-ridden, anxious, confused, and adrift in an alien environment as I am. I'm allowed. I don't believe. I have nothing to hope for. But you people claim you have a Savior. Why don't you look like you are saved?"

In Matthew 22 Jesus described the kingdom of God as a wedding feast. Do you really trust that you are going to a wedding feast that has already begun? Do you really believe that God loves you unconditionally and as you are? Are you committed to the idea that the nature of the world is to be a celebration? If you are, then in the words of Father John Powell, S. J., "Please notify your face."[365]

You have something to be happy about: God loves you for who you are. Christianity is not a moral code but a love affair.

WHATEVER GOD BACKS, SATAN ATTACKS

Today's Reading: 1 Thessalonians 2

Listen really carefully: whatever God backs, Satan attacks. In today's chapter Paul has a great desire to be with the Thessalonian Christians, but Satan fights to stop it from happening. I wonder how many things we have in our hearts to do that Satan fights against. Listen to Paul's desire and fight in 1 Thessalonians 2:18: "We really wanted to come. I myself tried several times, but Satan always stopped us" (CEV).

We have forgotten that we have an enemy who wants to disrupt our plans. Sometimes the best confirmation that our plans and desires are from God is Satan's attack on them. The last thing the devil wants us doing is the will of God.

Paul has a desire to go to this new church in Thessalonica, and Satan is bent on stopping the apostle from visiting. Sometimes Satan succeeds. Those last words of this verse remind us of the war we are in: "I tried several times but Satan always stopped us." These aren't the words of a one-hit wonder. This is the apostle Paul. And Paul tries a number of times and cannot seem to get through Satan's roadblocks.

C. S. Lewis was right when he said: "There is no neutral ground in the universe: every square inch, every split second is claimed by God and counterclaimed by Satan."[366] Always remember there is a counterclaim happening. Whatever God backs, Satan attacks. Or as Robert Murray McCheynne said, "I know well that when Christ is the nearest, Satan also is busiest."[367] The closer you get to what God wants you to do, the closer Satan comes in.

But some people don't believe in the devil. Two boys struggled with the problem of the devil's existence. As they walked home from Sunday school after hearing a message about the devil, one boy said, "What do you think about all this Satan stuff?" The other replied, "Well, you know how Santa Clause turned out. It's probably just your dad."[368]

In his classic work *The Screwtape Letters*, C. S. Lewis reminds us of two errors when it comes to Satan: "There are two equal and opposite errors into which our race can fall about the devils. One is to disbelieve in their existence. The other is to believe, and to feel an excessive and unhealthy interest in them.

They themselves are equally pleased by both errors and hail a materialist or a magician with the same delight."[369] You can give the devil too much or too little attention.

The Illustrated Bible Backgrounds Commentary of the New Testament gives us an insight to the enemy's tactics. The verb *enkoptō*, which literally means "to cut into," originally referred to the military practice of cutting up a road so as to make it impassable for a pursuing army. Paul wants his readers to know that his present absence from them is not due to his personal choice but to the activity of Satan, who, in typical military fashion, has destroyed the apostle's path back to Thessalonica.[370] "We are evidently no friends of Satan," says J. C. Ryle. "Like the kings of this world, he doesn't war against his own subjects. The very fact that he assaults us should fill our minds with hope."[371]

I want to challenge you. What is it that you have been trying to do lately and you are really convinced it's something God wants you to do but you can't seem to make it happen? Maybe you are being hindered by Satan from doing God's will like the apostle Paul was.

Maybe it's purity in a relationship. Maybe it's inconsistency in reading the Bible. Maybe it's going to church or serving at church. Perhaps it's forgiving an offense that is still lingering in your heart. Whatever it may be you have tried multiple times but have failed to gain any ground. What should you do? It may be time to launch a gnu attack.

There is a strange animal called a Gnu. When it catches sight of one of its predators, its enemies, it immediately drops down on its knees and, from that position, springs into the attack mode. Are you getting where I'm going here?

We need to practice a gnu way to fight.

We see our enemy putting up obstacles as he did for the apostle, and immediately we assume the gnu position and get on our knees and pray. That's how we fight.

Don't Be Deceived by the Packaging

Today's Reading: 1 Thessalonians 3

No one seems to wrap gifts anymore in boxes and wrapping paper. We use a gift bag and some colored tissue paper on top. If we forgot the occasion, whether it's a birthday or an anniversary, usually a gift card (which means *I forgot to shop*) lies beneath the tissue paper. Here in 1 Thessalonians 3, the apostle Paul shows us a special gift that we can easily miss because of the packaging and its wrapping.

At times I have prayed for things and never realized that the answer came in wrapping I never expected. We know Paul spent some months with this Thessalonian church and preached in their city. After being gone a few months, Paul sent Timothy to check on the church there. He wrote this letter to encourage them, because they faced false teachers, whom he did not want infiltrating the young church, as well as some difficult persecution. He knew that in the midst of those difficult times, they needed strength and encouragement "so that no one would be disturbed by these afflictions; for you yourselves know that we have been destined for this" (verse 3).

Those words, *disturbed by these afflictions*, are revealing. In fact, the actual word is *deceived*. I have learned that hard times can deceive people. Hard times can deceive us about God, deceive us about ourselves, and deceive us about life. We begin to believe the lies that say, *God doesn't love me. That's why I am going through this* and *These hard times are punishments for the bad things I have done. I'm the only one who goes through stuff like this. I am all alone.* It's the deception of hard times. When people go through difficulty, so does their faith.

So Paul sent to these young Thessalonian believers much-needed gifts: encouragement and strength. But the packaging was different. Listen to verse 2: "We sent Timothy, our brother and God's fellow worker in the gospel of Christ, to strengthen and encourage you as to your faith." God packaged strength and encouragement in a person—Timothy.

The movie *The Blind Side* chronicles a Christian family, the Tuohys, who took in a homeless young man, Michael Oher, and gave him the chance to reach his God-given potential. That homeless boy became the first-round NFL draft pick for the Baltimore Ravens in 2009. At a recent fundraiser, Sean Tuohy noted that the transformation of his family and Michael all started with two words. When they spotted Michael walking along the road on a cold November morning, Leigh Ann Tuohy uttered two words that changed their world. She told Sean, "Turn around." They turned the car around, put Michael in their warm vehicle, and ultimately adopted him into their family.[372] Hope was packaged for Michael Oher in the Tuohy family. Sometimes we don't recognize the packaging.

The Thessalonian church were about to discover their friend in their adversity. They just needed to be aware of God's packaging for this gift who was coming. Sometimes we ask for things and miss God's answer because of the packaging. We all need strength and encouragement every day. What does that answer look like? Paul told the church of Thessolonica that they needed strength and encouragement so "we sent Timothy." Timothy was to be their strength and encouragement.

That is why God places a high value of making sure we stay right with brothers and sisters. That person you are fighting with may contain your answer to prayer. Locked up in them may be your strength and encouragement for today. God's packaging of His answers is usually wrapped up in flesh and blood. How about the greatest "flesh and blood" packaging? Jesus.

Is there a friendship that needs to be repaired with an apology? You may be missing more than a friend, you may be missing your answer to your prayer. Make it a priority not only to call today but to understand that friendships are too valuable to let a hurt close them off.

John Maxwell tells about a Midwestern fair in which "spectators gathered for an old-fashioned horse pull (an event where various weights are put on a horse-drawn sled and pulled along the ground). The grand-champion horse pulled a sled with 4,500 pounds on it. The runner-up was close, with a 4,400-pound pull if hitched together. Separately they totaled nearly 9,000 pounds, but when hitched and working together as a team, they pulled more than 12,000 pounds."[373] As the strength of the horse pull shows, there is more power being part of the body of Christ than just being some loner Christian.

Your effectiveness multiplies when you are joined with the right people. Paul knew that he needed to put Timothy next to the Thessalonians so they would be able to pull a lot more, that Timothy would give them the encouragement and the strength they needed to pull the weight. The saying is true "that the quality of your life is determined by the quality of your relationships." There is another saying, a Zambian proverb, that is equally true: "When you run alone, you run fast. But when you run together, you run far."

In their gift of Timothy, the young church in Thessalonica received help to run far.

Ecclesiastes 4:12 says, "By yourself you're unprotected. With a friend you can face the worst" (MSG). That's a good gift.

Day 186

WAIT FOR TWO MARSHMALLOWS

Today's Reading: 1 Thessalonians 4

God's will is the exact place God wants you to be at the right time. It's being in the right relationship, the right job, living in the right city, reading the right book of the Bible. As Elisabeth Elliot said, "The will of God is not something you add to your life. It's a course you choose. You either line yourself up with the Son of God . . . or you capitulate to the principle which governs the rest of the world."[374]

First Thessalonians 4 teaches us something very valuable on understanding the will of God for our lives. God's will is the safest place on the planet. It is safer for me to be in the most anti-Christian country (such as North Korea) *in God's will* than it is to be living in a mansion in Cabo San Lucas *outside of God's will.* There is peace and safety and confidence in God's will, but it's not always easy. As missionary Joanne Shetler said: "God never said doing His will would be easy; He only said it would be worth it."[375]

But how do we know if something is God's will? I know of people who have tried flipping through the Bible and whatever passage they land on is what they are going to do. The story is told of a man who used this flip-open-the-Bible method to see what God wanted him to do in his life. The first verse he landed on was Matthew 27:5, which says Judas "went away and hanged himself." Since he was not sure how this verse applied to him, he flipped to another passage. The Bible fell open to Luke 10:37: "Said Jesus unto him, 'Go and do the same.'" The man was quite upset and did not know how he could ever obey that, so he decided to turn to one more place. Again he opened the Bible at random and to his horror his finger fell on John 13:27: "Jesus said to him, 'What you do, do quickly.'"

Not a good way to figure out God's will.

I think it is a lot simpler. The problem is that the will of God always seems to be this treasure hunt that everyone is on.

Where should I live?

What should be my career?

Should I go, should I stay?

What college?

Do I buy this house?

Do I rent this apartment?

Do I date this guy?

Do I marry this person?

We treat the will of God like God whispers it one time and if we miss it, we're left on our own to figure it out. I wonder if we don't know more of God's will for our personal lives, because we have not done what is clearly spelled out. Sometimes we don't get more specific future instructions because we have not obeyed what is clearly written for us right now.

There are two will-of-God verses that Paul clearly spells out for us in the Bible. We know this because Paul says, "for this is the will of God." Let's look at one today and one tomorrow. I believe if we follow these two verses, other future decisions will become clearer for us.

After reading each of the verses, ask yourself: Am I doing this? If you aren't, here's something to ponder: why would God entrust you with more if you won't do what is right before you?

Here is the clear will of God for our life: "For this is the will of God, your sanctification; *that is*, that you abstain from sexual immorality" (1 Thessalonians 4:3). Let's be really clear and define sexual immorality: it is having sex outside the boundaries of marriage.

"I love him" or "I love her" does not make sex outside of marriage right. "We are engaged" does not change what God has said. To engage before the marriage commitment is to sabotage your marriage before it happens. Why? The Bible says that "love is patient." That is the first definition of love in the long list. If you can't be patient till the wedding day, then love is suspect. The will of God says abstain from sexual immorality. You will prove your love to the person you love by your patience to do things the right way. And great things come from the fruit of the Spirit—patience.

Around 1970, Walter Mischel launched a classic experiment in which he left a succession of four-year-olds in a room with a bell and a marshmallow. If they rang the bell, he returned and they could eat the marshmallow. If, however, they didn't ring the bell and waited for him to come back on his own, they could then have two marshmallows.

In videos of the experiment, we can see the children squirming, kicking, hiding their eyes—desperately trying to exercise self-control so they can wait and get two marshmallows. Their performances varied widely. Some broke down and rang the bell within a minute. Others lasted fifteen minutes.

After the experiment, Mischel continued to follow and study them. The children who waited longer went on to get higher SAT scores. They got into better colleges and had, on average, better adult outcomes. The children who rang the bell quickest were more likely to become bullies. They received worse teacher and parental evaluations ten years on and were more likely to have drug problems by the age of thirty-two. Mischel concluded that children may be taught "that it pays to work toward the future instead of living for instant gratification."[376]

God is always thinking big picture. When God tells us to wait until marriage, it's because He realizes waiting for sex within those boundaries has really good things that happen for our future across the board—and we get to know more and more of His will for our lives.

Wait for two marshmallows. You get a lot more cool stuff in the future.

A PILLOW FOR YOUR HEAD

Today's Reading: 1 Thessalonians 5

My mentor R. T. Kendall said: "The happiest pillow on which you may rest your head is the knowledge of God's will. I cannot imagine a more miserable situation than consciously to be out of God's will."[377] Paul gives us two pillows to rest on in 1 Thessalonians. Those pillows are the clear will of God. And Paul makes it very clear that we know this is what God wants for us. My friend Winkie Pratney says, "Many say they can't get God's guidance, when they really mean they wish He would show them an easier way."[378]

Yesterday we looked at the first verse: "For this is the will of God, your sanctification; that is, that you abstain from sexual immorality" (1 Thessalonians 4:3). Sexual purity is God's clear will, that is pillow #1. Here is pillow #2: "In everything give thanks; for this is God's will for you in Christ Jesus" (1 Thessalonians 5:18).

Paul couldn't have stated God's will and guidance for us any clearer: sexual purity and thanksgiving in everything. Difficult verses to live out? Absolutely. Possible to live out? Absolutely. But not without God's help. Always remember, God will never ask us to do anything that He will not give us the power to obey.

Paul wrote to the church at Thessalonica about AD 54 while he was staying in Corinth. This was also the first letter of his fourteen Epistles Paul ever wrote. It was written mainly to Gentile converts, and was in effect, a design for discipleship, a practical primer on living the Christian life. So here in the fifth chapter of his first letter he ever wrote, he tells them, *in everything* give thanks. Paul did not say *for* everything but *in* everything. To say "for everything" would almost seem inhumane. No one can give thanks for everything, because some really horrible things happen to us. But when it gets hard, we *can* find thanksgiving *in* the situation. We can always find *something* to thank God for. And that's what Paul is telling us to do: in every situation find something to give thanks for.

How was your day? Terrible. I had a flat tire on the way to work. No. Give thanks in everything. We can thank God that He gave us a car to get a flat tire with, a job to pay for the car that we got a flat tire in, the jack in the back that was there when we got the flat, and breath that we still have because the flat tire did not go bad and hit any other cars causing a fatal accident.

Want to read the craziest I'm-thankful-in-everything scenario ever said? It has only been said in this place by only one man. Strange sounds, organs, all around him and here is the verse: "I will sacrifice to You with the voice of thanksgiving" (Jonah 2:9). *No big deal*, you think? It is a big deal when you realize who said that! Jonah—while he was in the belly of the whale. He gave thanks when he was inside a whale. If Jonah could say it where he was then you and I can be thankful in whatever situation we find ourselves.

Famous English Bible scholar Matthew Henry was once attacked and robbed. Afterward he wrote in his diary: "Let me be thankful, first, because he never robbed me before; second, although he took my purse, he did not take my life; third, because although he took all I possessed, it was not much; and fourth, because it was I who was robbed, not I who robbed."[379]

I believe it's God's will to thank Him before you ask Him. As Philippians 4:6 says, you are to make your requests known with thanksgiving." Thank Him before you ask Him. It will purge your asking. How does thanksgiving purge the ask? Thanksgiving reminds you of all that God has already given to you.

Former New York Yankees second baseman, Bobby Richardson, who is also a strong Christian, prayed at a meeting of the Fellowship of Christian Athletes. This was his short prayer: "Dear God, Your will: nothing more, nothing less, nothing else!"[380] Remember what Paul said, "*in* everything," not "*for* everything." That's the pillow R. T. Kendall speaks about.

In *The Hiding Place*, Corrie Ten Boom relates an incident that taught her this principle of being thankful in every situation. During World War II, she and her sister, Betsy, had been arrested for hiding Jews. They were both transferred to the concentration camp at Ravensbruck and found that their living quarters were infested with fleas, making a bad situation worse. She was complaining about it one day, when her sister reminded her of Paul's words to give thanks in everything. Then she challenged Corrie to give thanks for the fleas. But she made a choice to offer thanks for the fleas anyway. Later, she found out that the fleas had actually protected them from the assaults of the German soldiers.[381]

Christian poet George Herbert wrote these powerful words: "Thou who hast given so much to me, give me one more thing—a grateful heart!"[382]

GROW THROUGH IT NOT JUST GO THROUGH IT

Today's Reading: 2 Thessalonians 1

When the famed cellist Pablo Casals reached ninety-five years old, a young reporter asked, "Why do you still practice six hours a day?" To which Casals answered, "Because I think I'm making progress."[383]

Your goal is to make progress every day of your life. We call it growth. As John Newman said, "Growth is the only evidence of life."[384] That is true naturally and especially spiritually. The Thessalonian Christians were new Christians and more importantly growing Christians.

The Thessalonian church was under heavy persecution, yet continued to grow through it. This is important: they were not just going through it but growing through it. What a lesson for us. That when we are faced with difficult times, we remember that we can grow through them. Growth is not arrival, it's movement. Growth is not perfection but better.

The writer of the hymn, "Amazing Grace," John Newton, said it best: "I am not what I might be, I am not what I ought to be, I am not what I wish to be, I am not what I hope to be; but I thank God I am not what I once was, and I can say with the great apostle, 'By the grace of God I am what I am.'"[385]

Listen to Paul's words of commendation to these young Christians who were not what they used to be but growing:

> You need to know, friends, that thanking God over and over for you is not only a pleasure; it's a must. We *have* to do it. Your faith is growing phenomenally; your love for each other is developing wonderfully. Why, it's only right that we give thanks. We're so proud of you; you're so steady and determined in your faith despite all the hard times that have come down on you. We tell everyone we meet in the churches all about you. (2 Thessalonians 1:3-4, MSG)

These new believers were growing through hard times. They were growing in two areas: their love for others was developing wonderfully and their faith was growing phenomenally—the New American Standard Bible says, "your faith is greatly enlarged." And all of it happening in difficulty. He was basically saying, "Your faith is getting supersized." We know that word *supersize* because we know McDonald's. Supersize to us means bigger fries and bigger Coke. But it does cost to supersize. Paul was saying, "You paid the extra cost for the supersize of faith and it's evident."

What was the cost? That's the next verse: "Your perseverance and faith in the midst of all your persecutions and afflictions which you endure" (verse 4). Notice it says "persecution and affliction." Those two words are important. One is about the outside battles. The other is the mental battles. And Paul was commending them by acknowledging, "You are getting hit outside and inside and holding your own, because you are holding on to God."

A family-owned coat store in Nottingham, England, has a sign that hangs for all to see:

> We have been established for over 100 years and have been pleasing and displeasing customers ever since. We have made money and lost money, suffered the effects of coal nationalization, coat rationing, government control, and bad payers. We have been cussed and discussed, messed about, lied to, held up, robbed and swindled. The only reason we stay in business is we can't wait to see what happens tomorrow.[386]

It seems that the Thessalonians should have put that sign on their church. Tomorrow for the Thessalonians was phenomenal faith and developing love. Tomorrow for many is fearful but not for these new Christians. They were growing through their adversity.

A daughter complained to her father about how difficult things were for her. "As soon as I solve one problem," she said, "another one comes up. I'm tired of struggling."

Her father, a chef, took her to the kitchen where he filled three pots with water and placed each on a high fire. Soon the pots came to a boil. In one he placed carrots, in the second, eggs, and in the last, ground coffee beans. He let them sit and boil, without saying a word.

The daughter impatiently waited, wondering what he was doing. After a while, he went over and turned off the burners. He fished out the carrots and placed them in a bowl. He pulled the eggs out and placed them a bowl. He poured the coffee into a bowl. Turning to her he asked, "Daughter, what do you see?"

"Carrots, eggs, and coffee," she replied.

He brought her closer and asked her to feel the carrots. She did and noted that they were soft. He then asked her to take an egg and break it. After pulling off the shell, she observed the hard-boiled egg. Finally, he asked her to sip the coffee. She smiled, as she tasted its rich flavor.

"What does it mean, Father?" she asked.

He explained that each of them had faced the same adversity—boiling water—but each reacted differently. The carrot went in strong, hard, and unrelenting, but after being subjected to the boiling water, it softened and became weak. The egg was fragile. Its thin outer shell had protected its liquid interior, but after sitting through the boiling water, its inside hardened. The ground coffee beans were unique, however. By being in the boiling water, they changed the water.

He asked his daughter, "When adversity knocks on your door, which are you?"[387]

A GREAT PRAYER TO START YOUR DAY

Today's Reading: 2 Thessalonians 2

If you are a parent, you have most definitely heard these words from your children at one time or another, "But you said!" What that means is they are holding you to your word. Nothing is more incriminating than being quoted and held accountable. It seems that the only time they *do* listen is when it's a promise or commitment.

God is a Father and He who keeps His word loves to hear His children tell Him, "You said." I think that thrills the heart of God. In Hebrews 4:12, we are told that the Word of God is powerful. If you take God's powerful Word and pray it back to Him, that is exponential in power. Adding a "You said" to your prayer language gets God's attention just as a "you said" does for any parent. I don't think anything is more powerful than when you pray the Scriptures. You are just reminding God of what He told you.

I want to give you a great prayer to start your day. It's using God's words in prayer. It is basically saying, "If You said, then why *wouldn't* You hear and respond": "May Jesus himself and God our Father, who reached out in love and surprised you with gifts of unending help and confidence, put a fresh heart in you, invigorate your work, enliven your speech. (2 Thessalonians 2:16-17, MSG).

Consider the trilogy of requests: put a fresh heart in me, invigorate my work, enliven my speech. Let's briefly unpack each of these so we can spot it when God answers it in our day. That's called "watch and pray." If we ask for something, we have a responsibility to watch with expectancy.

First, ask God to put a fresh heart in you. *Fresh* is the word you would use when describing how you look when you've just returned from a two-week vacation. How do you freshen up your heart? How do you make your heart look as though it just got off vacation? Let your heart take a trip . . . a trip to heaven. Each morning let your heart take a trip into the presence of God. You cannot make that trip without coming out with a fresh heart.

Second, ask God to invigorate your work. The word *invigorate* means to give strength and energy to what you do. How does God invigorate your work? He has to refocus your attention on *who* you are doing it for. Listen to what the apostle says in Colossians: "Put your heart and soul into every activity you do, as though you are doing it for the Lord himself and not merely for others" (Colossians 3:23, TPT).

Your work is invigorated when you do it for Jesus. Every activity counts, not just church activities. Martin Luther King Jr. said it like this:

> If it falls your lot to be a street sweeper, sweep streets like Michelangelo painted pictures, sweep streets like Beethoven composed music. . . . Sweep streets like Shakespeare wrote poetry. Sweep streets so well that all the hosts of heaven and earth will have to pause and say: Here lived a great street sweeper who did his job well.[388]

Whatever your occupation—CVS cashier to TSA guard at the airport, police officer, first responder, teacher, or ambassador. Whether you work for the government or the church. May God invigorate your work. You work for *the* Boss, so you're doing it for Him.

Third, ask God to enliven your speech. The word *enliven* means to make your speech more entertaining, interesting, and appealing. When you open your mouth, you want life to come out. Not complaints, not ingratitude, just joy and encouragement.

As Proverbs 18:21 reminds us: Words kill, words give life; they're either poison or fruit—you choose" (MSG). Let's choose words of life today.

My prayer for you and me today is this: "God, put a fresh heart in us. Invigorate our work. And enliven our speech. In Jesus' name, amen."

Now go and have an amazing day!

GIVING MY QUARTERS AWAY EACH DAY

Today's Reading: 2 Thessalonians 3

I recently read this quote: "Isn't it funny how day by day nothing changes but when you look back, everything is different?"[389] The apostle Paul encourages us in our day by day in 2 Thessalonians 3. He reminds us that the day-to-day responsibilities and duties can be wearying but worth it in the long run: "Do not grow weary of doing good" (2 Thessalonians 3:13).

I don't know who said it but it is so true: "The years reveal what the days do not tell." That's what Paul is trying to tell us—that doing what's right and good every day without getting exhausted is our challenge.

Fred Craddock, in an address to ministers, caught the practical implications of how the day-to-day things matter when he said:

> To give my life for Christ appears glorious. To pour myself out for others . . . to pay the ultimate price of martyrdom—I'll do it. I'm ready, Lord, to go out in a blaze of glory.
>
> We think giving our all to the Lord is like taking a $1,000 bill and laying it on the table— "Here's my life, Lord. I'm giving it all."
>
> But the reality for most of us is that he sends us to the bank and has us cash in the $1,000 for quarters. We go through life putting out 25 cents here and 50 cents there. Listen to the neighbor kid's troubles instead of saying, "Get lost." Go to a committee meeting. Give up a cup of water to a shaky old man in a nursing home.
>
> Usually giving our life to Christ isn't glorious. It's done in all those little acts of love, 25 cents at a time. It would be easy to go out in a flash of glory; It's harder to live the Christian life little by little over the long haul.[390]

My prayer is this: "Jesus, help me to be consistent with my twenty-five cents a day. Teach me that faithfulness counts. Teach me not always to look for the big moment but to look for the little places where I can show charity—especially where no one is around and no applause can be heard, except a *Well done* whispered in my spirit." Those twenty-five-cent days are the day-today good decisions Paul is talking about. Not big exchanges of cash but little quarter decisions that pay off over time.

I want to tell you a cheese story. We know the guy but forgot about how a cheese delivery changed his life. He was doing a good thing for his dad and his brothers and because he did not get weary in submitting to his father, it changed the trajectory of his life. The delivery guy? David.

How did David start on the journey toward his destiny of eventually becoming king? A cheese delivery—saying yes to an errand his dad asked him to do:

> "Take these ten wedges of cheese to the captain of their division. Check in on your brothers to see whether they are getting along all right, and let me know how they're doing—Saul and your brothers, and all the Israelites in their war with the Philistines in the Oak Valley."
>
> David was up at the crack of dawn and, having arranged for someone to tend his flock, took the food and was on his way just as Jesse had directed him. (1 Samuel 17:18-20, MSG)

David's destiny started by simply doing a small errand for his dad. And he took the cheese out of his hand and put a sling and rock in it shortly after. But who knew? Don't get weary of doing good.

I believe entry ramps into your destiny starts with humble little tasks that don't even match what you want to do in the future. I really don't think David's dream was to be a Velveeta cheese delivery guy. But he was faithful in doing the little things. As Hudson Taylor said, "A little thing is a little thing, but faithfulness in a little thing is a big thing."[391]

Don't dismiss little things that are good. Many times the people who can defeat the giant are never selected because they hate cheese assignments. Don't be a cheese hater. You don't kill goliaths on goliath missions but on cheese missions. Cheese deliveries are the good things that Paul said may be small but good. It is doing something for others that will never get noticed or praised or seem significant enough to put on a resume. Don't try to find your destiny. Just say yes to small tasks and your destiny will find you. What you see as a cheese delivery, God sees further.

An unknown author powerful summarized the power of being willing to say yes to the small talks:

You know the world is a better place because Michelangelo didn't say,
I don't do ceilings.

The world is a better place because a German monk named Martin Luther didn't say, "I don't do doors."

The world is a better place, because an Oxford don named John Wesley didn't say, "I don't do fields."

Go from the beginning of the Bible to the end, and you will see over and over again the story of men and women who had servant hearts, minds, and spirits. And the world is a better place, because:

Noah didn't say, "I don't do boats."

Moses didn't say, "I don't do deserts."

Rahab didn't say, "I don't do hiding spies."

Ruth didn't say, "I don't do mothers-in-law."

David didn't say, "I don't do cheese."

Jeremiah didn't say, "I don't do weeping."

Amos didn't say, "I don't do speeches."

Mary didn't say, "I don't do virgin births."

Mary Magdalene didn't say, "I don't do feet."

Paul didn't say, "I don't do letters."

Jesus didn't say, "I don't do crosses."[392]

As Augustine said, "The last day is hidden that every day may be regarded as important."[393] So spend your quarter today.

GOD GOING OUT ON A LIMB

Today's Reading: 1 Timothy 1

Erwin Lutzer, author and long-time pastor of Moody Church in Chicago said, "There is more grace in God's heart than there is sin in your past."[394] This is something the apostle Paul knew and wrote about it in today's chapter:

> I thank Christ Jesus our Lord, who has strengthened me, because He considered me faithful, putting me into service, even though I was formerly a blasphemer and a persecutor and a violent aggressor. Yet I was shown mercy because I acted ignorantly in unbelief; and the grace of our Lord was more than abundant, with the faith and love which are *found* in Christ Jesus. (1 Timothy 1:12-14)

A. W. Tozer tells us how right Paul is:

> Sometimes I go to God and say, "God, if Thou dost never answer another prayer while I live on this earth, I will still worship Thee as long as I live and in the ages to come for what Thou hast done already." God's already put me so far in debt that if I were to live one million millenniums I couldn't pay Him for what He's done for me.[395]

The only currency we have to offer God for all He has done for us is thanksgiving. And sometimes we don't do well with gratitude. How can we get better? Here's a good place to start from Priscilla Maurice:

> Begin by thanking Him for some little thing, and then go on, day by day, adding to your subjects of praise; thus you will find their numbers grow wonderfully; and, in the same proportion, will your subjects of murmuring and complaining diminish, until you see in everything some cause for thanksgiving.[396]

The apostle Paul starts off by thanking God for putting him in the ministry. *The Message* says it like this: I'm so grateful to Christ Jesus for making me adequate to do this work. He went out on a limb, you know, in trusting me with this ministry" (1 Timothy 1:12). And just like Priscilla Maurice said, as he started thanking God, the list grew. After thanking God for trusting him with the ministry, his heart went into the past and realized that God had gone out on a limb to pick Paul to represent Him. Here is the limb God went out on for Paul: "Even though I was formerly a blasphemer and a persecutor and a violent aggressor. Yet I was shown mercy because I acted ignorantly in unbelief; and the grace of our Lord was more than abundant, with the faith and love which are *found* in Christ Jesus" (verses 13-14).

Paul used three words that built to a climax—*blasphemer* to *persecutor* to violent *aggressor*. What's crazy is how important our crazy past is. Instead of being tempted to hide it or ignore it, he shared it. Author Brennan Manning encourages us to do the same—to tell our terrible stories: "In a futile attempt to erase our past, we deprive the community of our healing gift. If we conceal our wounds out of fear and shame, our inner darkness can neither be illuminated nor become a light for others."[397] And as Warren Wiersbe reminds us: "The past is a rudder to guide you, not an anchor to drag you."[398]

That means Paul used his crazy past to guide his gratitude and thanksgiving. Maybe we don't think enough of our past and so our praise limps. Here is what Paul did. The thing that stands out in this passage is Paul's insistence on remembering his own sin in a very revealing ascending order. He piled up his words on top of one another to show the awfulness of what he had done and the kind of person he really was. Paul said he was an insulter of the church. He'd flung hot and angry words at the Christians, accusing them of crimes against God. Then he moved up to being a persecutor, taking every means to annihilate the Christian church. Then he moved up again and admitted he became a violent aggressor.

The word in Greek indicates a kind of arrogant sadism; it describes someone who is out to inflict pain for the sheer joy of inflicting it. Paul was showing us a dark heart. He had found delight in the suffering of other people, especially Christians. That was what Paul once was. Then Paul, amazed, said that God went out on a limb to put *him* in the ministry. That's definitely something to thank God about.

The Puritan pastor, Thomas Goodwin, wrote an insightful letter to his son:

When I was threatening to become cold in my ministry, and when I felt Sabbath morning coming and my heart not filled with amazement at the grace of God, or when I was making ready to dispense the Lord's

Supper, do you know what I used to do? I used to take a turn up and down among the sins of my past life, and I always came down again with a broken and a contrite heart, ready to preach, as it was preached in the beginning, the forgiveness of sins. I do not think I ever went up the pulpit stair that I did not stop for a moment at the foot of it and take a turn up and down among the sins of my past years. I do not think that I ever planned a sermon that I did not take a turn round my study table and look back at the sins of my youth and of all my life down to the present; and many a Sabbath morning, when my soul had been cold and dry, for the lack of prayer during the week, a turn up and down in my past life before I went into the pulpit always broke my hard heart and made me close with the gospel for my own soul before I began to preach.[399]

When we remember how we have hurt God, hurt those who love us, and hurt others, and when we remember how God and our neighbors have forgiven us, that memory must awake the flame of gratitude within our hearts. That's exactly what Paul did here in 1 Timothy. Let's read what Paul said after he recounted his awful past:

Grace mixed with faith and love poured over me and into me. And all because of Jesus. Here's a word you can take to heart and depend on: Jesus Christ came into the world to save sinners. I'm proof—Public Sinner Number One—of someone who could never have made it apart from sheer mercy. And now he shows me off—evidence of his endless patience—to those who are right on the edge of trusting him forever. (verses 14-16, MSG)

Paul's past was forgiven and now he was telling others the amazing forgiveness and mercy of God. Let's follow his example.

THE BEST WAY TO BE INVOLVED
IN POLITICS

Today's Reading: 1 Timothy 2

I want to help you get involved in politics. I knew that would get your attention. When it comes to being a Republican or a Democrat, let's be careful before labeling ourselves. I am of the school of C. S. Lewis, who said these important words about politics: "He who surrenders himself without reservation to the temporal claims of a nation, or a party, or a class is rendering to Caesar that which, of all things, most emphatically belongs to God: himself."[400]

Our heart, emotions, and energies first belong to God. We must be careful of giving these to a candidate to stay in office or to get one in office and give God less. So what part do we play as Christians in politics? There *is* a part we play, according to Paul, and its outcome is best for us:

> The first thing I want you to do is pray. Pray every way you know how, for everyone you know. Pray especially for rulers and their governments to rule well so we can be quietly about our business of living simply, in humble contemplation. This is the way our Savior God wants us to live. He wants not only us but *everyone* saved, you know, everyone to get to know the truth *we've* learned. [1 Timothy 2:1-4, MSG]

Wow! Our involvement is first on our knees.

I am grateful we have Christians in government. I am grateful we have chaplains in Congress. I am thankful we have men and women fighting for godly principles. But the best way we unify the church is not around a candidate but around a king—*the* King. The way we unify the church politically is by getting the church to pray. And notice, Paul was saying for those *in* office not for those to beat those who are in office. Whether or not we agree with their politics or policies, our responsibility is to pray for our leaders in local, in state, and even in the White House and on Capitol hill.

Paul says, "This is the way God wants us to live." What is our prayer? We are first to pray that they rule well. And if they don't, then pray more. The Passion

Translation says it like this: "Pray for every political leader and representative, so that we would be able to live tranquil, undisturbed lives, as we worship the awe-inspiring God with pure hearts. It is pleasing to our Savior-God *to pray for them*" (verses 2-3).

We pray for them "so that we would be able to live tranquil, undisturbed lives as we worship God." We are praying for our leaders so *our* lives can find peace and quiet instead of contention and division. Our government may be in the condition it's in because of the condition of prayer in the church. Call a prayer meeting for your church to pray for your local, state, and national leaders and see how many show up? That may be the reason we are in trouble—not because of a Republican president or a Democrat Congress or vice versa, but because of a non-praying church.

A prayerless church messes up our government more than the government messes up the government. Don't dismiss this. Why is this country everything but quiet when it comes to the political landscape? Because this prayer has not been answered, because this prayer has not been *offered*. The part we play in politics is to pray for our leaders—not the leaders we wish were there and not just the leaders we agree with. Let's for a moment remove the adjectives before the word *Christian*. There is no such thing as a Republican Christian or a Democrat Christian or an Independent Christian or a Libertarian Christian, we are *Christians*! Which means we pray regardless of the election and its outcome.

Why do we pray for our leaders? Paul says pray for this outcome: "This is the way our Savior God wants us to live. He wants not only us but everyone saved" (verses 3-4, MSG). The "everyone" here are the politicians. We pray for them two ways—that they would rule well and that they would become Christ-followers. That must be how we as Christians are first involved in politics. Anything else is a distraction and a disturbance. As W. Ian Thomas says, "Make sure it is God's trumpet you are blowing—if it's only yours, it won't wake the dead; it will simply disturb the neighbours."[401]

I want to wake the dead in DC. I want them to find Jesus.

Many years ago, government officials in The Hague invited Van Courtonne, a famous preacher in Paris, to preach in the State Church chapel. He agreed under the condition that all the government officials had to attend. They agreed, so he went and preached on "The Ethiopian" in Acts 8. Remember the Ethiopian eunuch was a government official on assignment. His sermon contained four points about the Ethiopian government official.

Remember the story? The Ethiopian had just visited Jerusalem and left with a scroll from Isaiah 53. Philip came alongside his chariot and explained what the man was reading. The government official became a Christian and ordered the chariot to stop and be baptized.

Now, here were Van Courtonne's points:

1. The Ethiopian was a government official who read the Bible: something rare.

2. He was a government official who acknowledged his ignorance: something rarer still.

3. He was a government official who asked a lesser person for instruction: something extremely rare.

4. He was a government official who got saved: the rarest thing of all.[402]

Let's get involved in politics. So let's get on our knees and pray.

We Have Been Using the Wrong Criteria for Hiring

Today's Reading: 1 Timothy 3

One of the toughest tasks for a church is choosing a pastor. One church was in this painful process, as the board kept rejecting applicant after applicant. Finally, frustrated with the board's *No one is good enough* attitude, one of the members submitted a bogus application to see what the board would do with it:

> Gentlemen: Understanding your pulpit is vacant, I should like to apply for the position. I have many qualifications. I've been a preacher with much success and also some success as a writer. Some say I'm a good organizer. I've been a leader most places I've been.
>
> I'm over fifty years of age. I have never preached in one place for more than three years. In some places I have left town after my work caused riots and disturbances. I must admit I have been in jail three or four times, but not because of any real wrongdoing.
>
> My health is not too good, though I still get a great deal done. The churches I have preached in have been small, though located in several large cities.
>
> I've not gotten along well with religious leaders in towns where I have preached. In fact, some have threatened me and even attacked me physically. I am not too good at keeping records. I have been known to forget whom I have baptized.
>
> However, if you can use me, I shall do my best for you.

The board member looked at the others on the committee. "Well, what do you think? Shall we call him?"

The board was appalled. "Call an unhealthy, trouble-making, absent-minded ex-jailbird? Are you crazy? Who signed the application? Who had such colossal nerve?"

The board member looked at them. "It's signed, the apostle Paul.'"[403]

Drop the mic. I think we have gone adrift from what a Christian leader looks like and have bought in to the lie of what we see in the media. In today's chapter, Paul gives criteria and qualities of what a pastor and deacons should have:

A pastor must be a good man whose life cannot be spoken against. He must have only one wife, and he must be hard working and thoughtful, orderly, and full of good deeds. He must enjoy having guests in his home and must be a good Bible teacher. He must not be a drinker or quarrelsome, but he must be gentle and kind and not be one who loves money. He must have a well-behaved family, with children who obey quickly and quietly. For if a man can't make his own little family behave, how can he help the whole church?

The pastor must not be a new Christian because he might be proud of being chosen so soon, and pride comes before a fall. (Satan's downfall is an example.) Also, he must be well spoken of by people outside the church—those who aren't Christians—so that Satan can't trap him with many accusations and leave him without freedom to lead his flock.

The deacons must be the same sort of good, steady men as the pastors. (1 Timothy 3:2-8, TLB)

If this is the criteria for hiring a pastor or selecting a deacon, I think we have been using the wrong grid and criteria. Some places have used the vote method instead of following this passage. Titus 1 adds a few more things, and they both comprise a powerful grid for pastoral leadership.

Paul lists twenty-five qualifications. Of the twenty-five, only one deals with preaching. Several translations, including the King James Version, says the pastor must be "apt to teach." I love that word *apt*. It sounds like he doesn't have to be an amazing preacher. Why? Because there are twenty-four other things churches have to look at. If this list is a good grid to start, that means "communicating" is 1/25 of the pastoral skill set, which is 4 percent. If the main thing we do in choosing a pastor is simply listen to their sermons, we may be in for a train wreck. Remember, I am speaking as a pastor. Preaching is hard work, but so are the other twenty-four things. I'm afraid we have exalted and been in awe of 4 percent in pastors but neither them nor churches ever examined the other 96 percent.

Think about some of the other things pastors are challenged with keeping in order:

- being free of greed
- keeping their households the priority
- being the husband of one wife
- being self-controlled
- remaining above reproach
- being prudent
- being hospitable.

Think of the challenge your leaders have to face to be an effective husband, father, and minister all at the same time. How do they schedule all of this? I have always said it's harder to be a pastor than a CEO of a Fortune 500 company. You can be a CEO and have a messed-up marriage. You can be a CEO and have messed-up kids. You can be a CEO and have a messed-up life. You can be a millionaire, an entrepreneur, a successful businessman and have everything in your life falling apart yet still have a job. This is what makes ministry different. If your personal life, your marriage, and your children are messed up, then you're out of a job. In fact, if only one of these areas are messed up, you're job is in jeopardy. Your pastor has got to give his attention to three priority areas of his life.

Therefore we need to find a way to help our pastors and leaders and not criticize them. So as a pastor and on behalf of my fellow pastors, let me say this: we need your help and we need your support. When someone says we are dropping the ball in one of those areas, it would help us if we can have a support system who says, *Let's pray for our pastor and find a way we can make him the best he can be.*

Every Sunday will not be a Billy Graham message. At times our marriages will need an oil change to get better. And our children will not always be the poster kids from child expert Kevin Lehman's books.

When you hire us, help us.

When you are disappointed by us, help us.

When we don't meet your expectations, help us.

How can you help your pastor? Yes, pray. And you can do more. Just to hear a word of encouragement or a board finding a way to give a pastor's family time off to recharge would be amazing. Remember that pastors are never off the clock. So they need your support.

THE ONE WORD THAT STOPS MOST OF OUR DREAMS FROM COMING TRUE

Today's Reading: 1 Timothy 4

How long does it take to become an expert in something? In the Development of Talent Project, Dr. Benjamin Bloom of Northwestern University studied the careers of world-class sculptors, pianists, chess masters, tennis players, swimmers, mathematicians, and neurologists. Across the board, he discovered that it takes between ten to eighteen years before someone can reach world-class competency.[404] The point of the study was that it takes time to be the best at whatever chosen career or path you aspire to.

In *Outliers*, author and researcher Malcolm Gladwell calls "becoming an expert" the ten-thousand-hour rule. How do you become the greatest band of all time? An expert in rock and roll? You work at it for ten thousand hours. Gladwell speaks about the Beatles seemingly instant success that many think happened on the Ed Sullivan show in one night. Gladwell says that's not the case. Before landing in America, they'd already been playing together for seven years. It was the band's ten-thousand hours of playing that made them who they were, not a night on American television.

They'd started out doing one-hour sessions, in which they performed their best numbers, the same ones, at every one. But then they were invited to play in Hamburg, Germany. While there, they played eight hours, seven days a week. Gladwell explains much of their ten-thousand hours:

> The Beatles ended up traveling to Hamburg five times between 1960 and the end of 1962. On the first trip, they played 106 nights, five or more hours a night. On their second trip, they played 92 times. On their third trip, they played 48 times, for a total of 172 hours on stage. The last two Hamburg gigs, in November and December of 1962, involved another 90 hours of performing. All told, they performed for 270 nights in just over a year and a half. By the time they had their first burst of success in 1964, in fact, they had performed live an estimated twelve hundred times. . . . Most bands today don't perform twelve hundred times in their entire careers. The Hamburg crucible is what set the Beatles apart.[405]

Gladwell considers that the key to success in any field is simply a matter of practicing a specific task that can be accomplished with twenty hours of work a week for ten years.

Paul gave this challenge to Timothy in *one word*:

Have nothing to do with worldly fables fit only for old women. On the other hand, discipline yourself for the purpose of godliness; for bodily discipline is only of little profit, but godliness is profitable for all things, since it holds promise for the present life and *also* for the *life* to come.
(1 Timothy 4:7-8)

Discipline! The grandmaster level chess player, a concert pianist, a high-level athlete all have the word *discipline* in common. The saying goes, "The distance from your dreams to reality is called discipline." This is why most people miss their dreams. The other side of an undisciplined life is disappointment.

Paul was telling Timothy that goal in discipline is godliness. Or putting it another way: "godliness" is not automatic. We have to work toward it. Getting born again? Christ did the work for us. Getting godly? We have to discipline ourselves. Listen to the passage from *The Message*: "Exercise daily in God—no spiritual flabbiness, please! Workouts in the gymnasium are useful, but a disciplined life in God is far more so, making you fit both today and forever."

I had a friend tell me one time that he was speaking to the boxing welterweight champion, who told him that he would set his alarm for 1 a.m. every night so he could get up and do one hundred sit-ups and one hundred push-ups. When my friend asked him why he would do that, he said, "I knew I was working while my opponent was sleeping, and I wanted the edge on him."

That's where ten-thousand hours comes from. Discipline and effectiveness, discipline and success travel together.

Theologian Henri Nouwen spoke about discipline for our spiritual lives: "Discipline means to prevent everything in our life from being filled up. Discipline means that somewhere we're not occupied, and certainly not preoccupied. In the spiritual life, discipline means to create that space in which something can happen that we hadn't planned or counted on."[406]

Jim Elliot was a modern-day missionary and martyr, who practiced ten-thousand-hour devotional living. He wrote these powerful words: "I may no longer depend on pleasant impulses to bring me before the Lord. I must rather respond to principles I know to be right, whether I feel them to be enjoyable or not."[407]

Discipline is focus. Discipline is work. Discipline puts blinders to things that are crying for our time and attention. Because Timothy joined Paul before AD 50 and Paul was writing in the early sixties, Timothy was at least in his mid-twenties and could well be in his early or mid-thirties. This term for "youth" (in verse 12) could apply up to the age of forty in that culture, although it usually applied especially to someone under twenty-nine. And the challenge to young Timothy was that he would have a lot of distractions in life, so it was important to get focused on the right thing.

Paul challenged Timothy about making his discipline about going to Planet Fitness and reminded him that disciplining ourselves physically isn't wrong or bad—it's just that there's a better discipline, and that is about pursuing eternal things. Listen to Paul's admonishment again: "Workouts in the gymnasium are useful, but a disciplined life in God is far more so, making you fit both today and forever" (verse 8, MSG).

No life ever grows great until it is focused, dedicated, and disciplined. Gary Player, one of the greatest golfers in the world, was known for his discipline. When he was 80 years old, he still got up every morning at 5 a.m. and did 1,300 sit-ups.[408] One day while hitting off the practice tees, he heard someone say, "I wish I could hit a ball like that." He turned around and said to the onlooker, "No, you don't. You know what it takes to hit a golf ball like [I do]? It takes getting up at 5:00 a.m. every morning to hit 1,000 balls until my hand bleeds, then I go to the clubhouse to bandage my hand, then go back and hit another 1,000 balls."[409]

We want the results but not the discipline. Godliness is the goal for us, says Paul, and discipline is the key.

LEARN TO BE AN EFFECTIVE COMMUNICATOR

Today's Reading: 1 Timothy 5

A truck driver had been hired to deliver fifty penguins to the state zoo. As he was driving his truck through the desert, his truck broke down. Three hours passed, and he began to wonder if his cargo would survive in the desert heat. Finally he was able to wave down another truck. He offered the driver five hundred dollars to take the penguins to the zoo for him, and the other driver agreed.

The next day, the first truck driver finally made it to town. As he drove, he was appalled to see the second truck driver walking down the street with the fifty penguins walking in a single-file line behind him! He slammed on his brakes, jumped out of his truck, and stormed over to the other trucker. "What's going on?" he shouted. "I gave you five hundred dollars to take these penguins to the zoo!" The other trucker responded, "I did take them to the zoo. And I had some money left over, so now we're going to see a movie."[410]

Miscommunication leads to complication and confusion. Just a little miscommunication can mean a lot of problems. In today's chapter, Paul gives us a lesson on effective communication. As author William H. Whyte so aptly said: "The great enemy of communication, we find, is the illusion of it."[411] Paul wants to remove the illusions for us. And his advice is priceless. He starts off 1 Timothy 5 with explaining how to communicate to people:

> Never speak sharply to an older man, but plead with him respectfully just as though he were your own father. Talk to the younger men as you would to much-loved brothers. Treat the older women as mothers, and the girls as your sisters, thinking only pure thoughts about them. (Verses 1-2, TLB)

This passage can so easily be passed over and we miss Paul's powerful lesson on how to communicate to different groups of people. All people don't hear the same way; ages and gender contribute to that. Paul tells us the importance of knowing who we are speaking to and how to speak to them. It's about knowing our audience.

I have had the privilege of doing chapels in different venues. I have spoken to MLB and NFL teams, and in those environments, I make sure I do certain things. The window is short, and I realize for the entire season, this is these professional players' church. I must not only respect their time but also must make sure I am making use of their time. Here are my two rules in these settings: lift up God's Word and lift up God's Son.

First, I always bring a physical Bible and read from it. Why? Isaiah 55:11 says, "My word shall never return void." That means better than a leadership principle or a pep talk, the best thing I can do for those players is give them a Bible principle, because it will always be productive. Second, I lift up God's Son. Jesus said in John 12:32, "If I'm lifted up I will draw men to Myself." When we don't lift up Jesus, then people are attracted to the wrong thing: us. And we don't have what they need.

The apostle Paul gave us his important chapel rules too when we are talking to certain groups of people. He said when we have to have a hard conversation with a person older than we are, harsh and hard talk must be dispensed with and we must take the posture of a son and see that person as a parent. This strategy goes if we're a supervisor with senior citizens on our staff to having to tell our elderly neighbor to keep their dogs off our lawn.

Plead with them as if they were your own father. He says the same treatment goes for elderly women. His plea about how we speak to our peers is much needed also in our generation. Young men talk to other young men as beloved brothers, as though they are our own flesh and blood. And when we see a young lady, we treat them as flesh and blood also and keep our thoughts pure about them. This is profound communication advice from Paul for all of us.

Warren Buffett, one of the wealthiest men in the world, was recently with some young entrepreneurs who asked him to share one piece of advice for twentysomethings who'd just graduated from college. He told them: "The one easy way to become worth 50 percent more than you are now—at least—is to hone your communication skills. . . . If you can't communicate, it's like winking at a girl in the dark—nothing happens. You can have all the brainpower in the world, but you have to be able to transmit it."[412]

First Timothy 5 keeps us from winking in the dark. Knowing how to talk to people is an art and hard work and there is much to consider. According to the *Harvard Business Review*, "The number one criteria for advancement and promotion for professionals is an ability to communicate effectively."[413]

Thanks to Paul, you can communicate effectively because of the tool he provided in 1 Timothy 5.

CAN CHRISTIANS BE RICH?

Today's Reading: 1 Timothy 6

There's a word in the game of football that keeps enduring—*Hut!* An article in *The New York Times* pondered why this word keeps hanging around:

> It is easily the most audible word in any football game, a throaty grunt that may be the sport's most distinguishing sound.
> Hut!
> It starts almost every play, and often one is not enough. And in an increasingly complex game whose signal-calling has evolved into a cacophony of furtive code words—"Black Dirt!," "Big Belly!," "X Wiggle!"—hut, hut, hut endures as the signal to move.
> But why? . . .
> "I have no idea why we say hut," said Philadelphia Eagles center Jason Kelce. . . . "I guess because it's better than yelling, 'Now,' or 'Go.'"
> Joe Theismann, the former Washington Redskins quarterback . . . reckons he shouted "hut" more than 10,000 times during games and practices. . . . "I've been hutting my way through football for 55 years—but I have no clue why."[414]

The article conjectures that "hut" may come from the military backgrounds of many early pro football players. But that's just a guess.

This is similar to what Christians believe and why. Many people have been told what to believe without the why or the rationale behind that belief or doctrine. And it's been around so long, they don't have a clue about the explanation.

The word *doctrine* means a set of beliefs or teachings from the Bible. Why do we believe what we believe? Or are we just saying *hut, hut* every Sunday and not knowing why? Will we get thousands of years into Christianity since the resurrection of Jesus and be asked why we say and do certain things and not have an answer?

Fortunately, we learn some answers in today's chapter, where Paul tells us the why. Paul takes a thirty-thousand-foot view of doctrine. He talks about doctrinal diversions but gives us one big statement. Here are Paul's important words:

> If anyone advocates a different doctrine and does not agree with sound words, those of our Lord Jesus Christ, and with the doctrine conforming to godliness, he is conceited *and* understands nothing; but he has a morbid interest in controversial questions and disputes about words, out of which arise envy, strife, abusive language, evil suspicions, and constant friction between men of depraved mind and deprived of the truth, who suppose that godliness is a means of gain. (1 Timothy 6:3-5)

There it is: the bombshell phrase, the thirty-thousand-foot view of why we believe: *doctrine conforming us to godliness.* To know if a belief system is true, the end result of our belief should make us godly, which means it should make us look more like Jesus.

Religion tries to get us to look like the club, the people on Sundays and in the pew. The goal is not to look like Sunday people but to lift our eyes a lot higher to heaven. Our goal is not to look like the person in the pulpit but the One who sits on the throne of heaven. That's what doctrine is supposed to do. It conforms us to godliness. D. Martyn Lloyd-Jones said, "If your knowledge of doctrine does not make you a great man of prayer, you had better examine yourself again."[415]

Paul wants to help us better understand how it plays out practically, so he offers the question "Can you be rich and a Christian?" as the test case. The answer is yes, absolutely. But Paul reminds us of some things in our lab work:

> Those who want to get rich fall into temptation and a snare and many foolish and harmful desires which plunge men into ruin and destruction. For the love of money is a root of all sorts of evil, and some by longing for it have wandered away from the faith and pierced themselves with many griefs. (Verses 9-10)

Paul challenges not being rich but the reason behind why we want to get rich. It's not the money but the motive that is destructive. If we want money we will fall into temptation and a snare to many foolish desires. That desire is so powerful that people have wandered from the faith.

But Paul says that you can be rich with the right motive. He doesn't stop there, though. Remember he says doctrine should conform us to godliness. We cannot say to Christians that we need to be rich or we need to be poor. That is religious. We *can* say to Christians that whether we are rich or poor, we must make sure we look more and more like Jesus.

If it's the prosperity doctrine telling people that gain is godliness, they are wrong. If it's another camp telling people that poverty like Mother Teresa is what God wants, that doctrine is just as bad.

Our goal in life is not to look like a rich televangelist or like a woman in India. Our goal is to look like the Man who died for our sins.

Paul continues by saying this to the rich people in regards to godliness:

Instruct those who are rich in this present world not to be conceited or to fix their hope on the uncertainty of riches, but on God, who richly supplies us with all things to enjoy. *Instruct them* to do good, to be rich in good works, to be generous and ready to share, storing up for themselves the treasure of a good foundation for the future, so that they may take hold of that which is life indeed. (Verses 17-19)

Those words are really for *all* of us: Do good. Be rich in good works. Be generous. Be ready to share.

Nineteenth-century preacher J. C. Ryle captured it well when he said: Doctrine is useless if it is not accompanied by a holy life. It is worse than useless: it does positive harm. . . . Something of "the image of Christ," which can be seen and observed by others in our private life, and habits, and character, and doings."[416]

Learning to Stop Before It's Too Late

Today's Reading: 2 Timothy 1

The apostle Paul gets three verses into Timothy's second letter as a young pastor and reminds him that serving God must be done with a clear conscience: "Timothy, I thank God for you—the God I serve with a clear conscience, just as my ancestors did. Night and day I constantly remember you in my prayers" (2 Timothy 1:3, NLT).

Serving God with a clear conscience. This is paramount in our relationship with God. For the most part a clear conscience helps us to know the voice of God. One of my dear friends and mentors Winkie Pratney said: "A clear conscience is absolutely essential for distinguishing between the voice of God and the voice of the enemy. Unconfessed sin is a prime reason why many do not know God's will."[417]

Your conscience is where you hear the whisper of God and feel the conviction of the Holy Spirit. The old saying goes, "Conscience does not keep you from doing anything. It just keeps you from enjoying it." I love a small boy's definition of what the conscience is: "something that makes you tell your mother before your sister does."[418] A clear conscience makes you stop before it's too late. It helps you to slam on the brakes before you say and do something that you will regret later.

So many people skip a clear conscience and keep going till consequences show up. And so many Christians assume it's okay to blow by the warning of their conscience and to continue on when really God has given us a mechanism to pause before moving forward.

Our goal is to have a clear conscience. There are different types of violated consciences in the New Testament, which are important for us to take note of. It comes after a conscience that was not kept clear:

- Paul warns Timothy in 1 Timothy 4:2 of a *seared* conscience.
- Paul tells Titus in Titus 1:15 to be aware of a *defiled* conscience.
- The writer of Hebrews in Hebrews 10:22 warns of an *evil* conscience.

I believe that every time we fail to keep our consciences clear, you border on a defiled or evil or even seared conscience. Do not dismiss conviction. It's the brake for moving forward into regret. Many of us have regrets because we did not respond to conviction. And so it's important for us to respond to conviction instead of waiting for consequences.

What makes us stop and pause? Conviction or being caught?

Conviction is when we feel something deep inside that is like an alarm telling us there is an intruder. Embarrassment will make us stop late, but *conviction* will go deeper to make us seriously pause early.

Have you ever been in the middle of a conversation and was about to say something that was not edifying about a person, something that was gossip, and you felt this feeling, *Don't say it*. That's God's warning mechanism for a clear conscience.

Don't finish that statement. Don't start that joke—it compromises who you are. Don't . . .

Stay in tune with the whisper of God. That will promote a clear conscience every single day, not just on Sundays at church. When you serve God seven days a week, you fight every day to keep a clear conscience.

There was a ship that had a regular route from California to Columbia. One day shortly before leaving for California, some drug dealers sent the ship's captain a message that offered him $500,000 to allow a small shipment of drugs to get through to the United States. The captain replied with a no. On his next three trips, they raised the offer each time until they reached $2 million. He hesitated, and then said, "Maybe." Then he contacted the FBI, which set up a sting operation, and the drug dealers were arrested. One of the FBI agents asked the captain, "Why did you wait until they got to $2 million before contacting us?" The captain replied, "They were getting close to my price."[419]

Do you have a price? Is it 20 percent off a coat or a dress using your friend's employee discount, which belongs to them and not you? But since they said they would buy it and you can pay them back, it must be okay? It isn't. Don't violate your conscience. Keep it clear. As A. W. Tozer said: "An honest man is strange when in the midst of dishonest men, but it is a good kind of strangeness."[420]

The story goes that Sir Arthur Conan Doyle, the author of the Sherlock Holmes novels, played a prank on five of the most prominent men in England. He sent an anonymous note to each one that said simply, "All is found out. Flee at once." Within twenty-four hours, all five men had left the country.[421] Their conscience wasn't clear.

What if you received that note? Would you have left or stayed?

WRITING YOUR FINAL LETTER

Today's Reading: 2 Timothy 2

Bill Bright has been one of the most influential Christian leaders of our generation. He and his wife, Vonette, founded Campus Crusade for Christ, which is now active in 190 countries, and consists of 26,000 staff members and an additional 553,000 trained volunteers, who work on campuses and in various settings around the world. Campus Crusade also produced the Jesus film that has been seen by more than 5.5 billion people to date, and the "I Found It" campaign, which swept the globe in 1975 and brought millions more to Christ. Bill also wrote more than one hundred books. He wrote his last one, *The Journey Home*, when he was slowly and painfully losing his battle with a debilitating illness called pulmonary fibrosis.

This is how his physician told him he didn't have much longer to live:

> He sat me down one day—Vonette and me—in his office and said, "You don't seem to realize what's happening to you. You're dying. It's worse than cancer. It's worse than heart trouble. We can deal with these in some measure, but nobody can help you with pulmonary fibrosis. You are going to die a miserable death. You need to get your head out of the sand and be prepared for it."
>
> So I said, "Well, praise the Lord. I'll see the Lord sooner than I'd planned."[422]

American poet W. H. Auden wrote, "Death is the sound of distant thunder at a picnic."[423] Think about that. While everyone is eating and enjoying the day, we all know there is an end. One Puritan writer said, "If you attempt to talk with a dying man about sports or business, he is no longer interested. He now sees other things as more important. People who are dying recognize what we often forget, that we are standing on the brink of another world."[424]

Second Timothy is the apostle Paul's "long journey home" book. This is number fourteen of Paul's letters. It's his last one. And it's investment into leaders and, more specifically, young leaders. Former United States Secretary of State, Henry Kissinger, said, "The task of the leader is to get their people from where they are to where they have not been."[425] This was the charge Paul gave Timothy:

> No soldier in active service entangles himself in the affairs of everyday life, so that he may please the one who enlisted him as a soldier. Also if anyone competes as an athlete, he does not win the prize unless he competes according to the rules. The hard-working farmer ought to be the first to receive his share of the crops. (2 Timothy 2:4-6)

In this challenge to Timothy, Paul used three images: a soldier, an athlete, and a farmer. With each of these images and examples, Paul specified something importantly inherent in each of them: to be effective.

Be a soldier. If you are in active service, you don't entangle yourself in the affairs of everyday life. Or as one version says it: "For every soldier called to active duty must divorce himself from the distractions of this world" (TPT). The soldier sees the big picture. He is not distracted by minutia, but is in it to please the One who enlisted Him. The soldier lives for his General.

Be an athlete. Compete according to the rules. There are no short cuts to winning. Paul is saying the prize is for those who keep the rules. With so many performance-enhancing drugs hitting professional athletes today, it's a perfect example of trying to cut corners to win. Winning in the Christian life has no short cuts. It may be a longer path and journey but God is doing something in your training.

Be a farmer. He is referred to as the hard-working farmer. Hard works gets results. The fruit of the farmer's labor is inevitable; a crop comes because of his commitment to that field. In God's Kingdom, it seems God gives promises, but they are not automatic. God gives the children of Israel the promised land but Joshua has to fight for it for seven years. Work hard and stay diligent.

Leadership calls for those who see the bigger picture, those who don't take short cuts, and those who work hard. One of my favorite writers is W. H. Griffith Thomas. He gave this priceless insight to young preachers is priceless: "Think yourself empty, read yourself full, write yourself clear, pray yourself keen—then enter the pulpit and let yourself go!"[426]

That's what Paul did for young Timothy.

THE LAST DAYS

Today's Reading: 2 Timothy 3

Biblical prophecy provides some of the greatest encouragement and hope available to us today. Just as the Old Testament is saturated with prophecies concerning Christ's first coming, so both the Old Testament and the New Testament are filled with references to the second coming of Christ. One scholar has estimated there are 1,845 references to Christ's second coming in the Old Testament, where seventeen books give it prominence. In the 260 chapters of the New Testament, there are 318 references to the second coming of Jesus. That means one out of every thirty verses talk about Jesus coming again. And twenty-three of the twenty-seven New Testament books refer to it. For every prophecy in the Bible concerning Christ's first coming, there are eight that look forward to His second coming![427]

Both of Paul's letters to Timothy speak of Christ's second coming. And in today's chapter, Paul warns Timothy about the condition of humanity just before Christ comes again. The prophetic words he gives to the young pastor are not only chilling but eye opening—because the condition he describes can be easily attributed to our culture today. That means we are closer than ever to the second coming of Jesus.

Billy Graham said, "Some years ago, my wife, Ruth, was reading the draft of a book I was writing. When she finished a section describing the terrible downward spiral of our nation's moral standards and the idolatry of worshiping false gods such as technology and sex, she startled me by exclaiming, 'If God doesn't punish America, He'll have to apologize to Sodom and Gomorrah.'"[428]

Consider what Paul says about what the planet will look like before Jesus comes:

> In the last days difficult times will come. For men will be lovers of self, lovers of money, boastful, arrogant, revilers, disobedient to parents, ungrateful, unholy, unloving, irreconcilable, malicious gossips, without self-control, brutal, haters of good, treacherous, reckless, conceited, lovers of pleasure rather than lovers of God, holding to a form of godliness, although they have denied its power. (2 Timothy 3:1-5)

Paul gives nineteen descriptions in verses 2-4 to distinguish what humanity will look like and how they will be controlled. What is striking is that five of them have to do with love. It is a misdirected love, a misconstrued love, a deceptive love. It's humanity not loving the One for whom they were created but finding a very bad substitute.

Look at what they love instead of God: self, money, pleasure. Then look at the other two: they are unloving or without love and not lovers of God. The phrase *without love* or *unloving* means *without true love*. It means that people today are not without love—it's just the wrong love.

Paul wants to warn Timothy that when people are not lovers of God, they will start to believe that "there is no God, and since there is no God, let us start loving other things—self, money, and pleasure."

But we also find hope in these verses. Notice what verse one tells us: "In the last days difficult times will come . . ." Paul is saying, *In the last days, Satan will unleash his worst—but God will unleash His best.*

Remember those words, *In the last days.* There is another section of Scripture that starts off with those words. It's found in Peter's sermon on the day of Pentecost in Acts 2:

> "IT SHALL BE IN THE LAST DAYS," God says, "THAT I WILL POUR FORTH OF MY SPIRIT ON ALL MANKIND; AND YOUR SONS AND YOUR DAUGHTERS SHALL PROPHESY, AND YOUR YOUNG MEN SHALL SEE VISIONS, AND YOUR OLD MEN SHALL DREAM DREAMS; EVEN ON MY BONDSLAVES, BOTH MEN AND WOMEN, I WILL IN THOSE DAYS POUR FORTH OF MY SPIRIT and they shall prophesy." (Acts 2:17-18)

Wow! That is so encouraging. That means the second coming of Jesus is not to discourage us but to encourage us. As the nineteenth-century preacher, G. Campbell Morgan said:

> To me the second coming is the perpetual light on the path which makes the present bearable. I never lay my head on the pillow without thinking that perhaps before the morning breaks, the final morning may have dawned. I never begin my work without thinking that perhaps He may interrupt my work and begin His own. This is now His word to all believing souls, "Till I come." We are not looking for death, we are looking for Him.[429]

Early on during World War II, the Japanese army stormed the Philippines and forced United States General Douglas MacArthur to leave the islands. Upon leaving the Philippines, General MacArthur declared his famous promise, "I shall return." And he did, walking ashore a victor at Leyte in the Philippines several years later.[430] There is a more famous "I shall return." This one from the Captain of the hosts, the Lord Jesus Christ, Who declared to His fearful band of disciples, "I will come again" (John 14:3).

WHY ARE PEOPLE STILL SICK WHEN JESUS HEALS?

Today's Reading: 2 Timothy 4

Let me give you an apostle Paul timeline. Paul's conversion is in Acts 9 around AD 34. Second Timothy is his last letter and that is in AD 67. He writes it thirty-three years after the day he met Jesus. Paul's entrance into the ministry is in Acts 13, in AD 48—fourteen years after his salvation experience on the road to Damascus. So he has been preaching and in full-time ministry for about two decades. Now two verses before he is about to pen his last words *ever*, he throws in a sentence of mystery: "Erastus remained at Corinth, but Trophimus I left sick at Miletus" (2 Timothy 4:20).

Paul couldn't leave well enough alone. He has to say something in regards to sickness and Christians. Only someone who has been in ministry for as long as the apostle can throw that sentence in his final letter. The Trophimus mystery is the mystery every Christian battles: why are people still sick when Jesus heals?

At some point in our lives we have asked those questions either for ourselves or others. Paul's seven words leave us hanging, longing for the answer: *But Trophimus I left sick at Miletus*. The man who God used to bring healing to people's lives leaves a seven-year companion sick in Miletus. Paul has healed people in Acts 14, 19, 20, and 28, but not 2 Timothy 4.

Paul heals others, but Trophimus he leaves sick. It doesn't seem to make sense. Everyone he heals in the book of Acts he does not know personally, but Trophimus he does. So why has he left this one sick at Miletus?

There is much speculation but no definitive answer. Some say divine chastisement. Some say he might not have had faith to be healed. And some put it on Paul: "Paul healed in Lystra and cast out demons in Philippi and wrought miracles in Ephesus but he failed with Trophimus."

We do not know the answer. Paul does a lot. But I like knowing that Paul's track record isn't perfect. There is a sick guy in Miletus.

Whatever the answer is, there are times we must leave Trophimus sick at Miletus. We may win many to Christ but not everyone. There is always one.

There are scores of answered prayers but there are some for whom God says no, and the prayer is like Trophimus, left without an answer.

Miletus is one spot on the map where a man was not healed. We will have our Miletus too. I am rather glad for Trophimus here in the Bible. I am helped by the fact that we don't have this unbroken record of successes and that everything Paul did was a success. I could not keep up with that. The great Baptist preacher Vance Havner said we must "leave room for Trophimus, allow for a Miletus to be somewhere along your journey."[431]

Some days are sick days. Some days are "I blew it" days. "One of the reasons why mature people stop growing and learning," says John Gardner, "is that they become less and less willing to risk failure."[432] Because someone didn't get healed doesn't mean we stop praying for people. Just because they did not respond the right way when we shared Jesus with them doesn't mean we stop telling people the Good News. I'm glad Trophimus is in the Bible. And we need to remember that Trophimus being left sick in Miletus does not diminish Paul or his work or his character.

Former figure skating Olympic gold medalist Scott Hamilton and his wife, Tracie, have four children, including two adopted form Haiti. While he was pursuing his success as a skater, he once said he dropped out of church involvement and started what he jokingly called "The Church of Scott." But through the love of his wife and other Christians, he came to a sincere faith in Christ. Rooted in his faith, Hamilton had an interesting take on dealing with personal sin and failure. In a 2018 *New York Times* interview, Hamilton said: "I calculated once how many times I fell during my skating career—41,600 times. But I got up *all* 41,600 times. That's the muscle you have to build in you—the one that reminds you to just get up."[433]

Trophimus in 2 Timothy 4 is a mystery. I really do think Paul prayed for his friend and believed for his friend's healing. But Trophimus was not healed. And that's okay, because I'm okay with having spots in my Christian walk with mystery. Evelyn Underhill said it like this: "If the Reality of God were small enough to be grasped, it would not be great enough to be adored."[434]

I think God leaves mystery moments in our faith walk, which means mystery in our faith walk doesn't have to necessarily bring doubt but it can inspire adoration. Doubt comes when we feel as though we are owed an explanation. Adoration comes when we realize we are involved with Someone way bigger than we are. Let's adore Him in the mystery.

MEN LIE, BUT GOD CANNOT

Today's Reading: Titus 1

A deacon sent in his apologies for the Sunday morning service, claiming that he was ill with the flu. One of the church members, however, said he had seen the deacon on his way to a baseball game. After the service, the minister visited the deacon. "Brother," he said. "I have information that you were not sick at all this morning, but went to watch a ball game." The deacon protested and was angry: "That's a vicious lie about me! I'll show you my *fish* to prove it!"

Men lie, but God doesn't. That's the message of Titus 1. And Paul wants that to be clear for the young pastor, Titus, who is dealing with a culture of lying and deceit on the isle of Crete, as he embarks on a mission in a new area for the gospel.

Consider some of the biggest lies ever told:

The check is in the mail.
I'll start my diet tomorrow.
Give me your number, and the doctor will call you right back.
One size fits all.
It's not the money, it's the principle of the thing.
Even though we are not seeing each other anymore, we can still be friends.
I've never done anything like this before.
This hurts me more than it hurts you.
Your table will be ready in a few minutes.
Open wide, it won't hurt a bit.[435]

A study done by researchers at Michigan State University found that the average number of lies people tell a day are 1.6—that means we lie about five hundred times a year![436]

A 2004 study at Temple University School of Medicine found that lying takes more brain energy than telling the truth. Researchers divided participants into two groups. They asked those in the first group to shoot a toy gun and then lie and say they didn't do it. Those in the second group watched what happened and then told the truth about it. An MRI machine indicated that the liars had to use seven areas of the brain in their response. By comparison, those who told the truth only used four areas of the brain.[437]

We serve a God who always tells the truth. In theology we call it the veracity of God. Titus 1 starts off with reminding us of this fact. Paul is writing to Titus who used to be his travel companion. Paul led Titus to Christ, which is why he calls him "my true child in the faith." Paul has left Titus at Crete to bring things in order there. And the first thing that Paul reminds Titus is that whatever God says is true because God cannot lie:

> From Paul, God's willing slave and an apostle of Jesus, the Anointed One, to *Titus*. I'm writing you to further the faith of God's chosen ones and lead them to the full knowledge of the truth that leads to godliness, which rests on the hope of eternal life. God, who never lies, has promised us this before time began. (Titus 1:1-2, TPT)

Paul is telling Titus that he know he left him in a place where a lot of lying is going on. And he tells Titus in verses 10-12 that Titus is surrounded by liars and deceivers. That is why Paul wants him to know one thing and the people there need to know it also: that God cannot lie. It's the veracity of God.

The word *veracity* means habitual truth. It means you always tell the truth. God not only tells the truth but designed us to do the same. He knows our body works better when we tell the truth. A *USA Today* article lists body signals of lying, which include: increased blinking and pupil dilation; a facial expression incongruous with what's being said; increased body movement (especially hand gestures); shorter sentences; more speaking pauses and errors; more negative words and extreme words.[438] Think about it. Why do lie-detector tests work? Authorities can tell we are lying because of our heart rate, sweat, tone of voice, and other factors that are all indicators that a person is lying. A lie-detector test figures out a person is lying by the reaction of their body—which shows that we were created to tell the truth!

God who cannot lie is a huge statement. That means God can be completed trusted. When God speaks, we can believe it.

When Paul says, "God cannot lie," he is making more than a statement. He is laying a foundational stone for Christianity. Our Christianity rises or falls on the veracity of God. The Bible is the Word of God. And if God cannot lie, then it is the truth of God. They are not just words spoken but truth spoken.

The assurance and comfort we have today as we do the 260 Journey is that every chapter we read we can believe, because God is telling the truth and we can believe Him. He is absolutely consistent with what He says and what He does. There are no fluctuations.

Paul ends the chapter by reminding Titus that even people will lie about serving Jesus. It's called *duplicity*—their words and actions don't match. It's dishonesty. Here is what Paul says: "They claim to know God, but by their actions they deny him. They are disgusting, disobedient, and disqualified from doing anything good" [Titus 1:16, TPT].

We serve a God who is the opposite of duplicitous, He is trustworthy. God is honest, He tells the truth, God cannot lie.

Day 202

ADVERTISING GOD AT WORK

Today's Reading: Titus 2

Do you have the happiest or the unhappiest job? Recently *Bloomberg Work Wise* put out a list of the happiest jobs in America, based on fulfillment, coworkers, supervisors, and balance of home and life. Here are the top five: firefighters topped the list, followed by machine operators, pediatricians, communication professors, and guidance counselors.

Bloomberg also listed the top jobs in which people are asking, "Is it 5 p.m. yet?" These are the jobs where lunch hour rescues them. They are: mail clerks and sorters are the first on the list, followed in order by court and municipal clerks, housecleaners, insurance claims and policy clerks, telemarketers.[439]

When talking about work, A. W. Tozer said: "We must do worldly jobs, but if we do them with sanctified minds, they no longer are worldly but are a much a part of our offering to God as anything else we give to Him."[440] In today's chapter Paul wants to teach us a lesson on work, regardless of which list we are on. And we find no better place to know how to sanctify our minds and make our job an offering to God than in Titus 2:9-10:

> Servants are to be supportive of their masters and do what is pleasing in every way. They are not to be argumentative nor steal but prove themselves to be completely loyal and trustworthy. By doing this they will advertise through all that they do the beautiful teachings of God our Savior. (TPT)

In Titus 2, Paul begins to give advice to a number of different groups. He speaks to the men and women who are part of AARP, he calls them older men and older women. Then he has advice for the young men and young women. And then Paul speaks to laborers who encompass all these groups. Author Dorothy Sayers, one of C. S. Lewis's literary friends said: "The only Christian work is good work well done."[441] That's our goal is: good work well done.

In their book, *The Edge of Adventure*, Keith Miller and Bruce Larson wrote, "If you are miserable or bored in your work, or dread going to it, then God is speaking to you. He either wants you to change the job you are in or—more likely—he wants to change you."[442] I think Paul helps us here, regardless of what job we have, and I think Titus 2 is a good place to start with wanting us to change. Paul says when we work the right way in our jobs, we advertise God the Savior through what we do, not what we say.

A lot of people like to talk, but it is those who *do* rather than talk who make the greatest impact. Former Notre Dame football coach Lou Holtz said: "When all is said and done, more is usually said than done."[443] Let's be a people who *do* more than say more.

Here is Paul's challenge for us, our on-the-job training:

- be supportive
- do what is pleasing in every way
- do not be argumentative
- don't steal
- prove to be completely loyal and trustworthy

Paul tells us to make those things our priority and we will be a walking advertisement for God. The Living Bible paraphrases that last part like this: "In this way they will make people want to believe in our Savior and God." We make God attractive by being a great employee. We witness for Jesus without even saying the name of Jesus.

Jesus alluded to this principle in the Sermon on the Mount: "Your lives light up the world. Let others see your light from a distance. . . . Let it shine brightly before others, so that the commendable things you do will shine as light upon them, and then they will give their praise to your Father in heaven" (Matthew 5:14-16, TPT).

Here it is in its simplicity. People see your good actions and attribute them to God in your life. It goes like this: your Christian faith should translate into good employee habits—show up on time, don't stealing, aren't argumentative, are loyal, are trustworthy. When you are a good worker, you makes God look good. Then eventually that opens the way for you to have a good God conversation with others about it. Talking to people about your faith is last, not first. Usually those who talk first have a lifestyle that messes up their conversation.

Charles Swindoll shares about an old story of Saint Francis of Assisi. One day Saint Francis said to one of his students, "Come with me. Let's go down to the village and preach to the people who need our Savior." Off they went.

Once at the gate they stopped, bent down to speak kind words to a crippled old man, and gave him a cool drink of water and a few coins. Then they saw some children playing with a ball out in the field, so they joined their game and had fun with the children. While they played, a lonely widow watching at her doorstep drew their attention. When they finished the game, they visited with her, bringing her a few words of cheer and encouragement. A fearful young man lurked in the shadows, ashamed of what he had done the night before. They prayed with him, spoke with him openly and freely about forgiveness, grace, and mercy, and they encouraged him to pursue a more productive future. On the way out of town, they stopped at a small store and greeted the merchant, asked about his family, and thanked him for his faithful work through the years.

Finally Saint Francis said, "Let's go back." The novice stopped and said, "But wait, when do we preach?" The older friar answered, "Every step we took, every word we spoke, every action we did has been a sermon."[444]

Imagine how well we could represent God if we approached our lives and work that same way?

Day 203

ACTIONS SPEAK LOUDER THAN WORDS

Today's Reading: Titus 3

Research experts tell us we communicate only 7 percent with our words, 38 percent with our tone of voice, and 58 percent with our actions.[445] This is why Paul emphasizes the word *deeds* to the young pastor Titus.

In today's chapter we are getting from the apostle Paul the last of the pastoral letters. His emphasis to Titus in chapter 3 and really throughout the entire Epistle is focused on the 58 percent. I imagine Paul feels like Benjamin Franklin who said, "Well done is much better than well said."[446] Basically, it is better to be a good doer than a good talker.

John Donne said: "Of all the commentaries on the Scriptures, good examples are the best."[447] Another word for *example* in the book of Titus is good deeds. The apostle Paul is really careful to tell us it's not the good deeds that make us Christians and get us to heaven: "He saved us, not on the basis of deeds which we have done in righteousness, but according to His mercy, by the washing of regeneration and renewing by the Holy Spirit" (Titus 3:5).

But it is good deeds that should be coming from God's people. He wants us to know that though we are *not* saved by good deeds, we pursue good deeds because they are the outflow of the work of God in our lives:

> Remind the people to be subject to rulers, to authorities, to be obedient, to be ready for every good deed. . . . This is a trustworthy statement; and concerning these things I want you to speak confidently, so that those who have believed God will be careful to engage in good deeds. These things are good and profitable for men. (Verses 1, 8)

Be ready for every good deed and *engage in good deeds*. Then he repeats in verse 14: "Our people must also learn to engage in good deeds to meet pressing needs, so that they will not be unfruitful." Again, he encourages us to engage in good deeds.

But these exhortations are not limited to Titus 3. In Titus 1:16, Paul tells Titus about people who know how to talk but not live: "They profess to know God, but by *their* deeds they deny *Him*, being detestable and disobedient and worthless for any good deed." Or as one Colin Morris put it, "Your theology is what you are when the talking stops and the action starts."[448]

Then Paul speaks about good deeds in chapter 2, two more times: "In all things show yourself to be an example of good deeds, *with* purity in doctrine, dignified. . . . Who gave Himself for us to redeem us from every lawless deed, and to purify for Himself a people for His own possession, zealous for good deeds" (verses 7, 14).

Zealous for good deeds.

It seems like "good deeds" is the emphasis Paul to giving to Titus: *Titus, let your people show their Christianity, not just speak it. You can preach a better sermon with your life than with your lips.*

Our challenge to live what we say. People will see with their eyes before they will listen with their ears. Our actions can bring someone closer to Jesus or be the very thing that turns them from Jesus.

Charles Banning was right when he said, "Too many of us have a Christian vocabulary rather than a Christian experience. We think we are doing our duty when we're only talking about it."[449] People may doubt what we say but they will believe what we do.

As the late British evangelist Gypsy Smith once quipped, "There are five Gospels: Matthew, Mark, Luke, John, and the Christian, but most people never read the first four."[450]

FORGIVEN BUT NOT FIXED YET

Today's Reading: Philemon 1

You can be forgiven of your past but still have an unfixed past. Forgiven and fixed are two different things, and sometimes people confuse them at salvation.

Being born again will change your relationship with God, but won't necessarily change your relationship with your family, the courts, the IRS, the law, a judge, a probationary officer, VISA, a collection agency, a halfway house, a bad marriage. At least not immediately. You are forgiven but not fixed yet.

Let me give you a scenario. If you robbed a bank and got saved after that, are you forgiven and really going to heaven? Yes. Are you going to jail? Yes. Are you now innocent since you are forgiven? Nope.

You are forgiven, but you may have a past that still needs fixed. You can be going to heaven and going to jail at the same time. God's forgiveness always exonerates in the courts of heaven, but not guaranteed in the courts on earth. Salvation forgives sin (past, present, and future) but it does not resolve them.

This is such an important issue that a whole book of the Bible is devoted to it. A twenty-five verse book, which is the best and most practical help on this issue—Philemon. The verses will pop off the page when I give you the background. We have three characters in the story: Paul, who is in prison, is the aged apostle and the writer of the letter; Philemon is a Christian who had a slave who ran away (and has the church in his house); Onesimus is the slave who ran away and who gets saved while he is trying to get lost among the residents in Rome.

In the first century, two million of the five million people in Rome were slaves. To purchase a slave was very expensive. There were 120 occupations for them—some were executives and had salaried positions; most slaves served between ten and twenty years and usually were free by the age of thirty. But if a slave ran away, it was like he was committing suicide. It was punishable by death or branding the letter "F" on his head, which stood for the Latin word *Fugitivus*.[451]

Bottom line: Onesimus ran away.

Bottom line: by law he can be killed or branded.

Paul knows this. Onesimus knows this. Philemon knows this.

While Paul is in prison in Rome, guess who he meets? Onesimus. And guess who Paul leads to the Lord? Onesimus.

Now we come back to our original thought: you can be forgiven but your past is still unfixed. So Paul has to write a letter and send Onesimus back to Philemon with that letter.

Listen to some of Paul's letter to Philemon. This is a masterpiece:

> I appeal to you for my child Onesimus, whom I have begotten in my imprisonment, who formerly was useless to you, but now is useful both to you and to me. I have sent him back to you in person, that is, *sending* my very heart, whom I wished to keep with me, so that on your behalf he might minister to me in my imprisonment for the gospel; but without your consent I did not want to do anything, so that your goodness would not be, in effect, by compulsion but of your own free will. For perhaps he was for this reason separated *from you* for a while, that you would have him back forever, no longer as a slave, but more than a slave, a beloved brother, especially to me, but how much more to you, both in the flesh and in the Lord. (Philemon 1:10-16)

Jesus has forgiven Onesimus. Will Philemon forgive Onesimus?

Paul doesn't mention the name Onesimus in the letter for nine verses. I want you to keep this in mind—this letter is being hand delivered. The Jerusalem postal service is not doing it, but the subject of the letter is Onesimus. I wonder if he knows exactly what is in the letter as he is coming back to Philemon.

Commentary writer William Barclay says, "Christianity never entitled anyone to default on debts."[452] Paul leads him to the Lord and then leads him to address his debt issue. The IRS. The police. The outstanding credit card and collection agencies—for the Christian all these have to be addressed with an Onesimus letter.

Don't call your irresponsibility a trial that God is going to get you through. Irresponsibility is fixed by integrity not a miracle. You address the unresolved not rebuke it. That's what the letter to Philemon teaches us.

Paul writes in verse 21 "I am confident as I write this letter that you will do what I ask and even more!" (NLT). Paul is saying, "You may be heating up the branding iron with the F on it. I'm asking you to put it down. I want you to forgive him—that's the F I want heating up in your heart."

Onesimus was useless when he was verse 11. He stole from Philemon in verse 18. But here's the game changer: he is now a brother in Christ, not just an employee.

Now the big question: what is the end of the story?

No one knows. The Bible does not tell us if Philemon forgives him or if Onesimus lives. I want to make a guess from something I saw in a church history book. In Earle Cains's *Christianity through the Centuries*, he writes:

> Some fifty years after Philemon was written, just on the heels of the apostles, was the church father Ignatius, martyr on the way to his death. He was allowed to write letters of encouragement and one of those letters was written to the church in Ephesus. And in that letter he makes mention of their pastor. His name? Onesimus.[453]

A coincidence or a miracle? Did the runaway slave become a pastor? Did the man who tried to hide out in Rome find himself leading the church in Ephesus? You may say, "That's a big stretch. That's a tall order." If an ex-murderer can write most of the New Testament letters, then I think this is feasible with God. Wait! That ex-murderer *is* the writer of this Philemon letter—the apostle Paul.

Jesus says it like this, "With people it is impossible, but not with God; for all things are possible with God" [Mark 10:27].

GOD DID A LORD NELSON

Today's Reading: Hebrews 1

At Trafalgar Square in London stands the 170-foot-high iconic Lord Nelson column. Resting on top of the pillar is Lord Nelson. It towers way too high for a passerby to distinguish his features and really know who it is. So about forty years ago a new statue, an exact replica of the original that is on top, was erected at eye level so everyone could see Lord Nelson way up there. Someone had the idea that if you want to know who is "way up there," we have to bring the exact representation down low enough for everyone to see.[454]

This also happened about two thousand years ago in a *very* big way. God transcends our ability to see Him for who He is. The eyes of our understanding cannot define or figure out His divine features. So God pulled a Lord Nelson for us. He set before us an exact representation, "the image of the invisible God." Now to know God, we must only look at Jesus. Here's what the writer of Hebrews tells us:

> In these last days he has spoken to us through his Son. God made his Son responsible for everything. His Son is the one through whom God made the universe. His Son is the reflection of God's glory and the exact likeness of God's being. He holds everything together through his powerful words. After he had cleansed people from their sins, he now holds the honored position—the one next to the majestic God [the Father] on the heavenly throne. (Hebrews 1:2-3, GW)

We live in a highly religious society today. I don't think America is godless; I think America has many gods. The issue is, what does America's god look like? One of the first things God did when He gave the Ten Commandments was to issue a warning from the very beginning about counterfeit gods. The Bible says this in Exodus 20 in the first commandment:

> You shall have no other gods before Me. You shall not make for yourself an idol, or any likeness of what is in heaven above or on the earth

beneath or in the water under the earth. You shall not worship them or serve them; for I, the Lord your God, am a jealous God. (Exodus 20:3-5)

Here is what stands out—that God gave the commandment against other gods not to pagans and idolaters but to Israel, the very people of God, a monotheistic people. Being religious never guarantees the worship of the true God. This was what we remember as we enter the book of Hebrews. Hebrews was written to religious people who were losing sight of Jesus. They were losing sight of the exact representation and likeness of God seen only in Jesus. And the book reminds them that God is in Jesus.

Divine truth must come from outside of us. It cannot be self-generated by us and come from within ourselves. Truth must be revealed by God to us. Without Jesus then we come up with our own version of God and thus the thousands of religions in the world who have self-defined God instead of letting God define Himself in Jesus. As Colossians 1:15 says, "We look at this Son and see the God who cannot be seen" (MSG). God is fully revealed in Jesus.

That's why any religion that doesn't give Jesus the honor that God gets is counterfeit. Jesus tells us, "The Son will be honored equally with the Father. Anyone who dishonors the Son, dishonors the Father, for it was the Father's decision to put the Son in the place of honor" (John 5:23, MSG). The Son is equally honored with the Father, because the Son is God in the flesh.

There are only two approaches to knowing God: one that begins with humans or the one that begins with God. Jesus is God's self-revelation. We know God only through Jesus. Lloyd C. Douglas was the author of the classic book, *The Robe*. He lived in a boarding house when he was a university student. He tells the story that when he lived on the first floor, he resided next to a retired music teacher, wheelchair bound and unable to leave his apartment. Every morning they had a ritual: Douglas came down the stairs, opened the man's door, and asked, "Well, what's the good news?" The other picked up his tuning fork, tapped it on the inside of his wheelchair, and said, "That is middle C! It was middle C yesterday, and it will be middle tomorrow. It will be middle C a thousand years from now. The tenor upstairs sings flat, the piano across the hall is out of tune, but my friend, *that* is middle C."[455]

Says Donald McCullough of the story: "The old man had discovered a constant reality on which he could depend, an unchanging truth to which he could cling. Jesus Christ is our tuning fork, ringing out middle C in a cacophonous world of competing truths; his pitch defines tonal reality and sets every other note in its proper place."[456]

Society may be flat. The church may be sharp. But as McCullough reminds us, "When we listen to middle C two things happen: the revelation of Jesus Christ both separates us from God and unites us to God."[457]

Astronomers observe stars with telescopes. Biologists examine cells with microscopes. Sociologists discover patterns of human behavior with surveys and interviews. Psychiatrists delve into the mind through conversation. Humanity can know God by the life and words of Jesus Christ. When we grasp the hand of Jesus, we meet God in Person.

RUNNING TO THE CRY

Today's Reading: Hebrews 2

My wife, Cindy, and I were sitting with our children's pastor some years ago. As we were talking in our living room, our four children were playing in the basement. All our kids were under the age of eight, so there was a lot going on. At that time the children's pastor was not married and had no children.

While we were talking we all heard a cry from the basement, but Cindy and I just kept talking. Finally he said, "Aren't you guys going to do something?"

"It's okay," we told him. "That's a 'You took my spot!' cry. It's all good."

We kept talking and then another cry came from the basement. We never flinched. He was unnerved. "Should we go check on them?"

"It's all good," Cindy and I said. "That's a bug cry."

We kept talking. Then a third cry came and we got up and left. He sat confused. "Where are you going?"

"That's an 'I'm hurt!' cry," we said as we rushed to the basement. "Someone hurt themselves and we need to go." Meeting postponed.

When you are a parent, you know the cry of your children. Hebrews 2 is about our Savior who knows the cry of His kids. Let's read this very encouraging passage:

> He had to be made like His brethren in all things, so that He might become a merciful and faithful high priest in things pertaining to God, to make propitiation for the sins of the people. For since He Himself was tempted in that which He has suffered, He is able to come to the aid of those who are tempted. (Hebrews 2:17-18)

The King James Version doesn't use the phrase, *come to the aid*. It uses a very old English word, "He is able to succor them." The word succor actually means *to run to the cry*. I think it's important to know that Jesus runs to the cry and not to the articulate. Sometimes all we have is a cry, and that moves our Savior to our rescue.

Psalms show us this over and over:

"In my distress I cried out to the Lord . . . my cry to him reached his ears." [Psalm 18:6, NLT]

"I love the Lord because he . . . heard my cry." [Psalm 116:1, NIRV]

"In my trouble I cried to the Lord, and He answered me." [Psalm 120:1]

David over and over uses cries for prayer. A cry is inarticulate but still has meaning. A cry is not grammatically correct, but it is understandable to God. A cry may be wordless but speaks with force and passion in the ears of God.

Tears are prayers. Tears talk when we can't. There's an old poem by John Vance Cheney that says in part, "The soul would have no rainbow had the eyes no tears."[458] Let me show you the rainbow of this verse. The writer of Hebrews was telling us that since Jesus became like us "in all things," He knows the cry and the pain of those things. He can recognize the emotions of situations that we forget Jesus became familiar with.

In *100 Days in the Arena*, David Winter recounts a horrific time in the early church when the Christians were being killed for their faith. He includes this prayer:

You give yourself with such total generosity, it might almost seem that you need us. There has never been a king like you ever before. You have made yourself available to everyone who needs you. Instead of high security, you have made yourself vulnerable even to those who hate you. [459]

What makes Jesus amazing is that our tears are enough to get His attention. It's not our experience, our vocabulary, our education, our position, or our finances. A cry is enough to make Him run to our help. There is no such thing as a bad prayer—even if it's just a cry.

Bruce Howell tells the story of a father and his young son and daughter went swimming in the Atlantic Ocean off New Jersey. Though they were all great swimmers, they got separated and the dad, looking around, realized that the tide was carrying them out to sea. He called out to his daughter, "I am going to shore for help. If you get tired, turn on your back. You can float all day on your back. I'll come back for you." He and the boy made it to shore and then set out on a frantic search for the girl. After four hours, they found her far out in the sea. She was calmly swimming on her back and wasn't frightened at all. The father was hugely relieved when the calm girl was finally back on shore.

Everyone wondered how she could be so calm. She said, "Daddy said he would come for me and that I could float all day, so I swam and floated because I knew he would come."[460]

This is what Jesus is all about. He will always come for us. He will always be there.

A Spoon Says a Lot

Today's Reading: Hebrews 3

Thomas Edison had very little formal education. In fact, he was only in school a few months before his mother pulled him out and began teaching him herself. She encouraged him in reading, writing, and arithmetic, and allowed him to pursue other interests that appealed to him. Always a curious boy, he was particularly fascinated with mechanical things and chemical experiments, which his mother encouraged.

How did it come about that his mother pulled him out of school? And why? According to a rare interview Edison gave to a now-defunct literary journal, *T. P. Weekly*, published on November 29, 1907, his mother's staunch support and belief in him made him the successful inventor he became:

> One day I overheard the teacher tell the inspector that I was "addled" and it would not be worthwhile keeping me in school any longer. I was so hurt by this last straw that I burst out crying and went home and told my mother about it. Then I found out what a good thing a good mother is. She came out as my strong defender. Mother love was aroused, mother pride wounded to the quick. She brought me back to the school and angrily told the teacher that he didn't know what he was talking about, that I had more brains than he himself, and a lot more talk like that. In fact, she was the most enthusiastic champion a boy ever had, and I determined right then that I would be worthy of her and show her that her confidence was not misplaced.[461]

Thomas Edison's mom spoke encouragement, life-giving words, into her son's life and gave us one of the greatest inventors in history. Because of her staunch belief in her son and her words about and to him, the world has the light bulb, phonograph, camera, telegraph, generators, microphones, alkaline batteries, cement, and a host of other things.

Words are powerful. As Mother Teresa said, "Words which do not give the light of Christ increase the darkness."[462] In today's chapter, the writer of Hebrews describes the heart challenge we all face and the antidote for it to be fixed:

> Take care, brethren, that there not be in any one of you an evil, unbelieving heart that falls away from the living God. But encourage one another day after day, as long as it is *still* called "Today," so that none of you will be hardened by the deceitfulness of sin. (Hebrews 3:12-13)

We are told that any one of us can find our heart moving into unbelief. The writer says that we are to be aware of that enemy. And before we can even be afraid, we are told there is an answer to it—encouragement. Encouragement is what keeps our hearts soft. That is the power of encouraging words. Those kinds of words don't just give us a Thomas Edison, they give us strong, faithful Christians.

Can I vent for a moment? I want to give you my pet peeve of "religious" encouragement. It's when people give you the preface before the encouragement. They say something like, "I don't want you to get a big head or get prideful, but you preached well, you sang well, your words were powerful." Their preface waters down their encouragement. I want to tell them, "You're not the pride police. Just say something nice without the caveat." People are so discouraged today, and a word of encouragement gets them in the game, so give someone a word of encouragement without your "concern" for their pride. Be more concerned of an unbelieving heart than a prideful heart. That means just say the good words.

More people fail for lack of encouragement, I think, than for any other reason. Encouragement is oxygen to the soul. We don't have enough encouragers out there. We need more encouragement in the home and in the church. Who knows what a word of encouragement could do for your spouse, your child, or the person you sit next to at your job. Just a "great job" could get someone through the day.

We need to make deposits into people's emotional bank accounts. It will help them finish their day, the week, their life well. Day-to-day encouragement. Send someone a text of encouragement. Make a quick Mom-and-Dad phone call and encourage them. The people you think don't need it because they always look happy are many times the ones who need it most.

A pastor friend told me about something that happened in his church. An elderly lady told him when he buries her that she wants a Bible and a spoon in her casket. He asked her why. She said, "At all the church fellowships I have been to over the last seventy-five years, when they come around after the dinner and give us spoons they are saying the best is yet to come—dessert. And when I die, I want people to know that the best is yet to come." Well, he'd heard the story before—it's been going around for years. But that's not the end of the story. My friend said there was a part B.

A little while later, he needed to step down from ministry for a season due to some personal issues. It was a hard year for that pastor to be attending the church he'd led for decades but who was now on the sidelines. After the year was up, he prepared for his first Sunday back. He was nervous and scared and wondered if the church would even want him back.

That first Sunday back, he stepped up to the pulpit and watched in amazement as the entire congregation stood. They didn't applaud. They held up spoons. They were encouraging him that the best is yet to come.

DOES JESUS REALLY UNDERSTAND WHAT I AM GOING THROUGH?

Today's Reading: Hebrews 4

The second most difficult book in the Bible to understand is Hebrews, because of its assumption that the reader is familiar with the Old Testament. It is dependent upon reader's understanding of the book of Leviticus and it is written to Jews who would know this book completely. The two key words in the book are *sacrifices* and *priest*. In today's culture, we are not familiar with the concept of priesthood and sacrifices.

The basic premise of Hebrews is that these Jews were getting tired of the battles that go along with being a Christian. The more secular the world becomes, the more at odds we appear to be. The more we are committed to Christ, the more we experience conflict and collision. Some of these Hebrew believers were being persecuted and even their property was being taken from them. These new Christians' wondered, *How can we make it? Is it worth it?* They were considering going back to the world and back to their old ways.

The author of Hebrews had one simple message to give them: Jesus. He wanted them to know they had a friend in high places who would get them through because He really understands what they were experiencing:

> We do not have a high priest who cannot sympathize with our weaknesses, but One who has been tempted in all things as *we are*, *yet* without sin. Therefore let us draw near with confidence to the throne of grace, so that we may receive mercy and find grace to help in time of need. [Hebrews 4:15-16]

That message is still true today: you are not alone. You have Someone with you and He is Someone who has been through what you are going through. *The Message* says it like this:

> We don't have a priest who is out of touch with our reality. He's been through weakness and testing, experienced it all—all but the sin. So

let's walk right up to him and get what he is so ready to give. Take the mercy, accept the help.

Wow! We serve a Jesus who has experienced it all. Why is this important? Charles Spurgeon said it well: "A Jesus who never wept could never wipe away my tears."[463]

Is this really true? Does Jesus understand what you are going through because He has been through it Himself? Jesus doesn't just know *what* you are going through, He knows what it's *like* to go through it. This makes Him a personal Savior. There is nothing you have gone through that He has not gone through in some form or fashion.

He understands what it is to be let down by friends.

He understands betrayal.

He understands fear and wanting to quit.

He knows the pain of losing loved ones.

He understands having someone close to Him murdered.

Just to name a few.

He found out what it's like to discover your life is on the clock. (Some hear it like this: "You have cancer; you have three months to live.")

He was a carpenter. He knows what it is to work a 9-5 job. He had deadlines and work orders.

He knew homelessness: Jesus said, "The foxes have holes and the birds of the air have nests, but the Son of Man has nowhere to lay His head" (Matthew 8:20).

Jesus knew what it's like to cry out to God and ask why when things got tough: He said on the cross: "My God, My God, why . . .?" (Matthew 27:46).

So what is the result of having this kind of Jesus? The writer of Hebrews tells us in the first word of the next verse: *Therefore*. It means, "here's the reason" I just told you what I told you. Hebrews 4:16 reads: "Therefore let us draw near with confidence to the throne of grace, so that we may receive mercy and find grace to help in time of need."

He says, now that you know you have a High Priest who understands the pain of life, what are going to do about it? And he gives the answer: "draw near with confidence to the throne of grace." The King James Version says we are to "come boldly." That says it all. In other words, we can approach God with frankness, bluntness. We can be open, plain, and daring—telling it like it is. We can have freedom in what we say. We can speak unreservedly. It's real talk. It is going to Jesus, not trying to impress Him, but telling him, "This is who I am, and this is what I am going through, and this is how I feel."

You say things like, "I am afraid," "I don't want to die," "I don't want to live," "I can't go on another day," "I'm through with this marriage."

The more you know Jesus, the more you can be real with Him. Jesus loves you as you are not as you ought to be. And He knows you! So you don't have to pretend with Him.

We can go to the throne boldly. Or as *The Message* puts it, "So let's walk right up to him and get what he is so ready to give." How can we do that? We have the Son who understands and will take us to the Father.

Did you know there was a time in American history when any citizen could go to see the president? At the end of the Civil War, a dejected Confederate soldier was sitting outside the grounds of the White House. A young boy approached and asked what was wrong. The soldier explained that he had repeatedly tried to see President Lincoln and had been unable to. He wanted to tell the president that his farm in the South had been unfairly taken by the Union soldiers. But each time he tried to enter the White House, the guards turned him away.

The boy motioned to the soldier to follow him. When they approached the guarded entrance, the soldiers came to attention, stepped back, and opened the door for the boy. He proceeded to the library where the president was resting and introduced the soldier to his father.

The boy was Tad Lincoln. He was the son of the President of the United States.[464]

The soldier had gained access to the president through the president's son. How much more should we rejoice in our access to the grace of the King of kings? We are connected to the Son and He can get us in to see the Father in tough times. The Son allows us to walk right up to Him.

TWO WORDS THAT DON'T SEEM TO BELONG TO EACH OTHER

Today's Reading: Hebrews 5

In talking about the power of mentoring, UCLA's great basketball coach, John Wooden wrote:

> [President Abraham] Lincoln fiercely believed in self-sufficiency, and in the maturity and character that struggles and hardships can bring. This lesson is so important for teachers and parents. It is only natural for us to want to shield our students and our children from anything that might possibly cause them hurt or to suffer or even to be uncomfortable. But some degree of pain is necessary for a person to become suited for the responsibilities that lay ahead.[465]

Pain is necessary. Those are true but tough words to swallow. In today's chapter we encounter a topic that is not often discussed in our culture. The writer of Hebrews speaks of a classroom that is often overlooked but more so avoided—the classroom of suffering. And we see that Father God was doing exactly what Lincoln and Wooden spoke about with His Son Jesus: "Although He was a Son, He learned obedience from the things which He suffered" (Hebrews 5:8).

Suffering and *learning*. These are words we don't normally associate together. Suffering and learning are partners, and they are integral in the life of Jesus.

Malcolm Muggeridge, one of the great British Christian writers, did not come to faith until later in life. His words on suffering and learning are powerful:

> Contrary to what might be expected, I look back on experiences that at the time seemed especially desolating and painful with particular satisfaction. Indeed, I can say with complete truthfulness that everything I have learned in my 75 years in this world, everything that has truly enhanced and enlightened my experience, has been through affliction and not through happiness.[466]

Amy Carmichael can attest to that. Carmichael was a missionary to India in the early 1900s. She was the originator of the safe house, rescuing young girls at a time when the world did not know about the horrific exploitation of them. She did this at the risk of her own life.

In 1932, Carmichael was badly injured in a fall, which broke her leg and twisted her spine, and which left her mostly bedridden and in constant pain for the next twenty years until her death. Rarely did she sleep through a night without waking up in pain. However, while bedridden, Carmichael wrote sixteen books that are filled with awe-inspiring revelation. All coming from a fall, sleepless nights, and back pain.[467] We could learn from her suffering.

Helen Keller said, "Although the world is full of suffering, it is also full of the overcoming of it."[468] Those are the learners. We try to avoid pain instead of learning from pain, which leads us to we waste our pain. A. W. Tozer was spot on when he said: "It is doubtful whether God can bless a man greatly until He has hurt him deeply."[469]

Our Daily Bread tells the story of A. Parnell Bailey who toured an orange grove where an irrigation pump had broken down. The season was in a drought, and the trees were beginning to die. Next Bailey visited another orchard where irrigation was used sparingly. "These trees could go without rain for another two weeks," the man giving Bailey the tour told him. "When they were young, I frequently kept water from them. This hardship and pain caused them to send their roots deeper into the soil in search of moisture. Now mine are the deepest-rooted trees in the area. While others are being scorched by the sun, these are finding moisture at a greater depth."[470]

That's what happens in pain, we learn to go deeper in God. Pain takes us deeper so we are not hurt by the pain but have learned to draw our resources from a place of depth. As Mildred Witte Struven explained: "A clay pot sitting in the sun will always be a clay pot. It has to go through the white heat of the furnace to become porcelain."[471]

I want to be porcelain. I want to come out of the struggle with depth and value that wasn't there before the struggle and pain.

Robert B. Hamilton's poem called "Sufferings" captures it well:

I walked a mile with Pleasure;
She chatted all the way;
But left me known the wiser
For all she had to say.
I walked a mile with Sorrow,

And ne'er a word said she;
But, oh! The things I learned from her,
When sorrow walked with me.[472]

FORWARD AND UPWARD IS OUR ONLY DIRECTION

Today's Reading: Hebrews 6

An old Presbyterian preacher named Clarence Macartney made a keen observation about airplanes and the Christian life:

> Between an airplane and every other form of locomotion and transportation there is one great contrast. The horse and wagon, the automobile, the bicycle, the locomotive, the speedboat, and the great battleship—all can come to a standstill without danger, and they can all reverse their engines, or their power, and go back.
>
> But there is no reverse about the engine of an airplane. It cannot back up. It dare not stand still. If it loses its momentum and forward-drives, then it crashes. The only safety for the airplane is in its forward and upward motion. The only safe direction for the Christian to take is forward and upward. If he stops, or if he begins to slip and go backward, that moment he is in danger.[473]

This is what the writer of Hebrews is speaking of in today's chapter:

> Leaving the elementary teaching about the Christ, let us press on to maturity, not laying again a foundation of repentance from dead works and of faith toward God, of instruction about washings and laying on of hands, and the resurrection of the dead and eternal judgment. (Hebrews 6:1-2)

Let us press on to maturity. Those are the words for moving forward and upward. It is the challenge of growth for the Christian. Always remember that maturity is not a gift, it is a journey. Inventor Rowland Hill once watched a child riding a rocking-horse and remarked, "He reminds me of some Christians. There is plenty of motion but no progress."[474]

Hebrews 6 is a plea for progress. It seems that these new Christians got stuck. The writer says we should know the foundational principles of faith, repentance, and laying on of hands, and that we should not stall out on these issues but press on toward maturity. As *The Message* so aptly puts it: "So come on, let's leave the preschool fingerpainting exercises on Christ and get on with the grand work of art. Grow up in Christ" (verse 1).

It is easy to confuse maturity with experience. Experience is a wonderful thing but not always the best teacher. There's nothing more tragic than when the years don't match the maturity.

A group of tourists were visiting a European village and walked by an old man sitting. With a patronizing tone, one tourist asked him, "Were any great men born in this village?" The old man replied, "Nope, only babies."[475] Every born-again believer starts life as a baby in Christ. Whether the new convert is six or sixty, that person is still a new Christian and needs to grow in the Lord. A baby Christian who has been saved for forty years is a tragedy. God intends for us to grow and mature so we can be a positive influence in the lives of others. Until we learn to dig into the meat of the Word for ourselves, we will never grow.

Amy Carmichael once penned these thoughts:

Sometimes when we read the words of those who have been more than conquerors, we feel almost despondent. I feel that I shall never be like that. But they won through step by step, by little bits of wills, little denials of self, little inward victories, by faithfulness in very little things. . . . No one sees these little hidden steps. They only see the accomplishment, but even so, those small steps were taken. There is no sudden triumph no spiritual maturity.[476]

That is the work of the moment. Maturity comes through taking small steps, introducing new habits, and stopping bad ones. In one *Peanuts* comic strip, Sally was struggling with her memory verse for Sunday, when she finally remembered, "Maybe it was something from the book of Reevaluation."[477] I think every time we read the Bible should be in the book of reevaluation for us to see if we are growing.

In most homes that have children present, you'll usually find a growth chart. It keeps track of each child's measurements. As a child ages, the body receives messages from the pituary gland in the brain that tells it to get moving, it's time to grow up. There's nothing the child can do to stop or start the growth, it happens naturally. I wish the same were true spiritually. I wish once we become a Christian, our growth becomes automatic, but it doesn't. There is no special gland to help us grow spiritually as Christians.

What if we did have a spiritual growth chart? If you could measure your spiritual growth in inches, how many inches have you grown in the last three to four years?

How much taller are you standing today spiritually from where you were last year?

What *does* growth and maturity look like? I think this story defines it for us.

A group of women who were studying the Bible together were puzzled by the words of Malachi 3:3: "He shall sit as a refiner and purifier of silver" (KJV). One of the ladies decided to call a silversmith to see if he could explain. That week she visited a silversmith and asked him to explain the process of refining silver. After he described the process, she asked, "Do you sit while the work of refining is going on?"

"Oh yes," he replied. "I must sit with my eye steadily fixed on the furnace. For if the time necessary for refining be exceeded in the slightest degree, the silver is sure to be injured."

At once she saw the beauty and comfort of the expression, *He shall sit as a refiner and purifier of silver.* As the lady was leaving the shop, the silversmith called her back with one more piece of information. "I only know when the process of purifying is complete by seeing my own image reflected in the silver."

As Joseph Exell explains:

Christ sees it needful to put His children into the furnace, but He is seated by the side of it, His eye is steadily on the work of purifying, and His wisdom and love are both engaged in the best manner for them. Their trials do not come at random. When Christ's image is reflected in us, His work of purifying is accomplished.[478]

There Is a Guarantee, You're Going to Make It

Today's Reading: Hebrews 7

Comedian Ray Romano said this about parenting: "Having children is like living in a frat house—nobody sleeps, everything's broken, and there is a lot of throwing up."[479] For us parents, this is so true. Let me tell you an "everything's broken" story.

When my son was little, he loved to color. One day while I was away from my laptop, my son decided to take his coloring skills to a new level. He grabbed a black Sharpie permanent marker and drew all over the screen. I walked into my office and caught him. I was frozen, not sure what to do other than plan my son's funeral. Then it hit me. My laptop was a Dell, and at the time, Dell had an amazing guarantee that if anything happened to the laptop, they would replace it. *No way that guarantee means a Sharpie and a two-year-old*, I thought, but figured I'd called Dell and told them the story. The customer service representative laughed and said they would ship out a new laptop in a day and I could use that box to send back to Dell the one my son signed. They did guarantee their product.

Hebrews 7 takes guarantees to a whole new level. This chapter compares the old covenant under Old Testament priests with the new covenant under the High Priest and Savior, Jesus. And the writer finally arrives at the guarantee portion of the covenant:

> This makes Jesus the guarantee of a far better way between us and God—one that really works! A new covenant. Earlier there were a lot of priests, for they died and had to be replaced. But Jesus' priesthood is permanent. He's there from now to eternity to save everyone who comes to God through him, always on the job to speak up for them. (Hebrews 7:22-25, MSG)

Jesus is the guarantee that the new covenant works and is better. Let me explain. When we are born again and come to God though Jesus Christ, we have a guarantee that we will make it to heaven. Under the old covenant a person was only as safe and secure as their next sin. And then they had to wait till the yearly sacrifice of the high priest for the sins of the nation of Israel. Under the new covenant, the writer tells us there is a guarantee. The Bible uses a comparable word to *guarantee*. It's the word *surety*. That word means a person who takes responsibility for another's performance of an undertaking. For example, their appearing in court or the payment of a debt. Remember the reality show *Dog, the Bounty Hunter*? He was a bail bondsman. When a person was released on bail money, but skipped appearing in court, Dog would hunt that person down to get that person to court.

That's why it's hard to be a backslider when our surety is Jesus. He comes after those who walk away from God, because He is the guarantee to get them not to court but to heaven. Jesus is the surety that we will make it to heaven. Jesus is, in a sense, your Dog, the bounty hunter. Ouch, I know that's hard to say, but He is. He has too big of an investment in you to lose you.

How does Jesus help you in that? That's where verse 25 explains an important point: "He is able to save fully from now throughout eternity, everyone who comes to God through him, because he lives to pray continually for them" (TPT).

Jesus is praying for you and me right now. And all of Jesus' prayers get answered. He is committed to getting us home. Robert Murray McCheyne said it like this: "If I could hear Christ praying for me in the next room, I would not fear a million enemies. Yet distance makes no difference because He is praying for me."[480]

The short life of the Old Testament priest made their guarantee weak, and the writer of Hebrews tells us that since our Great High Priest, Jesus *lives forever*, this warranty lasts that long. Puritan writer Thomas Watson shares this wonderful insight about our guarantee:

> When God calls a man, He does not repent of it. God does not, as many friends do, love one day, and hate another; or as princes, who make their subjects favourites, and afterwards throw them into prison. This is the blessedness of a saint; his condition admits of no alteration. God's call is founded upon His decree, and His decree is immutable. Acts of grace cannot be reversed. God blots out His people's sins, but not their names.[481]

I like guarantees! When we buy certain products, especially electronic products, or when we buy a car, that guarantee is important. In buying gifts we like to know about the guarantee. Does it say, "Satisfaction guaranteed or your money back!"?

God offers His Son Jesus as our guarantee. God backs up His promises with His Son. Every time we see the reenactment of that first Christmas, we are being reminded of God's guarantee. Think of it this way. If I made a promise to you, and you asked for some guarantee, some surety, that I would keep my promise, I would not hand over my son, Christian, and say, "Here's my son. He's yours until I keep my promises." That's outrageous. But in a sense, God did that. He gave us Jesus, His Son, as a guarantee, as a surety that He will do what He said. "Here's my Son, He's yours forever!" to guarantee that you and I will make it to heaven when life is over.

Jesus is our guarantee! God proved that He meant what He said. He signed it, sealed it, and sent the ultimate guarantee—the living Word. He is unchangeable. He guaranteed forever. No limitations. No fine print. No tricky words. Jesus is *the* guarantee—forever!

That's good news. You are going to make it home to heaven.

THE NEW COVENANT: NOT ME BUT GOD

Today's Reading: Hebrews 8

Why should you go to heaven?

I have asked many people that question. The number one answer I get is, "I am a good person." I remind them about what Jesus said. Jesus, who cannot lie, said that, "No one is good except God alone" (Mark 10:18).

And based on that person's answer . . . now two are good in the universe: God and that person. They start to see not only is that not the right answer, they start to see the futility of that answer. God the Father did not send His only Son to suffer horrifically on the cross so that you can do your best to get to heaven. The cross means more than that. Jesus did not die to get you to church. Jesus died to get you to heaven. You have no way to get to heaven on your own, you need help. You need a miracle. You need a new covenant. The old covenant put you in the driver's seat to do your best, and the Old Testament revealed that even at your best, it can't get you to heaven.

Hebrews 8 shows us the help and the miracle—it's the new covenant: "Now Jesus the Messiah has accepted a priestly ministry which far surpasses theirs, since he is the catalyst of a better covenant which contains far more wonderful promises!" (verse 6 TPT).

What is the "far more wonderful promises" of the new covenant? What makes this so different? It's what God says next in the form of two words. What follows verse 6 reveals the heart of God and offers us great help and hope. Those two words? *I will.*

Seven times in this chapter, God says, "I will." The new covenant is all on God. Where the old covenant was man trying to do better, the new covenant is God saying, *You can't, but I will.*

We live in a culture that embraces the *I will: I will* be better. *I will* get this right. *I will* be a success. *I will* be rich. *I will* get to heaven.

If you answer the question "How do I get to heaven?" with something *you do,* then the "I" of the "I will" is you. You can't be the "I." the "I" is the Son of God. It's what *He* has done for you in the new covenant. Martin Luther so powerful reminds us of this when he said: "What makes you think that God is more pleased with your good deeds than he is with his blessed son?"[482]

What follows the statement of "far more wonderful promises" is this (all quoted from the NIV):

"*I will* make a new covenant." (Verse 8)
"This is the covenant *I will* establish." (Verse 10)
"*I will* put my laws in their minds." (Verse 10)
"[*I will*] write them on their hearts." (Verse 10)
"*I will* be their God." (Verse 10)
"*I will* forgive their wickedness." (Verse 12)
"[*I*] *will* remember their sins no more." (Verse 12)

The new covenant is what God does for you, not what you do for God.

Another word for you being the "I" is *legalism*. You are working to make God like you and bring you to heaven. Legalism eliminates God's involvement in your life and puts it all on you. Legalism says that God will really loves you if you can change. As Tullian Tchividjian said, "The ironic thing about legalism is that it not only doesn't make people work harder, it makes them give up."[483]

That is when God says, *I have a better covenant for you.*

In *Mere Christianity*, C. S. Lewis said something that reminds me of the greatness of God's *I Will*. Digest these powerful words: "Christ offers something for nothing: He even offers everything for nothing. In a sense, the whole Christian life consists in accepting that very remarkable offer. But the difficulty is to reach the point of recognising that all we have done and can do is nothing."[484]

That's the new covenant.

What Happens After We Die?

Today's Reading: Hebrews 9

I was speaking to a major league baseball player once who was struggling with the idea of death. I told him, here is your anxiety about death, starting with the least and moving to the greatest anxiety:

- *The unlived life.* You didn't do your bucketlist—so many things you wish you would have done. You start to realize what you did do and how much time you wasted.
- *The regretful past.* This is going backward and wishing you could take back words and actions. You wish you would have let more things go, apologized more, spent more time with your kids and your family.
- *The gnawing possibility of accountability.* This causes the greatest anxiety. It is the eternity issue. Is there a heaven and hell? Am I accountable? Will God judge me? If so, *how* will God me?

The first two on that list deal with mortality. The final item on that list deals with immortality. Is there something after death? That causes people's anxiety to grow as they think, *Before I was only anxious about my last years on earth, but now I'm anxious about what is beyond and forever.*

We can brush off dreams unrealized. We can even brush off the stupid stuff we did that we wish we could take back. But eternity is different. Eternity keeps talking to us. And today's chapter gives us sobering reality check on it: "Every human being is appointed to die once, and then to face God's judgment" (Hebrews 9:27, TPT). *Everyone* will stand before God, either as our Judge or as our Redeemer. His role is determined by the choice we make on earth.

When CNN cancelled Larry King's interview show several years ago, King began obsessing with his death, becoming aware that there will come a day when he dies. But he doesn't believe in the afterlife, so each day he started taking four hormone pills for human growth, and plans to have his body frozen so that someday he will live again. He admits he knows "it's nuts," but at least he believes when he dies the potential of him being resurrected someday thanks to cryonics gives him some hope. Larry King says, "Other people have no hope."[485]

Our hope is not in extending life here but extending life on the other side in heaven. Larry King is trying to extend the wrong way. What he fails to understand is that eternity is too long to be wrong.

There's another who doesn't want to face eternity. In *The Last Word*, Thomas Nagel, professor of philosophy at New York University and an atheist, admits he doesn't want there to be a God:

> I speak from experience, being strongly subject to this fear myself: I want atheism to be true and am made uneasy by the fact that some of the most intelligent and well-informed people I know are religious believers. It isn't just that I don't believe in God and, naturally, hope that I'm right in my belief. It's that I hope there is no God! I don't want there to be a God; I don't want the universe to be like that.[486]

Those words are raw and honest, and I appreciate the professor's candor. But again, eternity is too long to be wrong.

In 1974 Muhammad Ali was set to box against George Foreman for the Heavyweight Champion title. While he was training, a father and his son, Jimmy, came to Ali's training camp, because he wanted to meet the Champ. When Ali discovered Jimmy was battling leukemia, he told him, "I'm going to beat George Foreman, and you're going to beat cancer." Two weeks later, Ali visited the boy, who was dying. Ali told him, and said to Ali, "Jimmy, remember what I told you? I'm going to beat George Foreman. You're going to beat cancer."

"No, Muhammad," Jimmy answered. "I'm going to meet God. I'm going to tell Him, you're my friend."[487]

Ali's kindness and name recognition throughout the world has always impressed me. But on the day of judgment, we can't count on name-dropping. The only name that will matter on that day is the name of Jesus. Even the Sportsman of the Century will stand before the true "The Greatest" and bow down.

Paul reminds us that "God highly exalted Him, and bestowed on Him the name which is above every name, that at the name of Jesus, EVERY KNEE WILL BOW, of those who are in heaven, and on the earth, and under the earth" (Philippians 2:9-10). What will you tell God when you meet Him? Can you honestly say when you do, "I know Jesus"?

The Bible says in 2 Corinthians 5:10 that "we must all appear before the judgment seat of Christ, so that each one of us may receive what is due us for the things done while in the body, whether good or bad" (NIV).

How can we be prepared for death? We need to remember that death starts eternity. So as C. S. Lewis reminds us, "Precisely because we cannot predict the moment, we must be ready at all moments."[488]

The saying goes like this: "Never fall in love with anything that can't go to heaven with you. The more important a matter is, the less you should postpone it. So claim the gift of eternal life immediately." Eternal life is a decision—one that cannot be delegated, and one that has a deadline. Today is the day of salvation.

WHY IS CHURCH SO IMPORTANT

Today's Reading: Hebrews 10

I have heard this question many times: "Do I have to go to church to be a Christian?"

The answer is obviously, "No, you don't have to go to church to be a Christian." But that's not the entire part of the answer. The end of the answer is this, "You *do* have to go to church to be a *growing* Christian." One of my dear friends says it like this: "Only weak people think they are strong enough to do the Christian life alone."

I grew up hearing and reciting Hebrews 10:25 as the reason for attending church: "Not forsaking the assembling of ourselves together" (KJV). But I love the way the Passion Translation opens the passage. It's much more profound and challenging:

> Discover creative ways to encourage others and to motivate them toward acts of compassion, doing beautiful works as expressions of love. This is not the time to pull away and neglect meeting together, as some have formed the habit of doing, because we need each other! In fact, we should come together even more frequently, eager to encourage and urge each other onward as we anticipate that day dawning. (Verses 24-25)

T. M. Luhrmann, professor of anthropology at Stanford, wrote an op-ed piece for the *New York Times* weekend edition several years ago called, "The Benefits of Church." Consider what she said about why going to church is good for you:

> One of the most striking scientific discoveries about religion in recent years is that going to church weekly is good for you. Religious attendance—at least, religiosity—boosts the immune system and decreases blood pressure. It may add as much as two to three years to your life.[489]

When we are connected to the church, we are better people. Think about it this way. Many members of the church can accomplish collectively what the same members cannot do individually. Think of an airplane. One hundred percent of it is made up of non-flying parts, but when we put them together, they can lift 175,000 pounds. How much can you bench by yourself? The power of the body of Christ is that together we can do the unimaginable.

The writer of Hebrews says that consistently not attending church is the *habit* of some. What a dangerous habit. If absence makes the heart grow fonder, then some people must really love church because they are absent a lot. Honestly, though? Absence makes the heart go wander.

Popular reformer and author R. C. Sproul said it brilliantly:

It is both foolish and wicked to suppose that we will make much progress in sanctification if we isolate ourselves from the visible church. Indeed, it is commonplace to hear people declare that they don't need to unite with a church to be a Christian. They claim that their devotion is personal and private, not institution or corporate. This is not the testimony of the great saints of history; it is the confession of fools.[490]

The writer of Hebrews goes on to explain why this habit is not healthy: "Because we need each other! In fact, we should come together even more frequently, eager to encourage and urge each other onward as we anticipate that day dawning" (verse 25, TPT).

The church's job is to encourage and urge each other onward. What a great job. The Amplified Bible, Classic Edition expands it even more with these words: "admonishing (warning, urging, and encouraging) one another." In a world and in a time that is so dark and discouraging, the church should be the place we go and come out better than we went in.

Russ Blowers, a minister in Indianapolis, knew the Rotary Club members would ask about his profession when he attended a local meeting. He didn't want just to say, "I'm a preacher," so when his turn came to introduce himself to the group, he said,

I'm with a global enterprise. We have branches in every country in the world. We have our representatives in nearly every parliament and boardroom on earth. We're into motivation and behavior alteration. We run hospitals, feeding stations, crisis-pregnancy centers, universities, publishing houses, and nursing homes. We care for our clients from birth to death. We are into life insurance and fire insurance. We perform spiritual heart transplants. Our original Organizer owns all the real estate on earth plus an assortment of galaxies and constellations. He knows everything and lives everywhere. Our product is free for the asking. (There's not enough money to buy it.).[491]

That's called the church. And it's amazing! Why would we skip it each week?

Day 215

CREATION VERSUS EVOLUTION

Today's Reading: Hebrews 11

Hebrews 11 is known as the faith chapter. We don't get but a few verses into this chapter when we are faced with creation. Which means that faith and creation go together. The writer of Hebrews says this in verse 3: "Faith empowers us to see that the universe was created and beautifully coordinated by the power of God's words! He spoke and the invisible realm gave birth to all that is seen" (TPT).

The writer jumps right into a twenty-first-century science classroom firestorm. The writer just says it like the first verse of the Bible does in Genesis 1.

Let me give you four false "facts" that homiletics students of West Coast Baptist College put together:

1. Books write themselves without the need of an author.

2. Cars build themselves without the need of a manufacturer.

3. Music composes itself into beautiful harmonies without the need of a composer.

Now, any kindergarten student could testify that the above three statements have as much truth to them as the flat-earth theory. However, countless university lecturers and professors are paid big dollars to promote the "reality" of this last false fact:

4. The whole universe came into being through a process of random chance and beneficial mutations, without any need of a Designer.[492]

The *true* fact of the matter is that evolution is just a big fairytale for grownups! The French Enlightenment philosopher Voltaire states it most simply: "If a watch proves the existence of a watchmaker but the existence of the universe does not prove the existence of a great Architect, then I consent to be called a fool."[493] The evolutionist's argument is so illogical, it really lends toward deception. There *is* a Designer of this wonderful universe: "In the beginning God."

Australian pastor J. Sidlow Baxter gives this powerful breakdown of the first verse of the Bible:

"In the beginning *God*"—that denies Atheism with its doctrine of *no* God.

"In the beginning *God*"—that denies Polytheism with its doctrine of *many* gods.

"In the beginning *God created*"—that denies Fatalism with its doctrine of *chance*.

"In the beginning God *created*"—that denies Evolution with its doctrine of infinite *becoming*.

"God created *heaven and earth*"—that denies Pantheism which makes God and the universe identical.

"God created *heaven and earth*"—that denies Materialism which asserts the eternity of matter.

Thus, this first "testimony" of Jehovah is not only a declaration of Divine truth, but a repudiation of human error.[494]

No one can get by the first verse of the Bible without having to submit to the authority of the Bible. Couldn't God have used evolution? That is a silly and intrusive question. God told us He didn't use evolution. He did everything in six days. Evolution needs more than six days. People reject the creation account because they don't want to deal with the God of Scripture. Evolution is hostile to the Word of God.

Ask people if they believe in a literal six days. If they conjugate that part of the Scripture, what will stop them from conjugating other parts of Scripture? If the culture can overturn to clear teaching the Genesis account, the culture can overturn any scriptural mandate. The Bible repeats the six days of creation from different parts of Scripture. It states it again in Exodus 20:11: "In six days the Lord made the heavens and the earth, the sea and all that is in them, and rested on the seventh day."

Proverbs 30:1 (msg) says, "The skeptic swore, 'There is no God! No God!—I can do anything I want!" But if you believe in Creation, then you have to face these maxims:

If I believe in creation, then I have a Creator.

If I have a Creator, then I have an Owner.

If I have an Owner, then I have accountability.

Evolution simply doesn't make sense. As G. K. Chesterton said, "It is absurd for the Evolutionist to complain that it is unthinkable for an admittedly unthinkable God to make everything out of nothing, and then pretend that it is more thinkable that nothing should turn itself into everything."[495]

In 2018, the famed physicist and atheist, Stephen Hawking, died at seventy-six years old. In his final book, *Brief Answers to the Big Questions*, he wrote:

When people ask me if a God created the universe, I tell them that the question itself makes no sense. Time didn't exist before the Big Bang, so there is no time for God to make the universe in. It's like asking directions to the edge of the Earth—the Earth is a sphere that doesn't have an edge, so looking for it is a futile exercise.

Do I have faith? We are each free to believe what we want, and it's my view that the simplest explanation is that there is no God. No one created the universe and no one directs our fate. This leads me to a profound realization: there is probably no heaven and afterlife either. . . . We have this one life to appreciate the grand design of the universe, and for that I am extremely grateful.[496]

Listen closely to what I am about to say. Stephen Hawking just became a believer one second after his death on March 14, 2018. Hawking died and saw the greatest mind ever: God. When will you become a believer? Will you be a too-late believer like Hawking?

Ravi Zacharias said, "To sustain the belief that there is no God, atheism has to demonstrate infinite knowledge, which is tantamount to saying, 'I have infinite knowledge that there is no being in existence with infinite knowledge.'"[497]

We think that since the bottom of every rock and tree does not have "made by God" that it's not. But that's why we have faith. Faith and creation go together.

Day 216

AM I IGNITABLE?

Today's Reading: Hebrews 12

Today's chapter ends with the shortest verse of the chapter and probably of the entire letter. It's about God's nature: "For our God is a consuming fire" (Hebrews 12:29). That's it, but that's enough.

God desires to set His servants on fire. He wants to consume them. One man He consumed with passion was Jim Elliot. Elliot was a missionary to a remote tribe of Auca Indians of Ecuador in the 1950s. **He was martyred alongside four other missionaries during Operation Auca on January 8, 1956.** After his death, his widow, Elisabeth, went on to impact many people through with her writings and her biography of Jim, called *Through Gates of Splendor* and *Shadow of the Almighty*, which later became a movie of his life called, *The End of the Spear.* Even though Jim died at age twenty-nine, he wrote. Thank God, Jim wrote. His journal and his biography are filled with spiritual gems, such as these two: "Father, make of me a crisis man. Bring those I contact to decision. Let me not be a milepost on a single road; make me a fork, that men must turn one way or another on facing Christ in me."[498] And "He is no fool who gives what he cannot keep to gain that which he cannot lose."[499]

But there's one statement he wrote in his journal that both challenged and convicted my soul and has affected me since the beginning of my ministry more than thirty years ago. I committed it to memory. It was something he wrote after his morning devotional reading of Hebrews. (Warning! Don't read this quote if you want to just stay where you are spiritually.) "[He makes] His ministers a flame of fire," he wrote. "Am I ignitible? God deliver me from the dread asbestos of 'other things.' Saturate me with the oil of the Spirit that I may be aflame. But flame is transient, often short-lived. Canst thou bear this, my soul—short life? In me there dwells the Spirit of the Great Short-Lived, whose zeal for God's house consumed Him. . . . 'Make me Thy fuel, Flame of God.'"[500]

Jim Elliot leaves us with two huge and penetrating questions: Am I ignitible? And what other things have been asbestos to keep me from being ignitible?

Since God is a consuming fire, I need to be, I *must* be ignitable. That is why I must bring judgment to everything I do, see, watch, have friendship with to this one standard: are those things asbestos? If I am not on fire for God, it's not God's inability to ignite me. So the question always haunts me, Am I ignitable?"

Every time the fire of God fell in the Bible, it was looking for something to fall on. In the Old Testament, it was looking for an animal sacrifice. But in the New Testament, it was looking for people. Fire fell on people on the day of Pentecost. As Tommy Tenney said, "If you want the fire of God, you must become the fuel of God."[501]

One of my favorite devotional writers, Samuel Chadwick, said this about the fire of God: "The soul's safety is in its heat. Truth without enthusiasm, morality without emotion, ritual without soul, make for a Church without power. Destitute of the Fire of God, nothing else counts; possessing Fire, nothing else matters."[502]

Am I Ignitable?

What things in my life is asbestos to retard the fire of God?

John Wesley said these words about the Methodist church he founded in the midst of revival: "My fear is not that our great movement, known as the Methodists, will eventually cease to exist or one day die from the earth. My fear is that our people will become content to live without the fire, the power, the excitement, the supernatural element that makes us great."[503]

Content to live without the fire? May it never be for any of us. I want to say with Jim Elliot to our God the consuming fire, "Make me Thy fuel flame of God."

Jim was right when he later wrote in his journal, "Forgive me for being so ordinary while claiming to know so extraordinary a God."[504] God is a consuming fire, and you and I need to be His fuel. Let's allow Him to consume us.

A Lot of Negatives
Can Equal a Positive

Today's Reading: Hebrews 13

Anything can happen before the year ends. You may meet your mate. You may get pregnant. You may graduate, start a new career, or move. You may have your first job interview. You may become an empty nester or attend your child's wedding or have your first grandchild. You may start attending a new church or you may start a new walk with God.

The bad stuff can come just as fast. You may get a divorce, have a miscarriage, deal with a foreclosure. You may get fired. The doctor may say you have cancer. Your child may become an atheist. You may experience the death of a spouse, a child, a parent, a close friend.

Nothing seems to be concrete or forever. And for all the change that happens in our lives, Hebrews 13 reminds us that despite change, there is One who does not change: "He hath said, I will never leave thee, nor forsake thee. So that we may boldly say, The Lord is my helper, and I will not fear what man shall do unto me" (Hebrews 13:5-6, KJV).

There is a tribe in South America that has an initiation rite for their young men when they turn twelve years old. One of the things they do is to take them into the deepest part of the jungle and leave them all night by themselves. It was their own father who had to lead them and leave them there for their dreaded night alone.

The boy would sit in fear all night listening to the ghoulish sounds of the forest. When the sun finally rose the next morning, the boy would look just a few feet away and would see that his father had been sitting there the entire time; he just didn't know.

The boy would ask, "Have you been there all night?" To which the father would reply, "Of course I was there all night. Do you think I would leave you alone? Do you think that I would have ever left you in this place alone?"[505]

God says the same thing that this South American father says. God says, "I will never leave thee, nor forsake thee." Hebrews 13:5 is a rare verse. It has been translated by many as simply, "He will never leave you nor forsake you." That is good English, but it is not good Greek in this instance. This verse contains an unusual triple negative. That is not good English (like "I ain't got no money"), but it is good Greek. It should actually be translated, "He will never, never, never leave us nor forsake us." In fact when the verse is complete, it has five negatives in total—reassuring the Christian believer that the Lord will never, ever, no not once, never forsake nor leave us. This is such a beautiful truth. God has promised never, no, not ever, never, to leave nor forsake us. That means a lot of negatives is a real positive for us Christians.

Jewish commentators believe it was a way of confirming the truth in the testimony of more than two witnesses. Jesus used that method often: "Verily, verily, I say unto you." One *verily* was not enough for Jesus.

When in conflict or hard times, our tendency is to ask the same question over and over. And it seems that God wants to make sure we get it immediately that He's not going anywhere and that He's here to stay for you.

When C. S. Lewis married the American Joy Davidman, and then soon found out that Joy was dying of cancer, Lewis wrote in *A Grief Observed* that he could have used a screaming room.[506]

Why do we feel that way? We feel that God is nowhere to be found. And like C. S. Lewis, we want to scream. But according to Hebrews 13:5, things may change, people may change, but God won't. He is always going to be there. That is a promise you can count on.

Gladys Aylward was a missionary to China in the early 1900s and was forced to flee when the Japanese invaded Yangcheng, the area where she lived. However, she was determined not to be the only one to make it to safety, so with only one assistant, she led more than a hundred orphans over the mountains toward, what was at that time, Free China. In *The Hidden Price of Greatness*, authors Ray Besson and Ranelda Mack Hunsicker, share the account:

> During Gladys's harrowing journey out of war-torn Yangcheng . . . she grappled with despair as never before. After passing a sleepless night, she faced the morning with no hope of reaching safety. A 13-year-old girl in the group reminded her of their much-loved story of Moses and the Israelites crossing the Red Sea.
>
> "But I am not Moses," Gladys cried in desperation.
>
> "Of course you aren't," the girl said, "but Jehovah is still God!"
>
> When Gladys and the orphans made it through, they proved once again that no matter how inadequate we feel, God is still God, and He can trust in Him.[507]

That's what the writer of Hebrews was telling us. When we face the conflict and difficult times and wonder, *Will God be with me? Will He abandon us?* the writer of Hebrews offers us the five negative promise that is a positive: "Never, positively not! It will never happen! It's unthinkable! There is not even the slightest possibility that it will ever happen!"

God *will* be with you.

More Valuable Than Rubies and Much Easier to Get

Today's Reading: James 1

In May 2012, a thirty-two-carat Burmese ruby-and-diamond ring—from the collection of Lily Safra, one of the richest women in the world—was sold at auction. The preauction estimate for the ring was $3 to $5 million, but the final sale price ended at $6.7 million. It is believed to be the most expensive ruby ever sold.[508] As valuable as rubies are, the Bible tells us there is something more valuable than that: wisdom. As Proverbs 8:11 says, "For wisdom is better than rubies; and all the things that may be desired are not to be compared to it" (KJV).

In today's chapter, James begins by telling us how to find this invaluable and rare jewel called wisdom. First we need to understand that wisdom is not simply information. I know a lot of intelligent people who are not wise. Being old is no guarantee of wisdom. And neither education nor experience alone make someone wise, although wisdom does include experience and education. And wisdom is not knowledge either. As former first lady Eleanor Roosevelt once said, "Never mistake knowledge for wisdom. One helps you make a living; the other helps you make a life."[509]

Knowledge speaks, but wisdom listens. As Doug Larson said, "Wisdom is the reward you get for a lifetime of listening when you would have preferred to talk."[510]

Each year in the United States 800,000 new books and 400,000 periodicals are published.[511] As Brian Buffini rightly said, "We are drowning in information and starving for wisdom."[512]

So what is wisdom and how do we get it?

Charles Spurgeon best defined it when he gave the difference between wisdom and knowledge: "Wisdom is the right use of knowledge. To know is not to be wise. Many men know a great deal, and are all the greater fools for it. But to know how to *use* knowledge rightly is to have wisdom."[513]

R. T. Kendall, who has been a spiritual father and mentor to me, also offers definitions of wisdom:

- Wisdom is saying or doing the right thing—at the right time!
- Wisdom focuses on knowing the next step forward in making decisions.

- Wisdom is to possess the ability to get things done.
- Wisdom [is] knowing what to do next.
- Wisdom is getting God's opinion.[514]

Kendall explains, "God *always* has an opinion on any matter. He therefore should be consulted first when we are wanting to know the next step forward."[515] God always knows the next step but is rarely asked. I have good news. Wisdom is not far away. And James 1:5 tells us where wisdom can be found. James says if you want wisdom, it's found in prayer: "If any of you lacks wisdom, let him ask of God, who gives to all generously and without reproach, and it will be given to him."

I think counseling has gone up in the church because prayer has gone down. We get counseling to gain wisdom when we could have started with God instead of an office. I think prayerlessness is an insult to God. Every prayerless day is a statement by a helpless individual that says, *I do not need God today*.

Baptist preacher Vance Havner said, "If you lack knowledge, go to school. If you lack wisdom, get on your knees."[516] Wisdom is available to those who ask God in prayer for it. That means wisdom and prayer go together. You can't have one without the other. No one who is wise is prayerless. And no one who is prayerless will ever be wise.

We will never attain wisdom apart from the presence of God. Colossians 2:3 says, "In him lie hidden all the treasures of wisdom and knowledge" (NLT). So He is our source and *the* source of wisdom. That means we can have an MBA or a PHD and still be D-U-M-B. Because if God is divorced from our lives, then we are divorced from the all-wise God. Every man of wisdom is a man of prayer. What God has joined together, let no man can put asunder . . . and in this case, the wise pray and the prayerful are wise.

Proverbs 13:20 "Walk with the wise and become wise" (NLT). So those who walk with God will have to be wise. Why? There is no one wiser than God. Walk with God. Talk with God. Listen to God. And watch how He rubs off on you.

I lived in Detroit for thirty years. I lived down the street from the first auto factory in the United States. There is a really cool story about that plant.

Henry Ford asked Charlie Steinmetz, an electrical genius, to build the generators for his automobile factory. One day the generators stopped working, and the repairmen couldn't figure out the problem. Ford called Steinmetz, who tinkered with the machines for a few hours and then hit the switch. Immediately the generators came to life. When Ford got the bill from Steinmetz, he was stunned. The amount was $10,000. When he asked why the bill was so high, Steinmetz replied: For tinkering with the generators, $10. For knowing where to tinker, $9,990. Ford paid the bill.[517] wisdom knows the exact spot to make things work. God is like Charlies Steinmetz, He knows how to make life work.

SMILE WHEN YOU DRIVE

Today's Reading: James 2

In *It Worked for Me,* former Secretary of State Colin Powell tells a story about a time he slipped out of his office and past the secret service agents and snuck down to the building's parking garage. He explains the set-up:

> The garage is run by contract employees, most of them immigrants making only a few dollars above minimum wage. The garage is too small for all the White House cars. The challenge every morning is to pack them all in. The attendants' system is to stack cars one behind the other, so densely packed that there's no room to maneuver. Since number three can't get out until number one and two have left, the evening rush hour is chaos if the lead cars don't exit the garage on time. Inevitably a lot of impatient people have to stand around waiting their turn. The attendants had never seen a Secretary wandering around the garage before; they thought I was lost. They asked if I needed help getting back "home."

He told them that he wasn't lost, but was just there to look around and chat. They seemed pleased. As they talked, Powell asked them, "When the cars come in every morning, how do you decide who ends up first to get out, and who ends up second and third?"

The attendants looked at each other with knowing looks and smiled. Then they explained their system. "When you drive in, if you lower the window, look out, smile, and you know our name, or you say 'Good morning, how are you?' or something like that, you're number one to get out. But if you just look straight ahead and don't show you even see us or that we are doing something for you, well, you are likely to be one of the last to get out."

Guess whose car was always first to get out? Colin Powell's![518]

Today's chapter talks about the importance of how to treat people for who they are and not what they possess. That was the challenge for this new church that James was addressing. It was parking-garage talk to the people, spoken like a secretary of state:

Listen to it.

My dear friends, don't let public opinion influence how you live out our glorious, Christ-originated faith. If a man enters your church wearing an expensive suit, and a street person wearing rags comes in right after him, and you say to the man in the suit, "Sit here, sir; this is the best seat in the house!" and either ignore the street person or say, "Better sit here in the back row," haven't you segregated God's children and proved that you are judges who can't be trusted?

Listen, dear friends. Isn't it clear by now that God operates quite differently? He chose the world's down-and-out as the kingdom's first citizens, with full rights and privileges. This kingdom is promised to anyone who loves God. (James 2:1-5, MSG)

Then a few verses down, James gives a name for this type of rule: the royal rule or royal law. Why is it royal? Because it was given by a King:

You do well when you complete the Royal Rule of the Scriptures: "Love others as you love yourself." But if you play up to these so-called important people, you go against the Rule and stand convicted by it. You can't pick and choose in these things, specializing in keeping one or two things in God's law and ignoring others. (Verses 8-10, MSG)

James starts off this chapter speaking to two words that are incompatible: *faith* and *favoritism*. Faith in Christ and prejudice toward people are contradictory. If there is no passion for Jesus, then there will be no compassion for people. The word *favoritism* in this verse is made up of two Greek words, which means *to receive the face*.

You receive someone based upon what you see (color, jewelry, clothing). This word is found in only three other places in the New Testament, and in every place, God is the subject and it tells us that God is not into judging people by their face. God shows no partiality or does not look at faces but hearts. Let's look at the three other passages:
- "For the Jew, then for the Gentile. For God does not show favoritism." (Romans 2:9-11, NIV)
- "You know that he who is both their Master and yours is in heaven, and there is no favoritism with him." (Ephesians 6:9, NIV)
- "If you do what is wrong, you will be paid back for the wrong you have done. For God has no favorites." (Colossians 3:25, NLT)

And then we come to James 2:1 and are told to do the same thing God does: don't judge people by the outward appearance: "My dear brothers and sisters, how can you claim to have faith in our glorious Lord Jesus Christ if you favor some people over others?" (NLT).

Then James tells a story with two different people showing up at a church meeting. One is rich and one is homeless. James warns the Christians about evaluating the externals and coming to a wrong conclusion. He said when we do that we became near sighted and don't see anything beneath the surface. Our criteria is flawed. The usher in James 2 does that and gives preferential seating to the rich and general-admission seating to the poor. One gets box seats, the other gets the floor.

If there is to be one place where there is to be no distinction or prejudice, it should be the house of God. Prejudice is inconsistent with God's method of seeing people. God does not look at a person's wallet or skin and say, "I want *that* person in My family." He does not look at the face, whether that face has Lancôme cream on it or is covered in dirt and grime.

Secretary of State Powell had more to his story. This is how finished:

Show more kindness than seems necessary, because the person needs it more than you will ever know. Don't just show kindness in passing or to be courteous. Show it in depth, show it with passion, and expect nothing in return. Kindness is not just about being nice; it's about recognizing another human being who deserves care and respect.[519]

Colin Powell sounds a lot like James 2.

WORDS MATTER

Today's Reading: James 3

If there is one book in the Bible that reminds us that our words matter, it is the book of James. In fact, the book of James has five chapters, and all five have something to say about the tongue. Let's sample a verse or two from each chapter.

From James 1: "Everyone must be quick to hear, slow to speak *and* slow to anger. . . . If anyone thinks himself to be religious, and yet does not bridle his tongue but deceives his *own* heart, this man's religion is worthless" (verses 19, 26).

From James 2: "Speak and so act as [people should]" (verse 12, AMPC).

From James 4: "Do not criticize one another, my friends" (verse 11, GNT).

From James 5: "Say only 'Yes' when you mean yes, and 'No' when you mean no, and then you will not come under God's judgment (verse 12, GNT).

You might think I skipped chapter 3. I didn't. James thought it wise to dedicate almost an entire chapter to the power of the tongue. Why? Because words matter. And that is James 3:

> Don't be in any rush to become a teacher, my friends. Teaching is highly responsible work. Teachers are held to the strictest standards. And none of us is perfectly qualified. We get it wrong nearly every time we open our mouths. If you could find someone whose speech was perfectly true, you'd have a perfect person, in perfect control of life.
>
> A bit in the mouth of a horse controls the whole horse. A small rudder on a huge ship in the hands of a skilled captain sets a course in the face of the strongest winds. A word out of your mouth may seem of no account, but it can accomplish nearly anything—or destroy it!
>
> It only takes a spark, remember, to set off a forest fire. A careless or wrongly placed word out of your mouth can do that. By our speech we can ruin the world, turn harmony to chaos, throw mud on a reputation, send the whole world up in smoke and go up in smoke with it, smoke right from the pit of hell.
>
> This is scary: You can tame a tiger, but you can't tame a tongue—

it's never been done. The tongue runs wild, a wanton killer. With our tongues we bless God our Father; with the same tongues we curse the very men and women he made in his image. Curses and blessings out of the same mouth! (Verses 1-10, MSG)

My friend, this can't go on. When James speaks about the tongue, he is telling us about our words. In the book of James, the tongue equals words. This is why it's important:

Your words influence (verse 1). James says not to rush into teaching because you are held to a higher standard. Why are teachers held at a high standard? Because you are influential at vulnerable moments of people's lives. You're getting a blank slate to write on.

Your words reveal maturity (verse 2). James says the best way to see how mature someone is is not to look at their age, if they have gray hair, or if they have experience, but to listen to them speak. Listen to their words, their talking.

I think wise people talk less, not more. As Proverbs 17:27-28 (TLB) says, "The man of few words is wise; therefore, even a fool is thought to be wise when he is silent. It pays to keep his mouth shut."

Your words make a difference. The tongue is little but its effect is big. James gives four illustrations of this: the horse and bridle (verse 3); the ship and the rudder (verse 4); the forest fire and the spark from a match (verses 5-6); the animal and the animal trainer (verse 7).

What do these word pictures mean? Something so small can cause great damage if not under control. The tongue is small but the tongue can cause a lot of damage. Hearing a comment can hurt people and ruin a friendship. Being called a name can sink into someone's soul that can make the person start believing the lie of that word. Hearing verbal abuse.

I've heard it said, "Light travels faster than sound. That's the reason most people appear to be bright till you hear them speak."

Words really do matter.

HOW TO PUT THE DEVIL ON THE RUN

Today's Reading: James 4

I was reading the story of a young man who had a call on his life to go on the mission field. The problem was that he still had an edge to him. He still an independent spirit, which came out by what he did and the way he spoke to others. When he went to his leader to ask him about his call to be a missionary, the leadership wisely said to him, "Before you can be a missionary you have to be *submissionary.*"[520]

I grew up in a church where binding Satan was a big deal and done often. We'd pray, and it was called spiritual warfare. Those words were supposed to distance us from the devil. In today's chapter, James gives us a way to put the devil on the run. James teaches us that binding is not done with the mouth but with the life, a life of submission: "Submit yourselves to God. Resist the Devil, and he will run away from you" (James 4:7, GNT).

Submission. It is a hard word but a powerful one. It is powerful enough to put the devil on the run, yet hard enough to make it part of our lives. *Submission* is a fighting word to the devil, and its power so easily missed by the Christian. Submission starts with recognizing authority, and then being willing to yield to that authority.

When you recognize God as *the* authority in your life, you are saying not only is God more powerful than you are, but He is wiser than you, and you yield to Him, believing God knows better than you too. I heard someone once say: "I can take more ground and advance with submission rather than ambition." Submission is powerful.

The unsubmissive person says "I choose what is good, best, and right for my life." The submissive person says, "I choose what God says is good, best, and right for my life."

The best way to "bind the devil"? Submit to God. We have so many Christians binding Satan over themselves, people, churches, and cities without a submissive spirit. Satan doesn't flee without a submissive spirit to God. It's impossible to resist the devil in any area if there is not a submission to God in every area. The greatest binding you can do is to always say yes to God.

Submission to God is the believers' way of binding Satan—keeping him out of their lives.

The truth of the matter is, speaking is always easier than lifestyle. But always remember that lifestyle gives authority to your speaking. They cannot be divorced from each other. Christian writer Edwin Cole says it like this, "Ability to resist temptation is directly proportionate to your submission to God."[521] For example, if we know the Word of God tells us not marry a non-Christian, and we decide our love for the person trumps the Word of God and we go ahead and marry that person, then we are not submissive to what God says.

Submission is not just obeying. Submission is not just doing what someone said. Submission is obeying with the right attitude. That's what makes submission difficult.

A mother ordered her disobedient son to sit in a corner. After a couple of minutes sitting, he told his mother, "I'm sitting down on the outside, but I'm standing up on the inside!" He obeyed, but he didn't submit.

I want to live a life that says yes to God with a smile on my face that He knows better.

Three-time World Series champion New York Yankee second baseman Bobby Richardson is an outspoken Christian. Before Mickey Mantle passed away, Bobby led him to the Lord. Bobby's prayer is a great prayer for all of us who want to bind the devil without saying, "I bind you, Satan!" It's the ultimate prayer of submission and the ultimate spiritual warfare prayer: "Dear God, Your will: nothing more, nothing less, nothing else!"[522]

Now that will put the devil on the run.

It Doesn't Work When You Chop It in Half

Today's Reading: James 5

Can you imagine what we would miss if we stopped short on verses in the Bible and just read half of them? What if we only quoted the second part of John 3:16: "Whoever believes in Him shall not perish, but have eternal life"? What makes it powerful is the first part: "For God so loved the world, that He gave His only begotten Son . . ." To know that God loves me and that He gave His only Son for me gives me the ability to believe in a God of love.

Devotional author Brennan Manning so insightfully said: "The temptation of the age is to look good without being good."[523] While everything looks good on the outside, we have a war waging on the inside. And no one knows about it.

How can I get free? How can I be healed? I heard someone say once, "If you want to be forgiven, confess your sins to God. But if you want to be healed, confess your sins to each other." James 5:16 is not only a powerful healing verse, but it is one of the most misquoted verses in the entire New Testament.

Let me give you the *misquote* first: "The effective prayer of a righteous man can accomplish much." I have heard this verse all my life in the church during prayer meetings. The problem is that those who said it chopped it in half. And when they did, it didn't quite work the way it's supposed to. This verse is not a prayer meeting verse, it's a healing verse.

Here is the actual: Confess your sins to one another, and pray for one another so that you may be healed. The effective prayer of a righteous man can accomplish much."

Just saying part B makes me the subject of the statement that righteous people praying get things done. But that is not what James was saying. He is telling me that I am not the righteous man. I am the struggling man in this verse.

James was challenging the church to transparency and confession of our struggle. And here was the challenge: if we can connect transparency with a righteous praying person, then healing is close by.

James was really clear on who we are to be honest with. The person we pick to come clean with is not necessarily our buddy, or our BFF. It could be . . . *only* if they are a godly person who knows how to pray and get answers from God. For my healing and freedom, I don't need you to know me, I need you to know God.

When James says, "Confess your faults one to another," two things are happening. First, he is creating humility in you and me and keeping sin in the open so it does not grow. Sin incubates in darkness. Sin grows in secrecy. There is no healing in hiding. And second, who we confess to is huge. He says the person we confess to better be able to pray. Get a praying righteous person.

For freedom, I need someone who is walking with God, not someone with a counseling degree. I don't care what your plaque or diploma says. The question on the floor is, "Are you a righteous person and are you a praying person?"

Here's a challenge for you today: Do you have someone in your life who meets the criteria of the second part of this verse? Your healing is connected to this important relationship.

Look for people who pray—not simply those who golf or do what you do. It's okay to find common denominators with friends. But friends don't necessarily mean this is your James 5:16- part-B relationship. When you meet someone who has a prayer life, latch on to them and meet with them. I would ask them to pray for you.

The words of pastor and theologian Dietrich Bonhoeffer are powerful as he speaks about confession of a struggle to a brother:

> A man who confesses his sins in the presence of a brother knows that he is no longer alone with himself; he experiences the presence of God in the reality of the other person. As long as I am by myself in the confession of my sins everything remains in the dark, but in the presence of a brother the sin has to be brought into the light.[524]

The mark of a healthy body is the ability to heal itself. The church is called the body of Christ. There are hurdles, struggles, and problems we all have that we can address and deal with when we have the right relationships in our lives. And James 5:16 tells us what our criteria must be for healing to come.

Let me date myself. I grew up with a television that started with a black screen and a dot that grew into the picture. We had a thing on top of the television set called rabbit ears, which was the antenna. There was no remote. To change the channels between the nine stations we got, the set had a dial, which many times we lost so we had to use pliers to turn the channels.

Boy, televisions have changed today. They are the size of a picture on your wall. And the clarity—they call it high def, 4K now. Every drop of sweat, the wrinkles in the skin, nothing is hidden. Just as high-definition (HD) television illuminates the blemishes and imperfections of those appearing on screen, living a high-definition life can expose both our strengths and weaknesses. And yet something liberates us when we go HD.

A revival started in the early church, because people went high def and confessed to one another: "Many of those who believed now came and openly confessed what they had done. A number who had practiced sorcery brought their scrolls together and burned them publicly. . . . In this way the word of the Lord spread widely and grew in power" (Acts 19:18-20, NIV).

The honesty of the saved challenged those in the occult. And transparency and confession started a revival.

I'm too exhausted to pretend. It takes too much work to pretend to be something I'm not. I don't have that kind of energy to be impressive. I just have enough energy to be real.

Confession is vulnerability and transparency. It tells everyone, *I'm on the team; I'm a fellow struggler and fighter just like you*. It's what makes us real. It allows us to tell others, "You have mistaken what the church really is. It's not a museum or a hall of fame. It is a hospital with a lot of sick people getting better. And you are looking at one of them."

Day 223

Precious Is a Rare Word

Today's Reading: 1 Peter 1

Seventeenth-century evangelist John Wesley was returning home from a service one night when he was robbed. Unfortunately for the thief, Wesley had only very little money and some Christian literature. As the robber turned to leave, Wesley said, "Stop! I have something more to give you." The surprised robber paused. "My friend," said Wesley, "you may live to regret this sort of life. If you ever do, here's something to remember: 'The blood of Jesus Christ cleanses us from all sin!'" The thief hurried away, and Wesley prayed for the man.

Years later, after a Sunday service, a man approached him. It was the robber! Only now he was a believer in Christ and a successful businessman. "I owe it all to you," said the man. "Oh no, my friend," Wesley said. "Not to me, but to the precious blood of Christ that cleanses us from all sin!"[525]

The word *precious* is not used of common things. We use it today when we are dealing with metals and stones. We refer to diamonds, rubies, sapphires, and emeralds as precious stones. And gold, platinum, and silver are our precious metals. They are precious because they are rare.

The Bible uses this word *precious* sparingly. There are only four things called precious in the Bible, and we find all of them in Peter's epistles: precious cornerstone (1 Peter 2:6); precious blood of Jesus (1 Peter 1:19); precious faith (2 Peter 1:1); and precious promises (2 Peter 1:4).

In today's chapter we focus on the precious blood of Jesus. Here are Peter's words to remind us of the power of the blood of Jesus and why it is precious to us as believers:

> You know that your lives were ransomed once and for all from the empty and futile way of life handed down from generation to generation. It was not a ransom payment of silver and gold, which eventually perishes, but the precious blood of Christ—who like a spotless, unblemished lamb was *sacrificed for us.*
>
> *This was part of God's plan*, for he was chosen and destined for

578

this before the foundation of the earth was laid, but he has been made manifest in these last days for you. It is through him that you now believe in God, who raised him from the dead and glorified him, so that you would fasten your faith and hope in God *alone*. (1 Peter 1:18-21, TPT)

The blood of Jesus does two things—and these are two big theological words—*expiation* and *propitiation*. Sometimes called atonement, *expiation* is what the blood does for us (it washes away our sin). Whereas *propitiation*, sometimes called satisfaction, is what the blood does for God (it turns away His wrath from us because the blood of His Son satisfies His justice).

R. T. Kendall explains it well: "Charles Spurgeon used to say there are two words you need in your theological vocabulary: "substitution" and "satisfaction." There is no gospel apart from these two concepts."[526] Jesus acted as our substitute. Substitution is that Jesus literally did everything on our behalf by His keeping the law for us and dying for us. This is why we put all our hope on Jesus and His death. And satisfaction means that God's justice has been completely and eternally satisfied by what Jesus did for us when He shed His blood.

Why is the blood of Jesus precious to us? "Eternally speaking, there are two ways whereby God punishes sin: the fires of hell and the blood of Jesus," R. T. Kendall says. "It's not a question of whether your sin will be punished; it's a question of how."[527] The blood of Jesus redeems you and me—not our hard work, not our tears, not our promises. The blood of Jesus is what God sees over our lives.

The story goes that reformer Martin Luther had a dream one night in which Satan visited him and began attacking him. Satan unrolled a long scroll, which held on it a list of Luther's sins, and showed it to him. Luther looked over the list, got to the end, and said, "Is that all?"

"No," said the devil, and produced a second scroll. And then a third.

After looking over all of his sins, Luther said, "You've forgotten something. Quickly write on each of them, 'The blood of Jesus Christ God's Son cleanses us from all sins!'" Satan, defeated, howled in protested and disappeared.[528]

When you are wondering if you have been really forgiven of your sin, you always have to go back to the blood Jesus. His blood was enough to satisfy God. When you doubt your salvation, you are putting the blood on trial.

Consider this powerful story about putting the blood on trial:

One night in a church service a young woman felt the tug of God at her heart. She responded to God's call and accepted Jesus as her Lord and Savior. The young woman had a very rough past, involving alcohol, drugs, and prostitution. But, the change in her was evident. As time went on, she became a faithful member of the church. She eventually became involved in the ministry, teaching young children. It was not very long until this faithful young woman had caught the eye and heart of the pastor's son. The relationship grew and they began to make wedding plans. This is when the problems began.

You see, about one half of the church did not think that a woman with a past such as hers was suitable for a pastor's son. The church began to argue and fight about the matter. So they decided to have a meeting. As the people made their arguments and tensions increased, the meeting was getting completely out of hand. The young woman became very upset about all the things being brought up about her past.

As she began to cry the pastor's son stood to speak. He could not bear the pain it was causing his wife to be. He began to speak and his statement was this: "My fiancée's past is not what is on trial here. What you are questioning is the ability of the blood of Jesus to wash away sin. Today you have put the blood of Jesus on trial. So, does it wash away sin or not?" The whole church began to weep as they realized that they had been slandering the blood of the Lord Jesus Christ. . . . If the blood of Jesus does not cleanse the other person completely then it cannot cleanse us completely. If that is the case, then we are all in a lot of trouble.[529]

What can wash away our sins? Nothing but the blood of Jesus. End of case!

Me Before DC

Today's Reading: 1 Peter 2

The people to whom Peter wrote the letters of 1 and 2 Peter were believers experiencing severe persecution under the reign and government of the Roman emperor Nero. Nero was a psycho and afflicted these believers with horrendous acts of evil. He threw women and children into the Coliseum for sport to be torn apart by lions. He impaled believers on stakes and burned them as human torches to light up his decadent evening parties. In fact, not long after Peter wrote his second letter, tradition states that Nero had him crucified upside down.

Martyrdom was not just a first-century problem, but is still happening today. According to the World Evangelical Alliance, more than 200 million Christians in at least 60 countries are denied fundamental human rights solely because of their faith.[530] Some estimates show that approximately 175,000 Christians have been martyred annually within only a few years, and if those trends continue, by 2025, an average of 210,000 Christians will be martyred annually.[531]

In his first letter, Peter wasn't just writing to the Christians but to Christians under heavy persecution from Nero. They were under a very oppressive government that was taking their lives because of their faith in Christ. And yet when Peter talks about getting rid of things, he isn't referring to Nero and his government but getting rid of stuff within each of us individually. This is so revealing of our society today. We want to rid our society of liberals or conservatives. Whatever side of the political aisle you sit on matters not, according to 1 Peter. For us today, Peter is sending a message to all of the church: *me before DC*.

While people are trying to get rid of politicians, we have forgotten to deal with ourselves. If Peter were alive today and living in America, he'd say, "You want to know corruption? Try living under Nero." Here is what Peter said in the midst of his horrible and dangerous first-century political landscape:

> Therefore, rid yourselves of all malice and all deceit, hypocrisy, envy, and slander of every kind. Like newborn babies, crave pure spiritual

milk, so that by it you may grow up in your salvation, now that you have tasted that the Lord is good. (1 Peter 2:1-3, NIV)

The first word of chapter 2 is *therefore*. Whenever we see "therefore," we need to ask, "What is it there for?" It should always make us go backward in Scripture. If you look at 1 Peter, chapters 2, 4, and 5 all begin with "therefore." We can't read the first verse of these chapters without the context of what came before it. For 2:1 to make sense, we have to read 1:17-25. The person "ridding themselves" here is a Christian, not a non-Christian trying to become a Christian.

Listen closely: You don't get rid of stuff to become a Christian. You get rid of stuff after you are a Christian. Once you become a Christian, you can't stay the same, as there must be growth.

In *God in the Dock*, C. S. Lewis was asked, "Are there any unmistakable outward signs in a person surrendered to God?" Lewis' response was epic. He said, "Take the case of a sour old maid, who is a Christian, but cantankerous. On the other hand, take some pleasant and popular fellow, but who has never been to Church. Who knows how much more cantankerous the old maid might be if she were *not* a Christian, and how much more likeable the nice fellow might be if he *were* a Christian?"[532]

Christianity is growth not perfection. I don't become a Christian and become perfect. I become a Christian and start growing.

I remember having the conversation with a Muslim husband whose wife just became a Christian and she was attending our church. He came to see me and was telling me that she was not a real Christian because she still had specific hang-ups in her life. I told this husband that becoming a Christian is the starting line, not the finish line.

We don't get good and come to Jesus. We come to Jesus and He makes us good.

Peter is telling you and me to get rid of malice, deceit, envy, and slander—not in DC but in you and me. We are on unbiblical ground when we want our politicians rid of slander, deceit, and hypocrisy but never deal with it in ourselves. The political climate today is not calling for impeachment but for introspection. Before we judge our leaders, let us judge ourselves on these matters. That's how Peter was. Peter was harsher on himself then he was on Nero's government. Although later in chapter 2 Peter *does* say something about our response to rotten politicians:

Make the Master proud of you by being good citizens. Respect the authorities, whatever their level; they are God's emissaries for keeping order. It is God's will that by doing good, you might cure the ignorance of the fools who think you're a danger to society. Exercise your freedom by serving God, not by breaking the rules. Treat everyone you meet with dignity. Love your spiritual family. Revere God. Respect the government. (1 Peter 2:13-17, MSG)

Unbelievable. Did you just hear what Peter said about the corruption of Rome? Respect the government. Respect the authorities. Any corruption you see today can't even compare to the corruption Peter and the early church were living under. And these are Peter's challenging words to us: respect them. He is sterner and stricter on his own spirit than he is on a rogue emperor. It's almost as if Peter is saying, "If there is a swamp to be drained, it starts with me and it's in me."

Me before DC.

DO YOU WANT TO SEE YOUR FAMILY GET SAVED?

Today's Reading: 1 Peter 3

The story goes that a lady approached Charles Spurgeon and told him that she felt called to the *ministry*. Spurgeon asked about her home and family. When he heard she had thirteen children, he exclaimed, "Well, praise God, not only has He called you to the ministry, but He's given you a congregation as well!"[533]

Our family is our first ministry priority.

But how do you win your family to Christ? Today's chapter is one of the most important sections of the New Testament that gives us brilliant advice on how to win family members to Christ.

But let me first tell you what was happening in the early church. Women were getting saved faster than the men. In fact, the women wrote to Paul in 1 Corinthians 7 asking if they should divorce their husbands since they were saved and their spouses were not. Paul told them, "Not so fast":

> If a woman has a husband who is not a believer and he is content to live with her, she should not divorce him. For the unbelieving husband has been made holy by his believing wife. And the unbelieving wife has been made holy by her believing husband *by virtue of his or her sacred union to a believer.* Otherwise, the children from this union would be unclean, but in fact, they are holy. And wives, for all you know you could one day lead your husband to salvation. Or husbands, how do you know for sure that you could not one day lead your wife to salvation? (1 Corinthians 7:13-16, TPT)

Wives, for all you know you could one day lead your husband to salvation. It seems once Paul got the women to stay with the unsaved spouses Peter stepped in. Here is the strategy he gave to win them to Christ:

> In the same way, you wives, be submissive to your own husbands so that even if any *of them* are disobedient to the word, they may be won

without a word by the behavior of their wives, as they observe your chaste and respectful behavior. (1 Peter 3:1-2)

Peter's advice to the women: stop using words; stop talking.

There comes a time when you must tell yourself, *They have heard the gospel message from me. Now they must see the effects of the gospel through my life and not just through my lips.*

It's time for them to see Christ, not just hear Christ. Preaching the gospel does not just need your voice, it is more powerful when it's shown through the other parts of your body.

I think Peter's words to these women are not just for ladies with unsaved husbands but for anyone with an unsaved family member whom they want to win to the Lord. I love Peter's words: *that they may be won without a word by the behavior of their wives.*

The way a son wins a father . . . the way a daughter wins a grandmother . . . the way a brother wins his sister . . . through behavior! They can watch the life of Christ as it comes through us in our attitudes, our commitments, and our actions.

A. W. Tozer said: "There are those rare Christians whose very presence is an incitement to you to want to be a better Christian."[534] I want to be that rare Christian. I think the same is true for those who are not Christians wanting to become a Christian because someone's life inspired them.

There comes a time that doing the dishes, being home at curfew when asked, respecting the rules of the home, showing wise stewardship over the family finances, and making family a priority preaches more than if you had a preacher in the home.

Peter was giving advice not just to women but to all saved family members who live in the house with unsaved family members. The first words of verse 1 are so important: "In the same way . . ." He was referring us to the verses in 1 Peter 2. The same way as . . . ?

Here is who Peter was referencing:

This is the kind of life you've been invited into, the kind of life Christ lived. He suffered everything that came his way so you would know that it could be done, and also know how to do it, step-by-step. He never did one thing wrong, not once said anything amiss. They called him every name in the book and he said nothing back. He suffered in silence, content to let God set things right. (1 Peter 2:21-23, MSG)

That's his answer: In the same way that Jesus faced the cross is the way we deal with our home life with unsaved family. Our example is Jesus.

Peter said that they can call us names—church boy, holier than thou, fanatic. Even then, we must be quiet with our words and not respond or retaliate. Well, we can retaliate . . . with good behavior, being content as we wait for God to set things straight.

There's a story about Alexander the Great, a great military general. One night during a campaign, restless and unable to sleep, he left his tent and walked around his soldiers' campground. As he wandered around, he came across a soldier on guard duty who had fallen asleep, a very serious offense. One, in fact, that could get him killed.

The soldier awoke as Alexander the Great approached him and immediately recognized who it was.

"Do you know what the penalty is for falling asleep on guard duty?" Alexander the Great asked the soldier.

"Yes, sir," the soldier responded, his voice quivering.

"Soldier, what's your name?" asked Alexander the Great.

"Alexander, sir."

Alexander the Great repeated the question: "*What* is your name?"

"My name is Alexander, sir," the soldier repeated.

A third time and more loudly, Alexander the Great asked, "What is your name?"

A third time the soldier meekly said, "My name is Alexander, sir."

Alexander the Great looked the young man in the eye. "Soldier," he said with intensity, "either change your name or change your conduct."[535]

Let our actions speak loudly of who Jesus is, so our family can see the difference.

THE PART OF FORGIVENESS NO ONE TALKS ABOUT

Today's Reading: 1 Peter 4

C. S. Lewis said, "Everyone thinks forgiveness is a lovely idea, until they have something to forgive."[536] That was certainly true for Corrie ten Boom.

The story is well-known, but I think it's a powerful illustration for us. Corrie and her family hid Jews during the Holocaust. The Nazis found out and put her entire family into the concentration camps, where they all died except Corrie. After World War II and her release, she traveled extensively telling her story and sharing the gospel.

In 1947 she was in Munich speaking about God's forgiveness and she saw a familiar face. It was one of the most cruel guards from the concentration camp she and her sister had been imprisoned in. Though she recognized him, he did not recognize her.

"You mentioned Ravensbruck in your talk," he told her after the service. "I was a guard there. . . . But since that time I have become a Christian. I know that God has forgiven me for the cruel things I did there, but I would like to hear it from your lips as well. Fraulein, will you forgive me?" He thrust his hand out to her.

She stood paralyzed. This man had been a monster; he had filled her with shame and misery every day. How could she preach forgiveness when she was staring into the face of someone she needed to forgive but couldn't. She did the only thing she knew to do, she prayed right there on the spot. *Jesus, help me! I can lift my hand. I can do that much. You supply the feeling*, she prayed silently.

"So woodenly, mechanically, I thrust my hand into the one stretched out to me. And as I did, an incredible thing took place," she said. Power surged through her. "I forgive you, brother!" she said and cried.[537]

When you forgive, you don't change the past but you sure do change the future. As poet William Blake said, "The glory of Christianity is to conquer by forgiveness."[538]

Corrie forgave the man but there is another part of forgiveness that often gets neglected. That part is what we look at in today's chapter. Peter's strategy on forgiving people is one of the most important lessons in relationships: "Above all, keep fervent in your love for one another, because love covers a multitude of sins" (1 Peter 4:8).

Love covers a multitude of sins.

When I am hurt by someone, I have two choices to resolve that hurt. Since forgiveness is not an option for me as a Christian, I have the choice of *how* I will forgive: I can confront it or I can cover it. Remember this about forgiveness: we base it on what God has done for us, not on what another person has done to us. That means, other person's apology, repentance, or admission of wrongdoing is not our motivation. Our forgiveness from God is our motivation. According to Ephesians 4:32, we forgive because we have been forgiven.

Peter wants us to cover the offense. And that fervent love is the prerequisite for that choice. We can't cover an offense because we don't want to confront a person, but we can cover a hurt because we fervently love someone. To cover a hurt is very biblical, meaning that not everything that is hurtful has to be an offense. We don't have to address everything every time we are offended. In fact, I think it's a sign of maturity to let certain things go. There are some things I think God wants us to absorb to show and extend mercy. Why? Because that is the only way to build our mercy account: As Jesus said, "Blessed are the merciful, for they shall receive mercy" (Matthew 5:7). There will come a day when we will need to withdraw from our mercy account and that can only happen if we showed mercy, not simply prayed for mercy.

Proverbs 19:11, NIV says there is honor in covering an offense: "A person's wisdom yields patience; it is to one's glory to overlook an offense."

The greatest people I know are not easily offended. Instead, they practice the habit of overlooking offenses. They take the high road, and give the offender the benefit of the doubt, and then they move on. They are magnanimous—high souled, able to overlook an injury or insult; rising above pettiness or meanness.

But what does having fervent love mean? Peter said that's the way to cover an offense. The word *fervent* is critical in this verse and means the willingness to be stretched out. This kind of hurts to say it, but the word was used of a torture device that would stretch its victims on the rack. Fervent love stretches you beyond your normal capacity.

Covering an offense is not based on the size of the offense but on the size of our heart. And if there is love there, fervent love. Solomon also talked about the concept of love covering an offense: "Love covers all transgressions" (Proverbs 10:12).

There is no chapter that best describes fervent love than 1 Corinthians 13:

Love is very patient and kind, never jealous or envious, never boastful or proud, never haughty or selfish or rude. Love does not demand its own way. It is not irritable or touchy. It does not hold grudges and will hardly even notice when others do it wrong (1 Corinthians 13:4-5, TLB)

What is love? It will hardly even notice when others do wrong. In order to cover an offense, we need love, fervent love, the love that stretches us.

I Don't Want to Be
the Devil's Next Meal

Today's Reading: 1 Peter 5

Puritan writer Thomas Brooks said: "If God were not my friend, Satan would not be so much my enemy."[539] In today's chapter, Peter warns that our enemy, the devil, prowls around us like a lion wanting his next meal: "Be of sober *spirit*, be on the alert. Your adversary, the devil, prowls around like a roaring lion, seeking someone to devour" [1 Peter 5:8]. Satan seeking to devour means he is on a mission to take down God's children.

There is a Bible study tool called "The law of first use." It can be a valuable tool when studying a topic in the Bible. It works by looking at the first time a word is used in the Scripture to see how it is used. If we applied it to *devil*, we'd find it first appears in Genesis 3. And the first thing the Bible ever says about the devil is this: "The serpent was the shrewdest of all the wild animals the Lord God had made" [verse 1, NLT]. This means that Satan is shrewd in Operation Devour. He shrewdly finds ways to devour people. Another Puritan writer, William Jenkyn said it like this: "He hath an apple for Eve, a grape for Noah, a change of raiment for Gehazi, a bag for Judas. He can dish out his meat for all palates."[540]

I do not want to be the devil's next meal.

I have learned some interesting things about lions when they are on the hunt to devour. We can learn some of Satan's tactics, since Peter describes the devil as a lion. Or as Paul says, "We are not ignorant of his devices" [2 Corinthians 2:11, NKJV]. for a hunt to be successful, a lion must first stalk close while undetected and then attack with a rush before the surprised prey has a chance to flee. A lion's prey know that a visible lion is a safe lion, because they are too slow to catch an animal alert to its presence. A herd of gazelle will allow a lion to walk past them at only a hundred feet away!

A second way lions hunt is that they catch whatever is easiest! They often kill the very young, sick, old, or the careless.

And finally, as Robert Simmons observed, "when the fire goes out, the lions move in."[541] When the fire of a camp goes out at night, this is a lion's signal to move in to devour its prey. Simmons tells the story of a doctor and his wife had traveled to the jungle in Africa. After a long flight from America and a full day of birdwatching and photography, they went to bed in their tent with a campfire outside. They had been warned to keep logs on the fire all night or the lions would come in. The fire was blazing hot when they fell into such a deep sleep that they failed to notice when the fire became smoldering embers. Under the guise of darkness, a lioness stuck her head into the tent and killed the doctor's wife.[542]

One of the ways we keep from becoming the devil's next meal is by keeping our hearts on fire for God. Remember in Luke 24:32 when the two men on the road to Emmaus realized, "Were not *our hearts burning* within us while He was speaking to us on the road, while He was explaining the Scriptures to us?" (emphasis added). Our hearts will stay on fire as God speaks to us through His Word. Every time we open God's Word, it's like putting another log on the fire.

Finally, when does the devil devour? Again Robert Simmons offers his insight: "Where stragglers roam, lions feed." These are animals out grazing alone. He says:

> In Africa, lions will lay out watching herds. Lions know their own strength, but he also knows the strength of numbers. When he looks at a herd of zebras, he knows if he attacks one and the herd stampedes, they would trample him. When he sees one rebelliously remove himself and independently feed away from the herd, that can be his next meal. When that zebra gets far enough away from the pack, the lion pounces, pulls it into the tall grass, goes for the jugular, and has begun eating the meat, before the herd even knew what happened. Stay in the strength of fellowship. Don't be a straggler and remove yourself from family of God. The lion is watching.[543]

One of the most powerful books on how Satan attacks the believers is called *The Screwtape Letters* by C. S. Lewis, which is the elaboration of the 1 Peter 5:8 passage. When Lewis wrote the book, he wrote it from the standpoint of the devil. There are three characters in the book. Screwtape is the senior demon training his young apprentice demon, Wormwood, on how to tempt a Christian. It was really a lesson in devouring. When Screwtape talks about the Enemy, he is referring to God. Every chapter are letters in the devilish art of devouring and making Christians fall and fail. The demon letters exchanged are haunting and accurate:

My dear Wormwood, . . .

All extremes, except extreme devotion to the Enemy, are to be encouraged. . . . A moderated religion is as good for us as no religion at all—and more amusing. . . . The safest road to Hell is the gradual one— the gentle slope, soft underfoot, without sudden turnings, without milestones, without signposts. . . . Surely you know that if a man can't be cured of churchgoing, the next best thing is to send him all over the neighbourhood looking for the church that "suits" him until he becomes a taster or connoisseur of churches. . . . The search for a "suitable" church makes the man a critic where the Enemy wants him to be a pupil.[544]

Wow, that is sobering. In fact, Peter said to *be sober*, and these devil words make me sober.

We are in a battle, but with God it's a battle we can win.

Day 228

NO KNOCKOFFS

Today's Reading: 2 Peter 1

A young man was at the zebra enclosure at the Cairo International Garden municipal park and noticed something wrong about the zebras. When he took a closer look he became convinced that the animals being touted as zebras were actually donkeys painted to look like zebras. He took a photo and posted his accusation on Facebook.

The photo gained the attention of a local news team, who contacted a veterinarian, who claimed that zebra snouts are usually black, and their stripes are more consistent and uniform compared to the striping on the animal in the photo, which also sported black smudging around the face. A zoo in Gaza also received similar accusations of donkey-painting in 2009. The zoo claimed they did it because of an Israeli blockade that prevented the zoo from purchasing actual zebras.[545]

Do you know what a knockoff is? It's the counterfeit of an expensive brand of anything. There are knockoff watches, pens, purses, sunglasses, almost anything. They have the same markings and the same logo and the same colors but they are the cheap versions of designer pieces. You buy them on the street instead of in the store. A knockoff Rolex is about $15. A knockoff Montblanc pen is about $10. A knockoff Coach purse is about $25. The knockoff has the same outward markings but lacks the craftsmanship. Knockoffs are exposed by time and use.

If it's real, it lasts.

If it's real, it can endure.

If it's real, you'll know it, because it doesn't diminish even when it faces harsh circumstances.

In today's chapter, Peter has something significant to say about the real thing. He starts off with comparing his faith and the new church's faith, which is separated by decades: "Simon Peter, a bond-servant and apostle of Jesus Christ, to those who have received a faith of the same kind as ours, by the righteousness of our God and Savior, Jesus Christ" (2 Peter 1:1).

He is writing to Christians who "received a faith of the same kind as ours." These words are significant. This epistle was written in AD 68, and Peter's time with Jesus was in the late AD 20s. Some forty years later, Peter makes this bombshell statement—that these believers' faith is the same kind as his. Think of this. He is telling them that they have the real thing, not some knockoff or second-rate faith." Think too of who is saying this. It is someone who talked with Jesus, saw His miracles, witnessed the transfiguration (Peter speaks about that at the end of this chapter), saw Christ die, saw Him after He rose again, ate a fish dinner with Him, and saw Jesus taken up in the ascension. And he tells these Christians forty years later that their faith in Jesus and his faith in Jesus is the same!

When I was a student at Baylor University, I did not have a lot of spending money. My father sent me $75 a month. I remember all these students walking around campus with Ralph Lauren Polos, and I desperately wanted one. The problem was that I did not have $32 to buy one. Then one day I saw a guy selling knockoff Polos on a street corner in Waco, Texas. They were only $5.

Now I get to be like everyone else, I thought, as I forked over $5 for a knockoff purple Polo. I noticed that the rider of the horse and the horse itself were slightly detached, but hey, it was only $5! I wore my Polo *one day* and then washed it. It went from a Large to a 2T. The wash shrunk it.

When it's real, it lasts. When it's real, time is not an enemy, it is a revealer.

Peter's and these Christians' faith are real. It can go through hard times, denial times (Peter knows about that), scared and cowardly times (Peter knows about that), and still come out the same. Hard times, harsh circumstances, persecution, tribulation—none of these will be able to take away that faith when it's real. And if anyone should know, it's Peter.

Peter knows it's the same, because these Christians are going through the persecutions of Nero. They are faced with death and yet their faith stays intact. That's the same kind of faith.

Two thousand years later, the faith that you and I have in Jesus Christ is the same as the apostle Peter's in the first century. Time doesn't shrink it or change it, it just reveals if it's real. We have a real faith that can and has stood the test of time.

No knockoff. We have the real thing.

We don't have to paint the donkeys, we've got the real zebras. We've got real faith.

RESCUED FROM BAD DECISIONS

Today's Reading: 2 Peter 2

"Y ou made your bed, now lie in it. Have you heard this phrase? It means, you made that decision, now you have to deal with its consequences." That is true if it weren't for the grace of God.

Today's chapter brings back Old Testament stories to the reader. Peter speaks about Noah, Sodom and Gomorrah, Balaam, and the character he introduces with an adjective I would never assign to him, righteous Lot. Not Lot, but *righteous* Lot:

> *If* He rescued righteous Lot, oppressed by the sensual conduct of unprincipled men (for by what he saw and heard *that* righteous man, while living among them, felt *his* righteous soul tormented day after day by *their* lawless deeds), *then* the Lord knows how to rescue the godly from temptation. (2 Peter 2:7-9)

When I read the story of Lot, I don't see him as righteous. Thank God I'm not God. I judge people too fast. It's easy to assign adjectives to people who God never sees and believes about them. The part of this verse that puzzles me about God, though, is that Lot is called righteous and God rescues him. But Peter explains and tells us why it's important to us.

He says that God rescued righteous Lot from Sodom and Gomorrah. Lot was being oppressed by the sensual conduct of unprincipled men. You might think, *This is a godly brother who got stuck in a really bad neighborhood that God had to burn down with fire from heaven.*

Not even close to the truth.

Lot *chose* to live in Sodom. Sodom was his *first* choice when Abraham, his uncle, said he could have any part of the land he wanted. Lot not only chose Sodom, but Genesis says, "He sat in the gate at Sodom" (Genesis 19:1, KJV). That means he was part of the government of the city. And despite all this, God showed off His graciousness by rescuing him from his really bad choice.

God didn't rescue a man who had something unfortunate happen to him. God rescued a man who made a really stupid decision. How many of us have made a bad decision before? How many of us are so thankful for the grace of God?

Nineteenth-century Bible teacher J. Wilbur Chapman said: "Anything that dims my vision of Christ, or takes away my taste for Bible study, or cramps me in my prayer life, or makes Christian work difficult, is wrong for me, and I must, as a Christian, turn away from it."[546]

Lot didn't think that way. And if we are honest, you and I have made decisions that violated Chapman's grid. So many times God rescues us before we are swallowed by our poor choices and decisions.

There are also times that God just vetoes bad decisions—in this case, bad prayers. One of the biggest atheists over the centuries was Robert Ingersoll. At a lecture, he opened his pocket watch for all the students to see and say, "I will give God five minutes to strike me dead for the things I said." When the five minutes were over, he shut the watch and said, "God did not retaliate because God does not exist." When evangelist Joseph Parker heard about the incident, he responded, "And did the gentleman think he could exhaust the patience of eternal God in five minutes?"[547]

God is bigger than our threats. Because God is love, God is patient. And because God is love and patient with us, He calls Lot righteous. Righteous has nothing to do with our perfection but with God's view of us. I can be the righteousness of God in Christ and an idiot at the same time.

I think many would think Lot should have perished in the fire of Sodom, but not God. Peter reminds us that God knows how to rescue the godly. Even if rescue means dragging a man out of danger when he is dragging his feet with no urgency. That was Lot's story during God's rescue plan. No gratitude from Lot, just an amazing gracious God rescuing.

After a wedding, the newlyweds contacted one of the guests to inform her that her present wasn't generous enough. The unnamed guest posted to a forum asking for advice after she was told her cash gift wasn't enough. She revealed how the couple, who had asked for cash gifts, had emailed to say, "We were surprised that your contribution didn't seem to match the warmth of your good wishes on our big day. In view of your own position, if you wanted to send any adjustment it would be thankfully received." The wedding guest assumed that the reference to her position was in regard to a recent inheritance she'd received.[548]

One thing you will never be able to say to God is, "I am surprised by your contribution, God. I suggest an adjustment."

When it comes to what we don't deserve, God gives crazy generous mercy and grace every day to us—even when we do stupid things. We need no adjustment from Him. Just a grateful heart because He rescues people when they make *really* bad decisions. Righteous Lot is amazing proof.

Be Careful Who You Hang With

Today's Reading: 2 Peter 3

A pastor was walking down a row of fine old Victorian homes in his neighborhood on a cold day when he spotted a young boy on the front porch of one of those homes. The old-fashioned doorbell was set high in the door, and the little fellow was too short to ring it despite his leaping attempts. Feeling sorry for the youngster, the pastor stepped up onto the porch and vigorously rang the bell for him. "And now what, young man?" inquired the minister. "Now," exclaimed the boy, "we run like crazy!"[549]

When I was a kid we used to call that "ring and run."

We have to be careful who we hang out with, because their issues may become our issues. What that pastor thought was just a kind deed for a little boy was actually making him an accessory to his mischief.

In today's chapter, Peter is appealing for us to grow but also connecting our growth to whom we are in relationship with:

> You therefore, beloved, knowing this beforehand, be on your guard so that you are not carried away by the error of unprincipled men and fall from your own steadfastness, but grow in the grace and knowledge of our Lord and Savior Jesus Christ. To Him *be* the glory, both now and to the day of eternity. Amen. (2 Peter 3:17-18)

One of the hardest decisions you will face in life is choosing whether to walk away or to try harder in a relationship. In verse 17, Peter is giving the green light for walking away so these new Christians don't fall from their own steadfastness. The Contemporary English Version says, "Don't let the errors of evil people lead you down the wrong path and make you lose your balance." You find firm ground and footing in your Christian life. If there is one thing that can knock you off your consistency, it is a poor relationship. Peter says unprincipled men can stunt your growth. That's why Peter warns about the negative influence of a relationship.

I remember this illustration from my youth group when I was growing up.

Our youth pastor put someone on top of a chair and someone down below him. He asked us, "Which is easier, for the person on the chair to pull the other up or for the person on the ground to pull him down?" The answer is easy. It is much easier for the person in the lower position to pull down the other than the person in the high position to pull the lower person up to where he is.

This is exactly what Peter is saying. You have those very same people in verse 17. And Peter is saying that we can lose our steadfastness if we don't let go of the unprincipled people in our lives, because they will pull us down.

There's an old but powerful visual illustration to this idea that says, "If you drop a white glove into the mud, the glove will get muddy but the mud will never glovey."[550]

Peter wants us to stay white and pure. As George Washington once wrote, "Associate yourself with Men of good Quality if you Esteem your own Reputation; for 'tis better to be alone than in bad Company."[551] Or consider William Gladstone's observation, "Choose wisely your companions, for a young man's companions, more than his food or clothes, his home or his parents, make him what he is."[552]

A relationship with two opposite people—one wanting to grow in God and the other living for themselves—is the recipe for two people living for themselves. There is an asterisk to this principle, which is given to us in 1 Corinthians 7, and which I have to make clear. This is not an approval for a divorce if one of the spouses is not a Christian. In fact, Paul is really clear that if you have a believer and an unbeliever married, God says He will let the believer be the principle influencer in that relationship and even protect the children. But when it comes to *friendships*, be careful and understand the unprincipled lives of others can have an adverse effect on you.

Have you ever thought about all the wonderful things you can do with apples? Of course, you can just eat them plain! But you can make juice, sauce, butter, pies . . . And if you keep them in a cool place, they can stay fresh for a month or more. But one thing can reverse the longevity of fresh apples—a rotten apple. All it takes is for one rotten apple to touch a fresh apple, and that fresh apple will turn rotten too. And if you have a bushel of apples, imaging how quickly the rot can spread? Before you know it, the entire basket of apples will be rotten—just because it started with that one rotten apple in here.[553]

You heard the statement, "One bad apple can spoil the whole bunch"?

Peter is really warning us about having bad apples in our circle of friends, or should I say, basket of friends.

Day 231

THE PREREQUISITE TO
A GREAT RELATIONSHIP

Today's Reading: 1 John 1

My wife and I have been married for more than two decades, and what she told me at the beginning of our marriage was both genius and biblical. Cindy said to me, "I will never complain or fight you on the amount of time you spend in the Word and in prayer. Because when you pray and read the Bible, you are a better husband, a better father, a better pastor, and a better man." My wife is a very wise woman.

Cindy and the apostle John give us the prerequisite for great relationships. Here's how John puts it: "If we keep living in the pure light that surrounds him, we share *unbroken* fellowship with one another, and the blood of Jesus, his Son, continually cleanses us from all sin" (1 John 1:7, TPT).

Fellowship with one another.

The word *fellowship* is a strong relationship word in the Bible. The word itself means "to share" and "to be in partnership with." Real fellowship is walking in agreement and in the same direction. In *The Living Church,* pastor and writer, John R. W. Stott provides the three components of true Christian fellowship: our common inheritance, our common service, and our mutual responsibility.[554]

Where does this fellowship start?

This is important: our fellowship with people is contingent on our walk with God. In order for there to be fellowship, according to 1 John 1:7, there must be light and blood. The light keeps everything open and accountable; the blood keeps everything forgivable if there is a sin encounter. When Cindy was urging me to my knees and the Bible, she was protecting our fellowship as husband and wife. There is no healthy thriving relationship without light and blood. We need light and blood to deal with sin, because sin is the corrupter of all relationships, starting with the most important one, with God.

Why is sin damaging to all relationships? Sin alters all relationships. The essence of sin is selfishness. It's always "me and mine" first, where God, who is without sin, thinks of you and me first.

In *Why Prayers Are Unanswered*, John A. Lavender retells a story about Norman Vincent Peale. When Peale was a boy, he found a cigar, so he slipped into an alley and lit up. It didn't taste very good, but it made him feel very grown up—until he spotted his father coming toward him. Knowing he'd get into trouble if his father caught him smoking, he quickly put the cigar behind his back and tried to act casual. Desperate to divert his father's attention, Norman pointed to a billboard advertising the circus. "Can I go, Dad? Please, let's go when the circus comes to town." His father's reply taught Peale a lesson he never forgot. "Son," he answered quietly but firmly, "never make a petition while at the same time trying to hide a smoldering disobedience."[555]

Light exposes sin. Blood forgives sin.

My walk with Jesus has direct bearing on my fellowship not only with my family but with all people. If I am walking in the light, then I have fellowship, John says.

What does it mean to walk in the light? It is to live a life that is scrutinized by the Spirit and that's open and honest to those around you. When there is no darkness, that means nothing is hidden.

When I am giving marital counseling and seeing that there is a great divide in the relationship between husband and wife, my first question to them is, "Tell me about your devotional life." While the couple is wanting to fix a toilet seat not put down, socks not picked up, and meals not on time, the real issue is light and blood. Inevitably I hear from them both that their time in the Word and prayer is nonexistent—and so is their relationship with each other.

Fellowship with one another is contingent on light that exposes our life, and blood forgives whatever is exposed. And when there is neither in our lives, then there is no healthy relationship in our lives. There is no shared life. There is no walking in agreement.

If we walk in the light as He Himself is in the light, then we have fellowship with one another. What God does in prayer and through His Word is that He gives us a common inheritance, common service, and a mutual responsibility.

In *The Pursuit of God*, A. W. Tozer brilliantly tells us how and why our relationship with God is imperative to healthy relationships:

Has it ever occurred to you that one hundred pianos all tuned to the same fork are automatically tuned to each other? They are of one accord by being tuned, not to each other, but to another standard to which each one must individually bow. So one hundred worshipers met together, each one looking away to Christ, are in heart nearer to each other than they could possibly be, were they to become "unity" conscious and turn their eyes away from God to strive for closer fellowship.[556]

When we walk with God, we walk successfully with each other, because we are tuning our lives to Him.

A Lawyer with an Open-and-Shut Case

Today's Reading: 1 John 2

Author and pastor Tony Evans once said:

> I spilled coffee on my suit pants recently. It did not matter whether I spilled it accidentally or intentionally. It stained my pants. There was a stain and it needed to be cleansed. But I don't let the fact that we have Tide detergent at home, a detergent that removes stains, allow me to dip my pants in coffee every day. I still try to avoid spilling stuff on my pants. No one says that since they have a washing machine and a dry cleaner, I can get as dirty as I want, do they? God knows every now and then coffee is going to spill, and He wants us to know that when it happens, we have a Cleanser. We have a spiritual washing machine. We have the blood of Jesus.[557]

In today's chapter, the apostle John wants to tell us about that spiritual washing machine and the blood of Jesus: "My little children, I am writing these things to you so that you may not sin. And if anyone sins, we have an Advocate with the Father, Jesus Christ the righteous; and He Himself is the propitiation for our sins; and not for ours only, but also for *those of* the whole world" (1 John 2:1-2).

There are two really important words here that every Christian must become familiar with: *advocate* and *propitiation*.

Let's start with *propitiation*. The word is one of the great words of the Bible, even though it appears only four times in the New Testament. The word was used to describe an Old Testament object in the holy of holies called the mercy seat. The mercy seat sat on top of the ark of the covenant with two cherubim. We were all reintroduced to it during *Raiders of the Lost Ark* and it's not in a warehouse in Washington DC nor at Area 51.

In the Old Testament times, the priests would put the blood of the animal sacrifice on top of the mercy seat. The blood on the mercy seat would cover the contents of the ark—the Ten Commandments, which the children of Israel were constantly breaking. Yearly when the priest would go in and ask forgiveness for the sins of the nation of Israel, God would look down and not see the disobedience of man but the blood of the sacrifice. Propitiation was made. That is exactly what Jesus did for us.

That's why *Advocate* is just as important. It was a court word, used of the person who spoke up for the accused. The word means to stand side by side, right next to the other person, the accused. When you are in a court of law and being accused of something, you, as the defendant, don't speak, the lawyer, the advocate, speaks for you. He understands the law and understands the case.

What John is trying to tell us is that when we sin, not if we sin, we have an Advocate, who has an open-and-shut case on our behalf. It's not how good we are or how many successful sinless days we have, it's that our Advocate, Jesus, shows the smoking-gun evidence of why we are innocent: His blood. His shed blood was spilled on our behalf. We don't say a word, because the blood speaks for itself. We are found innocent and propiated at that moment.

Charles Spurgeon tells us why this is beyond the courts of men and for the court of heaven and why being good or moral isn't enough: "Morality may keep you out of jail, but it takes the blood of Jesus Christ to keep you out of hell."[558] Like the old hymn says, "What can wash away my sin? Nothing but the blood of Jesus. What can make me whole again? Nothing but the blood of Jesus."[559]

As a Christian I am not sinless, but when I become a Christian, I will *sin less* and less. But I still sin and need something to fall on and into. We fall into our great Advocate, Jesus. After we get saved, we must not forget our greatest safety device, the blood of Jesus. We have an Advocate and that Advocate has an open-and-shut case. The best thing we can do is to keep our mouth shuts and let Him present that case to God on our behalf.

BETWEEN NOW AND KNOW

Today's Reading: 1 John 3

One of the greatest thrills for any violinist is to play a Stradivarius. Named for their creator, Antonio Stradivari, meticulously handcrafted these rare violins, which produce an amazing sound. So you can imagine the excitement of acclaimed British violinist Peter Cropper when, in 1981, London's Royal Academy of Music offered him a 258-year-old Stradivarius to play during a series of concerts.

But then the unimaginable happened. As Cropper walked onto the stage during a concert, he tripped and fell on the violin, breaking off the neck. Forget being embarrassed—he'd just destroyed a priceless masterpiece!

Cropper was inconsolable about what he'd done, and vowed to do whatever he could to make it right. He took the violin to a master craftsman in the vain hope that he might be able to fix it. A miracle happened, and the craftsman was able to repair it. In fact, he repaired it so perfectly that the break was undetectable—and the sound was exquisite.

The Academy was gracious enough to allow him to continue using the rare instrument. And for the remainder of the concert series, as Cropper played, he was reminded of the fact that what he once thought irreparably damaged had been fully restored by the hand of a Master craftsman.[560]

Our lives are the continual repair by the Master. That repair work has a name: sanctification. And one day, these broken lives will be a Stradivarius to God. Sanctification is what happens between *now and know*, between being born again and Jesus' coming again.

Here's what 1 John 3 says about *now and know*: "Beloved, now we are children of God, and it has not appeared as yet what we will be. We know that when He appears, we will be like Him, because we will see Him just as He is" (verse 2).

Now is the condition we are in presently. The broken violin. Broken by sin.

The *Know*—that's the end, when all the repairs are done and we will be like Jesus.

In between? That's the repair process called sanctification. We can compare the process of sanctification to an iceberg, which is almost 90 percent under water. As the sun shines on the iceberg, the exposed part melts, moving the lower part upward. In the same way, we are usually aware of only a small part of our sinfulness and need, which is all we can deal with at any one time. However, as the light of God's work in our lives changes us in the areas we know about, we become aware of new areas needing His work.

So put simply, sanctification is God's continual working on me, getting me closer to looking like Jesus. It's a good work, but it isn't an easy work. As D. L. Moody once said, "I've had more trouble with D. L. Moody than any other man I know."[561]

Devotional writer of the classic *My Utmost for His Highest*, Oswald Chambers said this about sanctification: "[Sanctification] will cause an intense narrowing of all our interests on earth, and an immense broadening of all our interests in God. Sanctification means intense concentration on God's point of view. It means every power of body, soul, and spirit chained and kept for God's purpose only."[562]

And F. F. Bruce speaks about the work of sanctification between now and know as imperative: "Those who have been justified are now being sanctified; those who have no experience of present sanctification have no reason to suppose they have been justified."[563]

Nineteenth-century writer J. C. Ryle even takes it to new level when he says: "The faith which has not a sanctifying influence on the character is no better than the faith of devils. It is a 'dead faith, because it is alone.'"[564]

My favorite book of the C. S. Lewis's Chronicles of Narnia series has always been *The Voyage of the Dawn Treader*. At one point in the book, the irritating antagonist Eustace Scrubb turned into a dragon because of his greed. But later we see Aslan the lion change him back to a boy. It is one of the most moving pieces of the Lewis stories—it made me literally cry. It is the perfect description of sanctification—the picture of the Lion of Judah scrapping those darn dragon scales off of us making us like children again. It's a powerful description between now and know:

> One night Eustace the dragon met a mysterious lion. The lion challenged him to "undress," to try to take off his dragon skin. He managed to peel off a layer but found he was still a dragon underneath. He tried repeatedly but made no further progress. The lion finally said: "You will have to let me undress you."
>
> I was afraid of his claws, I can tell you, but I was pretty nearly desperate now. So I just lay flat down on my back to let him do it. The

very first tear he made was so deep that I thought it had gone right into my heart. And when he had begun pulling the skin off, it hurt worse than anything I've ever felt. . . . Well, he peeled the beastly stuff right off—just as I thought I had done it myself the other three times, only they hadn't hurt—and there it was lying on the grass: only ever so much thicker, and darker, and more knobbly-looking than the others had been. And there was I as smooth and soft as a peeled switch and smaller than I had been . . . I had turned into a boy again.[565]

Sanctification is more than Christ's work for us, it is also the Spirit's work in us right *now*. And when that work is done, we *know* . . . we will be His Stradivarius.

Day 234

FIGHTING FEAR!

Today's Reading: 1 John 4

For many years when researchers asked Americans about their top fears, here is how Americans responded:

Their number 1 fear: public speaking.

Their number 2: death.[566]

Think of it. People would rather die than speak in front of people. That's especially an issue for Christians, because Christianity is very vocal: vocal in praise, vocal in witnessing, vocal in preaching. It's tough to be a silent Christian.

Fortunately, 1 John 4 provides an antidote, a simple prescription, to fighting fear: "There is no fear in love; but perfect love casts out fear, because fear involves punishment, and the one who fears is not perfected in love" (verse 18).

Perfect love casts out fear.

I don't cast out fear "in the name of Jesus." I don't bind it. Fear is removed by displacement. *Love* removes fear. Love casts it out, not me.

Fear is actually a love problem.

Two explorers were on a jungle safari when suddenly a ferocious lion jumped in front of them. "Keep calm," the first explorer whispered. "Remember what we read in that book on wild animals? If you stand perfectly still and look the lion in the eye, he will turn and run."

"Sure," replied his companion. "You've read the book, and I've read the book. But has the lion read the book?"[567]

Reading books and going to counseling does not seem to deal with fear when the lion is looking you right in the eye. But John says love fixes fear.

When I am afraid to speak to someone about Jesus, the truth is, I don't love them. In fact, I love me and my security and what that person thinks about me more than I love that person and their future and eternity! What an indictment.

The same is true when we have to correct someone. Think of it from a parent standpoint. If I refuse to correct my son or daughter, knowing their attitude or behavior is destructive, I am saying my refusal is because of fear, which is a love issue. I love being their friend more than their parent. I love keeping calm in my house. I love my peace and quiet, so I say nothing.

How about worship? When the Bible instructs me to lift holy hands and I just can't do it because I am self-conscious, isn't that fear? Fear of what others think of me? And fear is a love problem. I don't want to appear like a fanatic in front of people.

So how do we face fear?

I want you to think of a conversation that Jesus had with a very fearful man after His resurrection. Fear made him deny Jesus three times. His name was Peter, and the conversation was fixing fear with love. The apostle John captured the conversation in John 21:15-17:

> So when they had finished breakfast, Jesus said to Simon Peter, "Simon, *son* of John, do you love Me more than these?" He said to Him, "Yes, Lord; You know that I love You." He said to him, "Tend My lambs." He said to him again a second time, "Simon, *son* of John, do you love Me?" He said to Him, "Yes, Lord; You know that I love You." He said to him, "Shepherd My sheep." He said to him the third time, "Simon, *son* of John, do you love Me?" Peter was grieved because He said to him the third time, "Do you love Me?" And he said to Him, "Lord, You know all things; You know that I love You." Jesus said to him, "Tend My sheep."

The man Jesus was going to use to preach the first message of the church in Acts 2 was Peter. The man who couldn't even speak to a little girl without denying Jesus was now going to have to testify of Jesus *in the same place* he buckled in fear. What is revelatory about Jesus fighting Peter's fear is that Jesus never asked Peter, "Do you love sheep?" Jesus said, "Do you love me? Because if you love Me, then you will do the right thing for them."

So the first thing we have to do to deal with fear is to ask God to help us love Him, and loving others is a byproduct of that perfect love.

If you hear something often enough, you start to believe it's true. I heard this a lot growing up in the church: The words *fear not* appear 365 times in the Bible . . . one time for every day of the year. God put it in the Bible that many times so each day we face fear, we take one of the 365 for that day. A cool thought. So I decided to follow through and see if it's true.

Well here's the real story: it's not there 365 times! Not even close. Depending on the translation you are reading, it's there about 100 to 150 times.

Is it a letdown? Does it matter?

Here's the fact: if it was there once, that's all we need to see it in order not to fear again. Because with God, once is enough! If God, who cannot lie, said it once, that's enough! If God tells me not to fear in just one verse, I can believe it. I don't need it 364 other times.

Saying "fear not" 365 times a year does not release me from fear, but perfect love does. Because loves casts out fear.

So how can I love Jesus to fight fear? Today, I don't say to myself "fear not" to fight fear, but I pray this, "Jesus, help me to know how much You really love me. Because when I know how much You love me, I respond back in love. Perfect love is knowing You love me, and I in turn love You."

That's the next verse: "We love, because He first loved us" (verse 19). Love responds. His love for us makes us respond with love back to Him. There is something really perfect about that.

BE AN EXCLAMATION POINT NOT A QUESTION MARK

Today's Reading: 1 John 5

Next time you are in the airport I want you to notice something: observe the difference between passengers who hold confirmed tickets and those who are on a standby list. The ones with confirmed tickets read newspapers, chat with their friends, or sleep. The ones on standby hang around the ticket counter, pace, and wait to hear their names called to go to the front desk. Which is the signal they have a seat.

The difference in the two types of passengers is caused by the assurance factor. For the standby passengers, their whole day is one big question mark. Will they get on the plane? What time will they get home? How long will they have to wait?

There is nothing worse than living a travel day with one big question mark.

There is a travel day coming for every human being, and we have two destinations: heaven and hell. Let's talk about a confirmed ticket for eternal life. Can we really know for sure?

Today's chapter gives us that assurance to eternal life: "These things I have written to you who believe in the name of the Son of God, so that you may know that you have eternal life" (1 John 5:13).

If you ask someone the question, "Do you know if you are going to heaven?" and their answer is, "I hope so" or "I think I am," that person seems to have a standby ticket attitude with a confirmed ticket in hand. It's unbiblical and reveals an unread Bible. There is a whole book of the Bible to give them—and us—assurance. It is 1 John.

Verse 13 is so clear: "These things I have written . . . so you can know you have eternal life." John wants us to know we have a confirmed ticket and we can have a confirmed-ticket attitude.

He is saying to every Christian that we should not be a question mark but an exclamation point for God. And he helps us to do. We are not any more secure in Christ whether we have a big faith or a small faith—as long as we have a true faith. And true faith is this—that we believe in the Son of God. Every Christian should be able to say, "I know I am saved and going to heaven." Why? Edward Mote's lyrics from this old hymn tell us:

My hope is built on nothing less
than Jesus' blood and righteousness.
I dare not trust the sweetest frame
but wholly lean on Jesus name.[568]

One phrase always sticks out to me with this famous hymn: *I dare not trust the sweetest frame*. What does "frame" mean? We say things like "He is not in the right frame of mind." Webster's dictionary says that "frame" is a particular mood that influences one's attitude or behavior. And the songwriter says "I dare not trust it"—even when it's sweet. Even the sweetest frame will let us down. We are born again not because of how we feel but because of what Christ has done for you and me, and we believe He died for you and me.

A man once came to D. L. Moody and said he was worried because he didn't feel saved. Moody asked, "Was Noah safe in the ark?" "Certainly he was," the man replied. "Well, what made him safe, his feeling or the ark?" The inquirer got the point. "How foolish I've been!" he said. "It is not my feeling; it is Christ who saves!"[569]

If you follow or know anything about golf, you've probably heard names such as Arnold Palmer, Jack Nicklaus, and Tiger Woods. But have you ever heard of Doug Ford? He won the 1957 Masters. He never won again and he hasn't made the cut since 1971 (four years before Tiger Woods was born), but every year he is invited to play in the Masters. Why is Doug Ford invited? Because the Masters' rules include a lifetime invitation to every champion to play in the event. Although Ford only won the tournament once, hasn't qualified in nearly three decades, and hasn't been able to break par since 1958, he still gets to play in the tournament. One single occasion got him the forever invite.[570]

Our salvation is similarly linked to a single event. Christ's work on the cross was a one-shot deal. He died once so that all could live eternally. And when we decide to believe—that He lived the life we could not live, died the death we should have died, and been given a reward (heaven) we don't deserve, we can believe it. No more on standby. We have a confirmed ticket. And you can say with confidence, "I know I have eternal life."

A Simple Lesson that Saved Many a Relationship

Today's Reading: 2 John

In my library I have more than fifteen thousand books. I love books on preaching. Two preeminent nineteenth century preachers whose sermons are in my library are Charles Spurgeon (*Metropolitan Tabernacle Sermons*—sixty-three volumes) and Joseph Parker (*Preaching Through the Bible*). Both men had powerful churches in London at the same time. City Temple and Metropolitan Tabernacle were contemporaries and both doing amazing things. Though their books sit side by side on my bookshelf, the men in person seemed to have some issues with each other.

Joseph Parker published an open letter in the newspaper to express his concerns for his friend and colleague, Charles Spurgeon. The letter read, "Let me advise you to widen the circle of which you are the center. You are surrounded by offerers of incense. They flatter your weakness, they laugh at your jokes, they feed you with compliments. My dear Spurgeon, you are too big a man for this."[571]

Today's chapter, 2 John, may be a very short letter, but it has a huge message for Joseph Parker in the nineteenth century and for us in the twenty-first century. In John's small thirteen-verse letter, he ends it with these practical words that we all need to hear: "Though I have many things to write to you, I do not want to *do so* with paper and ink; but I hope to come to you and speak face to face, so that your joy may be made full" (verse 12).

Many believe 2 John was written to the same people that 1 John was written to. What is interesting is that when he starts off the letter "to the chosen lady and her children," some think he is writing to the church and not a mom and kids, that it was a metaphor for the bride of Christ. Regardless, the apostle wanted to say a number of things to these Christians.

John gives us this amazing practical advice: some things can be paper and ink and some things must be face to face. This is so good. And John delineates for us that all information is not disseminated the same way. I would like to put in my two cents to tell you what I think is face to face and what I think is ink and paper.

While I was attending the funeral of a loved one out of respect, a family member showed me something I could not believe. He pulled from his pocket a forty-year-old letter that was written to the deceased. A pastor had written the letter and in it shared some concerns and bad news with that person. I saw the letter's fold marks that were about to come apart from being opened and folded so many times over the years to show people the audacity of the preacher. This person, now deceased, was so angry with the letter and the pastor's insight on a situation that he'd carried it around for four decades. By the way, I read the letter and the preacher's words were true, but that is not the point. The point is that someone carried around a letter that infuriated him for forty years and now it's in the hands of a family member who I pray does not do the same.

Though the preacher's words were true, they did not belong on paper. Some things are paper and ink and some things are face to face.

Here is the rule: anything that is corrective or negative must be done face to face. Anything positive and encouraging can be done with paper and ink. Why? Posterity and longevity. Paper can be saved. Even for forty years.

I want people to hold onto a positive and encouraging text message or letter of uplifting words. I want them to be able to look at it again and again to bring joy and hope in tough times. I have done that before.

When something is hard and corrective, then do it face to face. People need to hear your tone, see your facial expressions, notice your tears, and be able to ask questions.

I wish Joseph Parker would have gone face to face with Spurgeon and not paper and ink. His concerns for a friend should have been done privately to help him. If he had something great to say about Spurgeon, then do an open letter. In Matthew 18:15, NIV Jesus tells us, "If your brother or sister sins, go and point out their fault, just between the two of you. If they listen to you, you have won them over." The goal is not to win an argument but to win back a friend.

Let's be clear. This was not just a nineteenth-century problem for Spurgeon and Parker. We have an issue with social media. It may not be literally paper and ink, but posting is the same. I would urge you to keep the same 2 John rule: if it's negative or combative, don't post. If it's encouraging and positive, post it.

You may ask, "But what if I am concerned about their point of view or stand on something?" Then show them love by going directly and privately to them, not writing about them.

I heard one of my pastor friends say: "If you are bolder on Facebook than in person, then you are a fraud." Wow, that is convicting.

John's first-century advice on face to face or paper and ink should have been heeded with two London pastors—and most definitely needs to be heeded in today's social media frenzy.

Thanks, John, for this amazing insight for us. Point taken and followed through.

I want you to notice I put that in ink.

THE GOAL EVERY PARENT IS SHOOTING FOR

Today's Reading: 3 John

Where parents used to rely on peers or their parents to help them navigate parenting challenges, such as bedtime, homework, and tantrums, many are now turning to parenting coaches. Many of these coaches charge between $125 to $350 a session and meet with parents—either in person, by phone, or over Skype—to set goals and develop a plan to reach them.

Parenting coaches, which is a more recent profession of just the past twenty years, has taken its place in the $1.08 billion personal coaching industry in the States. It seems more and more Americans choose to hire expert to help them improve every area of their lives—from parenting, to sleeping, to finances, to life in general.[572] Parents who invest that kind of money in this arena have one goal—joy. They want to see their children succeed, which in turn brings joy to their lives.

In today's chapter, the apostle John says something about spiritual parenting, which is true for all parenting: "I have no greater joy than this, to hear of my children walking in the truth" (3 John 1:4). There is no greater joy for a parent than to see their children succeed. Based on 3 John's passage, we understand that "succeed" means having our children walking with God.

The words of Jesus couldn't be clearer and more true when He said, "What does it profit a man to gain the whole world, and forfeit his soul?" (Mark 8:36). Having our children graduate college, get good grades, succeed in business, have a great marriage, have healthy grandchildren—they mean a lot, but not at the expense of not having a strong spiritual life. Our first priority as parents is their spiritual lives.

Steven Furtick, pastor of Elevation Church said, "My goal in parenting is to raise my kids to have a boring testimony. In other words, to stay out of trouble and love Jesus all their lives. It's just that I'd prefer that my kids change the world without having to have the world first change them. A person's testimony does not have to be spectacularly sinful to be significant."[573]

One of my dear friends told me, "You are only as happy as the child who is doing the worst." That means when one of my kids are not following God or going through a bad time, that is the watermark of joy for a parent.

How do you get the joy of knowing all your kids are walking in truth? It starts with you, not them. As T. D. Jakes said, "You can teach what you know but you can only reproduce what you are."[574]

That's why this article caught my attention several years ago:

> An annual Easter egg hunt attended by hundreds of children has been canceled because of misbehavior last year. Not by the kids, but by the grown-ups.
>
> Too many parents determined to see their children get an egg jumped a rope marking the boundaries of the children-only hunt at Bancroft Park [in Colorado Springs, Colorado] last year. The hunt was over in seconds, to the consternation of eggless tots and the rules-abiding parents.
>
> Parenting observers cite the cancellation as a prime example of so-called "helicopter parents"—those who hover over their children and are involved in every aspect of their children's lives—to ensure that they don't fail, even at an Easter egg hunt.[575]

Misbehaving children are usually the result of misbehaving parents. Your children need to see your life with God and your convictions. If they see you compromise or try to "get ahead," they will become disillusioned with religion, like a young Jewish boy who once lived in Germany.

His father, a successful businessman, moved their family to another German city, and then told the family that instead of attending the local synagogue, they were going to join the Lutheran church.

The boy, who had a deep interest in religion, was surprised and asked his father why the switch. His father answered that it was better for business, since so many Lutherans lived in the town, he could make good business contacts by attending the Lutheran church.

The boy became so disillusioned with his father that something died within him. The incident helped to turn him against religion. That young boy was Karl Marx, the father of Communism and the author of *The Communist Manifesto*, in which he called religion "the opiate of the masses."[576]

I wonder if history would have been different if Marx's father took God seriously and not as a business. Become serious about God and watch your children get serious about God.

If joy to you is hearing that your children are walking with God, as the apostle John said, then *you* walk with God the way you would want them to. As Francis Chan said, "Our goal as parents ought to be to help our kids become independently dependent on God."[577]

I like that.

Fight for What You Believe

Today's Reading: Jude

There's an old saying, "The question is not *if* we will defend the Christian faith, but how well." Such a true statement. And today's reading in Jude, though it's only one chapter, comes out swinging with it. Jude tells believers he wants to instruct them about this incredible salvation they enjoy together, but then goes into fighter mode:

> Dearly loved friend, I was fully intending to write to you about our *amazing* salvation we all participate in, but felt the need instead to challenge you to vigorously defend and contend for the beliefs that we cherish. (TPT)

The New American Standard Bible says, "to contend earnestly for the faith." These are important words for us and our children today as we live in a society where our religion, our values, and our beliefs are under attack. And we are enjoined by Jude not to sit back while this happens but to contend and defend.

Now the big question: how?

First let's deal with *what*. What kind of culture are we facing? What is the fight we are fighting? Here are two very important words about the culture we live in—*relativism* and *pluralism*. Relativism in morals and pluralism in beliefs. What does that mean?

Relativism means everyone's truth is equal. Personal preference trumps everything else. We hear phrases like *my truth*. Subjectivity trumps objective truth, and the individual and their "truth" is exalted over God.

Pluralism means all religions equal, so no one religion stands above another. There is no thought of examining a religion's validity. They are all equal—"whatever works for you." The enemy is Jesus' words that He is the Way, the Truth, and the Life.

Vince Vitale explained our pluralistic and relativistic culture like this:

Imagine being thrown into a game without knowing when it started, when it will finish, what the objective of the game is, or what the rules are. What would you do? You'd probably ask the other players around you to answer those four questions for you.

What if they responded with many different answers? Or what if they simply carried on playing, uninterested in your questions? . . .

Next, you look to a coach for help, but what if the coach was standing there, looking at the chaos, and yelling, "Great job, guys! You're all doing great! Keep going! We've got a first-place trophy waiting for all of you!"

Finally, you would turn to find the referee or umpire for definitive answers to your questions. But what if the players had gotten frustrated with the referee's calls and sent him home?

And now imagine the conversations about the game on the drive home. They would be completely meaningless.[578]

Rules and standards make the game meaningful and objective. But we are not in a game. When we live in a pluralistic culture, this is our reality. No wonder many people struggle to live a meaningful life! According to Vince Vitale, living in a pluralistic society means that we lose the answers to these four crucial questions:

- Origin—Where did I come from?
- Meaning—Why am I here?
- Morality—How should I live?
- Destiny—Where am I headed?[579]

So how are we to deal with this? I think the greatest way to contend for the faith is by constantly studying the authentic and the real. As Peter Kreeft brilliantly reminds us: "The more important a thing is the more counterfeits there are. There are no counterfeit paperclips or pencils, but plenty of counterfeit religions."[580]

Think about Kreeft's words and the counterfeits that are sold on the streets of major cities. There are no counterfeit Timex watches but Rolex watches. There are no counterfeit Bic pens but Montblanc pens. There are no counterfeit Target brands on the street, only Gucci, Coach, and Prada. Why? You counterfeit the expensive. And nothing gets counterfeited more than religion.

So how do we fight against counterfeits? My wife worked in the banking world for many years. In that world counterfeit money is obviously the enemy. How do they spot counterfeits?

When a bank teller is trained, they see nothing but the original 24/7. They become familiar with the markings, the feel, the smells of the real thing. Tellers never see counterfeits. Why? Because when you are familiar with the real thing, the phony is much easier to spot.

The same is true for us. We must become familiar with the real thing. The best way to defend the truth, the best way to contend for our faith is to know the real faith and the truth. Is that enough?

Charles Spurgeon said this:

> Suppose a number of persons were to take it into their heads that they had to defend a lion. . . . There he is in the cage, and here come all the soldiers of the army to fight for him. Well, I should suggest to them . . . that they should kindly stand back, and open the door, and let the lion out! I believe that would be the best way of defending him, for he would take care of himself. . . . And the best "apology" for the gospel is to let the gospel out. . . . Preach Jesus Christ and him crucified. Let the Lion out, and see who will dare to approach him. The Lion of the tribe of Judah will soon drive away his adversaries.[581]

God can defend Himself. So let us present the self-revealed God as He revealed Himself—not the twenty-first-century God, but the eternal, never-changing God.

From Cheap Praise to Real Praise

Today's Reading: Revelation 1

When music, lights, and atmosphere are what we need to get us to praise God, we have chosen cheap praise. Cheap praise needs props to inspire. Real praise needs a revelation.

In today's reading, we've reached the final book of the New Testament. Get ready for a roller coaster of a ride through the book of Revelation. The book's title and first words keep us centered and steady in a very controversial book: "The Revelation of Jesus Christ." The author, John, wants us to know throughout this book that we are not looking for events to happen but for a Person to come, Jesus. The word *revelation* actually means "unveiling." It's the unveiling of Jesus. And it is this unveiling that inspires us to praise.

Notice the praise that comes out of John when he speaks of three things Jesus does: "To him who loves us and has freed us from our sins by his blood, and has made us to be a kingdom and priests to serve his God and Father—to him be glory and power for ever and ever! Amen" (Revelation 1:5-6, NIV).

What are the three things that Jesus has done for us that inspire praise?

1. to Him who *loves us*

2. *freed us* from our sins by His blood

3. He has *made us* to be a kingdom and priests to God

Let this sink in. First, He *loves* us. We have this mischaracterization of God that if we can get rid of our sins and clean ourselves up, then God will really love us. Nothing can be further from the truth of Scripture. The word order is so important here in 1:5. He loves us before He frees us. He loves us dirty but loves us so much He won't leave us that way in our dirt. He loves *then* frees us. And thank God, He continues to set us free. Or to quote a familiar saying, "He loves us just the way we are, but He loves us so much that He won't let us stay that way."

Second John says He freed us from our sins by His blood. Every time we celebrate Memorial Day and remember the amazing sacrifice our soldiers made for this the greatest nation on the planet, I am reminded that freedom is not free. People paid with their lives to make us free. And nowhere does this price come out than in the freedom that Jesus gives us. He doesn't just love us, He frees us. His love was costly, which John emphasizes in these three words, *by His blood*. Our freedom from sin cost the Son of God His life.

Third, and finally, He made us kings and priests. We have three parts to what He desires to do in and through us: love, free, and make us. To be forgiven of sins is not the end of our journey. To make us kings and priests to God and Father is His goal and purpose.

Kings and *priests* are two Old Testament words that were used only of a special and exclusive group of people. A king had authority and a priest had access. And now John tells us because we are loved and free, we have access to God and authority in His name.

Then before John can go any further with this thought, he bursts into praise: "Has made us to be a kingdom and priests to serve his God and Father—to him be glory and power for ever and ever! Amen" (Revelation 1:6, NIV). When John realizes that God loves us, God frees us, and God makes him something we have no chance of becoming on our own, he also realizes he has a reason to praise God.

When you have a revelation of who Jesus is, you recognize praise is not limited to a building, a day of the week, or a time of the day. Praise is based on your knowledge of who God is and what God has done. Cheap praise needs props. Real praise needs a revelation. And the book of Revelation gives us plenty of fuel for praise.

I grew up during a time when praise and worship came out of the book that was in the back of the pew in front of us called a hymnal. Then when I went into ministry, cassette tapes from a group called Integrity Music gave us new choruses to sing. Then songs began to expand and change as churches and ministries started writing them. We started to sing the songs of Israel Houghton and Graham Kendrick from across the Pond. And now there is Hillsong, Elevation, and Bethel. While all of these changes are good, even good music is not enough. We need good revelation. I think that's why God saved the best for last.

For the remainder of our 260 journey, we are going to see Jesus unveiled. And when that happens, we won't need any music. We will simply be like John and shout out, "To him be glory and power for ever and ever! Amen."

You Didn't Lose It, You Left It

Today's Reading: Revelation 2

F amed classical cellist Yo-Yo Ma was in a rush to get from one side of Manhattan to the other for a quick appearance. So rushed in fact, that when he arrived at his destination, he paid his driver, exited the cab, and forgot to take his cello with him. He'd placed the cello in the trunk of the taxi. And the cello was priceless: handcrafted by Antonio Stradivari in 1733 in Vienna, Austria, it was valued at $2.5 million. Frantic, Ma began a desperate search, eventually finding the cab later that day parked in a garage in Queens—with the cello still in the trunk.[582]

Wow, talk about leaving something priceless inadvertently. In today's chapter, though, a church is accused of something more devastating—leaving their first love.

Revelation 2 and 3 are messages from Jesus to seven churches. Not every message is encouraging. In fact, they are convicting even two thousand years later. The first church God speaks to is the church of Ephesus:

> To the angel of the church in Ephesus write:
>
> The One who holds the seven stars in His right hand, the One who walks among the seven golden lampstands, says this: "I know your deeds and your toil and perseverance, and that you cannot tolerate evil men, and you put to the test those who call themselves apostles, and they are not, and you found them to *be* false; and you have perseverance and have endured for My name's sake, and have not grown weary. But I have this against you, that you have left your first love." (Revelation 2:1-4)

You have left your first love.

A few years ago I left my Kindle on a plane. I'd leaned it against the wall in the exit row by my seat. I was packing up my bag as we were landing and something said to me, *Put that in your backpack.* I didn't. I left a thousand books leaning against the wall of the plane. Let me be clear, I didn't lose it. I knew exactly where it was—seat 15C, flight #629 out of Atlanta.

Lost has no idea where it is. Lost means it fell out of a pocket, a car, a jacket.

The church of Ephesus left something bigger and more massive than a thousand books.

For all my life I have heard the wrong word used in this verse, which makes all the difference about the church of Ephesus. It's a verse that if anyone has been in the church for any amount of time, they have probably said it, heard it, or even quoted it. I have always said, "You have *lost* your first love." Not one version of the Bible puts "lost" in this verse. It is, "You have *left*."

Lost has the connotation of removing blame from the person, as in my "love for God" just got accidentally lost in the hustle and bustle of life. Let's be clear: Ephesus *left* it, Ephesus did not *lose* its first love. There is blame here. That's why they are not being challenged "to find it" but to repent for it. Repentance deals with responsibility.

Ephesus is the only church to have two different apostles write letters to it. In the book of Ephesians, Paul offers two prayers for the church, that they might have more light and more love. This was one of the few places Paul stayed for a length of time (three years). The church of Ephesus was first pastored by Apollos. Timothy then became the pastor (the first epistle to Timothy was while he was pastoring the Ephesus church; see 1 Timothy 1:3). Later on, John pastored the church. It was while he was in Ephesus that John was exiled to Patmos.

How do you lose your first love when your pastors were Apollos, Timothy, and John? How do you lose your first love when you had the apostle Paul hang with your church for three years? How do you lose your first love when you get two New Testament letters written to you?

Two thoughts:

First, Jesus says "you" left your first love. *You* means you have to take responsibility. It seems they fell in love with their successes and accomplishments—that's verses 2 and 3—but fell out of love with Jesus. This danger is subtle.

What's interesting is that the apostle Paul warned the Ephesian people in Acts 20:28, "Be on guard for yourselves." You, not demons, can be your worst enemy.

Second, the word *to leave* is a process word. It means to let expire. We have to renew certain things—our driver's license, our insurance, subscriptions, etc. So too our love for God will expire if we are not renewing it on a daily basis.

On October 11, 1775, the whaling ship *Herald* was fishing just off Greenland when it spotted another ship. When it got closer, it saw that even though the ship was sailing, its sails were tattered and hanging limply on the masts. The captain ordered a few of his men to board the other ship. What they discovered shocked them. Everyone on board the other ship, which they determined was the *Octavius*, a boat that had disappeared in 1761, was frozen to death. The ship had been sailing for fourteen years. Still moving but no one alive.[583]

That's what happens when we keep doing things and let our love for Jesus expire. It wasn't renewed. It starts when our conversations with God reduce to being on a need-to-talk basis or a once-a-week basis. Time spent in prayer become based more on convenience. We will see God on Sunday but not any other day.

My prayer is what Amy Carmichael prayed: "God hold us to that which drew us first, when the Cross was the attraction, and we wanted nothing else."[584]

WHEN MY OPINION AND MY REALITY ARE WORLDS APART

Today's Reading: Revelation 3

Some time ago Cindy and I were doing marital counseling for a couple who were struggling in their marriage. I asked a question I always ask in those types of counseling appointments. It is one of a reality and judgment so I can see how clear they are in their thinking. I asked the wife first, "Is there anything you can you do to help the marriage? What do you need to stop doing and what do you need to get better in?"

"I can't think of anything," she said. She was basically saying, *It's him, not me.* She misjudged herself really badly.

Today's chapter looks at a church that was in the same boat as this deceived wife. The church of Laodicea was miles apart between their opinion of themselves and the reality of their situation. This is what Jesus tells them:

> To the angel of the church in Laodicea write:
> The Amen, the faithful and true Witness, the Beginning of the creation of God, says this: "I know your deeds, that you are neither cold nor hot; I wish that you were cold or hot. So because you are lukewarm, and neither hot nor cold, I will spit you out of My mouth. Because you say, 'I am rich, and have become wealthy, and have need of nothing,' and you do not know that you are wretched and miserable and poor and blind and naked." (Revelation 3:14-17)

Paul gave the church at Rome a warning in Romans 12:3. Listen to these words, because Laodicea didn't: "Because of the privilege and authority God has given me, I give each of you this warning: Don't think you are better than you really are. Be honest in your evaluation of yourselves, measuring yourselves by the faith God has given us" (Romans 12:3, NLT). *The Message* says, "Don't misinterpret yourselves."

Now here is the Laodicean church who proudly said, *We are rich, wealthy, and need nothing.* That's their judgment of themselves. But the only opinion that counts is how God sees us. And in verse 17 we have both reality and opinion.

Listen to Jesus' reality: "You do not know that you are wretched, miserable, poor, blind, and naked."

Wow, can that be any different? Danish philosopher Soren Kierkegaard couldn't have said it more clearly: "It is so much easier to become a Christian when you aren't one than to become one when you assume you already are."[585] Nothing is more dangerous than a deceived Christian. Especially when the Spirit of truth resides in us.

How does my opinion of me match what Jesus assesses me to be? Am I Laodicea far off? Do I believe I'm rich when Jesus says I'm poor? Do I believe I don't need anything when Jesus says I am blind and naked?

Here is a great prayer for us to pray every day from David in Psalm 139:23 (MSG):

Investigate my life, O God,
find out everything about me;
Cross-examine and test me,
get a clear picture of what I'm about;
See for yourself whether I've done anything wrong—
then guide me on the road to eternal life.

I have learned that a number of factors can put me in the Laodicea category of misjudging myself:
- When I am not reading the Bible. James 1:23 says the Bible is a mirror. When I read it I can see the stuff out of place.
- When I am not praying. Prayer is where God talks and the Spirit convicts.
- When I am attending church but not being pastored. I have no one speaking to the areas that need to be tweaked and examined. I have surrounded myself with cheerleaders but no truth tellers.

The last thing God says to this church is profound. And I have read it wrong for years. Listen to Jesus: "Behold, I stand at the door and knock; if anyone hears My voice and opens the door, I will come in to him and will dine with him, and he with Me" (Revelation 3:20).

For decades I used to preach on the streets of the inner cities of America telling people that Jesus stands at the door of our hearts and is knocking today. We just need to let Him in. And I used to use Revelation 3:20 for the sinners. But Revelation 3:20 is not for the sinners. It's for the Christians who have really poor judgment. Jesus is knocking on the door of His own church.

But what is Jesus doing on the other side of the door? And how was Laodicea having church without Jesus in the building? That is sobering to consider. And it tells me that it still can happen and *is* happening. When Jesus is not on the inside, then I become the judge of me. And that is not good.

If you hear Jesus knocking, drop everything and answer the door, please.

Day 242

FAMILIARITY VERSUS INTIMACY

Today's Reading: Revelation 4

Pastor Gordon Lester says this about two important words:

> Familiarity and intimacy are not the same. Each has a value in life, certainly in married life, but one is no substitute for the other. If one is confused for the other, we have the basis for major human and marital unrest. In marriage, familiarity is inescapable. It happens almost imperceptibly. Intimacy is usually hard to come by. It must be deliberately sought and opened up and responded to. Familiarity brings a degree of ease and comfort. Intimacy anxiously searches for deep understanding and personal appreciation.[586]

These are not words for just the marriage relationship. These are two words for the most important relationship—our friendship with God.

Familiarity and intimacy can be defined like this: familiarity refers to knowledge, having information about someone. But for intimacy to happen, it doesn't stop at information; it needs to go further. When it comes to important things and people in our lives, if familiarity doesn't turn to intimacy then we face the danger of familiarity. Have you heard of this phrase, *Familiarity breeds contempt*? All the information you have does move you closer to the person.

Intimacy is not for every relationship, but it must be the threshold we cross in the important ones—especially in our relationship with God. Intimacy means closeness. It's a proximity word and a conscious effort to close the gaps between us. What I mean by closing the gaps is that all mysteries and hidden things are exposed. Intimacy knows the secrets and the motives. It's like the old saying, the best way to define intimacy is into-me-see.

That was God's invitation to John the revelator: *I want you to see deeper. I want to clear up some mystery for you. I am inviting you to intimacy.*

Here is the invitation:

After these things I looked, and behold, a door *standing* open in heaven, and the first voice which I had heard, like *the sound* of a trumpet speaking with me, said, "Come up here, and I will show you what must take place after these things." Immediately I was in the Spirit; and behold, a throne was standing in heaven, and One sitting on the throne. (Revelation 4:1-2)

John knew the Jesus on earth but intimacy calls for closing the gaps: *John, you are now going to see the Jesus you have never seen before. The Jesus in heaven. You knew the Jesus on the cross and the Jesus resurrected, but you have never experienced or seen the Jesus on the throne.*

Here's what happened to John. When he was in the Spirit, He saw the throne. The word *throne* is used eleven times in this short eleven-verse chapter. Eleven times! I think God was trying to show John something. John was shown an open door, but it was his prerogative whether he would go through or not. That was the choice of moving from being familiar with Jesus to being intimate with Jesus. And when the gap was closed between John on earth and Jesus in heaven, he saw a throne. Intimacy revealed Jesus on the throne.

That's what happens when we walk in the Spirit. I think the best New Testament phrase to describe intimacy with God is *walking in the Spirit*. To walk in the Spirit is to be in step with God, to walk in cadence with Him. Familiarity has moved to intimacy. To walk in the Spirit brings closeness and closes the gaps. When this happens, we see Jesus on the throne, the Jesus in charge, the Jesus who calls the shots. We see the sovereignty of Jesus.

The phrase *in the Spirit* is used often in the New Testament. Ephesians says pray in the Spirit, Philippians says worship in the Spirit, Colossians says love in the Spirit, and Galatians says walk in the Spirit. And when John was *in the Spirit* in Revelation 4, he saw a throne.

I think whether you are praying, worshiping, or walking in the Spirit, you see a throne. What does that mean? You see Jesus in charge and ruling. He has no rivals, He is the sovereign King.

When the United Nations headquarters was being built in New York City, there was some controversy as to whether a place of worship should be included in the building. One of the city's newspapers carried a cartoon depicting a huge hand (God's hand) and in the center of the hand was a small globe (the world). On top of the globe stood a group of little men from the UN in a heated argument. The caption read: "Do we have to invite Him as well?"[587]

Psalm 2 says God laughs in heaven at the arrogance of puny little sinful man.

If I were the UN, I would invite He who sits on the throne. Come to think of it, if I were in Washington DC and in our universities and public schools, I would invite Him and remember who holds the world, because He sits on the throne.

Washington DC is just a place. Heaven has a throne.

THE CURRENCY EXCHANGE

Today's Reading: Revelation 5

When I travel overseas, the first thing I have to look for in that new country is a currency exchange counter. I need to turn US dollars into the currency of that country. My currency doesn't work on their foreign soil. I can't use dollars when they only accept pesos or euros.

In today's reading, we are introduced to a currency that is required to live on eternal soil and a transaction that benefits the planet. The return or rate on the currency is unlike anyone has ever seen or heard. Listen to these words that John hears being sung in heaven: "They sang a new song, saying, 'Worthy are You to take the book and to break its seals; for You were slain, and purchased for God with Your blood *men* from every tribe and tongue and people and nation'" [Revelation 5:9].

Did you see the transaction?

"You [Jesus] purchased for God"—the transaction
"With Your blood"—the currency
"Men from every tribe and tongue and people and nation"—the product purchased, all humanity

The blood of Jesus was the currency that heaven accepted to purchase our redemption. The blood of Jesus is the only acceptable currency that allows me to go to heaven. If the value of an article is determined by the price paid for it, and Jesus died for you, then you can believe you are very valuable to God. Because God is not a foolish investor. Your worth to Him is the price of His precious Son's life.

The temptation of our times is to look good without being good. In other words, we try to use bogus currency that heaven, that foreign land, will not accept. We spend money and time trying to fix the outside thinking it will fix the inside. We suck and tuck and are still stuck and out of luck. The inside issue is the issue and the issue is a sin issue. The cross has revealed to good men that their goodness has not been good enough.

Men have tried for ages to get by on bogus currency. Let's see why this currency called the blood of Jesus is so important to understand. Jesus was punished for my sin, because sin had to be punished. His shed blood was the result of my sin and its payment for my sin.

If my sin was not transferred to Jesus than someone else has to pay for it. Why? Because it is a crime against God, and all crimes must be paid for. You and I would not be here if we had to pay for that crime against God. Someone had to die for committing crime against God—and it was Jesus who died in our place. But with one caveat: the One who died for me rose again!

Jesus' death is the acceptable payment, the currency for all of humanity. Why is sacrifice necessary for the atonement of sin? Because Justice demands it. A crime cannot be forgiven without a payment or just an "I'm sorry." We live in a time in which people try to pay the crime with the wrong currency and have never done the currency exchange.

Let me give you three currencies that God won't accept:

Currency #1: Sincerity. Some think that because they mean well that this is enough. But we have exchange for the blood of Christ.

Currency #2: Service. Some think that God owes them something because of their basic decency. That good people go to heaven and goodness is measured on a scale against their bad things, and if the scale tips in the good favor, then they're in. Doing good or being good is their currency. But we have to exchange for the blood of Christ.

Currency #3. Feeling sorry. Some think that if they feel bad for their sin and they cry, God knows their heart. The problem is that He does know our hearts, and the only remedy is a currency exchange, the blood of Jesus.

Romans 5:10 says, "we were reconciled to God by the death of His Son," not by men's currency of sincerity, service, or sorry. We can't leave Jesus out of the equation.

Recently I read the best mathematical equation ever: 1 Cross + 3 Nails = 4Given. That's the currency we need.

Consider this: who was the greatest sinner in human history? Hitler, Saddam Hussein, Bin Laden? Some say the Syrian president Bashar al-Assad. Some list serial killers Ted Bundy or Jeffrey Dahmer. Some say, the men who planned and acted out the events of September 11, 2001. But the greatest sinner in human history was Jesus.

He took all of their sins and ours at the same time to the cross. At some point between noon and 3 p.m. on that Friday two thousand years ago, God charged Jesus as "the" sinner of the planet, with every human sin on Him: "For

God took the sinless Christ and poured into him our sins. Then, in exchange, he poured God's goodness into us!" (2 Corinthians 5:21, TLB).

Why did He die? So you and I would not have to. That's why the most precious metal is *not* gold, silver, or platinum. It was four rusty nails.

Toward the end of the Civil War, when it was clear the North was going to win, Southerners had Confederate money that they realized was soon going to be worthless. Their currency wasn't going to be accepted, so they needed to figure out how to get US currency.

Right now, we Christians are living in the south (this world), and when Jesus comes He is going to take us north (heaven). The only currency that works up there is what has been transmuted into heavenly currency, the blood of Jesus. We need a currency exchange to live on that foreign soil. Calvary shows how far men will go in sin, and how far God will go for man's salvation. God always goes further, a lot further.

If you need to find a currency exchange counter for heaven, it's as close as asking Jesus to change you. And your currency gets exchanged when you choose to be born again.

Day 244

THE VOICE OF THE MARTYRS

Today's Reading: Revelation 6

Located in Washington DC is the iconic memorial to Thomas Jefferson. And written on the northeast portico of the memorial are these sobering and haunting words our country needs to read and digest again from one of our founding fathers: "Indeed I tremble for my country when I reflect that God is just; that His justice cannot sleep forever."[588]

Wow, that is sobering. God's justice will always be turned lose against sin. The best definition of sin I have ever read is from John Piper:

[Sin] is the glory of God not honored, the holiness of God not reverenced, the greatness of God not admired, the power of God not praised, the truth of God not sought, the wisdom of God not esteemed, the beauty of God not treasured, the goodness of God not savored, the faithfulness of God not trusted, the promises of God not believed, the commandments of God not obeyed, the justice of God not respected, the wrath of God not feared, the grace of God not cherished, the presence of God not prized, the person of God not loved.[589]

God's justice will judge sin. The problem is that, from our standpoint, it takes too long. Whenever we see sin and injustice, we want immediate recompense. The living asks for it and in today's chapter, we have another group asking for it. In Revelation 6 we hear the cry of the dead, but not just the dead—those who have died for their faith in Jesus. Listen to the cry of the martyrs when the Lamb broke the fiftth seal and we hear their hallowed voices:

When the Lamb broke the fifth seal, I saw underneath the altar the souls of those who had been slain because of the word of God, and because of the testimony which they had maintained; and they cried out with a loud voice, saying, "How long, O Lord, holy and true, will You refrain from judging and avenging our blood on those who dwell on the earth?" [Revelation 6:9-10]

Many believe early church father Tertullian said these famous words, "The blood of the martyrs is the seed of the church."[590] He argued that persecution actually strengthens the church; as martyrs bravely and willingly die for their faith, onlookers convert. In Christianity Today, Morgan Lee goes on to say:

Some 1,800 years later, restrictions on religion are stronger than ever. According to the Pew Research Center, 74 percent of the world's population live in a country where social hostilities involving religion are high, and 64 percent live where government restrictions on religion are high. Does this explain why Christianity is likewise growing worldwide?[591]

The Revelation 6 martyr's question is our question: "How long, O Lord, holy and true, will You refrain from judging and avenging our blood on those who dwell on the earth?" That is the question for the living and the dead. When is God going to put things right? When is God going to judge those who rightly deserve judgment?

Here is what I have learned about God and immediate judgment. First, God is patient. God is willing to wait. Second, God is willing to be misunderstood in delay. While men cry for "now," God sees the bigger picture as more important than answering our immediate cry. And third, there will be a day when God *will* make everything right; it just may not be the day on your calendar.

So God is patient. God can handle mischaracterization about Himself while He delays. And God will have the final word.

The book of 2 Peter gives such a great perspective to the *how long?* question the martyrs of Revelation 6 asked. The context of the answer is that people want Jesus to return quickly. They want that final judgment day to happen to show the mockers and skeptics that God is real and that they are going to get what's coming to them. But Peter explains God's reason for delay: "His 'delay' simply reveals his loving patience toward you, because he does not want any to perish but all to come to repentance" (2 Peter 3:9, TPT). *The Message* says it like this, "He's giving everyone space and time to change."

When we and the martyrs ask how long or why the delay in receiving justice, God wants us to understand that He is giving everyone space and time to change. God is willing to wait through mischaracterization, accusation, and our exhaustion and even death to bring as many people to heaven as He can. And I believe He is waiting on those who caused the injustice and the deaths.

Don't mistake God's patience for His absence. Patience is not the absence of action but the wisdom of knowing the right time to act. Thank You, God, for being patient not only with me but with all of humanity.

WORSHIP REACHES A CRESCENDO

Today's Reading: Revelation 7

I think we have mixed-up our priorities. Author Gordon Dahl agrees. Consider his observation: "Most middle-class Americans tend to worship their work, to work at their play, and to play at their worship. As a result, their meanings and values are distorted."[592] Worship is not an optional spiritual practice for Christians, it is a response to how we see God. A low view of God shows up in a view that worship is an inconvenience. A high view of God shows up as an automatic response to His worthiness.

The word *worship* literally means *worth-ship*. It's to see the true value of something or someone. It recognizes their worth. In today's chapter, we see something amazing happen with worship. The apostle John has multiple visions of worship happening in the heavens, but the one in chapter 7 seems to be the climax.

Before we look at that one, I need to take us on a worship journey in Revelation starting in chapter 1, so we can see how worship progresses. Starting in Revelation 1:6, we see two notes of praise: "He has made us to be a kingdom, priests to His God and Father—to Him be the glory and the dominion forever and ever. Amen" (Revelation 1:6). The two notes: *glory* and *dominion*.

Then in chapter 4, we see three notes of praise: "Worthy are You, our Lord and our God, to receive glory and honor and power; for You created all things, and because of Your will they existed, and were created" (4:11). The three notes: *glory*, *honor*, and *power*.

In chapter 5, we see four notes of praise: "Every created thing which is in heaven and on the earth and under the earth and on the sea, and all things in them, I heard saying, 'To Him who sits on the throne, and to the Lamb, *be* blessing and honor and glory and dominion forever and ever'" (5:13). The four notes: *Blessing, honor, glory*, and *dominion*.

Now we come to chapter 7, where the worship seems to reach a crescendo with seven notes of praise: "All the angels were standing around the throne and *around* the elders and the four living creatures; and they fell on their faces before the throne and worshiped God, saying, 'Amen, blessing and glory and wisdom and thanksgiving and honor and power and might, *be* to our God forever and ever. Amen'" (7:11-12). The seven notes: *blessing, glory, wisdom, thanksgiving, honor, power,* and *might* be to our God.

Wow! Worship reaches an apex in heaven. It seems that it kept building to this moment and those in heaven couldn't help themselves. Worship was *worthship* pouring out from them.

Heaven is where nothing but truth exists, maximum truth. The truth of who God is is unveiled. And since that happens, worship is the proper response. Everything is clearly seen in heaven. The price of salvation. The value of the Son of God coming to earth. What mercy and grace really is. All of these are unveilings, just to name a few.

When we see the true God and know the true God, we must worship God. Let me put it this way: if our idea of God, if our idea of the salvation offered in Christ, is vague or remote, our idea of worship will be fuzzy. The closer we get to the truth, the clearer becomes the beauty, and the more we will find worship welling up within us. That's why theology and worship belong together. If they are separated then theology is just a head-trip, and worship without truth is just an emotional experience as we enjoy singing or listening to songs about God. But heaven joins the truth of God and the emotion that He stimulates in our hearts to bring about a seven-note climax of worship.

In 1744, hymnwriter Charles Wesley, John Wesley's brother, was in Leeds, England, holding a prayer meeting in an upstairs room crowded with a hundred people. Suddenly the floor gave way and collapsed. Everyone crashed through the ceiling into the room below. The place was in obvious chaos, with people screaming or crying, while others sat in shock. But Charles, wounded and lying in a heap of rubble, cried out, "Fear not! The Lord is with us. Our lives are all safe." Then he broke out into a doxology of worship, singing, "Praise God from Whom all blessings flow."[593] While everyone else was viewing the damage, his heart responded with unshakable praise. He understood—as we must as well— that worship is based on the truth of God not on circumstances, good or bad.

THE DAY HEAVEN WAS SILENT FOR THIRTY MINUTES

Today's Reading: Revelation 8

You know a relationship is in trouble when silence occurs between the two parties. Nothing is worse than a silent home between husband and wife. I'm not condoning it, but yelling at each other is better than silence. At least people are voicing their opinions. But when silence occurs, it means, *I'm done talking. It's over.* Silence means the end is near.

After the Roman soldiers took Jesus into custody for His crucifixion, both Pilate and Herod questioned Jesus. We have his responses to Pilate. But when Jesus appeared before Herod, something eerie occurred. Here is how Luke recorded the scene:

> Herod was very glad when he saw Jesus; for he had wanted to see Him for a long time, because he had been hearing about Him and was hoping to see some sign performed by Him. And he questioned Him at some length; but He answered him nothing. (Luke 23:8-9)

But He answered him nothing.

Herod was an apostate. If Herod would not listen to John the Baptist's warnings and had him beheaded, he was not going to listen to Jesus. In fact, we are told that all Herod wanted was a sign performed, a trick to see. Herod had been wanting to see Jesus for a very long time and when he finally did, he received only silence! The only one talking in the room was Herod. He have the Son of God in his presence, the One whose very word created the ground he was walking on, and he was the only one talking. Silence from the Son of God.

And now in Revelation 8, we see that all of heaven has gone silent for thirty minutes. Do we understand the ramifications of this silence? For seven chapters heaven has been bursting with praise, and now everything comes to a screeching halt. All of the angels, elders, and four living creatures stop their worship.

The chapter prior shows that they are declaring that robes have been washed white in the blood of the Lamb. They are announcing in the last verse of chapter 7 that God shall wipe every tear from their eyes. And now in chapter 8, nothing:

> When the Lamb broke the seventh seal, there was silence in heaven for about half an hour. And I saw the seven angels who stand before God, and seven trumpets were given to them. Another angel came and stood at the altar, holding a golden censer; and much incense was given to him, so that he might add it to the prayers of all the saints on the golden altar which was before the throne. And the smoke of the incense, with the prayers of the saints, went up before God out of the angel's hand. Then the angel took the censer and filled it with the fire of the altar, and threw it to the earth. (Revelation 8:1-5)

When the Lamb broke the seventh seal, it caused silence. Why? That seal contains seven angels with seven trumpets, which are seven judgments about to be released on the earth. I think the silence is shock and awe by heaven's host. What they are about to see has never been witnessed before. Heaven has seen nothing but mercy and grace shown to the planet and all of humanity. But now, mercy and grace has run its course, and it's time for God to hold court on the planet and on its wickedness. It is earth's final judgment. It is the beginning of the end.

Heaven has never seen anything like this before. The mouths that had nothing but praise in them, now can say nothing at all at the breaking of the seventh seal.

What amazed me about this chapter is what seems to break the thirty-minute silence in heaven. It isn't an angel, an elder, or one of the four living creatures. It seems to be prayer—the prayers of the saints. There is no more prayer in heaven, only praise. So these prayers are coming from believers on the earth before the first trumpet sounds.

The power of these judgment trumpets are so awful, it silences heaven. But prayer is so powerful that it can end the silence in heaven and I believe protect the believer on earth.

Spurgeon said it best about the power of prayer:

> The power of prayer can never be overrated. They who cannot serve God by preaching need not regret it if they can be mighty in prayer. The true strength of the Church lies there. . . . If a man can but pray, he can

do anything! He that knows how to overcome the Lord in prayer, has Heaven and earth at his disposal.[594]

Prayer broke the silence in heaven because only prayer could. Prayer made the voice of ordinary mortals into a voice greater than angels. Keep praying those prayers. Heaven hears them.

WHAT WILL IT TAKE TO GET PEOPLE TO REPENT?

Today's Reading: Revelation 9

Not only was Thomas Jefferson our third president, in his retirement, he also founded the University of Virginia. Believing that students would take their studies seriously, he encouraged a more lax code of discipline. Unfortunately, some students took advantage and misbehaved, which turned into a riot. Professors who tried to restore order were attacked. The following day the university's board, of which Jefferson was a member, held a meeting with the defiant students. Jefferson began by saying, "This is one of the most painful events of my life," but couldn't continue because he was overcome by emotion and burst into tears. Another board member asked the rioters to come forward and give their names. Nearly everyone did. Later, one of them confessed, "It was not Mr. Jefferson's words, but it was his tears that broke us."[595]

Just as the students were moved by Jefferson's brokenness, so is God by ours. When we are truly broken and sorry for our sins, this leads to *repentance.* William Taylor describes true repentance like this: "True repentance . . . hates the sin, and not simply the penalty; and it hates the sin most of all because it has discovered God's love."[596]

The last few verses of today's chapter contain a response from mankind that still has me shaking my head, even though I have read this many times before. It leaves me dumbfounded.

Let me explain with background. When the seventh seal was broken in Revelation 8, there came out of that seal seven angels with seven trumpets with the most horrific judgment coming on the earth. Each trumpet was relegated for a disaster to judge mankind. Revelation 9 has the fifth and the sixth trumpet. The fifth plague on the earth came directly from the bottomless pit of hell. It was five months of absolute terror on the planet. It would be so bad that men would want to die, but John says these sobering words, "They will long to die but death flees from them." The sixth trumpet is an angel of death who kills a third of mankind. These trumpets are horrifying.

Why would this be important to describe and detail in this chapter? It's what happens at the end that is most mindboggling. Let's read what happens to two-thirds of the planet's population who are still alive after experiencing the judgments of trumpets six and seven:

> The rest of mankind who were not killed by these plagues still did not repent of the work of their hands; they did not stop worshiping demons, and idols of gold, silver, bronze, stone and wood—idols that cannot see or hear or walk. Nor did they repent of their murders, their magic arts, their sexual immorality or their thefts. (Revelation 9:20-21, NIV)

Twice it says that mankind still did not repent. The brazenness and the hardness of humans that the worst tragedy can hit the planet and yet they will still refuse to turn to God. Can a love for sin be that strong that people will not even repent?

Puritan writer Thomas Watson reminds us of the mistake of repentance: "Many think they repent, when it is not the offense, but the penalty troubles them."[597] Watson wants us to know that repentance has to do with wanting to stop sinning but many just want the penalty and result of their sin to stop. What will it take to get someone to repent? Based on Revelation 9, I know it's not catastrophe. Because it doesn't get more catastrophic than these trumpets.

Look what happened to people after September 11, 2001. The churches were filled, but it didn't last. Tragedy is not what makes people repent of their sin.

Repentance is a word not used much, if ever anymore, today in churches. If people would hear the word *repentance*, they might see it as puritanical or legalistic, when it is a surrendered will to God that hates sin so much that they want nothing to do with it, that there is a 180-degree turn from any known sin. No one described a repentant heart better than nineteenth-century orphanage director George Müller: "There was a day when I died . . . died to George Müller, his opinions, preferences, tastes and will—died to the world, its approval or censure—died to the approval or blame even of my brethren and friends—and since then I have studied only to show myself approved unto God."[598] That is a repentant and changed man.

Repentance by definition means a change of heart, to turn from. Repentance turns from the direction of sin and starts traveling toward God's direction. It seems that humanity in Revelation 9 wanted to continue in their sin more than turning toward God. Their murders, thefts, magic arts, and sexual immorality were worth continuing while still under judgment than asking God for mercy and grace. Sin is powerful!

How powerful? One Puritan writer said sin is so powerful that it made the devil the devil.[599]

These men in Revelation 9 are not just men in the tribulation who refuse to repent, I've seen it happen today. Where people hate the consequences but not the sin that caused it, so they don't repent. But if when you sin, your heart is broken, then there is hope.

Have you ever been going to a place where you needed the help of your GPS to talk the directions to you? The part I love about my phone's maps is that when I have been distracted or unfamiliar with an area and miss my turn, the voice doesn't say, "You are so dumb. I'm through helping you. Find someone else. Do what you want and stay lost if you're not going to listen." No, my GPS says, "Turn around when possible." And that's exactly what I do. And that's exactly what repentance is—we get to turn around when possible.

If you feel the Holy Spirit's conviction, turn around. It's possible.

You Can't Always Have Dessert, You Need Vegetables Too

Today's Reading: Revelation 10

David Wilkerson was a spiritual father to me. His investment in my life was so significant that I am in ministry today because of him. He is the founder of Teen Challenge, the author of *The Cross and the Switchblade*, and the founding pastor of Time Square Church, and he made an imprint on my life unlike anybody in my early years. From the investment of wisdom, finances, time, and opportunity, one thing I have today, which he gave me when he ordained me, was a New American Standard Bible that he signed in the front. He also included a verse from Revelation 10. Let's look at our passage for today, which includes the verse Wilkerson wrote in my Bible:

> The voice which I heard from heaven, *I heard* again speaking with me, and saying, "Go, take the book which is open in the hand of the angel who stands on the sea and on the land." So I went to the angel, telling him to give me the little book. And he said to me, "Take it and eat it; it will make your stomach bitter, but in your mouth it will be sweet as honey." I took the little book out of the angel's hand and ate it, and in my mouth it was sweet as honey; and when I had eaten it, my stomach was made bitter. (Revelation 10:8-10)

David Wilkerson was challenging me to be a man of the book. The book means the Bible. He was wanted me to understand that when we devour the Bible by reading it and studying it, there will be places in it that will be sweet and some places that will be bitter.

When John was being challenged to eat the book, it was not literally but figuratively. Eating meant study, read, and apply, not actually eat. I read this crazy story of someone who missed the point of Revelation 10. In the early 1900s, the Ethiopian emperor Menelik II grew ill. Believing the Bible could cure him, he ate pages of the Bible. He died in 1913 after eating the entire book of 2 Kings.[600] The book of 2 Kings is good but not good enough to eat all twenty-five chapters.

The Bible becomes bitter when truth troubles me, when it contradicts me. Then it's swallowing a bitter pill but a healthy one. When it's bitter, I am tempted to theologize the concepts away or to pass over it, but that's hard to do when you are eating the book.

E. Paul Hovey so insightfully said: "Men do not reject the Bible because it contradicts itself but because it contradicts them."[601] Those are the bitter sections.

But to be honest, there are a lot of sweet spots in the Word. And when you hit a sweet spot, there is nothing like it. A sweet spot is getting something from the Bible that you needed that day, that moment, for encouragement and hope. I can say without a doubt, the honey-sweet verses make the bitter verses palatable, because when I hit a bitter verse, one that is challenging my behavior and attitude, a verse that refuses to move for me, I remember all the sweet ones and realize I can't always have dessert but need vegetables too.

And that bitter verse isn't going to move, it's asking me to move.

An officer in the navy had always dreamed of commanding a battleship. He was finally given commission of the newest ship in the fleet. One stormy night, as the ship plowed through the rough water, the captain was on the bridge and spotted a strange light rapidly closing in on his own vessel. This was before radio, so he ordered the signalman to flash the message to the unidentified craft, "Alter your course ten degrees to the south." Only a moment passed before the reply came: "Alter your course ten degrees to the north." Determined that his ship would take a backseat to no other, the captain snapped out the order: "Alter course ten degrees—I am the Captain!" The response came back, "Alter your course ten degrees—I am Seaman Third Class Jones." Now infuriated, the captain grabbed the signal light with his own hands and fired off: "Alter course, I am a battleship." The reply: "Alter your course, I am a lighthouse."[602]

God's Word stands like a lighthouse for us. It directs us to alter our course at His direction both the sweet *and* the bitter parts.

No Shortcuts

Today's Reading: Revelation 11

Whenever I read Revelation 11, my mind goes back to the three temptations Jesus experienced in the wilderness that started His public ministry—especially to the third temptation.

Today's chapter reminds us that Satan will tempt us with the right outcome but with bad shortcuts getting there. Always remember the journeys God puts us on toward a desired end have our spiritual growth in it. One of those shortcuts that Satan has gotten so many to bow to has been immorality and fornication. Fornication is having sex outside of the covenant of marriage. The lie of immorality has been, *If I love you then I should sleep with you.* It's sabotaging the growth journey. Commitment and covenant are the prerequisites for intimacy, not love. Love leads us to commitment and covenant not to the bedroom. In the waiting period, we learn patience, we learn how to develop other important areas, we learn respect, and we learn what real love is. Immorality and fornication are shortcuts that will always hurt the future of a relationship because they are sin.

Jesus was tempted to take a shortcut when His ministry was launched with forty days of fasting and Satanic temptation. In order to see the magnitude of the Revelation 11 verse, we have to see the three temptations of Jesus, and key in on the third one.

In order for temptation to be temptation it has to attract us. It has to have something that we want. What was in it that attracted Jesus?

There were three satanic requests made to Jesus: make bread from stones, throw Himself off the pinnacle, bow before Satan.

Satan requested those things because he was asking Jesus for proof: *prove You are God's Son, prove the Bible is true, prove You don't want it now.*

In the first temptation, Satan is saying, the way to fix your own doubts/insecurity is by what you do instead of trusting what God says. God already told Jesus that Jesus is His beloved Son, so Satan said, "If You are the Son, turn these stones to bread."

In the second temptation, Satan quotes the Bible and wants Jesus to live out a misinterpretation of Scripture. He quotes Psalm 91 but not completely, telling Jesus to jump off the temple and the angels will rescue Him. But Psalm 91 isn't meant for random temple jumping. This is like what churches are doing by snake handling to prove Mark 16:18: "They will pick up serpents, and if they drink any deadly *poison*, it will not hurt them." It's dangerous and people have died. Don't jump without a full context.

Finally in the third temptation telling Jesus that He can have it all sooner than He thinks if He only takes a shortcut: "The devil took Him to a very high mountain and showed Him all the kingdoms of the world and their glory; and he said to Him, 'All these things I will give You, if You fall down and worship me'" (Matthew 4:8-9).

That's what Satan told Jesus. That's what Satan tells Jesus' children: "Bow down now and you can get what you what sooner." But what he doesn't tell us is by taking the shortcut, we lose the process and the maturity that comes in pain and affliction and patience.

These are some shortcuts: cheating on a test to cheating on a marriage, lying to get money, lying on an application, not tithing, exaggerating, plagiarizing, and the list goes on. The satanic proposal is that we should have it all *now*, and the only thing we have to do to get it is to bow. To Jesus he was saying that He could bypass suffering and the cross and the three years of ministry by bowing to his agenda and clock, not God's clock.

When you get it sooner than God's clock, you also get exhaustion, disappointment, strained or tainted character, and no joy.

The good news is that Jesus did not bow! Jesus did not take the shortcut!

But what about the kingdoms of this world? Now we enter into Revelation 11, the result of not bowing and taking the shortcut: "Then the seventh angel sounded; and there were loud voices in heaven, saying, 'The kingdom of the world has become *the kingdom* of our Lord and of His Christ; and He will reign forever and ever'" (verse 15).

Jesus got it all God's way. And heaven *got loud* with that statement.

Many times God's way is the long way, but it's the right way. Don't be afraid of it taking too long. When it's all said and done, I want heaven to get loud for you and me by not bowing when we have had every opportunity to take Satan's shortcut.

Day 250

SPIRITUAL WARFARE

Today's Reading: Revelation 12

Some years ago, I read an interesting book called *Military Misfortunes: The Anatomy of Failure in War* by Eliot A. Cohen and John Gooch, in which the authors noticed that throughout history defeat rises out of three basic features: the failure to learn, the failure to anticipate, the failure to adapt to changing conditions.[603] We are in a different war called spiritual warfare. And in today's chapter, we find one of the most descriptive places in all Scripture of this battle. We also see in these verses the battle lessons that Cohen and Gooch speak about—that we can learn about this battle, we can anticipate the enemy's movements, and we can have new weapons to adapt to his attacks.

Here is the battle we are in:

> There was war in heaven, Michael and his angels waging war with the dragon. The dragon and his angels waged war, and they were not strong enough, and there was no longer a place found for them in heaven. And the great dragon was thrown down, the serpent of old who is called the devil and Satan, who deceives the whole world; he was thrown down to the earth, and his angels were thrown down with him. Then I heard a loud voice in heaven, saying, "Now the salvation, and the power, and the kingdom of our God and the authority of His Christ have come, for the accuser of our brethren has been thrown down, he who accuses them before our God day and night. And they overcame him because of the blood of the Lamb and because of the word of their testimony, and they did not love their life even when faced with death. For this reason, rejoice, O heavens and you who dwell in them. Woe to the earth and the sea, because the devil has come down to you, having great wrath, knowing that he has *only* a short time." (Revelation 12:7-12)

We find so much in these verses about hell, heaven, and the believers. There is a battle going on against the soul of every Christian. This is the origin, the reason, the cast, and the results of spiritual warfare. We see all the descriptive words of the devil. He is called the dragon, the great dragon, the serpent of old, the devil, the accuser of the brethren, and Satan.

We learn that he and his angels were thrown out of heaven. They are fighting a war they can't win and they know the time is short, but that doesn't stop their devilish onslaught. They fight with great wrath and anger. And their target is God's church. The last verse of the chapter says, "The dragon was enraged with the woman, and went off to make war with the rest of her offspring, who keep the commandments of God and hold to the testimony of Jesus" (verse 17).

We are the offspring. And if we are the target, we need a weapon. But we don't get just *a* weapon, we get three weapons: "They overcame him because of the blood of the Lamb and because of the word of their testimony, and they did not love their life even when faced with death" (verse 11).

Here are God's three devil-winning strategies in order to overcome Satan:

First, the blood of the Lamb. This is a judicial weapon. Judicial means we have legal rights. The blood of Jesus is our assurance our sins are forgiven. In the long list of his names, the devil is called "the accuser of the brethren." He accuses us of our sins to try and get us to doubt that we are God's children. When we have been born again, the blood of Jesus goes over the doorposts of our hearts, just as the children of Israel needed to put it on their actual doorposts, so the angel of death would pass by. We are covered by the blood, Satan has to pass by, but not without throwing some fiery darts.

The second weapon is the word of our testimony. This is an evidential weapon. We have history from saints in the past that God delivers. When we read and hear about God's deliverance in His children's lives, this is a weapon. How do we use it? Like this: When we tell or hear testimonies, we are encouraged and know that if God did it for others, He can do for us as well.

The third weapon hardly gets mentioned: "They did not love their life even when faced with death." This is a sacrificial weapon. It's the realization that our lives are not our own, we have been bought with a price. We don't have to go into self-preservation mode, our timelines on earth are determined by God not by cancer, violence, or tragedy. We are on God's clock, and He determines our home-going date so we don't have to fear death.

As A. W. Tozer so powerful reminds us, "When God calls a man, he cannot die until he has done the work God has called him to do. If God calls a man to a work, and the man says yes, that man cannot die until that work is done. The man God calls is immortal until his work is done."[604]

Man doesn't decide our death, God does. That's why Jesus said, "No one has taken it away from Me, but I lay it down on My own initiative" (John 10:18).

Charles Spurgeon gives us this warning: "The trumpet still plays the notes of war. You cannot sit down and put the victory wreath on your head. You do not have a crown just yet. You still must wear the helmet and carry the sword. You must watch, pray, and fight. Expect your last battle to be the most difficult, for the enemy's fiercest charge is reserved for the end of the day."[605]

But something good comes out of this war and battle, as evangelist Smith Wigglesworth reminds us: "Great faith is the product of great fights. Great testimonies are the outcome of great tests. Great triumphs can only come out of great trials."[606]

This is a great fight we are in, but we will come out with great faith, great testimonies, and great triumphs because the Lamb of God gave us weapons in this war.

Day 251

Forty-Two Is an Important Number

Today's Reading: Revelation 13

If you are a baseball fan, the number 42 is an important number. It belonged to Jackie Robinson, the first African American to cross the racial lines and play major league baseball in 1947. That number has been retired from all MLB teams. This means that no future MLB player can ever wear Jackie's number. It commemorates the courage and bravery of what Jackie Robinson did for the game of baseball with the Brooklyn Dodgers. The number was retired in a ceremony, which took place April 15, 1997, at Shea Stadium to mark the fiftieth anniversary of Robinson's first game with the Dodgers.[607]

That number was important not just for baseball but for the racial divide in our country. It is also important and significant today and more so in the future for a different reason.

In today's chapter we look at something else important and significant for today and the future, where the number *forty-two* is seismic for the planet.

When we see the prefix *anti,* we immediately think it means "against" or "opposite." Consider some of these words with the anti prefix attached to it:

Anticlimax—the ending of something is disappointing, you expected more.

Antisocial—it's the opposite of being out going and inviting.

Anti-inflammatory—we older folks know about this, it's that which is against swelling in the human body and fights it.

But how about this disturbing one—*antichrist*?

Revelation 13 is the introduction to a character yet to be named in human history who is more evil than any one person who has ever walked the planet—the antichrist. Many believe that the beast from the beginning of this chapter refers to the antichrist. Let's read this chilling account of what is coming to the earth:

I saw a beast coming up out of the sea, having ten horns and seven heads, and on his horns were ten diadems, and on his heads *were* blasphemous names. And the beast which I saw was like a leopard, and his feet were like *those* of a bear, and his mouth like the mouth of a lion. And the dragon gave him his power and his throne and great authority. And *I saw* one of his heads as if it had been slain, and his fatal wound was healed. And the whole earth was amazed and *followed* after the beast; and they worshiped the dragon, because he gave his authority to the beast; and they worshiped the beast, saying, "Who is like the beast, and who is able to wage war with him?" There was given to him a mouth speaking arrogant words and blasphemies; and authority to act for forty-two months was given to him. And he opened his mouth in blasphemies against God, to blaspheme His name and His tabernacle, *that is*, those who dwell in heaven. It was given to him to make war with the saints. (Revelation 13:1-7)

Revelation 13 closes with the antichrist's mark of the beast, the number 666. Whenever you hear people talk about eschatology, the study of the end times, many like to speculate about this number and what it means. I grew up during a time when there was wild speculation about who the antichrist might be. Some even went as far as throwing out some names using the 666 as the key to unlock their identity. One name I heard growing up was Ronald Reagan. Why? His full name is Ronald Wilson Reagan. Every part of his name has six letters, thus ending up with 666. Seriously?

Nobody said it better about Revelation speculations than R. T. Williams: "Young men stay away from the subject of prophecy. Let the old men do that. They won't be around to see their mistakes."[608] Brilliant.

The things the apostle John detailed is scary and sobering. Let me give you three points of this time in the future.

First, it is disturbing to see the similarities between Christ and the antichrist. Listen to the language: ten diadems, like a lion, he has power and authority and a throne. And if you look closely at his head, it looks as if he has been slain. How deceptive this is. But no one can forget the beast's power comes from the dragon. What an awful combination—a beast and a dragon make an antichrist.

Second, the world is sucked in and duped by all of this. The *whole earth* is amazed and follows the antichrist. And they will worship the dragon and the beast. What insanity, before the tribulation, the world is made aware of the Lamb of God who died for them but not amazed and will not follow Him or worship Jesus. The satanic deception is awful.

Third, his job is to discredit the true and living Christ. He will speak blasphemies and arrogant words against God, His name, His tabernacle, and to all of His children who are in heaven. He will make war and inspire others on the planet to do the same.

Just as it seemed hopeless for African Americans ever to play in major league baseball until number forty-two paved the route, so *forty-two* gives hope again to humanity. Here is the hope in the midst of this planetary mayhem. Remember, God is the CEO of the universe, not Satan. Satan is not an independent power who can do whatever he wants. He is under God's rule and control. Satan is God's puppet. And as we see, here come number forty-two again!

God gives the beast *forty-two* months to wreak havoc. It will seem God is absent and not defending Himself or the saints in heaven, but this is all in God's plan in the end times. When we see all of these characteristics of the antichrist, it seems hopeless. But the part we cannot miss are these words: *authority to act for forty-two months was given to him*. This brings everything back to the reality of who is *actually* in charge.

Forty-two means God sets the boundaries. Forty-two means Satan is God's Satan and the beast and the dragon are not separate entities that call the shots. God says essentially, "Do your thing for forty-two months, then I will do My thing. And when I do My thing, your future is about to come to an end."

When I read these chilling details and remember forty-two, I'm always reminded of what E. Stanley Jones said: "When Satan attacks you, command him in the name of Jesus to bend his neck. On the back of it you'll find there's a nail-scarred footprint."[609]

Amen.

THE STRANGEST BEATITUDE

Today's Reading: Revelation 14

The Beatitudes are a unique part of Jesus' teachings from the Sermon on the Mount that all start the same way: "Blessed are . . ." Jesus said, "Blessed are . . ." nine different times in Matthew 5. The word *beatitude* actually means supremely blessed. It is a state of utmost bliss and happiness.

Here are some of Jesus' beatitudes:

"Blessed are the poor in spirit, for theirs is the kingdom of heaven" (verse 3).

"Blessed are those who mourn, for they shall be comforted" (verse 4).

"Blessed are the *meek*, for they shall inherit the earth" (verse 5).

"Blessed are the pure in heart, for they shall see God" (verse 8).

"Blessed are the peacemakers, for they shall be called sons of God" (verse 9).

But the strangest beatitude has to be in Revelation 14. It starts just like the Matthew 5 Beatitudes, but we would never think the word *blessed* belongs with the words that follow. It's radical, counterintuitive, and sobering:

I heard a voice from heaven, saying, "Write, 'Blessed are the dead who die in the Lord from now on!'" "Yes," says the Spirit, "so that they may rest from their labors, for their deeds follow with them." (Revelation 14:13)

Blessed are the dead.

Sounds morbid.

Blessed are the dead who die in the Lord from now on.

The Holy Spirit responds to this Beatitude and says, "Yes, so that they may rest from their labors."

We are part of a culture that is trying to stay alive the longest they can. Our culture says "Blessed are the living," yet God says here in Revelation 14, "Blessed are the dead." The world judges by the wrong standards; they don't have eternity in their minds and hearts. They are trying to stay alive and extend their life *longer* when they need it extended *forever*.

Blessed are the dead . . . with a very important attachment to it: "who die in the Lord." So that means that not all who die are blessed, happy beyond bliss.

Think of all the dying that happens every day. And blessedness is for those who die *in the Lord*.

There are more than 6 billion people on earth. On average, 60 million of them will die this year. That is 175,000 people dying every day, 8,000 people dying every hour; 200 people die every minute, 8 people die every second. It is unavoidable and undeniable, and one day, you will become one of these statistics. But not all will be blessed. Of the 175,000 who are pouring into eternity every day, there is a company who believe in Jesus and are on the *blessed* list.

As Robert Murray McCheyne wrote:

> There is no blessing on the Christless dead; they rush into an *undone* eternity, unpardoned, unholy. You may put their body in a splendid coffin; you print their name in silver on the lid; you may bring the well-attired company of mourners to the funeral in suits of solemn black; you may lay the coffin slowly in the grave; you may lay the greenest sod above it; you may train the sweetest flowers to grow over it; you may cut a white stone, and grave a gentle epitaph to their memory; still it is but the funeral of a damned soul. You cannot write *blessed* where God hath written "*cursed*."[610]

Mark 16:16 says, "Whoever believes and is baptized is saved; whoever refuses to believe is damned." *You cannot write "blessed" where God has written "damned."*

No three words could be more important to the living than *in the Lord*. That must be our goal, that when we die, we are "in the Lord." That's not the strangest beatitude but the ultimate beatitude. We are learning something about heaven and death with this beatitude. If the Holy Spirit is agreeing with the voice from heaven that "blessed are the dead who die in the Lord," then the ultimate happiness and bliss are not here but in heaven. Then death is not our enemy but our entrance into that joy.

One of the most amazing books I have ever read on the subject of dying is *Our Greatest Gift: A Meditation on Dying and Caring* by Henri Nouwen. It revolutionized my life and help me overcome any fear of death. Listen to how he starts the book:

> Is death something so terrible and absurd that we are better off not thinking or talking about it? Is death such an undesirable part of our

existence that we are better off acting as if it were not real? Is death such an absolute end of all our thoughts and actions that we simply cannot face it? Or is it possible to befriend our dying gradually and live open to it, trusting that we have nothing to fear? Is it possible to prepare for our death with the same attentiveness that our parents had in preparing for our birth? Can we wait for our death as for a friend who wants to welcome us home?[611]

Nouwen then tells us from the Bible that death is our enemy. First Corinthians 15:26 says that. But here's what is revolutionary. In Matthew 5:44, the same chapter with the Beatitudes, Jesus said, "Love your enemy." Nouwen says, "death included."

To befriend death makes death lose its sting. How does this happen? When we understand that death is not the end but the doorway to ultimate happiness into the presence and home of God Himself. C. S. Lewis spoke to it this way: "Our Father refreshes us on our journey with some pleasant inns, but will not encourage us to mistake them for home."[612] There is a longing for home, there is a call deep in the human spirit for more than life, as we know it can provide. What Lewis was saying to us was why would we want to stay forever at a hotel when we have a beautiful home waiting for us? Why long to stay here when something inside of us tells us God is preparing for us a place?

That's why blessed are the dead who die in the Lord. We no longer have to live in a hotel, we get to go home.

A Necessary Character of God We Don't Like to Mention

Today's Reading: Revelation 15

There is beauty in diversity and variety. Think about how diverse and beautiful America's landscape is. Parts of our country have mountains, deserts, forests, plains, and cities with skyscrapers. The diversity of landscape brings a balance that delights the eye.

The same is true for God. The smallest chapter of Revelation has very large concept in it. It's a word Christians rarely use anymore concerning God.

When we get stuck on part of the landscape of His character, we make God small, which allows unhealthy theology to arise from God. For instance, we know that God is love. That's what made God send His Son for our rescue: "God so loved the world that He gave His only begotten Son." I am grateful for God's grace and His mercy. His goodness is overwhelming at times.

But there's another aspect of God's character that makes us uncomfortable, so we just don't talk about it: the wrath of God. Today's chapter talks about it, so it's important for us to pay attention to it: "Then I saw another sign in heaven, great and marvelous, seven angels who had seven plagues, *which are* the last, because in them the wrath of God is finished" [Revelation 15:1].

The seven angels who have the seven trumpets have the most destructive judgment the planet has ever seen. John describes those as seven plagues because of their devastation. But the word that sums up these seven plagues from these seven angels and seven trumpets is the wrath of God.

As I mentioned in a previous day, when I was growing up, my Italian father had a statement that dealt with his wrath. When we were acting up at the dinner table and getting close to the edge of where judgment needed to come, my father would say, "The bag is getting full." That is how wrath works. It contains patience, warning, and then judgment. God has been sending warnings from the beginning of time and showing patience to the human race. Now Revelation shows when the bag has gotten full. Wrath does not come without thousands of years of warning, but it comes with people disregarding the warning and His patience.

What is the wrath of God?

When we think of wrath we think of anger, explosive anger. But this is not an accurate description of God's wrath. Revelation doesn't portray God losing it on the planet and going off on humanity. We see this kind of anger as irrational, the loss of self-control. Nothing could be further from the truth of this very important part of God. The best way to describe the wrath of God is by connecting it to God's hatred for sin. Revelation shows when God's patience reaches a limit and His calculated judgment comes with wrath against a planet that has rejected Him.

In *Free of Charge*, Croation theologian Miroslav Volf spoke about how early in life he disdained the idea of God's wrath and even rejected God for it. But part of his conversion to faith was in understanding how important God's wrath is and how it's connected to God's love. Listen to Volf describe it:

> Though I used to complain about the indecency of the idea of God's wrath, I came to think that I would have to rebel against a God who *wasn't* wrathful at the sight of the world's evil. God isn't wrathful in spite of being love. God is wrathful *because* God is love.[613]

The wrath of God is necessary if God is love. Because God's wrath is His righteous retribution against sin, the enemy of God. Because God is love and God is good, He can never *not* address evil and sin. How can a police officer be a good cop if he sees crimes committed and does nothing about it? Being a good police officer has a positive side to the law-abiding community but a negative side to the law-breaking criminal. The same is true for God. He is so good that when His wrath is released, He will separate sinners from saints in heaven and hell.

Tony Evans says, "God's wrath is not saying God is cruel but it is saying that God is just. In the same way you want the rapist locked up because you want justice that is what we are talking about, God must respond to the crime called sin. God must respond to sin based upon His nature."[614]

Let's look at Psalm 45:7 and we will see love and hate present in the same verse: "You have loved righteousness and hated wickedness." God hates sin because God loves righteousness. His hate is expressed through His wrath.

The book of Revelation reminds us that no one gets away with anything. God's wrath is God's justice. My father said, "The bag is full." Consider how Paul talked about it Romans 2:5: "Because of your stubbornness and unrepentant heart you are storing up wrath for yourself in the day of wrath and revelation of the righteous judgment of God." That's the best description of wrath and the book of Revelation. The storage unit of wrath is now full and unleashed.

In Psalm 7, David gives us a vivid picture of the wrath of God on evil:

Yet if the wicked do not repent,
you will not relent with your wrath,
slaying them with your shining sword.
You are the conqueror with an arsenal of lethal weapons
that you've prepared for them.
You have bent and strung your bow,
making your judgment-arrows shafts of burning fire.
(verses 12-13, TPT)

David says the patience of God is Him not releasing the bent bow that has been pulled back. The wrath of God is released because His mercy and grace have been ignored.

So here's the good news in the midst of all this wrath talk: the bow is still bent and hasn't been released. A bent bow means we can repent and ask for God's forgiveness. God is a God of wrath. And God is a God of mercy. The bent bow means we have time. Use this time to get right with God instead of waiting till the bag gets full.

We can experience angels worshiping in heaven or seven angels unleashing the wrath of God. How do we get the latter? Paul tells us in Romans 5:8-9:

Christ proved God's passionate love for us by dying in our place while we were still lost and ungodly! And there is still much more to say of his unfailing love for us! For through the blood of Jesus we have heard the powerful declaration, "You are now righteous in my sight." And because of the sacrifice of Jesus, you will never experience the wrath of God. (TPT)

Saved from the wrath of God through Jesus.

THE PARENTHESIS IS A LIFE PRESERVER

Today's Reading: Revelation 16

One of the scariest movies I have ever seen was not in a theater but in a church. It was called *A Thief in the Night*, and it was circulating in the 1970s about the end times. I knew I wanted to be ready for the rapture, the second coming of Jesus. I remember leaving that church service as an elementary student knowing full well in my heart that I needed to be ready for that day. I went on to read Hal Lindsey's *Late Great Planet Earth*. At that time they had it in a comic book form, and it was the clincher for me that I was going to be ready for Jesus to come back as a thief in the night.

If things could get any worse for earth and humanity, Revelation 16 tells us it does in the great tribulation. As if seven trumpets of disaster were not enough for the planet, God unleashes seven bowls of wrath into the earth, from bodily affliction to polluting rivers and water. What's interesting is that in the midst of these wrathful bowls of God's judgment, one theme keeps being shouted by the angels inflicting the punishment: "Righteous art Thou O Holy One." Their words remind us that God is not doing anything that we don't deserve—this is a day of wrath and judgment after millennia of mercy and patience.

These bowls are terrifying, as is men's response to the outpouring of God's wrath. Almost as many times as it says "God is righteous" after one of the bowls is poured out, it says as many times, "They did not repent so as to give Him glory." How corrupt is man by this time in his history?

The chapter ends with a name many of us are all familiar with. As if things can't get any worse, we are introduced to Armageddon, the place of the final battle on the planet. All that to say that in the midst of these horrific verses, a parenthetical statement shows up and stands alone in these passages, because the verse speaks to the *now* and not to the future: "('Behold, I am coming like a thief. Blessed is the one who stays awake and keeps his clothes, so that he will not walk about naked and men will not see his shame.')" (Revelation 16:15).

Verse 15 is a parenthetical life preserver for humanity now, right now before this chapter comes upon the planet with the wrath of God. When I say parenthetical, it's just a large word for parentheses, an insert of another thought, a little path from the original thought. But this is not a little diversion, this is deliverance from the wrath of God. It is as if John breaks from the vision and in terror of what is going to happen says to humanity, *This doesn't have to happen to you. Stay awake and ready for the rapture.* The parentheses show us John being overwhelmed and wanting to help us all.

The parentheses brings us to the rapture, the second coming of Jesus. The apostle John says that Jesus will come like a thief in the night, but this is not only John's description of the second coming of Jesus. Jesus says in Matthew 24 that this is the way it happens. In 1 Thessalonians 5:2, Paul uses the *thief-in-the-night* image. And in 2 Peter 3:10, Peter also says He will come like a thief. The thief-in-the-night day is the rapture. The rapture is Jesus coming physically a second time to the earth, not to redeem it but to start to judging it.

The rapture has two important days attached to it: the wedding day and the judgment day. The wedding day is the celebration of the "born again" dead and living all going to heaven. It's the final call, our reward of heaven. And the Bible calls it a wedding-day celebration. The second day is judgment day and it is God making all wrongs right. No one gets away with anything because of this day.

Every person will be judged for what they have done. Hitler and Saddam Hussein will be there. Stalin and Castro. People from your city and my city and from every place throughout the ages. Every person will stand before God.

In *Who Will Face the Tribulation?*, Tim LaHaye vividly imagined what the unexpected suddenness of the rapture will be like:

When Christ calls His living saints to be with Him, millions of people will suddenly vanish from the earth. An unsaved person who happens to be in the company of a believer will know immediately that his friend has vanished. There will certainly be worldwide recognition of the fact, for when over one-half of a billion people suddenly depart this earth, leaving their earthly belongings behind, pandemonium and confusion will certainly reign for a time.

A million conversations will end midsentence.

A million phones . . . will suddenly go dead.

A woman will reach for a man's hand in the dark . . . and no one will be there.

A man will turn with a laugh to slap a colleague on the back and his hand will move through empty air.

A basketball player will make a length-of-the-floor pass to a teammate streaking down the court and find there is no one there to receive it. And no referee to call it out-of-bounds.

A mother will pull back the covers in a bassinet, smelling the sweet baby smell one moment but suddenly kissing empty space and looking into empty blankets.[615]

Just as the Old Testament is saturated with prophecies concerning Christ's first coming, which we call Christmas, so both testaments are filled with references to the Christ's second coming. One scholar has estimated that there are 1,845 references to Christ's second coming in the Old Testament, where seventeen books give it prominence. In the 260 chapters of the New Testament, there are 318 references to the second coming of Christ. One out of every thirty New Testament verses speak about the Second Coming. Twenty-three of the twenty-seven New Testament books refer to the second coming of Jesus. For every prophecy in the Bible concerning Christ's first coming, there are eight that look forward to His second![616]

The first time He came, He came as an infant. The second time, He comes as the infinite. The first time He came in humility, deity in diapers. The second time, He comes in purple robes of royalty. The first time He came, men killed Him. The second time, every man will bow before Him.

Because He Wins, I Win

Today's Reading: Revelation 17

A few times in high school I had to fill in on the track and field team because some players were lost to injuries and the track coach pulled athletes from other school sports. I remember being asked to run a relay. I found it intriguing how these runners crossed the finish line on a close race. They leaned forward, sticking out their heads across their chests, because in that sport, milliseconds matter. And if the head crosses, the other parts of the body win too.

The Bible says in Colossians 1:18 that Jesus is the head of the body, which is His church. And as God's children, we are the body of Christ. He's the head and we are the body—that's the New Testament image. And as a runner wins the race with his head first, so is true with us spiritually. If the head crosses, the rest of the body wins. The book of Revelation reminds us the head of the body is crossing the finish line. And because He wins, you and I win!

Revelation 17 shows evil unleashed on the planet through the great harlot, Babylon, and the beast. This unholy trinity seems to launch on all-cylinders with one target in mind: the saints of God. In fact, their hatred for the saints is so intense, John describes it as "being drunk with the blood of the saints and with the blood of the witnesses of Jesus" (verse 6).

Then we read about the head. And wherever the head is, the body goes with it: "These [the unholy trinity of the harlot, the beast, and Babylon] will wage war against the Lamb, and the Lamb will overcome them, because He is Lord of lords and King of kings, and those who are with Him are the called and chosen and faithful" (Revelation 17:14).

I grew up in the church. We used terms and terminologies so often and frequently that I never knew context or reasoning, which has the capability of watering down the power of phrases. One of those phrases is *King of kings and Lord of lords*. We would say this about Jesus all the time. But to see it in the Revelation 17 context reminds me, this church boy, how powerful this phrase really is. What makes *King of kings and Lord of lords* powerful is the word that comes before it, *because*.

That word *because* is a subordinating conjunction, which means it connects two parts of a sentence in which one (the subordinate) explains the other. Part one of verse 14 says that these will wage war against the Lamb and the Lamb will overcome them. How? The answer is in the subordinating conjunction, *because*. *Because* He is the Lord of lords and King of kings. That phrase, which I heard in songs and sermons, is connected to the greatest victory in all human history—the Lamb defeats hell forever. Because no king and no lord is higher than Him.

But that's just part one of the subordinating conjunction. Without bogging us down with grammar, we get a conjunction within the subordinating conjunction. We read, "Because He is the Lord of lords and King of kings, and [because] those who are with Him are the called and chosen and faithful."

The good news for us is that *because* He wins, you and I win. Because the head crosses the finish line, the body gets the reward also. Because He is the King, you and I are royalty. Because He is the Lord, you and I are protected and provided for.

I was reading the story of someone that knew instinctively the power of the words *King of kings and the Lord of lords*. When Queen Victoria had just ascended her throne in the mid-1800s, as was the custom of royalty, she went to hear George Frideric Handel's *Messiah*, rendered by the London Royal Symphony. She had been instructed as to her conduct by those who knew royal protocol, and was told that she must *not* rise when the others stood during the "Hallelujah Chorus." When that magnificent chorus started and the singers were shouting "Hallelujah! Hallelujah! Hallelujah! for the Lord God omnipotent reigneth," witnesses of the event said she sat with great difficulty. It seemed as if she would rise in spite of the custom of kings and queens but contained herself. Finally when the oratorio came to that part of the chorus where the choir echoes the sopranos proclaiming Him "King of kings and Lord of lords" and as it kept modulating higher and higher, suddenly the young queen could no longer contain herself. She rose and stood with bowed head, as if she realized that a higher authority was being sung about and to at that moment. She realized He is the King of all kings and the Lord of all lords and so she must rise and declare it against all tradition and protocol. And Queen Victoria was right to do it.

King of kings and Lord of lords means there is no authority higher than the Lamb, and that is why every knee will bow and every tongue confess that Jesus is Lord. You can confess that now on your own or you will be forced to confess on the day of judgment. I choose now.

Babylon Talk

Today's Reading: Revelation 18

When Michael Bloomberg was still mayor of New York City, he announced he was stepping up his efforts beyond his role as mayor to battle a number of social issues, including fights against smoking and obesity, and for gun control. He detailed his plans in an interview in which he predicted his crusades against those issues would serve him well in the afterlife.

Then billionaire Bloomberg said, "I am telling you if there is a God, when I get to heaven I'm not stopping to be interviewed. I am heading straight in. I have earned my place in heaven. It's not even close."[617]

That is scary talk, Michael Bloomberg. That is Babylon talk.

What is Babylon talk? It's the prophecy in today's chapter of the fall of Babylon. But I don't think Babylon is Babylon at all.

The Revelation 18 Babylon has been the topic of so much eschatological speculation and guessing on who that actually is. I think that is dangerous and usually ends with the wrong assumptions. Scholars have guessed that it could be Rome or the United States. I don't see either. When people become sure on what the Bible calls mysteries, my antennae go up.

Why? I think Babylon is bigger than a localized and specific name of a city or country. It is a spirit of security that comes from wealth and influence and seeing no need of God for our forgiveness or help in getting to heaven. Fallen Babylon is the fall of humanism and every false foundation it is built upon—from science to affluence and influence, riches, power, and personality. Without God, Babylon will fall and always fail. Here is what John saw of what was considered Babylon the great:

> After these things I saw another angel coming down from heaven, having great authority, and the earth was illumined with his glory. And he cried out with a mighty voice, saying, "Fallen, fallen is Babylon the great! She has become a dwelling place of demons and a prison of every unclean spirit, and a prison of every unclean and hateful bird. For all the nations have drunk of the wine of the passion of her immorality, and the kings of the earth have committed *acts* of immorality with

her, and the merchants of the earth have become rich by the wealth of her sensuality."

I heard another voice from heaven, saying, "Come out of her, my people, so that you will not participate in her sins and receive of her plagues; for her sins have piled up as high as heaven, and God has remembered her iniquities. (Revelation 18:1-5)

Babylon was a specific Old Testament place. At one point at the height of her power, Daniel chapter 5 says the king of Babylon saw the finger of a man's hand write on the wall of his palace a message of judgment that needed someone to interpret. It was during a feast that the image crashed their Babylonian party. It was so frightening, the Bible says it affected King Belshazzar physically: "The king's face grew pale and his thoughts alarmed him, and his hip joints went slack and his knees began knocking together" (Daniel 5:6).

Daniel is called in to interpret the writing and says basically, "Babylon, your days are numbered and this kingdom is coming to an end." And the end for them happened that night with the invasion of the Medes and Persians.

The party was over in one night. And now in Revelation 18, the party is over again. But I don't think it's the same city again. I think it has to do with anyone, anything, any country, system, or government that feels no need of heavenly help.

The scary part is that Revelation 18 almost sounds like Daniel's interpretation from more than 2,500 years earlier. The Revelation Babylon party has a timed ending too. Twice in the chapter it says, "for in one hour your judgment will come" (verses 10 and 17).

Any system that tries to last without God is simply Babylon, be it a country, a person, a system, or a billionaire. Even if you are the best at these, your sins and forgiveness of them need God.

Let me give a word to those who have Babylon talk and left God out in their lives. Someone said it like this: "There are two ways whereby God punishes sin: the fires of hell and the blood of Jesus. These two things go together: the fires of hell and the blood of Jesus. It's not a question of whether your sin will be punished, it's a question of how." Remember, God always wins. Everyone who pronounces their power over God will fall like Babylon.

In the mid-1700s French humanist Voltaire at the end of his life had some Babylon talk. He declared that his writings would displace the Bible, and that in one hundred years the Word of God would be forgotten. You can't fight God or you will fall like Babylon. Here is what happened. Twenty-five years after

Voltaire's death, Voltaire's house became the printing center for the Geneva Bible society, and tens of thousands of Bibles were printed and sent from his house.[618] You can't mess with God. He always wins. Or as Allister McGrath said that many are "trying to exterminate God and finding out that he outlives his pallbearers."[619]

I wouldn't spend my time on trying to figure out if Babylon is an actual place in the tribulation future. I would spend my time making sure I am trusting in the only thing that can get me to heaven, the blood of Jesus.

Have you heard the story about the rich man who was determined to "take it with him" when he died? He prayed until finally the Lord gave in. There was one condition; he could bring only one suitcase of his wealth. The rich man decided to fill the case with gold bars that he'd invested in.

The day came when God called him home. One of the angels greeted him but told him he couldn't bring his suitcase.

"Oh, but I have an agreement with God," the man explained.

"That's unusual," said the archangel. "Mind if I take a look?"

The man opened the suitcase to reveal the shining gold bars. He thought gold would be good everywhere.

The angel was amazed. "Why in the world would you bring pavement with you?"

Revelation 21:21 tells us that gold is the pavement in heaven. Why trust in something that God says has no great value? Our greatest value is the blood of Jesus.

A Great Word to Use When Great Things Happen

Today's Reading: Revelation 19

For a number of chapters, we been through some dark moments, but now in today's chapter the hope bursts on the scene with loud shouting! It is God making all things right and heaven explodes in praise over it:

> After these things I heard something like a loud voice of a great multitude in heaven, saying, "Hallelujah! Salvation and glory and power belong to our God; BECAUSE HIS JUDGMENTS ARE TRUE AND RIGHTEOUS; for He has judged the great harlot who was corrupting the earth with her immorality, and HE HAS AVENGED THE BLOOD OF HIS BOND-SERVANTS ON HER." And a second time they said, "Hallelujah! HER SMOKE RISES UP FOREVER AND EVER." And the twenty-four elders and the four living creatures fell down and worshiped God who sits on the throne saying, "Amen. Hallelujah!" And a voice came from the throne, saying, "Give praise to our God, all you His bond-servants, you who fear Him, the small and the great." Then I heard *something* like the voice of a great multitude and like the sound of many waters and like the sound of mighty peals of thunder, saying, "Hallelujah! For the Lord our God, the Almighty, reigns." [Revelation 19:1-6]

Hallelujah! That's a great word to use when great things happen. Heaven shouted it! We see it here four times. A great multitude in heaven shouted it twice: "Hallelujah! Salvation and glory and power belong to our God." Then the twenty-four elders and the four living creatures said it, "Hallelujah." Then the bond servants said hallelujah so loudly that it sounded like Niagara Falls or thunder in the heavens.

What a great word. But what does *hallelujah* mean?

The word is an interjection, a part of grammar that is an interruption to a sentence. It is an emotional and, many times, a good interruption. It's a word that just pops out. It bursts out of the mouths because of joyful hearts. That happens in many of the psalms of the Old Testament. It's a Hebrew expression that means, "Praise Yahweh [the Lord]." We would translate the phrase as simply *praise the Lord*! It's a victorious shout.

In the New Testament *hallelujah* only occurs in Revelation 19 in the triumphant song of praise as heaven sings about God finally making things right and getting His banquet ready to celebrate. Here in this chapter all of humanity has been waiting for this day of judgment. God is avenging the wrongs done to His people.

It's a great word to use when something great happens. I think hallelujah does two things: it gives God the credit and it reminds me that He is good to me. We will get many hallelujah days now and will not have to wait until Revelation 19 to join heaven's chorus. It's important that God gets the credit for them. I love the simplicity of the word and the magnitude of it. It's an exercise that we should start using immediately.

When you have a good physical and all the numbers are healthy, throw out a hallelujah.

When your child has been in a car accident and the only thing busted up is a car but everyone is safe, throw out a hallelujah.

When you are reading the Bible and come across a verse that is exactly what you needed for that day, throw out a hallelujah.

When for some reason there is no rush-hour traffic coming home from work, throw out a hallelujah.

When the rent is paid . . .

When there is food on the table . . .

When the report cards are good . . .

When there is gas in the car . . .

When the sun is shining . . .

When you wake up in the morning . . . throw out a hallelujah! It's saying, "God, You get the credit. God, You are good to me."

There was a church that would not give God praise for anything. Every service they just sat there. No hallelujahs coming from this congregation—it was strictly a no-hallelujah church. The pastor knew he needed to do something epic to shake things up. He remembered what Jesus said in Luke 19:40: "If they keep quiet, the stones will cry out" (NIV). So one Sunday when the people came to church, they saw a giant boulder the pastor had rolled on to the stage. He'd spray painted on it, "If you don't, then I will."

Just remember, no matter how many praise God beside you and around you, they can't praise God for you. You must praise God for yourself. Let's start joining with heaven with some hallelujahs today. That is such a great word when great things happen. And great things are always happening!

THE DAY THE SAVIOR TURNS TO JUDGE

Today's Reading: Revelation 20

A young man was drinking heavily and decided to go for a swim at a California beach. Fortunately, an older man was watching the young man as he entered the water and saw that when he dove in, he did not come back up for air. The older man ran toward the struggling young man, dove into the water, and saved his life.

A few years later, that same young man was standing in court facing a sentence on drug charges. Suddenly, the young man realized the judge was the very same man who'd saved his life when he was drowning years earlier. He looked at the judge and said, "Sir, don't you recognize me? You saved my life a few years ago. Don't you remember?" The judge nodded and then looked at the young man. "Young man," he said. "Then I was your savior, but now I am your judge."[620]

While we are alive, Christ is available to all who will trust Him now as their Savior. But if we reject Him in this life, we will stand before the Lord and know Him only as our Judge. Savior or Judge—that decision is ours. What will we do with Jesus while we are alive?

If we do not choose Jesus as Savior, then Revelation 20 speaks about the setting and the court we will be in called the great white-throne judgment—in this final scene in human history where all will be judged.

This is what John the apostle saw:

I saw a great white throne and Him who sat upon it, from whose presence earth and heaven fled away, and no place was found for them. And I saw the dead, the great and the small, standing before the throne, and books were opened; and another book was opened, which is *the* book of life; and the dead were judged from the things which were written in the books, according to their deeds. And the sea gave up the dead which were in it, and death and Hades gave up the dead which were in them; and they were judged, every one *of them* according to their deeds. Then death and Hades were thrown into the lake of fire. This is the second death, the lake of fire. And if anyone's name was not found written in the book of life, he was thrown into the lake of fire. (Revelation 20:11-15)

The way we live here will have eternal, unchangeable, and profound consequences. Who we are today—and who we are becoming today—is preparing us for who we will be for all eternity. And only in this life can we impact our eternity.

There are two judgments in heaven: the great white throne and the judgment seat of Christ. The latter is for the saints of God who receive reward for their Christian life. The great white throne judgment is when it's all said and done. It's over for a person if they appear at this heavenly hearing.

A misconception is that while we are at the throne of God, that will determine whether we go to heaven or hell. Whether we go to heaven or hell is not determined in heaven, it is determined in this life right now. There is no opportunity to reroute our travel plans after we have died. One second after we die our eternal destination is unalterably fixed. If Christ has not bore our punishment in this life, then we must bear our own. As Matthew Henry tells us, "It ought to be the business of every day to prepare for our last day."[621]

Your attendance is mandatory at one of two judgments: the judgment seat of Christ or the great white throne judgment. This is an appointment humanity will keep. Which one you will be at will be determined by whether you are born again or not. If you are not born again, then you will be at this Revelation 20 great white throne judgment.

Here are the characteristics of this Revelation 20 judgment:

We will be judged fairly: no jury bias, no venue change, because none is needed.

We will be judged thoroughly: no loopholes and nothing missed on the evidence.

We will be judged impartially: all proceedings will be fair and no one can buy off the Judge.

We will be judged individually: no one will stand with us as us stand before the Judge of all the earth.

What makes this day incredible is the Savior of the world will become the Judge of the world. Jesus tells us that God will not judge us on that day, but the Son will: "For not even the Father judges anyone, but He has given all judgment to the Son" (John 5:22). The day the Savior turns to Judge.

When I think of John's description of this frightening day, my mind goes all the way back to the book of Genesis and a conversation Abraham had with the angel of the Lord. It was right before the judgment and destruction of Sodom and Gomorrah. In Genesis 18:25, Abraham made an eternal statement in question form: "Will not the Judge of all the earth do right?" The resounding answer to Abraham's question is yes!

During one of Billy Graham's final interviews, Diane Sawyer asked, "What do you hope [people] will say?" In other words she wanted to know how he would like to be remembered" He responded, "I don't want them to say big things about me. Because I don't deserve them. I want to hear one Person say something nice about me, and that's the Lord. When I face Him, I want Him to say to me, 'Well done, thy good and faithful servant,' but I'm not sure I'm going to hear it."[622] The humility of Billy Graham is staggering. I think he did hear those words a few years ago.

C. S. Lewis said this about that day: "Precisely because we cannot predict the moment, we must be ready at all moments."[623]

Day 259

Important Words to a Prostitute

Today's Reading: Revelation 21

Kimutchi will always have a place in my heart. She was a prostitute from the streets of Detroit who I led to the Lord. It was one of our initial conversations that forever has marked me. She used to call me Father Tim. She came to our church one day and said, "Father Tim, can you pray for me? I'm having a tough week."

"Sure, Kimutchi," I told her. But as I began to pray, she quickly interrupted me.

"No. You can't pray. I have no money."

I was puzzled. "What do you mean you have no money?"

She proceeded to tell me that certain pastors in town charge her $25 a prayer and then would give her a Bible passage, which she'd use for playing the lottery numbers. It was a religious scam much like the indulgences during the reformation, which Martin Luther railed against.

I explained that what they had been doing was wrong. Then I took Kimutchi to Matthew 7:21, which says, "Not everyone who says to Me, 'Lord, Lord,' will enter the kingdom of heaven."

Her eyes grew wide with amazement. "That's how you do it?" she said. "I never knew what that meant." When Kimutchi said that, she did not mean the meaning of the verse. She meant the actual numbers on the top of the page. She did not know that "7" meant the chapter and "21" meant the verse. Then she told me over and over, "Give me one I can look up." Then, "Give me another one." We took a journey through the Scriptures together until she finally she asked me, "Father Tim, if I give my life to Jesus, I won't have to be on the streets any longer? I won't have to sell myself any longer? And when I die, I won't have to cry every day like I do?"

And that's when I took her to today's chapter—a chapter that came to mean everything to a prostitute. Here's Kimutchi's final passage that she looked up and saw the numbers 21 and 1 in Revelation:

Then I saw a new heaven and a new earth; for the first heaven and the first earth passed away, and there is no longer *any* sea. And I saw the holy city, new Jerusalem, coming down out of heaven from God, made ready as a bride adorned for her husband. And I heard a loud voice from the throne, saying, "Behold, the tabernacle of God is among men, and He will dwell among them, and they shall be His people, and God Himself will be among them, and He will wipe away every tear from their eyes; and there will no longer be *any* death; there will no longer be *any* mourning, or crying, or pain; the first things have passed away." And He who sits on the throne said, "Behold, I am making all things new." And He said, "Write, for these words are faithful and true." (Revelation 21:1-5)

This is heaven. This is our reward. This is the climax of history. No more wars, no more pain, no more tears, no more funerals. No more cancer, no more taxes, no more racism, no more bills, no more rent, no more need for health insurance. Because God has made all things new.

Once when the great Scottish preacher and writer, George MacDonald, was talking with his family, the conversation turned to heaven. At one point one of his relatives said, "It seems too good to be true." To whom MacDonald replied, "Nay, it is just so good it *must* be true!"[624]

It is just so good it must be true. That is heaven. That's the place I wanted Kimutchi to know existed. And what makes heaven amazing is that "He will wipe away every tear from their eyes." God does that.

It's said that an Eastern Orthodox monk said these profound words about heaven: "For most Christians heaven is envisaged as a kind of postscript, an appendix to a book of which life on earth constitutes the actual text. But the contrary is true. Our earthly life is merely the preface to the book. Life in heaven will be the text—a text without end."[625]

Heaven is the text, not earth. C. S. Lewis's last words, *The Last Battle*, which end the seven-book series of *The Chronicles of Narnia* reiterates the monk's thoughts:

And for us this is the end of all the stories, and we can most truly say that they all lived happily ever after. But for them it was only the beginning of the real story. All their life in this world and all their adventures in Narnia had only been the cover and the title page: now at last they were beginning Chapter One of the Great Story, which no one on earth has read: which goes on forever: in which every chapter is better than the one before.[626]

They were beginning chapter one. It was the beginning of the real story. Lewis got it. The monk got it. I need to get it. Heaven is the text, not earth.

Listen to how the apostle Paul speaks about heaven: "There's far more here than meets the eye. The things we see now are here today, gone tomorrow. But the things we can't see now will last forever" (2 Corinthians 4:18, MSG).

Kimutchi got saved and stopped using her prostitute name and went back to using her given, Diane. She ended up marrying a deacon at another church who had a lawn mower retail shop. My last conversation with her on the phone is when she had only months to live because AIDS had set in from years of selling her body on the streets. This precious ex-prostitute is now in heaven. And in a place where she doesn't cry any longer and all her pain is gone. The words on the page have now become a reality to one of my favorite people in Detroit.

When I get to heaven, I will receive much joy when I see the face of Diane (formerly Kimutchi). Her face will be dry—dry from tears.

Day 260

REPETITION WAS ALWAYS A WARNING

Today's Reading: Revelation 22

Growing up in my house, if you heard Mom or Day say, "Don't make me say it again," you knew that was a clear warning—repetition was a warning. A warning that meant I wasn't listening to what they said the first time. It could be anything from "Clean your room" to how I said something to my sibling, not heeding the first warning shot would always call for the finale, "Don't make me say it again."

Today's chapter closes with repetition.

We've finally made it to number 260, the final chapter of the New Testament—Revelation 22. What a journey it has been.

As the New Testament closes, the apostle John speaks the same words three times. I believe because we forget how important they are. He quotes Jesus in verses 7 and 12: "I am coming quickly." Then he says it one final time: "He who testifies to these things says, 'Yes, I am coming quickly.' Amen. Come, Lord Jesus" (verse 20).

Repetition is always a warning for those who do not take it seriously. Repetition also means we weren't listening the first time, that we did not think it important enough to pause and ponder. Thus John is shooting us one last warning shot before the New Testament closes.

One of the ways the early-church Christians greeted and said goodbye to one another was to say, "Maranatha." That Aramaic word means "The Lord is coming" or "Come Lord Jesus." What a great challenge for us today to find a way to keep the *quick* coming of Jesus ever before us.

A gardener for a large estate in northern Italy was giving a tour to a visitor. He showed him through the castle and the beautiful, well-groomed grounds. The visitor commended him for the beautiful way he kept up the gardens. He asked, "When was the last time the owner was here?"

"About ten years ago," the gardener said.

"Then why do you keep the gardens in such an immaculate, lovely manner?"

"Because I'm expecting him to return," the gardener said.

"Oh, is he coming next week?"

"I don't know when he is coming," the gardener replied, "but I am expecting him today."[627]

In chapter 22, Jesus uses in the last chapter of Revelation the title He used in the first chapter of Revelation, "I am the Alpha and the Omega" (verse 13). He is the beginning and the end. Why does He use these two words or, actually, two letters? *Alpha* is the first letter of the Greek alphabet and *Omega* is the last letter of the Greek alphabet. Jesus is saying that He was there in the beginning of everything and He will be there at the end of everything. And now Jesus is really stressing the *Omega* part here. This is the ending for human history as we know it—judgment, hell, and heaven.

God only is Alpha and Omega. We are omega. That means we live forever beyond this life. In *Unveiling the End Times in Our Time*, Adrian Rogers said this about our omega part:

> When God created you with a soul, body, and mind, He made you in His image. You could no more cease to exist than God Himself could cease to exist. For all time, your soul will exist somewhere—either in heaven or hell. You have a life to live, a death to die, a judgment to face, and an eternity to endure either in heaven or in hell. And you will not miss hell and go to heaven unless you are twice born.[628]

Because He is coming quickly, we must be ready so the omega part is ready.

In Chicago many years ago, there was a nightclub called "The Gates of Hell" that was right downtown. Down the street from this nightclub was a church called Calvary Church. The story goes, that a young man wanted to go to that nightclub one evening, so he asked a stranger on the street, "Can you tell me how to get to The Gates of Hell?" The stranger replied, "Go right past Calvary and you'll come to the Gates of Hell."[629]

You can't get to hell without going past calvary. God made it possible for all humanity to avoid the gates of hell. Stop at Calvary and you will be ready for the coming of the Lord.

Charles Spurgeon preached something powerful more than a century ago, but it is still so important for us to heed today:

> At first He came as an Infant of a span long. Now He shall come—"In rainbow wreath and clouds of storm," the Glorious One. Then He entered into a manger, now He shall ascend His Throne. Then He sat upon a woman's knees. . . . Now earth shall be at His feet and the whole

universe shall hang upon His everlasting shoulders. Then He appeared the Infant, now the Infinite. . . . A stable received Him then. Now the high arches of earth and Heaven shall be too little for Him. . . .

Where now the carpenter's smock? Royalty has now assumed its purple. Where now the toil-worn feet that needed to be washed after their long journeys of mercy? They are sandled with light. . . . Where now the cry, "Foxes have holes and the birds of the air have nests but I, the Son of Man, have not where to lay My head"?

Heaven is His Throne. Earth is His footstool. . . .

Blind world, open your eyes while the thunderclaps of judgment make you start up in terror and amazement and look about you. His eyes are like flames of fire and . . . His head and His hair are white like wool, as white as snow. . . .

Bad men weep and wail because of Him. Good men cry, "All hail!" . . .

Let us suppose again the the Judgment Day has come and let us challenge the world to treat the Savior as it did before.

Now, then, Crowds, come and drag Him down, to hurt Him from the hill, headlong! Step forward, you Pharisees, and tempt Him and try to entangle Him in His words. Herodians, have you no penny now, that you may ask Him a difficult question to entrap Him? . . . Sadducees, have you no riddles left? . . . Smite Him on the cheek you soldiers . . . Set Him once more in the chair and spit in His face. . . . Have you not an old cloak to cast about His shoulders again? . . . Have you no songs, no ribald jests, and is there not a man among you that dares, now to pluck His hair? . . .

He was righteous at His first coming. . . . He shall be righteous at His second coming with the righteousness of supremacy. He came to endure the penalty, He comes to procure the reward. He came to serve, He comes to rule.

He came to open wide the door of Divine Grace, He comes to shut the door. He comes not to redeem but to judge. Not to save but to pronounce the sentence. . . . Oh, Jesus! How great the difference between Your first and Your second Advent![630]

He came then in poverty, now He will return as the King of kings and the Lord of lords. Maranatha. Come quickly, Lord Jesus!

ENDNOTES

1. John Maxwell, *Breakthrough Parenting* (Colorado Springs, CO: Focus on the Family, 1996), 180.
2. Journeys of Mary and Joseph Map, accessed September 24, 2019, https://www.biblestudy. org/maps/the-journeys-of-mary-and-joseph.html.
3. Brother Andrew, *God's Smuggler* (Bloomington, MN: Chosen, 2015), 60.
4. Max Lucado, "Baptism: The Demonstration of Devotion," accessed September 24, 2019, https://maxlucado.com/baptism-the-demonstration-of-devotion/.
5. Steven Furtick, *Crash the Chatterbox: Hearing God's Voice Above All Others* (Colorado Springs, CO: Multnomah, 2014) ,12.
6. C. S. Lewis, *The C. S. Lewis Collection: Biographical Works* (San Francisco: HarperOne, 2017), 344.
7. Thomas Watson, *Extracts from the Writings of Thomas Watson* volume 3, Hamilton Smith, ed. (Crewe, Cheshire, Great Britain: Scripture Truth, 2009), 58.
8. Bret Stephens, "Richest Country, Saddest People—Any Coincidence?," *Wall Street Journal*, March 9, 2007, https://www.wsj.com/articles/SB117341542798232054.
9. FROM A SERMON NT WRIGHT PREACHED
   I once heard theologian N. T. Wright say in a sermon, "The beatitudes of Jesus tell us that all the wrong people are going to be blessed; they are counterintuitive. God is turning everything upside down."
10. As quoted in John R. W. Stott, *Issues Facing Christians Today, Fourth Edition* (Grand Rapids, MI: Zondervan, 1984, 1990, 1999, 2006), 37.
11. Charles H. Spurgeon, *The Salt Cellars* (Fort Collins, CO: Delmarva Publications, Inc., 2017), 366.
12. Stephen Brown, "Toxic Pluralism," *Christianity Today*, April 5, 1993, 17, https://www.christianitytoday.com/ct/1993/april-5/editorials.html.
13. William Murdock, *Find Your Own Calcutta: Living a Life of Service and Meaning in a Selfish World* (Edinburgh, Scotland: WestBow Press, 2017), 6.
14. Martin Luther is attributed as saying, "I have tried to keep things in my hands and lost them all, but what I have given into God's hands I still possess." "Quotes," Bible.org, accessed November 11, 2020, https://bible.org/illustration/quotes-52.
15. Charles H. Spurgeon, as quoted in "The Comfort that Faith Brings, *The Christian Workers Magazine*, September 1919, vol 20, 54.
16. Oswald Chambers, "The Assigning of the Call," *My Utmost for His Highest*, September 30, https://utmost.org/the-assigning-of-the-call/.
17. Dietrich Bonhoeffer, *Dietrich Bonhoeffer Works, vol. 8, Letters and Papers from Prison,* letter no. 89 (Minneapolis: Fortress, 2009), 238.
18. Abraham Lincoln, in *New Encyclopedia of Christian Quotations*, compiled by Mark Water (Grand Rapids, MI: Baker Books, 2000), 764.
19. RICK WARREN ON TWITTER https://twitter.com/rickwarren/status/8660287646?lang=en
20. J. C. Ryle, *Expository Thoughts on the Gospel of Luke: A Commentary, revised edition* (Abbotsford, WI: Aneko, 1858, 2020), 161.
21. John Wesley, *The Works of the Rev. John Wesley: Volume 7* (New York: J & J Harper, 1826), 269.
22. John Newton, *The Amazing Works of John Newton* (Alachua, FL: Bridge-Logos, 2009), 338.
23. Author unknown.
24. As quoted in Philip Yancey, *Prayer: Does It Make Any Difference?* (Grand Rapids, MI: Zondervan, 2006), 283.
25. Keller, Timothy, *The Reason for God: Belief in an Age of Skepticism*, (New York: Dutton/ Penguin, 2008), 49.

26. E. Stanley Jones, *The Christ of the Indian Road* (Nashville: Abingdon, 1925, 1953), n.p.
27. Stephen Griffith, *Ruth Bell Graham: Celebrating the Extraordinary Life* (Nashville: Thomas Nelson, 2003), 177, 192.
28. As quoted in *The Christian Pioneer*, Joseph Foulkes Winks, ed. the 1856, 84.
29. C. S. Lewis, *Mere Christianity* (New York: Simon and Schuster Touchstone, 1996), 65.
30. I've heard this famous quote, "The last days are hidden so that every day would be regarded."
31. John Wesley, as quoted in "The Fragrant Basket," *The Christian Penny's Magazine*, vol X1 (London: John Snow, Paternoster Row, 1856), 276–277.
32. As quoted in Natalie Crowson, "Perfect Strangers: Christians Living Among Buddhists, Hindus, and Muslims," Lausanne World Pulse Arches, November 2007, https://www.lausanneworldpulse.com/research.php/856.
33. Quoted in "To the Preacher: The Idolatry of Intelligence by Leonard Ravenhill," Christian Life Today, accessed November 23, 2020, https://christianlifetoday.net/leonard-ravenhill.
34. Quoted in Ray Comfort, *The Word on the Street: How to Share the Gospel in the Open Air* (Newberry, FL: Destiny Image/Bridge-Logos, 2020), n.p.
35. John Bunyan, *The Pilgrims' Progress* (Philadelphia: Uriah Hunt, 1829), 209.
36. Mother Teresa, *In the Heart of the World*, (Novato, CA: New World Library, 1997), 57–58.
37. Dargan Thompson, "Jim Elliot Quotes that Will Change the Way You Think about Sacrifice," *Relevant*, January 8, 2016, https://www.relevantmagazine.com/faith/jim-elliot-quotes-will-change-way-you-think-about-sacrifice/.
38. Quoted in David Maraniss, "How Would the Legend Do Now?," *Washington Post*, January 27, 2000, https://www.washingtonpost.com/wp-srv/sports/nfl/daily/jan00/27/coaches27.htm.
39. Fred Rogers and Barry Head, *Mister Rogers Talks with Parents* (Pittsburgh: Family Communications, 1983), 183.
40. Noah Webster, as quoted in Robert J. Morgan, "How Do You Spell 'Cheerful'?," August 23, 2009, https://www.robertjmorgan.com/devotional/how-do-you-spell-cheerful/.
41. Merriam-Webster Dictionary, https://www.merriam-webster.com/dictionary/enthusiasm.
42. Os Guinness, *Renaissance: The Power of the Gospel However Dark the Times* (Downers Grove, IL: IVP, 2014), 40.
43. Andráe Crouch, "Through It All."
44. A. W. Tozer, as quoted in George Sweeting, *Who Said That?: More than 2,500 Usable Quotes and Quotations* (Chicago: Moody, 1995), n.p.
45. E. Paul Hovey, as quoted in Martin Manser, ed., *The Westminster Collection of Christian Quotations* (Louisville, KY: Westminster John Knox Press, 2001), 19.
46. Søren Kierkegaard, *Provocations: Spiritual Writings of Kierkegaard* (Walden, NY: Plough Publishing, 2014), n.p.
47. Marilyn Hickey, as quoted in J. Mark Copland, "Kingdom Pardon," *After This Manner, Pray*, (Alachua, FL: Bridge-Logos, 1992), accessed March 9, 2020, prayerlinksministries.com/SampChap.htm.
48. As quoted in John A. Lavender, *Why Prayers Are Unanswered* (Carol Stream, IL: Tyndale, 1980), n.p.
49. Maltbie D. Babcock, "This Is My Father's World," 1901, public domain.
50. C. S. Lewis, *The World's Last Night and Other Essays*, *The Essential C. S. Lewis*, Lyle W. Dorsett, ed. (New York: Scribner, 2017), 390.
51. Marty Duren, "Five Pitfalls to Avoid When Teaching on the End Times," *Facts & Trends*, August 10, 2017, httsp://factsandtrends.net/2017/08/10/5-pitfalls-avoid-preaching-end-times/.
52. C H Spurgeon, *Sermons on Prayer: 40 Powerful Sermons to Ignite Your Prayer Life*, Kindle edition, locations 3757–3762.
53. Halford Edward Luccock, *Halford Luccock Treasury* (Nashville, TN: Abingdon Press, 1963), 255.
54. James S. Stewart, *The Strong Name* (London: Hodder and Stoughton, 1973), n.p.

55. From the *New International Bible Dictionary*.
56. As quoted in Edythe Draper, Draper's Book of Quotations for the Christian World (Carol Stream, IL: Tyndale, 1992), entry 9846.
57. Maggie Malach, "How Did the Standing Ovation Originate?" Mental Floss, August 3, 2018, https://www.mentalfloss.com/article/89214/how-did-standing-ovation-originate. Jim Reineking, "Twenty-Five Fascinating Facts about Cal Ripken's Record Streak," USA Today, May 30, 2017, https://www.usatoday.com/story/sports/mlb/2017/05/30/cal-ripken-consecutive-games-streak-fascinating-facts/102281920/.
58. Hudson Taylor, as quoted in Daniel L. Akin, *Ten Who Changed the World* (Nashville, TN: B&H, 2012), 152.
59. Timothy J. Keller, "Reason for God: The Exclusivity of Truth," The Viritas Forum at the University of Chicago, 2008; *A Place for Truth: Leading Thinkers Explore Life's Hardest Questions*, Dallas Willard, ed., (Downers Grove, IL: InterVarsity, 2010), 61.
60. David A. Smart, *Coronet*, vol 24, issue 3, 1948, 6.
61. Charles R. Swindoll, *The Continuation of Something Great: Jesus' Teaching and Training of the Disciples: A Study of Luke 7:1–10:37* (Nashville, TN: Thomas Nelson, 1995), 18.
62. This had just been through personal research and not knowing the source exactly. This is in my own words however.
63. This had just been through personal research and not knowing the source exactly. This is in my own words however.
64. Barbara Bowen, *Strange Scriptures that Perplex the Western Mind: Clarified in the Light of Customs and Conditions in Bible Lands* (Grand Rapids, MI: Eerdmans, 1944), 23–24.
65. Emphasis in the original.
66. Raghav, *Motivating Thoughts of Abraham Lincoln* (New Delhi, India: Prabhat Prakashan, 2016), Kindle edition.
67. Brennan Manning, *The Wisdom of Tenderness: What Happens When God's Fierce Mercy Transforms Our Lives* (San Francisco: HarperSanFrancisco, 2002), 78.
68. John M. Darley and C. Daniel Batson, "From Jerusalem to Jericho: A Study of Situational and Dispositional Variables in Helping Behavior," *Journal of Personality and Social Psychology*, 1973, vol 27, no 1, 100–108.
69. Martin Luther King Jr., *Strength to Love: Sermons from Strength to Love and Other Preachings* (Boston: Beacon Press, 1963), 26.
70. Mary McGinty, "Holiday Shoppers Plan to Spend 4 Percent More This Year," National Retail Federation, October 24, 2019, https://nrf.com/media-center/press-releases/holiday-shoppers-plan-spend-4-percent-more-year.
71. Leia Mendoza, "Get Some Cash for Those Unused Gift Cards," *Kearney Hub*, February 23, 2012, https://www.kearneyhub.com/news/local/get-some-cash-for-those-unused-gift-cards/article_d278234e-5e2a-11e1-965a-001871e3ce6c.html.
72. Mendoza, "Get Some Cash."
73. A. W. Tozer, *That Incredible Christian*, as quoted in A. W. Tozer, *Pursuit of God: A Thirty-One Day Experience*, compiled by Edythe Draper (Camp Hill, PA: Wing Spread Publishers, 1995), day 6.
74. Calvin Coolidge, "Veto of Salary Increase: 2/4/1916," "Early Speeches (1890–1918)," Calvin Coolidge Presidential Foundation, https://www.coolidgefoundation.org/resources/early-speeches-1890-1918-6/.
75. J. Oswald Sanders, *A Spiritual Clinic* (Grand Rapids, MI: Discovery House, 1958), n.p.
76. John Wesley, as quoted in John R. Tyson, *The Way of the Wesleys: A Short Introduction* (Grand Rapids, MI: Eerdmans, 2014), 170.
77. Mother Teresa, "Mother Teresa Quotes," Catholic Online, accessed March 20, 2020, https://www.catholic.org/clife/teresa/quotes.php.
78. Hannah Ritchie, "How Many People Die and How Many Are Born Each Year?," Our World in Data, September 11, 2019, https://ourworldindata.org/births-and-deaths.

79. Medindia Content Team, "World Death Clock," accessed March 20, 2020, https://www.medindia.net/patients/calculators/world-death-clock.asp.

80. I HEARD RICK HAGANS SAY THIS IN A SERMON

81. I HEARD RICK HAGANS SAY THIS IN A SERMON

82. W. H. Auden, as quoted in Ashton Applewhite, Tripp Evans, and Andrew Frothingham, *And I Quote, Revised Edition: The Definitive Collection of Quotes, Sayings, and Jokes for the Contemporary Speechmaker* (New York: Thomas Dunne Books, 2003), 177.

83. "Frequently Asked Questions," Cryonics Institute, accessed March 20, 2020, https://www.cryonics.org/about-us/faqs/.

84. Thanks to great information from Kenneth Bailey, *Jesus Through Middle Eastern Eyes: Cultural Studies in the Gospels* (Downers Grove, IL: InterVarsity, 2008).

85. Billy Graham, as quoted in Pamela Rose Williams, "Billy Graham Quotes: Twenty-two Great Sayings," What Christians Want to Know, accessed March 21, 2020, https://www.whatchristianswanttoknow.com/billy-graham-quotes-22-great-sayings/.

86. Dietrich Bonhoeffer, *Life Together* (Norfolk, UK: SCM Press, 1954), 17.

87. Gladys Bronwyn Stern, BookBrowse, accessed March 27, 2020, https://www.bookbrowse.com/quotes/detail/index.cfm/quote_number/466/silent-gratitude-isnt-much-use-to-any-one.

88. George Herbert, as quoted in David Self, *Somebody Once Said: An Anthology of Quotations for Preachers and Speakers* (London: SPCK, 2004), 76.

89. Steven Furtick, "The Highest Level of Living—Steven Furtick Blog," December 20, 2010, https://www.facebook.com/notes/messiah-college-foundation-inc/the-highest-level-of-living-steven-furtick-blog/166845206690904/.

90. Søren Kierkegaard, as quoted in *Brian Bell Commentary on the Bible*, StudyLight.org, accessed March 27, 2020, https://www.studylight.org/commentaries/cbb/luke-21.html.

91. Don Stewart, "Why Is the Bible Divided into Chapters and Verses?" Blue Letter Bible, accessed March 27, 2020, https://www.blueletterbible.org/Comm/stewart_don/faq/bible-special/question8-why-is-the-bible-divided-into-chapters-and-verses.cfm.

92. Dwight Lyman Moody, "Christ Seeking Sinners," *Addresses: Revised by Himself* (Albany, NY: D. R. Niver & Co., 1875), 48.

93. Charles Haddon Spurgeon, Spurgeon at His Best: Over 2,200 Striking Quotations from the World's Most Exhaustive and Widely-Read Sermon Series (Grand Rapids, MI: Baker, 1988), 166–167.

94. Ravi Zacharias, *Cries of the Heart: Bringing God Near When He Feels So Far* (Nashville, TN: Thomas Nelson, 1998, 2002), 66–68.

95. C. S. Lewis, as quoted in Zacharias, *Cries of the Heart*, 66.

96. "Henry Ford," Bits & Pieces, March 3, 1994, 1–2, as quoted in SermonSearch, accessed March 27, 2020, https://www.sermonsearch.com/sermon-illustrations/2664/henry-ford/.

97. Kenneth W. Harl, Roman Economy, 300 B.C. to A.D. 700 (Baltimore, MD: The Johns Hopkins University Press, 1996), 177.

98. Robert Murray M'Cheyne, as quoted in *The Monthly Herald: A Religious Miscellany and Intelligencer of the English Churches of the Calvinistic Methodists*, vol 1(London: R. Hughes and Son, 1858), 200.

99. Søren Kierkegaard, as quoted in Tony Campolo, *Stories that Feed Your Soul* (Grand Rapids, MI: Baker, 2010), introduction, n.p.

100. Though the story is unconfirmed, the point of it is important enough that I wanted to share it.

101. Vance Havner, as quoted in Michael Catt, *Prepare for Rain: The Story of a Church that Believed God for the Impossible* (Fort Washington, PA: CLC Publications, 2007), 160.

102. Vance Havner, *All the Days* (Grand Rapids, MI: Revell, 1976), 32.

103. Napoleon Bonaparte, as quoted in William J. Federer, *America's God and Country: Encyclopedia of Quotations* (St. Louis, MO: Amerisearch, 2000), 463.

104. George Campbell Morgan, *The Morning Message: A Selection for Daily Meditation* (London: Hodder and Stoughton, 1906), 17.

105. Patrick Morley, *I Surrender: Submitting to Christ in the Details of Life* (Brentwood, TN: Wolgemuth & Hyatt, 1990), 14.

106. C. S. Lewis, *The Problem of Pain* (SanFrancisco: HarperOne, 1996), 54.

107. "Billy Sunday Fights Sin," Preaching Today, accessed April 1, 2020, https://www.preaching-today.com/illustrations/2004/february/14808.html.

108. John Charles Ryle, *Expository Thoughts on the Gospels,* vol. 1 (London: William Hunt and Company, 1865), 161.

109. Ron Marshall, "How Many Ads Do You See in One Day?," Red Crow Marketing, Inc., September 10, 2015, https://www.redcrowmarketing.com/2015/09/10/many-ads-see-one-day/.

110. Larry Crabb, *Finding God* (Grand Rapids, MI: Zondervan, 1993), 17.

111. Halford Edward Luccock, *Halford Luccock Treasury* (Nashville, TN: Abingdon, 1963), 218.

112. Corrie ten Boom, Corrie ten Boom Museum, May 16, 2016, https://www.facebook.com/corri-etenboommuseum/photos/a.321655254518249/1318762261474205/?type=1&theater.

113. Oswald Chambers, *My Utmost for His Highest: Classic Edition* (Grand Rapids, MI: Discovery House, 2017, 1963), July 7.

114. Matt Wild, "Just a Flesh Wound: Nine Fun Facts about That Time Theodore Roosevelt Was Shot in Milwaukee," *Milwaukee Record*, February 20, 2017, https://milwaukeerecord.com/city-life/flesh-wound-nine-fun-facts-theodore-roosevelt-shot-milwaukee/.

115. Dorothy Leigh Sayers, *Christian Letters to a Post-Christian World* (Grand Rapids, MI: Eerdmans, 1969), 15.

116. Bono, as quoted in Michka Assayas, *Bono: In Conversation with Michka Assayas* (New York: Berkley, 2005, 2006), 223.

117. *Kansas City Star*, as quoted in Edward K. Rowell, ed., *1001 Quotes, Illustrations, and Humorous Stories for Preachers, Teachers, and Writers* (Grand Rapids, MI: Baker, 1996), 542.

118. Donald W. McCullough, *The Trivialization of God* (Colorado Springs, CO: NavPress, 1995), 13.

119. Quoted in McCullough, *Trivialization of God*, 14.

120. Charles Haddon Spurgeon, "The Form of Godliness without the Power," *The Metropolitan Tabernacle Pulpit*, vol 35, June 2, 1880, The Spurgeon Center, https://www.spurgeon.org/resource-library/sermons/the-form-of-godliness-without-the-power#flipbook/.

121. Charles Colson, *Tough Questions about God, Faith, and Life: Answer to the Difficult Questions Teens Ask* (Carol Stream, IL: Tyndale, 2000, 2006), 93–94.

122. Colson, *Tough Questions*, 94.

123. *Reader's Digest*, May 1996, 156.

124. SermonCentral, October 18, 2000, https://www.sermoncentral.com/sermon-illustra-tions/1158/someone-asked-c-s-lewis-why-do-the-righteous-by-mark-hensley.

125. C. S. Lewis, *The Four Loves* (New York: Harcourt Brace, 1960, 1988), 140.

126. Don Stewart, "Why Is the Bible Divided into Chapters and Verses?," Blue Letter Bible, accessed April 8, 2020, https://www.blueletterbible.org/Comm/stewart_don/faq/bible-special/question8-why-is-the-bible-divided-into-chapters-and-verses.cfm.

127. Amy Standen, "Life on The Gate: Working on the Golden Gate Bridge 1933–37," KQED, April 27, 2012, https://www.kqed.org/quest/36106/life-on-the-gate-working-on-the-golden-gate-bridge-1933-37.

128. Charles H. Spurgeon, The New Park Street Pulpit (Grand Rapids, MI: Zondervan, 1964), 258.

129. Jim Rohn, Facebook, April 25, 2014, https://www.facebook.com/OfficialJimRohn/posts/there-are-only-3-colors-10-digits-and-7-notes-its-what-we-do-with-them-thats-imp/10154052025455635/.

130. Louis Giglio, Twitter, July 23, 2012, https://twitter.com/louiegiglio/status/227506945869881344?lang=en.

131. Louis Lallemant, *The Spiritual Doctrine of Father Louis Lallemant* (London: Burns & Lambert, 1855), 84.

132. Charles Swindoll, *The Grace Awakening: Believing in Grace Is One Thing. Living It Is Another* (Nashville, TN: Thomas Nelson, 1990, 1996, 2003, 2010), 111.

133. Bryan Chapell, *Holiness by Grace: Delighting in the Joy that Is Our Strength* (Wheaton, IL: Crossway, 2001), 80.

134. Oswald Chambers, *The Oswald Chambers Devotional Reader* (Nashville, TN: Thomas Nelson, 1990), 164.

135. Quoted in *The Quotable Oswald Chambers*, David McCasland, ed. (Grand Rapids, MI: Discovery House, 2008), n.p.

136. Dwight Longenecker, "C. S. Lewis, Science Fiction, and Why Jesus Walked through Walls," April 14, 2018, https://dwightlongenecker.com/c-s-lewis-science-fiction-and-why-jesus-walked-through-walls/.

137. Rusty Wright, "Carrying the Second Bulb," SermonCentral, May 10, 2007, https://www.sermoncentral.com/sermons/carrying-the-second-bulb-rusty-wright-sermon-on-discipleship-106462.

138. "Abraham Lincoln Quotes," HistoryNet, accessed April 10, 2020, https://www.historynet.com/abraham-lincoln-quotes.

139. Robert H. Schuller, *Tough Times Never Last, but Tough People Do!* (Nashville, TN: Thomas Nelson, 1983), 98.

140. R. T. Kendall, *It Ain't Over Till It's Over: Persevere for Answered Prayers and Miracles in Your Life* (Lake Mary, FL: Charisma House, 2015), 34.

141. William Secker, *The Nonsuch Professor in His Meridian Splendour: Or, The Singular Actions of Sanctified Christians* (Oxford: J. C. Pembrey, 1877), 27–28.

142. Persecution in the Early Church," Religion Facts, November 19, 2016, http://www.religionfacts.com/persecution-early-church.

143. John R. W. Stott, *The Message of Romans: God's Good News for the World* (Downer's Grove, IL: InterVarsity, 1994), n.p.

144. Quoted in John T. McNeill, *Calvin: Institutes of the Christian Religion* (Louisville, KY: Westminster John Knox, 1960, 2006), 1520.

145. E. V. Hill, *A Savior Worth Having* (Chicago: Moody, 2002), 31–32.

146. C. S. Lewis, *God in the Dock* (Grand Rapids, MI: Eerdmans, 1970), 267.

147. Shaw's Reply to Judge Neil, *The Weekly Freeman*, September 6, 1919, Quote Investigator, https://quoteinvestigator.com/2018/07/24/lunatic-shaw/#return-note-19210-3.

148. Rick Warren, Facebook, March 29, 2011, https://www.facebook.com/pastorrickwarren/posts/10150178454855903.

149. Glenda Kwek, "Death of the Angel of The Gap: The Man Who Saved the Suicidal from Themselves," *Sydney Morning Dispatch*, May 14, 2012, https://www.smh.com.au/national/nsw/death-of-the-angel-of-the-gap-the-man-who-saved-the-suicidal-from-themselves-20120514-1ymle.html.

150. John Watson, pen name Ian MacLaren, *Congregationalist*, In Brief, January 6, 1898, vol 83, issue 1, as quoted in the Quote Investigator, accessed April 11, 2020, https://quoteinvestigator.com/2010/06/29/be-kind/.

151. D. Martyn Lloyd-Jones, *God's Ultimate Purpose: An Exposition of Ephesians 1:1-23* (Grand Rapids, MI: Baker, 1998), 395.

152. Jerry Bridges, *The Discipline of Grace Study Guide: God's Role and Our Role in the Pursuit of Holiness* (Colorado Springs, CO: NavPress, 1994, 2006), 18. Emphasis in the original.

153. Bill Thrasher, *A Journey to Victorious Praying: Finding Discipline and Delight in Your Prayer Life* (Chicago: Moody, 2003), 78.

154. Louis Lallemant, *The Spiritual Doctrine of Father Louis Lallemant* (London: Burns & Lambert, 1855), 84.

155. Quoted in *Religion, Culture, and Sustainable Development*, Roberto Blancarte Pimentel, Robert Charles Ellion, Robert Holton, et al, vol 2 (Oxford, United Kingdom: Eolss Publishers, 2010), 293.

156. A. W. Tozer, *The Root of the Righteous* (Chicago: Moody, 1955, 1986), 189.

157. Thomas Watson, *A Divine Cordial*, (London: Thomnas Parkhurst, 1663), accessed April 13, 2020, http://www.digitalpuritan.net/Digital%20Puritan%20Resources/Watson,%20Thomas/A%20Divine%20Cordial.txt.

158. Grandma Joy, *Grandma Joy's Hope for Hurting Women* (Shippensburg, PA: Destiny Image, 2006), 143–44.

159. Quoted in Debbie McDaniel, "Forty Powerful Quotes from Corrie ten Boom," Crosswalk.com, May 21, 2015, https://www.crosswalk.com/faith/spiritual-life/inspiring-quotes/40-powerful-quotes-from-corrie-ten-boom.html.

160. C. S. Lewis, *The Grand Miracle: And Other Selected Essays on Theology and Ethics from God in the Dock* (New York: Ballentine, 1970), 5.

161. Often misattributed to G. K. Chesterton. Émile Cammaerts, *The Laughing Prophet: The Seven Virtues and G. K. Chesterton* (North Yorkshire, England: Methuen, 1937), 211.

162. John Wesley, *Journal of John Wesley*, March 28, 1741, accessed April 15, 2020, https://ccel.org/ccel/wesley/journal.vi.iv.v.html.

163. Caleb Thomas Winchester, *The Life of John Wesley* (New York: Macmillan, 1912), 165.

164. Quoted in *Pearson's* magazine, vol 47, July 1921, 78, https://books.google.com/books?id=-Ef367y2t0AC&pg=PA28&dq=I+have+never+in+my+life+learned+anything+from+any+man+who+agreed+with+me.%E2%80%9D&hl=en&newbks=1&newbks_redir=0&sa=X-&ved=2ahUKEwivyd2K8uroAhXPWcOKHUSzC7kQ6AEwBnoECAcQAg#v=onepage&q=I%20have%20never%20in%20my%20life%20learned%20anything%20from%20any%-20man%20who%20agreed%20with%20me.%E2%80%9D&f=false.

165. William Penn, "Part 2: Of Jealousy," *Some Fruits of Solitude*, Harvard Classics, accessed April 16, 2020, https://www.bartleby.com/1/3/217.html.

166. Martha Tarbell, *Teachers Guide to International Sunday School Lessons for 1912* (New York: Fleming H. Revell, 1911), 440, accessed April 16, 2020, https://www.google.com/books/edition/Tarbell_s_teacher_s_guide_to_the_Interna/GCbuAAAAMAAJ?hl=en&gbpv=1&d-q=martha+tarbell&printsec=frontcover.

167. R. T. Kendall, *Jealousy: The Sin No One Talks About* (Lake Mary, FL: Charisma, 2010), 100.

168. "Temple of Artemis at Ephesus," GlobalSecurity.org, accessed April 16, 2020, https://www.globalsecurity.org/military/world/europe/temple-of-artemis-at-ephesus.htm.

169. Andrew Murray, *The Full Blessing of Pentecost: Your Greatest Need, The Spirit's Unlimited Supply* (Fort Washington, PA: CLC, 2005), "Introduction."

170. Corrie ten Boom with Jamie Buckingham, *Tramp for the Lord: The Story that Begins Where The Hiding Place Ends* (Fort Washington, PA: CLC, 1974), 63.

171. Charles Swindoll, *Come before Winter and Share My Hope* (Sisters, OR: Multnomah, 1985, 1988, 1994), n.p.

172. Quoted in Tryon Edwards, *A Dictionary of Thoughts* (New York: Cassell, 1891), 436.

173. Alice Morse Earle, *The Sabbath in Puritan New England*, Project Gutenberg, accessed April 16, 2020, https://www.gutenberg.org/files/8659/8659-h/8659-h.htm#chap06.

174. Hannah Ritchie and Max Roser, "Age Structure," Our World in Data, September 2019, https://ourworldindata.org/age-structure.

175. Louie Giglio, AZ Quotes, accessed April 16, 2020, https://www.azquotes.com/author/22501-Louie_Giglio/tag/sin.

176. David Jeremiah, *Slaying the Giants in Your Life* (Nashville, TN: Thomas Nelson, 2001), 105.

177. Charles Swindoll, *Swindoll's Living Insights: New Testament Commentary, Acts* (Carol Stream, IL: Tyndale, 2016), n.p.

178. Brennan Manning, *The Ragamuffin Gospel* (Colorado Springs, CO: Multnomah, 1990, 2000, 2005), 9.

179. "Redeem the Time," Precept Austin, July 26, 2019, https://www.preceptaustin.org/redeem_the_time.

180. William Penn, *Some Fruits of Solitude* (London: Headley Brothers, 1905), 16.
181. Halford Luccock, *Halford Luccock Treasury* (Nashville, TN: Abingdon, 1963), 263.
182. "Redeem the Time," Precept Austin.
183. A. W. Tozer, Twitter, March 31, 2014, https://twitter.com/tozeraw/status/450641803595628544.
184. Mother Teresa, unverified.
185. William Barclay, *The Daily Study Bible Series, Revised Edition* (Louisville, KY: Westminster Press, 1978), n.p.
186. Peggy Noonan, "Still, Small Voice," *Crisis* 16, no. 2, February 1998, 12–17, https://www.catholiceducation.org/en/faith-and-character/faith-and-character/still-small-voice.html.
187. Ibid.
188. R. A. Torrey, "Anniversary Sermon," *The Christian Workers' Magazine*, vol 11, August 1911, 591–592.
189. Ibid.
190. Quoted in Frederick B. Wilcox, ed., *A Little Book of Aphorisms* (New York: C Scribner's Sons, 1947), 51.
191. "Forum of Appius," Biblia, accessed April 18, 2020, https://biblia.com/factbook/Forum-of-Appius.
192. Jay W. Belle Isle, "When Is a 'Friend' Not a Friend? Florida Court Defines Facebook Friendships," LegalReader, September 7, 2017, https://www.legalreader.com/when-is-a-friend-not-a-friend-florida-court-defines-facebook-friendships/.
193. Martin Schönfeld and Michael Thompson, "Kant's Philosophical Development," *The Stanford Encyclopedia of Philosophy*, Winter 2019, https://plato.stanford.edu/entries/kant-development/.
194. *The Methodist New Connexion Magazine and Evangelical Repository*, 1874, 61, https://www.google.com/books/edition/The_Methodist_new_connexion_magazine_and/JxEEAAAAQAAJ?hl=en&gbpv=1&dq=isaac+newton+and+atheist+friend&pg=PA61&printsec=frontcover.
195. Haddon Robinson, "Blending Bible Content and Life Application," Haddon Robinson and Craig Brian Larson, eds., *The Art and Craft of Biblical Preaching: A Comprehensive Resource for Today* (Grand Rapids, MI: Zondervan, 2005), chapter 77.
196. Paulo Coelho, Twitter, November 29, 2017, https://twitter.com/paulocoelho/status/935852120636608512?lang=en.
197. Quoted in Alex Murashko, "Exclusive Rick Warren: 'Flat Out Wrong' that Muslims, Christians View God the Same," *The Christian Post*, March 2, 2012, https://www.christianpost.com/news/exclusive-rick-warren-flat-out-wrong-that-muslims-christians-view-god-the-same-70767/.
198. Joseph Telushkin, *Words That Hurt, Words That Heal, Revised Edition* (New York: Harper Collins, 2019).
199. June Bingham, *Courage to Change: An Introduction to the Life and Thought of Reinhold Niebuhr* (New York: Charles Scribner's Sons, 1961), chapter 1.
200. "What's Wrong with the World?," The Society of Gilbert Keith Chesterton, April 29, 2012, https://www.chesterton.org/wrong-with-world/.
201. Charles Finney, "The Effect of Sin and Disobedience," *The Gospel Trumpet*, July 31, 1913, 467, https://www.google.com/books/edition/The_Gospel_Trumpet/RFBFAQAAMAAJ?hl=en&gbpv=1&dq=%E2%80%9CSin+is+the+most+expensive+thing+in+the+universe%22&pg=PA467&printsec=frontcover.
202. "How Many People Died in World War 2?," History on the Net, https://www.historyonthenet.com/how-many-people-died-in-world-war-2; *Mein Kampf*, Reading Length, accessed November 23, 2020, https://www.readinglength.com/book/isbn-1682040216.
203. A. W. Tozer, A. W. Tozer Classics, Twitter, January 10, 2014, https://twitter.com/TozerAW/status/421758015943888896.

204. Smith Wigglesworth, *The Teachings of Smith Wigglesworth: Ever Increasing Faith and Faith that Prevails* (Pantianos Classics, 1924), 17.

205. Edna Butterfield, as told in "The Toaster," Bible.org, accessed April 19, 2020, https://bible.org/illustration/toaster.

206. Timothy L. O'Brien, "Buffett to Give Bulk of His Fortune to Gates Charity," *New York Times*, June 26, 2006, https://www.nytimes.com/2006/06/26/business/26buffett.html?th=&emc=th&pagewanted=print; Associated Press, "Buffett Donation to Double Gates Foundation Yearly Spending," Fox News, June 26, 2006, updated January 13, 2015, https://www.foxnews.com/story/buffett-donation-to-double-gates-foundation-yearly-spending.

207. C. H. Spurgeon, "Lama Sabachthani?" sermon delivered March 2, 1890, *Metropolitan Tabernacle Pulpit* (London: Passmore & Alabaster, 1890), 144.

208. Ravi Zacharias, Twitter, November 20, 2013, https://twitter.com/ravizacharias/status/403333034134364161?lang=en.

209. R. C. Sproul, *The Holiness of God* (Carol Stream, IL: Tyndale, 1985, 1998), 159.

210. Charles W. Colson, *Political Action: A Bible Study* (Colorado Springs, CO: NavPress, 1988), 41.

211. Saint Augustine, *Confessions*, R. S. Pine-Coffin, trans. (New York: Penguin, 1961).

212. Watchman Nee, *The Normal Christian Life* (Fort Washington, PA: CLC, 1957, 2009), n.p.

213. William Cowper, "Olney Hymn 29: Exhortation to Prayer," https://www.poemhunter.com/poem/olney-hymn-29-exhortation-to-prayer/.

214. Brennan Manning, *Abba's Child: The Cry of the Heart for Intimate Belonging* (Colorado Springs, CO: NavPress, 1994, 2002, 2015), 154.

215. Charles Haddon Spurgeon, *Spurgeon's Sermons: Volume 6:1860* (Woodstock, ON: Devoted Publishing, 1860), 390.

216. Corrie ten Boom, *I Stand at the Door and Knock* (Grand Rapids, MI: Zondervan, 2008), 155.

217. David Qaoud, "Charles Spurgeon on The Sweet Sovereignty of God," Gospel Relevance, June 22, 2015, https://www.gospelrelevance.com/2015/06/22/charles-spurgeon-on-the-sovereignty-of-god/.

218. C. S. Lewis, *Mere Christianity*, in *The Complete C. S. Lewis Signature Classics* (San Francisco: HarperOne, 1952, 2002), 121.

219. Andy Stanley, *Deep and Wide: Creating Churches Unchurched People Love to Attend* (Grand Rapids, MI: Zondervan, 2012, 2016), n.p., Emphasis in original.

220. W. A. Criswell, *With a Bible in My Hand* (Nashville, TN: Broadman, 1978), 38.

221. Adapted from Max Lucado's statement, "God loves you just the way you are, but he refuses to leave you that way," *A Heart Like Jesus* (Nashville, TN: W Publishing, 2003), 4.

222. Source Unknown.

223. D. L. Moody, *Dwight Lyman Moody's Life Work and Gospel Sermons*, Richard S. Rhodes, ed. (Chicago: Rhodes & McClure, 1907), 433.

224. Oswald Chambers, *Biblical Psychology: Christ-Centered Solutions for Daily Problems* (Grand Rapids, MI: Our Daily Bread, 1962, 1995, 2014), n.p.

225. Quoted in "Miscellaneous Quotes," Bible.org, accessed April 19, 2020, https://bible.org/illustration/miscellaneous-quotes.

226. Edythe Draper, *Draper's Book of Quotations for the Christian World* (Carol Stream, IL: Tyndale, 1992), 57.

227. Quoted in Edward K. Rowell, ed., *1001 Quotes, Illustrations, and Humorous Stories for Preachers, Teachers, and Writers* (Grand Rapids, MI: Baker, 2008), 24.

228. Barbara Woodhouse, *No Bad Dogs: The Woodhouse Way* (New York: Fireside, 1978, 1982), 59.

229. Celsus, *True Discourse*, as quoted in Vernon Grounds, "What Are You Worth?," *Our Daily Bread*, August 29, 1998, https://odb.org/1998/08/29/what-are-you-worth/.

230. R. C. Sproul, *Knowing Scripture* (Downers Grove, IL: InterVarsity, 1977), 17.

231. John Wooden and Don Yaeger, *A Game Plan for Life: The Power of Mentoring* (New York: Bloomsbury, 2009), 16.

232. Wooden and Yaeger, *Game Plan*, 11.

233. Quote investigator, accessed April 20, 2020, https://quoteinvestigator.com/2010/12/21/doing-good-selfless/#more-1761.

234. Albert Einstein, "The World as I See It," *Living Philosophies* (New York: Simon & Schuster, 1931), 3, accessed April 20, 2020, https://history.aip.org/history/exhibits/einstein/essay.htm.

235. Charles Swindoll, *Hope Again* (Nashville: Thomas Nelson, 1996).

236. Donald Coggan, *Paul: Portrait of a Revolutionary* (Chestnut Ridge, NY: Crossroad, 1985), 75.

237. Hermine Saunders, "Saunders: A Humorous Nun's Prayer for Aging Gracefully," *Carroll County Times*, April 13, 2019, https://www.baltimoresun.com/maryland/carroll/opinion/cc-lt-saunders-041419-story.html.

238. Jim Cymbala, "Faith in and for the Holy Spirit," August, 2, 2016, http://m.blog.daum.net/urmymt/1867?np_nil_b=-2.

239. A. W. Tozer, Twitter, January 8, 2015, https://twitter.com/tozeraw/status/553290706593513472?lang=en.

240. Quoted in Mark Stallard, *Kansas City Chiefs Encyclopedia: Third Edition* (New York: Sports Publishing, 2013), lxiv.

241. Keith Green, "Oh Lord, You're Beautiful," © 1980, Birdwing Music.

242. Jayson Blair, "N.Y.U. Library Scofflaw Taken Out of Circulation," *New York Times*, October 6, 1999, https://www.nytimes.com/1999/10/06/nyregion/nyu-library-scofflaw-taken-out-of-circulation.html.

243. Steven Furtick, "The Highest Level of Living," Steven Furtick blog, Facebook, December 21, 2010, https://www.facebook.com/notes/messiah-college-foundation-inc/the-highest-level-of-living-steven-furtick-blog/166845206690904/.

244. As quoted in Cheri Fuller, *The One Year Praying through the Bible* (Carol Stream, IL: Tyndale, 2003), October 28.

245. C. S. Lewis, *The Four Loves* (New York: Harcourt, Brace, Jovanovich, 1960), 169.

246. Robert L. Hubbard, *The NIV Application Commentary: Joshua* (Grand Rapids, MI: Zondervan, 2009), 582. Slightly amended from R. A. Stedman, *Body Life* (Glendale, CA: G/L Publications, 1977), 23.

247. Sheena Iyengar, "How to Make Choosing Easier," Ted Summaries, December 6, 2014, https://tedsummaries.com/2014/12/06/sheena-iyengar-how-to-make-choosing-easier/.

248. William Barclay from his New Daily Bible Study Commentary on II Corinthians

249. Stephen R. Covey, *The Wisdom and Teachings of Stephen R. Covey* (New York: Free Press, 2012), n.p.

250. Quoted in Rick Warren, *The Purpose-Driven Church: Every Church Is Big in God's Eyes* (Grand Rapids, MI: Zondervan, 1995), n.p.

251. Quoted in Lauren Barlow, ed. *Inspired by Tozer: Fifty-Nine Artists, Writers, and Leaders Share the Insight and Passion They've Gained from A. W. Tozer* (Ventura, CA: Regal, 2011), 133.

252. Quoted at Forbes Quotes, accessed April 20, 2020, https://www.forbes.com/quotes/4679/.

253. Quoted in Joel Augustus Rogers, *World's Great Men of Color*, vol. 2 (New York: Touchstone/Simon & Schuster, 1947, 1975, 1996), 467.

254. H. A. Ironside, *Expository Notes on the Gospel of Matthew* (New York: Loizeaux Brothers, 1948), n.p.

255. Jim Elliot, *The Journals of Jim Elliot,* Elizabeth Elliot, ed. (Grand Rapids, MI: Baker, 2002), 174,

256. Elizabeth Elliot, Shadow of the Almighty: The Life and Testament of Jim Elliot (Peabody, MA: Hendrickson, 2008), 345. Emphasis in the original.

257. George Santayana, *The Life of Reason: Or the Phases of Human Progress* (New York: Charles Scribner's Sons, 1920), 284.

258. Wayne Grudem, *Bible Doctrine: Essential Teachings of the Christian Faith* (Grand Rapids, MI: Zondervan, 1999), 90.

259. "Great Is Thy Faithfulness," Thomas Obadiah Chisholm, ©1923, 1951 Hope Publishing, public domain as of 2018.
260. Buzz Aldrin, "Guideposts Classics: When Buzz Aldrin Took Communion on the Moon," *Guideposts*, October 1970, https://www.guideposts.org/better-living/life-advice/finding-life-purpose/guideposts-classics-when-buzz-aldrin-took-communion-on-the-moon.
261. Eric Metaxas, "Communion on the Moon: July 20th, 1969," Eric Metaxas blog, July 19, 2014, http://ericmetaxas.com/blog/communion-moon-july-20th-1969/.
262. Stefan Pociask, "Why Do Canadian Geese Fly at Night?," Quora, March 2, 2018, https://www.quora.com/Why-do-Canadian-geese-fly-at-night/answer/Stefan-Pociask.
263. Arthur T. Pierson, "Seed-Thoughts and Gold Nuggets for Public Speakers," *The Homiletic Review: Vol. XLI* (New York: Funk and Wagnalls, 1901), 448.
264. Authors unknown.
265. Cheryl Lavin, "What Is Love? Out of the Mouths of Babes," *Chicago Tribune*, September 23, 2001, https://www.chicagotribune.com/news/ct-xpm-2001-09-23-0109230461-story.html.
266. Thomas à Kempis, *The Imitation of Christ*, Robert Jeffery, trans. (New York: Penguin, 2013), chp 15.
267. James Packer, Your Father Loves You (Carol Stream, IL: Harold Shaw, 1986), March 10.
268. C. S. Lewis, *God in the Dock* (Grand Rapids, MI: Eerdmans, 1970), 49.
269. Skip Heitzig, *The Daily God Book Through the Bible: A Bird's-Eye View of the Bible in a Year* (Carol Stream, IL: Tyndale, 2010), May 14.
270. "The Great Violinist, Niccolo Paganini Willed His Violin," SermonCentral, June 18, 2007, https://www.sermoncentral.com/sermon-illustrations/60553/the-great-violinist-niccolo-paganini-willed-his-by-sermoncentral.
271. Jackie Pullinger with Andrew Quicke, *Chasing the Dragon: One Woman's Struggle against the Darkness of Hong Kong's Drug Dens* (Bloomington, MN: Chosen, 1980).
272. Erwin Raphael McManus, *Seizing Your Divine Moment: Dare to Live a Life of Adventure* (Nashville: Thomas Nelson, 2002), 109–112.
273. K. Connie Kang, "Commitment to Tithing Is Now Rare," *Los Angeles Times*, May 31, 2003, https://www.latimes.com/archives/la-xpm-2003-may-31-me-religtithe31-story.html.
274. R. T. Kendall, *The Thorn in the Flesh* (London: Hodder & Stoughton, 1999), n.p.
275. Charles Henry Brent, *With God in the World: A Series of Papers* (New York: Longmans, Green, and Co., 1899), 82.
276. Walter Wink, *The Powers that Be: Theology for a New Millenium* (New York: Galilee/Doubleday, 1998), 185.
277. John M. Drescher, *Spirit Fruit* (Independence, MO: Herald Press, 1974), 60.
278. Bill Waterson, *Calvin and Hobbes*, GoComics, January 14, 1987, https://www.gocomics.com/calvinandhobbes/1987/01/14.
279. Quoted in Ernest Ogbozor, "Martin Luther King Jr.," The Love and Forgiveness Project, December 31, 2013, https://blogs.shu.edu/diplomacyresearch/2013/12/31/martin-luther-king-jr/.
280. Lewis Smedes, *Forgive and Forget: Healing the Hurts We Don't Deserve* (New York: Pocket Books, 1990), 168.
281. C. S. Lewis, @CSLewisDaily, Twitter, February 15, 2015, https://twitter.com/cslewisdaily/status/567005808588640257.
282. Rick Joyner, "MorningStar Prophetic Bulletin #63," MorningStar TV, accessed April 21, 2020, https://prod.morningstarministries.org/publications/anchor-soul.
283. WILLIAM BARCLAY FROM HIS NEW DAILY BIBLE STUDY COMMENTARY ON II CORINTHIANS
284. "The Love of Christ," Bible.org, accessed April 21, 2020, https://bible.org/illustration/love-christ.
285. J. C. Ryle, *Expository Thoughts on the Gospels: For Family and Private Use: St. Luke* (Ipswich, England: William Hunt, Stream Press, 1856), 257.
286. Howard Hendricks, *A Life of Integrity: Thirteen Outstanding Leaders Raise the Standard for Today's Christian Men* (Sisters, OR: Multnomah, 1997), 173.

287. Eugene Peterson, *A Long Obedience in the Same Direction: Discipleship in an Instant Society*, twentieth anniversary edition (Downers Grove, IL: InterVarsity, 1980, 2000), 29.

288. Patrick M. Morley, *I Surrender: Submitting to Christ in the Details of Life* (Nashville: Wolgemuth & Hyatt, 1990), 14.

289. Charles M. Schulz, Peanuts, https://www.peanuts.com/comics/.

290. Rachel Cruze, *Love Your Life, Not Theirs: Seven Money Habits for living the Life You Want* (Brentwood, TN: Ramsey Press, 2016), 209.

291. Anonymous, "Quotes," Bible.org, accessed April 21, 2020, https://bible.org/illustration/quotes-52.

292. D. Martyn Lloyd-Jones, *Studies in the Sermon on the Mount* (Grand Rapids, MI: Eerdmans, 1959), 366–367.

293. Anonymous, "I Have Bad News," The Stories, accessed April 21, 2020, http://thestories.site/i-have-bad-news/.

294. Quoted in *The Westminster Collection of Christian Quotations*, compiled by Martin H. Manser (Louisville, KY: Westminster John Knox Press, 2001), 122.

295. Quoted in Robert J. Morgan, *One Hundred Bible Verses Everyone Should Know by Heart* (Nashville, TN: B&H, 2010), 145.

296. Donald Miller, *Blue Like Jazz: Nonreligious Thoughts on Christian Spirituality* (Nashville, TN: Thomas Nelson, 2003), 110.

297. Karl Menninger, *Menninger Quarterly* (University of California, 1960), 14.

298. Elisabeth Elliot, *Shadow of the Almighty: The Life and Testament of Jim Elliot* (Peabody, MA: Hendrickson, 1958, 1989), 17.

299. Author Unknown.

300. Danny Sullivan, "Google Still World's Most Popular Search Engine by Far, but Share of Unique Searchers Dips Slightly," Search Engine Land, February 11, 2013, https://searchengineland.com/google-worlds-most-popular-search-engine-148089.

301. Adam Bryant, "Walt Bettinger of Charles Schwab: You've Got to Open Up to Move Up," *New York Times*, February 4, 2016, https://www.nytimes.com/2016/02/07/business/walt-bettinger-of-charles-schwab-youve-got-to-open-up-to-move-up.html?rref=collection%2Fcolumn%2Fcorner-office&action=click&contentCollection=business&region=stream&module=stream_unit&version=latest&contentPlacement=1&pgtype=collection&_r=1.

302. D. Martyn Lloyd-Jones, *God's Ultimate Purpose: An Exposition of Ephesians 1:1-23* (Grand Rapids, MI: Baker, 1998), 395.

303. Quoted in *Brian Bell Commentary on the Bible*, StudyLight.org, accessed April 22, 2020, https://www.studylight.org/commentaries/cbb/luke-21.html.

304. Eugene Peterson, *The Contemplative Pastor: Returning to the Art of Spiritual Direction* (Grand Rapids, MI: Eerdman's, 1989, 1993), 125. Emphasis in the original.

305. Quoted in "Shannon L. Alder Quotes about Test," accessed April 22, 2020, http://topfamousquotes.com/shannon-l-alder-quotes-on-test/.

306. "Torch-Race," Ancient Olympics, accessed April 22, 2020, http://ancientolympics.arts.kuleuven.be/eng/TC002eEN.html.

307. Rick Warren, @RickWarren, Twitter, July 28, 2014, https://twitter.com/rickwarren/status/493649682845818880?lang=en.

308. From a Sermon Preached by Winkie Pratney

309. "Content of Belief Is Important," Bible.org, accessed April 22, 2020, https://bible.org/illustration/content-belief-important.

310. Quoted at Quote Investigator, April 18, 2019, https://quoteinvestigator.com/2019/04/18/staircase/.

311. Ravi Zacharias, @RaviZacharias, Twitter, February 25, 2014, https://twitter.com/ravizacharias/status/438507269613813760.

312. C. S. Lewis, "Is Theology Poetry?," *The Weight of Glory* (San Francisco: HarperOne, 1949, 1976, 1980), 140.

313. Buck O'Neil with Steve Wulf, *I Was Right on Time: My Journey from the Negro Leagues to the Majors* (New York: Simon & Schuster Paperbacks, 1996), 2–3.

314. Dinesh D'Souza, *What's so Great about Christianity*, also listed as *What's So Great about God: A Reasonable Defense of the Goodness of God in a World Filled with Suffering* (Carol Stream, IL: Tyndale, 2013), 64.

315. Author unknown.

316. Ed Miciano, *Fooling Ourselves with Fig Leaves: Confusing Religiosity with Righteousness* (Eugene, OR: Wipf & Stock, 2016), 78.

317. Quoted in J. Gerald Suarez, "Career Coach: Focus on What You Want," *Washington Post*, July 7, 2013, https://www.washingtonpost.com/business/capitalbusiness/career-coach-focus-on-what-you-want/2013/07/03/42b5a4ac-e25e-11e2-a11e-c2ea876a8f30_story.html.

318. Lee Roberson, *The Gold Mine: A Rich Collection of Stories, Poems, and Illustrations from One of America's Best Preachers* (Murfreesboro, TN: Sword of the Lord Publishers, 1996), 74.

319. Paul Chappell, *A Firm Foundation: Building a Household of Faith on the Unchanging Principles of the Word of God* (Lancaster, CA: Striving Together Publications, 2004), 74.

320. "Mother Prays for Near-Impossible Gift," *Taipei Times*, May 11, 2002, https://www.taipeitimes.com/News/taiwan/archives/2002/05/11/0000135554.

321. David Mikkelson, "Special Olympics Linked Arms Race Finish, Snopes, March 28, 2001, https://www.snopes.com/fact-check/special-olympics-linked-arms-race-finish/.

322. *Communicator*, InSight, Syncrude Canada Lld., Communications Division, 6. As quoted in "If 99.9 Percent Is Good Enough, Then . . .," Bible.org, accessed April 22, 2020, https://bible.org/illustration/if-999-percent-good-enough-then-%E2%80%A6.

323. James Merritt, *Nine Keys to Successful Leadership: How to Impact and Influence Others* (Eugene, OR: Harvest House, 2002, 2008, 2011), 56.

324. Brennan Manning, *The Ragamuffin Gospel* (Colorado Springs, CO: Multnomah, 1990, 2000, 2005), 65.

325. Brian Kohout, "Perfection Required for Acceptance at Stanford University," Preaching Today, accessed April 22, 2020, https://www.preachingtoday.com/illustrations/2018/july/perfection-required-for-acceptance-at-stanford-university.html; "http://www.collegesimply.com/colleges/california/stanford-university/admission/.

326. D. Martyn Lloyd-Jones, *Living Water: Studies in John 4* (Wheaton, IL: Crossway, 2009), 500.

327. Dorothy L. Sayers, *Christian Letters to a Post-Christian World* (Grand Rapids, MI: Eerdmans, 1969), 15.

328. Glenn Van Ekeren, Speakers Sourcebook II: Quotes, Stories, and Anecdotes for Every Occasion (Upper Saddle River, NJ: Prentice Hall, 2002).

329. C. S. Lewis, *Mere Christianity* (New York: Macmillan-Collier, 1960), 55–56.

330. Corrie ten Boom with Jamie Buckingham, *Tramp for the Lord: The Story that Begins Where the Hiding Place Ends* (Fort Washington, PA: CLC, 1974), 55.

331. Luis Palau, *Experiencing God's Forgiveness* (Sisters, OR: Multnomah, 1984), as quoted at Bible.org, accessed April 23, 2020, https://bible.org/illustration/clara-barton.

332. As quoted in Alister E. McGrath, *Zondervan Handbook of Christian Beliefs* (Grand Rapids, MI: Zondervan, 2005), 27.

333. C. S. Lewis, "On Forgiveness," *The Weight of Glory* (San Francisco: HarperOne, 1949, 1976, 1980).

334. Andy Stanley, *It Came from Within: The Shocking Truth of What Lurks in the Heart* (Colorado Springs, CO: Multnomah, 2006), 144.

335. Paul Middleton, ed., *The Wiley Blackwell Companion to Christian Martyrdom* (Hoboken, NJ: Wiley & Sons, 2020), 416–417.

336. Oswald Chambers, *The Quotable Oswald Chambers*, David McCasland, ed. (Grand Rapids, MI: Discovery House, 2008).

337. A. W. Tozer, *Life in the Spirit* (Peabody, MA: Hendrickson, 2009), 24.

338. "D. L. Moody Was Once Asked Why He Urged Christians," Sermon Central, accessed April 23, 2020, https://www.sermoncentral.com/sermon-illustrations/2970/d-l-moody-was-once-asked-why-he-urged-christians-by-owen-bourgaize.

339. "The Redwood Forest and the Role of Water," Exploring the Eel River Valley, accessed April 23, 2020, https://sunnyfortuna.com/explore/redwoods_and_water.htm.

340. H. B. Charles Jr., *It Happens After Prayer: Biblical Motivation for Believing Prayer* (Chicago: Moody, 2013), n.p.

341. Carey Nieuwhof, "CNLP 268: Luis Palau on His Friendship with Billy Graham, How Evangelism Has Changed, and How to Be More Alive at Age 84 than Most 24 Year Olds," Carey Nieuwhof Leadership Podcast, accessed April 23, 2020, https://careynieuwhof.com/episode268/.

342. Quoted in *Dictionary of Quotations from Ancient and Modern, English and Foreign Sources*, James Wood, ed. (London: Frederick Warne and Co., 1899), 43.

343. Quoted in Mike Yaconelli, *The Door Interviews* (Grand Rapids, MI: Zondervan, 1989), 230.

344. Quoted in Brian Bell Commentary on the Bible, Luke 21, StudyLight.org, accessed April 25, 2020, https://www.studylight.org/commentaries/cbb/luke-21.html.

345. C. S. Lewis, *Grief Observed* (San Francisco: HarperOne, 1961, 1996), 28.

346. C. S. Lewis, *Mere Christianity* (San Francisco: HarperOne, 1952, 1980), 49.

347. Quoted in Tricia Goyer, *The One Year Book of Amish Peace: Hearing God's Voice in the Simple Things* (Carol Stream, IL: Tyndale, 2013), 79.

348. John Ortberg, *The Me I Want to Be: Becoming God's Best Version of You* (Grand Rapids, MI: Zondervan, 2010), 122. Emphasis in the original.

349. Quoted in Cal Samra and Rose Samra, *More Holy Humor: Inspirational Wit and Cartoons* (Nashville, TN: Thomas Nelson, 1999,), 142.

350. Often misattributed to C. S. Lewis, possible attribution is to either Lou Holtz or Lena Horne. See William O'Flaherty, "[CCSLQ-11] Load that Breaks," Essential C. S. Lewis, August 11, 2018, http://www.essentialcslewis.com/2015/11/07/load-that-break/.

351. "An Average Person's Anxiety Is Focused On . . .," Bible.org, accessed April 25, 2020, https://bible.org/illustration/average-person%E2%80%99s-anxiety-focused-on%E2%80%A6.

352. *National Lampoon's Van Wilder*, Myriad Pictures, 2002, IMDb, accessed April 25, 2020, https://www.imdb.com/title/tt0283111/quotes/?tab=qt&ref_=tt_trv_qu.

353. C. S. Lewis, *The Collected Letters of C.S. Lewis, Vol. III, Narnia, Cambridge, and Joy, 1950–1963*, Walter Hooper, ed. (San Francisco: HarperSanFrancisco, 2007), 111. Emphasis in the original.

354. Jon Winkelman, "Christ at the Center," Illustration Exchange, July 9, 2015, https://illustrationexchange.com/illustrations?category=541.

355. Charles Haddon Spurgeon, *A Defense of Calvinism*, accessed April 25, 2020, https://books.google.com/books?id=XWOmI9sXdKkC&printsec=frontcover&dq=%E2%80%9CI+believe+there+will+be+more+in+heaven+than+in+hell.+If+you+ask+me+why+I+think+so,+I+answer,+because+Christ+in+everything+is+to+have+the+preeminence+(Col.+1:18),+and+I+cannot+conceive+how+he+could+have+the+preeminence+if+there+are+to+be+more+in+the+dominions+of+Satan+than+in+paradise+of+God.%E2%80%9D&hl=en&newbks=1&newbks_redir=0&sa=X&ved=2ahUKEwjNoPSGgYTpAhXIQs0KHUQWAkUQ6AEwAnoECAIQAg#v=onepage&q=more%20in%20heaven&f=false.

356. *A Treasure of Bible Illustrations* (Chattanooga, TN: AMG, 1995), 1.

357. Jon Courson, "Colossians: Background to Colossians," *Courson's Application Commentary: New Testament*, vol 3 (Nashville, TN: Thomas Nelson, 2003).

358. Quoted in Barry Minkow, *Down, But Not Out: Ten Steps for Rebuilding Your Life, Your Career, and all that Other Stuff* (Nashville, TN: Thomas Nelson, 2006), 157.

359. Tullian Tchividjian, *Jesus + Nothing = Everything* (Wheaton, IL: Crossway, 2011).

360. Rick Renner, *Sparling Gems from the Greek: 365 Greek Word Studies for Every Day* (Tulsa, OK: Harrison House, 2003), January 1.

361. Curtis Hutson, "Deciding Questionable Things for the Christian," accessed April 25, 2020, https://www.jesus-is-savior.com/BTP/Dr_Curtis_Hutson/questionable_things.htm.

362. Thomas Keneally, "How Good People Got that Way," *New York Times*, September 8, 1988, section 7, 18, https://www.nytimes.com/1988/09/04/books/how-good-people-got-that-way.html.

363. William Sloane Coffin, *Credo* (Louisville, KY: Westminster Knox, 2004), 6.

364. Brennan Manning, *The Ragamuffin Gospel* (Colorado Springs, CO: Multnomah, 1990, 2000, 2005), 11.

365. Brennan Manning, *Souvenirs of Solitude: Finding Rest in Abba's Embrace* (Colorado Springs, CO: NavPress, 2009), 26.

366. C. S. Lewis, *The Lion, the Witch and the Wardrobe*, as quoted in Art Lindsley, "The Lion, the Witch and the Wardrobe, *Knowing & Doing*, C. S. Lewis Institute, Winter 2005, 6, https://www.cslewisinstitute.org/webfm_send/466.

367. Robert Murray McCheynne, *The Postman: A Paper for the People and House to House Evangel*, December 1881, 7, https://books.google.com/books?id=oh0FAAAAQA-AJ&pg=RA23-PA7&dq=When+Christ+is+nearest,+Satan+also+is+busi-est.&hl=en&newbks=1&newbks_redir=0&sa=X&ved=2ahUKEwj_18qqvoTpAhVYK80KHX-AICtAQ6AEwBHoECAIQAg#v=onepage&q=When%20Christ%20is%20nearest%2C%20Satan%20also%20is%20busiest.&f=false.

368. Dale W. Decker, "Satan and Santa, in Craig Brian Larson and Phyllis Ten Elshof, eds., *1001 Illustrations that Connect: Compelling Stories, Stats, and News Items for Preaching, Teaching, and Writing* (Grand Rapids, MI: Zondervan, 2008), 467.

369. C. S. Lewis, *The Screwtape Letters* (SanFrancisco: HarperOne, 1942, 1996), ix.

370. Clinton Arnold, ed., *Zondervan Illustrated Bible Backgrounds Commentary: Romans to Philemon* (Grand Rapids, MI: Zondervan, 2002), 125.

371. John Charles Ryle, *Holiness: Its Nature, Hindrances, Difficulties, and Roots* (Peabody, MA: Hendrickson, 2007), 72.

372. *In Other Words*, as quoted in "Two Words, Ministry 127, access April 25, 2020, https://ministry127.com/resources/illustration/two-words.

373. John Maxwell, *Developing the Leaders Around You*, in *Maxwell 2 in 1* (Nashville, TN: Thomas Nelson, 1995), 223.

374. Elisabeth Elliot, in a speak delivered at Urbana '76, as quoted in J. Mack Stiles and Leeann Stiles, *Mack and Leeann's Guide to Short-Term Missions* (Downers Grove, IL: InterVarsity, 2000), 57.

375. Quoted in Jim Ayer and Janene Ayer, *Your Daily Journey to Transformation: A 12-Week Study Guide* (Hagerstown, MD: Review and Herald, 2013), 130.

376. David Brooks, "Marshmallows and Public Policy," *New York Times*, May 7, 2006, https://www.nytimes.com/2006/05/07/opinion/07brooks.html.

377. R. T. Kendall, "R. T. Kendall Quotes, Jar of Quotes, accessed April 25, 2020, https://www.jarofquotes.com/view.php?id=the-more-conscious-gods-presence-more-i-feel-like-being-myself-less-conscious-his-presence-more-i-feel-i-need-to-prove-myself-r-t-kendall.

378. Winkie Pratney, "Knowing God's Will," Last Days Ministries, March 20, 2012, https://www.lastdaysministries.org/Groups/1000087738/Last_Days_Ministries/Articles/By_Winkie_Pratney/Knowing_Gods_Will/Knowing_Gods_Will.aspx.

379. Quote Search, Beliefnet, accessed April 25, 2020, https://www.beliefnet.com/quotes/evangelical/m/matthew-henry/matthew-henry-meditating-on-the-theft-of-his-wall.aspx.

380. Quoted in Ron Kincaid, *Praying for Guidance: How to Discover God's Will* (Downers Grove, IL: InterVarsity, 1996), 73.

381. Corrie ten Boom, *The Hiding Place* (Peabody, MA: Hendrickson, 1971, 1984), 218–219.

382. Quoted in David Self, *Somebody Once Said: An Anthology of Quotations for Preachers and Speakers* (London: SPCK, 2003), 76.

383. "I Feel that I AM Making Daily Progress," Quote Investigator, February 12, 2014, https://quoteinvestigator.com/2014/02/12/casals-progress/.

384. Quoted in *Coleridge and Newman: The Centrality of Conscience* (New York, NY: Fordham University Press, 2004), 60.

385. Quoted in Martin H. Manser, ed., *The Westminster Collection of Christian Quotations* (Louisville, KY: Westminster John Knox, 2001), 153.

386. Dave Kraft, *Leaders Who Last* (Wheaton, IL: Crossway, 2010), 43.

387. Coral Ridge Presbyterian Church Communicator, vol 11–12, accessed April 25, 2020, https://books.google.com/books?id=A6LtAAAAMAAJ&q=The+egg+was+-fragile.+Its+thin+outer+shell+had+protected+its+liquid+interior,+but+after+sitting+through+the+boiling+water,+its+inside+hardened.+The+ground+coffee+beans+were+unique,+however.+By+being+in+the+boiling+water,+they+-changed+the+water.+He+asked+his+daughter,+%E2%80%9CWhen+adversity+knocks+on+your+door,+which+are+you?%E2%80%9D&dq=The+egg+was+-fragile.+Its+thin+outer+shell+had+protected+its+liquid+interior,+but+after+sitting+through+the+boiling+water,+its+inside+hardened.+The+ground+coffee+beans+were+unique,+however.+By+being+in+the+boiling+water,+they+changed+the+water.+He+asked+his+daughter,+%E2%80%9CWhen+adversity+knocks+on+your+door,+which+are+you?%E2%80%9D&hl=en&newbks=1&newbks_redir=0&sa=X&ved=2ahUKEwjcstPFi-YXpAhXCK80KHS5uDPIQ6AEwCHoECAcQAQ.

388. Martin Luther King Jr, "What Is Your Life's Blueprint?" speech given at Barratt Junior High in Philadelphia, October 26, 1967, quoted in Seattle Times, accessed April 25, 2020, https://projects.seattletimes.com/mlk/words-blueprint.html.

389. Often misattributed to C. S. Lewis. Author unknown, quoted in Harold Isbell, *Every Life Is a Story that Deserves to Be Told: True Stories about Life's Ups and Downs* (Bloomington, IN: Xlibris, 2008, 2012), 127.

390. Quoted in Craig Brian Larson, ed., *750 Engaging Illustrations for Preachers, Teachers, and Writers* (Grand Rapids, MI: Baker, 1993, 1996, 1998, 2002), 471–472.

391. Quoted in Os Guinness, *The Call: Finding and Fulfilling God's Purpose for Your Life* (Nashville, TN: Thomas Nelson, 1998, 2003, 2018), 249.

392. Multiple author sources. Quoted at "The Heart of Servants, "Fred Jordan Missions," accessed April 25, 2020, http://legacy.fjm.org/news_events/media_center/take_3/20091002.html.

393. As quoted in *The Homiletic Review*, volume 72 (New York: Funk & Wagnalls, 1916), 218.

394. Erwin W. Lutzer, *Putting Your Past Behind You: Finding Hope for Life's Deepest Hurts* (Chicago: Moody, 1990, 1997), 45.

395. A W Tozer, *Tozer on the Almighty God: A 365-Day Devotio*nal (Chicago: Moody, 2004), December 17.

396. Quoted in Daniella Whyte, *365 Days of Thanking God: Cultivating a Heart of Everyday Thanks* (Dallas, TX: Torch Legacy, 2010), Day 89.

397. Brennan Manning, *Abba's Child: The Cry of the Heart for Intimate Belonging* (Colorado Springs, CO: NavPress, 1994, 2002, 2015), 12.

398. Warren W. Wiersbe, "Learn from the Past," Bible.org, accessed April 26, 2020, https://bible.org/illustration/learn-past.

399. Quoted in Charles R. Swindoll, *The Mystery of God's Will: What Does He Want for Me?* (Nashville, TN: Thomas Nelson, 1999), chap. 7.

400. C. S. Lewis, *The Weight of Glory: And Other Addresses* (San Francisco: HarperOne, 1949, 1976, 1980), 53.

401. Quoted in Gordon S. Jackson, ed., *Quotes for the Journey, Wisdom for the Way* (Eugene, OR: Wipf and Stock, 2000), 117.

402. R. Kent Hughes, *Second Corinthians: Power in Weakness* (Wheaton, IL: Crossway, 2006), chap. 25.

403. Author unknown, Abigail Van Buren, "'Perfect' Clergyman Is Only Human," *Chicago Tribune*, March 19, 1988, https://www.chicagotribune.com/news/ct-xpm-1988-03-19-8803020042-story.html, submitted to "Dear Abby" by C. W. Kirkpatrick, Union Church of Christ, Ludlow, MA.

404. Marcus Buckingham and Curt Coffman, *First, Break All the Rules: What the World's Greatest Managers Do Differently* (New York: Simon & Schuster, 1999), 184–185.

405. Malcolm Gladwell, *Outliers: The Story of Success* (New York: Little, Brown and Company, 2008), 42–50.

406. Henri Nouwen, *A Spirituality of Living: The Henri Nouwen Spirituality Series* (Nashville, TN: The Upper Room, 2011), 16.

407. Quoted in Dargan Thompson, "Jim Elliot Quotes that Will Change the Way You Think about Sacrifice," *Relevant*, January 8, 2016, https://relevantmagazine.com/god/jim-elliot-quotes-will-change-way-you-think-about-sacrifice/.

408. Derek Lawrenson, "Gary Player Is 80 on Sunday but Still Does 1,300 Sit-Ups a Day and Never Shoots More than His Age . . . No Wonder He Still Gets a Kick Out of Life," *The Daily Mail*, October 29, 2015, https://www.dailymail.co.uk/sport/golf/article-3295850/Gary-Player-80-Sunday-does-1-300-sit-ups-day-never-shoots-age-No-wonder-gets-kick-life.html.

409. Marty Osborn, "What Are You Willing to Do to Be Successful?," Marty's Minute, August 26, 2019, https://www.martys-minute.com/post/what-are-you-willing-to-do-to-be-successful.

410. "The Helpful Client," The TaxBook Message Board, posted by Veritas, August 5, 2006, https://forum.thetaxbook.com/forum/discussion-forums/main-forum-tax-discussion/2801-the-helpful-client.

411. Often misattributed to George Bernard Shaw. William H. Whyte, "Is Anybody Listening?" *Fortune*, 1950, 174, https://quoteinvestigator.com/2014/08/31/illusion/#note-9667-1.

412. Quoted in Catherine Clifford, "Billionaire Warren Buffet: This Is the 'One Easy Way' to Increase Your Worth by 'At Least' 50 Percent," CNBC, December 5, 2018, https://www.cnbc.com/2018/12/05/warren-buffett-how-to-increase-your-worth-by-50-percent.html.

413. As quoted in John Maxwell, *Everyone Communicates, Few Connect: What the Most Effective People Do Differently* (Nashville, TN: Thomas Nelson, 2010), 4.

414. Bill Pennington, "Hut! Hut! Hut! What?," *New York Times*, January 31, 2018, https://www.nytimes.com/2018/01/31/sports/football/quarterback-signals-hut.html.

415. Quoted in Jason C. Meyer, *Lloyd-Jones on the Christian Life: Doctrin and Life as Fuel and Fire* (Wheaton, IL: Crossway, 2018), chp 9.

416. J. C. Ryle, *Holiness* (Lafayette, IN: Sovereign Grace, 2001), iii, v.

417. Winkie Pratney, "Knowing God's Will," Last Days Ministries, March 20, 2012, https://www.lastdaysministries.org/Groups/1000087738/Last_Days_Ministries/Articles/By_Winkie_Pratney/Knowing_Gods_Will/Knowing_Gods_Will.aspx.

418. Craig Kingsley, in "Think and Grin," *Boys' Life*, March 1979, 82.

419. Gene Haraldsen, "Defeating Temptation," July 2002, http://www.sermoncentral.com/sermon.asp?SermonID=30170 – ship captain illustration.

420. A. W. Tozer, *Living as a Christian: Teachings from First Peter* (Grand Rapids, MI: Baker, 2009), chp 14.

421. John Baker, *Life's Healing Choices: Freedom from Your Hurts, Hang-ups, and Habits* (New York: Howard, 2007), 103.

422. Bill Bright, *The Journey Home: Finishing with Joy* (Nashville, TN: Thomas Nelson, 2003), foreword.

423. Quoted in Ashton Applewhite, Williams R. Evans III, and Andrew Frothingham, *And I Quote: The Definitive Collection of Quotes, Sayings, and Jokes for the Contemporary Speechmaker*, revised edition (New York: Thomas Dunne Books, 2003), 177.

424. William Law, *A Practical Treatise upon Christian Perfection*, as quoted in Craig Brian Larson, ed., 1001 *Quotations that Connect: Timeless Wisdom for Preaching, Teaching, and Writing* (Grand Rapids, MI: Zondervan, 2009), 141.

425. Quoted in Lolly Daskal, "The 100 Best Leadership Quotes of All Time," *Inc.*, April 3, 2015, https://www.inc.com/lolly-daskal/the-100-best-leadership-quotes-of-all-time.html.

426. W. H. Griffith Thomas, *Through the Pentateuch: A Chapter-by-Chapter Study* (Grand Rapids, MI: Kregel, 1985), 9.

427. *Today in the Word*, April 1989, 27.

428. Billy Graham, "Billy Graham: 'My Heart Aches for America,'" Billy Graham Evangelistic Association, July 19, 2012, https://billygraham.org/story/billy-graham-my-heart-aches-for-america/.

429. Quoted in David Jeremiah, *What to Do When You Don't Know What to Do* (Colorado Springs, CO: David C. Cook, 2015), 254.

430. William M. Leary, ed., *We Shall Return!: MacArthur's Commanders and the Defeat of Japan, 1942–1945* (Lexington, KY: University of Kentucky Press, 1988, 2004), 8.

431. Vance Havner, *Truth for Each Day: Meditations for Every Day of the Year* (Grand Rapids, MI: Fleming H. Revell, 1960), n.p.

432. Tim Hansel, *Eating Problems for Breakfast: A Simple, Creative Approach to Solving Any Problem* (Nashville, TN: Word Publishing, 1988), 32.

433. Juliet Macur, "Scott Hamilton Was Demoted as an Olympic Broadcaster. Don't Feel Sorry for Him," *New York Times*, February 18, 2018, https://www.nytimes.com/2018/02/18/sports/olympics/figure-skating-nbc-scott-hamilton-.html.

434. Evelyn Underhill, *Lent with Evelyn Underhill* (London: Continuum, 1964, 1990), 24.

435. Bits & Pieces, December 9, 1993, 12–13. As quoted in "Lie," Sermon Illustrations, accessed April 26, 2020, http://www.sermonillustrations.com/a-z/l/lie.htm.

436. Kim B. Serota, Timothy R. Levine, and Franklin J. Boster, "The Prevalence of Lying in America: Three Studies of Self-Reported Lies," accessed April 26, 2020, https://msu.edu/~levinet/Serota_etal2010.pdf.

437. Staff Writers, Lying, Telling Truth Use Different Parts of Brain, *Los Angeles Times*, December 4, 2004, https://www.latimes.com/archives/la-xpm-2004-dec-04-sci-briefs4.1-story.html.

438. *USA Today*, as quoted in "Lie," Sermon Illustrations, accessed April 26, 2020, http://www.sermonillustrations.com/a-z/l/lie.htm.

439. David Rovella and Alexander McIntyre, "Firefighters Are the Happiest Workers in America, *Bloomberg Work Wise*, July 17, 2019, https://www.bloomberg.com/news/articles/2019-07-17/which-jobs-make-people-the-happiest-in-america.

440. A. W. Tozer, *The Crucified Life: How to Live Out a Deeper Christian Experience* (Grand Rapids, MI: Baker, 2011), chp 3.

441. Quoted in Tom Nelson, *Work Matters: Connecting Sunday Worship to Monday Work* (Wheaton, IL: Crossway, 2011), 29.

442. Keith Miller and Bruce Larson, *The Edge of Adventure: An Experiment in Faith* (Nashville, TN: Word, 1974), 127.

443. The saying goes, "When all is said and done, more is usually said than done."

444. Charles R. Swindoll, *Insights on 1 & 2 Timothy, Titus* (Carol Stream, IL: Tyndale, 2014), 327.

445. Philip Yaffe, "The 7 Percent Rule: Fact, Fiction, or Misunderstanding," *Ubiquity*, October 2011, https://ubiquity.acm.org/article.cfm?id=2043156.

446. Quoted in Barlett Jere Whiting, *Early American Proverbs and Proverbial Phrases* (Cambridge, MA: Harvard University Press, 1977), 113.

447. Quoted at AZ Quotes, accessed April 26, 2020, https://www.azquotes.com/quote/1406504.

448. Quoted in Martin H. Manser, ed., *The Westminster Collection of Christian Quotations* (Louisville, KY: Westminster John Knox, 2001), 375.

449. Charles F. Banning, quoted at Daily Christian Quotes, access April 26, 2020, https://www.dailychristianquote.com/charles-f-banning/.

450. Quoted in Bobby Conway with Jeff Kinley, *The Fifth Gospel: Matthew, Mark, Luke, John . . . You* (Eugene, OR: Harvest House, 2014), 9.

451. William Barclay, *The Letters to Timothy, Titus, and Philemon* (Louisville, KY: Westminster John Knox, 1965), 304. See also Laurie Venters, *Recovering Runaways: Slave Catching in the Roman World*, July 2019, https://openaccess.leidenuniv.nl/bitstream/handle/1887/74843/Recovering%20Runaways%20-%20Slave%20Catching%20in%20the%20Roman%20World%20.pdf?sequence=1.

452. Barclay, *Letters to Timothy*, 319.

453. Earle Cains, *Christianity through the Centuries*

454. Donald McCullough, *The Trivialization of God: The Dangerous Illusion of a Manageable Deity* (Colorado Springs, CO: NavPress, 1995), 63. As quoted in "Lowering the Lord Nelson Statue," Sermon Illustrations, The Pastor's Workshop, accessed April 26, 2020, https://the-pastorsworkshop.com/sermon-illustrations-2/sermon-illustrations-eyes/.

455. Tim LaHaye, Jerry B. Jenkins, and Frank Martin, *Embracing Eternity: Living Each Day with a Heart toward Heaven* (Carol Stream, IL: Tyndale, 2004), 121.

456. McCullough, *Trivialization of God,* 66–67. As quoted in Richard Osborn, "Finding Middle C: How God Works in All Those Meetings," Adventist Review, 2000, accessed April 26, 2020, https://www.adventistreview.org/archives/2000-1536/middlec.html.

457. Ibid.

458. John Vance Cheney, quoted in *The Treasure of American Sacred Song: With Notes Explanatory and Biographical* (London: Henry Frowde, 1896), 277.

459. David Winter, *100 Days in the Arena: One Hundred Dynamic Readings from Great Men of the Early Church* (Carol Stream, IL: Harold Shaw, 1977), 4.

460. Quoted in John Bergh, "Claim the Name," sermon given on April 8, 2011, Sermon Central, https://www.sermoncentral.com/sermon-illustrations/79183/father-s-day-by-sermoncentral?ref=TextIllustrationSerps.

461. Thomas Edison, *T. P.'s Weekly*, November 29, 1907, as quoted in Alex Kasprak, "Did Thomas Edison's Mother Lie About a Letter Expelling Him from School?," Snopes, December 1, 2016, https://www.snopes.com/fact-check/thomas-edisons-mom-lied-about-a-letter-expelling-her-son-from-school/.

462. Quoted in Susan Conroy, *Mother Teresa's Lessons of Love and Secrets of Sanctity* (Huntington, IN: Our Sunday Visitor, 2003), n.p.

463. Charles Haddon Spurgeon, *Sermons of Comfort and Assurance* (London: Marshall, Morgan & Scott, 1963), 60.

464. Steve Triplett, "Pastoral Commentary: Access to the Father," *Kiowa County Signal*, March 23, 2019, https://www.kiowacountysignal.com/news/20190322/pastoral-commentary-access-to-father.

465. John Wooden and Don Yaeger, *A Game Plan for Life: The Power of Mentoring* (New York: Bloomsbury, 2011), 79.

466. Malcolm Muggeridge, in *Homemade*, July 1990, quoted in "Learning through Afflictions," Bible.org, accessed April 27, 2020, https://bible.org/illustration/learning-through-afflictions.

467. Gene Fedele, *Heroes of the Faith* (Gainesville, FL: Bridge-Logos, 2003), 230.

468. Quoted in "Minute with Maxwell," The John Maxwell Team, accessed April 27, 2020, https://www.johnmaxwellteam.com/2020-helen-keller-2/.

469. A. W. Tozer, *The Root of the Righteous*, (Chicago: Moody, 1955, 1986), 165.

470. *Our Daily Bread*, as quoted in "Deep Roots," Bible.org, accessed April 27, 2020, https://bible.org/illustration/deep-roots.

471. Quoted in Michael Neale and Vernon Whaley, *The Way of Worship: A Guide to Living and Leading Authentic Worship* (Grand Rapids, MI: Zondervan, 2020), https://books.google.com/books?id=b1WeDwAAQBAJ&pg=PT86&lpg=PT86&dq=%E2%80%9CA+clay+-pot+sitting+in+the+sun+will+always+be+a+clay+pot.+It+has+to+go+through+the+white+heat+of+the+furnace+to+become+porcelain.%E2%80%9D&source=bl&ots=DEc8J4o-geV&sig=ACfU3U14R2acsWuJv9pOAW6KRzrcJKoxwg&hl=en&sa=X&ved=2ahUKEwi88v7s-gInpAhXfTQIHS4pAQkQ6AEwD3oECAgQAQ#v=onepage&q=%E2%80%9CA%20clay%20pot%20sitting%20in%20the%20sun%20will%20always%20be%20a%20clay%20pot.%20It%20has%20to%20go%20through%20the%20white%20heat%20of%20the%20furnace%20to%20become%20porcelain.%E2%80%9D&f=false.

472. Robert B. Hamilton, quoted in *Farm Journal*, volume 41, March 1917, 209, https://books.google.com/books?id=RS5HAAAAYAAJ&pg=PA209&dq=I+walked+a+mile+with+Pleasure;+She+chatted+all+the+way;+But+left+me+known+the+wiser+For+all+she+had+to+-say.&hl=en&newbks=1&newbks_redir=0&sa=X&ved=2ahUKEwjGwsHBgonpAhVFUK0KHXB-

KATQQ6AEwAXoECAAQAg#v=onepage&q=I%20walked%20a%20mile%20with%20
Pleasure%3B%20She%20chatted%20all%20the%20way%3B%20But%20left%20
me%20known%20the%20wiser%20For%20all%20she%20had%20to%20say.&f=false.

473. Quoted in Stephen Arterburn and Bill Farrel, *The One Year Devotions for Men on the Go* (Carol Stream, IL: Tyndale, 2004), 178.

474. Martin Ralph DeHahn, *Bread for Each Day* (Grand Rapids, MI: Zondervan, 1981), 11.

475. Leonard Ravenhill, *The Last Days* newsletter, as quoted in "Only Babies," Bible.org, accessed April 27, 2020, https://bible.org/illustration/only-babies.

476. Quoted in Dana M. Harris, *Today in the Word*, September 21, 2008, https://www.todayin-theword.org/issues/2008/9/devotions/21/.

477. Quoted in "The Book of Reevaluation," Ministry 127, accessed April 27, 2020, https://ministry127.com/resources/illustration/the-book-of-reevaluation.

478. Joseph S. Exell, *Biblical Illustrator Commentary: Isaiah–Malachi*, vol 3 (Harrington, DE: Delmarva, 2015), n.p.

479. Quoted in Stephanie A. Sarkis, "Thirty Quotes on Parenting," *Psychology Today*, September 25, 2012, https://www.psychologytoday.com/us/blog/here-there-and-every-where/201209/30-quotes-parenting.

480. Quoted in Erik Raymond, "If I Could Hear Christ Praying in the Next Room, I Would Not Fear a Million Enemies!" The Gospel Coalition, May 1, 2011, https://www.thegospelcoalition.org/blogs/erik-raymond/if-i-could-hear-christ-praying-in-the-next-room-i-would-not-fear-a-million-enemies/.

481. Thomas Watson, *All Things for Good: An Exposition of Romans 8:28* (Shawnee, KS: Gideon House, 2015), n.p.

482. Quoted in Erwin Lutzer, *Ten Lies About God: And How You Might Already Be Deceived* (Nashville, TN: Thomas Nelson, 2000), 35.

483. Tullian Tchividjian, *One Way Love: Inexhaustible Grace for an Exhausted World* (Colorado Springs, CO: David C. Cook, 2013), 91.

484. C. S. Lewis, *Mere Christianity*, in *The Complete C. S. Lewis Signature Classics* (San Francisco: HarperOne, 1952, 1980, 2002), 121.

485. Mark Leibovich, "Larry King Is Preparing for the Final Cancellation," *New York Times*, August 30, 2015, https://www.nytimes.com/2015/08/30/magazine/larry-king-is-preparing-for-the-final-cancellation.html.

486. Thomas Nagel, *The Last Word* (New York: Oxford University Press, 1997), 130–131. Also quoted in "Atheist Admits that He Doesn't 'Want There to Be a God,'" Christian Worldview Press, July 28, 2014, http://christianworldviewpress.com/atheist-admits-that-he-doesnt-want-there-to-be-a-god/.

487. Asrar Chowdhury, "Muhammad Ali: Little Jimmy's Friend," *Daily Star*, September 24, 2015, https://www.thedailystar.net/shout/echoes/muhammad-ali-little-jimmys-friend-147676.

488. C. S. Lewis, *Essential C. S. Lewis*, (New York: Scribner, 2017), 390.

489. T. M. Luhrmann, "Opinion: The Benefits of Church," *New York Times*, April 21, 2013, https://www.nytimes.com/2013/04/21/opinion/sunday/luhrmann-why-going-to-church-is-good-for-you.html.

490. Robert Charles Sproul, *The Soul's Quest for God* (Carol Stream, IL: Tyndale, 1993), 151.

491. Max Lucado, *Traveling Light: Releasing the Burdens You Were Never Intended to Bear*, deluxe edition (Nashville, TN: Thomas Nelson, 2001), 33.

492. The homiletics class of West Coast Baptist College, "Four False Facts," Ministry 127, accessed November 23, 2020, https://ministry127.com/resources/illustration/4-false-facts.

493. Quoted in Paul D. Wegner, *The Journey from Texts to Translations: The Origins and Development of the Bible* (Grand Rapids, MI: Baker Academic, 1999), 28.

494. J. Sidlow Baxter, *Explore the Book* (Grand Rapids, MI: Zondervan, 1960), n.p.

495. Quoted in "The Un-Apologist," Christian History Institute, accessed April 27, 2020, https://christianhistoryinstitute.org/magazine/article/chesterton-un-apologist.

496. Stephen Hawking, *Brief Answers to the Big Questions* (New York: Bantam, 2018), 38.

497. Ravi Zacharias, @ravizacharias, Facebook, July 15, 2013, https://www.facebook.com/ravizacharias/posts/to-sustain-the-belief-that-there-is-no-god-atheism-has-to-demonstrate-infinite-k/10151464540701813/.

498. Quoted in Elisabeth Elliot, *Shadow of the Almighty: The Life and Testament of Jim Elliot* (San Francisco: HarperSanFrancisco, 1958), 59.

499. Elliot, *Shadow*, 247.

500. Elliot, *Shadow*, 58–59.

501. Tommy Tenney, *The God Chasers: "My Soul Follows Hard After Thee"* (Shippensburg, PA: Destiny Image, 1998), 65.

502. Samuel Chadwick, *The Way to Pentecost* (Fort Washington, PA: CLC, 1932, 2000), 15.

503. Quoted in John Wesley: 500th Anniversary of Christian Reformation, accessed April 27, 2020, https://www.learnofchrist.org/today-restoration-begun-anew.html.

504. Quoted in Dargan Thompson, "Jim Elliot Quotes that Will Change the Way You Think about Sacrifice," *Relevant*, January 8, 2016, https://relevantmagazine.com/god/jim-elliot-quotes-will-change-way-you-think-about-sacrifice/.

505. Father & Son in South America
"Of course I was there all night. Do you think I would leave you alone? Do you think that I would have ever left you in this place alone?"

506. Quoted in J. P. Moreland and Tim Muehlhoff, *The God Conversation: Using Stories and Illustrations to Explain Your Faith* (Downers Grove, IL: InterVarsity, 2007), 21.

507. As quoted in Dutch Sheets and Chris Jackson, *Praying through Sorrows*, (Shippensburg, PA: Destiny Image, 2005), 182.

508. Anthony DeMarco, "Lily Safra's Jewels for Hope Auction Fetches $38 Million, Sets Two Records," *Forbes*, May 14, 2012, https://www.forbes.com/sites/anthonydemarco/2012/05/14/lily-safras-jewels-for-hope-auction-fetches-38-million-sets-2-records/#51a6e8d2f06d.

509. Quoted in Erika Andersen, "Ten Quotes from the 'First Lady of the World,'" *Forbes*, January 10, 2013, https://www.forbes.com/sites/erikaandersen/2013/01/10/10-quotes-from-the-first-lady-of-the-world/#5ddc9996272b.

510. Quoted at Sermon Central, accessed April 27, 2020, https://www.sermoncentral.com/sermon-illustrations/11111/wisdom-by-paul-fritz?ref=TextIllustrationSerps.

511. Steven Piersanti, "The Ten Awful Truths about Book Publishing," Berrett-Koehler Publishers, September 26, 2016, https://www.bkconnection.com/the-10-awful-truths-about-book-publishing.

512. Quoted in "400: Brian Buffini Says We Are Drowning in Information and Starving for Wisdom," The Ziglar Show, accessed April 27, 2020, https://www.awarebc.com/podcast/400-brian-buffini-says-we-are-drowning-in-information-and-starving-for-wisdom/.

513. Quoted in *Correct Mental Attitude* (Buffalo, NY: Frontier Press, 1916), 68.

514. R. T. Kendall, *In Pursuit of His Wisdom: How to Get God's Opinion on Any Matter* (Lake Mary, FL: Charisma, 2015), 3, 5–6.

515. Kendall, *In Pursuit*, 6.

516. Quoted in Michael Catt with Amy Parker, *Courageous Teens* (Nashville, TN: B&H, 2012),157.

517. Today in the Word, Moody Bible Institute, April 1990, 27. Quoted in "Knowing Where to Tinker," Bible.org, accessed April 27, 2020, https://bible.org/illustration/knowing-where-tinker.

518. Colin Powell with Tony Koltz, *It Worked for Me: In Life and Leadership* (New York: Harper, 2012).

519. Powell, *It Worked*.

520. I've heard it said, "Before you can be a missionary, you have to be submissionary."

521. Quoted in Phil Cooke and Jonathan Bock, *The Way Back: How Christians Blew Our Credibility and How We Get It Back* (Nashville, TN: Worthy, 2018),

522. Quoted in Ron Kincaid, *Praying for Guidance: How to Discover God's Will* (Downers Grove, IL: InterVarsity, 1996), 73.

523. Brennan Manning, *The Ragamuffin Gospel: Good News for the Bedraggled, Beat-Up, and Burnt Out* (Colorado Springs, CO: Multnomah, 1990, 2000, 2005), chp. 7.

524. Dietrich Bonhoeffer, *Life Together: New Edition* (London: SCM Press, 2015), 91.

525. "John Wesley and the Thief: The Power of God's Word," Sermon Index, accessed April 28, 2020, http://www.sermonindex.net/modules/newbb/viewtopic.php?topic_id=23203&forum=44.

526. R. T. Kendall, *Why Jesus Died: A Meditation on Isaiah 53* (Grand Rapids, MI: Monarch, 2011), 115.

527. R. T. Kendall, "How Does God Punish Sin?," *Charisma*, accessed April 28, 2020, https://www.charismamag.com/spirit/1524-devotionals/by-love-transformed/8078-how-does-god-punish-sin, excerpted from *The God of the Bible*.

528. Kurt E. Koch, *Occult Bondage and Deliverance: Counseling the Occultly Oppressed* (Grand Rapids, MI: Kregel, 1970), 110.

529. "The Blood," accessed April 28, 2020, https://bible.org/illustration/blood.

530. Art Babych, "Christianity: The Most Persecuted World Faith," *Messenger of Saint Anthony*, March 30, 2003, https://www.messengersaintanthony.com/content/christianity-most-persecuted-world-faith.

531. David B. Barrett and Todd M. Johnson, *International Bulletin of Missionary Research*, January 2002, as quoted in "World Evangelism Facts, Walking with Jesus Ministries, accessed April 28, 2020, https://www.wwj.org.nz/world-evangelism-facts.

532. C. S. Lewis, *God in the Dock* (Grand Rapids, MI: Eerdmans, 1970), 49.

533. Source unknown, "Spurgeon: Lady with Thirteen Children Felt Called to the Ministry," Family Times, accessed April 28, 2020, https://www.family-times.net/illustration/Ministry/202283/.

534. A. W. Tozer, *Experiencing the Presence of God: Teachings from the Book of Hebrews* (Minneapolis, MN: Bethany, 2010), 170.

535. Wayne Rice, *Hot Illustrations for Youth Talks: 100 Attention-Getting Stories, Parables, and Anecdotes* (Grand Rapids, MI: Zondervan, 1993), 18.

536. C. S. Lewis, *Mere Christianity* (New York: Macmillan, 1943, 1945, 1952, 1060), 104.

537. Corrie ten Boom and Jamie Buckingham, *Tramp for the Lord: The Story that Begins Where the Hiding Place Ends* (Fort Washington, PA: CLC, 1974), 55–57.

538. William Blake, *The Complete Poetry and Prose of William Blake*, David V. Erdman, ed., (Berkeley, CA: University of California Press, 1965, 1981), 201.

539. Thomas Brooks, *The Complete Works of Thomas Brooks: Nichol's Series of Standard Divines: Puritan Period* (London: James Nisbet and Co., 1866), 367.

540. I. D. E. Thomas, *The Golden Treasury of Puritan Quotations* (Simpsonville, SC, Christian Classics Foundation, 1999), 76. Quoted in John M. Strohman, *Application Commentary of the Gospel of Matthew: 2015 Revised Edition* (Pierre, SD: Cross Centered Press, 2012, 2013, 2014), 562.

541. Robert Simmons, "Where Lions Feed," Sermon Central, February 28, 2002, https://www.sermoncentral.com/sermons/where-lions-feed-robert-simmons-sermon-on-endurance-43796?page=1&wc=800.

542. Ibid.

543. Ibid.

544. C. S. Lewis, *The Screwtape Letters* (San Francisco: HarperOne, 1942, 1996), 32, 46, 61, 81–82.

545. "Zoo Accused of Painting Donkeys to Look Like Zebras," CBS News, July 27, 2018, https://www.cbsnews.com/news/donkey-painted-zebra-cairo-international-garden-park-zoo-accused/.

546. Quoted in Ford C. Ottman, *J. Wilbur Chapman: A Biography* (Garden City, NY: Doubleday, 1920), 322.

547. Quoted in *The Church School Journal*, vol 47, January 1915, 41, https://books.google.com/books?id=unwzAQAAMAAJ&pg=PA41&dq=and+did+the+gentleman+think+he+could+exhaust+the+patience+of+the+eternal+God+in+5+minutes%E2%80%9D&hl=en&newbks=1&newbks_redir=0&sa=X&ved=2ahUKEwivwaen9ovpAhVFZc0KHfnrBWYQ6AEwAnoECAMQAg#v=onepage&q=and%20did%20the%20gentleman%20think%20he%20

could%20exhaust%20the%20patience%20of%20the%20eternal%20God%20in%20 5%20minutes%E2%80%9D&f=false.

548. Lydia Willgress, "Wedding Guest Asked by Bride for a 'Bigger Contribution' After Giving Her a £100 Cheque," Telegraph, May 11, 2016, https://www.telegraph.co.uk/news/2016/05/11/ wedding-guest-asked-by-bride-for-a-bigger-contribution-after-giv/.

549. "Illustrations Help Make Memorable Messages," BibleStudyTools, accessed April 28, 2020, https://www.biblestudytools.com/pastor-resources/illustrations/illustra- tions-help-make-memorable-messages-11567002.html.

550. Anonymous, "Inspirational Quotes," accessed April 28, 2020, http://www.inspiration. rightattitudes.com/authors/unknown/.

551. "The Rules of Civility: Rule No. 56," Mount Vernon, accessed April 28, 2020, https://www. mountvernon.org/george-washington/rules-of-civility/article/associate-yourself-with- men-of-good-quality-if-you-esteem-your-own-reputation-for-tis-better-to-be-alone- than-in-bad-company/.

552. Quoted in Walter Dudley Cavert, Remember Now . . . : Daily Devotional Readings for Young People (Nashville, TN: Abingdon-Cokesbury, 1944), 161.

553. "Bad Company Corrupts Good Character," Free Bible Lessons, accessed April 28, 2020, http://freebiblelessons.net/object-lessons/bad-company-corrupts-good-character?utm_ source=feedburner&utm_medium=feed&utm_campaign=Feed%3A+FreeBibleLessons+%- 28Free+Bible+Lessons%2C+Object+Lessons+and+Sermon+Illustrations%29.

554. John R. W. Stott, The Living Church: Convictions of a Lifelong Pastor (Downers Grove, IL: InterVarsity, 2007), 91–93.

555. John Allan Lavender, Why Prayers Are Unanswered (Carol Stream, IL: Tyndale, 1980), 23.

556. A. W. Tozer, The Pursuit of God (Dallas, TX: Gideon House, 2017), 38.

557. From a Sermon by Pastor Tony Evans

558. Quoted in Walter B. Knight, Knight's Treasury of 2,000 Illustrations (Grand Rapids, MI: Eerdmans, 1995), 94.

559. Robert Lowry, "Nothing But the Blood," 1876, public domain.

560. Albin Krebs and Robert Thomas, "Notes on People; Music to His Ears," New York Times, October 3, 1981, https://www.nytimes.com/1981/10/03/nyregion/notes-on-people-music-to- his-ears.html.

561. Quoted in C. L. Wallis, ed., A Treasury of Sermon Illustrations (Nashville, TN: Abing- don-Cokesbury press, 1950), 254.

562. Oswald Chambers, My Utmost for His Highest: Classic Edition (Grand Rapids, MI: Discovery House, 1927, 1935, 1963), February 8.

563. F. F. Bruce, The Letter of Paul to the Romans: An Introduction and Commentary (Grand Rapids, MI: Eerdmans, 1963, 1985), 135.

564. J. C. Ryle, Holiness: Its Nature, Hindrances, Difficulties, and Roots (Peabody, MA: Hendrick- son, 2007), 22.

565. Quoted in Timothy Keller, Counterfeit Gods: The Empty Promises of Money, Sex, and Pow- er, and the Only Hope that Matters (New York: Penguin, 2009), 122–123.

566. Joel Comm, "How to Overcome the Fear of Public Speaking in Five Minutes," Inc., December 3, 2015, https://www.inc.com/burt-helm/how-be-great-remote-manager.html.

567. Anonymous, "Has the Lion Read the Book?," Bible.org, accessed April 28, 2020, https://bible. org/illustration/has-lion-read-book.

568. Edward Mote, "On Christ the Solid Rock," 1834, public domain.

569. "Not My Feeling," Bible.org, accessed April 28, 2020, https://bible.org/illustra- tion/1-john-511-13.

570. Jim McCabe, "World Gold Hall of Fame member Ford Dies at 95," PGA Tour, May 15, 2018, https://www.pgatour.com/news/2018/05/15/doug-ford-obituary.html.

571. Quoted in W. Y. Fullerton, Charles Haddon Spurgeon: A Biography, The Spurgeon Archive, accessed April 28, 2020, https://archive.spurgeon.org/misc/bio16.php.

572. Erica Pearson, "Parenting Coaches? Frazzled Families Pay for Advice," *Star Tribune*, November 12, 2018, https://www.startribune.com/parenting-coaches-frazzled-families-pay-for-advice/500206461/.

573. Quoted in "From Pastor Steven's Site: My Goal in Parenting," ekidz, December 6, 2012, http://elevationekidz.com/from-pastor-stevens-site-my-goal-in-parenting/; J. L. Martin, "My Goal in Parenting by Steven Furtick," March 30, 2011, http://daddy4ms.blogspot.com/2011/03/my-goal-in-parenting-by-steven-furtick.html.

574. T. D. Jakes, @BishopJakes, Twitter, October 3, 2015, https://twitter.com/bishopjakes/status/650358536204062720.

575. Associated Press, "Aggressive Parents Force Cancellation of Colorado Town's Easter Egg Hunt," *New York Daily News*, March 26, 2012, https://www.nydailynews.com/news/national/agressive-parents-force-cancellation-colorado-town-easter-egg-hunt-article-1.1051091.

576. Adrian Rogers, *Ten Secrets for a Successful Family: A Perfect Ten for Homes that Win* (Wheaton, IL: Crossway, 1996), 38.

577. Francis Chan, @crazylove, Twitter, June 30, 2015, https://twitter.com/crazylove/status/615986923165904896.

578. Vince Vitale, "The Questions of Pluralism," Ravi Zacharias International Ministries, accessed April 29, 2020, https://www.rzim.org/read/just-thinking-magazine/the-questions-of-pluralism-jt-25-3.

579. Ibid.

580. Peter Kreeft

581. Charles Haddon Spurgeon, *The Complete Works of C. H. Spurgeon, Volume 42: Sermons 2446–2497* (Fort Collins, CO: Delmarva, 2013).

582. Katherine E. Finkelstein, "In Concert, Searchers Retrieve Yo-Yo Ma's Lost Stradivarius," *New York Times*, October 17, 1999, https://www.nytimes.com/1999/10/17/nyregion/in-concert-searchers-retrieve-yo-yo-ma-s-lost-stradivarius.html.

583. Ian Harvey, "The Mystery of the Octavius: An 18th-Century Ghost Ship Was Discovered with the Captain's Body Found Frozen at His Desk, still Holding His Pen," *The Vintage News*, November 28, 2017, https://www.thevintagenews.com/2017/11/28/frozen-at-his-desk/.

584. Amy Carmichael, *Gold Cord: The Story of a Fellowship* (Fort Washington, PA: CLC, 1932, 1996, 2013), chp 2.

585. Brian Bell Commentary on the Bible, StudyLight.org, accessed April 29, 2020, https://www.studylight.org/commentaries/cbb/luke-21.html.

586. Gordon Lester, *Homemade*, vol 4, no. 11, quoted in "Familiarity Vs. Intimacy," Bible.org, accessed April 29, 2020, https://bible.org/illustration/familiarity-vs-intimacy.

587. UN cartoon caption

588. "Quotations: Thomas Jefferson Memorial Inscriptions," National Park Service: Thomas Jefferson Memorial, accessed April 29, 2020, https://www.nps.gov/thje/learn/photosmultimedia/quotations.htm.

589. John Piper, "Sin Prefers Anything to God," Desiring God, April 8, 2015, https://www.desiringgod.org/interviews/sin-prefers-anything-to-god.

590. Quoted in Richard Sibbes, *The Complete Works of Richard Sibbes*, vol 3 (London: James Nisbet and Co, 1862), 530.

591. Morgan Lee, "Sorry, Tertullian," *Christianity Today*, December 4, 2014, https://www.christianitytoday.com/ct/2014/december/sorry-tertullian.html.

592. Gordon Dahl, *Work, Play, and Play in a Leisure-Oriented Society* (Minneapolis, MN: Augsburg-Fortress, 1972), 7.

593. Matt Redman and Beth Redman, *Finding God in the Hard Times: Choosing to Trust and Hope When You Can't See* (Bloomington, MN: Bethany, 2005), chp 5.

594. Charles Haddon Spurgeon, "A Young Man's Vision," *Metropolitan Tabernacle Pulpit*, vol 14, April 16, 1868, The Spurgeon Center, https://www.spurgeon.org/resource-library/sermons/a-young-mans-vision#flipbook/.

595. *Today in the Word*, March 29, 1993. Quoted in "Thomas Jefferson's Tears Touched the Rioting Students' Hearts," Family Times, accessed April 29, 2020, https://www.family-times.net/illustration/Brokenness/202448/.

596. William M. Taylor, *Moses: The Law-Giver* (New York: Harper & Brothers, 1879), 92.

597. Thomas Watson, *Discourses on Important and Interesting Subjects: Being the Select Works of the Rev. Thomas Watson*, vol 1 (Glasgow, Scotland: Blackie, Fullarton, & Co, 1829), 354.

598. Quoted in Arthur T. Pierson, *George Müller of Bristol* (London: James Nisbet & Co., 1899), 367.

599. This quote is attributed to a puritan writer: "Sin is so powerful that it made the devil the devil."

600. Historical Nonfiction, July 13, 2014, https://historical-nonfiction.tumblr.com/post/91666381802/ethiopias-emperor-menelik-ii-believed-that-the.

601. Quoted in Martin H. Manser, ed., *The Westminster Collection of Christian Quotations* (Louisville, KY: Westminster John Knox, 2001), 19.

602. James S. Hewett, ed., *Illustrations Unlimited: A Topical Collection of Hundreds of Stories, Quotations, and Humor for Speakers, Writers, Pastors, and Teachers* (Carol Stream, IL: Tyndale, 1988), 208.

603. Eliot A. Cohen and John Gooch, *Military Misfortunes: The Anatomy of Failure in War* (New York: Free Press, 1990), 26.

604. A. W. Tozer, *Voice of a Prophet: Who Speaks for God?* (Bloomington, MN: Bethany, 2014).

605. C. H. Spurgeon, *Besides Still Waters: Words of Comfort for the Soul*, Roy H. Clarke, ed. (Nashville: Thomas Nelson, 1999), 2.

606. Peter J. Madden, *The Wigglesworth Standard* (New Kensington, PA: Whitaker House, 1993).

607. History.com editors, "MLB Retires Jackie Robinson's Number," History, November 12, 2019, https://www.history.com/this-day-in-history/mlb-retires-jackie-robinsons-number-42.

608. Quoted in R. T. Kendall, *Holy Fire: A Balanced, Biblical Look at the Holy Spirit's Work in Our Lives* (Lake Mary, FL: Charisma, 2014), 171.

609. Quoted in Stephen Seamands, *Wounds that Heal: Bringing Our Hurts to the Cross* (Downers Grove, IL: InterVarsity, 2003), 91.

610. Robert Murray McCheyne, *The Works of the Late Rev. Robert Murray McCheyne* (New York: Robert Carter, 1847), 148. Emphasis in the original.

611. Henri Nouwen, *Our Greatest Gift: A Meditation on Dying and Caring* (San Francisco: HarperOne, 1994), xii–xiii.

612. C. S. Lewis, *The Problem of Pain* (San Francisco: HarperOne, 1940, 1996), 116.

613. Miroslav Volf, *Free of Charge: Giving and Forgiving in a Culture Stripped of Grace* (Grand Rapids, MI: Zondervan, 2005), 139.

614. Tony Evans, *Theology You Can Count On: Experiencing What the Bible Says About . . . God the Father, God the Son, God the Holy Spirit, Angels, Salvation, the Church, the Bible, the Last Things* (Chicago: Moody, 2008).

615. Tim LaHaye, *Who Will Face the Tribulation?: How to Prepare for the Rapture and Christ's Return* (Eugene, OR: Harvest House, 2003), 37.

616. *Today in the Word*, April, 1989, 27. Also, David Jeremiah, "The Second Coming of Christ," *David Jeremiah* blog, accessed April 30, 2020, https://davidjeremiah.blog/the-second-coming-of-christ/.

617. Jeremy A. Peters, "Bloomberg Plans a $50 Million Challenge to the N.R.A.," *New York Times*, April 16, 2014, https://www.nytimes.com/2014/04/16/us/bloomberg-plans-a-50-million-challenge-to-the-nra.html?hp&_r=0.

618. John Pritchard, "Bible Sunday," Bible Society, accessed April 30, 2020, https://www.bible-society.org.uk/content/get_involved/bible_sunday/2016_resources/Bible-Sunday-Sermon-notes.pdf.

619. Alister McGrath, *Doubting: Growing Through the Uncertainties of Faith* (Downers Grove, IL: InterVarsity, 2006), 9.

620. Larry Petton, "Savior or Judge?," Sermon Central, January 14, 2014, https://www.sermon-central.com/sermon-illustrations/83588/savior-or-judge-by-dr-larry-petton.

621. Matthew Henry, *Directions for Daily Communion with God: In Three Discourses Shewing How to Begin, How to Spend, and How to Close Every Day with God* (London: Golden Lyon, 1715), 127.

622. ABC News, "Billy Graham, in His Own Words, about Facing Death and the Lord," YouTube, February 21, 2018, https://www.youtube.com/watch?v=5vOk9e9Qll4.

623. C. S. Lewis, *The World's Last Night* (Orlando, FL: Harcourt, 1988), 107.

624. Greville MacDonald, *George MacDonald and His Wife* (New York: Dial Press, 1924), 172.

625. Quoted in George Every, Richard Harries, and Kallistos Ware, eds., *The Time of the Spirit: Readings through the Christian Church* (Crestwood, NY: St. Vladimir's Seminary Press, 1984), 162.

626. C. S. Lewis, The Last Battle, quoted in Leland Ryken and Marjorie Lamp Mead, *A Reader's Guide Through the Wardrobe: Exploring C. S. Lewis's Classic Story* (Downers Grove, IL: InterVarsity, 2005), 115.

627. J. Vernon McGee, *Thru the Bible: Genesis through Revelation* (Nashville, TN: Thomas Nelson, 1984).

628. Adrian Rogers with Steve Rogers, *Unveiling the End Times in Our Time: The Triumph of the Lamb in Revelation* (Nashville, TN: B&H, 2004, 2013), 58.

629. Adrian Rogers, *Unveiling the End Times in Our Time: The Triumph of the Lamb in Revelation* (Nashville, TN: B&H, 2013), 48.

630. Charles H. Spurgeon, "Two Advents of Christ," December 22, 1861, in *Spurgeon's Sermons Volume 8: 1863* (Woodstock, Ontario, Canada: Devoted Publishing, 1863), 30–32.